DISCARDED

DISCARDED

Images and Empires

Images and Empires

Visuality in Colonial and Postcolonial Africa

EDITED BY

Paul S. Landau

AND

Deborah D. Kaspin

UNIVERSITY OF CALIFORNIA PRESS
Berkeley   Los Angeles   London

University of California Press
Berkeley and Los Angeles, California

University of California Press, Ltd.
London, England

© 2002 by the Regents of the University of California

Parts of chapter 7 were first published in Henry J. Drewal, "Mermaids, Mirrors, and Snake Charmers," *African Arts* 21, 2 (1988): 38–45, 96. Part of chapter 9 was first published in Catherine Hodeir and Michel Pierre, *L'Exposition coloniale, 1931: La mémoire du siècle* (Paris: Éditions Complexe, 1991). Chapter 12 has been adapted from material incorporated in Eric Gable, "Appropriate Bodies: Self through the Other in Manjaco and Portuguese Representation," *Visual Anthropology Review* 14, 1 (1998): 3–19.

Library of Congress Cataloging-in-Publication Data

Images and empires : visuality in colonial and postcolonial
Africa / Paul S. Landau and Deborah D. Kaspin, editors.
    p.   cm.
Includes bibliographical references and index.
   ISBN 0-520-22948-7 (cloth : alk. paper) — ISBN 0-520-22949-5 (paper : alk. paper)
   1. Visual anthropology—Africa.   2. Visual sociology—Africa.
3. Africa—Colonization.   4. Postcolonialism—Africa.   5. Africa in art.   6. Africa in literature.   7. Africa in mass media.
I. Landau, Paul Stuart, 1962–   II. Kaspin, Deborah, 1953–
   GN645 .I43 2002   2001008248
   301′.096—dc21   CIP

10 09 08 07 06 05 04 03 02
10 9 8 7 6 5 4 3 2 1

The paper used in this publication meets the minimum requirements of American National Standard for Information Sciences–Permanence of Paper for Printed Library Materials, ANSI Z39.48-1984. ∞

CONTENTS

LIST OF ILLUSTRATIONS   /   *vii*
PREFACE   /   *xi*
ACKNOWLEDGMENTS   /   *xv*

Introduction: An Amazing Distance: Pictures and People in Africa
Paul S. Landau   /   1

1. "Our Mosquitoes Are Not So Big": Images and Modernity in Zimbabwe
   Timothy Burke   /   41

2. The Sleep of the Brave: Graves as Sites and Signs in the Colonial Eastern Cape
   David Bunn   /   56

3. Tintin and the Interruptions of Congolese Comics
   Nancy Rose Hunt   /   90

4. Cartooning Nigerian Anticolonial Nationalism
   Tejumola Olaniyan   /   124

5. Empires of the Visual: Photography and Colonial Administration in Africa
   Paul S. Landau   /   141

6. Portraits of Modernity: Fashioning Selves in Dakarois Popular Photography
   Hudita Nura Mustafa   /   172

7. Mami Wata and Santa Marta: Imag(in)ing Selves and Others in Africa and the Americas
   Henry John Drewal   /   193

8. "Captured on Film": Bushmen and the Claptrap of Performative Primitives
   Robert J. Gordon   /   212

9. Decentering the Gaze at French Colonial Exhibitions
   Catherine Hodeir   /   233

10. The Politics of Bushman Representations
   Pippa Skotnes / *253*
11. Omada Art at the Crossroads of Colonialisms
    Paula Ben-Amos Girshick / *275*
12. Bad Copies: The Colonial Aesthetic and the Manjaco-Portuguese Encounter
    Eric Gable / *294*

    Conclusion: Signifying Power in Africa
    Deborah D. Kaspin / *320*

BIBLIOGRAPHY / *337*
LIST OF CONTRIBUTORS / *371*
INDEX / *375*

ILLUSTRATIONS

1.1 "Urban bioscope," Northern Rhodesia (Zambia), ca. 1907 / *44*

1.2 A scene from *Philemon the Footballer*, 1952 / *46*

1.3 Advertisement for Lifebuoy soap, 1960s / *50*

2.1 Map of the Eastern Cape / *59*

2.2 Bernard Picart, "Les funerailles des Cafres et Hottantots" (1729) / *63*

2.3 Robert Jacob Gordon, "Hottentot chief's grave" (1779) / *63*

2.4 King Cetshwayo's corpse (1884) / *69*

2.5 Henry Butler, "The Epitaph" (1837) / *74*

2.6 Thomas Baines, *The Death of Colonel Fordyce* (detail) / *76*

2.7 "Graves in the Winterberg" (1853) / *77*

2.8 "Fingoes viewing the body of Chief Sandile" / *79*

2.9 Sandile's grave / *80*

2.10 Godlonton candelabra (detail) / *81*

2.11 George Hay, "Sandili," *carte de visite* / *83*

3.1 Welded silhouette by Lubumbashi railway worker, ca. 1970. / *95*

3.2 "Le match de Jako et Mako" by Louchet / *99*

3.3 "Vision de guerre" by Narib / *101*

3.4 Congolese soldier in fez cap / *101*

3.5 "Les enchaînés" by SAV / *102*

3.6 "Les aventures de Mbumbulu" by Masta / *104*

3.7 "Mbu et Mpia.... espiègles Kinois" by P. M'Bila / *107*

3.8 "Apolosa moniteur" by Sima Lukombo / *115*

4.1 Akinola Lasekan, "Foreign Capitalist" / *127*

4.2 Akinola Lasekan, "Eternal Servitude?" / *128*

4.3 Akinola Lasekan, "Democracy versus Communism" / *130*

4.4 Akinola Lasekan, "Nigerian Nationalism" / *131*

4.5 Akinola Lasekan, "A Suggestion" / *132*

4.6 Akinola Lasekan, "Thin Wall of Lies Smashed" / *133*

4.7 Akinola Lasekan, "Leaving Us at the Mercy of the Big Wolf?" / *134*

4.8 United Africa Company, "Joseph Learns Something New" / *136*

4.9 United Africa Company, "The Gang Have Been Captured" / *137*

4.10 United Africa Company, "Joseph Talks to the Chief" / *138*

5.1 Advertisement for Banania / *143*

5.2 "Lake Chrissie San" from Raymond Dart's "Gallery of African Faces" / *151*

5.3 "The Authentic Sculpture," frontispiece in Margery Perham's *Ten Africans* / *153*

5.4 "Ndebele Warriors," ca. 1890 / *160*

6.1 Amateur portrait of a well-dressed person, illustrating *sañse* / *174*

6.2 Sotiba fashion show / *182*

6.3 Wall in an atelier of an old tailor, Dakar / *184*

6.4 Wedding photo of a bride with guests in a living room / *186*

6.5 Seated guests at a naming ceremony / *187*

7.1 Snake charmer chromolithograph / *196*

7.2 Water spirit headdress, Bonny, Nigeria / *199*

7.3 Contemporary Igbo shrine to Mami Wata / *201*

7.4. Mrs. Margaret Ekwebelam and her shrine / *202*

7.5 Mami Wata clay sculptures / *204*

7.6 Clay Mami Wata wearing costume jewelry / *205*

7.7 Contemporary "Saint Martha," manufactured object / *207*

7.8 Henry Drewal's personal altar to Mami Wata / *209*

8.1 N!ai, from *N!ai, The Story of a Kung Woman* (dir. John Marshall, 1980) / *213*

8.2 C. L. H. Hahn, "Dr. Cadle and two average size Kalahari Bushmen" / *217*

9.1 Senegalese weaver and apprentice / *235*

9.2 Senegalese jeweler's workshop / *236*

9.3 "Le gaz aux colonies" / *239*

9.4 French Western African Pavilion, Paris, 1931 / *243*

9.5 "Coco Banania et les poissons-volants" / *245*

9.6 Former Cameroon-Togo pavilion, Paris / *249*

10.1 Diorama of hunter-gatherer camp, South African Museum, Cape Town / *254*

10.2 /Xam from the Prieska district, 1910 / *257*

10.3 Paintings of animals and plants / *258*

10.4 *Miscast* installation, main room / *265*

10.5 Another view of *Miscast* installation, main room / *265*

10.6 *Miscast* installation, section of semi-circle of resin casts / *266*

10.7 Part of the *Miscast* installation / *267*

11.1 Carved royal altar tusk, late nineteenth century / *283*

11.2 Drawing by Joanne Wood, detail of tusk in fig. 11.1 / *284*

11.3 Omada wood carving of a European shopkeeper, part of a box / *286*

11.4 Drawing of Omada carving of young girl with tray / *287*

11.5 Omada wood carving of a European / *288*

11.6 Omada wood carving criticizing European manners / *289*

11.7 Omada carved chair depicting a drunk European / *290*

12.1 Photograph of a scarified Manjaco woman, by Artur Martins de Meireles / *297*

12.2 Two Manjaco ancestor posts, one by Jon Biku Pinambe / *298*

12.3 Art deco lithograph of "village scenes" from António Carreira's ethnographies / *301*

12.4 Photographs from Artur Martins de Meireles, *Mutilações étnicas dos Manjacos* / *304*

12.5 Cluster of Manjaco ancestor posts / *306*

12.6 Manjaco ancestor posts by Uut / *308*

12.7 Manjaco ancestor posts by Soga Mendes / *309*

12.8 Cluster of Manjaco ancestor posts, including some by Jon Biku Pinambe / *310*

PREFACE

This volume stems from a meeting of interested scholars, called "Images and Empires in Africa," organized by us, Paul Landau and Deborah Kaspin. Yet it represents much more than a publication of those conference papers. Both of us wrote commentaries on most of the papers, combining our own critiques with the remarks of our able discussants who spoke at the conference. Most of our authors then rewrote their essays to reflect the planned integrity of the book, and eleven of those essays were selected and edited again, and illustrations were settled on. Paul Landau wrote an extended introduction to the abiding issues in the burgeoning scholarship behind the project as a whole. He also contributed a separate chapter on the subject of photography in Africa. Deborah Kaspin wrote a conclusion addressing the problems of culture and power that our authors variously describe.

We thank our initial participants and, most of all, the contributors to this book for bearing with us through this long process.

Landau's initial concept for the conference and for this book derived from his prior work on images in the history of southern African evangelism. When missionaries used pictures or slides, they received unpredictable responses. Iconic images sometimes became focuses of different interpretations and revealed important epistemological conflicts beneath the surface of colonial contact. In the conference, Landau wanted to consider the visual image as a particular mode of expression in Africa, in much the same way that texts and orality have been problematized. The meaning of any communicative medium, including iconic images, is arguably a product of what Stanley Fish calls its "interpretive communities."[1] If there are histories of text (writing and printing, for instance), and of orality (folktales and oral traditions, for instance), then perhaps there could be a history of images in the same vein.

Kaspin came to the project with a background in the cultural politics of Chewa ritual and Nyau masquerades. Like Landau's evangelical pictures, Nyau has been differently interpreted, and energetically contested, by the several factions created by colonial and postcolonial politics. More mundane practices, from the shapes of houses to the cut of clothing, are similarly implicated in contests of cultural authority. As a teacher, Kaspin found that these images—along with films, photos, maps, advertising, and so on—elicited students' interest in the politics of meaning in a way that oral and textual media alone could not.

We share the premise that Africans have the major role in shaping their histories and their presents. Both of us strongly felt that such a focus on Africans was missing from too many studies of "colonial discourse." We therefore disavowed the fashionable idea that Western analyses of Africans' expressions must primarily be self-reflective. On the other hand, we also explicitly rejected the contrary notion that art and expression somehow "speak" their original intentions directly, in an unmediated way.

THE CONFERENCE

We began planning for the conference in 1996. The invitation to submit proposals to the meetings laid out the essential framework we would later rely upon in making this anthology. We suggested not only that pictures and sculptures might be seen as elements of colonialism in Africa, but also that they continue to mark and express the inequalities that typify the postcolonial condition today:

> Participants are invited to treat examples of subaltern, hand-wrought, or artistic images, and official, consumer or colonial images, in a single regional, social and historical context.... In New Crossroads, South Africa, wall murals of up-raised fists, and the government's cartoon pamphlets, both spoke to the single issue of the tricameral parliamentary elections. In the 19th century Cape interior, foragers and pastoralists painted caves with scenes of white men on horseback, and photographers helped define the stereotype of "bushmen" who were then identified as the artists of those same paintings. In central Africa, Africans produced tourist art to reflect European expectations, while imperial hygiene films depicted African life to Africans themselves. In West Africa, studio photographers supplied twin-cult duplicate photos to urbanites, while twin-cult statuary was collected by Westerners; sculptors fashioned deities wearing pith helmets while European images of whites as Christ appeared in Sunday schools. Figurative images thus played an important role in mediating relationships between the colonizer and the colonized, the state and the individual, the global and the local.[2]

As a working hypothesis, we suggested that

> Imperial depictions of Africans created ideal forms that fit, discursively, into the administrative apparatus; African depictions of Europeans sought to understand, deny and control Europeans' authority. Since many Africans were and are not literate, pictures also represented an important medium of communication. Africans saw whites on butter wrappers, cheap posters of *The Last Supper*, and 1940s Spencer Tracy films: just as whites understood Africans through *Natural History Magazine*, *Tarzan* and *King*

Solomon's Mines. Images were and are artworks, instruments of hegemony, hidden transcripts, and anonymous or surreptitious speech. "Images and Empires" seeks a unified perspective on the circulation of meanings growing out from these images and operating between them.

We received a great many fine proposals for papers. While the great majority of them could not be accommodated in the limited framework of three days of meetings, they showed us that we had tapped into a young and vigorous field of scholarship. The conference was held at the Henry Luce Center for International and Area Studies at Yale, from February 14 to 16, 1997. Our presenters came from the United States, Canada, Europe, and Africa. The twenty original participants and their papers, in order of presentation, were as follows:

Bennetta Jules-Rosette (University of California at San Diego), "Interrogating Modernity: Representation and Reappropriation in Zairian Popular Painting and Tourist Art."

Bogumil Jewsiewicki (Université Laval, Canada), "Visual Archeology of Zairian Modernity and Political Culture: Popular Images of P. E. Lumumba, 'Belgian Colony' and 'Chains of Slavery.'"

Nancy Rose Hunt (University of Arizona), "*Tintin au Congo* and Its Colonial and Post-Colonial Reformulations."

Enid Schildkrout (American Museum of Natural History, New York), "Mangbetu Sculptural Art and the Texts of Herb Lang."

Robert Gordon (University of Vermont), "Don't Look At Me Now: Death Is Dancing Me Ragged."

Keyan Tomaselli and Arnold Schepperson (University of Natal, South Africa), "Something Old, Something Borrowed: A Marriage of Past and Present Monumental Images in South African Television Advertisements after May 1994." Presented by Tomaselli.

Timothy Burke (Swarthmore), "'Our Mosquitoes Are Not So Big': Images in the Making of Mass Communication in Colonial Zimbabwe."

Judy Seidman, with C. Schaer, E. Potenza, and M. Smithers (Images of Defiance Poster Collective, Johannesburg), "Join the New Struggle: Images of AIDS in South Africa." Presented by Seidman.

Eric Gable (Mary Washington College), "Appropriate/Inappropriate Bodies: Manjaco Portuguese Interfigurations at the Climax of Colonialism."

Paula Ben-Amos Girshick (Indiana University at Bloomington), "Omada Art at the Crossroads of Colonialisms."

Hudita Mustafa (Harvard), "Portraits of Modernity: Popular Photography and Desiring Selves in Dakarois Fashion."

Samba Diop (State University of New York at Buffalo), "Mutual Representations in Colonial Senegal (1900–1960): The Image of the African Native in the French Press and the Native's Perception of the European in Popular Paintings."

David Bunn (University of the Western Cape, South Africa), "The Sleep of the Brave: Graves as Sites and Signs in the Colonial Eastern Cape."

Pippa Skotnes (University of Cape Town, South Africa), "The Politics of Bushman Representations: A Diorama, an Archive and an Art Exhibition."

Carol Muller (University of Natal, South Africa), "The Book, Badge, Bride, Bell and BMW: Hybridity of Image and Empire in South Africa's *Ibandla LamaNazaretha*."

Keith Snedegar (Utah Valley State College), "Mapping Heaven and Earth: A Stereographic Projection of British Astronomy and Khoisan Cosmology onto the Intellectual Culture of 19th-Century Cape Town."

Christraud Geary (National Museum of African Art, Washington, D.C.), "Betwixt and Between: Postcard Representations by Western and African Photographers."

Catherine Hodeir (Institut d'Études politiques de Paris), "Decentering the Gaze at the French Colonial Exhibitions."

Tejumola Olaniyan (University of Virginia), "Cartooning Nigerian Nationalism."

Henry Drewal (University of Wisconsin-Madison), "Mami Wata and Santa Marta: Imaging Selves and Others in Africa and America."

The conference was introduced by Paul Landau. Commentary on the papers was offered by Susan Vogel, Christopher Miller, Robert Harms, James Scott, and Deborah Kaspin. At the time all of us were affiliated with Yale University.

NOTES

1. Stanley Fish, *Is There a Text in This Class?* (Cambridge, Mass.: Harvard University Press, 1980).

2. One or two phrases have here been altered in order to avoid repetitions.

ACKNOWLEDGMENTS

There are a number of people and institutions without whom this book would not have been possible. First the institutions. Yale University and many departments and programs at Yale contributed to the success of the conference and we thank them. We wish also to acknowledge the precedent set by the Southern African Research Program (SARP), and we are grateful for the use of SARP funds in order to finance the southern Africanist panels at the conference, convened under SARP's aegis. We therefore also wish to acknowledge the Ford Foundation, the source of those funds. Finally, the Office of the Dean of the College and Arlene McCord generously supplied us with additional funding when we needed it most.

Many individuals also helped us. At Yale, Ian Shapiro of the Political Science Department lent his voice to the idea of a conference at an early and critical stage, and without his initial intervention, it would have died on the vine. David Apter of the Program in African Studies and Robin Winks of the History Department also threw their support behind us. Without David's subsequent aid at certain key moments, we would again have failed. Donna Perry was our tireless assistant, who took care of a great many logistical issues. John Moore Crossey continually sent us bibliographic information tailored to the theme of the conference, an amazing service that will now be greatly missed at Yale, since he has retired as the Africanist librarian. Moore also organized an exhibition from Yale's Africana holdings in pictures, cartoons, and postcards, which ran in February 1997 in Sterling Memorial Library on Yale's campus. Susan Vogel hosted a gathering for the participants and contributors at the Yale Art Gallery. We thank her also, and Christopher Miller, Robert Harms, and James Scott, for their illuminating commentaries on the papers in their respective panels.

For subsequent intellectual engagement during the preparation of the introduction and conclusion, we would like to thank Rory Bester, Timothy Burke, Emily

Epstein Landau, Patricia Hayes, Eric Gable, Kira Hall, Catherine Howard, Peter Marks, Peter Miller, Santu Mofokeng, Andrew Perchuk, Donna Perry, Pippa Skotnes, Laura Wexler, and our two anonymous readers at the University of California Press. In the long preparation of the book, we have been gratifyingly encouraged and efficiently assisted by Monica McCormick.

Introduction

An Amazing Distance: Pictures and People in Africa

Paul S. Landau

"Truly here are real savages by our standards; for either they must be thoroughly so, or we must be; there is an amazing distance between their character and ours."[1] Michel de Montaigne makes this observation in his essay "Of Cannibals." His point, especially apparent in the word "amazing," is that the derogatory European appraisal of Brazilian indigenes as "savages" is ironic. For while European "civilization" has left behind the valor and moral simplicity of the classical past, the Brazilian "cannibals" have not, and are pure of heart. The argument is made mostly by implication, especially in the consistency with which Montaigne quotes King Pyrrus, Plato, Aristotle, Zeno, and other such luminaries in describing the "cannibals": Plato for instance would have seen mankind's Golden Age in them, and the cannibal language resembled Greek. "Of Cannibals" can be read as an early formulation of a theory of what some modern writers call "alterity," the idea that certain kinds of interactions tell people who they are and who most certainly they are not.[2]

This book is about Africans, not about Brazilians, and in fact, about Africans and visual mimesis. Our authors come from various fields, but each chapter focuses on visual images as they were deployed in their contexts of apprehension. Most of the chapters juxtapose two different kinds of images, in the sense of the editors' suggestion that essays compare "African" iconographies and readings, with "European" ones. More accurately, their discussions can be said to concern "the global and the local." They embrace advertising and folk art; colonist and indigene; photography and funerary sculpture; film and dance; public spectacle and private behavior; and international and street cartooning, among other topics. By focusing on the intersections between such domains, the authors, as a group, make several related arguments, demonstrating that images change depending on who is looking at them and showing how images have both underwritten, and undermined, the hierarchies that governed colonial Africa. Most interesting to me, the chapters in this book all reveal how people use images to draw together previously inchoate social meanings from their *own* societies, and then how they use them to "recognize" people from *other* societies. Our contributors are smart enough to know that any kind of dualism is an inadequate model for human interaction. Nonetheless, and this is my point, they all contemplate the same "amazing distance" remarked upon by Montaigne. It seems as if images lend themselves particularly to doing so.

"Image" is a very forgiving word, even a promiscuous one. In a basic sense, an image means a picture, whether the referent is present as an object, or in the mind. At the same time, a picture, in the sense of a sign that resembles—"a picture is *of* something"—cannot really be in the mind, as a moment's reflection will show.[3] Thus, if we begin thinking about the subject matter of this book in a limited sense, with the idea of an "image of Africa," it should be acknowledged that this image really consists of a set of ideas associated with Africa (albeit ones that, perhaps, also embody visual components).[4] Montaigne's essay is again a good guide. It reminds us that the history of the European view of non-European peoples has always reflected Europeans' history of imagining themselves.

Patently such was the case with Europe's general knowledge of Africa before the nineteenth century. Armchair geographers reached into what was a rather shallow archive of reports, glimpses, and rumors accumulated over past centuries, and the "Africa" they fabricated derived from Western demands and prejudices. We might call the resulting collage—the "image" of Africa that, in fact, still survives today—an "image-Africa," paralleling Edward Said's discursive "Orient" constructed by European travelers.[5] The history of the development of the image-Africa would include *The Periplus of the Erythraean Sea* (75 C.E.), with its cryptic description of tall trading men; the temporary location of Prester John in Nubia or Ethiopia; the visibility of the pilgrimage of Mansa Musa, emperor of Mali; the white spaces on the Mappa Mundi, and Guy Tachard's and Peter Kolben's woodcuts of Bushmen posed like Socrates. It would account for dark invocations of witchery and fetishism "from" Africa; the popularity of Leo Africanus's narratives; the ancient mystique of the "Mountains of the Moon," and the idea of the Hamites. It would brace us for a reading of two of the volumes of the massive eighteenth-century *Universal History*. The image-Africa's permutations might be seen as implicitly charting the rise of sixteenth-century Europe out of Asia's shadow, the colonial encroachments of the Portuguese and the Dutch, and the prospects of swift gain along the Ivory, Slave, and Gold coasts.[6] Its accretion of images and figments and blanks either followed the contours of the familiar or detoured into obscenity, exoticism, and incomprehension.

At the height of the African slave trade, the image-Africa underwent a change. Joseph Miller has called the transatlantic commerce in human beings the "way of death." Its effect on the West's picture of Africa was also pernicious, as the degradation of millions of Africans soured the Western imagination of their places of origin.[7] The contrary response was to assert the commonality of the slaves' humanity. The freedman Olaudah Equiano went further than this and effectively recapitulated Montaigne's cannibal trope in "Of Cannibals." Equiano grasped that even if Westerners could not see contemporary Africans as their equals, they might still be led to understand Africans as embodying the essence of Europe's ancestors, and so he drew an analogy between "the manners and customs of my countryman and those of the Jews before they reached the Land of Promise . . . [in other words,] the Israelites in their primitive state. . . . As to the difference of colour between the Eboan Africans and the modern Jews," he continued, "I shall not presume to account for it."[8]

Equiano was asking his European readers to project aspects of their imagined past selves into the void of their knowledge about Africa. He knew they could not understand his own Igbo-speaking people on Igbo ("Eboan") terms, because they had no idea what those terms were, and possibly no desire to know.[9] But just like Montaigne's "cannibals," the Igbos held within them a critical part of Europe's most authentic self. In the history of the circulation of images in and about Africa, this mode of interpretation consistently recurs: the substitution of what is familiar and internal for what is alien. Westerners' visualizations of Africa did this, and Africans' visualizations of Westerners did it too.

In the fullness of the West's nineteenth-century engagement with Africa, the slave era's harsh views were fragmented. Of the many varieties of observations that jostled against one another, several again reflected Montaigne's ironic reversal. It was maintained that Africans were children; that the present day in Africa was somehow the primitive past of the West; and yet, conversely, that the ancient history of Africa belonged to the biblical past of the West.[10] Wild men of the dark forests and magical pygmies were linked with lost Egyptian tribes and forgotten cities. Maybe, some imperialists thought, Africans could attain the same level of civilization as Europeans. Perhaps, however, others felt, they should be discouraged from wanting to. European theorists ranked subsets of humanity from fauna up to Caucasian, informing the evangelical and military engagement of Africans from Isandlhwana to Kumase.[11]

In all this mixed-up thinking, the images of Africans and Europeans both repelled one another and overlapped. The West's distancing of the image-Africa was met again and again by a sense of slippage toward it, or even a congruence with it. When one of Montaigne's "cannibals" was captured in internecine battle, he typically challenged his mortal enemies to eat him, taunting them that his own body had been nourished by the blood of his captors' ancestors. "These muscles. . . . Savor them well; you will find in them the taste of your own flesh," he would say.[12] Just as the absorbed ancestors of the cannibal's opponent were part of the very stuff of the cannibal, Montaigne finds traces of "our" (or at least his) ancestors inside the "savages." He announces "an amazing distance between their character and ours" and locates classical virtues in theirs, not ours. In the same way, Equiano, by asserting the Igbos' similarity to the Hebrews of antiquity, dared Europeans to savor "the taste of your own flesh." For if the past of the West was mixed with the present of Igboland, slavery was also a form of cannibalism. In the chapters to come, while images are shown to behave in all sorts of ways in all sorts of different situations in colonial and postcolonial Africa, this dizzying, self-devouring, "us-them" reversal recurs over and over again.

When Christian travelers encountered slave traders and plantations in Central and West Africa, they reacted in horror and attributed what they saw to an extreme "otherness" of essence, to the irreducibly "barbaric" character of "Arabs" (actually Swahili) or Africans. They did not know or did not credit that the slave trade and the importation of European firearms had destabilized new African polities; nor that the subsequent abolition of the Atlantic slave trade had cheapened slaves in Africa without shutting off their supply.[13] Toward the end of the nineteenth century, when the providential benefit of slavery in the Americas was no longer argued, Central Africa's garrisoned states and the incorporation of slave carriage into legitimate commerce in West Africa continued to reinforce European prejudices. All the while, Westerners accumulated a library of knowledge about Africa, developed ethnological comparisons, and applied their misprisions of Darwinism to them. As African identities were essentialized in terms drawn from the growing image-Africa of these paper representations, a science of bodies and races emerged and became a sourcebook of biological arguments for African inferiority. The "amazing distance" became a chronological gulf: Africans lived in a past era, which had accidentally been mislaid in the present.[14]

Such were the ideas and assertions of the learned. In comparison, the late Victorian public's ideas about Africa were probably more nuanced.[15] A host of material entered the corpus of the image-Africa as the nineteenth century drew to a close in the form of explorers' accounts, sentimental missionary vignettes, promotions, tales of hunting exploits, and yellow press reports of military campaigns, all aimed at the burgeoning middle class. Some of this reflected the concerns and ideas of Africans in an imprecise way, but not much. Once-popular accounts have today been forgotten: not only explorers and missionaries, but boys'-adventure writers (Rockwood, Henty, Lloyd, and other lesser lights) also "visited" Africa. Those authors who participated in inventing the modern best-seller are still remembered today. David Livingstone's *Missionary Travels and Adventures* sold 70,000 copies in 1857, and Henry Morton Stanley's *In Darkest Africa* sold 150,000 in its English 1890 edition alone. Teddy Roosevelt, Frederick Selous, and other hunters were widely read, and Rider Haggard's sensational novels, which drew on South African history, had a broad impact. Like Montaigne's Brazil, the image-Africa of Stanley and Haggard was at once part of Europe's glorious past and the antithesis of Europe's refined present.[16]

During the twentieth century, the "archive" of both visual and textual Africana grew, but the image-Africa became even simpler and flatter in its resonances. Edgar Rice Burroughs, one of the most successful novelists of his century, fixed the image of Africa in the American imagination as a jungle playground for masculine innocence. Laurens van der Post helped distill the modern image of the mystical Bushman as a sort of Jungian self of his white readers.[17] Despite the forward march of scholarship on Africa from the 1930s on, the Western public today is by and large left with decontextualized vision-bites of the continent and its peoples. Steamy jungle, arid savannah, Stanley and his bearers, Livingstone in a cauldron, the wise Bushman squinting in the Kalahari sun, bronze bodies, spears, lions, witch doctors and bones, tom-toms and war cries, wild-eyed rites and wildebeest on the plains, all hang in front of Africa like a theatrical scrim. They reproduce themselves over and over again, fade into the dark, the squalid, the starving child and the refugee camp, the irrational war cry, before returning in fresher forums: Saturday morning cartoons, *Star Wars* movies, and television commercials. The release and subsequent recollection of visual tropes replenish the tableau in an unending spectacular cycle of images already partially familiar to Western viewers.

Unlike the discursive field that "is" other parts of the imperial world—for instance, the Muslim Orient—the image-Africa lives on almost solely in picture form. This notwithstanding an African literary canon stretching back centuries in Sahelian, Sudanic, and coastal East Africa. The African "savage" is the inarticulate twin of overcivilized "man." North Africa, as an adjunct of the Mediterranean world, has been conspicuously excepted from this effect: in the Sahara, Beau Geste makes his way among all-too-human scoundrels, but in "darkest Africa," the society scion Greystoke grows up as a monosyllabic Tarzan of the apes.[18] In contrast to the cacophony of the bazaar and the music of the harem, sub-Saharan Africa appears muted and speechless, deriving almost entirely from descriptions *of* Africa and Africans, and pictures *of* Africa and Africans.[19]

Items of visual media were therefore critical to the image-Africa. Colonial-era cinema, stereoscopic slides, tobacco-package inserts, Senegalese postcards, *Tintin* comic strips, half-tone news photographs, colonial exhibitions, *Natural History Magazine*, animal trophies, and mounted spears and shields all informed it. The serious investigation of visual signs in the experience of colonialism has only just begun. Christraud Geary has written a pathbreaking study of photographs from the kingdom of Bamun, Cameroon, and Andrew Roberts has directed scholars' attention to photography in Africa as an historical source.[20] Annie Coombes has produced an innovative work on the evolution of Victorian and Edwardian modes of seeing Africa in museums and colonial exhibitions.[21] Jan Nederveen-Pieterse has written a general overview of images of Africa and African Americans, and James Ryan has published a history of photography in the British empire.[22] Pascal Blanchard and the Association Connaissance de l'histoire de l'Afrique contemporaine have archived, exhibited, and commented on colonial images throughout francophone Africa.[23] And as Pippa Skotnes discusses in this volume, her important exhibition *Miscast* visually deconstructed the conditions of the making of the peculiar South African "archive" that has kept Bushmen at "an amazing distance" for so long.[24]

Of course, even in a banal sense, as Ulf Hannerz writes, "distances, and boundaries, are not what they used to be."[25] High-speed travel, television, and the Internet have all trivialized "the distinction between the propagation of images or waves and that of objects or bodies."[26] And so Montaigne's "amazing distance" may be shrinking, too. Nowadays it is fashionable to claim alterity and similarity at one and the same time. Western television commercials are rife with South African Bushmen, elderly Australian Aboriginals, Tibetan monks, Vietnamese fishing people, Maasai and Ovahimba pastoralists, and so on, a particularly mediated form of "imagined nostalgia."[27] They proclaim the globalization of information and the (supposed) blurring of ethnic and class distinctions as they sing the praises of a software company, a cellular phone, or a sports utility vehicle. The effect is jocular, a disruption of visual knowledge, a "creolization" of the exotic. Have these insouciant people so consumed the culture of *their* alter-egos, that they have become them?[28] No. They are entirely *visual* beings, straight out of the pages of the *National Geographic* magazine in a pediatrician's waiting room. Their projection serves to hide the reliance of major manufacturers on the labor of their kind: cheap, brown-skinned, Third World. Thus once again images of people in the postcolony serve as interfaces for an oscillation of perspective, from one end to the other of the "amazing difference": from alterity, to shared identity, and back again.

Of course, while there is always an "us" and "them," neither pronoun stands consistently on any one side of a permanent divide. Us and them change their shapes with the ingestion and expulsion of all sorts of constellations of people.[29] The chapters in this volume deliberately consider Africans' images alongside Europeans', but also quite varied Africans' descriptions, interpretations, and distributions of images among themselves—both within and beyond the venues provided by colonial and postcolonial state structures. None of our essays make the mistake of assuming the primacy of "ethnicity" for Africans' identities; nor do any of them treat Africans' creativity or responsiveness as somehow discernibly "African."

BRIDGING AFRICAN ART

"No poem is intended for the reader, no picture for the beholder, no symphony for the listener," Walter Benjamin wrote.[30] It should be obvious to all that Africans have a long history of art and aesthetics behind them, whether Westerners have understood them or not. Saharan sandstone bas-reliefs, Nok statuary from Nigeria, and rock paintings and the Lydenberg heads from South Africa all instantiate traditions that can no longer be comprehended in their original circumstances. And even when we turn to African art being produced today, it still must be faced that the situation of its widest public, who are upper-middle-class Westerners, obscures the dense cluster of meanings in much of it. Africans' images can never simply be addressed "on their own terms," since those terms do not readily present themselves. Art is a compression of culture. It is no surprise that anthropologists use terms like "translation" or even "conversion" to describe the process of committed scholarly engagement with another culture, of imagining (in Paul Ricoeur's phrase) "oneself as another."[31] The process seems so absolutely improbable.

What about attending to unknowable forms in the medium of one's own culture? Since this is what we all do, it must be a genuine form of appreciation! With hindsight, it is clear that mistakes have been made. As Annie Coombes has pointed out, African art is a fairly new category. Until recently masks and staffs and other "ritual objects" were housed in ethnographic collections like the Horniman, the Pitt-Rivers, and the Mayer museums, and a body of knowledge was created through them. Since the regrouping of such artifacts as "art," Western art historians have produced new insights, and the essays in this book draw on them. Even the now outmoded framework of "tribal" art has permitted knowledge that no serious student of visuality can reject. And while the simple attribution of artistic styles to ethnic groups may be unsupportable, one can presently speak of Yoruba or Chokwe sculptural trends, just as of Flemish or Venetian art traditions.[32] The idea of an African art history also serves to alert us that most of the illustrations in this book show objects of (sometimes considerable) monetary value. Images are not only cherished for what they signify. In this sense, if in no other, paintings, sculptures, and photographs may well be approached together as artworks.

Nonetheless this book does not approach images as art per se. Nor is there any comparison of African art with European art in the following chapters, and the reader may well wonder why. The reason is that neither the things Westerners see as art in Africa, nor the processes that give rise to them, share a single coherent status in Africa. One of our contributors addressed this problem some years ago in an excellent review essay.[33] By examining various social-science approaches to African art, Paula Ben-Amos (Girshick) raised the question of what it is exactly that has tied together African art as a category of study. After all, as V. Y. Mudimbe remarks, "what is called African art covers a wide range of objects introduced into a historicizing perspective of European values since the eighteenth century."[34] In most cases, Western collectors not only appropriated African objets d'art in the figurative sense but did so literally as well. In its curatorial organization, the African art museum, like the ethnographic collection before it, corresponds less to any African category than to the history of colonial expropriation. It offers its audience, in Maurice Merleau-Ponty's words, "a false consciousness, a thief's consciousness."[35] The film *Les statues meurent aussi* (1953) criticized the expropriation and exhibition of Malian statues in Western museums and was censored by the French government in 1955. Mali is still suffering from the rampant thievery of its art works from archaeological sites today.[36] As if to obscure such provenance, collections of African art were given coherence under the rubric "primitivism" (a synonym for "colonized"), an ideology which reached its apogee in the early 1980s. Many holdings still have no other unity now, even as the principles of "authentic primitive art" collapse.

It may be that the West's classification of forms in African art can only proceed by ignoring the content of that art. In a recent essay, Mamadou Diawara traces the African art object from its web of "libation, sacrifice, prayer" to its *re-sacralization* in the "temple" of the museum; there it is revealed in "the new ritual, that of being shown." In Bamako, Mali, the local museum cannot fully achieve this transformation, and many Mande people are afraid to visit it: they do not just see a mask, they are sucked into its world. Diawara's keen insight is that the aesthetic love of "culture," as an object, only commences when the terrors generated from within the culture subside.[37] On the other hand, we must not view such meanings as "mystical" or "fetishistic." The assignation of "religion" to the making of art follows only from the derisory view that all precolonial African practices are somehow religious. Descriptions such as "ritual object," "occult figure," and most of all "fetish," often mean nothing more than that art collectors had little idea how objects were supposed to be used.[38] The way in which religion is supposed to have infused African culture is precisely how Leo Frobenius, the influential German anthropologist and photographer, saw *art* as "manifest in every aspect" of African culture.[39] In such arguments what is being remarked upon is nothing more than the inappropriateness of a category. At the same time, as Nelson Graburn, Bennetta Jules-Rosette, and others have demonstrated, the inappropriate category "art" has midwived the vocation of African tourist-artists with their copious output.[40]

The unfittingness of Western categories—such as "art"—has been apprehended both by anthropologists and Africanist art historians. Robert Farris Thompson promulgated the recognition that "African art" was something in motion, alive, with duration and rhythm, not something contemplated at a viewer's leisure. Johannes Fabian and Ilona Szombati-Fabian adopted the concept of "genre" from folklore in order to surmount the aestheticizing implication of "art" and to accentuate the ramifications of audiences. In a brave and insouciant little book, David Hecht and A. Maliqalim Simone represent similar material as "African micropolitics."[41] Henry and Margaret Drewal have discussed the performance of beholding art in Africa, which underlines the fact that quietly lighting a mask behind a piece of plexiglass falsifies the piece itself. Zoe Strother has recently emphasized the history of Pende dance over the history of transitions in the visual forms of masks, and this in a book called *Inventing Masks*.[42] Mary Jo Arnoldi and Kris Hardin opted to shift the field of inquiry from art to "material culture." Susan Vogel, who long held the formalists' position that there are indeed universal criteria for judging quality in all art, rejected in her show *Africa Explores* the usual distinction between colonial, hybrid pieces and "authentic," precolonial pieces created by tribes in pristine styles. In her more recent show on Baulé (Côte d'Ivoire) art, Vogel advocated contextualizing African art in local African aesthetic systems. Visitors were alerted to the privilege of seeing certain objects when they encountered rooms "restricted" to viewers of only one sex, or glimpsed a mask in the semi-darkness. Her award-winning book *Baulé* fosters a productive tension between Western aesthetic description and such very different sorts of evaluations by Baulé informants.[43]

Such a dynamic may nonetheless still conceal problematic hierarchies, in which African aesthetics are "regional" or "traditional," and Western tastes are universal. As Anthony Appiah points out, the attribution of cosmopolitanism to market-driven Western curators is hilariously undercut by their own narrow-minded statements.[44] Mudimbe directly addresses the problem of "popular art" within curatorial frameworks in his book *The Idea of Africa,* and shows how standard classifications have little room for the African artist as metacritic. For instance, Marshall W. Mount distinguishes among traditional, Christian-influenced, tourist, and high art of modern technique. Noting that Mount's taxonomy is based on inconsistent criteria, beginning with the notion of "authentic" art, Mudimbe argues instead that there are three contemporary trends: art inspired by tradition ("to bring the past among us"), art searching for a "modern aesthetic," and popular art, which *reinterprets* the high culture behind the first two, commenting upon it for the benefit of local patrons. One thinks of the wall murals of Dakar, which blend images of the Statue of Liberty with an iconified image of the Mouride *tariqa* founder Amadou Bamba. Or the vernacular concrete sculptures fronting *asafo* women's cults in Ghana. Or paintings in Kinshasa and Lubumbashi that depict scenes of martyrdom, resistance heroes, and deities of wealth and good fortune. One thinks of painted backdrops to West African studio portraits or movie posters; ribald cartoons in the opposition newspapers of Douala, Cameroon; and Koffi Kouakou's witty carvings of lap-top computers and shoes.[45] All of which, more or less, comment on the death of authenticity.

It is not hard to think of examples of African art that confound even Mudimbe's classification: Koffi Kouakou, for example, sells his carvings in the international marketplace; and what do we make of the appropriation of African barbershop signs and other ordinary objects by collectors? But let us agree with Mudimbe that the aesthetic hierarchies into which African art has been projected foreclose on potential understandings of it. The trouble is not that Africans have no idea what art is, nor is it appropriate to say the European concept of art is too limited for what Africans do.[46] It is only that the exhibitory view of art, from decoration to subversion, a painted rose to a Marcel Duchamps urinal, is not a good definition of what we are interested in here.

We require a different framework altogether with which to hold together our various discussions of European and African image-making. How might we view the production of popular comics in Kinshasa, Congo (Nancy Hunt, this volume), which stand in tension with Western comic strips and yet follow their markets?[47] The resemblance of Manjaco grave posts to caricatures of colonial officials (Eric Gable)? The great importance that indigent women in Dakar attribute to photos of themselves arrayed in the finest borrowable *couture* (Hudita Mustafa), or the mockery of the innovative court carvers in the Edo Kingdom of Benin (Paula Girshick)? The only coherent framework for Xhosa grave sites (David Bunn), typological colonial photography (Paul Landau), the commercial products set on shrines of Mami Wata (Henry Drewal), and the filmed gestures of Bushmen in game preserves (Robert Gordon) is that they all deal with visual phenomena.[48] And so it is good to ask what a visual representation is—especially in a cross-cultural context such as this book.

THE NATURE OF THE IMAGE IN DIVERSE SETTINGS

"Let us take Africa as she is, and try and see what her people are like. She has no smooth and easy history, each race has its past. What is this history? Not being set down in writing, documents for our information are lacking," says a 1957 photo album, a *Guide Bleu* for French Africana.[49] Where we lack written history, it says, where we find silence in Africa, we can rely on pictures, which can somehow tell us even about the history of something as intangible as a "race." Can pictures indeed speak so meaningfully to us? What do they say?

In order to answer such questions, we must begin by noting that resemblance and signification are separate concepts. A painting, for instance, shows a woman in tears. Whether she is part of an advertisement for antihistamines or a condemned sixteenth-century Italian noblewoman is secondary. The standard theoretical treatment in this regard is C. S. Peirce's distinction between the index, the symbol, and the icon. The first of these, the *index*, is a contiguous form of signification. It is motional, causal, or gestural: the sign emanates, as a trace or pointer, from what it denotes, and so can be read back to it.[50] In this volume, a small graveyard near Albany in the Eastern Cape indexes the plight of white settlers (David Bunn); animal trophies and ethnographic photographs index game and people (Paul Landau), and resin body casts (Pippa Skotnes) both index and resemble the African women's bodies from which they were made.[51] *Symbolic* signification, the second type, is a matter of arbitrary assignment. In writing and speech, meaning is conveyed simply through habitualized conventions: there is no necessary bond between the sounds pronouncing the word "table" and a table, and it is only through past usages that the relationship has come to be. Finally, in contrast to both indexing and conventional symboling, pictorial or *iconic* signs are held to work by resembling what they denote. They share visual properties with what they sign for: Adam's hand on the ceiling of the Sistine Chapel looks like a hand, and a thirteenth-century Ife bronze head looks like a head.

As it happens, this tripartite distinction has been seriously questioned. Peirce himself recognized the complex interplay between these modes and draws a distinction between resemblance and signification: when that bird pecked at Xeuxis's famous painting of a bunch of grapes, it was acting out of hunger, not aesthetic admiration.[52] Some critics have then proceeded to argue that icons actually operate in much the same way as conventional symbols do. An early move toward such a position came with Erwin Panofsky's influential critique of perspectival representation; he suggested that perspective was merely a symbolic convention for representing depth, and not a copy of the real. Ernst Gombrich expanded the ramifications of the view in his celebrated treatise on the "language of art." When one looks carefully at that language, he argued, the distinction between "natural" (iconic) and "arbitrary" (symbolic) signs breaks down.[53] In Gombrich's view, it is, for example, necessary to learn the conventions inhering in sculpture before being able to recognize even Michelangelo's *David*. Art functions by relying on visual "terms of art": one must know the "language" of picturing for a given genre before one can see what is actually pictured. The learning process is often hidden in culture and goes largely unnoticed.

The same argument has also been extended to photographs: their apparent realism has been considered by some scholars to be purely a product of convention.[54] Often enough, when scholars have questioned the transcultural "transparency" of photography, and even the idea that photographs signify through resemblance, they have looked for evidence in colonial contexts—such as Africa. Following Gombrich's *Art and Illusion*, M. H. Segall, D. T. Campbell, and M. J. Herskovits together reviewed visual perception among "primitive people" in 1966. Because primitives often cannot interpret what photographs signify without being shown how, they reasoned, it follows that photographs must employ arbitrary conventions that Westerners have naturalized among themselves. Similarly, noting that "primitive" peoples who had never seen photographs apparently do not know what to make of them, Nelson Goodman argues that the photographic sign must be deciphered like any other. In a widely cited article, Allan Sekula again has recourse to Herskovits's examples to make the same point: the photograph is an arbitrary sign.[55]

Wherever we come down on the question of whether Africans could or could not read "naturalistic" visual signs before being habituated to them, however, *the debates themselves* naturalize a host of imbalances in colonial and postcolonial relationships. Even as their results revealed that key aspects of iconic signification are themselves really matters of politics, custom, and culture, the experiments undertaken by Herskovits and his colleagues prefigured colonized people as people who lacked, and therefore could highlight, something called "naturalistic conventions." But as W. J. T. Mitchell tells us, the very idea of natural (iconic) signification may have been elaborated at least partly in opposition to the category "non-Western art," "ritual objects of pagan, primitive cultures . . . [in their] 'stylized' or 'conventional' modes." In interpreting Africans' imagery as "ritualistic," Mitchell suggests, Westerners call attention to what they cannot recognize in themselves. He argues in effect that "spirits" are hidden in the highly mimetic images so common in the West. The "natural sign" is a fetish or an idol, in the same way that some African sculptures, which provoked charged behaviors in their home environments, were understood as fetishes by Western collectors (more about this below).[56] The edifice of nature (icon) versus culture (conventional symbol) has effectively blocked out more interesting questions of power, politics, and thought in the colonial world.

Consider three short examples concerning the relationship between imagery and money. One: A missionary in the 1870s wrote that many black South Africans felt of the queen of England that "she can only be an image on the money . . . not a real person." What were the roots of those doubts? Is it justifiable even to consider what they might be, without looking at the meanings of British sterling as it cropped up on the Highveld after the opening of the diamond fields at Kimberley? Two: A schoolboy named Anton Lembede, later the intellectual leader of the African National Congress Youth League in South Africa, wrote an "essay on money" in about 1927, saying: "Money is a small coin, a small wheel bearing the picture of the King's head. Round this head is an inscription—head of the King of England—George V. You can go to any store. If you present this coin the storekeeper gives you whatever you want."[57] Here the head of the king becomes a kind of passbook, and text validates image. The young Lembede understood commerce as a form of social regulation. Is this relevant to his notion of "naturalism"? Three: In the 1990s, platinum miners in South Africa claimed that some of their co-workers were disappearing underground and resurfacing after several weeks with mysterious "writing" on their bodies. A mine spirit had fed them "clay," which X rays revealed in picture form; the writing instructed mine authorities to release them and pay them a generous severance package. Now, in one sense, the ideas about photographic truth and captions in this example are simple misunderstandings about X rays and silicosis. Is it important here that there was a massive strike at the same mine shortly after the interview invoking these claims was recorded?[58]

The idea that Africans, Melanesians, and Aboriginals can reveal the hidden mechanisms of Western representation because they "have" or "do not have" certain aptitudes thus needs to be joined to another fact. The West has muted, observed, put to work, and classified those peoples, and rarely engaged them as equals. In South Africa, the "National Institute for Personnel Research" showed photographs to "illiterate, relatively primitive Africans" in order to see whether they could estimate three-dimensional distances; its conclusion was that Africans and Indians lacked "pictorial depth perception" because of "cultural" reasons.[59] This is balderdash. When colonial power is naturalized, the "primitive" visual sense is wrongly imagined to be some sort of definable category—one that is, tellingly, cultish and overschooled and naïve and unschooled all at the same time.[60]

Power is therefore hidden in "ways of seeing." Pierre Bourdieu has further argued that the license to appreciate and evaluate the worth of images in the Western world—in other words, the exercise of taste—is surreptitiously determined by the viewer's class status. In this view, an investment in an expropriated mask or statue and the sentiment that a photograph of African girls is a good one, both serve materialist interests. Status and privilege, according to Bourdieu, continue to affect all subsequent meanings for such images in the West, even subversive ones. By way of illustration here, we might think of the immense differences among various "tribal masks," the statuary in the Musée de l'Homme in Paris, and the semi-nude Senegalese girls in Edmond Fortier's photographs. All these influenced Pablo Picasso in his painting of *Les Demoiselles d'Avignon* (1907). Picasso "understood" them as signifying together, coherently: they meant the reverse of bourgeois refinement, the exaltation of sexual license. Ninety years later, the magical mask in Jim Carrey's lowbrow film *The Mask* (1997) means much the same thing. Such consistency derives from the perpetuation of colonial and class relations to the present era.[61]

Bourdieu has got hold of a large truth, but the relationships between interpretation and power in Africa were and are, often, more multisided than his analysis suggests. A central question of this volume is how we can begin to understand the jostling between the various realms of collection and approval that competed with one another: sacred and profane (Bunn, Skotnes, Drewal, Gordon, Gable); ethnographic, reportorial, and artistic (Girshick, Olaniyan, Landau, Skotnes, Gordon); even authentic and kitsch (Hodeir, Hunt, Drewal). All of the essays in this book pay attention to the particular political contexts of ways of seeing in Africa. The first two, "'Our Mosquitoes Are Not So Big,'" by Tim Burke, and "The Sleep of the Brave," by David Bunn—chapters 1 and 2—treat aspects of the variances in interpretations of shared images and intertwined signs, in southern African settler colonies.

In both the Eastern Cape and in Southern Rhodesia, power and status were ultimately mortal worries for much of the population. Burke examines the relationships among images, advertising, and refigurations of "modernity" in the latter (today's Zimbabwe). He reveals the considerable effort that businesses made to figure out the ways whites and Africans would react to commercial advertisements. The picture of an infant on Stork Margarine wrappers, for instance, was apparently understood by some Africans to indicate that the product contained baby fat. Whites reacted nervously to such "mistakes," since they pointed out something disturbing about their own taken-for-granted world: the "public slippage between the surface of things" and what lay underneath. Different periods saw different theories of African perception; Colgate and Raleigh and Bayer influenced Africans and, in turn, reacted to them. Advertisers' accounts of "African" interpretations were not neutral, if only because they displaced whites' recognitions of the seductive danger of images in their own lives. By rooting iconography in economic and social relationships, Burke usefully reproblematizes the idea of "difference" between the visual senses (and sensibilities) of Africans and Europeans.

David Bunn argues that the interplay of tombs and gravesites formed a history of competing "sepulchral representations" on the very landscape of the Eastern Cape. The modes of burial and the means of memorialization used by Xhosa and by settlers were in constant dialogue with one another, just as in the case of black and white Zimbabweans' mutual misinterpretations. In the course of the violent colonial history of the eighteenth- and nineteenth-century Eastern Cape, English settlers dislodged graves from their "illocutionary" places in Xhosa memory and made them into spatial markers. Along the way, Bunn argues, Xhosa people's perceptions of the indexes and icons of death also transformed settlers' perceptions. Here no one could mistake perception for a value-free activity. Opposing alliances of men sought to protect, respect, make visible, hide, or ruin burial places and graves; they defiled and inscribed corpses, painted burial mounds for reproduction in alarmist English journals, and made soldiers into bas-relief miniatures cut in stone. Focusing especially on representations of the death of the Xhosa chief Sandile, Bunn demonstrates that the fury of Africans, and of whites, paradoxically created a cross-talk of informed interpretation, not only about new representational forms, but about authority, pollution, and citizenship.

IMAGE AND TEXT

Burke and Bunn show how habituations to representational conventions have had contested and turbulent histories. Yet, as I have pointed out, iconicity also has a rather passive, objective dimension, that of *resemblance*. It is possible for a small child to be "fooled" by a wax figure, or for a first-time spectator to be nauseated by the roller-coaster ride in the pioneering film *Cinerama*. Even if the conventions of painting, film, or sculpture need to be learned, visual mimesis may still be self-evident. Panofsky recognized the necessity of distinguishing between illusion and symboling, and separated the initial denotation of an image, which he called "pre-iconographic," from the reading of conventions that relate it to specific themes. "Signifying" in this view depends on experience. Consider the following vignette, reported by Henry Methuen, a traveler in Bechuanaland in the 1840s: "[T]here were in Mr. Moffat's house two good likenesses of himself and his lady, on first beholding which, the Bechuanas were struck with amazement; saying that they were glad that the originals of the pictures were both present else they should have concluded that these were their ghosts, or their skins stuffed."[62]

The contemplation of pictures by Tswana ("Bechuana") observers in this example cannot be disentangled from the prestige of Robert and Mary Moffat, the white missionaries, the assertion of status involved in displayed portraits, and the condescension of Methuen's reportage. Yet the Tswana were in fact unfamiliar with the portrait as a thing in itself. While they at once noted some kind of resemblance to the Moffats, it is by no means clear that they fathomed the general situation of the images at all. These Tswana had never encountered a surface as a fragment of dimensional space, but they had encountered John and Mary Moffat.[63] The essence of the mimetic image, this distinction has been called its "double reality," in that it is simultaneously a part of a plane, and a section of real space.[64]

In the situation described above, Methuen perhaps tried to tell the Tswana what the pictures were. Text or voice can indeed substitute for experience and can convert resemblance into representation—turning, in other words, Panofsky's "pre-iconographic" denotation into iconography.[65] In this case, "European painters have this skill" or "the Moffats sat for a long time while they were copied" was very likely given in explanation. Mark Twain, having seen Guido Reni's painting of a sixteenth-century Italian noblewoman, *Beatrice Cenci the Day before Her Execution*, commented: "It shows what a label can do. If [observers] did not know the picture, they would inspect it unmoved, and say, 'Young girl with hay fever; young girl with her head in a bag.'"[66] For Twain, as for the Tswana, the text in the painting's label elevated what could already be distinguished in some fashion, to a more specific variety of sign. The picture's meaning would otherwise have been guesswork.

In this volume, chapters 3 and 4 offer extended analyses of iconic media that make no bones about relying on text: political cartoons and comic strips (in French, *bandes dessinées* or "BDs"). Along the way, their authors, Nancy Hunt and Tejumola Olaniyan, confound any attempt to distinguish African from European forms of representation. While recently in Nairobi, in a rather dingy local travel agency, I found myself staring at a poster: "Remember your first time in Africa?" it asked, above a picture of a lad paging through *Tintin au Congo*. Nancy Hunt takes on this tiny giant in *"Tintin* and the Interruptions of Congolese Comics," placing her discussion in opposition to the suggestion Deborah Kaspin and I sent to our contributors (which was to focus on a "single locale [and] two forms of representation").[67] Instead, she describes BDs as a single medium, a complex, transnational social and historical field, with a core vocabulary that has proved remarkably able to traverse multiple locales. Congolese illustrators appropriated elements of Hergé's *Tintin*, and especially the famous *Tintin au Congo*; and Hunt traces an uneven trajectory through Kinshasa painting, postwar Congolese-drawn BDs such as *Mbumbula* and *Mbu and Mpia*, to the international success of Chéri Samba's paintings and Barly Baruti's BD, *"Eva K,"* and the low-end street BDs in Lingala.

Almost by definition, comics include text. Printed words identifying the funny brown characters in *Tintin au Congo* as Africans could not prevent some Congolese/Zaireans from identifying with Tintin and putting his perspective to new uses. On the other hand, by fixing meaning in an image, text can greatly reduce the free play of its interpretation. After all, the very word "stereotype" comes from the plate that laid down print on the pages of newspapers like *La Croix du Congo* and the *West African Pilot,* an important Nigerian newspaper. Tejumola Olaniyan argues that the consuming fervor of "the mirror stage of nationalism" drove the prodigious output of the *Pilot*'s cartoonist, Akinola Lasekan. On behalf of the National Council of Nigeria and the Cameroons (NCNC), Lasekan evolved an accessible style derived almost entirely from European and American newspapers of the 1930s and 1940s; ironically enough in light of European perceptions of Nigerian sculpture, Lasekan explained his choice with the remark "African people seem to prefer realistic art." Quite unlike Hergé, who adopted the minstrelsy rubrics of the same era (what Hunt calls "a global iconography used to depict black people"), Lasekan employed a heavy-lined "graphic realism," in Olaniyan's words, another sort of global iconography, to economize on his use of text and further bring home his meaning. What strikes me is how relentlessly mythified Lasekan's symbology nonetheless was, how much it relied on clichés. Even when he labels a figure "Zik," for the NCNC leader Azikiwe, the figure is also a shepherd threatening to abandon his flock. The United Africa Company's comic strips were technically derivative and reactionary but were filmic and narrative. Lasekan spoke in stylized visual proverbs, in a suitable international style.

OSCILLATIONS AND IDENTITY

Iconic images do not dictate to us. As Twain's remark about Guido Reni's painting shows, the conceit that titles are irrelevant to the expressive message of artworks is a pretense of high art. Captions at the bottom of lowly news photographs are even more important.[68] Even if we accept purely iconic signification as a theoretical possibility, it is awfully rare in practice. Museums have wall text, comics have dialogue, photographs have eager owners, paintings have titles, video has sound—and experts are always ready with narratives and theories. Nor is it only through conventional (vocal or alphabetic) signification that viewers are aided in interpreting images: indexical elements offer less obvious help. Knowing that a Rockefeller *called* an African mask "art," like knowing that a Rockefeller *donated* a Rothko to an exhibition, at least disposes audiences to pay attention. In photography, blurring or strobe-light effects (and in film, slow motion) do not accord with the perception of moving subjects, but they come from the circumstances of visual capture and so add "realism." Rosalind Krauss has even argued that the photograph is fundamentally an indexical sign, not an iconic one. In her view, the "quasi-tautological" relationship it posits between signified and signifier mandates textual captions to a far greater degree than painting, which more easily accommodates visual symbols.[69]

The trouble is, when an image is passed from situation to situation, from predicament to predicament, the conventional signs that once went with it fall by the wayside. A common feature of many of the visual signs discussed in this book is their mobility. Chapters 5 through 8 focus on images especially as they were shifted away from their original performative or ceremonial context. As they entered alien circuits of information and exchange, images often arrived without any linguistic accompaniment.[70] In fact, when observers adjusted and manipulated the identity of represented figures, they relied on the relative mobility of images, and the relative immobility of signifiers that worked by convention. It was the momentary parting of resemblance, or "mimesis," from signification, which allowed an image to be invested with relevance, and often, with key parts of the observer's own world.

Chapters 5 through 8 all treat this process in one way or another. They each discuss the relationship between mimetic representation, and the construction of dialogues between the self and the "other." In chapter 5, "Empires of the Visual" (Paul Landau), I contextualize the production of colonial photographs of Africans in the political economy of indirect rule. I argue that hunting and shooting established a technology and a discourse that subsequently accommodated the visual typing of African ethnic groups. The catalogue of recognizable peoples that informed colonial administrations operated largely, I suggest, through distance, which allowed Europeans to project various qualities into images. The "realism" of colonial photography was itself colored by the *practice* of photography, which changed from something that happens in a studio to something that happens "instantly" at the hands of the shooter. Instant "capture" furthermore reinforced the indexical character of the chemical reaction that froze the visible world on film and vouchsafed its reality.

The indexical nature of photography can itself even become a trope for verification. In southern Africa, the concept of the "photo" can express facticity even when no specific photograph exists. Photos have become stand-ins in important ceremonies for distant kin or friends.[71] In one southern African account of Luther's objections to Catholicism that I know of, Luther "took a bottle of ink and threw it in the Pope's direction," a notion which nicely captures the centrality of text in the Reformation, but the proof that the ink stained the wall was "some of the people have a photograph."[72] The leader of the "Ghathlian Church," a small movement in the 1920s in South Africa, wrote in a letter to the editor of *The Negro World*: "All I [can] do is to spread the opinion of the United Negro Improvement Association and get books of its photos to spread this spirit of the new Negro."[73]

Once the truth claims of photography had been advanced, they could also be manipulated. The same Mark Twain who noted the indeterminacy of Guido Reni's painting—a histamine attack or grief—in 1905 extolled the reportorial power of the photograph in a satirical pamphlet, *King Leopold's Soliloquy*, in which Leopold blames the exposure of his tyranny in the Congo on "the incorruptible *Kodak*... the only witness I have encountered that I couldn't bribe."[74] Yet the Portuguese government supplied dozens of photographs to its pavilions in the 1931 Paris Colonial Exposition, illustrating the wonderful benefits of Portuguese colonialism in Angola and Mozambique. A careful reading of the pictures reveals children working in a cigarette factory and a somber African driving a tractor over an already-harvested field.[75] In Ghana, portrait photographers supply elaborate backdrops, painted with television consoles, refrigerators, or fancy cars, not as visual trickery but to supply "a mask of cool."[76]

In this volume, chapter 6, "Portraits of Modernity," recounts the manipulations of photography in the latter sort of context. There are, as of yet, very few histories of ordinary Africans' creation and deployment of photographs.[77] In Dakar, as Hudita Mustafa shows us, women go to extraordinary lengths to create images of themselves wearing expensive, often borrowed, clothing. They strike poses aimed at projecting a precise form of double in the frame of the photograph, so that a poor woman can "look like the President's wife."[78] Mustafa's analysis suggests that in these staged photos, several interpretations of women find concurrent expression: as objects of male desire, bearers of patriarchal decorum and prestige, and at the same time, independent and competitive individuals. In West Africa generally, "there is a strong tradition of remembering events by clothes and clothes by photographs," and photographers often start out as tailors.[79] The "double reality" of photographs is manipulated, and the photograph as a façade indexes another façade: dress. In the same vein, we might think of the Bamun king Njoya's wearing of locally manufactured German uniforms and Hausa royal garb; of South African "Zionist" Christians' adaptations of clerks' uniforms; or even African youth's T-shirts emblazoned with pictures of their heroes. All are assumptions of the signs of power.[80] When Dakar women "dress" themselves photographically, when they distance themselves from their daily lives in images, they create alter-ego selves.

In order to draw conclusions about the intention of signs—to make signification out of resemblance—we need as many clues as possible. The elements of a Kuba statue that make it *of a king* are akin to the title that explained Guido Reni's painting to Mark Twain; those elements are located in a visual vocabulary of Kuba conventions, which may or may not be intelligible in a museum, depending on the "reading" knowledge of the beholder. In any and all cases, however, the elements of the nose, mouth, and eyes, the relationship between the position and shape of the limbs, all correspond to a person's body rather more closely than a cooking pot, a cat, or a mountain. The images and indexical signs of Africa pitched and rolled in oceans of speech, were hung in cathedrals of text, and winked and vanished in great tapestries of historical knowledge; but in the absence or mistaking of such contexts, interpretation nevertheless proceeded apace. The results have sometimes been astonishing. A Kongo *nkisi* became an African fetish on a Portuguese slaving ship, an ethnographic item in a museum of natural history, and a work of art in a gallery. Leonardo's *Last Supper* has been copied and recopied in Africa by hand and in halftone: versions of it hang in the homes of strict Methodists in South African townships and grace the rear of dozens of Nigerian buses. The first Apollo landing stimulated "trucker gossip" in the Tio kingdom that "the Americans" were going to hide the moon with a Coca-Cola sign and disrupt human and natural fertility: a prescient understanding, given the numbing ubiquity of Coke signs in Africa today. In these cases, previous usages are reworked in a way that erases the distinction between misprision and evaluation.[81]

The unfamiliar is not only malleable but also potent. A picture of a Sri Lankan may speedily take on deep meaning for a Ghanaian Twi-speaker. A note written in Sinhala (a Sri Lankan language) could not do this—even if the Twi-speaker knew as little of the intentions of the writer as of the colorist. Icons are polysemic: their resembling aspect is itself what allows interpretations to differ from one another, and sometimes to oppose one another. Much like ideologies, icons weave different audiences together and link mutually incompatible interpretations, all of which will be held to be legitimate. Such is one theme in chapter 7, "Mami Wata and Santa Marta," by Henry Drewal. A successful German circus master and keeper of exotic beasts, Carl Hagenbeck, included in his show a woman from the "East," possibly a Sri Lankan. Hagenbeck had a chromolithograph made of her as an Oriental snake charmer. The picture reached West Africa, where many people apparently understood it as a reflection of something they already knew, a deity of personal ambition. This "Mami Wata" was associated with foreigners and water, and so fish, and via synecdoche, snakes. In making the snake charmer picture their own, Twi-speakers (among others) subsequently reimaged Mami Wata in its form. If the lithograph had been but a written text, no West African could have appropriated even part of its meaning without a translation. The history of the chromolithograph involves a break in the continuity of text and speech, while history of the idea of Mami Wata connects ever-new speakings with metamorphosing images. The picture of Hagenbeck's employee was but one: Drewal ends his chapter by considering her American incarnation, Santa Marta.[82]

Recall Montaigne's "amazing distance." Seeing a picture of a Sri Lankan snake charmer as Mami Wata required such a distance from Ceylonese-looking people. Seeing a picture, or a woman, as "an African" similarly relied on distancing, since otherwise such a picture would resolve into a more particular identity. Indeed, generic African identities were and are supplied to Western consumers merely by recycling their prior gleanings of the image-Africa. States and businesses have choreographed spectacles (Hodeir) and distributed caricatures (Hunt), required performances of "public transcripts" (Landau) and overt role-playing (Burke).[83] Perception was inseparable from power, which is what decided which Africans were "authentic" representatives of their kind, and which were "bad copies" of others (Gable). In chapter 8, "Captured on Film," Robert Gordon discusses the way that Khoe and San speakers in southern Africa have, for so long, performed the role of "Bushmen." Gordon moves from the era of German photographic ethnography in the nineteenth century, through the filmed "Denver Africa Expedition" of 1925, to N!xao's starring role in the 1981 film *The Gods Must Be Crazy*.[84] Because the expressive "dance" is a critical mode of being and expression among many Kalahari-dwellers, Gordon uses it as a metaphor to argue that the people labeled "Bushmen" have long participated—for better or worse—in performing their filmic, doppelgänger selves. In other words, Bushmen improvise steps in a negotiated choreography. Like impoverished people in the way of tourists all over the world, they conduct interpretations of their lives toward the learnt idea of authenticity in order to survive in an inauthentic world.

EXHIBITIONS AND INSTALLATIONS

The frequent imposition of identity in the colonial milieu relied on more than the fact that representations of Africans did not simply "work" by resembling something else. In any environment in which people have power over those they depict, identity is a critical node of struggle and compromise. Perhaps such struggle can most clearly be seen in colonial "theater," in which living Africans themselves (who clearly resemble Africans!) can be representations of identities that they are supposed to hold "naturally," but do not. In chapters 9 and 10, Catherine Hodeir and Pippa Skotnes discuss the relationships between exhibition and mimesis in the charged contexts of colonial and postcolonial politics. Like Gordon, Hodeir describes a situation in which Africans *perform* Europeans' prior ideas of them. In her chapter, "Decentering the Gaze at French Colonial Exhibitions," she shows us how Senegalese men and women portrayed the "Senegalese" of the image-Africa in the Paris exhibitions of 1889 and in 1931. They occupied Hollywood-lot "streets" and proto-Disney confabulations of West African architectural styles; they acted out the ideology of primitivism and innocence, and, as seamlessly as possible, the ameliorative effects of the French civilizing mission. The collective narrative resulted from careful performances by Africans in Paris who rode the metro and took cigarette breaks. Hodeir focuses on the exhibitions from several angles, revealing the motives and methods of their construction, and undermining their iconography in the process.

In chapter 10, "The Politics of Bushman Representations," Pippa Skotnes writes retrospectively as the curator of the most controversial post-apartheid museum exhibition, "Miscast: Negotiating the Presence of the San." The visual displays in the exhibit were recontextualized into widely varying discourses, including acclaim, complaint, humility, irritation, and trauma. One person's view that a picture was of a "bandit," another's that it was of a "victim," and a third's that it was "of a /Xam forager" might each be defended.[85] In critiques at the time, even rare considerations of Skotnes's intention as the artist in no way hindered people's interpretations of her work as they saw fit. In her own thinking, Skotnes was influenced by Lucy Lloyd, a nineteenth-century linguist who collaborated in transcribing /Xam myths and traditions; and in her essay here, Skotnes juxtaposes Lloyd's archive with the museological and medical "archive" of body castings, artifacts, and brutal photographs of "Bushmen." But in the wake of "Miscast," Skotnes was herself accused of imposing an externally derived identity on "Bushmen," either that of victim or sensual object.

Skotnes herself is forced to conclude that she could not predetermine all the meanings her installation would convey. As we have seen, such changefulness is a general feature of images as they cross borders. Suggestions that a figure is an Igbo Mbari statue or a god of thunder do not rule out its reading as a white colonial officer. A "Kota" reliquary figure appears both in a dark corner of a men's association in Gabon and a street vendor's spread in front of the Museum of Modern Art in New York.[86] Because images involve both resemblance, and conventional associations rooted in experience, they are bound to be differently interpreted by different audiences.[87]

DEPERSONALIZING OTHERS

In his pioneering book *The Savage Hits Back,* Julius Lips noted that European artists most commonly depicted Africans as "unspecified figures." In contrast, he pointed out, African artists showed Europeans as individuals, and indicated their nationality, status, and even their personal character in their artworks.[88] In fact, in almost all pictorial traditions, regardless of the national origin of the artist, only those persons recognized as powerful or relevant attain the full status of named individuals (see Landau, Gordon, and Hodeir, this volume). The same was sometimes true when Africans depicted Europeans. Sixteenth-century Benin guild artists represented white people mainly as generic "Portuguese," who became in their bas-reliefs figures supportive of (or ancillary to) the Benin court. This was much as they were in life.[89]

In chapter 11, "Omada Art at the Crossroads of Colonialisms," Paula Ben-Amos Girshick investigates how a lesser-known group of carvers in the nineteenth-century Edo kingdom of Benin (Nigeria) represented Portuguese men just as the balance of power in Benin began to shift. In delightful sculptural reliefs, these young artisans, called Omada ("bearers of the king's sword"), took advantage of their casted status to widen the space for their personal creativity. The Omada depicted Europeans and their material accoutrements on doors, boxes, stools, and chairs. Their iconography sometimes ridiculed white men in Edo idioms, but it also betrayed a new and uneasy sense that Europeans' possessions were powerful objects. At the same time, the situation of the Omada placed them at a sufficient distance from Europeans so that the personal identities of the "Portuguese" could disappear. Girshick argues that the Omada's "in-between" stature, their position at the fulcrum between the high-status Edo hierarchy and increasingly importunate foreigners, gave them their license. It allowed them to evade the sacred strictures associated with guild sculptors and create a more charged commentary on political change.

In chapter 12, "Bad Copies," the last essay before Deborah Kaspin's Conclusion, Eric Gable offers an example of a *mutual* repudiation of individual stature, a mutual gesture of distancing, disdain, and appropriation. Like David Bunn, Gable examines the interplay between the resilient politics of African chiefdoms and the insistent hegemony of Europeans. He discusses how a Portuguese colonial administrator, Artur Martins de Miereles, created an illustrated archive of the bodies of thousands of African women. Miereles's effort to capture the image of the "traditional" part of Manjaco society in twentieth-century Portuguese Guinea (Guinea-Bissau) focused on the scarification of women's torsos. He catalogued 56 percent of the Manjaco's bodies, over 42,000 people, and photographed hundreds of women. Retrograde, feminine, authentic, naked, and collective, Miereles's pictures suggest the quintessence of the image-Africa.

The Manjaco first evaded and then chafed against colonial rule. They also sought to copy its parts for their own purposes. The "smart Manjaco" who dressed in fashionable clothes and lived in urban settings appeared to Miereles as "bad copies" of Europeans. They were too close to the observing European self, and so insufficiently Manjaco. In contrast to Montaigne's Brazilian cannibals, these persons discomfited Portuguese rulers by resisting the "amazing distance" between civilized and savage, defying Miereles's attempts to transform them into embodiments of difference. Most fascinating of all, some Manjaco created a parallel to Miereles's attempts to record their nameless selves in his anthropological project. They carved deindividuated "Portuguese colonials" as wooden posts in commemoration of chiefly ancestors. The Manjaco were eclectic in their borrowings, Gable tells us; they were not cargo cultists, not obsessed with European capacities; with their "European" markers staked at the margins of physical life, they were simply exercising their right to copy. They reworked themselves on their boundaries with images—much as they had done, in another fashion, by scarifying their bodies.

MAGIC, AUTHENTICITY, DOUBLENESS, AND ECSTASY

Miereles was after the impossible. No one can measure and freeze what he sees as another's authenticity. Even grasping it for a moment feels almost impossible, since its reality is predicated on distance. When the *photograph* captures authenticity, then, having been taken at close quarters, it tends to erase authenticity from whatever it pictures. Such an image is then relevant only because it shows something that no longer exists. What happens when the meaning of an image is the disappearance of its subject? It becomes magical. The early photographs of South African Bushmen, as discussed by Gordon, clearly have this quality (see also the essays by Mustafa and Drewal in this volume). Seventeenth-century users of the "magic lantern" understood the same principle when they claimed they could commune with spirits of the dead. And in 1839, the photographic pioneer Fox Talbot called photography "natural magic," seeing in it "the character of the *marvellous*."[90] In discussing the impact of a photograph of himself and his mother, Roland Barthes suggests we "keep in mind the *magical* character of the photographic image." In West Africa, photographers were long called "image magicians," and even today, "studio names such as Magic Photo Studio or Mr. Magic" are common.[91]

In discussing this magic, let us remember the odd notion that "savages" and "primitives," people in other words on the other side of the "amazing distance," also seem to *possess* magic powers. This goes for faraway rural peoples, for elves, Pygmies, leprechauns, Bushmen—and from some past African perspectives, Europeans. "Primitive" people are uncanny imitators (see Gordon, Hodeir); they are in touch with spirits; they shamelessly traffic in pretend magic.[92] When George Eastman introduced a camera costing a dollar, he named it the Brownie, after the lilliputian people called "Brownies" by the children's author Palmer Cox.[93] Surely a magical people called "Brownies" also gestures to the brown Bushmen or brown Pygmies of the image-Africa, whose remote alterity made them the perfect foil for hi-tech wizardry.[94] In this unexpected and circuitous way, the "double reality" of the mimetic image, its startling ability to be and not be at once, again bridges the "amazing distance" between the civilized self and the savage other. That's "the magic of Kodak."

Just like other aspects of iconicity, the "magic" of mimesis is subject to the effects of interpretive hegemony. We can ground the point by considering the treatment by some Baulé women of certain small sculptures that Susan Vogel glosses as "spirit husbands." All images routinely imply presences beyond themselves to *some* observers without revealing them to *others*. "Spirit husbands" are one such case. Baulé women marry them, care for them, and are troubled by them. One might say here that the image (the sculpture) has a presence beyond itself as an object of wood and paint. At first glance perhaps this looks like a peculiar feature of "tribal" art, or of African magic. But it is really no different from the "double reality" of the photograph: that it is simultaneously a flat design, *and a section of the real:* simultaneously an object and its referent, to at least some interpreters. The special care given to spirit husbands (and spirit wives), the way they are tended and hidden from public view, seems to derive only from the deepest meanings of husbandhood and wifehood in the culture of their living spouses. It is the signification of the statues.[95]

When such items are removed from the matrix of interaction in which they signify, when they are appraised under florescent light in air-conditioned galleries, then their prior meanings become spirits or specters. It often happens that the thing pictured or referenced is important for its fragility or evanescence. Its scaffolding, its "belief system," collapses on the shores of the modern world. At that moment, the mask, sculpture, or photograph that represents this thing at once becomes a fetish or a magic trinket. The "spirit" presence of a "spirit-husband" figure, once it is described in this way, is something that must be "believed in" by Baulé women (with the implication that they are wrong). Such women then take their places beside credulous Zimbabweans (Burke), hushed visitors to graveyards (Bunn), naïve spectators in a colonial fair (Hodeir). They are like the Malians who are afraid to look at a mask at a Bamako art museum. When Walter Benjamin discussed the vanishing "auras" of artworks in the "age of mechanical reproduction," he was alluding to just such spirits. In short, recognizing a specter presupposes its superannuation as natural meaning in life.[96]

The aura of a *person* means either personality or ghost, does it not? In Africa, these are often kindred concepts: the essence of personhood and the chimerical reflection of the outward self. It was frequently the second phenomenon, the human image, that was thought to survive after death as a "ghost." In Zulu, for instance, *isithunzi* means reflexive self, double, or image, and it is often given as "shadow."[97] When it was used in ways that missionaries recognized as referencing the past, the same notion became "ancestor" (*idlozi*). Similar to *isithunzi*, the word *modimo* in Tswana located a person as a fading but ever more powerful and inclusive memory, a "shade."[98] Note the association between image and self in these ideas, a matter that also occupies David Bunn in his discussion of South African spirits and grave images (this volume).[99] On the western side of the continent, one finds a similar variety of image and essence. Explaining the relationship between *Ibeji* dolls, twins, and photographs, a Yoruba spiritualist interviewed by Hecht and Simone called "Mr. Deja Vu" said, "When you snap [photograph] ... someone, you are looking at a picture of the soul of that person, not the person. . . . That is why, when one twin dies, we snap the other and we find the dead twin again."[100] Behrend and Wendl tell us that "in many African languages, the word for (photographic) "negative" is the same as for "ghost or dead spirit," and (to return once more to "shades") that photos have been in many places integrated into ancestor veneration.[101]

Yet Henri Junod, in his grand ethnography of "the Thonga" (an ethnic group his orthographic standards helped to construct), remarked that Thonga people did not really know the category "soul" at all. Instead of soul, Junod found a Thonga word that correlated with "Breath, viz., something of the nature of the wind, the shadow, the image, the external likeness, or fashion of man as opposed to his flesh." Quite obviously, these listed ideas are widely differentiated in English. As a result of their semantic affinity in Thonga, the human being is a "double" and can be "unsheathed" by witches or even, under some circumstances, by a photographer ("the magic of Kodak" once again). Thus when Thonga observers were shown a lantern slide of their people, they cried out, "That is how they illtreat us when they take our photographs!"[102] Now, one might still chuckle at this, since the projections were after all "just images." But one might also try to understand the manner in which the Thonga were correct. Europeans had long associated the double-natured image with magic. If they denied it in the milieu of colonial administration, if they located its magic only among children and "natives," they did so because they had failed to transform imagery completely into common sense. Moreover, they always cherished their ability to manipulate signs of all sorts—textual, aural, pictorial, and numerical ones. When it came time to make policy, they even seemed to privilege the importance of images over tangible people. The Thonga were perceptive.

As both Gordon and Burke remind us (this volume), colonial censors consistently banned cinematic scenes of Africans kissing or drinking: evidently they held it as a principle that Africans would read themselves into the diegesis of the shadowplay. Fritz Kramer does indeed notice this kind of "identification" in Africa, referring to it as an "ecstatic" and (for him) nonrational beholding of difference. In his challenging book *The Red Fez,* Kramer argues that in small-scale African societies, when mysterious "outside" presences possess people or things, what in fact is happening is that people are adopting alterity ("otherness") through mimesis ("imitation"), and so are empowering themselves. He views such imitation as an empirical activity, a sort of tactile phenomenology; and so he pronounces it utterly devoid of specters or spirits.[103] Ecstatic (beside-the-self) imitation is "realism" in the same sense, according to Kramer, that Honoré de Balzac's writing is realism: it so full of perceptions, of "suggestive, intuitively grasped images" that they simply "overwhelm" the self.[104]

This might also remind us of the Sudanese Zār, or the Niger Hauka cult, in which people perform, in altered states of being, as powerful others. Whether or not we call such ecstatic behavior "realism," it may certainly have real effects on the social relations of men and women.[105] The cowboy "Bills" gang in Zaire borrowed from Gene Autry, and gangsters in South African townships emulated Spencer Tracy. As Drewal tells us (this volume), an Ewe person in Ghana likewise can adopt the guise of a Mossi or Hausa foreigner—or the image of Mami Wata— not by mulling it over but by "engaging" it. Such an argument might be tied to Theodore Adorno's claim that true understanding is not dispassionate, but instead "engages the specific experience of a matter . . . [in a] relatedness to the object."[106] As an example, Adorno refers to one's submission to a work of art as giving way to "the compulsion of its structure." This "losing oneself" in dis- or different embodiments may be violent (as for instance in the disturbing Hauka episodes Jean Rouch filmed in *Les maîtres fous*), or somnambulant. But unless we distinguish "engagement" from understanding and empathy, which are functions of protracted interaction, we risk falling into the same mysticism that infused Picasso's milieu when he intuitively "engaged" African art.[107] Sculpting a drunken foreigner (Girshick), dressing up as a rich woman (Mustafa), gazing upward at a film (Burke), and miming "African" blacksmithy (Hodeir) need not involve any sort of "understanding." Nor does the donning of blackface. In twentieth-century Cape Town,

"Coloured" people still trouped in blackface in a "Coon Carnival." In Ghana, Africans did so. In Zaire (Hunt), artists reworked comic-book minstrelsy for new purposes. None of these instances of blackface required much knowledge of American blacks. On the other hand, they were not about ridiculing blacks either. The reuse of minstrelsy was about wealth, cool, and danger from a sort of image-America (or *image*-France); of songs and adventures; of automobiles and black celebrities. The high prices that Michael Jordan T-shirts fetch in Kenya's outdoor markets indicate that minstrelsy is alive and well as of this writing.[108]

The fact is that imagic appropriations, however tendentious they are, often create new versions of the self. Through that self, they channel preexisting forces, whether of anticolonial rage, monetary greed, or adolescent posturing. Sometimes, however, the effect fails to take. The images fail to work, and encounters remain a puzzle.

We have already seen how visual interpretations can be rerouted by hidden conventional symbols that signify in untoward ways, such as (perhaps) in the case of the United Africa Company's comic strips (Olaniyan), whose conventions marked them as manipulative, or "Stork" brand margarine (Burke), which accommodated a profound suspicion of colonial authority. But the removal of *self* from signification altogether is a different matter, and ends the alteric relationship completely. Montaigne's cannibal disgorges his enemy, ceasing to be his alter-ego because he no longer contains any part of him. The image of an "other" becomes "a mere image," a naked sign; the chain is broken, and the prior "meaning" of a sign becomes spectral, illusory, or just phony. Thus in a remarkable sermon, the South African Griqua leader A. A. S. Le Fleur scolded his parishioners in the late 1920s:

> Pentecost is no reality to the Ministry of today, the spirit of God is lost and the spirit of sects race or colour, has taken its place. This is the age, church without God, [so God becomes] ... a sort of show *more the nature of a cinema imaginary*, ... for to them Jesus is a stranger, the spirit of God, a mere shadow.[109]

A "mere shadow" here is the opposite of the Thonga's notion of the "shadow" as one half of our double-nature. Le Fleur's "shadow" is what is left when aura dies, when cynicism sets in. "Unity is a picture in the air," says a bitter Zimbabwean survivor of President Mugabe's purges of the 1980s. "What colour is it? What shape is it?"[110] In 1879, a band of Jesuits passed through Shoshong, a town in Bechuanaland (now Botswana); they carried a painting of figures which, they hoped, would provoke Africans to lose themselves (as Adorno says) in "the compulsion of its structure." The imaging of oneself as another, as I noted at the beginning of this essay, is describable as "conversion." In this case no one converted.

> For two days the entire population of Shoshong came along to admire our picture of Christ. But they were shocked at seeing a Zulu, a Matebele and a Becwana in adoration at the foot of the cross. *They were unable to understand how or why these Blacks were there.* We could not make them realize that this symbolized the calling to the faith.... In desperation, we feel that we shall have to alter the figures in the picture.[111]

The Jesuits presumed that their image was an adoration of Christ. But in Barthes's sense it was "literature," meaning it signified no real thing at all. It was not even a "picture of Christ" in the usual sense; it was a parable, a word-picture in iconic signs, in which the *faith* was personified in Christ, and the hoped-for future of the faith was signaled by the trio of African "types." The Panofskian "pre-iconographic" representation of the picture—in which it resembled four individuals in the same space—ran counter to the intended message of the picture.

The point here is not that visual signs of a mixed nature were beyond the normal ability of Africans to understand. Rather, when an observer is said to *mis*read an image, it can only be that he is not at home with the "aspect" (to use Wittgenstein's word) or with the "*langue*" (to use Saussure's) in which it is constrained to signify. He would have to learn that aspect by habit, or else as a set of rules, in order to arrive at a "proper" interpretation. Yet, as we have also seen, for an image to invite the widest audience into its fold of meanings, its beholders must not be *too* familiar with its components. They should, in fact, glimpse those elements from across a chasm: perhaps from across Montaigne's "amazing distance." Thus in the case of the picture in Shoshong, the Jesuits had to "alter" the Africans in it to render them sufficiently "other," perhaps lightening their skin, or clothing them differently. The figures could then become "types" and not particular persons to black southern African observers.[112]

The "amazing distance" is a tricky distance. Standing too close leads to scorn ("bad copies") or misunderstandings. Standing utterly outside a sign's ambit can detach its referents, which then become fictive. The Baulé spirit husband becomes a mere wooden figurine, taken as more than that only by deluded people. In fact, things are no different on this side of the Atlantic. "Do millions of consumers believe a sneaker is somehow imbued with the spirit of their hero?" writes one skeptic about the American success of Nike-brand athletic shoes. "I am forced to conclude that I have no idea why Michael Jordan sells so many sneakers."[113] Or so many T-shirts in Nairobi. When such habits are formulated and stated as propositions beyond the whole "aspect" of their usage, they can safely be termed false, even if millions of consumers remain inside Nike's world, and some Baulé people still keep spirit spouses, and their habits are all logical enough. (Let it be noted that the accounting of images as doubles for the self is not therefore only a phenomenon in acephalous African societies. Indeed, it supports the economy of the Western world.)[114] People fathom alterity, and encounter ecstasy, through images: they want to become wealthy, comfortable, loving, loved, sexy, famous, or just other. Who is to say whether they succeed?

Every unit of meaning, and not just every image, is a public crossroads of histories of interpretation. In the realm of the visual, decontextualized icons sometimes reveal this with sudden clarity. Not only Lady Liberty, but also Mickey Mouse stands beside Cheikh Amadou Bamba in a Senegalese wall-mural graffito. Spiderman works together with Anansi, the mythical Akan spider-trickster, in a Ghanaian comic strip. An ancestral marker looks like a colonial officer. "James Bond" becomes an ancestor figure in East Africa. More often, however, the ships of variant interpretations trawl past each other quietly, unflagged as to their origins. Was not James Bond also a type of deity to American boys?[115] "Rambo" has been adopted in different ways by populations in Sierra Leone, Benin City, and Angola, but the figure had a bigger impact in New York and Los Angeles.[116] The intersections of global and local interpretations need not all be ostentatious ones. The West African deity Ogun has "many faces," which vary from place to place, so that he has a different persona depending on where he is beheld. Each version of Ogun can be seen as a front for a larger unity, or as a separate discourse—just like a movie star.[117]

Everywhere there are images, there are also struggles over what ultimately is real, and what is representational. Some such struggles are profound, others are comical. We shall see how positions vary, and vary legitimately, on different "sides" of images: the adaptation of *Tintin* to carry social messages in Congo (Hunt), the defacing of grave sites as an act of war between Xhosa chiefs and English military men in the Eastern Cape (Bunn), the attempt by a Portuguese officer to replace Manjaco people with images of their women's bodies (Gable). In all such contests, a fundamental point of contestation is where to delineate the real. Could an "African" ride the metro at the turn of the century (Hodeir)? Were not "tribes" a social reality under colonial rule (Landau)? Among the criticisms of the South African "Miscast" exhibition (Skotnes), the most interesting was the notion that the displayed body casts "were," in effect, the grandparents of some observers.

It is only right that we have trouble separating images from reality. Mimetic images seem attracted to that "amazing distance" that marks alterity, that limns the borderlands of the ego, and the "double reality" of mimetic images resonates discomfitingly with our sense of selfhood. Indeed, a picture in this book, and you, the reader of the book, are both *in* the world, and embracing *of* wider parts of the world, at one and the same time.[118] The image possesses an address and yet encompasses territory far beyond it; it is simultaneously opaque and transparent, "there and not-there" at the same time; ultimately, it is uncontained. These same attributes describe consciousness. It is hoped that the following essays help make sense of this unsettling correspondence, perhaps not in the well-fitted vocabulary of nineteenth-century Thonga or Zulu observers, but nonetheless.

NOTES

1. Michel de Montaigne, "Of Cannibals," Essay 31 in *Complete Essays*, trans. Donald M. Frame (Stanford, Calif.: Stanford University Press, 1958), 158.

2. For a fascinating if not entirely convincing discussion of the origins of this relationship, see Tzvetan Todorov, *The Conquest of America: The Question of the Other* (1984; Norman: University of Oklahoma Press, 1999). The best history of the "noble savage" concept is offered by Anthony Pagden, *The Fall of Natural Man: The American Indian and the Origins of Comparative Ethnology* (1982; New York: Cambridge University Press, 1986). See also Michel de

Certeau, "Montaigne's 'Of Cannibals': The Savage 'I,' " in *Heterologies: Discourse on the Other,* trans. Brian Massumi (Minneapolis: University of Minnesota Press, 1986), 67–79. I am, of course, aware that Montaigne's real subject in "Of Cannibals" is his fellow Europeans.

3. Ludwig Wittgenstein, cited by Ray Monk, *Ludwig Wittgenstein: The Duty of Genius* (New York: Free Press, 1990); I cannot recover the page reference.

4. Philip Curtin, *The Image of Africa* (Madison: University of Wisconsin Press, 1975).

5. Edward Said, *Orientalism* (New York: Vintage Books, 1978).

6. James Blaut, *The Colonizer's Model of the World: Geographical Diffusionism and Eurocentric History* (New York: Guilford Press, 1993); M. Van Wyke Smith, " 'The Most Wretched of the Human Race': The Iconography of the Khoikhoin (Hottentots), 1500–1800," *History and Anthropology* 5, 3–4 (1992): 285–330; Philip Curtin, *The Image of Africa* (Madison: University of Wisconsin Press, 1975), esp. 23, citing Bryan Edwards, *The History, Civil and Commercial, of the British Colonies in the West Indies* (2d ed., London: John Stockdale, 1794), 2: 60–79; *The Periplus Maris Erythraei,* ed. Lionel Casson (Princeton, N.J.: Princeton University Press, 1989); and *An Universal History, from the Earliest Account of Time* (London: T. Osborne, 1747–68), with articles by George Sale, George Psalmanazar, Archibald Bower, George Shelvocke, John Campbell, John Swinton, and others. There were exceptions to the generally deprecatory way of depicting Africans, in pictures of royalty, and in Caspar the "black" of the three magi. See also *The Voyages of Cadamosto and Other Documents on Western Africa in the Second Half of the Fifteenth Century,* ed. G. R. Crone (London: Hakluyt Society, 1937; Nendeln, Liechtenstein: Kraus Reprint, 1967), cited in Peter Mark, *Africans in European Eyes: The Portrayal of Black Africans in Fourteenth- and Fifteenth-Century Europe* (Syracuse, N.Y.: Maxwell School of Citizenship and Public Affairs, Syracuse University, 1974), 66–68; Frank Snowden Sr., *Blacks in Antiquity* (Cambridge, Mass.: Harvard University Press, 1970), and Jean Devisse and Michel Mollat, *From the Early Christian Era to the "Age of Discovery,"* vol. 2 of *The Image of the Black in Western Art* (New York: Morrow, 1979); Paul Landau, "With Camera and Gun in South Africa: Constructing the Image of Bushmen, ca. 1880–1940," in *Miscast: Negotiating the Presence of Bushmen,* ed. Pippa Skotnes (Cape Town: University of Cape Town Press, 1996), 129–41.

7. This is the classic argument of Eric Williams, *Capitalism and Slavery* (Chapel Hill: University of North Carolina Press, 1944); see also George M. Frederickson, *The Black Image in the White Mind: The Debate on Afro-American Character and Destiny, 1817–1914* (Hanover, N.H.: University Press of New England / Wesleyan University Press, 1971); and Seymour Drechsler, "The Ending of the Slave Trade and the Evolution of European Scientific Racism," in *The Atlantic Slave Trade: Effects on Economies, Societies, and Peoples in Africa, the Americas, and Europe,* ed. Joseph E. Inkori and Stanley Engerman (Durham, N.C.: Duke University Press, 1992), 361–96; and for an excellent recent overview of the relationship between slavery and images of Africans, see David Brion Davis, "Constructing Race: A Reflection," *William and Mary Quarterly,* 3d ser., 54, no. 1 (January 1997): 6–16, and the essays published in that issue. And Joseph Miller, *Way of Death: Merchant Capitalism and the Angolan Slave Trade, 1730–1830* (Madison: University of Wisconsin, 1988).

8. Olaudah Equiano, "The Interesting Narrative of the Life of Olaudah Equiano, or Gustavus Vassa, The African. Written by Himself," in id., *The Interesting Narrative and Other Writings,* ed. Vincent Carretta (New York: Penguin Books, 1995), 43–44.

9. Equiano's narrative first appeared in 1787. Mainstream Protestants of the day commonly reflected on their own putative similarity to biblical Jews (David Waldstreicher, pers. comm., April 1999). Vincent Caretta has recently (and cautiously) cast doubt on whether

Equiano, or Gustavus Vassa, as he was known for most of his life, was born in Africa or in the Carolinas, which makes his comparison even more interesting; see Carretta, "Olaudah Equiano or Gustavus Vassa? New Light on an Eighteenth-Century Question of Identity," *Slavery and Abolition* 20, 3 (1999): 96–105.

10. Curtin, *Image*.

11. By locating the "true church" somewhere on the African continent, for example, Swedenborgians amplified the idea that Africans lived especially "spiritual" lives. Curtin, *Image*, 39; Patrick Brantlinger, "Victorians and Africans: The Genealogy of the Myth of the Dark Continent," in *"Race," Writing, and Difference* (Chicago: University of Chicago Press, 1986), ed. Henry Louis Gates Jr., 185–223; Ann McClintock, "Maidens, Maps, and Mines: The Reinvention of Patriarchy in Colonial South Africa," *South Atlantic Quarterly* 87, 1 (Winter 1988), 146–92; Martin Bernal, *Black Athena: The Afroasiatic Roots of Classical Civilization* (New Brunswick, N.J.: Rutgers University Press, 1987), esp. vol. 1, *The Fabrication of Ancient Greece, 1785–1985*, chs. 4 and 7; Saul Dubow, *Scientific Racism in Modern South Africa* (Cambridge: Cambridge University Press, 1995); and Jean-Bernard Ouedraogo, "Scénographie d'une conquête: Enquête sur la vision plastique d'un colonial," *Cahiers du LERSCO: Iconographie et Sociologie* (1991). Hermann Wittenbergh's forthcoming work on the capture of African landscapes into biblical and classical terminology will prove significant here.

12. Montaigne, "Of Cannibals." This is also a reworking of transubstantiation.

13. Brantlinger, "Victorians and Africans"; see also Patrick Manning, *Slavery and African Life* (Cambridge: Cambridge University Press, 1990), and Paul Lovejoy, *Transformations in Slavery: A History of Slavery in Africa* (Cambridge: Cambridge University Press, 1983).

14. "At Harvard... in a museum[,] a series of skeletons [were] arranged from a little monkey to a tall well-developed white man, with a Negro barely outranking a chimpanzee. Eventually in my classes stress was quietly transferred to brain weight and brain capacity, and at last to the 'cephalic index.'" W. E. B. Du Bois, "On Being Ashamed of Oneself (1933)," in *The Oxford W. E. B. Du Bois Reader*, ed. Eric J. Sundquist (New York: Oxford University Press, 1996).

15. The 1890 Stanley Africa Exhibition, for example, avoided many of the stereotypes very much in evidence now: see Annie E. Coombes, *Reinventing Africa: Museums, Material Culture and Popular Imagination in Late Victorian and Edwardian England* (New Haven, Conn.: Yale University Press, 1994).

16. Carolyn Hamilton, *Terrific Majesty: The Powers of Shaka Zulu and the Limits of Historical Invention* (Cambridge, Mass.: Harvard University Press, 1998), argues for the sustained influence of Africans' concerns in colonial stereotypes of the Zulu. On travel writing generally, see Mary Louise Pratt, "Fieldwork in Common Places," in *Writing Culture: The Poetics and Politics of Ethnography*, ed. James Clifford and George E. Marcus, 27–50 (Berkeley and Los Angeles: University of California Press, 1986); and Pratt, *Imperial Eyes: Travel Writing and Transculturation* (London: Routledge, 1992); Laura Ann Stoler, *Race and the Education of Desire: Foucault's History of Sexuality and the Colonial Order of Things* (Durham, N.C.: Duke University Press, 1995); Brantlinger, "Victorians and Africans."

17. For *Tarzan*, ignore Kenneth Cameron's empty analysis of the many Tarzan movies in his *Africa on Film* (New York: Continuum Press, 1994), and see Gail Bederman, "*Tarzan* and After," in her *Manliness and Civilization: A Cultural History of Gender and Race in the United States, 1880–1917* (Chicago: University of Chicago Press, 1995), who points out that the writ-

ten Tarzan was a "killer of many black men" (in Tarzan's words), an emphasis missing from the filmic Tarzans. For van der Post, see, e.g., Alan Barnard, "Laurens van der Post and the Kalahari Debate," in *Miscast: Negotiating the Presence of Bushmen*, ed. Pippa Skotnes (Cape Town: University of Cape Town Press, 1996), 239–47; and we await Edwin Wilmsen's fuller study.

18. Despite the quip about Africa beginning at the Pyrenees, for most Westerners Africa refers to latitudes south of the Sahara.

19. For a recent summary of our advances in knowledge about (mainly precolonial) African history, see Joseph C. Miller, "History and Africa / Africa and History," *American Historical Review* 104, 1 (1999): 1–32. See also Said, *Orientalism;* Percival Christopher Wren, *Foreign Legion Omnibus: Beau Geste, Beau Sabreur, Beau Ideal* (New York: Grosset & Dunlap, 1925); Edgar Rice Burroughs, *Tarzan of the Apes* (1912; New York: Ballantine Books, 1983); Malek Alloula, *The Colonial Harem* (Minneapolis: University of Minnesota Press, 1986).

20. Christopher M. Lyman, *The Vanishing Race and Other Illusions: Photographs of Indians by Edward Curtis* (New York: Pantheon Books, 1982); Christraud M. Geary, *Images of Bamun: German Colonial Photography at the Court of King Njoya, Cameroun, West Africa 1902–1915* (Washington, D.C.: Smithsonian Institution Press, 1988). Andrew Robert's pioneering work on photography and film archives includes *Photographs as Sources for African History: Papers Presented at a Workshop Held at the School of Oriental and African Studies, London, May 12–13, 1988*, ed. Andrew Roberts (London: SOAS, 1988); and id., "Review Article: Photographs and African History," *Journal of African History* 29 (1988): 301–11. See also *The Raj: India and the British, 1600–1947*, exhibition catalogue, ed. Christopher Bayly (London: National Portrait Gallery, 1991), esp. Christopher Pinney's essay, "Colonial Anthropology in the 'Laboratory of Mankind' "; David Prochaska, "Fantasia of the Phototeque: French Views of Colonial Senegal," *African Arts* 24, 4 (1991): 40–47; and Nicolas Thomas, *Colonialism's Culture: Anthropology, Travel, and Government* (Princeton, N.J.: Princeton University Press, 1994).

21. Coombes, *Inventing Africa*, and Raymond Corbey, "Ethnographic Showcases, 1870–1930," in *The Decolonization of the Imagination: Culture, Knowledge and Power*, ed. Jan Nederveen-Pieterse and Bhikhu Parekh (Atlantic Highlands, N.J.: Zed Books, 1995), 57–80; Sylviane Leprun, *Le théâtre des colonies: Scénographie, acteurs et discours de l'imaginaire dans les expositions, 1855–1937* (Paris: L'Harmattan, 1986); Catherine Hodeir and Michel Pierre, *L'Exposition coloniale, 1931: La mémoire du siècle* (Paris: Éditions Complexe, 1991); and Robert Rydell, *All the World's a Fair: Visions of Empire at America's International Expositions, 1876–1916* (Chicago: University of Chicago Press, 1984). See also Grace Sieberling with Carolyn Bloore, *Amateurs, Photography and the Mid-Victorian Imagination* (Chicago: University of Chicago Press, 1986); and Roy Flukinger, *The Formative Decades: Photography in Great Britain, 1839–1920* (Austin: University of Texas Press, 1985).

22. Jan Nederveen-Pieterse, *White on Black: Images of Africa and Blacks in Western Popular Culture* (New Haven, Conn.: Yale University Press, 1992); James Ryan, *Picturing Empire: Photography and the Visualization of the British Empire* (Chicago: University of Chicago Press, 1997), and Alloula, *Colonial Harem*.

23. Pascal Blanchard et al., eds. *L'autre et nous: Scènes et types* (Paris: Syros / Association Connaissance de l'histoire de l'Afrique contemporaine, 1995).

24. Allan Sekula, "The Body and the Archive," in *The Conquest of Meaning: Critical Histories of Photography*, ed. Richard Bolton (Cambridge, Mass.: MIT Press, 1989), 343–89. Skotnes insists on her own entrapment in the "politics of [her] own knowledge," to quote her wall text (which quotes the anthropologist Greg Dening). That may, of course, be so, but her exhibit nevertheless also attempted to contextualize the creation of colonial knowledge about so-called Bushmen.

25. Ulf Hannerz, *Transnational Connections: Culture, People, Places* (New York: Routledge, 1996), 3 (thanks to John Comaroff for introducing me to Hannerz's work); and see Arjun Appadurai, *Modernity at Large: Cultural Dimensions of Globalization* (Minneapolis: University of Minnesota Press, 1996).

26. Paul Virilio, *The Aesthetics of Disappearance* (New York: Semiotext(e), 1991), 74; see also id., *Speed and Politics* (New York: Semiotext(e), 1986), quoting Paul de Kock (1842): "The railroad is nature's true magic lantern." Major motion pictures that betray a sense of anxiety about visual reality include *Terminator* (1993) and *Terminator Two* (1996), *The Net* (1997), *Dark City* (1997), *Lawnmower Man* (1997), *The Game* (1998), *The Truman Show* (1998), *The Matrix* (1999), *Existenz* (1999), *Ed TV* (1999), and *The Sixth Sense* (1999).

27. Appadurai, *Modernity*, 77. I refer to the international business elite, to the conjunction of the Northern and Western hemispheres in the so-called First World, and to the likely position of most readers as "the West," for the sake of simplicity.

28. See Catherine Lutz and Jane Collins, *Reading National Geographic* (Chicago: University of Chicago Press, 1993); Landau, "With Camera and Gun in South Africa"; and Hannerz, *Transnational Connections,* 66. The predicament of "civilized natives" is a political analogue to what Mary Douglas has famously described as the discomfort generated by "matter out of place" in *Purity and Danger: An Analysis of the Concepts of Pollution and Taboo* (1966; reprint, New York: Routledge, 1992).

29. There are exceptions—the work of Tobias Wendl, Heike Behrend, Vera Viditz-Ward, and Birgit Meyer being a few.

30. Walter Benjamin, "The Task of the Translator," in *Illuminations: Essays and Reflections,* ed. Hannah Arendt (1968; New York: Schocken Books, 1969), 69.

31. Paul Ricoeur, *Oneself as Another* (Chicago: University of Chicago Press, 1992).

32. The cataloguing of affinities between workshops and artists in tribal domains results in a confusion of tribe and style. Rejecting this was the emphasis of Jan Vansina's important book *Art and History in Africa* (Madison: University of Wisconsin, 1984), and see also Paula (now Girshick) Ben-Amos, *The Art of Benin* (London: British Museum Press, 1995); the more "traditional" Africanist art history of such scholars and curators as (to take a few anglophone examples) Philip J. C. Dark, William Fagg, Marshall Mount, Frank Willet has also, of course, been terribly important.

33. Paula Ben-Amos, "African Visual Arts from a Social Perspective," *African Studies Review* 32, no. 2 (September 1989): 1–53.

34. Ibid., 3, and Ben-Amos's citation of V. Y. Mudimbe, "African Art as a Question Mark," *African Studies Review* 29, 1 (1986): 3–4.

35. Maurice Merleau-Ponty, *The Prose of the World* (Evanston, Ill.: Northwestern University Press, 1973), 72, quoted in V. Y. Mudimbe, *The Idea of Africa* (Bloomington: Indiana University Press, 1994), 67; and see 58. See also Guy Brett, *Through Our Own Eyes: Popular Art and Modern History* (London: GMP Publishers, 1986). On the problem of thievery, see *Plundering Africa's Past,* ed. Peter R. Schmidt and Roderick J. McIntosh (Bloomington: Indiana University Press, 1996).

36. For the fall of "authentic primitive art" after 1984, see Shelly Errington, *The Death of Authentic Primitive Art and Other Tales of Progress* (Berkeley and Los Angeles: University of California Press, 1998), who also offers an extended discussion of the discursive construction of meaning in "tribal art" in general. Chris Marker and Alain Resnais's film *Les statues meurent aussi* is discussed in Manthia Diawara, *African Cinema: Politics and Culture* (Bloomington: Indiana University Press, 1992), 23. Scholars of African art no longer subscribe to the

idea of a "pure" (anti-hybrid) art. See *Unpacking Culture: Art and Commodity in the Colonial and Postcolonial Worlds*, ed. Ruth B. Phillips and Christopher B. Steiner (Berkeley and Los Angeles: University of California Press, 1999).

37. Mamadou Diawara, "Le cimitiere des autels, le temple des tresors: Reflexions sur les musées d'art Africains," *Jahrbuch der Wissenschaftskolleg zu Berlin* (Berlin: Wissenschaftskolleg, 1997). Cf. David Freedberg, *The Power of Images: Studies in the History and Theory of Response* (Chicago: University of Chicago Press, 1989).

38. William Pietz discusses the fetish as both a projection of European categories of thought in the mercantile era into African culture, and as a theory of African thought, in William Pietz, "The Problem of the Fetish, I," *Res* 9 (1985): 5–17; "The Problem of the Fetish, II: The Origin of the Fetish," *Res* 13 (1987): 23–45; and "The Problem of the Fetish, IIIa: Bosman's Guinea and the Enlightenment Theory of Fetishism," *Res* 16 (1988): 105–23. See also Wyatt MacGaffey, "Dialogues of the Deaf: Europeans on the Atlantic Coast of Africa," in *Implicit Understandings: Observing, Reporting, and Reflecting on the Encounters Between Europeans and Other Peoples in the Early Modern Era*, ed. Stuart B. Schwartz (Cambridge: Cambridge University Press, 1994), 249–67.

39. Christopher Miller in *Theories of Africans: Francophone Literature and Anthropology in Africa* (Chicago: University of Chicago Press, 1990) tells us that Frobenius saw Africa as marked by a "rough, austere" art, which was in essence the "pure" Africa leaving no room for (in Miller's words) "disjuncture or agency." Frobenius influenced Leopold Senghor, who also came to imagine "Africa" as "an idealistic vision." Senghor quoted from Leopold Senghor, "Les leçons de Léo Frobenius," *Présence africaine* 3, 3 (1978): 147–48, and Leo Frobenius, "Die Kunst Afrikaner," *Der Erdball* 3 (1931): 90, both cited by Christopher Miller, *Theories of Africans*, 17. W. E. B. Du Bois also articulated an anticolonialism that, like *négritude*, reversed, without erasing, many of the images of nineteenth-century colonial writers; see *The Oxford W. E. B. Du Bois Reader*, ed. Sundquist, 624.

40. Robert Brain, *Art and Society in Africa* (New York: Longman, 1980), quoted in Mudimbe, *Idea of Africa*,

41. David Hecht and A. Maliqalim Simone, *Invisible Governance: The Art of African Micropolitics* (New York: Autonomedia, 1994); Ilona Szombati-Fabian and Johannes Fabian, "Art, History, and Society: Popular Painting in Shaba, Zaire," *Studies in the Anthropology of Visual Communication* 3, 1 (1976), and "Folk Art from an Anthropological Perspective," in *Perspectives in American Folk Art*, ed. Ian M. G. Quimby and Scott T. Swank (New York: Norton, 1980).

42. Robert Farris Thompson, *African Art in Motion: Icon and Act in the Collection of Katherine Coryton White* (Los Angeles: University of California Press, 1974); Thompson, *Flash of the Spirit: African and Afro-American Art and Philosophy* (New York: Random House, 1983; Vintage Books, 1984); and see Johannes Fabian, *Remembering the Present: Painting and Popular History in Zaire* (narrative and paintings by Tshibumba Kanda Matulu) (Berkeley and Los Angeles: University of California Press, 1996). See also Henry Drewal and Margaret Drewal, *Gelede: Art and Female Power among the Yoruba* (Bloomington: Indiana University Press, 1983); Z. S. Strother, *Inventing Masks: Agency and History in the Art of the Central Pende* (Chicago: University of Chicago Press, 1998); and Mary Jo Arnoldi and Chris Hardin, "Efficacy and Object: Introduction," in *African Material Culture*, ed. Mary Jo Arnoldi et al. (Bloomington: Indiana University Press, 1996), 1–28.

43. *Africa Explores: Twentieth-Century African Art*, ed. Susan Vogel (New York: Center for African Art; Munich: Prestel-Verlag, 1991); Susan Vogel, "Always True to the Object, in Our Fashion," in *Exhibiting Cultures: The Poetics and Politics of Museum Display*, ed. Ivan Karp and

Steven D. Lavine (Washington, D.C.: Smithsonian Institution Press, 1991); and id., *Baulé: African Art, Western Eyes* (New Haven, Conn.: Yale University Press, 1997). And see also Vansina, *Art and History,* and Sidney Kasfir, "African Art and Authenticity: A Text with a Shadow," *African Arts* 25, 2 (1992): 41–53.

44. Kwame Anthony Appiah, *In My Father's House: Africa in the Philosophy of Culture* (Oxford: Oxford University Press, 1992), 137–39, scathingly discusses Susan Vogel's organization of a 1987 show.

45. Marshall W. Mount, *African Art: The Years Since 1920* (1973; Bloomington: University of Indiana Press, 1989), and Susan Vogel, "Introduction," in *Africa Explores;* and V. Y. Mudimbe, *Idea of Africa,* 160–62. For wall murals, see Mamadou Diouf, "Fresques murales et écriture de l'histoire: Le *Set/Setal* à Dakar," *Politiques africaines,* June 1992, 41–54, and David Hecht and A. Maliqalim Simone, *Invisible Governance,* esp. ch. 6. See also Samba Diop, "Mutual Representations in Colonial Senegal (1900–1960): The Image of the African Native in the French Press and the Native's Perception of the European in Popular Paintings" (paper presented at the Images and Empires conference). For the Ghanaian form called the *posuban,* see Fritz Kramer, *The Red Fez: Art and Spirit Possession in Africa* (New York: Verso Press, 1993), 210–11. And see Bogumil Jewsiewicki, "Collective Memory and Its Images: Popular Urban Painting in Zaire: A Source of 'Present Past,'" *History and Anthropology,* 2 (1986), and id., "Painting in Zaire: From the Invention of the West to the Representation of the Social Self," and Susan Vogel, "Inspiration and Burden," in *Africa Explores,* 114–75, and 236 (and Cat. 86). In the Congo case, Fabian agrees that interactions between local audiences and artists create art, although he himself contracted the art he analyzes in Fabian, *Remembering the Present.*

46. Robert Faris Thompson, commentary, ACAS, New Orleans, 1998.

47. Achille Mbembe, "The 'Thing' and Its Doubles in Cameroonian Cartoons," in *Readings in African Popular Culture,* ed. Karin Barber (Bloomington: University of Indiana Press, 1997), 151–63. My view reflects that of Pierre Bourdieu, *Distinctions: A Social Critique of the Judgement of Taste* (London: Routledge, 1986), who points out inter alia that the elevation of photographs of ordinary objects and situations, over special ones, is a characteristic of the aspiring classes, 34–36.

48. The way in which this volume moves away from "art" as a category is in an important sense prefigured by *African Material Cultures,* ed. Mary Jo Arnoldi et al.; see especially the introduction by Kris L. Hardin and Mary Jo Arnoldi.

49. Robert Delavignette, introduction to the photographic album *French Equatorial Africa* (photographs by Michel Huet, Michel Mako, and Pierre Ichac, with notes by Jacques Vulaines) (Paris: Hachette, 1957), 21; a translation of *Afrique équatoriale française,* Les Albums des Guides bleus 29 (Paris: Hachette, 1957). For the *Guides Bleu,* men exist only as "types." Roland Barthes, "The Blue Guide," in *Mythologies* (Paris: Seuil, 1957).

50. Indexical interpretations have always been important in Western scholars' understanding of African-wrought objects: the use of organic materials, blood, grasses, and so on has especially come to their attention. The reasons for this are complex, but one might note that material indexing is implicitly suggested as the tribal equivalent of Western iconic signification, in the sense that both are "natural" representations of larger fields of meaning.

51. C. S. Peirce, "The Icon, Index, and Symbol," in *Collected Papers of Charles Sanders Peirce,* ed. Charles Hartshorne and Paul Weiss (Cambridge, Mass.: Harvard University Press, 1931–58), vol. 2.

52. Thanks to Brigitte Miriam Bedos-Rezak for her insightful remarks here. Major critiques of Peircean thought have come from Saussure, Barthes, and others. Umberto Eco

would get rid of the notion of the iconic sign, but he concedes that some things can perhaps look like other things (Eco, *A Theory of Semiotics* [Bloomington: Indiana University Press, 1976], 216). See also W. J. T. Mitchell, *Iconology: Image, Text, Ideology* (Chicago: University of Chicago Press, 1986), 17.

53. Erwin Panofsky, "Die Perspektive als 'symbolischen Form,'" *Vorträge der Bibliothek Warburg* 4 (1924–5): 258–331, cited in Martin Jay, "Scopic Regimes of Modernity," in *Vision and Visuality*, ed. Hal Foster (Seattle: Bay Press, 1988), 5; Ernst Gombrich, *Art and Illusion* (Princeton, N.J.: Princeton University Press, 1956). Gombrich subsequently "clarified" his position in order to limit its less supportable implications: see his "Image and Code: Scope and Limits of Conventionalism in Pictorial Representation," in *Image and Code*, ed. Wendy Steiner (Ann Arbor: University of Michigan, 1981), 11, cited in Mitchell, *Iconology*, 65.

54. Nelson Goodman, *Languages of Art: An Approach to a Theory of Symbols* (1968; Indianapolis: Hackett, 1976); Roland Barthes, "Rhetoric of the Image," in *Image-Music-Text* (New York: Hill & Wang, 1977); and Mitchell, *Iconology*. It must be noted here that C. S. Peirce himself classed the photograph as an indexical, not an iconic, form of signification, because the photograph is an imprint of the real left on a sensitive surface. For more on this point, see my discussion of captions, later in this Introduction. See also Rosalind Krauss, *The Originality of the Avant Garde and Other Modernist Myths* (Cambridge, Mass.: MIT Press, 1985), "Notes on the Index 2," 210–11, citing Peirce, "Logic as Semiotic: The Theory of Signs."

55. I am somewhat caricaturing the complex arguments in M. H. Segall, D. T. Campbell, and M. J. Herskovits, *The Influence of Culture on Visual Perception* (New York: Bobbs-Merrill, 1966); in fine, they argue against the sort of naïve cultural relativism afflicting other studies set in colonial contexts (32, 52 ff.). Goodman, *Languages of Art*. See also Allan Sekula, "On the Invention of Photographic Meaning," in *Thinking Photography*, ed. Victor Burgin (London: Macmillan, 1982), 84–109. Sol Worth and John Adair reckoned with the issue by giving their camera to Navajo people in the film *Through Navajo Eyes* (1972); see the discussion by Jacques Aumont, *The Image* (London: British Film Institute, 1997), 94–95.

56. Vogel, *Baulé* (I return to Baulé spirit husbands at the end of this essay); Mitchell, *Iconology*, 90–91, 113. My brief comments on Herskovits dovetail with criticisms from others who have argued that he erred primarily by divorcing cultures from their historical context in the New World. My colleague Stephan Palmié's forthcoming *Wizards and Scientists: Explorations in Afro-Cuban Modernity and Tradition* (Durham, N.C.: Duke University Press, 2002) offers a critique in this regard. Mitchell is quite aware of the relativistic usage of "fetish" to depict what *other* people do and cites Patrick Brantlinger's "Victorians and Africans," *Critical Inquiry* 12, 1 (September 1985), 205. For *idol* he is also drawing on usages in Karl Marx, *The German Ideology* (1845–47) and Sir Francis Bacon, *The New Organon* (1620). My thoughts here are strongly conditioned by Wittgenstein's works, especially (to put things perhaps too succinctly) by his effort to avoid the common error of confusing customs with rules. See *Philosophical Investigations* (New York: Blackwell, 1958), part 1.

57. *Freedom in Our Lifetime: The Collected Writings of Anton Muziwakhe Lembede*, ed. Robert R. Edgar and Luyanda ka Msumza (Athens: Ohio University Press, 1996). The quotation comes from the memory of Lembede's teacher at Inkanyezi Catholic school, Sister Sibeko, and may reflect her own thoughts. Lembede was about fourteen.

58. University of the Witwatersrand, Historical Collection, CPSA AB 2259/Gd1.1, William Crisp, vol. 1, Crisp to Aunt Polly, Thaba Nchu, 1/6/1872; and interviews conducted by Mpho Matebula for Paul Landau, Phala Mines, August 1996.

59. Saul Dubow, *Scientific Racism in Modern South Africa* (Cambridge: Cambridge University Press, 1995), 236–40. Aumont, *Image*, 17, 20, 43, has pointed out that other studies of vi-

sual perception have shown that movement is required for recognition, and that the perception of space particularly relies on the movement of the observer, or memories of such movement. *The Influence of Culture on Visual Perception* by Segall et al. aims in the direction of the dynamic I am stressing.

60. W. J. T. Mitchell argues that the debate over the relative weight of image or word in producing iconic signification is itself a displaced contest between ideologies touting nature or culture, respectively. See Mitchell, *Iconology*, 44 and passim.

61. In other words, it is not only that taste indexes status but that status defines good taste through such indexing. See Pierre Bourdieu, *Distinctions*, and id. et al., *Photography: A Middle-Brow Art* (1965; Stanford, Calif.: Stanford University Press, 1990). Phillips and Steiner come dangerously close to sneering at the hoi polloi in their critique of the populist amalgamation of "ethnic art" in *Unpacking Culture*, 18. On Picasso, see Marilyn McCully, "The Fallen Angel?" review of *The Picasso Papers*, by Rosalind E. Krauss, *New York Review of Books*, April 8, 1999, 18–24; and Anne Baldassari, *Picasso and Photography: The Dark Mirror* (Houston: Houston Museum of Fine Arts / Flammarion, 1997), also cited by McCully; and see Philippe David, ed., *Inventaire général des cartes postales Fortier* (Saint-Julien-du-Sault: Fostier, 1986–87). In Otto Preminger's film *Bunny Lake Is Missing* (1965), a tribal mask signifies sexual voyeurism.

62. See Paul Landau, "The Illumination of Christ in the Kalahari Desert," *Representations* 45 (Winter 1994).

63. Learned perception is a matter of moving about and deriving information from the constantly shifting sum of one's activities, but a visual frame in a painting or photograph cannot be shifted to make way for independent observations of the section of real space represented, which was new to the Tswana in the 1840s. This argument draws heavily on Terence Wright, "Photography: Theories of Realism and Convention," in *Anthropology and Photograph, 1860–1930*, ed. Elizabeth Edwards (New Haven, Conn.: Yale University Press, 1992), citing James Gibson, *The Senses Considered as Perceptual Systems* (Boston: Houghton Mifflin, 1966), and *The Ecological Approach to Visual Perception* (Boston: Houghton Mifflin, 1979); Wright's discussion of the implications of Gibson's work is particularly good (24–28). And see, additionally, Suren Lalvani, *Photography, Vision, and the Production of Modern Bodies* (Albany: State University of New York Press, 1996), 5.

64. Aumont, *Image*, 40: this "double reality" has been mostly discussed for the photograph, but there is no reason to exclude realistic painting.

65. Theodore K. Rabb and Jonathan Brown, "Image and Text," *Journal of Interdisciplinary History* 17, 1 (Summer 1986): 1–6.

66. The example is expanded from Mitchell, *Iconology*, 44, citing Mark Twain, *Life on the Mississippi* (1883; reprint, New York: Reader's Digest, 1987), 262.

67. Hunt is here provocatively quoting the editors' invitation to the meetings in which these papers were first delivered.

68. Certainly, captions have been all but ignored in histories of photography: Patricia Hayes, personal communication, December 1997.

69. Terrence Wright, "Photography," points out that phenomena like blurring segue into convention with accustomed encounters, 27. The photograph's power to convince relies in large part on our implicit or explicit knowledge about how it was produced: as a physicochemical reaction to light. As noted in n. 54 above, C. S. Peirce classed photographs as indices. In a well-known two-part essay, Rosalind Kraus draws attention to the critical importance of indexing in Western abstract expressionism in producing apparently "self-referential" artworks. Like photography in this regard, such painting is composed solely

of the gesture that produces it. See her *The Originality of the Avant Garde and Other Modernist Myths* (Cambridge, Mass.: MIT Press, 1985), esp. "Notes on the Index 1" and "Notes on the Index 2," citing (inter alia) André Bazain and Roland Barthes.

70. Michael Taussig explores this process in his book, *Mimesis and Alterity* (New York: Routledge, 1993).

71. Heike Behrend and Tobias Wendl, "Photography: Social and Cultural Aspects," in *Encyclopedia of Africa South of the Sahara*, ed. John Middleton (New York: Scribner, 1997), 409–15.

72. Oral History Project, University of Witwatersrand, interview of Miss Nkwapa Ramorwesi by Mmantho Nkotsoe, May 25, 1982, Phokeng, "Bophuthatswana," South Africa. The concept of a "written record" can work the same way among the nonliterate.

73. Joseph Masagha [Masogha], "South African Agent," *Negro World*, September 27, 1924. Thanks to the historian Robert Hill.

74. Twain himself supplied nine pictures of rubber-gatherers with their hands cut off: Gore Vidal, "Twain on the Grand Tour," *New York Review of Books*, May 23, 1996, 26. For the best recent treatment of the atrocities in the Congo, see Adam Hochschild, *King Leopold's Ghost: A Story of Greed, Terror and Heroism in Colonial Africa* (Boston: Houghton Mifflin, 1998).

75. The more one knows, of course, the more one can read the contrivances in photographs, e.g., the famous Stalinist images from which purged Bolsheviks were excised. On the rich set of photographs published in *Albuns fotográficos e sescrítivos da colónia de Moçambique*, with photos by José dos Santos Rufino (Hamburg: Broschek & Co., 1929), see Eric Allina, " 'Fallacious Mirrors': Colonial Anxiety and Images of African Labor in Mozambique, ca. 1929," *History in Africa* 24 (1997): 9–52.

76. Philip Kwame Apagaya's photographs in this vein may be seen in *Snap Me One! Studiofotografen in Afrika*, ed. Tobias Wendl and Heike Behrend (Munich: Prestel, n.d. [1998?]), 52–63, "Shama/Ghana." See also Tobias Wendl and Nancy Du Plessis, "Future Remembrance: Photography and Image Arts in Ghana," film (Institut für den Wissenschaftlichen Film, 1997). Thanks to Birgit Meyer for alerting me to this. Her forthcoming work on local video-cinema in Ghana is fascinating.

77. However, see David, ed., *Inventaire général*; Guggenheim Museum, *In/Sight: African Photographers, 1940 to the Present* (New York: Guggenheim Museum, 1996); Steven Sprague, "Yoruba Photography: How the Yoruba See Themselves," *African Arts* 12, 1 (1978): 52–59, 107; *Snap Me One!* ed. Wendl and Behrend, and Vera Viditz-Ward, "Photography in Sierra Leone, 1850–1918," *Africa* 57, 4 (1987): 510–17.

78. The quotation is a citation from an earlier draft of Mustafa's paper.

79. See Kerstin Pinther, " 'Wenn die Ehe eine Erdnuß wäre . . . ' Über Textilien und Fotografie in Afrika," and also Tobias Wendl, "Francis K. Honny," in *Snap Me One!* ed. Wendl and Behrend, 36, 74 (in German), and quotation, English, from the unpublished "Proposal for an Exhibition" (1998), 3.

80. Geary, *Images from Bamun*; Jean Comaroff, *Body of Power, Spirit of Resistance* (Chicago: University of Chicago Press, 1985), 242; see also *Clothing and Difference: Embodied Identities in Colonial and Post-Colonial Africa, Bodies, Commodity, Text*, ed. Hildi Hendrickson (Durham, N.C.: Duke University Press, 1996).

81. Errington, *Death of Authentic Primitive Art*, 4, puts this very well: "Discourses create objects. . . . [In other words, they] materialize and narrativize categories by creating institutions and using media that illustrate, support, confirm, and naturalize their dominant ideas." See also MacGaffey, "Dialogues of the Deaf." For the almost accurate prognostication about the Coca Cola sign, see Jan Vansina, "Venture into Tio Country: Congo, 1963–1964," in *In*

Pursuit of History: Fieldwork in Africa, ed. Caroline Keyes Adenaike and Jan Vansina (Madison: University of Wisconsin Press, 1996), 117: Coke executives refer to Coke signs' overexposure as "the red rash."

82. I am aware that the chromolithograph appears in this book as a 1955 print with Hindi on it, but I am highlighting Sri Lankan language as a comparison to the appropriated "Ceylonese" image. See also Tobias Wendl, *Mami Wata: Oder ein Kult zwischen den Kulturen* (Munster: Lit, n.d. [1991?]); and Charles Gore and Joseph Nevadomsky, "Practice and Agency in Mammy Wata Worship in Southern Nigeria," *African Arts* 30, 2 (Spring 1997): 60–69, 95. The latter authors grant less importance to the lithograph for the wider Mami Wata cult than does Drewal. "Mami Wata" is a genre in the same way the "Chevrolet Impala" is a genre: such names describe not only a particular car, but also every car in the long history of a brand in its shifting market, even if late models share not even a chassis with earlier ones.

83. James Scott, *Domination and the Arts of Resistance: Hidden Transcripts* (New Haven, Conn.: Yale University Press, 1990). *Africans on Stage: Studies in Ethnological Show Business*, ed. Bernth Lindfors (Bloomington: University of Indiana Press, 1999), was published after this essay was drafted, but the essays by Zoe Strother, Neil Parsons, and Veit Erlmann are relevant to this discussion.

84. See also Robert J. Gordon, *The Bushman Myth: The Making of a Namibian Underclass* (Boulder, Colo.: Westview Press, 1992), 225 nn. 1 and 2. For another view of N!xao, the star of *The Gods Must Be Crazy*, see the photographs and text in Paul Weinberg, *In Search of the San* (Johannesburg: Porcupine Press, 1997).

85. It is easier to deal with "archives and artifacts that 'don't talk back,'" than with representatives of ethnic communities, who may be hostile or have their own political agenda that is not in harmony with the position of the museum curator," Anna Laura Jones notes in "Exploding Canons: The Anthropology of Museums," *Annual Review of Anthropology, 1993* 22 (1993): 215. Jones goes on to advise taking the counsel of representative groups. For what it is worth, I see Jones's advice as a recipe for banality.

86. Herbert Cole, *Icons: Ideals and Power in the Art of Africa* (Washington, D.C.: Smithsonian Institution Press, 1989), on a sculpture of Amadioha god of thunder, 56–57; Kramer, *Red Fez* discusses similar figures; for "Kota," see Vansina, *Art and History in Africa*, 31–32, 80, and Gable, this volume.

87. Sometimes context arises in unexpected ways: a Congolese displays national feeling by owning an oil painting of Patrice Lumumba in her living room; it is significant if it hangs beside a reproduction of *The Last Supper*. See Fabian, *Remembering the Present*, and Bogumil Jewsiewicki, "Corps interdits: La représentation christique de Lumumba comme rédempteur du peuple zaïrois," *Cahiers d'Études africaines* 141–42, 36 (1996): 113–42.

88. Julius E. Lips, *The Savage Hits Back* (1937; New Hyde Park, N.Y.: University Books, 1966). See also Fritz Kramer, *Red Fez*, 255. The reality of identity complicates the matter, however, as, for instance, Enid Schildkrout, Jill Hellman, and Curtis Keim, show in "Mangbetu Pottery: Tradition and Innovation in Northeast Zaire," *African Arts* 22, 2 (February 1989): 38–47, 101, and other work on the *statuettes colons*, figurines in Western dress made in Congo for the international market. These figures are interesting precisely because they do *not* specify the individual nature of Euro-Americans (tourists and so forth), and they include Africans too.

89. In Mustafa's essay, women wish to showcase their conformity to idealized modes of personal expression. See also Sprague, "Yoruba Photography."

90. I have written about the magical character of the camera's progenitor, the magic lantern (or slide projector) in Landau, "Illumination of Christ in the Kalahari Desert." Fox

Talbot: see Don Slater, "Photography and Modern Vision: The Spectacle of 'natural magic,'" in *Visual Culture,* ed. Chris Jenks (New York: Routledge, 1995), 227. Slater also discusses the conundrum of modernity and magic in photography.

91. Roland Barthes, "Rhetorique de l'image," *Communications* 4 (1964): 42, cited and translated by Rosalind Krauss, *Originality of the Avant Garde,* 211; Behrend and Wendl, "Photography: Social and Cultural Aspects," *Encyclopedia of Africa South of the Sahara,* 3: 413.

92. My thoughts here are very influenced by Taussig, *Mimesis and Alterity,* esp. ch. 14, which explores the irreducible "magic of mimesis." But see Hunt's and Gable's arguments, this volume.

93. On the Brownie, see the Eastman House Museum exhibit, "The History of the Camera," in Rochester, New York. "Brownie" is recorded earlier as a term meaning a benevolent goblin in Scotland (*Oxford English Dictionary,* s.v.). Eastman may also have been inspired to name his camera after Robert Brownell, who designed many of his camera bodies, but a public recognition of others was uncharacteristic of him.

94. Image-fixing borrows the cult value of the alter-ego of the self, who is therefore foreign, childish, or primitive. The very "types" who, as we have seen, reflexively defined naturalism by virtue of their lack of it, now become the sign for the mystery of naturalistic mimesis. Similarly, Walt Disney's Mickey Mouse (first appearing in "Tugboat Willy"), appears to have been formed from a caricature of early Jazz Age black vaudevillians.

95. Vogel, *Baulé,* 246 ff.

96. This again is why Mitchell argues that spirits are hidden in the highly mimetic images so common in the West, in Mitchell, *Iconology,* 90–91, 113; and see Walter Benjamin, "The Work of Art in the Age of Mechanical Reproduction," in *Illuminations: Essays and Reflections,* ed. Hannah Arendt (1968; New York: Schocken Books, 1969), 217–52. The point about specters is made differently by Ludwig Wittgenstein, "Remarks on Frazer's *Golden Bough,*" I, 1931 (MS 110), and II, ca. 1948 (MS 143), in Ludwig Wittgenstein, *Philosophical Occasions, 1912–1951,* ed. James Klagge and Alfred Nordman (Indianapolis: Hackett, 1993).

97. Axel-Ivar Berglund, *Zulu Thought Patterns and Symbolism* (Uppsala: Swedish Mission Institute, 1976), 85 ff.

98. Ibid.

99. The "historical testimony" of the person's existence, distilled and recalled as his or her image after corporeal death: cf. Benjamin, "Work of Art," 233.

100. Hecht and Simone, *Invisible Governance,* 123. See also Sprague, "Yoruba Photography," and *Snap Me One!* ed. Wendl and Behrend.

101. Behrend and Wendl, "Photography: Social and Cultural Aspects," 411.

102. Henri Junod, *The Life of a South African Tribe* (2d ed., New Hyde Park, N.Y.: University Books, 1962), 2: 362–63; see also Patrick Harries, "Exclusion, Classification and Internal Colonialism: The Emergence of Ethnicity among the Tsonga-Speakers of South Africa," in *The Creation of Tribalism in Southern Africa,* ed. Leroy Vail (London: James Curry; Berkeley and Los Angeles: University of California Press, 1989), 82–117. Taussig, *Mimesis and Alterity,* 102, shows the "implicitly sacred nature of image-making" (103) with the example of a Cuna (Panama) text in which *purba,* double or image, was alternately translated as "spirit."

103. Lienhardt writes that the deities of the Dinka may be thought of as "the images of human *passiones,*" using the Latin concept "*passiones*" to describe "events" such as anger and desire. Geoffrey Lienhardt, *Divinity and Experience: The Religion of the Dinka* (Oxford: Oxford University Press, 1961), 150, cited in Kramer, *The Red Fez;* see also Strother, *Inventing Masks.*

104. Kramer's intention is to counterpose Balzac's "ecstatic" knowing (which *pace* Nietzsche he calls "demonic") with "the doctrine of decorum evoked by the story of Jesus." Kramer, *Red Fez*, 253–55.

105. Janice Boddy, *Wombs and Alien Spirits: Women, Men and the Zar Cult of Northern Sudan* (Madison: University of Wisconsin Press, 1989).

106. Ibid.

107. Jean Rouch, *Les maîtres fous* (1956); Paul Stoller, "Regarding Rouch: The Recasting of West African Colonial Culture," in *Cinema, Colonialism, Postcolonialism: Perspectives from the French and Francophone World*, ed. Dina Sherzer (Austin: University of Texas, 1996), 65–79; and see Nwachukwu Frank Ukadike, *Black African Cinema* (Berkeley and Los Angeles: University of California Press, 1994), 48–52.

108. I admit that Adorno would be horrified at the connections I am drawing, and further, that he was thinking about music, not visual art. Kramer, *Red Fez*, passim; and Jean Comaroff, *Body of Power, Spirit of Resistance*; Boddy, *Wombs and Alien Spirits*. For African cowboys, I rely on notices of forthcoming or recent work by Pieter Remes, Kolanga Molei, and Didier Gondola, and discussion from Edward Alpers and Charles Ambler, via H-Africa, the e-mail discussion network cited above; for South Africa, see Shamil Jeppie and Bill Nasson, "'She preferred living in a cave with Harry the snake-catcher': Towards an Oral History of Popular Leisure and Class Expression in District Six, Cape Town, c. 1920s–1950s," in *Holding Their Ground: Class, Locality and Culture in Nineteenth- and Twentieth-Century South Africa*, ed. Philip Bonner (Johannesburg: Ravan Press, 1989), 285–306; Ezekiel Mphahlele, *Down Second Avenue* (New York: Anchor Books, 1971); anything by Nat Nakasa; or Mike Nicol's elegiac compendium, *A Good-Looking Corpse*. For West African blackface, see Catherine Cole, "Reading Blackface in West Africa: Wonders Taken for Signs," *Critical Inquiry* 23 (1996): 183–215, and forthcoming work by Emmanuel Akyempong; and, finally, personal observation, Nyanza, Kenya.

109. E. M. S. LeFleur Collection, UNISA, Pretoria. Circulars, A. A. S. Lefleur, "Griqua Independent Church of S.A. [Christmas] Greeting." N.d. (prob. late 1920s); this is an exact quotation, but with my emphasis added.

110. Jocelyn Alexander, "Dissident Perspectives on Zimbabwe's Post-Independence War," *Africa* 68, 2 (1998): 175, quoting Mawobho Sibindi.

111. H. Depelchin and C. Croonenberghs, *Journey to Gubulawayo: Letters of Fr. J. Depelchin and C. Croonenberghs, J.J., 1879, 1880, 1881* (Bulawayo, Zimbabwe: Historical Facsimiles, 1979), 133.

112. The same misprisions occurred in other colonial forums. According to an account in the *Nyasaland Times* cited by Megan Vaughan, for instance, the screening

> of a hygiene film lecture by the Durban City Health Department at a convention of native chiefs ended in uproar when one of the characters acting the part of a man suffering from venereal disease was recognized by the chairman. "That is my nephew", he cried in astonishment. "What is he doing in a film like this? I never knew he had been sick." "He's related to me too" called out the General Secretary . . .

The man suffering from venereal disease was recognized as a specific and named person, not a "type," and no "identification," no "ecstatic possession" of the viewers transpired. The audience understood the conventions of cinema, but the "double reality" of the actor-as-image fell away, and the audience was left looking only at a movie of a man's nephew. Vaughan, *Curing Their Ills*, 187. See also the example on p. 194. In film theory, emotion is the key element to participation in the narrative life of a protagonist; see Aumont, *Image*, 79.

113. Steve Landsberg, "The $10 Billion Man," *New York Times,* January 24, 1999, A21. The sense of "skepticism and self-correction" is, of course, accommodated by advertisers as ironic or "knowing" sensibility.

114. Like rock painting in Bushman communities in the Kalahari, advertising joins transformation and signification in one moment. Cf. J. David Lewis-Williams, *Believing and Seeing: Symbolic Meanings in Southern San Rock Paintings* (New York: Academic Press, 1981).

115. Paula Ben-Amos, "African Visual Arts from a Social Perspective," 45. Ian Fleming's character James Bond and some other Western icons have become ancestor figures in East Africa (pers. comm., Richard Waller and Dorothy Hodgson, August 1998; and see Henry Drewal, this volume). Drewal tells us elsewhere that the Hagenbeck chromolithograph was regarded by devotees as a "photo" of Mami Wata, in "Mermaids, Mirrors, and Snake Charmers: Igbo Mami Wata Shrines," *African Arts* 21, 2 (February 1988): 39.

116. See Paul Richards, *Fighting for the Rain Forest: War, Youth and Resources in Sierra Leone* (Portsmouth, N.H.: Heinemann, 1996), 48–60; Marissa Moorman, "Film, Gender and the Nation in Postcolonial Angola: On the Possibilities of Cinema as an Historical Source" (forthcoming); Gore and Nevadomsky, "Practice and Agency"; and see Brian Larkin, "Indian Films and Nigerian Lovers: Media and the Creation of Parallel Modernities," *Africa* 67, 3 (1997): 406–40.

117. Sandra T. Barnes, "The Many Faces of Ogun," in *Africa's Ogun: Old World and New,* ed. id. (Bloomington: Indiana University Press, 1989), 2 and passim. Perhaps not coincidentally, this book and Barnes's book share two contributors. The Ugandan spirit mediums called "Cwezi" also had different shapes in different historical discourses, yet they were "one" phenomenon, and have been considered as "living" art icons: see Renée Tantala, "Verbal and Visual Imagery in Western Uganda: Interpreting the 'Story of Isimbwa and Nyimawiru,'" in *Paths Toward the African Past: African Historical Essays in Honor of Jan Vansina,* ed. Robert W. Harms et al. (Atlanta: ASA Press, 1994), 223–43. Tantala explicitly connects the Cwezi idea to Jan Vansina's understanding of continuity in iconography in African art; see Vansina, *Art History in Africa,* 101 ff.

118. See Ricoeur, *Oneself as Another.*

Chapter 1

"Our Mosquitoes Are Not So Big": Images and Modernity in Zimbabwe

Timothy Burke

In 1990, I asked Roger Dillon, a long-time Zimbabwean advertiser who was the owner of a small marketing firm, whether he had ever seen an example of African audiences misinterpreting or misunderstanding an advertisement of some kind. Dillon, who specialized in mobile cinema vans and billboards, thought about it for a minute and then told me two stories. The first concerned the experiences of an acquaintance who had worked for the Rhodesian government as a health officer. On one occasion, Dillon said, the man had gone to the Zambezi Valley to talk to remote villages about malaria prevention. Equipped with several large drawings, a demonstration mosquito net, and a two-foot-long papier-mâché mosquito, he explained the transmission of the disease and suggested some possible strategies for its prevention. At the conclusion of his talk, the villagers thanked him but gently suggested that his ideas did not apply in their area, because their mosquitoes were so much smaller. In her book *Curing Their Ills: Colonial Power and African Illness*, Megan Vaughan cites an almost identical story told by a staff member of the Colonial Film Unit.

Dillon's second tale involved his experiences showing films to African audiences at mining compounds and in rural areas. At one such screening of a documentary on World War II, Dillon said, the audience arose screaming in fright when footage of planes strafing the ground was shown, and many of them fled the room. Again, this echoes many of the anecdotes discussed by Vaughan in her discussion of colonial films about hygiene. As Vaughan notes, these kinds of tales "abounded on the colonial circuit and were clearly told with great glee."[1] Why were they a genre, a common colonial story?

Some of the repetition here may simply be the literal truth: George Pearson, the man who tells the story about the mosquito in Vaughan's book, may actually have been Dillon's unnamed acquaintance, or at the least, may have been connected to him. Nevertheless, the currency and popularity of such stories clearly stretched beyond any one group of colonial individuals. The temptation is to treat these tales straightforwardly as a form of imperial apocrypha, tall tales whose popularity was due largely to their racist lampooning of the deficient interpretative skills of Africans, parallel to stories about African incompetence with machinery or middle-class African faux pas with European manners. This was certainly part of their appeal to white storytellers.

Another possibility is that these stories were elaborated versions of real events, that Africans in fact did interpret modern visual genres of representation as terrifyingly mimetic, that Africans did not understand the visual grammar of such materials and reacted in ways that Europeans saw as humorous or inappropriate. I think this too is absolutely on target. Africanist scholars are accustomed to discussing the complicated historical transactions and misrecognitions between Europeans and Africans regarding literacy and writing.[2] The historical evolution of various styles and technologies of visual representation within modern Western societies have been intrinsically just as complex, and their introduction to colonial Africa no less so. Of course, African audiences had surprising, sometimes violent, sometimes whimsical, reactions to visual media and imagery circulating during the era of colonial rule: how could it have been otherwise?

I want to review both of these interpretations in relation to visual materials and mass communication in twentieth-century Zimbabwe, with particular attention to early experiments in colonial cinema for African audiences and to the later development of advertisements directed at Africans. In so doing, I also want to explore a third way of thinking about such stories. White settlers and administrators were not merely amused by African reactions to films, posters, and the like. Whites were just as likely to express anxiety, uncertainty, and even fear about such reactions. For every whimsical story of Africans running in terror from a movie screen, there was an advertiser nervously commissioning a scientific study on the supposedly different physiological basis of African color vision. For every humorous anecdote about giant mosquitoes, there was a surveillance report by a policeman about the behavior of African audiences in urban movie houses. Whether fearful or bemused, white onlookers were never certain what Africans saw or how they saw it.

Part of their confusion was produced by the familiar ideological and cultural defense mechanisms among colonizers, which actively maintained the alterity of their African subjects. I argue that, to an equal extent, uncertainty about African audiences and their reception of visual materials was caused by uncertainty among whites about their own interpretative skills. New styles and technologies of visual representation unnerved Europeans to the same extent that they puzzled or alarmed Africans. Though whites often claimed mastery of the visual, their stories about Africans were sometimes a technique for laundering fears and anxieties about the impact that new styles of visual representation were having on their own lives. At the end of the day, these stories were ultimately part of a larger, albeit somewhat fractured, discussion between Africans and Europeans about the dangers and benefits of modern visual technologies. These stories were the tip of an iceberg, a deeply embedded and shared reaction to modern visual genres and forms.

THE UNEASY VISUAL

If we were to catalogue the core narratives to emerge out of Western colonial expansion since the sixteenth century, stories about Western modes of visual representation and their effect on non-Western peoples would surely figure prominently. "The native who fears that the camera will capture his soul" and "The native who fails to recognize himself in the mirror" are iconic tales that recur again and again in the Western imaginary. Some Africanists have discussed the actual colonial encounters that animated such narratives. For instance, Paul Landau has described the use of a magic lantern, an early form of image projector, in the early 1920s in colonial Botswana by Ernest Dugmore, a London Missionary Society preacher; and Christraud Geary has chronicled the role played by photography in the German colonial administration of Cameroon.[3]

The introduction of cinema to African audiences in British territories provides a valuable and relatively fresh opportunity to examine a similar colonial experience with visual representation.[4] It came only a few decades after film's appearance in metropolitan societies. From the moment of its invention, film has provoked intense anxieties in every society exposed to it, and we should not suppose that white colonizers were any less anxious about the general power of cinema merely because they were colonizers. Cinema combined, in the minds of many onlookers, the presumed mimetic powers of photography with the imaginative plasticity of literature and painting. It could bring the fantastic to life, make the unreal or impossible into truth, grant images a power they had never had before. Such a prospect was unnerving and exciting enough in itself, but of peculiar concern in a colonial situation. If whites themselves were not certain what to make of film, then what would Africans do? If cinema could make Frankenstein come to life, powerfully reproduce the Russian Revolution, or convince an audience that the image of a train was actually going to hit them, then could it not depict something that to African audiences might suggest (and thus help create) a remade social order?

The introduction of cinema to Africans in British territories was therefore handled with extreme care, and subjected to a good deal of semi-official scrutiny and surveillance. For example, the Bantu Educational Cinema Experiment, sponsored by the International Missionary Council, showed a variety of films to African audiences in East Africa between 1935 and 1937, mostly instructional films of different kinds. The "Experiment" recorded Africans' reactions to several versions of the same films, in order to elicit responses to variations of particular images and sequences. The supervisors of the project assumed, for the most part, that African reactions to the visual language of film would be fundamentally different than those of white audiences.

Figure 1.1. "Urban bioscope," Northern Rhodesia (Zambia), ca. 1907. Photo no. 6319b, National Archives of Zimbabwe (NAZ). Courtesy NAZ.

In some cases, they felt satisfied that they had accurately understood and anticipated African interpretations of films and were able to edit various movies until they conveyed the appropriate instructional message (though the project also struggled with considerable technical difficulties that interfered with this process of correction). For example, one film that tried to be a "slap-stick comedy" in which a young boy played pranks on his elders, produced both laughter and consternation. Upon investigating, the unit found that the concern was emanating from older members of the audience who thought that it was disturbing to show such disrespectful behavior, "even though the boy had a beating at the end."[5]

In other cases, however, the film unit was relatively baffled by audience reaction or deeply concerned about persistent misreadings. In one instance, a film about a progressive chief who tries to bring education to his district showed one scene in which the chief falls ill and is brought to a hospital, where he faints. Later, the chief arrives back home, cured in the nick of time, to save a schoolteacher from having to undergo a poison ordeal at the hands of a witch doctor. Audiences persistently assumed that the chief had died in the hospital and that the man who showed up later in the story, dressed in new clothes, was another, different, chief. The film unit resorted to reading an explanation through a microphone during the airing of the film, but it remained, in their judgment, a failure due to the audience's persistent refusal to recognize the chief as the same character. Another film experimented with dramatizing a local folktale called "The Hare and the Leopard" and made use of African actors dressed as anthropomorphic animals. The film was not a success with audiences. One viewer summed up a prevalent complaint by saying, "[T]he animals were merely human beings."[6]

The unit producers sometimes explained such misunderstandings by arguing that Africans had defective or reduced interpretative skills that were especially evident in dealing with visual material, capacities that would need to be investigated and specially catered to before instructional films for African audiences could be successful. At the same time, they often acknowledged the validity of African readings and misreadings of the films shown by the unit, attributing them in some cases to visual or conceptual errors on the part of the film producers but also to the legitimate exercise of interpretation by the audiences. After the showing of one film about a theft, debates often broke out among audience members about the fate of the thief and about the appropriateness of colonial law. In the first version of the story, the thief was killed by falling from a tree; in the second version, he was taken off by an African policeman, while his victim deposited his recovered money right away in the Post Office Savings Bank.[7] Audiences debated whether the thief should die—many assumed that his fall from the tree was deliberately caused by his pursuer, not by an accident—and argued about which court system should have jurisdiction in the case; many felt that the thief should be punished by a chief, not the European courts. Although the film producers described the assumptions about the thief's death as a "misunderstanding," it is also clear that they understood audience reactions as being legitimately predicated upon the film's content, and more

Figure 1.2. A scene from *Philemon the Footballer*, 1952. Central African Film Unit, photo no. 22390, NAZ. Courtesy NAZ.

important, on the content of African experience in colonial society. When Africans reacted with shock, surprise, or confusion to the capacity of moving images to conflate the imaginary and the real, the producers often conceded the legitimacy of these reactions without necessarily engaging in racist condescension.

When they made such concessions, they did so in part because their cinema experiment aroused concern among white and Indian audiences as well, often premised on the same apprehension about the ability of the cinema to transform reality through its uniquely powerful representational technology. In the case of the film about the thief, some Europeans who saw the movie told the unit that no film portraying crime or violence should be shown to Africans for fear that such a film would create the behavior it sought to censure.[8] Europeans and Africans watching a film on agricultural planning had a split reaction when a buffoonish African character realizes late in the film that he forgot to plant seeds in his well-tilled and watered garden: whites laughed, Africans did not. In the same film, Indians objected strenuously to a scene showing an Indian merchant overcharging an African customer, while Europeans objected to a scene showing a European farmer who mistreated his laborers and to the use of an African actor's voice to represent the voice of another European planter later in the film.[9] What is striking about the reaction to this and many of the other films shown by the unit is that African interpretations of the language and meaning of film were often closely mirrored or echoed by the reactions of other colonial audiences. All social groups were often unnerved or startled by the mimetic capacities of the cinema, concerned about the power of visual representation not only to reflect but to transform social relations in colonial society. Indeed, in many cases, Africans, Europeans, and others were critical precisely because the camera translated social reality into cinematic images, transforming unspoken understandings about everyday life into a discomforting mirror that demanded some response.

The same pattern marked similar experiments with cinema in colonial Southern Rhodesia (Zimbabwe) from the late 1910s to the early 1940s. African audiences were watched, both openly and in secret, for their reactions to films. At the same time, the reactions of whites to movies, especially during World War II, were sometimes of equal concern to government officials and various civic groups and were watched closely as well.

Local efforts by the Rhodesian state and by civic groups like the Boy Scouts to supervise cinema for Africans were particularly provoked by the recommendation of a metropolitan commission in the 1930s that no distinction between African and European audiences be made in the case of films. However, surveillance and official concern about Africans and the cinema had been prevalent in Rhodesia since the end of World War I. As one Rhodesian official typically concluded, "for the Native, there is a wealth of opportunity for misunderstanding even our simple domestic melodramas. Incident is everything to the Native, and unless the subject deals quite definitely with an artistic development based on his own psychology, a wrong impression is bound to be created."[10]

Between 1917 and 1940, Rhodesian police officials reported a number of incidents they found distressing while surveilling African audiences. During one newsreel that showed a white beauty queen, "thrills of delight" were heard, and an unspecified but apparently disturbing "noise" was heard whenever kissing appeared on the screen.[11] Another movie showed an African stealing roller skates from his former employer, a skating rink, after he is sacked for disturbing a white woman skater. The skates are brought back to his rural homestead, where he explains that these are "the things that amuse the white man." A police sergeant charged with investigating this film immediately requested it be taken out of circulation, as it was "very much appreciated by the natives, as was evident from the laughter."[12] In another instance, a Roman Catholic missionary who showed films in townships assured police that "should anything of an objectionable nature be shown... I immediately shut the film off and continue further on."[13]

Censorship of this sort aimed at Africans was hardly exceptional: the British South Africa Company's local authorities and later administrators were perpetually wary about African access to a wide range of materials, from Garveyist tracts to flyers for patent medicines and fancy clothing. However, visual materials, especially film, aroused particular anxiety. That concern was primarily explained, just as in other instances, as a concern for the deficient interpretative powers of Africans or about their alien cultural sensibilities. But just as in other instances, the extent to which official fears about African audiences were echoed by concerns about white audiences was often remarkable. One official file leapt from the need to exercise selective censorship of films for African audiences to a long harangue about the appeal of movies to Europeans of "limited mentality," arguing that regular patrons of movies favored "spectacularity, sensationalism and maudlin sentimentality," and that they were unable to appreciate films either in terms of messages or in terms of art.[14] Having delivered these remarks, the author of the report immediately segued back to the inability of Africans to properly understand cinema.

In another instance, a 1942 report about the exhibition of war newsreels to white farmers near Chinhoyi, northwest of the capital, the supervisor of the film unit complained to the minister of internal affairs that white audiences were indifferent to or actively scornful of the movies.[15] White audiences in southern Africa also demanded that images of the Rhodesian African Rifles (an all-black unit) bearing arms be deleted from wartime films.[16] At the end of a lengthy correspondence between government officials and filmmakers about the making of a film on Cecil Rhodes entitled *There Lies Your Hinterland*, Prime Minister Godfrey Huggins scrawled at the bottom: "History should be presented factually down to the last detail. In other words, fiction and fact should not be mixed. I also realize if this were done it would probably ruin the movie business."[17]

These sentiments have a certain bitter hilarity coming from the pen of a prime minister of Southern Rhodesia. Dominant elites expressed concern that films mixed "fiction and fact" in a uniquely powerful manner, not only for African audiences, however, but also for whites of "low mentality," children, and other people in England. Members of these audiences expressed the same concern. Africans probably did at times run from images of strafing planes or make appreciatively naughty noises at white beauty queens, just as white audiences sought and feared cinematic spectacle or nervously examined cinematic representations of their own vigorously sanitized history of colonial conquest.

The historical development of visual advertising directed at Africans provides further insight into these issues, while also illuminating the historical specificity of different visual media. Print advertisements, billboards, and similar promotions directed at white Rhodesians appeared almost immediately after the founding of the colony in 1890. Similar advertisements explicitly directed at African consumers emerged in the 1920s, and their propagation was marked by profound uncertainties from that point on. Some of these problems had relatively little to do with questions about visual representation and more to do with an imagined relationship between consumption and citizenship, more to do with local struggles between factions of capital interested in suppressing African wages and manufacturing capital's interest in African purchasing power. Advertising to Africans acknowledged their considerable and constantly growing centrality to the colonial economy as consumers, a fact most white Rhodesians were unprepared to accept.

But many of the furtive debates among marketers and between marketers and groups of concerned whites about African advertising were animated by concerns specifically related to the relationship between visual representation and colonial hegemony. At the same time that the cinema was a growing concern, in the 1920s, civic groups publicly requested that the Rhodesian government regulate images seen on posters in stores and other public locations in colonial Salisbury, because Africans might be intercepting messages intended for white consumers and might act inappropriately as a result.[18] Many businesses responded positively to these requests, and the government also passed a law in 1929 that heavily restricted visual advertisements of any kind in rural reserve areas.[19] As in the case of cinema, the primary fear expressed by whites was that to reproduce a particular image was, in some fashion, to make what it showed into reality. For example, one Anglican cleric complained early in the colonization process that pictures showing mission Africans in fancy European clothing—a common genre—were not based on reality, but acknowledged that the pictures were helping to create such fashions where they had not existed.[20]

Print advertising directed specifically at Africans began to appear in colonial Zimbabwe in the 1930s. Once it became relatively common, many whites warily examined such ads both for images that showed Africans things they should not be allowed to see, such as white women portrayed as objects of desire, and for images that represented a social world dramatically out of line with colonial reality. The former appeared only rarely, as advertisers were acutely conscious of white sensibilities in this regard, but the advertisers I interviewed told me that they often had to fend off complaints in the latter category. Of course, this underscores that it was not just Africans who were surreptitious spectators of images meant for whites, but the other way around as well. Printed images displayed in public and semi-public forums, unlike cinema or written materials, do not necessarily betray their audiences, which is part of what makes them unnerving in situations where cultural hegemony rests on fragile underpinnings.

Print advertisements used throughout southern Africa often portrayed Africans achieving some high social and economic standing through the wise use of some commodity, particularly from the 1950s to the 1970s. One campaign for Castle Lager, for example, showed Africans fly-fishing in the mountains and picnicking next to their car, transposing black men and women directly into images that had initially featured white subjects. Campaigns for Ambi, a skin lightener, featured a wealthy African couple relaxing at Victoria Falls and a light-skinned African doctor reviewing charts, contrasted with his dark-skinned janitor. Other campaigns were careful to show African achievements as more suited to the standards of colonial society: a regular series of print ads for Lifebuoy soap showed African men in a variety of "appropriate" work settings, including mining, bricklaying, clerking, and teaching.

Moreover, even in those cases where advertisements made implicit promises of social advancement to Africans that were clearly unrealistic, standard visual tropes that predated the advent of print advertisements in Africa were still extensively adapted for use in colonial society. For example, ads for toiletries aimed at Africans

Figure 1.3. Advertisement for Lifebuoy soap, *Bantu Mirror*, September 10, 1960.

frequently tapped into one of the oldest themes in modern advertising, a theme with deep roots in Victorian England and the United States, namely, the fantasized power of a good soap to turn blacks into whites. These were not subtle ads: one version, promoting Gossage's Soap, showed a caricatured African whose face was half white and half black, with the caption "Soap Makes Black White."[21] But these were also images that could never appear in this form in colonial Africa itself. They would have been massively transgressive. As a shorthand description of the cleansing power of a soap, making use of Africans as a symbol while appealing to white metropolitan consumers, they were fine. As a promise to Africans that they might literally become white, they were impossible to accept. The basic trope—toiletries can lighten you and fulfill some social aspirations—thus remained the same, but the content of the image often changed, to show Africans becoming lighter, but not "white."

MISINTERPRETATIONS

Advertisers worried a great deal about images and their interpretation by Africans. Elsewhere, I have recounted in detail the general concern of advertisers about communicating with African audiences.[22] Virtually every individual aspect of advertising intended for African audiences was scrutinized for the possibility that it might contain a fatal miscommunication or error of some kind. The sensibilities of African consumers and of wary white onlookers alike figured into the calculus of marketing teams as they designed print campaigns. But nothing made these professionals more anxious than the visual component of print advertisements. As professional conventions governing transnational or cross-cultural advertising grew in importance around the world during the 1950s, they had an immense impact on the outlook and practice of advertising professionals in southern Africa. At the outset, such conventions argued that pictures had an immediacy and inherent transcultural currency that made them the ideal medium for conveying advertising messages in a wide variety of cultural settings. Pictures, in contrast to words, were believed to have universal power. Most advertising apocrypha about cross-cultural blunders and disasters turned on poor translations or the dual meaning of words, like the selling of the Chevrolet Nova in Latin America ("Nova" being turned into *no va*, or "doesn't go") or the translation of "Coke adds life" into Chinese, allegedly becoming "Coke brings your dead ancestors back to life" in the process. Many First World professionals argued that the ability of a picture to make real some proposition about the power of a commodity was not usually subject to such textual miscommunications. (They no longer so argue, and the general consensus today is that visual communication across cultures should be approached with as much caution as any other form of communication, or perhaps more.)[23]

Professionals in southern Africa never accepted the then-conventional wisdom. Even in the 1950s, their most time-honored anecdote about the dangers of cross-cultural advertising concerned an image rather than words. An ad for Raleigh bicycles that showed a young African boy fleeing a lion on his bicycle had led to a precipitous drop in Raleigh sales among Africans in some parts of the region, it was said. The explanation was that Africans had interpreted the advertisement to mean that lions would chase you if you bought a Raleigh bicycle. From the outset, advertisers wondered what Africans saw and how they saw it, what kinds of perceptions Africans brought to pictures and especially colors.

As in the case of the cinema experiments, advertisers sometimes had a racist understanding of African perceptions, seeing them in terms of a lack, an absence, or an incapacity. Color was a particular concern among advertisers working with the "African market": many were concerned that particular colors were seen as "taboo" by African viewers.[24] Some of this obsession was laundered through scientific racism: advertisers commissioned studies that allegedly "proved" that Africans lacked the same range of color vision that whites had. Later on, similar studies understood the difference in cultural, rather than biological terms, but the core proposition remained in place.[25] I encountered the continuing power of this idea myself while interviewing a South African advertiser who had worked in Zimbabwe for many years. Africans, he argued, reacted very differently than whites to pictures, particularly to brightly colored ones, which tended to overwhelm and frighten them. Leaning over with a conspiratorial air, he informed me that he had a theory about this reaction, based on his long experience. Africans spent most of their lives in the dark, he explained—their rural huts were dark, townships were dark, mines were dark—so bright images "excited" them.

This advertiser was perhaps unusual in the racist absurdity of his views and in the persistence of those views (most professionals in southern Africa have dropped the more overtly racist underpinnings of their practice with alacrity in recent years). However, the foundation of such a view lies fairly deep within professional practice in the region. What made the whole matter even more difficult for advertisers was an equally fundamental assumption that pictorial display was the most powerful technique for reaching and transforming African consumers. This is precisely what made images so dangerous: they were understood as far more powerful than words in dealing with a population assumed to be essentially nonliterate and mostly without access to radio. The potential consequences from a misunderstanding were grave, but so too were the potential benefits from a successful campaign. J. E. Maroun, an advertiser active in the 1950s and 1960s, a man who was unusually blunt in his admission that his profession's goal was to transform the innermost self of Africans, held that the single most powerful and effective way to do this was simply to picture an African using a new product in a new manner.[26]

Just as in the case of cinema, stories also abound about African misrecognitions of the language of print advertising and of commodity packaging. One example involves the image of a baby on the wrapper for Stork Margarine, which apparently was taken by some Africans to signify that the margarine was made from rendered baby fat. During interviews in Harare, several individuals recounted stories about small changes in the packaging of cigarettes that they took to signal a secret reduction in the quality of the tobacco. Local Colgate-Palmolive executives told me that changing the image of a brand is approached with great reluctance in southern Africa for exactly this reason. Campaigns announcing that a product is "new" and "improved" are very rare in comparison with the Euro-American context. I assume that these stories, like stories of Africans running from cinema screens, have some empirical truth to them, even though they are also told and retold as humorous apocrypha by those who have never come into personal contact with these incidents.

Such reactions suggest once more that Africans themselves have sometimes been uneasy about the power of modern technologies of visual representation to transform everyday life. In numerous conversations, particularly with older individuals, I was told how underwear advertisements in newspapers have created immorality and licentiousness among young people. Many also blamed the Zimbabwean government's promotional campaigns against AIDS for creating loose sexual behavior. By picturing sexuality, these images are held to create the behavior they envision. However, advertising images also have had immense appeal and fascination for many African viewers for much the same reason, as a set of novel and powerful propositions about how life looks elsewhere and how life could look at home.

And once again, whites' uncertainties about the meaning of pictures to African onlookers, whites' fears that the potentially surreptitious gaze of Africans might intercept images in public space, have not only reflected whites' desire to maintain social control over Africans. Such discomfort has also been rooted in whites' concerns about the power of advertising to transform their own desires and their own sense of self through new technologies of visual representation. In this regard, advertising is a fundamentally different than film. Anxieties about the cinema have centered on its technologically driven capacity to make the imaginary come to life; anxieties about advertising, especially about the visual dimension of advertising, center on its capacity for subverting the free will of its targets. Indeed, one of the best known and most widespread genres of opposition to advertising centers on its visual components: the paranoiac writings of Wilson Bryan Key and his fellow travelers about "subliminal images" in advertising.[27] Familiarity with the idea of subliminal images in advertisements, even among those highly skeptical about the idea, is nearly universal around the world: I even had several interviewees in the townships of Harare loosely describe an approximation of this phenomenon.[28] The wide currency of the concept has something to do with its correspondence to the lived experience of viewing advertisements: many people feel as if they have been compelled to purchase a commodity or pursue an action by representational mechanisms that they cannot quite perceive or identify. This sense was, I think, as common among white audiences in colonial Zimbabwe as it was in the United States or Europe. Concern over African responses to posters, billboards, and print advertisements was a way to defer or displace these deeper anxieties. Modern visual advertising proposed a new kind of disconnection between the surface of things and a hidden truth underneath; it required that viewers routinely accept and be motivated by a representation that they know to be a lie. When Africans "failed" to see that the picture of a baby on the surface of a margarine wrapper had no relationship with the substance inside, that the baby's image was arguably a lie and, at the least, a major slippage between representation and reality, they called into question the whole of advertising practice and indeed, the whole of modern modalities of viewing and understanding visual material. If whites laughed at African responses, it was a rather nervous sort of laughter.

The fact that fears about the power of new technologies of representation could be deferred at all is what makes this a study of a specifically colonial situation. Colonial southern Africa was (and southern Africa still remains) a deeply censorious place, a place where police sat in darkened movie theaters taking notes on the noises that Africans made in response to the action, where concerned individuals furtively scanned African newspapers looking for images that portrayed inappropriate social ambitions, where self-conscious state censors specified with great precision that magazine pictures of semi-nude women must have their nipples erased, and so on. In colonial southern Africa, the racialized distribution of power and the nature of the colonial public sphere allowed for the deferral of the impulse for censorship substantially onto a subaltern group, with the usual consequences in terms of social control and regulation, burdened by the usual quotient of racist thought and practice. But underneath it all, pictures—whether they were on a screen or in a newspaper—both excited and repelled the whole of colonial Zimbabwean society, Africans and Europeans alike. Such sensations were unevenly represented and reported in public discourse, to be sure, but the advent of new kinds of visual media also underscored the complicated and convoluted manner in which modernity was a mutually forged artifact in colonial southern Africa.

NOTES

1. Megan Vaughan, *Curing Their Ills: Colonial Power and African Illness* (Stanford, Calif.: Stanford University Press, 1991).

2. The most recent and interesting treatment of this subject is Paul Landau, *The Realm of the Word: Language, Gender, and Christianity in a Southern African Kingdom* (Portsmouth, N.H.: Heinemann, 1995).

3. Paul Landau, "The Illumination of Christ in the Kalahari Desert," *Representations* 45, Winter (1994): 25–39; Christraud Geary, *Images from Bamun: German Colonial Photography at the Court of King Njoya, Cameroon, West Africa, 1902–1925* (Washington, D.C.: Smithsonian Institution Press, 1988).

4. A forthcoming work by James Burns should vastly expand our understanding of the history of colonial cinema in southern Africa.

5. L. A. Notcutt and G. C. Latham, *The African and the Cinema: An Account of the Work of the Bantu Educational Cinema Experiment during the Period March 1935 to May 1937* (London: Edinburgh House Press for the International Missionary Council, 1937), 39.

6. Ibid., 48.

7. Ibid., 33.

8. Ibid., 34.

9. Ibid., 46–47.

10. National Archives of Zimbabwe (NAZ), S 2784/3/A-2, Cinema Censorship, "Cinema Report."

11. NAZ S 2784/3/A-2, Cinema Censorship, Sgt. A. G. Horn, British South Africa Police to chief superintendent, June 1927.

12. NAZ S 2784/3/A-2, Cinema Censorship, detective sergeant to superintendent, July 1917.

13. NAZ S 2784/3/A-2, Cinema Censorship, Tilman Esser, St. Patrick's Church, to British South Africa Police, 1927.

14. NAZ S 2784/3/A-2, Cinema Censorship, "Cinema Report."

15. NAZ S 482/240/39.

16. NAZ S 482/240/39, information officer to minister of information, November 1941.

17. NAZ S 482/240/39.

18. NAZ SA 5/1/5, Salisbury Chamber of Commerce Minute Books, 1921–31.

19. See NAZ S 2390/751/39, Department of Native Affairs, Correspondence re: Regulation of Advertisements, 1927–32.

20. G. W. H. Knight-Bruce, *Memories of Mashonaland* (London: Edward Arnold, 1895), 149.

21. For more on this subgenre of advertisement, see Anne McClintock, *Imperial Leather: Race, Gender, and Sexuality in the Colonial Contest* (New York: Routledge, 1995), ch. 5; Jan Nederven-Pieterse, *White on Black: Images of Africa and Blacks in Western Popular Culture* (New Haven, Conn.: Yale University Press, 1992); and Thomas Richards, *The Commodity Culture of Victorian England* (Stanford, Calif.: Stanford University Press, 1990), ch. 3.

22. Timothy Burke, *Lifebuoy Men, Lux Women: Commodification, Consumption and Cleanliness in Modern Zimbabwe* (Durham, N.C.: Duke University Press, 1996), ch. 7.

23. Paul Messaris, *Visual Persuasion: The Role of Images in Advertising* (Thousand Oaks, Calif.: Sage Publications, 1997), 91–125.

24. One black professional, Nimrod Mkele, found himself having to reassure white colleagues that there were no colors that carried negative connotations for Africans with the exception of the color black, whose negative meaning, he noted, was "universal." See Nimrod Mkele, *Advertising to the Bantu: Second Advertising Convention in South Africa* (Durban: Society of Advertisers, 1959), 134.

25. See A. P. van der Reis, *The Response of Urban Blacks to Colours* (Pretoria: Bureau of Market Research, 1980), for one more recent example.

26. J. E. Maroun, "Second Address, 'Bantu Market' Session," in *Third Advertising Convention in South Africa: The Challenge of a Decade* (Johannesburg: Statistic Holdings, 1960), 133.

27. See Wilson Bryan Key, *The Clam-Plate Orgy, and Other Subliminal Techniques for Manipulating Your Behavior* (Englewood Cliffs, N.J.: Prentice-Hall, 1980), and other works by the same author.

28. Tapera household, Kambuzuma Township, Harare, May 18, 1991.

Chapter 2

The Sleep of the Brave: Graves as Sites and Signs in the Colonial Eastern Cape

David Bunn

This essay discusses the representational power of graves in the Eastern Cape region of colonial South Africa between 1840 and 1880. Under conditions of extreme violence in this period, something of a reciprocal exchange developed between British and Xhosa forms of memorialization. Evidence of this convergence may be found in the increasing visibility of Xhosa graves as topographical features, and a widespread obsession with the idea of the disinterred corpse.

THEORIES AND SEPULCHERS

What does a grave represent? There is considerable disagreement between anthropologists and art historians on this question. First and foremost, a tomb is usually understood to be a chamber for the corpse, a receptacle in which the body undergoes its silent transformation through deliquescence into dust. But for those who remember the departed, the grave is also a place to be visited. At the graveside, in homage or in mourning, one seems closer to the tangible presence of the dead below. At a second order of remove, moreover, this sense of presence may also come to be associated with the political role of the dead citizen living on in the memory of the public. For this reason, many historically important graves become reembellished and elevated into monuments associated with the maintenance of civil society.

For the eighteenth-century European imagination, as we shall see, graves were signifiers with a landscape function. Many of them were designed for visual impact, appearing over the horizon for an approaching observer and appealing, in epitaphs, to a new class of sympathetic citizens for whom funeral monuments were a fashionable occasion for meditation. Significantly, as graves became places to visit and signs to be read, they were also displaced from urban churchyards. In the first quarter of the nineteenth century, the Euro-American rural cemetery movement adopted and popularized the idea of picturesque grave landscapes in a countryside setting. Cemeteries became places to wander, meditate, or picnic.[1]

Broadly speaking, there are thus two general categories of explanation for sepulchral representation. The first is that the grave is a *sign*, consisting of a signifier such as a headstone, epitaph, or marble slab, associated with a signified, the idea of the memorialized departed. But this explanation is also rather awkward. A grave can never be a pure sign in the semiotic sense. The relationship between signifier and signified is not, in the end, an arbitrary one, as it is in linguistics, precisely because most people also associate the grave with the presence of the dead. When we speak of graveyards being haunted by restless spirits, or of grief-stricken mourners who prostrate themselves upon tombs, we are also speaking about the grave as a point of access to other worlds. Mortuary signs are unusual in that they *have presence*; for this reason, they are less like signs and closer to what Charles Peirce and later Roland Barthes called *indexes*. Just as for Peirce a photograph is indexical because it has a "motivated" relationship to the real, stemming from the actual exposure of the photographic plate, so too the grave is associated with the literal proximity of human remains and the lingering spiritual presence of the dead.[2] Its placing is also fixed rather than symbolically flexible, for if the headstone is moved away from the presumed last resting place of the corpse, it becomes a different sort of monument altogether.[3]

As every elegiac poet knows, tombs are not mute. Within the English topographical verse tradition, graves are, first and foremost, markers of arrest, points at which a freely wandering subject on an imaginary landscape circuit is addressed and cast into a meditative mood. In Gray's "Elegy," for instance, the speaker pauses before a rural churchyard, to make the following observation about the relationship of discursive dependency between tombs and sympathetic mourners: "On some fond breast the parting soul relies, / Some pious drops the closing eye requires: / E'en from the tomb the voice of Nature cries" (ll. 89–91). This crying out of the grave—one might even call it ventriloquism—also has an important ideological function. Emerging at a time of massive rural peasant displacements, the topographical elegy imagines the rural cemetery as an extension of the organic, precapitalist village community in need of paternalistic care.[4] These conventional forms of ideological naturalization were then transported, with significant regional adjustments, into the writing of English colonial settlers around the world.

By far the most significant wave of English immigration to the Eastern Cape was the group known as the 1820 Settlers. Envisaged as a solution to frontier instability abroad, and civil unrest and overpopulation at the time of the Peterloo massacre in England, this settlement scheme involved joint-stock parties of emigrants who were settled in the Zuurveld district (later called Albany), between the Bushmans and the Great Fish River, centered on the present-day town of Grahamstown. Within two years, all but six hundred of the original five thousand settlers had been forced to abandon farming and move to towns.[5]

With the arrival of the 1820 settlers in the Eastern Cape, local land and property relations were substantially changed. Most visibly, new spatial linkages developed between defensible sites: colonial forts and signaling stations, with their attendant military rayons; emerging settler villages like Bathurst and Salem; fortified farmhouses; and a network of churches with walled graveyards. All these played a role in the development of the settler public sphere, and churches were particularly important in the regulation of rhythms of visiting and gathering that make up the spatiotemporal experience of community.[6] "Virtually every well-to-do emigrant," says Crais, "hoped to establish a landed estate in the Cape Colony," and this desire was communicated in an obsession with the idea of the Eastern Cape as a picturesque landscape dotted with pleasing rural architectures.[7] But there are significant differences between the metropolitan and colonial representation of churchyard monuments. Ruins and sepulchers in colonial South Africa cannot function primarily as points of meditative attraction, as they are also always signifiers of *violence in the present*. For every picturesque church, for every hoary gravestone, there is the counterexample of the pillaged farmhouse and the disinterred corpse. Thus while the poetry of the settler Thomas Pringle refers extensively to the figure of the Whiggish, elegiac wanderer, he is only too frequently unable to distance himself from the memory of violence. Traveling through the Kat River region, for instance, he pauses before the remnants of an old mission: "a roofless ruin, scathed by flame and smoke". "[A] baboon," he concludes, "with jabbering cry doth mock / The pilgrim passing in a pensive mood."

Despite these setbacks—the appearance of the baboon in the ruin—there is a strong association between graveyards and an emerging Eastern Cape settler public sphere. In a smug commemorative sermon delivered at Bathurst in 1845, the Reverend John Ayliff paid homage to the Pilgrim Fathers of the settlement. With frequent reference to the Providential colonization of New England, this address marks the point at which the first generation of white settlement thinks of itself in the past and future tense. Secure in the knowledge of a network of linked church sites at Salem, Clumber, Kowie, Cuylerville, Grahamstown, and elsewhere, with the flower-bedecked Methodist chapel in Bathurst at its heart, Ayliff is able to construct a founding narrative for the settlement, symbolized by the patriarchal grave: "Today, in which we commemorate twenty-five years of adversity and prosperity—today, at the grave of our Fathers, let our enmities cease."[8] With its litany of references to church sites within riding and walking distance of one another, the sermon offers a foundational account of the spatially coherent and ideologically secure community. Graves, in this view, have a *centripetal* address; instead of appealing to the individual Liberal wanderer, they evoke the emerging, collective subject of settlement. In the shadow of the graveyard, a new enunciative position appears for the likes of John Ayliff. Not only is he able to speak with confidence about the meaningful settler past but the future holds consequent promise, as though the burial of the first patriarchs were an act of insemination as much as of memorial.

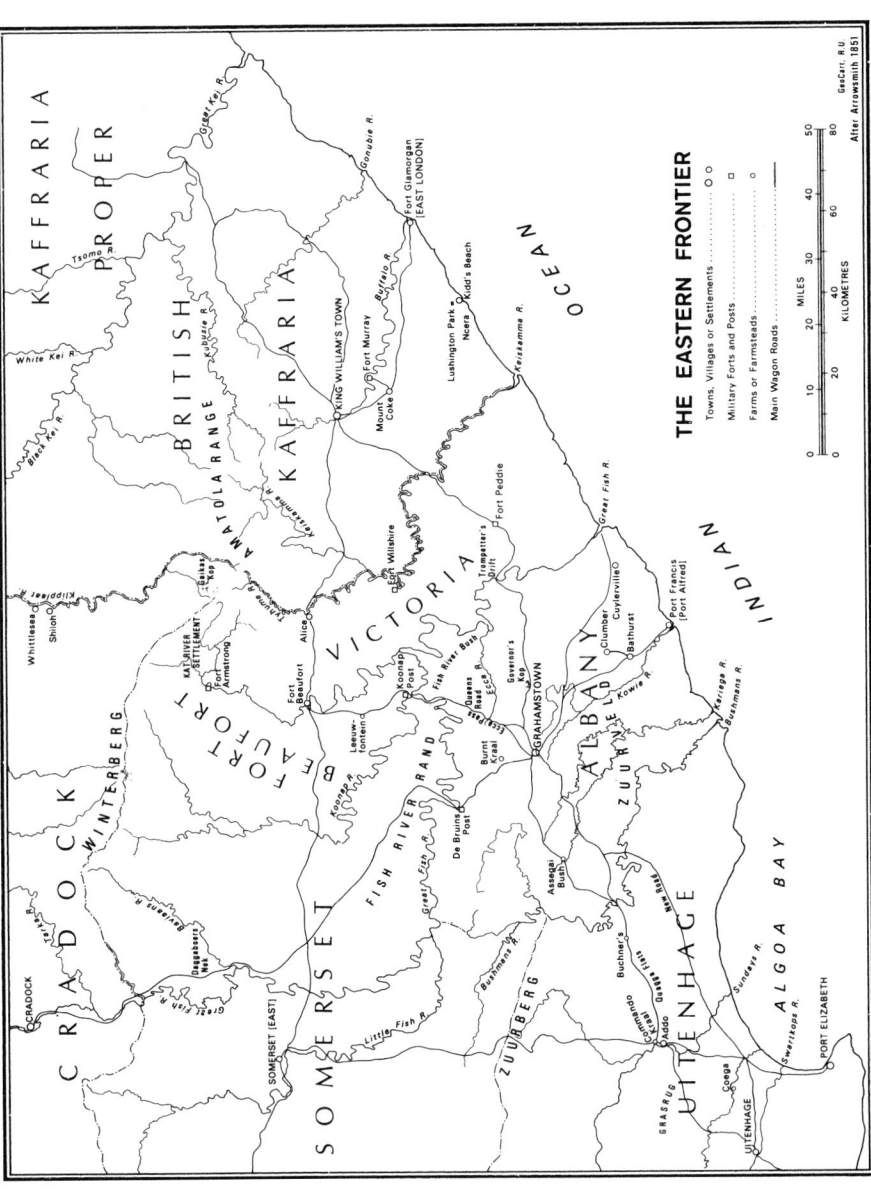

Figure 2.1. Map of the Eastern Cape. *The Albany Journals of Thomas Shone*, ed. Penelope Silva (Cape Town: Maskew Miller Longman for Rhodes University, Grahamstown, 1992).

ON THE MELANCHOLY OF THOMAS SHONE

Graveyards like those in Bathurst and at Salem were an important visual analogue of the idea of white settlement itself. As rows of gravestones fanned out and the second generation returned to tend the graves of the founders, so genealogy itself was dramatized, with the graveyard as a metonymy for the new settler identity in its landscape context. Each headstone, therefore, functioned both as an individual sign, and in a visible syntactical association with neighboring monuments. But this functioning of sepulchral symbolism also depended on control over the *indexical* nature of the settler grave: that sense of the grave full of the presence of the corpse and haunted by the manner of its death. Management of the idea of violent death was one of the key preoccupations of Albany memorials.

Consider the melancholy example of Thomas Shone. A working-class Cockney, Shone had the additional distinction of having spent time as a prisoner in France during the Napoleonic Wars. While incarcerated, he was helped by French Freemasons, who lovingly tattooed his body with complex Masonic symbols. Coincidentally, when Shone and his family emigrated to Albany in 1820, they intruded on a domain where bodily embellishment was perhaps the chief representational language. This was an area heavily contested by Ngqika Xhosa, who claimed ancestral grazing rights and access to pits where cosmetic clays were dug. Soon the settlers began to lose cattle to raids. After crop failure left the Shones impoverished, they moved in 1828 to join the Nottingham party on the Lushington River, "made up of 36 farms, grouped around a central 'village' area (market place and chapel ground) named Clumber."[9] This centripetal arrangement meant that Shone's new property virtually adjoined the church, and it was within walking distance of Bathurst. Catastrophe visited the family again between 1832 and 1841. In November 1832, eleven-year-old Elizabeth Shone was raped and murdered while out herding cattle. Five years later, Thomas's beloved wife Sarah died, and four years after that, his eldest son drowned.[10]

This catalogue of horrors was not as unusual as it might sound. What is important for our purposes, though, is the sequence of symbolic funeral practices that followed the death of the two Shone women. Young Elizabeth was buried in the Methodist graveyard at Clumber. In a pathetic memorial poem written for her, a neighbor, William Elliott, drew attention to the fate of the child's body, using the familiar epitaphic trope of prosopopoeia, as though making the child speak from the grave:

> Beneath this cold clod lies my pereshing clay.
> On yonder green hills was my life taken away
> And abused unto death in a barbarous way,
> While my body in blood it was rol'd.
> When the Kaffer he seized me, to escape I try'd;
> I struggled, I Mourn'd, 'Have pitty', I cried,
> But the Monster, he stab'd me: I bled and I died,
> Then my body he thrust in a hole.[11]

Here the mourner's attention is drawn through a series of deictic rhetorical markers to the location of the murder on "yonder green hills," as well as to the brutal treatment of the body "thrust in a hole." It is an epitaph intended not for consolation, but for the incitement of outrage. Implicit in the poem is a warning that the superficially picturesque encircling landscape is a place of deep menace.[12]

Shone's *Journal* also shows evidence of the deeply traumatic effect of his wife's death. His writing is punctuated by references to the periodic labor of mourning. A careful record is kept of the cutting of the tombstone; the carving of the epitaph, letter by letter; the painting of the stone and the fencing of the tomb, a process that occupied the distraught father of six orphans for some seven months. Moreover, there is evidence that Shone disliked the pompous religiosity of the Bathurst Methodist community. Unlike the many surrounding graves in the Clumber churchyard that speak of exemplary suffering, the force of God's will in the world, or the allegory of successful settlement, Sarah Shone's resorts to the older vocative appeal of the English country churchyard. It calls out to strangers rather than the insensitive audience of local patriarchs: "Ah! Stranger", the epitaph beckons, "had it been your lot to know / the worth of her whose relics sleep below / In silent sorrow o'er this grave you'd bend / and mourn."[13]

It is customary to think of graves in terms of memorialization and of the past. But if we view them as landscape features, with a particular discursive address to an imagined subject, they appear to have a different temporality. In fact, graves usually address civil society in the future tense. That is to say, their ability to function within the general syntax of mourning depends on the presumption of a stable civil society in the future, administered by those with roughly the same attitudes to the body and to property. For the majority of Methodist graves, this entails reference to the metaphor of sacrifice and providential death. For Thomas Shone, no such communal understanding exists. His wife's grave establishes a far less secure enunciative position, preferring instead to trust to the "stranger" in the future.

ARTICULATED SPACES

Tensions around grave representation in this period may also be explained by the fact that settlers had disrupted the entire *habitus* of the western Xhosa, an experiential landscape clustered with sites of symbolic significance. Recent historians have argued that the nine wars fought in the nineteenth-century Eastern Cape together constitute "the longest and most damaging conflict maintained between the white man and the black man in Africa."[14] Typically, this conflict involved intense periods of close-quarter fighting, followed by guerrilla skirmishing and cattle raiding; its overall effect was the catastrophic eastward displacement of the Ngqika Xhosa across the Fish River from the lush riverine valleys they had once occupied. At first, these displacements were sporadic; and the Xhosa answered by regularly sweeping back across the frontier. Later, however, the full force of the imperial war machine, supported by settler and Mfengu irregulars, was ranged against chiefs like

Maqoma and Sandile. By the late 1870s, the remaining coherent elements of the Ngqika polity had been shattered, with remnants driven as far east as Transkei. Historically Ngqika regions like the verdant Kat River valley were given over to Khoikhoi and Mfengu allies of the British.

The Zuurveld heartland of the Ngqika was heavily inscribed with symbolic meaning. It was crossed by transhumance routes, tributary zones associated with cattle clientage, and traditional hunting domains.[15] Visible signs of an older Ngqika presence existed if you knew how to look for them: there were grain pits, excavations, and indistinct grave sites, sometimes indiscernible among hut ruins. Throughout the region, moreover, there were physical features associated with performative meaning: particular trees associated with rainmaking, rivers used in river ceremonies, and the strange, ubiquitous stone cairns known as *isivivane*, at which passers by would pause and add pebbles. Landscape, in this mode, was a domain of performative inscription, or, as Nancy Munn describes it, of the "practice of locatedness," in sharp contrast to the writerly and specular habits of the settlers.[16]

My main concern here is with the period 1850 to 1880, during which time colonial authority was directly imposed, reinforced with a gridlike system of spatial control and substantial "reserved" areas.[17] After the seventh frontier war (the War of Mlanjeni), the area east of the original colonial boundary, between the Keiskamma and Great Kei River, was proclaimed the colony of British Kaffraria. The region was divided into "counties," and an older treaty system was replaced by direct colonial administration.[18] By midcentury, therefore, there was a complex overlapping of symbolic zones, several of which were centered on significant Xhosa chiefs' graves, which began to appear as features on British maps. To understand the significance of this phenomenon, and the evolution of an intricate reciprocity between British monumentality and Xhosa grave practices, it is necessary to look more closely at the semiology of Xhosa burial in this period.

ABAPHANTSI: "THOSE WHO ARE BELOW"

While there are many disparaging accounts of Nguni mortuary practices in the early colonial period, actual descriptions of grave monuments are quite rare. One of the earliest is Bernard Picart's 1729 copperplate engraving for *The Ceremonies and Religious Customs of the Idolatrous Nations,* which depicts a "Kaffir and Hottentot" funeral, with a procession of mourners carrying a corpse, shown wrapped and bound in fetal position, into a cave tomb. Some years later, in the 1779 journal of Robert Jacob Gordon—a remarkable Dutch linguist and observer—there are two significant representations of interment. In the first, a Khoikhoi corpse is displayed ready for burial. Already stiffened into its crouched position, the body is about to be wrapped in its kaross. Further on in the journal, there is a sketch of a "Hottentot chief's grave." "When a rich Hottentot dies," says Gordon, "many cattle and sheep are slaughtered and eaten at his grave. The bones and joints are left there as a memorial."[19] This is perhaps one of the earliest European representations of the memorial stone cairns

Figure 2.2. Bernard Picart, "Les funerailles des Cafres et Hottantots." Copperplate engraving in Bernard Picart, *Ceremonies et coutumes religieuses de peuples idolatres representées par des figures dessinées de la main de Bernard Picard* (Amsterdam: J. F. Bernard, 1729). Courtesy Library of Congress.

Figure 2.3. Robert Jacob Gordon, "Hottentot chief's grave" (1779). From the journal of Robert Jacob Gordon, MS. AG.7146.95, National Archives, Cape Town.

referred to by Nguni peoples as *isivivane*, and one of the very few illustrations of southern African grave monuments as landscape features.

To white settlers and soldiers accustomed to vertical grave markers, Xhosa burial sites were indistinct features. Moreover, missionary propaganda against heathen bodily practices contaminates most early European descriptions of Nguni graves, making it difficult to trace the material history of mortuary practices. As if this were not enough, contemporary historians have consistently exaggerated the problem of burial in Nguni society, suggesting that there was an inability on the part of Xhosa metaphysics to come to terms with the material fact of death. "There was," says Jeff Peires, "something missing in Xhosa religion, a gap through which some of the central ideas of Christianity were able to infiltrate."[20]

Peires's suggestion that there is a lacuna in Xhosa metaphysics is echoed by similar statements in most of the major twentieth-century ethnographies of southern Nguni mortuary ritual. Monica Hunter's influential *Reaction to Conquest* announces that "the Pondo have a great distaste for speaking of anything connected with death," while others such as W. D. Hammond-Tooke and Eileen Jensen Krige and Jacob Krige describe Nguni avoidance rituals that mark the corpse as a dangerously polluting force.[21] Despite such influential opinions, none of these accounts reveal the presence of a significant metaphysical aporia that is altogether different from others elsewhere. Instead, southern Nguni burial practices simply underline the materiality of relations between the living and the dead, a materiality that post-Enlightenment European Christianity was seeking to mask. Recall that graveside vigils in Victorian popular literature reflect a highly developed bourgeois sense of what constitutes individual personhood. However, this does not mean that the grave is no longer a traumatic site. On the contrary, sharp distinctions between notions of proper bereavement, on the one hand, and destructive melancholia (especially as that term came to be applied to the condition of women's grief) reveal the extent to which it was necessary to control the influence of the dead over the living. After all, the early Victorian period in England is also a period in which haunted graves, risen corpses, and a thousand other Gothic stereotypes belie any attempts to stabilize notions of bereavement. The unquiet grave is one of the key figures of romantic rebellion in the period.[22]

Bearing the Gothic counterexample in mind, the differences between European and Nguni notions of the unquiet grave are minimal. There are, however, significant variations in the way corpses are imagined to speak back to the living. In Harriet Ngubane's account of Zulu funeral ritual, for instance, the corpse continues to exert a dangerous power over the life of the community. It exerts a negative influence, which has asymmetrically gendered effects. At the moment of death, a door opens between the quotidian and the world of the spirit; it is a threatening vortex that has the potential to harm the community. Women, as the center of reproductive continuity, are especially subject to pollution at this time: "a woman as a 'mother of birth' (*umdlezane*) and a 'mother of death' (*umfelokazi*)," says Ngubane, "is also dangerous because she is impure."[23]

Thus despite the insistence by early ethnography that European and African grave practices do not resemble one another, the differences they describe have more to do with class and gender than ethnicity. To this day, many peasant communities in Europe treat the grave as a dangerous, yawning opening with vertiginous appeal. Nadia Seremetakis's description of mortuary ritual in the Inner Mani in Greece is a case in point: "[W]hen ritual procedures are not observed, the corpse can be reanimated and enter the domain of the living as an autonomous entity, a revenant, introducing pollution into the social order. The corpse that has not been properly cleansed and subjected to various prophylactic procedures . . . can 'drag' . . . the living into the domain of the dead."[24]

Once we reduce the differences between European and Xhosa grave practices, it is hard to explain precisely what it was in southern Nguni burial ritual that was so unsettling to settlers and missionaries. Most obviously, the idea of burial beginning a transactional process in which the everyday is opened to the world of the ancestors has no exact correlative in Christianity. Even in contemporary Xhosa belief, the dead appear to pass into a transitional realm in which they are other but nevertheless accessible: after a time, they change their state and are referred to as *abaphantsi* ("those who are below").[25] Several ritual processes enable the passage of the corpse from one state to another, and these are highlighted by the presence of distinct lexical items in the Xhosa language. Thus, for instance, a distinction is frequently made between timely death *(ukugoduka, ukuhamba)*, expressed in terms of a metaphor of travel; and violent death.[26] Moreover, the recent dead are referred to as *umfi*, and the corpse itself as *isidumbu* (in Zulu *isithunzi*), the latter signifying the fact that decomposition is not yet complete.[27] Thereafter, within a year or so of mourning, in the manner of the classic Hertzian paradigm, the *ukubuyisa* ceremony signals the entry of the departed into the realm of the ancestors, where they have a special mediating power.[28] The departed, by now, have changed their nature. In Zulu, they are described as part of the community of *amadlozi*, to whom one appeals in times of crisis or propitiation.

What is most significant about precolonial and contemporary Xhosa funerary practices, is precisely this emphasis on the corpse *as an event*, moving through the process of decomposition and through a discursive transition in the life of the community. Moreover, while the corpse itself changes state, it continues to have a dangerous power, and disturbance of a grave site was and is associated with the significant unleashing of malevolent forces. Throughout the nineteenth and early twentieth centuries, in Xhosa and Zulu communities, chiefs' grave sites were ritually guarded—sometimes for a period of years—by appointed elders with a specially selected funeral herd of cattle.[29]

In nineteenth- and twentieth-century Xhosa society, burial marked a process by which the individual passed into community memory. Like burial everywhere, its final stage, as Maurice Bloch and Jonathan Parry put it, involved "the reassertion of society manifested by . . . the belief that the soul has been incorporated into the society of the dead and has settled down."[30] However, there was one additional and distinctive feature of Xhosa burials that was utterly unlike those of the settlers. Unlike the grave of Richard Gush at Salem, or that of Sarah Shone at Clumber, which stand as visible signifiers within an architectural discourse of headstones, most Xhosa graves *were not obvious landscape features*. Whether elders were buried at designated sites in the cattle byre, in deliberately ruined funeral huts, or in community graveyards, the grave site was, literally, a matter of communal memory, rehearsed in oral poetry. Moreover, graves were frequently incorporated into the spatiotemporal fabric of the living homestead. Heinz Kukertz's structuralist analysis of gendered space in one Mpondo *umzi* (homestead), has shown how graves are an integral but invisible part of this system.[31] Elders are buried on the perimeter of the cattle byre, in a mirroring relationship to the main house. Senior men and women sit near the door of the hut, in order, as one informant put it, that they "should see 'those down below' *(lo mnutu makbone abaphantsi)*." "Even if overgrown with bush," Kukertz continues, "the graves remain 'in sight.'" Throughout southern Africa, ethnography that is sensitive to questions of spatiality reveals evidence of communities planning village architecture in relation to the need to "watch over" the invisible graves of elders.[32]

Mpondo homesteads encompass the hierarchized spaces of burial, with men interred close to the center of symbolic power in the cattle byre and the gendered interior spaces of huts mirroring the division of sepulchral space. This doubling of grave site and *umzi* resembles the pattern of "double obsequies" first identified by Robert Hertz in which there are two stages to funeral transformation: "the first disposal is associated with the time-bound individual and the polluting aspects of death, and the second with the regenerative aspects which re-create the permanent order on which traditional authority is based."[33] Grave spaces thus recapitulate the patriarchal lineages reflected elsewhere in the habitus, with elaborate *hlonipha* (avoidance) rules governing gendered access to these territories. In fact, in some Nguni communities, there is a metonymic splicing together of terrain and tradition made possible by the continuing power of elders' graves. Monica Hunter called attention to the spatial articulation of new kraals with old grave sites over several generations: "[T]he owner of an *umzi* is buried at the entrance to his kraal *(isibaya)*, the old kraal pulled down, and a new one erected, the grave being under the fence at the middle of the back of the new kraal."[34] In other words, the spatiotemporal center of the community lifeways is the patriarch's grave, which frequently determines the very migration of architectures across the landscape.[35]

Throughout southern Africa, graves were places of power associated with lineal continuity. Unlike many European sepulchral traditions, however, this did not necessarily entail the erection of visible monuments. As Terence Ranger has shown, missionaries like David Livingstone complained that nowhere in the whole of Central Africa was there a single "stone of remembrance" to be found.[36] To summarize, then, what is different about Nguni graves is that they generally had a distinct symbolic relationship to topography, one that did not involve a metaphoric association between visible monumentality and ethics. When the Zulu king Cetshwayo died in 1884, his wrapped body was taken in slow ceremonial procession to a burial site in the Nkhandla forest. Prevented from interring the chief in the ancestral ground of the emaKhosini valley, his followers prevailed on the community of Lukungu to watch over the grave site in a grove of trees.[37] The funeral wagon was broken up and the pieces scattered over the site, thus adding the signs of disunity and disrepair to the subtle funerary markers. Many other royal graves existed only in this tenuously visual state. It required an understanding of oral tradition, and of local patterns of avoidance, to "read" vegetated thickets or ruined huts as places of burial.

Not all colonial writers responded negatively to the idea of grave erasure; as we shall see, the most vituperative comments on Xhosa graves were from missionaries. Administrators like Frank Brownlee, on the other hand, purported to have admired the last resting place of Chief Rharhabe: "His grave is in the soft red soil at the foot of great grey boulders. There the mourners planted twigs from the tombo tree—the wild fig. Those twigs are now grown into stately shade-giving trees. . . . Those not knowing rest under their shade, those knowing approach the spot . . . and respectfully place a small stone on the cairn that is there." In Brownlee's description, there is a revealing wistfulness verging on envy ("the soft red soil," the "great grey boulders") for the apparently natural association of topography and community lifeways that enfolds the chief's body. The same affective interest is apparent in his account of Pondomise river burials, a form of ritual, mortuary practice in which the bodies of chiefs were staked to the riverbed to be eventually washed away. "Respect" for the invisible, watery grave is signaled, says Brownlee, by red-blanketed women allowing their skirts to trail in the water as they move from stepping-stone to stepping-stone.[38]

The contrast between two orders of grave observance, the one visible, the other discursive and symbolic, is at its most intense for ethnographers when they deal with African graveside rituals associated with ancestor worship. In 1943, far from the Eastern Cape, Eileen Krige recorded from her informants that certain Lobedu graves were imagined by the community to be responsible for dissipating rain clouds: "As soon as the vapour-laden air reaches the grave, it stops or dissolves in the wind and it is even believed that the corpse, thrusting up an arm, waves it about to cause the wind that drives away the rain."[39] It was precisely this sort of strong contrast, between the grave as vertical sign on the one hand, and on the other as a place associated with gendered power exerting its influence over the spatiotemporal rhythms of a community, that produced clashes in the nineteenth-century Eastern Cape. In one community, the grave marker is seen as the visible, symbolic axis of a landscape circuit, in turn associated with the property-owning sensibilities of English settlers; in the other, it is part of an invisible field of symbolic force, exerting a grid of charged influence over the asymmetrically gendered lifeways of neighboring communities. Out of the different rhetorics of burial, one more specular than the other, there emerged a powerfully neurotic form of nineteenth-century missionary discourse, that took as its focus the fear of the neglected frontier grave.

MISSIONARY CONCERNS

Eighteenth-century European accounts of Xhosa burial frequently describe graves as "abandoned." John Barrow, for instance, speaks with measured revulsion about the interment of chiefs "deep in the dung of their own cattle." Several others echo his sentiments.[40] But it is not just disgust at the treatment of corpses that moves these visitors. Equally disturbing to them is the apparent *erasure* of the grave site as a visible memorial. For Ludwig Alberti (1802–6), cattle-byre burial was the first step in a process of effacement: "Thereupon a number of oxen are driven into the kraal and are kept moving around until the surface of the grave is no longer distinguishable from the rest."[41] The horror of pagan burial, therefore, is that it sometimes ceases to be a form of visible inscription altogether; it may no longer be likened to a type of writing. European gravestones, on the other hand, were a manifestation of public ethics: they spliced together, in epitaph and graveyard, notions of ethical attentiveness with landscape semiotics.

In many missionary texts, the abandonment of corpses to hyenas becomes a key signifier of moral neglect: "Oh! To see th' unburied heaps, / On which the lonely moon-light sleeps! / The very vultures turn away, / And sicken at so foul a prey; / Only the fierce hyena stalks / . . . . At midnight and his carnage plies."[42] It is indeed likely that corpses of commoners were sometimes laid out for disposal by scavengers.[43] Nonetheless, by midcentury, this missionary antagonism toward Xhosa mortuary practices had swelled into the most hysterical forms of propaganda. Harriet Ward, one of the most opinionated bigots of the period, offers this account of Ngqika burial: "[There] are instances every day," she says "of parents, husbands and wives, dragging their unfortunate sick, in the last mortal agony, into the bush." "I also heard from a respectable missionary," she continues, "that a poor child was buried three times by its mother, and each time burst the earthly trammels of the grave, and returned home."[44] Of course, such descriptions tell us more about changing Victorian conceptions of the body and embodied subjectivity than they do about the Ngqika. Given the bizarre fashion in England and on the Continent at the time for devices rigged to graves that would warn, with an elaborate bell and pulley system, in the event of a still living person being prematurely entombed, these claustrophobic grave nightmares tell us much about how subjectivity was becoming somatized.[45]

For missionaries, visible graves were one of the most concrete signifiers of Xhosa conversion. This was true not only in the case of individual headstones, but also in the allegorical implications of a neatly arrayed "native graveyard" spreading alongside the mission station itself. Missionaries, to put it another way, have a stake in the politics of landscape best emblematized by their interest in the spread of rectilinear architectural features, which are imagined to replace the disorder of the pagan habitus.[46] At the same time, the more visible the *individual* native grave, the more distinct its monumental pretensions, the more likely it was that its architects had Christian sympathies. For this reason, throughout nineteenth-century missionary

Figure 2.4. King Cetshwayo's corpse (1884). Engraving by Charles Edwin Tripp. First published in *The Graphic,* March 22, 1884. Thanks to Ian Knight.

records, obsessive attention is paid to the representational detail in Ngqika burials. Such ceremonies were highly ritualized events. Most eyewitnesses agree that precolonial chiefs' graves (*idlaka*) were round, deep holes "with a recess . . . in the wall at the bottom, big enough to take the body in a squatting position with the knees drawn up to the chin."[47] In general, the body was wrapped in a kaross, or sewn animal-skin sleeping mat, and placed on a bed of stones in the grave recess, its face turned toward the cattle kraal. This form of burial was widely in use throughout southern Africa and was not restricted to Nguni communities.[48] Perhaps the most spectacular late-nineteenth-century example of the traditional form was in Cetshwayo's burial, a ceremony that I have already referred to. A number of eyewitnesses recall how the king's corpse was allowed to stiffen into a fetal crouch before being placed in its ceremonial resting place. Moreover, in the treatment of the body, and the digging of the circular tomb, deliberate metaphoric associations between birth and death are made. "The hut with the corpse and mourners together within it," says Ngubane, "symbolizes the confinement hut as well as the womb itself."[49] Missionaries cared little for these symbolic associations between graves and the womb of the community. They were more interested in the metonymic association between vertical grave markers and the idea of access to transcendence.

All variations from the Nguni burial paradigm were symbolically significant to missionaries. The use of visible memorial inscriptions, prominent grave cairns, rectilinear grave design; the centralization of the body at the bottom of the pit, the use of a coffin, the absence of grave ornaments; all these were taken to be signs of the advance of a new ethical order of Christian care. However, for the Xhosa themselves, the semiology of abandonment—ruined huts, overgrown grave sites, broken pots, and selective avoidance of the grave site—was an important means by which the dead, as a metaphysical force, passed out of the material world, into the memory of the community. Thus the very process of forming ancestors frequently involved a resistance to visible inscription and the deliberate ruin of domestic order.

DEATH COMES TO EMGWALI

Perhaps the most extraordinary record of contradictions around bodies and burials in the colonial Eastern Cape may be found in the journal of the Reverend Tiyo Soga, the first ordained Xhosa Presbyterian minister. As Freud reminded us, the ability to redirect the psychic damage caused by bereavement onto a new internal object of mourning is one of the keys to psychic health.[50] For sensitive proselytizers like Soga, however, signs of profound grief among the Xhosa single out individuals as targets for conversion. One such example is the case of a "bereaved Fingo" the priest describes in a published letter. When the distraught man appears, he is weeping, and has his right hand resting on the crown of his head, with the head itself slightly inclined. "This attitude," says Soga, "to the Caffres indicates great grief and dejection of spirit."[51] The Mfengu man is someone whom tragedy has cast into a new subjective mold: grieving after the death of his wife and children, he appears to be in a state of inconsolable melancholia. As such, he is, as it were, hybridized by death, caught between the old somatic domain of "Caffre" body language and a new form of individual grief. Of course, Soga is quick to remind the man of the comfort of the Resurrection, to which the man gives the following strange reply: "Do you know (he asked me) why you find me in this place? Here I buried them. I came to weep at the graves. I did it purposely. I did it because we have a belief among us that if a friend comes to weep at the grave of a friend, it will not be long until he follows. I would go after them if I could."[52] Moving between two orders of mourning, the older, collective patterns of grave avoidance or propitiation, and a new expressive language of individual grief characteristic of the postromantic subject, the man becomes victim to destructive melancholia. What in another context would be a quite conventional form of meditative landscape experience (visiting the grave of a loved one), here becomes a suicidal repetition-compulsion.

An even more important account of the etiology of burial practices and grave signification may be found in Soga's description of the death of Namba, son of Maqoma, the greatest Xhosa military strategist of the nineteenth century. After the

War of Mlangeni, and the catastrophic cattle killing movement of 1853–57, which devastated the entire Xhosa nation, most significant chiefs and their followers were penned into barren, circumscribed zones. The rebellious Maqoma was condemned to twenty-one years on Robben Island.[53] In Soga's eyewitness record of Namba's last hours, the dying chief mourns the fact that he leaves his family "without a ploughing field" (that is to say, landless), and without friends "among the red blanketed" (that is, those who resist missionary dress and dictates).[54] Distanced from his followers, who had been resettled in the Crown Reserve, with his father suffering a lonely exile on Robben Island, Namba seems doomed to an incoherent and lonely funeral. Soga witnesses pathetic attempts by the family to muster a burial party, but locals refuse to participate, and the ceremony descends into chaos. At the last moment, Maqoma's half brother Chief Anta arrives to take charge of the ceremony. He proceeds to go against custom by simply ordering particular individuals to perform the ceremony. To one he exclaims, "Because we are still living yet our children are dying—I kill you today. Die with my children."[55] The translation is awkward here; nevertheless, this may be an echo of the chief's attempt to appoint a grave watcher, for the rigors of living near the grave and tending to it for a year or more in such a desolate region may have been tantamount to a type of living death.

Namba's burial serves as a reminder of the fact that chiefs' graves played an important role in the symbolic coherence of the Ngqika polity. For most communities, the quiet repose of the chief's bones in a known, orally memorialized, but inconspicuous site was a crucially gendered signifier of patriarchal continuity. For the Ngqika, therefore, a grave could best be described as having an illocutionary existence *as its first order of meaning*, existing fundamentally within the domain of community oral histories and local avoidance rituals. That is, the function of a grave might be compared to what in linguistic terms is referred to as a "performative utterance." Even though chiefs' graves are not obvious landscape features, they have an importance existence both in the rhetorical practices of the community and in the invisible divisions of symbolic space in the immediate vicinity of the site. Above all else, a grave imposes an idea of lineal continuity on the surrounding community. This helps to explain a prophetic remark by Chief Anta. Faced with the divisive squabbling at Namba's graveside, he declares: "[Namba] does not have a grave anymore, you people broke it up."[56] It is to this new figure, of the grave disrupted, the corpse torn from the earth, that the colonial imagination now turned. The remainder of this essay examines some examples of symbolic exhumation, moving from the world of missionaries to that of soldiers and administrators.

VIOLENCE AND VISIBILITY

Two contending theories of the representational power of graves started to influence each other in the colonial period. Xhosa burial sites became increasingly implicated in the British understanding of graves as visible landscape signifiers, associated with ideas of individual citizenship, male subjectivity, and property ownership. Conversely, British soldiers' graves became linked to the Xhosa understanding of the corpse as a source of pollution and the tomb as a reminder of lineal authority.

Colonialism does not have an entirely autonomous representational field. Instead, in seeking to image its authority, it is forced into a magpie borrowing from other indigenous visual lexicons, which are made available in what Mary Louise Pratt calls the "contact zone."[57] Mortuary symbolism is an important part of that exchange, and this alone helps to explain why Xhosa chiefs' graves seem to become increasingly visible topographical features by the 1840s. In fact, it is in this period, when the Ngqika Xhosa were finally alienated from their Amatolas heartland, that we find the young chief Sandile first using his father's grave as a point of reference in his debate with the new colonial administrators: "Why am I severed from the grave of my father? The inheritance of a chief is not cattle, it is lands and men."[58] This is an extremely telling remark, for it suggests that by now Sandile and others were using references to graves as a means of speaking back to the abstract, masculinized disciplinary systems of cartography and colonial land division. What is evident, too, in this exchange, is that there are crucial differences between the representational function of the grave in military or administrative discourses on the one hand, and those of missionaries on the other. In fact, it is precisely because the graves of elders and chiefs represent the invisible order of patriarchal authority that they are easily absorbed into the conservative, masculine rhetoric of colonial administrators. This is clearly demonstrated by the example of Chief Nqeno, who, on his deathbed, persuaded Commissioner John Maclean to ensure that he was given a British military funeral. Nqeno did this for extremely complex reasons, not least of which may have been an attempt to cement an alliance between his son Stockwe and the colonial authorities.[59] When, during the Sixth Frontier War, a British garrison descended upon Stockwe's Great Place, firing huts and crops, something extraordinary occurred. The commanding officer, H. Somerset notes in his dispatch of June 8, 1846: "I destroyed the Chief's kraal, leaving the burial hut of the late Chief, Eno [*sic*], untouched."[60] Thus begins a new order of symbolic exchange *between men* around graves in the Eastern Cape, one centering on either respect for or humiliation of the last resting places of local leaders, depending on the state of their alliances with the colony. As a system of informal empire begins to emerge, and administrators become more involved in the manufacture and control of customary law, so too there is increasing topographical reference to chiefs' graves. To take the idea one step further, the emergence of the monumental Xhosa grave may be the result of a need for a shared language of administration.

It was during the War of Mlanjeni (1850–53), however, that the figure of the violated grave took on crucial ideological significance. On Christmas Day 1850, combined Ngqika forces attacked the fortified villages of Woburn, Auckland, and Juanasburg, which ringed the Chumie Mission. In a subsequent British government inquiry into the causes of the war, the Reverend Henry Renton told a dramatic tale of how the followers of Chief Tyali had watched with growing outrage from one side of the Tyumie river as military settlers despoiled the land on the opposite bank they still considered their own. In a form of spatial articulation characteristic of the colonial period, the village of Woburn had been built alongside Tyali's Great Place, and the chief's grave was in the immediate vicinity; it was marked on 1850 maps of the layout of the village.[61] Renton describes what happened next:

> After its location the men of [the village of Woburn] . . . dug up the grave, to get possession of the saddle, and bridle, and guns, and what not. . . . On the other side of the river, *by a spot that could command a view*, was the great place of his widow, and his heir, and the great men of his tribe; and this act of outrage, I was assured by the missionaries, had excited the Kaffirs . . . to an extent that could not be supposed.[62]

Clearly, the desecration of a chief's grave in full view of his widow flew in the face of propaganda about how colonialism protected its native subjects. While we may never know the full import of what happened at Woburn, it is significant that by now the rifled grave and the disturbed corpse had become visible signs of colonial violence. An interesting index of converging mortuary rhetorics is the fact that the Xhosa are described as occupying a site "that could command a view" of the grave. The Xhosa, it is suggested, are being taught a lesson about graves as topographical features within a landscape system.

COLONEL FORDYCE EXHUMED

Having considered the peculiar mortuary interests of missionaries, and the very different monumental concerns of colonial administrators, let us now turn to focus on the military. There is, one might say, a special problematic associated with military graves. During the nine main wars that wracked the colonial Eastern Cape, the Xhosa were driven from plains to mountain fastnesses, and from fertile valleys to high forests. Throughout the nineteenth century, there were additional skirmishes between the Xhosa and settlers determined to take advantage of the unsettled frontier by expropriating African cattle. These raids against African "cattle thieves" were supported by the military. Gradually, as losses accrued on both sides, a new rhetoric begins to emerge, focused on the disposition of enemy bodies. In the 1830s, we find Captain Henry Butler mocking the ignominious death of a "Kafir borderer." Aside from the mock epitaph provided by Butler, there is no funeral monument for this "accomplished liar and enterprising thief [who was] deservedly the idol of his tribe." No mourners attend his final moments, for "the Hyaena and the Vulture alone witnessed his dying agonies and inherited his carcase."[63] Here, of course, two entirely different rhetorics of burial are in complete antagonism. For the Xhosa, there was a particular evil associated with the corpses of those who died in battle, a negative force that could attach itself to others. For this reason, the battlefield dead were frequently left unburied. For the British military, the abandonment of corpses is a sign of primitive moral inferiority and lack of soldierly camaraderie.

Figure 2.5. Henry Butler, "The Epitaph" (1837). Courtesy MuseumAfrica, Johannesburg, image 52/655. Reproduced by permission.

With the irruption of widespread, all-consuming warfare such as that which emerged in the Eastern Cape in 1850, violence enters the fabric of daily life, including the order of representation. By 1850, I believe, a different epistemic order had established itself, one in which dead bodies, unburied, torn apart, or significantly mutilated, had become important *as a means of communication* between warring forces.[64] At its most brutal, this language of the corpse meant that enemy bodies were often deliberately mutilated or inscribed, left hanging in trees, displayed in ranks by the roadside, laid out in town squares, or arranged decapitated and truncated in horrific displays for returning troops.

The high point of the Eighth Frontier War was the Waterkloof campaign, an extended guerrilla offensive waged by British and colonial forces against the Ngqika under Maqoma in the wooded fastnesses of mountains west of Fort Beaufort. For the Waterkloof Xhosa, the British dead were instruments to be deployed within a general language of resistance. When one colonial burial party returned from its grim labor, they were confronted by irate Ngqika warriors: "[W]hen they saw us in the valley below, their anger knew no bounds, and dragging out the dead bodies which we had placed in graves, they flung them into the air, and over deep ravines after us."[65] Ultimately, to avoid such indignities to the British dead, officers like Mackay took to camouflaging newly dug graves in the Waterkloof.

Maurice Bloch has called attention to the ideological nature of references to pollution in funerary rites: "In the representation of the funerary ritual individuality is what decomposes and is what has to be thrown out so that the ideological order can be created as an emotional force by first stressing pollution and then getting rid of it." That is to say, insofar as funeral rituals stage individuality in negative terms—in manifestations of grief and weeping, for instance—they also, by implication, recreate the symbolic presence of the collective community once mourning is overcome. It is for this reason, Bloch concludes, that warring parties sometimes try to prevent their opponents from burying the dead: "[B]y stopping one's enemies from performing the funeral rituals one diminishes their power."[66] He calls this practice "negative predation." However, given the fact that mutilation or humiliation of the enemy dead is also often associated with castration, I would suggest that such contests over bodies have much to do with the language of masculinity.

A logic of mutilation and exhumation seems to have been at work during the Eighth Frontier War. However, on the side of the British, class distinction became an important factor in ensuring the security of grave sites. On November 6, 1851, Colonel Fordyce, one of the most senior and respected officers on the frontier, was shot and killed in the Waterkloof. Thomas Baines's painting of this event records not simply its historical significance, but also its shock value.[67] Trauma is distributed across the figures in the painting, and a dulling of affect is evident in the repeated motif of common soldiers bowed by exhaustion and grief standing in knots around their dying officers and subalterns.

When Fordyce died, he was first buried in a simple grave at the nearby military settlement of Post Retief. Now officers' graves stand at the intersection of various

Figure 2.6. Thomas Baines, *The Death of Colonel Fordyce* (detail). Courtesy William Fehr Collection, Cape Town. Reproduced by permission.

contradictions. Subject to the variable whims of metropolitan parliaments, military force is sometimes quite unevenly applied: regiments return home, commanders are disgraced, troops are rotated, and there is no certain stock of mourners for the military sepulcher. Moreover, without attendant mourners or a sympathetic, surrounding civil society, there is the horrible possibility that the soldier's grave site will be forgotten and cease to function discursively, the corpse within truly returning to dust. Such a threat undermines the entire order of imperial representation and its inscriptional ability, for with the withering away of mourning, it is as though all monuments to the benevolent extension of empire are confronted with the lie of empire. For this reason, perhaps, in many pictorial views of far-flung soldiers' graves in journals like the *Illustrated London News*, lonely burial mounds usually have attendant guards, with bent heads, posed over them.[68] For the grave to survive, it is as though it has to remain part of a landscape organized as a specular field, with attendant and observing consciousnesses.

For Victorian mourners, death appears to have been more bearable if it could be perceived to have had an inscriptional effect, as though, ideally, the loss of another consciousness should be marked on the landscape like a lightning bolt. When Fordyce died, his regiment immediately marked the spot by means of carving the Ordnance Broad Arrow on a tree.[69] Descriptions of the Fordyce tragedy were

Figure 2.7. "Graves in the Winterberg," *Illustrated London News,* April 16, 1853. Courtesy South African Library.

widely disseminated in the British press. However, for colonial painters like Thomas Bowler, eager to cash in on the taste for views of these foreign battle sites, the isolated Waterkloof location was a problem. All significant traces of violence had disappeared. Bowler's way out of the dilemma was to use an imaginative form of prosopopoeia, harking back to the paradigm of elegiac wandering. In his painting *Mount Misery,* Fordyce's death site is indeed visited by a community of mourners: stray groups of mountain reedbuck, reminiscent of the roe deer of English parklands, act as prosthetic mourners, pausing in their free passage through the landscape as though called to primitive consciousness by the presence of an invisible epitaph.

Without a community of mourners, all that will save an officer's memory in a foreign country is the continued application of military force to guarantee the integrity of the grave.[70] In the end, when memorialization could not be assured for senior officers' graves, their bodies were often simply shipped home. For all the sad rhetoric about beloved leaders and the democracy of common graves, the systematic order we know as class demanded that the bodies of the officers buried at

Post Retief be removed. At the insistence of fellow members of their Masonic Lodge (like many British officers and administrators of the time, Fordyce and Carey were Masons), the three now considerably decomposed bodies were dug up, placed in lead-lined coffins, and marched one hundred kilometers or so back to Grahamstown, escorted by a regimental guard of honor with drums and pipes. In Grahamstown, two of the officers were buried with Masonic ceremony. The third, Captain Gordon, was interred in the Roman Catholic cemetery. Within ten years, the location of his grave had been lost.[71] Fordyce was not even allowed to rest in peace in Grahamstown. His bones were exhumed again and shipped back to his ancestral Scotland.[72]

A MONUMENT AT ISIDENGE

Thus far, we have been examining broad changes in the semiology of Eastern Cape graves, in the context of increasing violence and a deep fear, on the part of British authorities, of grave erasure. In May 1878, at the end of the War of Ngcayecibi (1877–1878), the Ngqika chief Sandile, leading opponent of British colonial rule after his brother Maqoma, was killed in the Pirie bush.[73] His body was left to decompose for two days before being pointed out to British authorities by an informer. This was the symbolic end of the resistance of the Xhosa nation, for Sandile was widely regarded as the last chief with sufficient authority to pose a threat to the stabilization of the frontier.

What is most striking about the death and burial of Sandile is that it reveals quite distinct representational languages used by settler and military authorities. Of the several eyewitness accounts of the body and the funeral, none is more graphic than that of George Hay, who also sketched the corpse for the *Cape Mercury*. Hay describes how Sandile was given a strangely distorted version of a military funeral. Eight Mfengu soldiers bore the body to the grave on their guns, and the traditional hollow square of troops was formed, yet rifles were not reversed in the normal tribute. Shortly before the filling of the grave, Commandant Schermbrucker made a speech, "principally addressed to the ... natives present," saying:

> [Sandile] has been killed by our volunteers and has been denied the honours which are usually accorded even to an enemy. Had he fallen on the side of his Queen ... he would have been buried in a manner befitting his rank. This is the last chief of the Gaikas; let his life and death be a warning to you.... Instead of being lords and masters in the country they once owned, [Sandile's followers] will now be servants.[74]

Schermbrucker uses the threat of a humiliating burial to remind the Mfengu volunteers of the need for colonial loyalty. London accounts of the burial were, however, entirely different, concentrating instead on the decency of the final rites. An illustration in the *Graphic* draws a melodramatic contrast between the ethical instincts of a British officer and the fetishistic understanding of Mfengu soldiers, apparently only too eager to mutilate and disgrace the corpse.[75]

Figure 2.8. "Fingoes viewing the body of Chief Sandile." *The Graphic*. Volume and date unknown.

As far as performances go, Sandile's burial was meant to dramatize the ability of colonial administration to guarantee civil protection for even the most pagan body, guarding it even from primitive self-neglect. But what is more important for our purposes is the bizarre architecture of the grave in which the corpse was finally laid. It is what one might call a "trophy grave," where the body of the chief is captured for the purposes of symbolic reburial in a manner calling to mind the superiority of white administration. On Schermbrucker's instructions, the Ngqika leader was buried between the bodies of Trooper Dicks of the Wodehouse True Blues, and Trooper Hillier of Gormon's Horse. Reportedly, the commander explained that he put the troopers there "to keep the blackguard quiet."[76] In death, the troopers are permanently deployed like toy guards or pillars. This strangely deliberate triangulation of graves is reminiscent, too, of the deep ambiguity expressed by colonial authorities toward Sandile's living body. While arch-racists like the *Grahamstown Journal*'s editor Robert Godlonton and his supporters caricatured Sandile as a drunken beast, they were also intrigued by his picturesque wildness, producing a contradiction visible in the monumental candelabra presented to Godlonton on his retirement. Imperialist ideology, in such instances, stands in a complex relationship to fantasy: conquest is also predicated on a deep, erotic attachment to the idea of chiefly authority and feudal bodily relations, figured as the body bent in submission or arrogantly resistant.[77]

Figure 2.9. Sandile's grave. Photo by David Bunn.

What the Sandile monument demonstrates, once again, is the rather contradictory role of graves in symbolizing the spread of European ethics and modernity. Care for the neglected native grave in the colonial context is another example, therefore, of how the "belatedness of the black man" is demonstrated in terms of white ontology, to use Homi Bhabha's phrase. As an outrider of modernity, imperialist administration is seen to extend ethical attention into the premodern world, and this serves to universalize and dehistoricize conceptions of the liberal subject of law. Nevertheless, this narrative is itself inhabited by several contradictions. First, the desire to depict protected native graves is linked to an increasingly gendered form of referencing between colonial authorities and male chiefly elites that eventually results in the establishment of an elaborate system of native customary law. Secondly, the increasing visibility of Xhosa chiefs' graves in the nineteenth century also has its origins in a fantastical imperialist admiration for the idea of dynastic chiefly power. For a certain class of white administrators, a number of whom would have been driven into overseas service because of primogeniture inheritance rules, the spectacle of an apparently archaic order of male power, invested with supposedly fetishistic ideas of service to chiefly authority, was deeply intriguing. Schermbrucker invoked this fantastical authority when he deployed his soldiers' bodies as imaginary guards for the dead chief. Thus the regimental hierarchies of the British military, focused on the emblematic difference

Figure 2.10. Godlonton candelabra (detail). Executed by Joseph Angell. Courtesy of the Albany Museum, Grahamstown. Photo by Hepburn and Jeanes.

between commissioned and noncommissioned ranks, converge with a fantastical idea of Xhosa chieftainship, producing a composite monument.

So the proximity of the chief's memorial to those of the watchful soldiers enables a visual allegory about the benevolent discipline of empire. This redeployment of the symbolic power of a grave for new ideological purposes is a strategy we shall see over and over again from now on, and it produces an effect of ideological *amplification,* in which the value of one sign system is magnified by a visual association with another. Increasingly, after midcentury, as Xhosa chiefs' graves become more visible, they become associated with the nostalgic rhetoric of military monumentality. Late Victorian public memorials everywhere make extensive use of the figure of the vanquished native chief. In specifically military memorials, it is associated with a nostalgia for premodern face-to-face heroic combat.

Surprisingly, Sandile's burial was the occasion for the release of far more surplus affect than that demonstrated in the official trophy grave. In stark contrast to the picture in the *Graphic,* Eastern Cape settlers circulated a very different image of the defeated chief among themselves. George Hay's original eyewitness sketch of the mutilated body was made into a popular *carte de visite,*[78] which takes us full circle in our understanding of the language of the risen corpse in the colonial Eastern Cape. For the settler imaginary, Hay's image was a satisfying icon: with the chief's remains permanently exhumed, exhibited in the rounds of settler visiting, permanently in a state of decay, forever humiliated, the image participated in the logic of revenge. For settlers, therefore, it is as though the link between ideology and the imaginary was not through the erotic so much as through the death drive.

My focus thus far has been on issues of violence and representation. To some extent, this masks the often ambiguous attitude that settlers had toward frontier war. Far from simply dreading the repeated conflicts, male settlers often found in them opportunities for advancement: cattle and large parcels of land could legitimately be expropriated from the displaced Xhosa. This ambiguity around the whole question of war is mirrored in contradictory attitudes toward the body of the enemy. Sandile was, in a sense, a necessary signifier for the discourse of settlement, and the circulation of his death image is thus far more than a simple act of gloating. In fact, the very popularity of the image suggests the presence of a collective process rather like that in Freud's descriptions of melancholia, in which there is an inability to give up the lost object and "the pleasure principle seems actually to serve the death instincts."[79] In other words, the photograph of this partially consumed body dramatizes the inability of the settler imaginary to relinquish the corpse for burial. To do so, would mean that it ceases to function as a signifier within the temporal logic of settlement narratives that demand potential future enemies. Ironically, therefore, this mutilated figure comes to satisfy the logic of the death drive itself in a process of disavowal. In such psychic economies, Freud suggested, the ego "wants to incorporate [the] object into itself . . . [as though] by devouring it."[80]

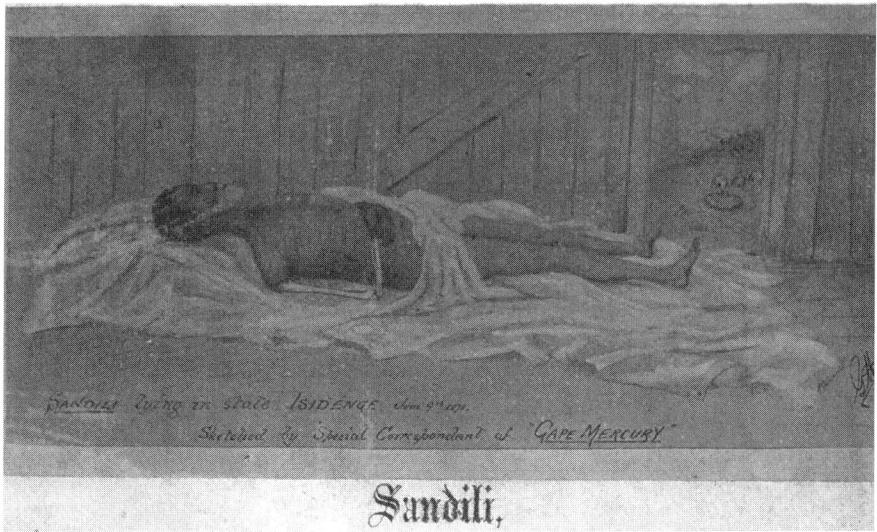

Figure 2.11. George Hay, "Sandili," *carte de visite*. Courtesy of the Albany Museum, Grahamstown.

In the end, though, Sandile's grave no longer operates as a landscape sign addressed to a potential community of mourners. Rather, its indexical function came to be emphasized. Just as the trophy military grave failed to satisfy the desires for revenge of the Stutterheim settlers, so too its iconography failed to take root in the imagination of the Xhosa themselves. Throughout the late nineteenth and early twentieth centuries, rumors abounded that the monument at Isidenge marked an empty grave. Still today, many local villagers believe that Sandile's body was secretly buried in a cave above the forest, or that parts of the body were taken as souvenirs to England.[81] Despite the presence of ghostly guards to guarantee the integrity of this monument, it has no illocutionary address, and is not served by community memorialization. For the majority of South Africans, therefore, Sandile's spirit continues to walk abroad.

NOTES

The financial assistance of the Centre for Science Development (HSRC, South Africa) toward this research is hereby acknowledged. Opinions expressed and conclusions arrived at are those of the author and not necessarily those of the Centre. Research for this paper was also made possible by a grant from the University of the Western Cape. Furthermore, I am greatly indebted to Jane Taylor, Steven Robins, Dell Upton, Roz Morris, Mark Auslander, and Martin Hall for their constructive criticism, and to Paul Landau and Deborah Kaspin for their illuminating editorial suggestions. My Eastern Cape fieldwork was made easier by extensive assistance from Khaya Matyobeni (who produced fine translations of Mqhayi for me), Drusilla Yekela, Moose van Rensburg, Reverend Zolile August, Denver Webb, Sitati Gitywa, Colin Coetzee, Manton Hirst, Lita Webley, William Jervois, and the Cory Library. My thanks also to Jean Beater of the National Monuments Council. The Cory Library, Rhodes University, Grahamstown, made available the following unpublished Sources: MP 39 (Map of Wobum); Cory Library MS 6646 ("The Massacres in 1850..."); GH 28/71, C. Brownlee to J. Maclean; Tim Stapleton, interview with Chief Lent Maqoma, October 22, 1991; and British Parliamentary Papers, "Correspondence Relevant to the Fate of the Kafir Tribes on the Eastern Frontier (1847)." Newspapers consulted included the *Daily Despatch; Imvo;* and the *Weekend Post.*

1. David Charles Sloane, *The Last Great Necessity: Cemeteries in American History* (Baltimore: Johns Hopkins University Press, 1991), 46–49.

2. See Charles Peirce, "Logic as Semiotic: The Theory of Sign," in *The Philosophy of Peirce: Selected Writings,* ed. Justus Buchler (New York: Harcourt, Brace, 1940), 98–119. For a brief, lucid account of motivated signs, see also Norman Bryson, *Vision and Painting* (New Haven, Conn.: Yale University Press, 1983), 52.

3. Neo-Durkheimian social theory has generally avoided discussion of graves as representational forms. Instead, like its nineteenth-century antecedents, it usually associated them with the performance of socially significant mortuary rites. "Durkheimian theory," explains Nadia Seremetakis, "localizes death in a specific culture as a determined component of an overarching social organization" (*The Last Word: Women, Death and Divination in Inner Mani* [Chicago: University of Chicago Press, 1991], 13). Most of the influential recent ethnographies of mortuary practice continue this trend toward seeing the grave simply as a site of representative ritual performance. In Robert Hertz's classic analysis (*Death and the Right Hand* [1906], trans. Rodney and Claudia Needham [Aberdeen: Cohen & West, 1960]), funerary ritual is the means by which the shock of individual death is dissipated through a renewed understanding of community identity. For this reason, he introduces the influential notion of the double funeral, in which, as Maurice Bloch and Jonathan Parry describe it, there is a phase of disaggregation "followed by a phase of reinstallation...from which the collectivity emerges triumphant over death" (*Death and the Regeneration of Life,* ed. Maurice Bloch and Jonathan Parry [Cambridge: Cambridge University Press, 1982], 4.) Bloch and Parry themselves favor his description of the "reassertion of the social order at the time of death" (p. 6). Thus even in the most sophisticated ethnographic analyses of homologies between mortuary practice and lineal authority, there is little emphasis on the grave as a spatial or inscriptional phenomenon.

Recently, especially with the impact of the anthropology of practice, there has been a more sustained attempt to explore the landscape functioning of graves. For instance, Seremetakis's nuanced study of exhumation rituals in Inner Mani veers sharply away from the Hertzian paradigm. Another key recent development has been the understanding of graves as sites of hybrid representation. Outstanding among these studies are Marilyn Ivy's *Discourses of the Vanishing: Modernity, Phantasm, Japan* (Chicago: University of Chicago Press, 1995), and John Pemberton's *On the Subject of "Java"* (Ithaca, N.Y.: Cornell University Press, 1994), both of which examine the changing function of monumental tombs in various attempts to establish the legitimacy of the modernizing states such as Japan and Indonesia.

4. Of the many fine recent studies of the politics of English topographical poetry, Alan Liu's *Wordsworth: The Sense of History* (Stanford, Calif.: Stanford University Press, 1989) is perhaps the most instructive.

5. Clifton Crais, *The Making of the Colonial Order* (Cambridge: Cambridge University Press, 1992), 92.

6. For three very different views of patterned movement and meaning in the colonial context, see Yvonne Brink, "Places of Discourse and Dialogue: A Study in the Material Culture of the Cape during the Rule of the Dutch East India Company, 1652–1795" (Ph.D. diss., University of Cape Town, 1992), 20–24; and David Bunn, " 'Our Wattled Cot': Mercantile and Domestic Space in Thomas Pringle's African Landscapes," in *Landscape and Power*, ed. W. J. T. Mitchell, 127–74 (Chicago: University of Chicago Press, 1994); and Nancy D. Munn, "Excluded Spaces: The Figure in Australian Aboriginal Landscape," *Critical Inquiry* 22 (Spring 1996): 446–65.

7. Crais, *Making of the Colonial Order*, 91.

8. Rev. John Ayliff, *Memorials of the British Settlers of South Africa* (Grahamstown: Godlonton, 1985), 42.

9. *The Albany Journals of Thomas Shone*, ed. Penelope Silva (Cape Town: Maskew Miller Longman for Rhodes University, Grahamstown, 1992), 17, 21.

10. Ibid., 24–25.

11. Ibid., 93.

12. The extent to which the surrounding countryside was imprinted with a sense of menace is graphically illustrated in *The Reminiscences of Thomas Stubbs*, ed. W. A. Maxwell and R. T. McGeogh (Cape Town: A. A. Balkema, 1978). Acknowledging his intimate knowledge of the terrain and of guerrilla warfare, the Royal Engineers prevailed on the settler Stubbs to help them compile a map. "In doing so," he says, "I drew a line through the map [and remarked] 'on this path, my father was murdered—on this one Johnstone was murdered, on this one Anderson was murdered and on nearly all someone had been murdered' " (p. 147).

13. *Albany Journals of Thomas Shone*, ed. Silva, 215.

14. Noël Mostert, *Frontiers: The Epic of South Africa's Creation and the Tragedy of the Xhosa People* (New York: Knopf, 1992), xxix.

15. Several excellent recent works have helped to paint a fuller picture of the Ngqika sense of place in this period. Among others, see J. B. Peires, *The Dead Will Arise: Nongqawuse and the Great Xhosa Cattle-Killing Movement of 1856–7* (Johannesburg: Ravan Press; Bloomington: Indiana University Press, 1989); Crais, *Making of the Colonial Order;* Timothy Stapleton, *Maqoma* (Johannesburg: Jonathan Ball, 1994); and Mostert, *Frontiers*. My own forthcoming *Land Acts: Modernity, Representation, and the Making of South African Space* deals extensively with this issue.

16. Nancy Munn, "Excluded Spaces: The Figure in Australian Aboriginal Landscape," *Critical Inquiry* 22 (Spring 1996): 450.

17. J. S. Bergh and J. C. Visagie, *The Eastern Cape Frontier Zone, 1660–1980: A Cartographic Guide for Historical Research* (Durban: Butterworths, 1985), 48.

18. The evolution of this controlling matrix is well documented in Bergh and Visagie, *Eastern Cape Frontier Zone*. By the 1850s, magistrates had come to displace chiefly authority; *amatakhati* (native councilors) had been installed; chains of forts and signaling towers had been linked; trigonometrical surveys had been completed; and mission stations had been reinforced with surrounding military villages.

19. Picart, *The Ceremonies and Religious Customs of the Idolatrous Nations;* and Patrick Cullinan, *Robert Jacob Gordon, 1743–1795: The Man and His Travels at the Cape* (Cape Town: Struik, 1992), 108.

20. Peires, *Dead Will Arise*, 31.

21. Monica Hunter, *Reaction to Conquest* (London: Oxford University Press, 1936), 231; W. D. Hammond-Tooke, *Bhaca Society* (Cape Town: Oxford University Press), 1962; and Eileen Jensen Krige and Jacob Krige, *The Realm of a Rain Queen: A Study of the Pattern of Lovedu Society* (London: Oxford University Press, 1943).

22. For example, when in Emily Brontë's *Wuthering Heights* ([1847; New York: Oxford University Press, 1987], 290), Heathcliff digs his way down toward Catherine Earnshaw's corpse, he suddenly feels the warm breath of his dead beloved on his cheek: "as certainly as you perceive the approach to some substantial body in the dark, though it cannot be discerned, so certainly I felt that Cathy was there, not under me, but on the earth."

23. Harriet Ngubane, *Body and Mind in Zulu Medicine* (London: Academic Press, 1977), 84, 88.

24. Seremetakis, *Last Word*, 64.

25. In the section that follows, I am frequently dependent on the contemporary ethnographic detail collected by Gordon Ndodomzi Zwide in "Burial and Funeral Practices in the Ciskei: An Enquiry Into Present-Day Practices and Associated Ideas" (M.A. thesis, University of Fort Hare, 1984). In addition, I have learnt a great deal from my research assistant and friend Khaya Matyobeni, without whose intimate knowledge of the landscape practices and oral history of the Stutterheim region, this project would not have been possible.

26. Zwide, "Burial and Funeral Practices," 69.

27. Ibid., and John Middleton, "Lugbara Death," in *Death and the Regeneration of Life*, ed. Bloch and Parry, 137.

28. Zwide, "Burial and Funeral Practices," 70; Ngubane, *Body and Mind*, 50; and Matyobeni, pers. comm. For Hertz, see note 3.

29. The best-documented case of grave watchers appointed to attend a chiefly grave is that of Cetshwayo in 1884. See John Laband, *Rope of Sand: The Rise and Fall of the Zulu Kingdom in the Nineteenth Century* (Johannesburg: Jonathan Ball, 1995), 368.

30. *Death and the Regeneration of Life*, ed. Bloch and Parry, Intro., 4.

31. Heinz Kukertz, *Creating Order: The Image of the Homestead in Mpondo Social Life* (Johannesburg: Witwatersrand University Press, 1990). See also Patricia Davidson, "Material Culture, Context and Meaning" (Ph.D. diss., University of Cape Town, 1991), 52–54, for an analysis of the progressive migration of homesteads across the landscape, in relation to the burial of chiefs in cattle byres.

32. Kukertz, *Creating Order*, 289. In a period of fieldwork in Matabeleland, Steven Robins recorded the efforts of local villagers rebuilding a homestead to enable a better "view" of the almost invisible graves of elders. Robins, pers. comm.

33. *Death and the Regeneration of Life*, ed. Bloch and Parry, intro., 11, citing Robert Hertz, "A Contribution to the Study of the Collective Representation of Death," in id., *Death and the Right Hand*.

34. Hunter, *Reaction to Conquest*, 228. See also Davidson, "Material Culture, 50–54.

35. Over the past decade of African studies, there has been a significant revolution in the understanding of graves as sites and signs. Bloch and Parry's *Death and the Regeneration of Life* contains key examples of this new scholarship. Outstanding among recent studies that examine graves in their landscape context is Terence Ranger's work on the Zimbabwean Matopos hills; see esp. his " 'Great Spaces Washed with Sun': The Matopos and Uluru Compared," in *Text, Theory, Space: Land, Literature, and History in South Africa and Australia*, ed. Kate

Darian-Smith et al. (New York: Routledge, 1996), 157–71, and "Taking Hold of the Land: Holy Places and Pilgrimages in Twentieth-Century Zimbabwe" (paper presented at conference on "Culture and Consciousness in Southern Africa," September 1986); and Jean Comaroff's groundbreaking ethnography of the Tswana, *Body of Power, Spirit of Resistance* (Chicago: University of Chicago Press, 1995). There have also been several intriguing attempts to see African graves as the sites for counterhegemonic negotiation of modernity. For instance, Deborah Kaspin's reading of Nyau mortuary ritual as an attempt to regain "representational authority" defines the graveyard as "a halfway point, lying between parallel worlds, linking the village to the bush and to the spirit world beyond the grave," in Kaspin, "Chewa Visions and Revisions of Power: Transformations of the Nyau Dance in Central Malawi," in *Modernity and Its Malcontents: Ritual and Power in Postcolonial Africa*, ed. Comaroff and Comaroff (Chicago: University of Chicago Press, 1993), 41. There is also Brad Weiss's exploration of Haya burial, which describes the grave "as a site which encompasses the horizon of the past which has created it, and the future which ensures it," because the occasion of the return of the body to the land is a way of binding agnates and reinforcing claims to residential farms: see Weiss, " 'Buying Her Grave': Money and AIDS in Northwest Tanzania" (seminar paper, Department of Anthropology, University of Chicago, 20–23); and David William Cohen and E. S. Atieno Odhiambo's *Burying SM: The Politics of Knowledge and the Sociology of Power in Africa* (Portsmouth, N.H.: Heinemann, 1992), in which it is claimed that the occasion of the struggle over the body of S. M. Otieno "brought into an organized dispute setting the entire moral ground of Luo beliefs about death and Luo funeral practices" (59). The controversy around Otieno's burial site reveals the crucial role played by graves in symbolizing political authority, and it also shows how the idea of the "unsettled" burial may be deployed as a figure of resistance.

36. Ranger, "Taking Hold of the Land," 4.

37. Laband, *Rope of Sand*, 368, 480, nn. 3 and 4.

38. W. T. Brownlee, *Reminiscences of a Transkeian* (Pietermaritzburg: Shuter & Shooter, n.d.), 23–24; "Burial Places of Chiefs," 23.

39. Krige and Krige, *Realm*, 275.

40. John Barrow quoted in Marly Louise Pratt, *Imperial Eyes: Travel Writing and Transculturation* (London: Routledge, 1992); Margaret Shaw and N. J. van Warmelo, "The Material Culture of the Cape Nguni (Part 4)," *Annals of the South African Museum* 58 (March 1988), 202–4; 757.

41. *Ludwig Alberti's Account of the Tribal Life & Customs of the Xhosa in 1807, Translated by Dr. William Fehr from the original manuscript in German of The Kaffirs of the South Coast of Africa* (Cape Town: A. A. Balkema, 1968), 95.

42. Andrew Steedman, *Wanderings and Adventures in the Interior of Southern Africa*, vol. 1 (London: Longman & Co., 1835; reprint, 1966), 199.

43. Similar practices are recorded for the Maasai. The ritual exposure of Parsee corpses for disposal by vultures was a much discussed phenomenon in Anglo-Indian colonial writing.

44. Harriet Ward, *Five Years in Kaffirland*, vol. 1 (London: Henry Colburn, 1848), 197, 198.

45. Philippe Ariès, *The Hour of Our Death* (New York: Knopf, 1981), 562.

46. Comaroff and Comaroff, *Of Revelation and Revolution*, 1: 204; Ranger, "Taking Hold of the Land," 9–10.

47. Shaw and van Warmelo, 822.

48. Ranger, "Taking Hold of the Land," 10.

49. Ngubane, *Body and Mind*, 85.

50. Sigmund Freud, *The Standard Edition of the Complete Psychological Works of Sigmund Freud*, translated under the general editorship of James Strachey (London: Hogarth Press and the Institute of Psycho-Analysis, 1953–74), vol. 14: *On the History of the Psycho-Analytic Movement, Papers on Metapsychology and Other Works*, 243.

51. Tiyo Soga, *The Journal and Selected Writings of the Reverend Tiyo Soga* (Cape Town: Balkema, 1983), 89.

52. Ibid., 90.

53. Stapleton, *Maqoma*, 194.

54. Soga, *Journal*, 156.

55. Ibid., 159.

56. Ibid.

57. Pratt, *Imperial Eyes*, 7.

58. GH 28/71, C. Brownlee to J. Maclean; quoted in Peires, *Dead Will Arise*, 62.

59. Mostert, *Frontiers*, 880.

60. Ibid., 151.

61. As shown in Cory Library MP 39, Map of Woburn. I am grateful to Colin Coetzee for drawing my attention to this map.

62. *Imperial Blue Book* (Cape of Good Hope: Govt. Printer, 1847), 381, evidence of H. Renton; emphasis added.

63. Henry Butler, "The Epitaph" (1837), MuseumAfrica, Johannesburg, image 52/655.

64. For an extensive analysis of this language of corpses, see David Bunn, "Morbid Curiosities: Mutilation, Exhumation, and the Fate of Colonial Painting" (forthcoming).

65. James Mackay, *Reminiscences of the Last Kafir War* (Grahamstown: Richards, Glanvile & Co., 1871), 28.

66. Maurice Bloch, "Death, Woman and Power," in *Death and the Regeneration of Life*, ed. Bloch and Parry, 224, 228.

67. Thomas Baines, *The Death of Colonel Fordyce* (1852).

68. *Illustrated London News*, "Graves in the Winterberg."

69. R. A. Wilmot, *A Cape Traveller's Diary* (1856; Johannesburg: Ad. Donker, 1984), 31.

70. The only individual soldier's death sites recorded on colonial maps of the Eastern Cape are those of Fordyce and Lieutenant Bailey. The record of their passing has only been inscribed because military outposts, namely, Fort Fordyce and Bailey's Grave, sprang up at these locations.

71. *The Reminiscences of Amelia de Henningsen*, ed. Margaret Young (Grahamstown: Maskew Miller Longman, 1989), 140.

72. In piecing together this sequence of events, I have relied mainly on contemporary sources, such as Captain W. R. King, *Campaigning in Kaffirland* (London: Saunders & Otley, 1853), 146–60; Mackay, *Reminiscences*, 117, 154; and *Reminiscences of Amelia de Henningsen*, ed. Young, 140.

73. See Mostert, *Frontiers*, and Stapleton, *Maqoma*, for this history.

74. George Hay, who also sketched the corpse for the *Cape Mercury*, was the artist.

75. Anon. illustration in *The Graphic*, "Fingoes Viewing the Body of Chief Sandile."

76. Jack H. French, "The Death and Burial of Sandile," *Coelacanth* 18, 1 (April 1980): 43.

77. This point relies on an understanding derived from Slavoj Žižek's revision of Althusser, in *Tarrying With the Negative: Kant, Hegel, and the Critique of Ideology* (Durham, N.C.: Duke University Press, 1993).

78. George Hay's original eyewitness sketch, Sandile's Corpse.

79. J. B. Pontalis, *Frontiers in Psychoanalysis: Between the Dream and Psychic Pain* (New York: International Universities Press, 1981), 102.

80. Freud, *Standard Edition*, 14: 249–50.

81. See Drusilla Yekela, "The Sandile Dynasty" (South African Museums Association Annual Conference, Eastern Cape Branch, paper, October 1985). Further attention was drawn to such rumors during the time of intensive press coverage of the hunt for Hintsa's head by Nicholas Gcaleka. For a detailed discussion, see Shula Marks, "Rewriting South African History; or, The Hunt for Hintsa's Head" (University of Natal History Seminar paper, April 1996).

Chapter 3

Tintin and the Interruptions of Congolese Comics

Nancy Rose Hunt

"... sounds like he was—what was it again? I completely forgot, although I read about it once in the Tintin comics."
"No [that's not it]. That I saw in the book Tintin au Congo. ... Those are notions that were brought [here], notions ..."
—TSHIBUMBA (a Zairean painter) to Johannes Fabian, 1973

"That he [Tshibumba] aligns me with Tintin *is not a gentle jibe.*"
—FABIAN, *Remembering the Present*, 1996

Colonial imagery could be sadistic. Sadism can produce laughter. Not only the European viewer finds such mocking funny. The colonized, especially the middle figure enmeshed in mimetic predicaments (and confronted by the "corporeal quandary ... faced by the [colonial] subject when obliged to identify with an image which provides neither idealization nor pleasure"),[1] laughs at minstrelsy-inspired caricatures, too. The abjectness of these blackface rubrics basic to imperial popular culture produces unease in us, their contemporary viewers.[2] It is through such encumbrances that we can begin to fathom the ambivalent semiotics of colonial comics and their parodic disruptions.[3]

TINTIN IN BELGIUM

Visit a Brussels BD shop—BDs are *bandes dessinées,* or comics—or a BD gallery-opening in Charleroi, and ask about African comics or BDs.[4] *Tintin au Congo,* the only Tintin album not translated into English,[5] will come right up. Yet most Belgian BD-ists (BD collectors) will also reel off a string of series titles that have included a volume or more situated in Congo-Zaire.[6] These albums range from post-1960 refabrications of colonial icons and scripts to subtle, historically contextualized *bandes dessinées* for adults.[7] If the BD-ist you ask is up to date, and most pride themselves in being so, he or she will also tell you to buy the most recent volume of the crossover Congolese cartoon artist Barly Baruti's *Eva K.,* a glossy, stylized thriller about an African political prisoner of the 1990s battling tropical art thieves in a fictional dictatorship not unlike Mobutu's Zaire.[8]

Although you may not learn anything about comics published locally in Congo-Zaire, any Belgian can tell you plenty about Tintin, including his infamous voyage to colonial Congo. *Tintin au Congo* is notorious for its depiction of animal slaughter and its caricatured representation of the black body: "Basically, it's all to do with rubbery lips and heaps of dead animals," according to Sue Buswell, Tintin's editor at the British publisher Methuen.[9] The iconic bodies quoted other caricatures in advertisements selling tropical products and tropical climes, and this cannibal humor in turn was based on minstrelsy rubrics that had been in wide circulation for decades. The racialized humor of *Tintin* is elemental, largely arising from contradictory pairings and episodes of misrecognition. After a parakeet lands Tintin's dog Milou in the ship infirmary, for instance, the near-human pet mistakes a *nègre* carpenter, entering the room with saws, for his doctor and is terrified. A pitch black Congolese youth is known as "Snowball." He is busy reading a copy of the *Petit Vingtième*, the Brussels-based children's newspaper for whom Tintin—and Hergé—worked, as Tintin and Milou arrive by ship to a cheering Congolese crowd. A Congolese dandy refuses to help upright his derailed train after it collides with Tintin's stuck car; this indignant passenger does not want to get dirty. If the idea of a clean *nègre* is a joke, so perhaps was that of a newspaper-reading Congolese. Other jokes are just silly. The gangster car thief disguises himself as priest. An old pygmy is mistaken for a child. To make a film about giraffes, Tintin dresses up like one. Finally, the young boy-scout-like prankster of a reporter joins the latex of two rubber trees to create a gigantic slingshot for launching rocks at enemies. Tintin's Congo embraced animals and diamond wealth; cars and trains; international reporters; missionary priests; Chicago gangsters; and primitive, domesticated, and dandified Congolese. Colonial modernity appeared as farce, an entertaining charade of contradictory mixtures in a mixed and mixed-up world. The central narrative turns around the absurd alliance between a white villain—successively stowaway, car thief, and Al Capone–allied Chicago gangster—with a Congolese "witch doctor," who envies the instant prestige of Tintin, an innocent white man hero whose dog companion is declared a chief by Congolese.

Many have discussed this early newspaper-commissioned comic strip, with its weak storyline and not yet developed Tintin character, as an anomaly in the oeuvre of Belgium's BD hero par excellence. Tintin was born in Brussels in 1929, the brainchild of Georges Rémi, or, as he is better known, Hergé (a pseudonym based on the backward pronunciation of his initials, G.R.). Hergé also was born in Brussels, and he grew up drawing stories in pictures and scouting. His first comic series appeared in *Le Boy-scout belge* in 1926. A year earlier, at the age of eighteen, Hergé was already working for the Catholic nationalist newspaper *Le Vingtième Siècle: Journal catholique et national de doctrine et d'information*, directed by the resolute and energetic Abbé Norbert Wallez. When in 1928 this priest decided to create a weekly supplement for children, *Le Petit Vingtième*, he put Hergé in charge. Within a couple of months, Hergé had created Tintin, a youth with an almost blank face, a striking quiff of hair, and a fox terrier named Milou.

BD critics and biographers have reconstructed Hergé's colonial library, his specifically Congolese repertoire of icons, and the instructions he received from his procolonial priest of a boss in 1929.[10] Abbé Wallez insisted that Hergé, who was eager to move his hero Tintin from adventures in Russia to more in America as soon as possible, first take time to promote the civilizing mission of the Congo. If Wallez had a colonial mission, he also had a marketing one. Tintin's trip to the Congo was the first time this comic figure was used in advertising—for Brussels's biggest department store of products for colonists. Tintin's supposed return from the Congo to Belgium in 1931 was another occasion for this priest-publisher to promote the colonial enterprise and the cartoon hero he helped Hergé invent. Wallez organized two homecoming stunts in Brussels with actors posing as the returning Tintin. "Congolese bearers" and "a menagerie of wild animals hired from a circus" escorted Tintin and Milou. Crowds of children demanded "their share of an insufficient supply of sweets and African souvenirs. When the performance was repeated in Liège, there was a near riot. Wallez was delighted."[11] So were the Belgian children.

Hergé's original black-and-white Congo album, *Les aventures de Tintin: Reporter du Petit "Vingtième" au Congo*, has been easy to find in Belgium since its facsimile republication in 1983. The color album, *Tintin au Congo*, has been widely available since it reappeared under a 1974 copyright. This substantially revised and abbreviated version first made its way into print in 1947,[12] at a time when Hergé and his crew were redoing and standardizing all of Tintin's adventures for a postwar audience requiring new gloss and color. The Hergé industry Europeanized the original black-and white version. Most famously, Tintin's original geography lesson about "your fatherland, Belgium" to a mission classroom of Congolese became an impartial arithmetic session. The new version also replaced the use of Brussels street vernacular by Congolese natives with a standardized *petit nègre* speech, although it did not reform the caricatured, cannibal humor representation of the black body.[13]

Hergé is often credited with being the father of Belgian (and Belgo-French) BDs. He transformed European serial visual stories by no longer separating text from images as description; for the first time, as in American comics since 1896, he began inserting text as action within talking balloons situated inside the sequential drawings.[14] Hergé also changed comics with his *ligne claire* ("clean line") style, which combined "very iconic characters with unusually realistic backgrounds."[15] His highly abstract hero became a transcendent, naïve, boy-scout-like do-gooder of a reporter of about sixteen years in age. Tintin never aged, never submitted a story, never loved a woman, but he traveled the world, from Russia to Congo to America to China and beyond, even going to the moon in 1954.

Hergé and Tintin are as basic and everyday to a common Belgian national imaginary as Magritte paintings or mussels with fries, no small feat in a country ever more fractured by linguistic boundaries, especially since the Belgian state was federalized. Indeed, the cuisine, the monarchy, and Tintin comics join Belgium's postcolonies, corruption scandals, wartime occupations, and Sabena Airlines as some of the few widely resonant forms of imagining Belgium as a nation.[16] Tintin is, of course, a global icon and business, too. More than 120 million books have been sold in almost forty languages. There are now Tintin stores in most major European cities, and the French think of Tintin as French.[17] But no one needs a Tintin store to find Hergé products in Belgium. Even news-and-tobacco shops have BD sections with Tintin subsections, selling at least one if not both versions of *Tintin au Congo*. Full sets of Hergé's oeuvre are also available in numerous specialist BD shops of Belgium's cities and towns. As in Tintin shops in Brussels, London, and Paris, the albums are sold beside Tintin posters, postcards, key rings, T-shirts, and calendars. Most of these products can be purchased with Hergé's standardized colonial icon, where the youthful reporter and his dog set out in their car with their African "boy," movie camera, and gun for slapstick adventures in the Congo.

TINTIN IN AFRICA, OR "NOT A GENTLE JIBE"

Pierre Halen has suggested that *Tintin au Congo* was not colonial because Hergé never went to the Congo.[18] Yet King Leopold II never went to his Congo either. Authorship and the author's location of writing do not determine audience, identification, and available readings—nor reprinting and translation decisions. Hergé's publisher in the United Kingdom, Methuen, refused to translate *Tintin au Congo* into its English-language Tintin album line. Hergé also grew embarrassed by the album's colonial paternalism, racist caricatures, and slaughter of wildlife. One version goes that he was "not keen to keep the book on sale in later years, but the continued commercial success of the story won him round."[19] Another alludes to a "fairly large period of disgrace" when *Tintin au Congo* was "difficult to track down. It was a period of often painful decolonization and the book did not seem particularly relevant."[20] While one version alternates between the colonial banning and the commercial quarantining of *Tintin au Congo* in the late 1950s, another is that *Tintin au Congo* sold better in Congo-Zaire than anywhere else. Harry Thompson reported in 1991: "The biggest market of all was in the Belgian Congo, and it continues to sell in great numbers in independent Zaire today. Zairian children, it seems, consider it an honour that Tintin included their country in his list of those meriting a visit."[21] This latter rendition has had many wondering about the comic strip's reception by Congolese, the apparent esteem by which this comic series, notorious in the West for its exaggerated imperial blackface rubrics, has been held within the Congo itself.

Less obvious within existing treatments has been how important it became to the Hergé-Casterman enterprise to prove the acceptability of *Tintin au Congo* to postcolonial Congolese.[22] Hergé played an active role in "giving" the later 1947 version of *Tintin au Congo* to Congolese in late 1969 (as he must have as well in agreeing to have several other of his color albums published in serial form in the pages of *Zaïre*, a semi-glossy news magazine published in Kinshasa). *Zaïre* hailed its republication of *Tintin au Congo* as a publishing coup and holiday gift that would bring pleasure to thousands of readers and their children. The editors stated that "the whites"—they also referred to them as the "colonial authorities"—had stopped the circulation of *Tintin au Congo* in the late 1950s so as not to offend Congolese.[23] *Zaïre* had undertaken a survey to see what Congolese "from seven to seventy-seven years" thought. Most, the editors reported, considered Tintin as "an integral part of their patrimony," even a "national hero." Moreover, Congolese were finding "material there by which to ridicule the whites 'who saw them like that!' " The next issue's installment of pages reminded readers to carefully save the entire series so that they could assemble and bind the complete story.[24]

A Congolese intellectual based in Italy, Baudouin-Freddy Kasongo, wrote a letter to the editors questioning the politics of a publishing decision that would reinforce colonized mentalities in his home country. He condemned *Tintin au Congo* as a "vast imaginary venture," which was "packed with prejudices against the black man and stinks of an out-of-date and scandalous paternalism."[25] The editors scoffed at the criticisms of this censorious Congolese named after the Belgian king: "Congolese youth don't have complexes [are not *complexés*], and it's in this perspective that we decided that this series . . . would amuse the youth of Congo."[26] Tintin worship continued to be endorsed in this Mobutiste magazine in pre-authenticity Zaire. When Neil Armstrong took his first steps on the moon in 1970, *Zaïre*'s editors printed an image of Tintin walking on the moon from Hergé's 1954 album, and the lead story was titled: "Armstrong: 15 years after Tintin." An interview with Hergé and a special drawing as a New Year's gift for *Zaïre* readers followed.[27] About this same time, Congolese youth began dancing Apollo dances, and a new comic character named Apolosa—perhaps Congo-Zaire's most popular and subversive ever—was born on Kinshasa's streets.[28]

A former railroad employee in Lubumbashi welded spitting silhouettes of Tintin and Milou out of a thick iron wire some time before 1973, when a Belgian professor remarked on the beautifully crafted BD hero and his dog on a visit to the caricaturist's home. When the same historian was leaving Zaire a few years later, the son of this spontaneous BD sculptor presented the outline shapes as a departure gift. When the carefully wrapped silhouettes subsequently went through security at the Lille airport in a plastic bag, the agents recognized Tintin and Milou on their X-ray screen and laughed. The same wire figures were later produced by a jury member at the doctoral defense of a French student who mistakenly suggested, echoing the wish of Baudouin-Freddy Kasongo, that *Tintin au Congo* was so racially offensive that it had been censored in Zaire since independence.[29]

That Tintin has become an icon and a commodity in francophone Africa is apparent in Abidjan, where Tintin albums and souvenirs produced by the Belgian publisher Casterman are available in one major bookstore. Locally sculpted *colon* figures depicting Tintin are for sale in tourist curio shops, too, alongside European

Figure 3.1. Welded silhouette by Lubumbashi railway worker, ca. 1970. Courtesy Jean-Luc Vellut.

colonist and African colonial doctor, lawyer, big man, and *tirailleur* figures. "Who buys these?" I asked recently in Abidjan, pointing to the Tintin colon statues. "Belgians" was the immediate response. Tintin images are also for sale in anglophone Africa. When I asked who bought Tintin colon sculptures in Accra, I received the same semi-joking answer: "Belgians." T-shirts celebrating Tintin in Zanzibar and Dar es Salaam were likewise for sale in Tanzanian tourist shops in the late

1990s,[30] and "Tintin au Congo" paintings were readily available in Brazzaville in 1996.[31]

Tintin au Congo has become a postcolonial joke—in Zaire and beyond—about the Western visitors interested in colonial nostalgia and jungle adventure tales.[32] Tintin figures are also much more than a postcolonial joke in Congo-Zaire. Zairians in Brussels told me in 1996 how *Tintin au Congo* albums were eagerly sought, though difficult-to-find collector items among the middle class. Not only do children love reading these adventures, Blaise-Pascal Baruani told me, but parents also buy the album for their children if they can to show them the colonized world their parents once lived in and how Europeans imagined Congolese subjects.[33] In 1996, the creative writer and literary critic Yoka Lye was imagining Tintin figures all over Mobutu's Zaire. He used the metaphor for naïve urban Zairian intellectuals who were romanticizing rural life as home and tradition as well as for the latest boy scout figures without borders—refugee workers, doctors, and journalists—who land as heroes and are airlifted out when they are ready for their stories to end.[34]

"That he aligns me with *Tintin* is not a gentle jibe," Johannes Fabian admitted about his ethnographic "confrontation" of 1973 with the popular historical painter Tshibumba Kanda Matula. That Tshibumba was "an avid reader of Hergé's comics" is significant. So, too, is the fact that *Tintin au Congo* had become vital to local understandings of "colonial discourse." Yet Tshibumba's ungentle alignment was also a way of poking fun at the anthropologist's categories and earnestness, of teasing Fabian that his habits of consuming and reproducing serial images and dialogues, as well as his appearances and disappearances by airplane, made him too just one more Tintin.[35]

VIEWING A COLONIAL ARCHIVE

It would be nice to know exactly *how* Congolese had access to Hergé comics prior to 1973. One can surmise that *Tintin au Congo* must have found its way onto coffee tables and children's beds in Belgian homes, into bookshops catering to Europeans, and perhaps into libraries and kiosks catering to Congolese. Belgians who were living in the Belgian Congo would have had copies of BD albums and *Tintin* and *Spirou* magazines.[36] Yet how and when these Belgian BDs came into "native" hands is not clear, even if affective and surreptitious moments in domestic service relationships would have represented opportunities for looking and reading, borrowing and theft.

Bogumil Jewsiewicki evokes the walls and living rooms of Congolese urban subjects, asserting that "pictures cut from magazines and catalogues, have decorated Zairian homes since at least 1920." Yet with what kinds of images did people decorate their walls, we should ask. Certainly, we need to know more about what colonists read and viewed. Yet we should not assume that what Congolese consumed were always items "discarded by whites," that only urbanized Congolese had access to such screens of blackness, and that such imagery "exposed" only "the authoritarianism of industrial mass culture." Jewsiewicki's chronology on Congolese interior decoration—"only" magazine and catalog illustrations from the 1920s, still photographs from the 1940s, and paintings from the 1970s—is surely too circumscribed. It seems unlikely that "African urban culture" was really "crushed during the 1930s."[37] The evidence below suggests that visual culture at least flourished during this decade, and not only in cities, but wherever newspapers traveled.

What access did Congolese have to comics? Did they glimpse BDs in shops or schools? Did they draw comics themselves? Here I focus on the production of caricatured images in newspapers and periodicals published in the Congo, drawing on a small portion of Jean Berlage's bibliography of some 600 titles.[38] Such an exercise places the colonial-minstrelsy rubric of Tintin within a larger context. It also reveals a wide circulation of forms, multiple producers and authors, and motivated icons and meanings. My first questions were simple: What was out there? And, how was the body figured within these images? The "recursive iconic elements and symbols"[39] that I trace are those of a cannibal-humor-derived, highly abstracted, cheerful blackface figure and his counterpart, an indignant dandy figure. Each of these is a male figure, although their gender meanings differ. I also ask how subject identification was formed. Was it involuntary or did it allow for multiple identifications and readings? What kinds of quandaries and refusals did such identifications produce?

Scott McCloud suggests that there are two central aspects to comics. One is at the level of the cartoon, the single frame that makes up a comic strip or sequence of panels.[40] The other aspect is the contiguity of the sequential form. Comics, he says, are composed of cartoons (icons) used to represent a person, place, or thing. The key characteristic of a cartoon is "amplification through simplification." It abstracts an image through simplifying its form, meanwhile accentuating a particular meaning. These abstractions *permit* reader-identification with a character or an object. Most comics use cartoons for characters, "for the world within."[41] Tintin is such an abstract figure, McCloud explains, that the world within (him, the subject) remains quite open to multiple readings. Hergé's *ligne claire* combination, which combined realism and abstractions,[42] allowed readers to travel the globe and planet with his boy scout, while masking themselves in the oblique character of Tintin. What happens if we turn McCloud's logic toward the blackface characters in Congolese comics? One wonders if the historical context of colonial racism, segregation, and minstrel imagery obliged Congolese to identify with the iconic characters who figure in the rest of this chapter. A key question needs to be considered in future research. As Congolese increasingly intervened in the production of blackface- and dandy-related icons, and as the contexts of viewership changed over time, did readers remain subjected, involuntarily identifying with de-idealizing screens of blackness? When and how did identification grow more polysemic, opening comics to writerly readings, infringements, and inversions?

THE ICONS AND AESTHETICS OF INTERWAR CONGO

The first *Tintin au Congo* comics appeared in 1930–31, we saw, in a Belgian Catholic newspaper's special children's supplement published on Sundays in Brussels. The first cartoons produced by Congolese appeared in 1933 in a Congolese Catholic newspaper published on Sundays in Leopoldville. *La Croix du Congo*, published by the Scheutist congregation of missionary priests, was one of the first newspapers to try to create a Congolese readership. Its news items alternated between French and Lingala, and it included special stories, articles, amusements, and comic strips for African readers.

On September 3, 1933, "Le match de Jako et Mako," appeared beneath a blow-by-blow account by Gabriel Elongo of a July football match between two Stanleyville teams with ever-so-Belgian names, the Count of Flanders and the Duke of Brabant. Elongo listed each player's Congolese name, noting that Alexis Njolo replaced Antoine Sindano after a knee injury.[43] The cartoon's "composition" (text) was by Louchet, while the "linocut"[44] was by Paul Lomami of Kinshasa.[45] The six frames in the single panel depict two figures kicking a ball between them under a palm tree; the text explains that they are members of a soccer team preparing for Sunday's game. Jako and Mako are monkeys perched in a tree watching this game of kicking and stopping this "round machine" of a ball. When Pierre and Paul leave to rest, Jako and Mako come down from the tree with a coconut as their ball. When Mako kicks the coconut and Jako blocks the shot with his head, they shriek in pain. This first Congolese comic strip, at least partly produced by a Congolese, is about the dangers of mimicry. Like Tintin, "Jako and Mako" was for the young at heart, was published by priests, and had an educational goal, while poking fun. Pierre and Paul appear as whites, counterposed to the two aping monkey figures who climb out of the tree as Africans. Given the comic form and the colonial context, including the ubiquity of blackface rubrics that animalized blacks as near apes, this visual reading is the dominant one. Only the text ("Pierre and Paul are preparing for Sunday's match") and additional context (Elongo's report) allow the viewer to alter this reading. The text, if read, allows the spectator to shift among the alternative—visual and textually mediated—readings provided by the comics-plus-segregated-text form, thus to shift from the visual reading of white (man) versus black (monkey) to the textually mediated one of middle / "not quite" colonized, with a European name, versus low / "quite" colonized, with a Congolese name.[46]

Little attention has been paid to the range of ironic representations of the body available in francophone colonial worlds. Some were slapstick; some were wry. Some were for adults; some were for children. Often this divide was a European-African one, too, as if all Africans are children. Some icons were in the form of advertising; some made fun of advertising. Some teased about European colonial life; some laughed at the colonized; some did both at the same time. In the interwar period, Europeans—and Congolese—may have been saturated with the icons of colonial cannibal humor (including *Tintin au Congo*'s

Figure 3.2. "Le match de Jako et Mako" by Louchet, with linocut by Paul Lomami, from *La Croix du Congolais* (Kinshasa) 7 (September 3, 1933): 4.

blackface abstractions), yet these were not the only icons available, nor the only aesthetic. This was also the heyday for a more "high culture," sometimes surrealist fashion for *l'art nègre*.

Comics about colonial dandy figures date back as far as the 1890s in Belgian colonial publications. In the 1920s, cartoons in colonial newspapers were rare, and those that did appear tended to be European imports.[47] By 1930, minstrel jokes began to appear independently of colonial ads. "Jim, Jim," a mammy figure says to her son with big lips and curly hair in a cartoon called "Illusion": "You will always be the white sheep of the family."[48] European colonial life, however, was cosmopolitan, even if differently so in Kinshasa (Leopoldville) than in Elisabethville. By 1931, a multilingual weekly called *Cosmo-Kin* appeared, with special attention paid to cultural news and the international, multilingual nature of Kinshasa life and its jazz-filled nightlife.[49] An exhibition of art made by Congo-based European painters received much attention, while advertisements featured Josephine Baker films and jazz clubs. Comic blockprint-based drawings by "Narib" with "Linos by *Cosmo-Kin*" were a regular feature. One featured a nocturnal scene of bar life in the middle of Lent with tipsy candles and tipsy white men and one white woman listening to an African jazz band. Another was a parody of an ad for whiskey and soda, served by a quick, stylish Congolese waiter to a smiling white man, all with an art deco feel. Yet another teased about the city's smells with an image of a group of colonial-helmeted Europeans donning World War I gas masks in a Kinshasa street; they were busy rescuing a friend who had passed out from the pungent odor of salted fish, dropping helter-skelter from the large, overfilled sack of a hurried African porter.[50]

A taste for this kind of wry colonial image soared in the 1930s in journals as diverse as this cosmopolitan, Leopoldville literary magazine and *Le Coq Chante*, a missionary publication for Congolese Mongo. *Le Coq Chante* did not carry publicity, rather only Church news and catechist writings, but it did include whimsical linocut art about colonial life—a Congolese soldier, a whirling trumpet player in a uniform, a smoker. There was no text. These were not cartoons that made viewers laugh; their abstracted icons produced ironic smiles, whimsical affection. They were not exaggerated, blackface stick figures, even though the technology relied on black and white impressions to create a wry, sometimes even sensuous aesthetic.[51]

La Croix du Congo began to appear every Sunday in 1932. *Ngonga*, the *Journal des Indigènes du Congo Belge*, or *Barua ya Watu wa Kongo Beleji*, began to appear every Saturday in Elisabethville in 1933. *La Croix du Congo* was a Catholic publication, and part of it was published in Lingala. *Ngonga* was directed and owned by A. Verbeken, an honorary district commissioner in Katanga; it appeared with texts in French and Swahili, as well as carnal blackface advertisements,[52] and cartoons by "SAV." One SAV cartoon, "Elégances du dimanche," shows a dandified, sexualized African woman with handbag, tight short dress, and umbrella walking with such allure in front of Salomon & Co's open shop that even a tennis-racket-clutching dandy figure pauses to take a look. Another shows a group of chained

Figure 3.3. "Vision de guerre" by Narib, in *Cosmo-Kin* (Kinshasa) 1, 16 (April 19, 1933): 16.

Figure 3.4. Congolese soldier in fez cap, in *Le Coq chante* (Coquilhatville) 4, 27 (October 1, 1939).

Figure 3.5. "Les enchaînés" by SAV, *Ngonga* (Elisabethville) 1, 29 (December 15, 1934): 2.

prisoners being knocked against trees and one another because one of them has tried to run away.[53]

Neither "Jako and Mako" or *Tintin au Congo* is similarly sadistic. Tintin's fanciful, self-mocking adolescent humor is always wholesome. There are no women and no sexuality in Tintin comics, even if colonial relations are problematized in *Tintin au Congo*.[54] Likewise, the figures in "Jako and Mako" were neither the sensuous, ironic bodies of colonial art blockprints nor the sexualized or terrorized ones of SAV's cartoons. Jako and Mako are slapstick figures who caricature the male gender, the black race, and the predicaments of mimicry in the colony.

The aesthetic range of the interwar years included room for accidents, space for surprise, even the surreal playing with the debris of war to cope with smelly Kinois fish. Still, there were at least two different styles at work, whether visible in different newspapers or mediated by different cities.[55] In Leopoldville (Kinshasa), *Cosmo-Kin* wished to be roaring with its jazz, its wild, cosmopolitan scenes suggesting that colonial splendor could be fun and urbane. Meanwhile, *La Croix du Congo* provided children's play for Congolese, further separating them from this segregated world of European leisure. In Elisabethville, the bilingual newspaper's reading publics were multiracial; *Ngonga* provided sexualized and colonial adult humor for Congolese and Europeans alike, while poking ambivalent fun at the ordeals of colonial confinement.

POSTWAR 1: *MBUMBULU*

One of the first comic strips explicitly produced for Congolese was the *Adventures of Mbumbulu*. It appeared in the state-published (although missionary-influenced) photographic magazine for Congolese, *Nos Images*, which circulated widely in the colony's four major vernacular languages from 1946 on. *Nos Images* severed typical links between listening and reading publics in the Congo. Anyone who could see could "read" *Nos Images*' photographic and cartoon texts. Packed with photographs, this biweekly was in a sense the Belgian Congo's *Life* magazine. Readers could send in photos of themselves, and many of these were published.

Mbumbulu became the newspaper's mascot from its first issue, when the front page announced that his adventures would soon begin. His highly abstract, blackface image, with oversized white lips and eyeballs and a white circle of a nose, was used to advertise subscriptions and send holiday wishes. For the first forty-two episodes, *Mbumbulu* was signed by "Masta," a pseudonym likely chosen as parody by Frère Marc, the first of the four graphic artists—and the only missionary—who drew the series drawings.[56] The "Masta" signature disappeared with the forty-fourth issue of *Nos Images* in 1951, just as the images lost their *ligne claire* aesthetic for a busy, muddied look. By 1954 (with issue no. 83), the BD series carried a new title, *The Adventures of the Mbumbulu Family*. Mbumbulu had grown up, becoming not only father but grandfather, enmeshed in a purposive narrative in search of a didactic plot.

Mbumbulu announced that he was a *farceur*—a practical joker—in the first of Masta's episodes, and he acted like an indignant dandy in the second. When he went hunting with his white boss in the third, he accidentally hit him with an arrow in his behind. In the fourth, he thought he had come across a new magic pen, and he ended up squirting some onlookers, including a European boss, with ink. After these first few episodes, space to ridicule colonial authority figures disappeared. The controlling intentions of Masta's images became blunter as Mbumbulu's adventures turned to the classic didactic tropes of Belgian colonial propaganda: the dangers of excessive drinking and the virtues of saving money, marrying in a church, and turning over a good share of one's wages to one's wife. Mbumbulu, the colonized Good Samaritan, receives colonial medals for his righteous deeds; he fathers accomplished, colonial-trained children. By their close, Mbumbulu's "adventures" had settled down into a colonial how-to strip demonstrating a model, modest *évolué* family.

Mbumbulu, like most colonial BDs of the time, did not integrate text and images through the use of talking balloons. Instead, explanatory texts ran below each cartoon frame. The text remained superfluous, usually underlining the visual point, quite unlike the textual additions of Jako and Mako that enabled new readings. Mbumbulu remained a colonial-made, bumbling, minstrel-like *petit nègre* figure. He had many of the slapstick, repetitive, and narrative-weak characteristics of *Tintin au Congo*. He did not speak, and he was a solitary *farceur*—was no Milou, no Mako, no Pilipili. Yet *Mbumbulu* was in many ways a semiotic diminutive of *Tintin au Congo*. While there are no car thefts in Mbumbulu's adventures, a toy car crashes

Figure 3.6. "Les aventures de Mbumbulu" by Masta, in *Nos Images* (Kinshasa) 1, 3 (September 15, 1948).

and bicycles are plentiful. One *Mbumbulu* episode is about a bicycle theft; another features a too-stylishly embellished one. Tintin drives a car; Mbumbulu rides a bicycle. The first, more comical episodes, created by Frère Marc, were also similar to *Matamata and Pilipili*, a popular burlesque missionary-produced film series reminiscent of Laurel and Hardy and produced with Congolese actors in Luluabourg.[57]

Catholic missionaries were keen to produce educational fictional forms for and about Congolese subjects, and several priests became involved in the production of narrative, fictional films for Congolese spectators such as *Matamata*.[58] Whereas Mbumbulu is an authoritarian husband and father,[59] Matamata is harassed by his domineering wife, who chases after him on payday, hitting him and reproaching him for wasting his wages in bars. The next payday, Matamata dutifully gives her his pay in front of their *évolué* house. Other comic episodes have Matamata and Pilipili defying colonial authority, even running away from chasing Congolese police. Matamata enjoys the prestige of reading newspapers, but it makes him an absentminded father. One day his wife tells him to take the children for a walk. As he pores over the pages of *La Croix du Congo*, each child wanders off and gets into trouble without his noticing. One by one they disappear; his baby crawls out of the pram, and a European baby climbs in instead.[60] *Mbumbulu*, except in its first few episodes, does not come near the humor of these spoofs.[61]

Immediately after *Mbumbulu* ended, with its 125th episode in December 1955, the series was reprinted as an album. Readers of *Nos Images* were advised to hurry to buy one because few of the 9,000 copies printed were left, and the many ads for it show a beaming *évolué* couple reading theirs together. Does the narrative of Belgian colonial officials censoring *Tintin au Congo* relate to the disappearance of *Mbumbulu*? There is no evidence of a Congolese reading and viewing public ever objecting to this de-idealizing screen of blackness. Nor did blackface rubrics disappear. *Nos Images* readers had access to new comics especially designed for them. The adventures of Mayele ("Clever") and how he built a house, for example, were equally derivative of minstrel icons and equally patronizing in their didacticism. Others in *L'Antilope*, a children's paper, were Congolese-drawn animal stories. All—in racial terms—were milder than *Mbumbulu*.

THE FIFTIES: A CONGOLESE SUPERMAN AND AN INTERRUPTED COMIC STRIP

Klim ads by Borden showed a male domestic worker beneath a talking cow; the strip detailed how to mix the powdered milk. Blue Band featured a young boy, Makasi, and the bread and margarine sandwiches his mother made him to make him strong while swimming. Youthful Léon cures a migraine after his boss, the white owner of a truck repair shop, suggests Aspro tablets. Such comic-based advertisements, common in Congolese newspapers and magazines, were among the comics produced by Europeans and intended for Congolese in the 1950s. The blockprint aesthetic declined, at least in newspapers and magazines, although it survived as a feature of some colonial novels.

The new phenomenon of comics for Congolese gave birth in 1957 to a Congolese Superman called Sao, drawn by Paul Merle. "Adventure and bravery with Sao the advocate who vanquishes and redresses wrongs [*le justicier*]" appeared in the "Actualités africaines" (African news) pages of the Elisabethville paper *L'Avenir*. Sao is a loyal colonial subject who punishes vice; he even helps a white storekeeper solve a theft problem. He is portrayed as a handsome black man, with noncaricatured facial features and a hypermuscular body, and wears a Supermanlike outfit of tight-fitting shorts, belt, and singlet, with metal wrist bands. Blackface rubrics hardly disappeared, however. If the dandy figure as embodied by Sao lost his transgressive indignation, the cannibal was infantilized and domesticated. Sao made his debut at the same time as "the joyous dwarf . . . Tshibamba," an abstract, thick-lipped, happy circus elf of a figure wearing a checkered suit and bowtie. We need only read Patrice Lumumba's defiant statement at independence in order to recall that Congolese *évolués* had become very sensitive to icons and texts comparing colonized black men to monkeys. *Sao* was an early compromise. It made room, for the first time, for a hyperbolic, phallic, black masculinity.

In the 1950s, the rare BDs drawn by Congolese resembled comic strips more than Paul Lomami's linocuts did. In 1953, well before *Mbumbulu* ceased, the first Congolese-drawn BD since Lomami's 1932 "Jako and Mako" appeared. Like the latter, *Mbu and Mpia* was printed in *La Croix du Congo*. P. M'Bila was the "native illustrator" of this series about the escapades of a rascally pair of twins, not unlike Hergé's Brussels urchins Quick and Flupke.[62] M'Bila drawings were rudimentary, accompanied by a nonballooned explanatory storyline. Each episode had three panels. Few of the drawings—and none of the frames—were inherently comic, even if proportion was often distorted (perhaps unintentionally).

Whereas the white colonial superego is always in the background in *Mbumbulu* in the shape of the author's pseudonym "Masta," in *Mbu and Mpia*, European figures and ethics disappear. The story begins one Sunday in Kinshasa. The mischievous twins, who wear shorts and caps and have Kikongo names, are bored because they can't find any birds to shoot at with their slingshots Suddenly, they hear the voice of Pierre Monoko, shown wearing his tie on the other side of the urban residential enclosure: "Undoubtedly another palaver with his wife . . . poor Paulina; she has already seen plenty with her nitwit of a husband . . . what else is she going to undergo?" Mbu and Mpia approach, witnessing the couple's spat. Mbu and Mpia don't like the pretentious Monoko, who is shown shaking his finger at his wife as she goes off to buy food to prepare for him.

The twins decide to play a memorable trick on this arrogant—and Tshilubaspeaking—*évolué*. Perched on a chair, Monsieur Monoko practices a speech that

Mbu et Mpia.... espiègles Kinois

Figure 3.7. "Mbu et Mpia.... espiègles Kinois" by P. M'Bila, in *La Croix du Congolais* (Kinshasa) 27, 16 (April 26, 1953): 4.

he hopes will lead to his election as president of "The Flower of Kasai," the parodic name of an ethnic association of Luba residents. While Monoko continues his preparations, shaving over a large china bowl in his backyard, young Mbu takes aim. His slingshot is much smaller than Tintin's was, but the stone shatters Monoko's shaving bowl. Furious, the half-shaved Monoko chases after the twins. The two Bakongo pranksters hide behind a policeman in a red fez cap. He defends them against the ridiculous-looking Monoko, his razor in hand and his black face still covered with white soap. A colonial soap joke about the impossibility of cleaning—whitening—a *nègre* is embedded in this image.[63]

The young villains continue playing pranks of this sort for another ten episodes. They leave the policeman with a calabash hanging from his behind, before wrapping up a brick as a mysterious gift for the speech-preparing Luba upstart from Kasai. Again furious, Monoko aims the brick at these young scoundrels. He misses. They apologize. Satisfied, the pompous Monsieur Monoko goes off to search for his speech, hoping to persuade these trickster boys to leave him alone. They prepare a new escapade, involving the chair and a rope. Perhaps the idea was to make Monoko tumble to the ground when he next mounted the chair to practice his speech, but there is no next frame! Instead, the editors reported in the next issue that the strip had to be interrupted because the "native illustrator" had failed to supply his drawings: "We hope that the interruption will not last long."[64]

M'Bila's illustrated sequential story never reappeared. Perhaps his defection—or removal?—was due to the very plot he was enmeshed in producing. The red-fezzed city policeman may have been the butt of one prank. However, Mbu and Mpia direct most of their farcical scorn at the finger-waving, brick-hurling, tie-wearing, speech-inclined colonial parvenu Monoko. This ostentatious *évolué* is a

Luba (while his wife shops in a Bakongo market at Camp Cito). The text implies that the two young pranksters are members of an urban gang of thieves. Regardless, the pair make fun of a rising *évolué* ethnic group of immigrant urban elites in a colonial story where all the characters—husband and wife, Mbu and Mpia, and the policeman—are Congolese.[65]

The relationship between text and image was also more complicated than in *Mbumbulu*. It was the accompanying text, more than the images themselves, that made this strip dangerous. Because the images are weak, unable to carry a central storyline, the text more than supplements the images; its specificities exceed them. Perhaps the editors stopped the *Mbu and Mpia* series because it seemed to be encouraging juvenile delinquency. But it was the text that insisted that readers understand the pranks against Monoko as ethnic mockery. Was the interruption a missionary decision? Or did M'Bila stop producing the work because he became frightened? At the time he ceased producing his drawing, the editors identified M'Bila as the "native illustrator"? Who was writing the script? And which came first? We shall never know. But we might surmise that it became untenable for two unruly boys to poke fun and aim slingshots at the ostentation of an *évolué* in 1953 and dangerous to valorize anti-Luba "juvenile delinquency" as fun. The fact that a blackface soap joke adds to the ridicule of Monoko also reminds us of how stock an icon this had become in Congolese visual vocabularies.

POCO RETURNS

Try to find an educated—even semi-educated—francophone African who has not heard of Tintin. Try to find a Nigerian or Ghanaian, never mind an American, who does not express surprise at the glossy, colorful, witty, sequential graphic novels coming out of francophone Europe and Africa. The first major African graphic novelists are coming out of Kinshasa, Libreville, Abidjan, and Dakar. And French and Belgian cultural agencies are helping to create comic artists, just as their predecessors produced novelists and water-colorists in the interwar and postwar periods.[66]

There has been an explosion of comic forms produced in the Congo since independence, ranging from development comics, to the use of serial, caricatured juxtapositions in popular paintings, to Mobutu's life story, to ephemeral street comics. Multiple circuits, markets, and sites of authorship are implicated in the production and consumption of comics, especially those of postcolonial Congo. Anyone can scribble cartoons. Some scribbles approach art. What makes its way into print is an indication of at least minimal access to printing presses or photocopying machines, drawing tools, and consumers. BDs, wherever they get reproduced, wherever they circulate, have markets. Not all readers or viewers are purchasing consumers, but sales determine audiences as well as creation and publication decisions. Unless BDs are produced as gifts, as schoolbooks, or as development handouts, that is, and this kind of production has not been slender. Indeed, one of the most important publishers of postcolonial BDs by Zairians since 1981 has been the Belgian "cooperation and development" agency, the Administration générale de la coopération au développement (AGCD). Even more important has been Congo-Zaire's largest publisher, Saint Paul Afrique, a Catholic-owned press with the only chain of bookstores and the most reasonable prices in the country. They, like their Catholic counterparts worldwide encourage and publish BDs "*à bon Dieu.*" (Brussels's monumental basilica promotes its BD shop and research center as you enter the cathedral doors!)[67]

Hergé went out of his way to produce the impression in 1969 that Congolese wanted *Tintin au Congo* reprinted. *Zaïre* also published other Tintin albums in serial form in the early 1970s (including *Le Temple du soleil* and *Les 7 boules de crystal*). Tintin has had institutional and economic legacies on the cultural production of Congolese-created BDs—in and outside of Congo-Zaire—ever since. Barly Baruti's first major album, for example, resembles *Tintin au Congo*, and he created *La voiture! C'est l'aventure* while doing an internship in the Hergé Studios in Brussels in the mid 1980s. Both are African detective-like adventure stories replete with animals, automobiles, and chases after wicked men. Race is much less central in Baruti's album than class pretensions, destitution amid colonial debris, and abuse of wealth and power.[68] In 1978, youth using the library of Kinshasa's French Cultural Center tended to go there to read BDs.[69] Tintin albums were certainly available. In the 1980s, wealthier Kinois youth were finding a rental market for their most recently imported BD albums.[70]

Hergé and his largesse also fostered the careers of two of the major Congolese cartoon artists, Mongo Sisé and Barly Baruti. Not until 1972 did *Zaïre* begin to publish its first BDs written and drawn by a Zairian. Mongo Awai Sisé revived the missionary-invented, fat-and-thin colonial movie buffoons as his own cartoon figures, and *Zaïre* was the first to publish these *Aventures de Mata Mata et Pili Pili* (e.g., "Le chèque" in 1972 and "La poudre de chasse" in 1975).[71] By the early 1980s, Mongo Sisé was receiving his first contracts from the Belgian cooperation funds of the AGCD.[72]

Baruti seems at first glance to be Mongo Sisé's heir as the most successful cartoonist of development contracts. In quite similar ways, the talents of these two cartoonists came to the attention of the AGCD and were pushed forward by internships at the celebrated Hergé Studios. These BD-for-development contracts and visits to Belgian BD-dom enabled them to enrich their contacts with Belgian—and European—cartoonists. Each went on to publish their own humorous adventure BD albums. Whereas Mongo Sisé devoted a BD to Mobutu in a Kinshasa weekly at one point, Barly Baruti moved to Kinshasa about 1990, just after democratization began and a liberalized press appeared. Virtually all official Belgian cooperation in the city but a single francophone Belgian cultural center had closed down. Baruti benefited from this young Belgian cultural milieu, interested in promoting culture as (sometimes subversive) "development." His activities in encouraging youth to make BDs, like the BD association he helped found, became suspect. There were seven BD associations and some sixty cartoonists in Kinshasa at the time. Some work leaned toward the didactic; health-related NGOs and anti-AIDS funds tended to support these. Other BDs treated popular urban lore, especially those by Mfumu'eto. Many Congolese novelists aspire to high culture, but only the low-brow popular novelist Zamenga was turning to BDs, including an intriguingly ironic one (drawn by Masioni) about a white man who becomes the triumphant hero of a crowd of Zairian women after teaching them about the dangers of skin-lightening cream and encouraging pride in their black skin.[73]

Ephemeral street comics were fairly common in Mobutu's Zaire, and youth consciousness and BD speech underlay the military raids on BD artists and associations in 1991. Looting was both random and highly strategic, and the BD association to which Baruti belonged and his home were both pillaged by soldiers. He is nonetheless, in the eyes of many, an African success story as a comic strip artist. His internship at the Hergé Studios led to the publication of the first BD album in color by a Zairian cartoonist. Shortly after he came to live in Belgium in 1992, Brussels's francophone daily, *Le Soir*, ran a small feature on him.

Barly Baruti's Lokele father, of distant "Arab" descent, was named "Livingstone" at birth.[74] He was a painter and, at least in his son's eyes, a well-heeled professional who worked for international organizations based in Kisangani, with a private library of books (and BDs) at their home. In 1996, Baruti lived on the outskirts of Brussels, was cutting his first musical CD, finishing the third volume of *Eva K.*, and affiliated as an active *animateur* with Ti Suka, an unusual, nonprofit Brussels "culture and development" association. As well as assisting Ti Suka with the politicized BD contest *Concours BD 96 Bruxelles-Kinshasa*,[75] Baruti was also finding an international, primarily Belgian audience for the prize-winning *Eva K*. This lavishly produced album cost around BEF 450 (about U.S.$15) a copy, so only Zaire's slender class of ruling thieves would have been able to afford it at the time.

CATHOLIC AUDIENCES

Hergé once wondered why he received so much fan mail from India.[76] In Madagascar, a Jesuit priest informed him, schoolchildren filed past a volume of *Tintin* displayed under glass, a missionary turning over a new page each day.[77] We cannot, of course, trace such adoration to *Tintin au Congo* and the effects of its continuing circulation within and outside of Congo-Zaire. Nor is Baruti the only Congolese comic artist with a transnational career. Maurice Kalibiona, a Belgian-born cartoonist of Congolese descent, went on a pilgrimage to Medjugorge in Bosnia-Herzegovinia in the early 1990s (just before the war began) and became a Catholic witness of Virgin Mary apparitions and cartoonist in one go, producing two BD albums about his transnational religious experience.[78]

The first Congolese-authored BD in *La Croix du Congo* may be long forgotten. But the Catholic theme has remained central to cultural production in postcolonial Congo-Zaire, as any Mudimbe reader knows. Readers of the most popular

Congolese novelist, Zamenga, know so, too; most of his over twenty novels, stories, BDs, and poems have been published by Saint-Paul Afrique.[79] Saint-Paul Afrique even has its own BD line, consisting of Congolese folk tales, biblical stories, and a historical series about Congolese-named saints.[80] A Catholic strand first met a BD strand in the Congo with Tintin, and this squeaky clean world traveler is still alive in Congolese imaginations and quotations. Less well known is the role of Catholic mission priest-publishers and filmmakers and the subversive potential of some of the twinned, farcical figures that they and their protégés helped create: Jako and Mako, Mbu and Mpia, and Matamata and Pilipili.

Comics produced in the Congo began to appear in Belgian colonial newspapers from the late 1920s on, and Congolese had access to these media, especially *La Croix du Congo*. Congolese began drawing and imitating European forms, including comic strips. Belgian officials and missionaries also sought ways to *steer* Congolese eyes toward publications created and meant for them. Such *steering* became more directed with the appearance in 1946 of the official lay publication for natives, *Nos Images*, and its didactic, blackface-based *Mbumbulu* cartoon. The range of comics in circulation, however, was wide. An American boy who grew up in South Africa was able to pick up a Batman comic book in a Matadi hotel in 1945, as if he had never seen American comics before.[81] Yet Catholic (or Catholic-influenced) newspapers dominated the production of BDs. In 1956, *La Croix du Congo* was reserializing one of the Tintin comic series, *L'étoile mystérieuse*. This Catholic newspaper also featured a puzzlelike game, asking if readers could remember in which Tintin album different characters had appeared. If the colony's Catholic Congolese reading public was not recollecting Tintin and his adventures, it was at least being encouraged to do so.[82]

MIRRORS AND CAMERAS, SCREEN AND GAZE

A *New York Times* journalist recently expressed surprise at the enigmatic Congolese fondness for Tintin that he uncovered during a visit to Kinshasa. "How could Tintin possibly be popular?" he wondered, while repeating a familiar canard: *Tintin au Congo* had once been so detested that it was banned.[83] The assumption behind this naïve wonder is akin to the surprise of realizing that native colonial Africans who watched Tarzan movies did not find them offensive, at least when they watched them in a colonial-based viewing situation (of a segregated African audience). These colonial subjects identified themselves with the hero Tarzan, not with the degraded savages of these jungle adventure films. Yet, as Frantz Fanon and Kaja Silverman have suggested, the context of spectatorship can dramatically shift the meanings of screen (mirror), gaze (camera), and the ever-lurking white look, and thus shift the sense of necessity "to identify with an image which provides neither idealization nor pleasure." Fanon's personal example is of traveling to the colonial metropole of Paris, where he realized in a movie theater that he was being observed through "images of a stereotypically menial blackness" even before the film began.

These not-yet filmic "representation[s] from which any subject would recoil . . . turn[ed] into a 'mirror,' and induce[d] a highly unpleasurable redefinition." His "violent corporeal redefinition," a "decomposition . . . precipitated by an obligatory identification with an intolerable imago," was "experienced through the fantasy of the body in bits and pieces."[84]

As *Mbumbulu*'s reformulations of Tintin's colonial vocabulary suggest, colonial cartoons intended for natives signified colonizing control and diminution, achieved in part through a colonial gaze and, in no small way, through bicycles. *Tintin au Congo* cartoons placed a camera center stage. This device was capable of capturing giraffe shots as well as filmic evidence about the plots of the gangster and witch doctor team. When cartoons became didactic messages for Congolese subjects, the fact of a colonial gaze—and the possibility of a writerly reading—was no longer represented within the cartoon through a camera and movie screens. Ironic references to colonial screens of blackness disappeared. Instead, the gaze became transcendental and omniscient, removed from the text. Only a readerly (singular, coerced) reading became possible. Likewise, when the central jester figure turned from Tintin to Mbumbulu, the other-gazing camera became a self-reflecting mirror. There was no gangster, no witch doctor, no plot. The focus turned to bicycle-riding, monkey-resembling Mbumbulu. Gaze was no longer ironized through a weapon-reminiscent camera. Nor did Mbumbulu's self-reflexivity produce a public spectacle of viewership in BD frames. The viewing situation instead appeared as a solitary frame of Mbumbulu facing into an obligatory, de-idealizing mirror with a puzzled expression, asking himself: "Who am I?" In *Mbumbulu* comics, we saw, a screen of menial blackness as self became the only necessary reading. Rather than a teasing camera of a gaze—"a synecdoche for lucidity" in Pierre Halen's words[85]—Mbumbulu's view, like the reader's view of him, was obliged to see this other in the mirror of a comic *as* self.

There is also a mirror in *Mbu and Mpia*, but it is Monoko's shaving mirror. Mbumbulu's mobility is limited to a bicycle; he has no car. In *Mbu and Mpia*, Monoko's social mobility extends to a speech; yet like all the signs of Monoko—his speech and chair, his shaving mirror, his porcelain bowl and razor—the performance of this discourse is a joke. Monoko's receipt of a brick wrapped as a gift is likewise a mean, violent prank, just as the image of Monoko falling off his chair of a stage would have been if the storyline had gotten that far.

INTERTEXTUALITY AND STREET COMICS, OR, WHY BOTHER?

The explosion of street comics in Kinshasa from 1968 or so on, an explosion in which Chéri Samba took part,[86] cannot be told without returning to the kinds of source material that I have discussed here. Congolese colonial comics also give us a capacity to read postcolonial images intertextually. And such an archival entry onto potential identifications and rejections is necessary if the silencing of

Mbumbulu in explicit memory and the celebration and appropriation of Tintin is to be explained. The contrast in the remembering of Mbumbulu partly derives from a novel context of spectatorship—postcoloniality—where suddenly the possibility of identifying with the hero—whether Tarzan or Tintin—is immersed in a new positioning of laughter. Tintin permitted laughter with and at the subject as self. *Mbumbulu* only allowed laughing *at*, while the subject imposed a de-idealizing self, even if the drawings themselves served as models of juxtaposed sequential art that schoolchildren like Barly Baruti copied so as to learn formal comic drawing techniques.[87]

The cultural production of Congolese BDs within and outside of Congo-Zaire remains a neglected popular art, while the academic literature on painting grows ever bigger. Jewsiewicki has noted the use of cartoon panels in Congolese popular painting, especially by Chéri Samba of Kinshasa, who once drew cartoons.[88] Fabian has wondered about the comic-like juxtaposed sequential nature of Tshibumba's historical painting series.[89] Each of these specialists in Congolese vernacular art has, therefore, suggested that more attention should be paid to forms of "leakage" among media and genres.[90]

Four assumptions and one question have guided the small selection of comics discussed here. First, we must attend to the wider genre of images, caricatures, and semi-caricatures that were part of colonial literatures—including newspapers and periodicals—written by and for Europeans in the colony. Second, ironic, affectionate representations of the black body represent a striking difference from blackface caricatures and deserve special care, especially since these alternative *art nègre*–like conventions predated and postdated the cannibal-like humor of Tintin. Third, we need to take into account the kinds of caricatures and cartoons that European colonials explicitly made for colonial subjects, since such visual steering tells us about conventions of appropriateness and the mimetic desires of colonial pedagogy. Finally, it is important to consider when and how Congolese were allowed to draw and publish caricatures. How did their themes, rubrics, and bodily figurations relate to these other genres?

My central question is: Who skirts—or escapes—the blackface iconic rubric, and when? A central theme of steering within colonial mimicry was how to produce a proper, not quite/not white, semi-civilized native: a good middle figure. The liminality of this figure went along with corporeal reconfiguration, that is, with either the laughter that surrounded the icon of the cannibal-with-his-cooking pot or the indignant, exaggerated dandy figure. Mbumbulu as dandy figure never knew indignation, just ostentatious parading in fancy clothes. Mbumbulu could never escape the blackface rubric, even if he was billed as semi-civilized. And unlike Matamata and Pilipili, he has no comic counterpart. His liminality is condensed into a solitary figure; he is a *petit nègre* objectified.

An indignant dandy figure is part of *Tintin au Congo*'s humor; it is he who in the name of cleanliness refuses to help upright a derailed train. And this dandy is juxtaposed to more noble savages, while the cannibal with cooking pot becomes the witch doctor villain. But the central comic figures are the incongruous European pair: Tintin and Milou. Although *Tintin au Congo* also has its share of practical jokes and a gigantic slingshot, *Mbu and Mpia* took inspiration from another of Hergé's comic strips as well, the Brussels street urchins Quick and Flupke.[91] The indignant dandy figure of *Mbu and Mpia*, Monoko, is mocked and simultaneously ethnicized by a comical pair of Kinshasa street boys. The good middle figure of colonial steering—a Luba speech writer—becomes stark antihero in this Congolese-created comic strip.

What has happened to the indignant dandy and cannibal figures in postcolonial street comics? There is space for two of these parodic reformulations here, both from Jean-Pierre Jacquemin's collection. By the early 1970s, a comic book subculture was thriving among youth in urban Zaire. The first issue of *Jeunes pour Jeunes* appeared about 1968, after a Catholic priest decided that it would be interesting to publish BDs in the "Hindubill" argot.[92] *Jeunes pour Jeunes* became *Kake* in the early 1970s, when it began to feature Sima Lukombo's BDs, including his character the "immortal Apolosa."[93] Apolosa, "a comic character still made use of today," is a *flic*—a cop—whose "picaresque adventures marvelously incarnated the country's humor."[94] Apolosa seems to have had more than one incarnation. Sima Lukombo also drew (while Inampunde wrote) "Apolosa moniteur" (Teacher Apolosa). This Apolosa is a realistically drawn, hairy mouthed, clownlike schoolteacher who speaks broken French and proposes a lesson in verb conjugation as though it were a tempting, lustful act. His snobbish, sophisticated students laugh at him, while one sketches cartoonlike images of him. Another flaunts his fingernails and perfect French, while threatening to tattle to his father if he cannot ask his question.[95]

"Apolosa moniteur," with its unevolved savage of a teacher, simultaneously plays with and mocks blackface rubrics and colonial education. The teacher becomes an apelike savage, while the elite student is more of the indignant figure. The blackface rubric is rendered realistically rather than abstractly; amplification through simplification disappears just as the apelike image becomes tied to the almost—but not at all "quite"—white man figure, the dubious bearer of colonial education, dispensing deranged French language and Belgian colonial history lessons. Should we call this postcolonial cannibal humor?

As striking in Jacquemin's collection are two 1990 installments of a BD 'zine by Mfumu'eto about a sugar daddy big man. Here, the cannibal figure reappears as sorcerer and dandy at one and the same time, while the pretentious big man figure is domesticated into a sexualized, predatory snake. (Mfumu'eto tends to comment on current political events; another of his cartoons is about the airplane that crashed into a Kinshasa market.) This man with sumptuous car transforms himself into a boa in his bedroom and proceeds to consume not Milou but his sexual prey, a young married woman who, missing the cash of sexual transactions, has eagerly accepted his invitation home. The sequel begins with images depicting Kinois readers eagerly buying "Super-choc" 'zine no. 2 in order to find out if the story is true. True and ongoing it is, they find out. The woman-eating boa is

Figure 3.8. "Apolosa moniteur," drawings by Sima Lukombo and text by Inampunde, in *La Revue des Jeunes* (Kinshasa), no. 25 (n.d.; ca. 1973), 23.

now vomiting up his meal as cash. Bills—dollars?—by the hundreds fill his bedroom as shocked city people read the unfolding news.[96]

Age-old sorcery idioms of ingestion, power, wealth, and malevolent human agency are implicit in this cartoon. Yet as Barly Baruti said to me about his own take on sorcery, unjust wealth, and sexual conquest in *L'aventure! C'est la voiture*, "These are everyday Zairian realities. These things happen every day." One of the very few Congolese artists to conjure up the meanings of this sexualized, money-mad period of Mobutu's final years is Yoka Lye.[97] I know no writer who has better expressed the collective mentality that underlines such imagery of a powerful, big man consuming—devouring as food—women/sex in order to produce his obscene, bodily derived wealth. "Of course, he symbolizes Mobutu," Jacquemin said in a Brussels restaurant of the boa/man cartoon figure, while a Kinoise named Bijoux broke into unmanageable laughter. It was not laughter of denial or contempt but rather of unexpected recognition and fantastic amusement.

NOTES

I am grateful to Barly Baruti and Tshibanda Wamuela Bujitu, who agreed to interviews in Brussels on December 18, 1996, and January 13, 1997; Vincent Romain, who combed through colonial newspapers and magazines in Brussels in search of comics for me; Blaise-Pascal Baruani, who helped me fathom Congolese fondness for Tintin; Jean-Luc Vellut and his father for their Tintin and Hergé memories; Bob White for his Mfumu'eto comics; and Marie-Hélène de Wilde for keeping me up to date on Barly Baruti. I also owe much to the Belgian cultural critic Jean-Pierre Jacquemin, a key *animateur* of Congolese studies in Brussels, for sharing his insights and extensive 1980s–1990s Congolese BD collection with me. His 1986 essay remains one of the best treatments of Congolese and other francophone African comics, and one can only hope that he will update and expand it soon; see Jean-Pierre Jacquemin, "BD africaine: Masques, perruques," in *L'année de la bande dessinée 86–87*, ed. Stan Berts and Thierry Groenstein (Grenoble: Éditions Glénat, 1986). Otherwise, there is precious little on the subject of Congolese comics; see Paul Herman, "Bande dessinée et Congo: De la passion au flirt discret," in *Zaïre 1885–1985: Cent ans de regards belges* (Brussels: Coopération par Éducation et la Culture, 1985); and the brief Barly Baruti and Jacquemin essays in *Un dîner à Kinshasa: Concours BD 96 Bruxelles-Kinshasa* (Brussels: Édition Ti Suka asbl, 1996).

1. I draw throughout this essay on the feminist film critic Kaja Silverman's rereading of Lacan's mirror stage and "bodily ego" in light of Frantz Fanon's *Black Skin, White Masks*. See Kaja Silverman, *The Threshold of the World* (New York: Routledge, 1996), 27–31, esp. 27.

2. On the performance of blackface rubrics within colonial life, see Nancy Rose Hunt, *A Colonial Lexicon: Of Birth Ritual, Medicalization, and Mobility in the Congo* (Durham, N.C.: Duke University Press, 1999).

3. See Kaja Silverman, *The Subject of Semiotics* (New York: Oxford University Press, 1983). I pay attention to the motivated signs and subjections of these semiotics and draw on Silverman's use, for reading film, of Roland Barthes's distinction between readerly and writerly readings; ibid., 242–50. My understanding of "ambivalence" owes much to Homi Bhabha; see his "Of Mimicry and Man: The Ambivalence of Colonial Discourse," *October* 28 (1984): 125–33.

4. BD is the shorthand for *bande dessinée*, French for comic strips and albums, a genre well recognized as an art form since the 1960s in the francophone world, where there is a considerable and differentiated market of fictional album series for adults; the latter are often called "graphic novels" in the anglophone world.

5. Methuen, Hergé's U.K. publisher, "always steadfastly ignored it" (Harry Thompson, *Tintin: Hergé and His Creation* [London: Hodder & Stoughton, 1991], 42). Yet the color album *Tintin au Congo* was published in many other languages, including a Swahili edition printed by mission priests in Usumbura (Bujumbura, Burundi), Pierre Assouline notes in *Hergé: Biographie* (Paris: Plon, 1996), 348. Assouline provides no date, but the name "Usumbura" dates it as a colonial publication. According to the Bibliothèque royale de Belgique (see http://opac.kbr.be/), Casterman—not Methuen—published an English edition of the original black-and-white album in 1991: *The Adventures of Tintin, Reporter for "Le Petit Vingtième" in the Congo* (Tournai: Casterman, 1991).

6. Congo-Zaire or Congo-Kinshasa (as distinct from Congo-Brazzaville, formerly part of French Equatorial Africa) was known as the Congo Free State from 1885 to 1908; the Belgian Congo from 1908 to 1960; the Republic (and the Democratic Republic) of Congo until 1971; and Zaire from 1971 until 1997, when Laurent Kabila renamed the country the Democratic Republic of the Congo. This chapter alternates been Congo and Zaire, as well as Congolese and Zairian, as appropriate.

7. See, notably, Pierre Halen, "Le Congo revisité: Une décennie de bandes dessinées 'belges' (1982–1992)," *Textyles*, no. 9 (1992): 291–306; and Anouche Martirossiantz, "L'Afrique centrale vue par la bande dessinée: Notes de lecture," in *Papier blanc, encre noire: Cent ans de culture francophone en Afrique centrale (Zaïre, Rwanda, et Burundi)*, vol. 2, ed. Marc Quaghebeur, E. van Balberghe et al. (Brussels: Éditions Labor, 1992), 627–41. See, too, Christian Jannone, "Les hommes-léopards et leurs dérivés dans la bande dessinée," in *L'autre et nous: Scènes et types*, ed. Pascal Blanchard et al., 197–200 (Paris: Association Connaissance de l'histoire de l'Afrique contemporaine and Syros, 1995); Edouard François, "Raoul et Gaston, le mythe africain," *Phénix: Revue internationale de la bande dessinée*, no. 13 (1970): 31–35; Michel Pierre, "Un certain rêve africain," *Les cahiers de la bande dessinée*, no. 56 (February–March 1984): 83–86.

8. Frank Giroud and Barly Baruti, *Eva K.*, vol. 1: *Les hommes du train;* vol. 2: *Amina* (Toulon, France: Soleil/MC Productions, 1995–96). Frank Giroud, a well-known French cartoon scriptwriter (*scénariste*), collaborated with Baruti on this (thus far, two-part) graphic novel. Since then they have turned to the Swiss publisher Glénat with a new album series—not set in Africa—called *Mandrill*.

9. Buswell in the *Mail on Sunday*, November 27, 1988, quoted in Thompson, *Tintin*, 38.

10. Pierre Halen, "Tintin, paradigme du héros colonial belge? (A propos de 'Tintin au Congo')," in *Tintin, Hergé et la belgité*, edited by Anna Soncini Fratta (Bologna: Cooperativa libraria universitaria editrice Bologna, 1994); Marie Rose Maurin Abomo, " 'Tintin au Congo,' ou la stratégie d'une démarche coloniale," also in *Tintin, Hergé et la belgité*, 57–73; Philippe Chanson, *Tintin au Congo, c'est quand même un peu GROS! Une relecture critique de l'imagerie nègre en perspective créole* (Cartigny: Tribune Libre, 1995); Assouline, *Hergé;* Thompson, *Tintin;* Frederic Soumois, *Dossier Tintin: Sources, versions, themes, structures* (Brussels: Jacques Antoine, 1987); and H. van Opstal, *Tracé RG: Le phénomène Hergé* (Brussels: Lefrancq, 1998).

11. Thompson, *Tintin*, 41. See, too, Assouline, *Hergé*, 52–53.

12. Hergé, *Les aventures de Tintin: Reporter du Petit 'Vingtième' au Congo* (Tournai, Belgium: Casterman, 1982 [facsimile of the original edition, Brussels: Éditions du Petit 'Vingtième,' " 1931]); and Hergé, *Les aventures des Tintin: Tintin au Congo* (1946; Paris and Tournai, Belgium:

Casterman, 1974). These dates come from examining the currently available versions; Rosella Grillenzoni gives 1937, 1946, and 1970 for the first through third editions of Casterman's *Tintin au Congo*, in "Bibliographie Hergé," in *Tintin, Hergé et la belgité*, edited by Anna Soncini Fratta (Bologna: Cooperativa libraria universitaria editrice Bologna, 1994).

13. On cannibal humor, see Hunt, *Colonial Lexicon*.

14. Hergé's biographers have not failed to notice that it was Léon Degrelle, the leader of the Belgian francophone fascist (Rexist) movement during World War II, who handed Hergé his first examples of American comics in the 1920s. Degrelle brought them home with him after a trip to Mexico; Assouline, *Hergé*. Whether Hergé was himself fascist has been the subject of considerable debate. Some point to his anti-Semitic comics, some to *Tintin au Congo*, some to his friendship with Degrelle, and many to his work for *Le Soir*, a collaborationist newspaper, during the war. Most biographies moderate with the word "naïve."

15. "This combination allows readers to *mask* themselves in a character and safely enter a sensually stimulating world." These are Scout McCloud's words; see his *Understanding Comics: The Invisble Art* (New York: HarperPerennial, 1994), esp. 42–43, 54.

16. The key source on Tintin, *belgité*, and *belgitude* are the conference papers published by a center for francophone Belgian literature in Bologna. Ruggiero Campagnoli's distinction between *belgité* (francophone Belgian-ness) and *belgitude* (Belgian-ness without a linguistic distinction) was rejected by Marcel van de Kerchove, who insisted on seeing the global vision and Belgian provincialism that were combined in Hergé's pre-1960 BDs as a "mirror of a predominant Belgian mental universe." See Ruggero Campagnoli, "Présentation du quatrième numéro de *Beloeil*"; and Marcel van de Kerckhove, "Tintin en voyage: Une vision 'belge' des mondes exotiques?" in *Tintin, Hergé et la Belgité*, ed. Anna Soncini Fratta (Bologna: Cooperativa libraria universitaria editrice Bologna, 1994), 7–13, 25–37, esp. 38.

17. Charles de Gaulle once told André Malraux: "In the end, you know, my only international rival is Tintin." Jean-Marie Apostolidès, *Les métamorphoses de Tintin* (Paris: Seghers, 1984), 13, as cited in Fedwa Malti-Douglas and Allan Douglas, *L'idéologie par la bande: Héros politiques de France et d'Egypte au miroir de la BD* (Cairo: Centre d'études et de documentation économique, juridique et sociale,1987), 13. And in 1999—the year of Tintin's seventieth birthday—the French National Assembly debated whether and how to recognize Tintin, given the debate over his procolonialist, anti-Semitic, and collaborationist past. Norimitsu Onishi, "Tintin at 70: Colonialism's Comic-Book Puppet," *New York Times*, January 8, 1999, 4.

18. Halen, "Tintin, paradigme," 43–44. Thus Hergé was unlike Fernard Dineur, a Belgian cartoonist who authored *Tif et Tondu au Congo* in the 1930s after living in the colony; see Fernard Dineur, *Tif et Tondu au Congo belge* (Brussels: Éditions Jonas, 1979).

19. Thompson, *Tintin*, 41–42.

20. Benoît Peeters, *Tintin and the World of Hergé* (London: Methuen, 1989), 31.

21. Thompson, *Tintin*, 41.

22. Assouline is the most detailed in his *Hergé*, 348–49. Peeters's comment within his Hergé industry-produced book reveals the kind of impression Hergé or this enterprise did want to create: "But amusingly it was in a Zairean magazine that the story reappeared for the first time and from then on the quarantine of *Tintin au Congo* was over. From 1970, it was once again easy to obtain" (Peeters, *Tintin*, 31).

23. It is more likely that the publisher withdrew it from circulation to avoid bad press.

24. "Editorial: Tintin revient au Congo," *Zaïre*, December 29, 1969, 3; see too, "Tintin et Hergé débarquent," ibid., 61–67. Pages of the 1947 album were printed unchanged. In

the late 1960s, Hergé received a letter from a missionary in Kinshasa, Père Lannoy, seeking permission to whiten the black skin of the devils in *L'oreille cassée* before publishing the series in his journal *Afrique chrétienne* so that he would not have to contend with Congolese asking him why angels were white and devils black (Assouline, *Hergé,* 343).

25. "Tintin au Congo" in the letters to the editor, *Zaïre,* August 17, 1970, 5.

26. Ibid. Baudouin became a household word in the Congo from at least the time that the young Belgian king toured the Congo in 1955.

27. Benedicte Vaes and Ignace M'Boma, "Rendez-vous chez Tintin," *Zaïre,* January 11, 1971, 26–39.

28. On Apolosa, see below.

29. Jean-Luc Vellut, personal communications, December 1996 and March 2000.

30. They seemed "bloody racist, & hilarious, too"; Jon Glassman, personal communication, September 30, 1999.

31. Personal communication with accompanying slides from the art historian Joanna Grabski, then of the University of Indiana, 1996.

32. So ubiquitous has this joke become that even Sabena and Casterman have been able to reappropriate the icon in their marketing. On Sabena, see Onishi, "Tintin at 70." See, too, *Les carnets de route de Tintin: L'Afrique noire* (Tournai, Belgium: Casterman, 1992), a *Tintin au Congo* retake refashioned as an introductory guide to the continent.

33. Blaise-Pascal Baruani, Brussels, January 12, 1997; at the time, Baruani was doing research on attitudes to AIDS in Brussels's Congolese neighborhood, Matonge, at the time.

34. Yoka Lye, *Lettres d'un Kinois à l'oncle du village,* in *Cahiers Africains* 15 (Brussels: Institut Africain; Paris: L'Harmattan, 1996).

35. Johannes Fabian, *Remembering the Present: Painting and Popular History in Zaire* (Berkeley and Los Angeles: University of California Press, 1996), 301–6, 305 n. 13, 312.

36. Tintin and Spirou are household words in Belgium. They refer first to these comic figures, created in 1929 and 1938 respectively, yet also to the competitive comic journals named after them (*Le Journal de Spirou,* created in Charleroi in 1938, and *Le Journal de Tintin,* created in Brussels in 1946); they also refer implicitly to the two major schools of Belgian comics, the Charleroi, or Marcinelle, and the Brussels, or Hergé, school. For such basic history of Belgo-French BDs, see Claude Moliterni, Philippe Mellot, and Michel Denni, *Les aventures de la BD* (Paris: Découvertes Gallimard, 1996); and the excellent Annie Baron-Carvais, *La bande dessinée* (Paris: Presses universitaires de France, 1985).

37. Jewsiewicki only mentions book illustrations and engravings in old travel books. Bogumil Jewsiewicki, "Painting in Zaire: From the Invention of the West to the Representation of Social Self," in *Africa Explores: Twentieth-Century African Art,* ed. Susan Vogel (New York: Center for African Art, 1991), esp. 131, 135, 137, 142, 145, and 148.

38. Jean Berlage, *Répertoire de la presse du Congo belge (1884–1958) et du Ruanda-Urundi (1920–1958)* (Brussels: Commission belge de bibliographie, 1959).

39. Fabian, *Remembering the Present,* 191.

40. Some say a comic is only a comic if talking balloons are integrated into the visual caricatures as action and dialogue. Some say that it is the serial nature of a strip that makes for comics. In this essay, I have not limited BDs to a humorous storyline told in panels nor to Scott McCloud's more inclusive definition of "juxtaposed sequential art." I have also included single comic illustrations so as to broaden my tracing of recursive iconic forms.

41. McCloud, *Understanding Comics.*

42. A style not yet fully developed when Hergé created *Tintin au Congo.*

43. "Le match de Jako et Mako," with "Composition Louchet" and "Lino Paul Lomami (Kinshasa)," *La Croix du Congo* 7 (September 3, 1933): 4; and Gabriel Elongo (Stanleyville), "Correspondance de Stanleyville. Match Comte de Flandre—Duc de Brabant," ibid.

44. I assume a "linocut" was a linoleum cut made on the basis of the drawing and thus was closely related to a blockprint technically. I gloss the two forms here as the blockprint genre.

45. Paul Lomami Tchibamba disappeared for about twenty years from the reading public's view after playing a role in making the first Congolese comics. By the 1950s, he had become one of the Congo's premier *évolués* and its first prize-winning novelist. Lomami never mentioned his foray into comics when he won the Grand Prix littéraire for his novel *Ngando* during the 1948 Colonial Fair in Brussels. He took his peers to task instead for suggesting that he might be interested in the prize money rather than in the sake of "art." In addition to being a creative writer, Lomami was an active writer in *La Voix du Congolais*, who identified with colonial power. See Hans-Jürgen Lüsebrink, " 'Le Congo belge s'ouvre à la littérature': Impact et contexte historique des concours littéraires de *La Voix du Congolais* en 1940–1951," in *Littératures de Congo-Zaïre. Actes du colloque international de Bayreuth, 22–24 juillet 1993*, ed. Pierre Halen and Janos Riesz (Amsterdam: Rodopi, 1995), 204.

46. "Not quite" is a reference to Homi Bhabha's fertile "not quite/white" formulation, so useful for condensing the ambivalences—the subjections and desires—of colonial mimicry and translation. The shorthand I include here plays with the rigidities of official colonial categories—*évolués* and *indigènes*—and of subalternist academic categories by introducing the terms "middles" and "lows."

47. See, e.g., the imported cartoons with European themes in the "L'actualité humoristique" section of the Elisabethville paper, *L'Étoile du Congo*, May 20 1922; or *L'Essor du Congo*, no. 558, January 1930.

48. "Illusion," *Essor du Congo* 3, no. 653, May 16, 1930.

49. This *"hebdomadaire polyglotte,"* with material printed in French, English, Italian, and Portuguese, was edited by M. Dubois and J. Laxenaire; it only lasted for a few years.

50. *Cosmo-Kin*, 1931–32.

51. *Le Coq Chante*, 1938–48.

52. Simba beer ad; *Ngonga,*, 1934–35.

53. SAV cartoons; *Ngonga*, 1934–35.

54. Benoît Denis, "L'Afrique à l'Amérique: L'odyssée mentale des héros chez Hergé et Céline," in *Tintin, Hergé et la belgité*, ed. Anna Soncini Fratta (Bologna: Cooperativa libraria universitaria editrice Bologna, 1994).

55. The distinctiveness of Lubumbashi and Kinshasa urban cultures needs more research. Jewsiewicki has called Kinshasa painting "comic-strip-inspired" as opposed to Lubumbashi painting, which is more "historical," although the contrast seems to be a Samba vs. Tshibumba one. See Bogumil Jewsiewicki, *Chéri Samba: The Hybridity of Art / L'hybridité d'un art* (Westmount, Quebec: Galerie Amrad African Art Publications, 1995), and "Painting in Zaire," 149.

56. The only evidence on authorship is in the album version, where the front matter indicates that the book is intended for "Congolese youth" and that the book is the "fruit" of work done by a team, members of the personnel of the Services d'Information du Gouvernement Général du Congo belge. Credit for conceptualization and editing are given to R. R. Antoine, R. J. Antoine, J. Collard, J.-M. Domont, A. Scohy, and E. Warnier. It adds: "The drawings were executed successively by Frère Marc, M. A. Carpentier, Mlle Brebant,

Mme Colette." Frère Marc (Victor Wallenda) was an artist and missionary who went to the Congo as a member of the Institut des Frères des Ecoles Chrétienne, a teaching congregation, in 1939. He taught sculpture classes in 1943 at the École Saint-Luc de Gombe-Matadi, a professional school; the student art exhibitions that he organized were so successful that he was asked to relocate the school to the capital, where it became the Académie des Beaux-Arts de Léopoldville in 1957. See Joseph-Aurélien Cornet, "Histoire de la peinture zaïroise," in id et al., *Soixante ans de peinture au Zaïre* (Brussels: Les Éditeurs d'art associés, 1989).

57. The filmmaker, Father Van Haelst of the Scheutist order, became Congo's "Father Cinema." Up until that time, most films available to show to Congolese were American imports, and Van Haelst thought that their pace was too rapid for Congolese subjects. Yet Congolese were "born actors" in his mind, so why not put one of the mission's machete-wielding grass cutters to good use? Of his 150 some films, more than a dozen were Matamata and Pilipili comedies. See the film/video by Tristan Boulard, *Matamata et Pilipili* (Brussels: Libération Films? 1996), 55 min. (available from African Library of Cinema, California Newsreel), and Francis Ramirez and Christian Rolot, *Histoire du cinéma colonial au Zaïre, au Rwanda et au Burundi* (Tervuren, Belgium: Musée royale de l'Afrique centrale, 1985), 39, 269, 271, 311, 368.

58. Ramirez and Rolot, *Histoire du cinéma colonial au Zaïre.*

59. In various episodes, Mbumbulu "accidentally" batters his wife with a ladder, reprimands her for looking at *Nos Images* rather than tidying up, and smacks his children.

60. Boulard, *Matamata et Pilipili.*

61. Yet Mbumbulu did become a movie.

62. "Mbu et Mpia .... espiègles Kinois," illustrated by P. M'Bila, first appeared in *La Croix du Congo* 21, 13 (April 5, 1953): 1. The nineteenth and last episode appeared in *La Croix du Congo* 21, 32 (August 23, 1953): 3. Monoko suggests to the policeman that the two *brigands* might belong to the *compagnie Kitunga* in episode 9.

63. In addition to advertisements that used this trope, a colonial proverb went: "A blanchir un nègre, on perd son savon." Robert Detry, *Les mots français désignant les noirs du Congo belge (1920–1945),* Mémoire en philologie romaine, Université Catholique de Louvain, 1965, 107. Bakongo, or Kongo, unlike Luba were from the lower Congo (including Kinshasa) region.

64. The language was ambiguous; P. M'Bila was *restant en défaut.*

65. On the history of the Luba, see Bogumil Jewsiewicki, "The Formation of the Political Culture of Ethnicity in the Belgian Congo, 1920–1959," in *The Creation of Tribalism in Southern Africa,* ed. Leroy Vail (Berkeley and Los Angeles: University of California Press, 1989).

66. Jacquemin discusses such institutional postcolonial patronage for comics in his "BD africaine." Jewsiewicki provides fascinating material on Kinshasa-based Belgians who were Chéri Samba's major patrons in his *Chéri Samba.* For the Lubumbashi postcolonial expatriate academic-as-art consumer scene, Fabian's book of and about Tshibumba's paintings is revealing. Not until 1945 did Belgian colonists take a serious interest in the drawings of Congolese children; Jean Leyder, *Le graphisme et l'expression graphique au Congo Belge* (Brussels: Société royale belge de géographie, 1950). For colonial forms of patronage for graphic arts, see also Jean-Luc Vellut, "La peinture du Congo-Zaïre et la recherche de l'Afrique innocente," *Bulletin des Séances de l'ARSOM* 36, 4 (1990): 663–59.

67. The Petit Musée de la BD Chrétienne was publicized in 1996 with a cartoon image of the Basilique du Sacré-Coeur raising welcoming hands and saying in a BD balloon, "2000 bandes dessinées en toutes langues." Brother Roland Francart is in charge; see his *La BD chrétienne* (Paris: Éditions du Cerf, 1994).

68. Barly Baruti, *La voiture! C'est l'aventure* (Brussels, 1985?).
69. Mata Masala, "Zamenga," 245.
70. Jacquemin, "BD africaine," 186.
71. Mongo Awai Sisé, *Les aventures de Mata Mata et Pili Pili: Le portefeuille* (Kinshasa: Mongoproduction and Ed. Mama-leki, 1978), and *Le Boy: Les aventures de Mata Mata et Pili Pili* (Ecaussines, Belgium: Euraf Éditions, 1982).
72. Mongo Awai Sisé, dessinateur, *Bingo en ville, Les aventures d'un enfant africain* (Brussels: AGCD, 1981), and *Bingo à Yama-Kara: Les aventures d'un enfant africain* (Brussels: AGCD, 1982).
73. B. Zamenga, scènariste, and Masioni, dessinateur, *Belle est aussi ma peau noire* (Zaire: Éditions Zola-Nsi, n.d. [1995?]). See, too, B. Zamenga, scènariste, and Alain-Mata and A. Mushabah 'Mass, dessinateur, *Pourquoi tout pourrit chez nous?* (Luozi, Zaire: Zola-nsi, 1992).
74. This would have aligned him with the more powerful, early Zanzibari colonizers of the region, known locally as BaTambatamba. Jewsiewicki notes the importance of establishing a "professional and spiritual genealogy" among urban painters (Jewsiewicki, "Painting in Zaire," 141).
75. Baruti drew the spectacular cover—Mobutu at dinner—to the published results of the contest, *Un diner à Kinshasa: Concours BD 96 Bruxelles-Kinshasa* (Brussels: Édition Ti Suka asbl, 1996).
76. See Peeters, *Tintin*.
77. Pol Vandromme, *Le monde de Tintin* (Paris: La Table Ronde, 1994), 101.
78. Maurice Kalibiona, *Marie reine de la paix* (Louvain-la-Neuve, Belgium: Éditions du Moustier, 1989), which was translated into five languages, and *Le triomphe du coeur immaculé de Marie* (Marquain, Belgium: Éditions Hovine, 1993). According to an authority on Catholic BDs, Kalibiona's albums "please youth" and contain an "African sensibility"; see Francart, *La BD chrétienne*, 75.
79. In 1993, Zamenga had more than 23 published works, including novels, poetry, essays, stories, some which were illustrated as BDs. His *Carte postale* of 1974, reprinted eight times by Saint-Paul Afrique, sold some 50,000 copies; Catherine M. Mata Masala, "Zamenga Batukezanga: Anatomie d'un succès populaire," in *Littératures de Congo-Zaïre: Actes du colloque international de Bayreuth, 22–24 juillet 1993*, ed. Pierre Halen and Janos Riesz, *Matatu* 13/14 (Amsterdam: Rodopi, 1995), 242, 245. On his conversion to Catholicism and his own press (Éditions Zabat, for works not published by Saint-Paul Afrique), see Nadine Fettweis, "Le phénomène Zamenga," in *Papier blanc, encre noire: Cent ans de culture francophone en Afrique centrale (Zaïre, Rwanda, et Burundi)*, vol. 2, ed. Marc Quaghebeur, E. van Balberghe et al. (Brussels: Éditions Labor, 1992). See, too, Wyatt MacGaffey, "Zamenga of Zaire: Novelist, Historian, Sociologist, Philosopher, and Moralist," *Research in African Literatures* 13 (1982): 208–15.
80. On this genre, see Jacquemin, "BD africaine"; and *Bande dessinée et Tiers monde*. Special issue of *Vivant Univers*, no. 367 and *Coccinelle: La BD à bon dieu. Revue d'information et d'analyse sur la bande dessinée*, no. 11 (January–February 1987).
81. Drury L. Pifer, *Innocents in Africa: An American Family's Story* (London: Granta Books, 1998), 324.
82. *La Croix du Congo* began to publish *L'étoile mystérieuse* on May 20, 1956; it continued through July 21, 1957. José Lobeya was the chief editor at the time. The puzzle advertisement appeared on July 15, 1956.
83. Onishi, "Tintin at 70."
84. All quotations come from Silverman's important rereading of Fanon in her *Threshold of the World*, 27–31.

85. Halen, "Tintin, paradigme," 40.

86. See Jacquemin, "BD africaine," 190. The magazine was *Bilenge,* not exactly a successor to *Jeunes pour Jeunes* and *Kake,* but more of a disco-music magazine featuring BDs, not unlike *Disco-Magazine,* which included five BD supplements under the title *Yaya.*

87. In 1992, Baruti recalled "devouring" colonial *Mbumbulu* cartoons as a boy, alongside American and Belgian comics strips, furiously copying as he went. He was more circumspect when I spoke with him in Brussels in December 1996, wary of simplistic conclusions about models and inspirations that this earlier newspaper quotation might inspire. The *Mbumbulu* album had survived in his father's library. Barly Baruti, interview with Colette Braeckman in *Le Soir.* "Barly Baruti: Dessiner envers et contre tous à Kinshasa," *Le Soir,* n.d. [1992?]; from Marie-Hélène De Wilde's Congolese comics file, with many thanks.

88. Jewsiewicki, "Painting in Zaire," 145.

89. Fabian, *Remembering the Present,* 305 n. 13.

90. Karin Barber, "Popular Arts in Africa," *African Studies Review* 300 (1987): 1–78, 105–32.

91. Perhaps, as Jacquemin suggests, a Congolese Hergé enthusiast also sent his version of a "Quick et Flupke" cartoon in Lingala to *Le Petit Vingtième* in the late 1920s (Jacquemin, "Jeunes pour Jeunes," 20).

92. Jacquemin stated 1964 in 1987 (in his "BD africaine," 190) and 1968 in 1996 (in his "Jeunes pour jeunes"). Tshibanda was among those who told me, disapprovingly, that the first popular BD magazines, carrying names like *Rasta* and *Jeunes pour Jeunes,* encouraged juvenile delinquency because the balloons featured characters speaking "Hindubill," a coded youth language that playfully deforms French orthography and grammar (Tshibanda Wamuela Bujitu, Brussels, December 1996). Tshibanda's work—if compared to Mongo Sisé's or Baruti's—does suggest that popular art from Lubumbashsi or Shaba may well be more "historical" than the more ludic BDs of Kinshasa. I am unable to give Tshibanda's work the attention it deserves here; he is a social psychologist with books on social problems like prostitution to his name, who has adopted the form of comics (Nsenda Kibwanga has done the drawings) to popularize this work. See Tshibanda Wamuela Bujitu and Nsenga Kibwanga, *Alerte à Kamongo ou un accident dans la mine* (Lubumbashi: Éditions Lanterne and Imprimerie Saint Paul, 1989), and *Les refoulés du Katanga* (Zaire [Brussels?]: Impala, n.d. [1995?]).

93. Jacquemin, "Jeunes pour jeunes et compagnie . . . ," 20–21; and Barly Baruti, "Souvenirs, avenirs . . . ," 12–13, both in *Un diner à Kinshasa: Concours BD 96 Bruxelles-Kinshasa* (Brussels: Édition Ti Suka asbl, 1996).

94. Jacquemin, "BD africaine," 190.

95. Sima Lukombo, dessinateur, and Inampunde, scènariste, *Apolosa moniteur, La Revue des Jeunes,* no. 25 (n.d. [ca. 1973; cost in kuta: "10 K à Kin and 15 K à l'intérieur"]), 21–27.

96. Mfumu'eto, "Nguma ameli Muasi na Kati ya Kinshasa," *Mensuel de Bandes Dessinées* 1, no. 1 (Kinshasa: Éditions Mpangala Original and Offest MGS, April 1990 [cost in zaires: 150 Z]), and "Nguma ameli Muasi na Kati ya Kinshasa," *Mensuel de Bandes Dessinées et de Détente* 1, Super Spécial Choc no. 2 (Kinshasa: Offest MGS and Union Chrétienne, Le journal des petits pour l'éducation et le savoir vivre, [May?] 1990).

97. Yoka Lye was born in Kinshasa in 1947; he has won literary prizes for his plays and stories and is the author of many essays on cultural questions. In 1995, he was rector of the Institut Universitaire Cardinal-Malula.

Chapter 4

Cartooning Nigerian Anticolonial Nationalism

Tejumola Olaniyan

Akinola Lasekan (1916–74) was Nigeria's pioneer political cartoonist. From 1944 through the early 1960s, Lasekan published editorial cartoons nearly every single day. This legendary prolificacy is explicable if we carefully piece the historical puzzle together. Lasekan was part of the new clamorous nationalism that gripped the country from the 1940s on. He worked during the pivotal period of nationalist struggles for Nigerian independence, a period when nationalism had the aura of divinity and the nationalists of its anointed saints. The virulent competition among the nationalist parties for legitimacy is another no less significant catalyst. Lasekan the cartoonist was a major part of the mammoth anticolonial nationalist political machinery of his employer and mentor, Nnamdi Azikiwe (1904–96), distinguished Pan-Africanist, a preeminent Nigerian nationalist, leader of the first and for more than a decade the only countrywide Nigerian anticolonial political party, the National Council of Nigeria and the Cameroons (NCNC), and the first indigenous governor-general and commander-in-chief of independent Nigeria. Lasekan was convinced he was working at a momentous period in history, and he threw himself headlong into his political project. I suggest that only the "mirror stage of nationalism," that stage of burning passion and unquestioned self-justification that an anticolonial nationalism goes through before it gains the nation's rulership, could explain Lasekan's prodigious exertion.[1]

Partly out of conviction and partly out of devotion to his mentor, Lasekan's ideology closely follows that of Azikiwe: a blend of liberal democratic, welfarist, and socialist precepts forged by the master in the crucible of black racial protests and cultural renaissance in the United States of the 1920s and 1930s, where Azikiwe was studying, and in the context of the obscene injustices in colonial Africa. This blend was couched in the language of pan-African racial nationalism.

Azikiwe's return to Nigeria in the interwar years profoundly energized Nigerian nationalism and decisively reoriented it away from the reformism of older figures like Herbert Macaulay to a strident call for total Africanization. His *Renascent Africa* (1937), designed to rouse Africans to their historic responsibilities in overthrowing the colonial order, became the nationalist bible for a whole generation across the continent. But what is a radical nationalism without an appropriate propaganda organ? Perhaps more important to the spread of Azikiwe's fame and brand of nationalism was his highly successful newspaper, the *West African Pilot*.[2] Emboldened by the hypocrisies of colonial rule, the *Pilot* was influenced in its uncompromising radical stance by the black American militant press of the period. It introduced a new urgency to nationalist demands totally in tune with the yearnings of the swelling group of educated young Nigerians impatient with the gradualism of Macaulay and his generation. Some scholars have credited the newspaper with being "the most crucial single precipitant of the formative Nigerian awakening." This was the party newspaper for which Lasekan worked for over two decades. The conceptual universe of Lasekan's cartoons is anchored on three broad polemical axes: (1) colonialism is not simply unjust but also unnatural; (2) nationalism is a necessity that is self-evident and thus needs no justification; and (3) the NCNC is Nigeria's only true nationalist party, and Nnamdi Azikiwe, Nigeria's leader.[3] From these come the specific thrust of individual cartoons: the first authorizes attacks against the colonizers from all imaginable angles (economic exploitation, political domination, the hypocrisy and racism of colonial policies, inflation, unemployment, and so on); the second underwrites the messianism of the cartoons' anticolonial nationalism; and the third wages a relentless war of legitimation against other parties, especially the Action Group headed by Obafemi Awolowo.

For the iconographic resources to prosecute the all-out war, Lasekan drew on a wide spectrum of sources, from the culturally indigenous to the colonial and European. He was, however, working in a medium, cartooning, that had no indigenous provenance but was part and parcel of the colonial modernity that defined his historical context. All his models were European. And so, even with domestication, many of the borrowed visual codes advertise their foreignness. One of the most obvious is the symbolization of "freedom," "independence," or "democracy" as woman, which has more to do with European history than Nigerian. But this was not necessarily a problem for Lasekan's audience, for, from the highest to the lowest strata, that audience was bonded together in one gigantic process of Westernization, in which the Western foreign and strange was often quickly learned and assimilated. Thus even though a critic of European cultural imperialism, Lasekan also contributed substantially to that imperialism's consolidation by the repeated broadcast of its visual codes in sensuous and interpellative (i.e., subjectifying) artistic form. But this paradox was not Lasekan's alone; it was what effectively structured the colonial experience wherever the colonized, even to speak against the colonizer, had to use the tools of the latter; it was a process of constructing subjectivity from subjection, agency from subordination.

Lasekan's conventions of physiognomic representation, especially musculature and the equation of largeness with hierarchical dominance, have strong indigenous resonance, but they were also common in the cartoons published in many British *(Daily Mirror, Daily Express, Daily Herald, News Chronicle,* and *Evening Standard)* and American *(Washington Post)* newspapers of the 1930s and 1940s. His dramatic use of contrast between light and dark, and sumptuous labeling, are owed wholly to these Euro-American cartoonists. Ample though his indebtedness was, it was far from wild, for Lasekan was very particular about his aesthetic preferences as an African artist. For one thing, he was against anything outside of realism—"the largest number of African people seem to prefer realistic art," he argued—and poured scorn on "abstract styles" because they afford "charlatans the greatest opportunity to hide their mediocrity under the guise of modernism."[4] Realism in Lasekan's cartoons manifests itself in the comparatively ample degree of iconicity of the images. There is usually a wealth of visual details. Very often, the human subjects are easily recognizable public officials, or made recognizable according to the generic features of "race," ethnicity, or profession. Typical stereotypes include the bloated white colonizer, the muscular black nationalist, the scrawny, overexploited worker, the gaunt and ragged poor "common" man or woman. Lavish labeling or commentary practically clarifies any lingering obscurity. Because the cartoons grant the viewer such an express visual access without much intellectual challenge, they are generally viewer-friendly and so were quite popular with readers of the *West African Pilot.*

But Lasekan did not start out as the comparatively iconic cartoonist he was later exclusively defined as being. His earliest cartoons, such as "Foreign Capitalist," are stylized and largely conceptual, and apart from words in the speech balloons, labels and a lengthy explanatory narrative beside or below the cartoon panel are the other viewer-friendly features.[5] Otherwise, the cartoon panel is needlessly cluttered; the preponderance of light or white areas gives the impression of starkness; the lines that make up the images are overly straight and severe and far less dynamic than in his later works; and the letters look as if carved laboriously and clumsily out of wood or stone. Although the cartoons are far less iconic, they are by no means lacking in radical nationalist rhetoric. I suppose then that a problematic Lasekan must have confronted at the time was conveying a radical populist pedagogy—the type to wake up a "nation" to a new dawn, as NCNC iconography repeatedly communicated—in a more or less abstract form, a form he believed to be elitist, "un-African," and antagonistic to progressive mass politics.

An attempted realism was Lasekan's solution. His cartoons began to be more iconic. The starkness gave way to more detailed and visually richer images, with more dramatic and nuanced deployment of possible shades from light to dark. The wordy explanatory narrative outside the cartoon panel became obsolete and was discarded, as the increasingly iconic images say and clarify more with graphics. The use of word balloons gave way to a neater and spatially more economical

Figure 4.1. Akinola Lasekan, "Foreign Capitalist," *West African Pilot* (Lagos), August 30, 1944.

placement of a character's speech close to that character, without encasement. A hand-lettering style in harmony with the now more supple and dynamic lines of the images replaced the earlier gawky lettering. The speeches did not reduce significantly in the new aesthetic dispensation, and neither did the extensive use of labels and placards—in fact, it could be said that Lasekan never completely trusted graphic images alone to convey exactly what he wanted, mainly because images, by their very nature, are more susceptible to fanciful interpretations than words. The young idealistic nationalist simply could not afford such a luxury in what appeared to him to be an implacably "Manichean" context.[6] It is this understanding of the colonial relation as one structured by inexorable opposition that organizes the tripartite division I identified earlier as defining the conceptual universe of Lasekan's cartooning.

THE UNNATURALNESS OF COLONIALISM

For Lasekan, it is not simply that colonialism is tyranny, injustice, exploitation, and other staple expletives of standard nationalist rhetoric, but that it is fundamentally

Figure 4.2. Akinola Lasekan, "Eternal Servitude?" *West African Pilot* (Lagos), December 19, 1950.

unnatural. According to this logic, that the stranger should be the lord over the indigene, that the European should be the master of the African in Africa, is nothing but a sign of the world turned upside down. The most popular political institutionalization of this discursive logic is, of course, Marcus Garvey's slogan "Africa for the Africans." But it would be unwise to take the simplicity of the formulation for granted. The resort to heavy-handed positivism here in the language of a supposed natural order of things is a clever strategy to provoke in the colonized an anticolonialist sentiment with a reserve of self-righteousness so deep that it will never stop for a moment to doubt itself. Its subversive potential is limitless, for what it implies is that if colonialism is "unnatural"—meaning an anomaly—then the most "natural" thing in the world to do is put an end to it. It also means that the unnatural order, precisely because it is unnatural, is sustained and sustainable only by abnormal means, by "dint of a great array of bayonets and cannons," in Fanon's words—the brute, vulgar power of the colonizer.[7] From this conceptual anchor, individual cartoons are freed to pillory colonialism and its retainers on a variety of matters—political, economic, administrative, judicial, moral, religious, and so on.

Perhaps no Lasekan cartoon better represents the unnaturalness of colonial rule than the one whose title is, most appropriately, a rhetorical question, "Eternal Servitude?" Centered in the rectangular frame is a muscular black man, on whose shoulders sits an older, bald-headed white man. The white man, "Imperialist," holds over his own head a capacious umbrella labeled "Imperial Prestige." The black man, "African Colonial," looks up at the white man with a querulous, agonized expression, and the latter responds: "I quite appreciate your agitation for freedom, but frankly you'll admit that it is very difficult to part voluntarily with a loyal servant." African Colonial is bearing his Imperialist burden along "Imperial Highway," a name that resonates ominously with the cartoon's title, as if Lasekan's real meaning, simultaneously a statement and a rhetorical question, is "Highway to eternal servitude?"

Although Imperialist is supposed to be sitting on the shoulders of African Colonial, his weight and most of his torso is actually rather low. In fact, the cartoon does give the impression of the colonizer as sitting on the back rather than the shoulders of the colonized. On this score, Lasekan draws upon a conception of unnaturalness with deep local provenance. In the first place, back porterage is a gendered practice in most parts of Nigeria, because it is done only by women. Secondly, it is a nurturing practice, as it is the main way women carry their infants as they go about their daily business. Which is to say that it is only children who are so carried. That the African colonial man is forced into a role of the African woman is, to the nationalist, a lamentable feminization of African muscular virility. There is also a violent age reversal, as it is the youthful African who bears the older, languorous exploiter in this struggle to the death. To make matters worse, the man is not carrying a child, that figure of guarantee of both familial and national futures for whom all today's struggles are worth their "last drop of blood," but a bald-headed vulture who is determined precisely to make that future impossible. Back porterage, which in the natural cultural order of things is nurturing and life-affirming, becomes, in the unnatural order of colonial rule, a thwarted, blood-sucking, murderous practice.

In "Democracy versus Communism," which works in a similar way, the historical subtext is the hypocrisy of Winston Churchill in keeping his stranglehold on the colonies—here he is bloated from feeding off them—while fighting for freedom in Europe against Josef Stalin. (He stands on a figure labeled "Coloured People," and his words, illegible here, are "You are a warmonger!") Stalin's riposte is to unfurl a scroll proclaiming "Equality and Freedom of All Peoples," a principle formulated and agreed to by President Franklin D. Roosevelt of the United States and Churchill at the height of World War II in 1941, but which Churchill later, infamously, qualified as applicable only to European states and not the colonies.[8] Hence, in the cartoon, Churchill hides behind his back the Atlantic Charter in which the principle is inscribed.

Figure 4.3. Akinola Lasekan, "Democracy versus Communism," *West African Pilot* (Lagos), January 26, 1951.

THE NECESSITY OF NATIONALISM

If colonialism is unnatural, then the colonized need no more justification than this to overthrow it. In the world of Lasekan's cartoons, anticolonial nationalism is a necessity with a self-evident status. Of course, Lasekan is in good company here, and indeed, the NCNC, and especially its religious wing, the National Church of Nigeria, often made ample use of that famous first document of anticolonial nationalism, the American Declaration of Independence, composed by Thomas Jefferson and others.[9] It is this self-righteous self-evidence that underwrites the pervasive messianic discourse with which the cartoons unselfconsciously adorn nationalism. Anticolonial nationalism is the "inextinguishable fire of the human soul," as a cartoon bearing that legend would have it. While the "imperialist" fails to quench the vibrant, burning fire of "Nigerian nationalism" with the water of "imprisonment" (of nationalists), "Father Nigerianus," an old sage some Olympian height away in a tree, looks on with the self-assured patience of a destined winner. His expression perfectly matches his philosophical rumination on nationalism: "The fact is, it is an immortal fire which no earthly element can extinguish." And in an untitled cartoon in 1950, a foregrounded giant, "The Blackman," pur-

Figure 4.4. Akinola Lasekan, "Nigerian Nationalism: The Inextinguishable Fire of the Human Soul," *West African Pilot* (Lagos), January 8, 1954.

sues "imperialists," ant-sized in the background, out of the frame and presumably out of Africa. Their panicky prayer, "Lord have mercy on our souls!" is apparently too banal to be effective.

Lasekan knew very well that the univocal voice against colonial rule he gave to the nationalists was more of a wish than a reality. In fact, that careful orchestration of unanimity could be read as a monumental desire—artistically, that is, symbolically—to order a reality different from the factious and ideologically disparate nationalisms that he saw. He saw party politics, the only means by which independence struggles could be fought and won in the circumstances, as an unnecessary dissipation of nationalist energy that only bought more time for the colonizer. The garish way he represents partisan party politics is apparently designed to leave no room for doubt about its counterproductivity. Party politics is a solidarity-destroying monster, and Lasekan's "suggested" solution is literally spelled out in "A Suggestion."[10]

Figure 4.5. Akinola Lasekan, "A Suggestion," *West African Pilot* (Lagos), June 13, 1951.

THE TRUE PARTY, THE TRUE LEADER

One meaningful historical irony is that even as Lasekan maligned party politics in cartoon after cartoon, he never ceased his partisan glorification of the National Council of Nigeria and the Cameroons as the country's only truly national and nationalist party, and Azikiwe as the nation's messiah. Inaugurated in 1944, and until 1957 "the leading all-Nigerian nationalist organization," the NCNC was the first political party to have a national rather than merely regional spread.[11] The party long defended pan-Nigerian and transethnic politics, even as the British, through the many constitutions, continued to foist an ethno-regional political structure on the country. Of course, like the parties with firm ethno-regional bases and no national pretensions such as the Action Group and Northern Peoples Congress, the NCNC too would quickly master the game of ethnic politics, and invoke and accept its privileges, even while accusing other parties of "tribalism."[12] For Lasekan the NCNC could do no wrong. It was the party that, like its symbol, the rooster, heralded a new dawn with its crowing, a new dawn of "One Nigeria, One Constitution," in contrast to the other parties—"tribalists" all—whose quest for power at any cost led them to campaign for a loose federation of the regions with a weak federal government. The NCNC's nationalist sincerity is the sharp knife that rips through the "[p]ropaganda wall" of "reactionary nationalists" in

Figure 4.6. Akinola Lasekan, "Thin Wall of Lies Smashed," *West African Pilot* (Lagos), October 5, 1955.

"Thin Wall of Lies Smashed." Azikiwe, the party leader and deliverer-saint, appears in another cartoon as the only fitting husband for dainty "Miss Independence."[13] Lasekan's nationalist is always male, and his work is marked by a surfeit of significations of woman as desire, as the object of competition between colonizers and the colonized and among the colonized—all males. In this masculinist vision, Lasekan's African woman, standing for abstractions such as "freedom," "independence," "Nigeria," is always mute and neutral, meaning *outside* the historical antagonisms being waged by the men.[14]

For Lasekan, Azikiwe's "sincere nationalism" is a protective armor against the arrows of both the "imperialist" and the local "careerist," as one cartoon puts it. Thus in another cartoon, "Leaving Us at the Mercy of the Big Wolf?" the Nigerian masses are no more than sheep without their lord and shepherd when Azikiwe feigns at retiring from politics. This cartoon is merely one of the more striking among the many in the grand project to beatify Azikiwe. The imperialist wolf lies in ambush on the "Road to Independence Pasture Land," while a flock of sheep labeled "Nigerians" look back anxiously at "Zik."

On the other hand, the Action Group, NCNC's main political opponent, is often represented as a monster sowing tribalism, disunity, and all kinds of unspeakable

Figure 4.7. Akinola Lasekan, "Leaving Us at the Mercy of the Big Wolf?" *West African Pilot* (Lagos), January 2, 1951.

horrors in the body politic. The Action Group's leader, Obafemi Awolowo, a distinguished legal luminary and a notable advocate of federalism as the only just way to deal with the country's untamable political differences, is repeatedly portrayed as a breaker of Nigerian unity, and the name of his party often altered to "*Auction* group."

It remains a matter of great historical interest that neither the NCNC's opponents—the colonial rulers or other nationalist parties, particularly the Action Group—ever responded in like manner. The Action Group's newspaper, the *Nigerian Tribune*, was established in 1949, but it did not begin to have regular cartoonists until well after independence. The colonial government's "silence" might be easier to understand. It was part of a carefully cultivated attempt to avoid giving the NCNC any legitimacy by mud-wrestling with it in the cartoon pages of the popular press. Indeed, Lasekan once complained in a cartoon of the hypocritical Olympian detachment of the colonial establishment, as if it were a neutral entity in the matter of decolonization. Whatever low opinions the colonizers had of the militant nationalists—and there were reams of them—were expressed only in the colonial records. The government newspaper, the *Daily Times*, published "cartoons" all right: the British comics series "Bruin, Pingo and Percy," was a favorite and appeared with great regularity, perhaps to palliate colonial desire for less hot and humid and "more homely" climes, with such titles as "Where is the North Pole?" and "It's all snow!"

But there was a comic strip worthy of note that was political in an oblique sense and subtly responded to nationalist demands. *Joseph's Holiday Adventure*, published in the *Daily Times* between 1955 and 1956, was probably the first comic strip with indigenous characters and subject matter. And although it ran nearly daily for more than fifteen months, it was billed as an "advertiser's announcement," so that the artist remains unknown today. While clearly responding to nationalist demands for the reform of the colonial economy, it was designed, both in story line and visual language, to appeal largely to the young. Although published in the government newspaper and representing the closest response in the visual medium to the Lasekan/NCNC challenge, its connection with the government was anything but straightforward, because it was issued by a private enterprise, the famous colonial multinational United Africa Company (UAC).

The connection between the UAC and the colonial regime may not have been straightforward, but the nationalists, despite all protests to the contrary by colonial administrators, always refused to make any sharp distinction between the two. As James Coleman rightly notes, the nationalists saw only a "close association between alien political control and an alien economic oligopoly."[15] And for good reason, because colonial economic and trading policies were regularly fashioned by the colonial government to ensure the domination of, and maximum profits for, the foreign companies. In fact, nationalist economic complaints especially targeted the companies' exploitive and monopolistic conducts, refusal to employ Nigerians, and racist and discriminatory hiring practices.

The UAC had been a dominant force in the Nigerian economy since 1930. It garnered over 40 percent of Nigeria's import-export trade by the end of that decade, and by the end of the 1940s, it controlled 43 percent of all Nigerian nonmineral exports on behalf of that notorious leech of the Nigerian farmer, the Marketing Boards. "In large measure, African resentments and grievances stemmed from the concentration of economic power in the hands of expatriate firms, particularly the major firm, the United Africa Company," Coleman observes. The UAC subsequently teamed up with other European companies to form the Association of West African Merchants (AWAM), which controlled about two-thirds of Nigeria's trade. "This near-totality of economic power exercised by a small group of European firms, together with apparent governmental support or toleration of that power," writes Coleman, "gave rise to the popular image of alien collusion and exploitation."[16] After detailing the unbridled exploitation of Africans by the companies, Walter Rodney concludes with laconic plainness: "In a way, the companies were simply receiving tribute from a conquered people."[17] *Joseph's Holiday Adventure* was an ideological effort by the UAC to represent itself in a different light and to make its existence and activities in Nigeria seemingly coextensive with nationalist goals: the end of job discrimination, employment of more Nigerians at

Figure 4.8. United Africa Company, "Joseph: Joseph Learns Something New," *Nigerian Daily Times,* January 6, 1956.

the managerial level, economic prosperity, and general economic modernity.[18] The comic has no storyline as such that is followed with any consistency. It is, partly as the title says, an adventure story, and partly detective fiction. Thus in both genre matters as well as visual economy—the detailed realism of the images, the melodramatic use of extremes of light and dark, and a deliberate, almost ostentatious use of the line—it closely follows two popular internationally circulated American comics of the period: *Tarzan* and *Superman*. In the resulting hybrid, what is really important are the moral-laden episodes rather than an explicit expository plot, although there is a thin link of continuity between the episodes, namely, Joseph's encounter with a notorious gang of thieves, led by the terrifying Scarface. As both an adventure story and a sort of crime thriller, the comic strip is full of action and suspense and street-smart language, all appealing ingredients to the adolescents of Joseph's age, although adults of various classes are—secondarily—targeted too.[19]

For all its action and excitement, the pace of the comic strip is extremely controlled, even to the point of rigidity, for the cartoon panels—as indicators of spatiotemporal passage—very rarely number more than four of even size in any issue.[20] It is as if the UAC divined that it could not afford to let its message get lost in the spell of a thrilling action narrative. In spite of the variety of episodes, the structure within each one rarely changes: the young Joseph is involved in a trying circumstance, which he ultimately overcomes. His heroism, honesty, defense of law and order, respect for constituted authority, and above all, unquestioned belief in the good things the UAC is doing shine brilliantly forth. He and his uncle, Samson, an employee of the UAC, who hopes to soon become a manager, are frequently involved in similar circumstances with similar outcomes. Most of the information about the UAC comes from Uncle Samson.

In the opening adventure, which ran for five days, Joseph discovers a small box in the hollow of a tree and picks it up to turn it in to the police. He is soon hotly pursued by two thieves, who have apparently hidden their loot in the box. Joseph easily floors them with blows and karate chops. Other thieves from the same gang appear and Joseph adroitly escapes. He then meets Uncle Samson, who praises

Figure 4.9. United Africa Company, "Joseph: The Gang Have Been Captured," *Nigerian Daily Times*, March 22, 1956.

him, saying, "We want clever boys like you in the U.A.C." Uncle Samson also, as the title of this last installment of the episode says, teaches Joseph "something new." The old thing Joseph knows is that "My friend says they [the UAC] don't give good jobs to Africans." The "new" thing that Uncle Samson teaches him is "That's not true! I've got a good job. I'll soon be manager! Four times as many of us are managers as when you were born fifteen months before the war." Ever the nice, credulous boy, Joseph promptly responds, "I didn't know that—I must tell my friend." We can easily imagine what good things about the UAC Joseph will tell his friend. In another installment, Joseph is congratulated for helping the police to capture the gang. And in "Joseph Talks to the Chief," a local chief thanks Joseph for protecting his daughter, while Joseph marvels at the many new buildings the UAC has put up, which, he says, quoting his uncle, "enrich our country."

The comic strip carefully erects a complete identity of interests between the UAC and various segments of Nigerian society: workers, such as Uncle Samson; prospective workers and managers, such as young Joseph; indigenous chiefs and the towns they govern; and law enforcement agents. As a multinational company interested mainly in exploiting the colonies, it is not surprising at all that these groups fall into the two main categories crucial to the unfettered reign of colonial capitalism: exploitable labor, whether current or projected (Joseph and Samson), and the agents of discipline and coercion (the police and the chief). Those who obstruct the progress of colonial capital are either damned (the gang of thieves) or totally ignored (the nationalists). The UAC may not have been owned by the British colonial government, but it certainly served its interests.

With the benefit of hindsight, it is difficult not to say that the circumstances of history—meaning, really, the conditions of a grossly unjust world—favored the colonial government and the UAC more than the nationalists. The UAC, through its products, profoundly altered the consumption patterns of Nigerians, so that their purchases became significantly more outward-directed. Certainly, the nationalists acquired political power, but colonial economic interests became more entrenched than ever, so that the nationalists could not chart the economic path of their own new nation.

Figure 4.10. United Africa Company, "Joseph: Joseph Talks to the Chief," *Nigerian Daily Times*, April 19, 1956.

There is a popular saying, attributed to Kwame Nkrumah, that Azikiwe was fond of repeating and that aptly captures the spirit of Lasekan's cartoon corpus, indicating both the depth and limitation of the nationalist vision: "Seek ye first the political kingdom and all things shall be added to it." The problematic is both aesthetic and political. In his cartoons, with the righteous impatience of militant nationalism, Lasekan transformed human beings from political animals into distilled political positions. The UAC, in its cartoons, produced from a political program idealized human beings with personal ambitions.

We have then two different entities fighting for the "soul" of the nation in the context of empire, both using images. Although no two agendas could be more opposed, popular cartooning was the medium for both as they competed to capture popular aspirations. Lasekan and the nationalists attempted to free the nation from the colonial empire through nationalist cartooning. The UAC and the colonial government mocked, or "cartooned" nationalism, in the patient knowledge that battles are won and lost in the belly.

NOTES

1. R. Radhakrishan, "Nationalism, Gender, and the Narrative of Identity," in *Nationalisms and Sexualities*, ed. Andrew Parker et al., 77–95 (New York: Routledge, 1992), makes a useful distinction between nationalism in "antagonistic" and "protagonistic" phases. What I call the "mirror stage" here would closely approximate the "antagonistic" with its resolute sense of conviction and moral and historical right to overthrow the colonizers (85–86).

2. James S. Coleman contends in *Nigeria: Background to Nationalism* (1958; Benin City: Broburg & Wistrom, 1986) that Azikiwe's

> combative and provocative journalism was the principal source of his fame and power.... His was the first major effort to Nigerianize journalism. The Nigeria-wide circulation of his *West African Pilot*... was crucially significant in the spread of racial consciousness and ideas of nationalism in the interior. Nigerian political activity was still Lagos-centered, but Nigerians throughout the country were for the first time permitted the stimulation of vicarious participation.

At its inception in 1937, this paper, described as "an instant public success," topped the circulation supremacy of the *Daily Times*'s 6,000 with its own 9,000 readers. See Fred I. A.

Omu, *Press and Politics in Nigeria, 1880–1937* (Atlantic Highlands, N.J.: Humanities Press, 1978), 87.

3. On Azikiwe's influences and political ideology, see Ray Ofoegbu, "Azikiwe's Intellectual Origins," in *Azikiwe and the African Revolution,* ed. Michael S. O. Olisa and Odinchezo M. Ikejiani-Clark (Onitsha, Nigeria: African-Rep Publishers, 1989), 53–71; and M. S. O. Olisa, "Azikiwe's Political Ideas: The Dream of the African Revolution," in ibid., 72–89. Benedict Anderson discusses the contributions of "print capitalism" to the origins and spread of nationalism in *Imagined Communities: Reflections on the Origin and Spread of Nationalism* (London: Verso, 1983), 38–49. See also Coleman, *Nigeria: Background to Nationalism,* 223 (quotation), and 220–24.

4. See Roy Douglas, *The World War, 1939–1943: The Cartoonists' Vision* (London: Routledge, 1990), and David Low, *A Cartoon History of Our Times* (New York: Simon & Schuster, 1939); and Akinola Lasekan, "Problems of Contemporary African Artists," *Kurio Africana: Journal of Art Criticism* (Ile-Ife, Nigeria) 1, 1 (1989), 31–32, reprinted from an unstated earlier source, probably 1960s. I am referring specifically to cartoons, because Lasekan knew—in his capacity as a cartoonist rather than as a painter, which he also was—that a technical gap exists between realism as artistic philosophy and as cartooning practice. For if realism emphasizes the representation of reality as empirically observed, cartooning is defined precisely by some measure of distance to actuality, often achieved by caricaturing, by amplification through simplification. In other words, realist practice in painting is not the same as in cartooning. Embodied in cartooning is a simultaneously prescriptive and proscriptive challenge, in which to be most naturalistic is to lose its caricaturing essence, while to be too "abstract" is to lose referential power. On the graphic representation of the "picture plane" and the several possibilities between the poles from a survey of actual practices of cartoonists, see Scott McCloud, *Understanding Comics: The Invisible Art* (Northampton, Mass.: Kitchen Sink Press, 1993), 52–53.

5. The lengthy explanatory narrative was one of the hallmarks of the great American artist Rube Goldberg in his famous series of the 1930s, "Inventions of Professor Lucifer Butts." See Thomas Craven, *Cartoon Cavalcade* (New York: Simon & Schuster, 1943), 235–36.

6. Frantz Fanon, *The Wretched of the Earth* (New York: Grove Press, 1963), 41.

7. Ibid.

8. Ibid., 36. For Roosevelt, see Olisa, "Azikiwe's Political Ideas," 76.

9. Coleman, *Nigeria: Background to Nationalism,* 302–3.

10. Under the rubric "Coalition Party," the placard reads as follows:

Pre-Independence Programme
1. Suspension of Present Political Bodies.
2. Formation of a Country-wide Coalition Party to Expedite Independence.
Post-Independence Programme
1. Resuscitation of Political Parties.
2. Full Scale Development of the Country.

11. Ibid., 265, 264–95.

12. A succinct account of rivalries among the nationalist parties is given by Kunle Lawal, "Britain and Nationalists' Conflicts in Nigeria in the Age of Transfer of Power: 1948 to 1960" (African Studies Association conference paper, 1992). Perhaps indicative of how far ethnic politics in Nigeria have gone, there has not been another instance of a Yoruba cartoonist (like Lasekan) working single-mindedly for an Igbo political leader (like Azikiwe) whose principal opponent was a Yoruba.

13. In the cartoon (not shown), the husband/Azikiwe figure is labeled "United Nigeria" and stands between a man in a top hat labeled "Papa U.K." and "Miss Independence." "United Nigeria" is saying: "Papa, who has to decide when I'm to marry, you or I?" (Lasekan, "The Big Question," n.d.)

14. "In the fight against the enemy from the outside, something within gets... repressed and "woman" becomes the mute but necessary allegorical ground for the transactions of nationalist history" (Radhakrishnan, "Nationalism, Gender, and the Narrative of Identity," 84).

15. Coleman, *Nigeria: Background to Nationalism*, 81.

16. Ibid., 80, 81; and Walter Rodney, *How Europe Underdeveloped Africa* (Washington, D.C.: Howard University Press, 1972), 168–70.

17. Ibid., 158.

18. Anderson, in *Imagined Communities,* shows in suggestive ways the strong affinities between religious imaginings, which are, characteristically, willfully ahistorical, with nationalist imaginings (17–25).

19. I have benefited here from Ernest Mandel's insightful study *Delightful Murder: A Social History of the Crime Story* (Minneapolis: University of Minnesota Press, 1984).

20. Generally, the greater the number and the smaller the size of the panels, the faster time and space pass; while the lesser the number and the bigger the size of the panels, the slower the time-space change.

Chapter 5

Empires of the Visual: Photography and Colonial Administration in Africa

Paul S. Landau

> *Many of our people were killed in this fight. I saw four of my cousins shot. . . . One was hit between the eyes; another here, in the shoulder; another had part of his ear shot off. We made many charges but each time we were beaten off, until at last the white men packed up and retreated. But for the Maxims [machine guns], it would have been different. The place where we have been making the film is the very place where my cousins were killed.*
> —NDANSI KUMALO, who played the Ndebele king Lobengula in the film *Rhodes* (1936)

There were two interfaces for Westerners' contacts with Africans during the colonial era. The first was actual: trading, working, having sex, sharing a joke or a beer; policing, killing, and negotiating; requesting, releasing or denying consents and licenses, paying taxes; prevaricating, appealing, judging, and so on. The second was virtual: the paper-thin barrier composed of photographs, words on stationery, and images projected onto screens. Both interfaces supported a kind of two-way traffic, as the essays in this book show. Nonetheless the second one most often positioned Europeans as observers of Africans. In fact, it was only by way of the written word and of the printed image that most Europeans knew anything at all about the places their countrymen were busy ruling.

No one doubts that writing became an indispensable tool in European empires. Consider, for example, the subject of real estate. Sub-Saharan Africans fully understood that various kinds of rights in land could be granted and denied. What was foreign to most of them was the embodiment of rights in paper representations of the landscape: maps, title deeds, morgen counts, written laws, and so forth. A constant appeal to the treaties signed by agents of mercantile companies and nineteenth-century chiefs was novel. Ultimately Europeans' familiarity with and enforcement of the conventions governing the use of all these signs gave them an insurmountable advantage. After the establishment of European overrule, carbon copies, telegraphy, typewriters, and printing continued to be critical to the everyday functioning of colonial institutions. Mimeographed directives depersonalized demands. Pamphlets of "native law" and court reports legitimized jurisprudence. Triplicate forms validated transactions, secured funding, and stabilized institutional memories. Back in the Colonial Office in London, the printed signs that administrators shuffled around on their desks served them more surely than living people for conveying their wishes. One dispatched them and went to lunch.

The other medium for colonialism's representational encounter was the image. Unlike the published and printed word, the mechanically reproduced image relied on contemporary developments in technology: cameras, celluloid film, half-tone screens. Daniel Headrick's widely read book *The Tools of Empire* discusses various inventions in the nineteenth century that permitted Europeans to extend their imperial power; he describes breech-loading rifles, Gatling guns, steamships, and quinine as indispensable colonizing tools. In much the same way, it might be argued, the technologies for producing images were tools of empire too. Headrick discusses the great changes brought about by the laying of submarine cables. Between Africa and various Western metropoles those lines transmitted not only written words (and later, speech), but also "wire-service" pictures.[1] Other images traveled more slowly, by ship or by airplane, but chromolithographs, lantern slides, stereoscopy, private photographs, cinema, and thousands of postcards all crossed great distances. All of them bore images of the new imperialism that were otherwise inaccessible to various Western publics.[2]

What exactly all those images displayed is, of course, something else. The way Africans were pictured and the selection of which pictures circulated—and where— were the results of many individual decisions, and they cannot be reduced to a formula. Moreover, while pictures appear very specific in their denotations, they are vulnerable—even more than are texts—to widely varying interpretations. In other words, if photography became a concrete tool of empire, it is also true that the apparent meaning of particular photographs is a slippery matter. This essay seeks to unite these two ideas into a single approach to understanding the role of photography in the colonial era in Africa.

THE RESOLUTION OF CATEGORIES

"Who but I should sing of you, your brother in arms, in blood?" Leopold Senghor wrote of the *tirailleurs Sénégalais,* French colonial African troops whose image had been used in advertisements for a cocoa breakfast drink. "I will tear down the *banania* smiles from every wall in France."[3] The hallmark of the mid-Victorian age was the "impulse to classify nature and man into types,"[4] and the African soldier, before he became a logo, had been a type: staunch, dependable, loyal, French, and disposable. This sort of reductiveness was not by any means applied only to blacks or Africans. Robert Knox, Pierre Paul Broca, John Beddoe, and most famously Linnaeus and later Gobineau, all sought to arrange, rank, and essentialize all humankind, "Caucasians" included. Each of their efforts relied on an assumption: that a useful classificatory scheme must be capable of being indexed by visible signs of difference.[5]

Figure 5.1. Advertisement for Banania, a brand of cocoa breakfast drink. © Bestfoods France.

Martin Jay has referred to the results of such synechdochic connections as constituting "empires" of visualization.[6] The simile of "empire" is more than appropriate, for while Broca and Knox were debating the relative purity of humanity's various distinct types, the (British East India) "Company School" of painting, in that empire called the Raj, was reducing India's humanity to visual categories.[7] Just as zoologists and botanists drew and catalogued species from life, so such painters depicted peoples. Emblematic types were not necessarily caricatures. The mid-Victorian British Pre-Raphaelites, for instance, praised the benefits of painting from nature, and when Holman Hunt sought to render biblical scenes with "complete visual and archaeological correctness," he scrutinized the faces of living residents of Palestine. Yet he too must have thought in terms of a catalogue of human variety when he wrote to Dante Gabriel Rossetti, "Think how valuable pictures of the social life of the tribes of men who are in this age undergoing revolutions would be in aftertimes."[8]

Photography arrived at this juncture. Painters soon used photographs in their studies, and by the end of the nineteenth century, the simpler product of camerawork eclipsed the labors of reportorial painting.[9] Allan Sekula has argued that the photograph was first imagined as a tool for recording possessions. He calls this its "repressive" function. Henry Fox Talbot's third plate in his pioneering 1844 book *The Pencil of Nature* was of "articles of china," an image that could be produced in court as evidence of ownership. But very soon, Sekula suggests, photography also became a mode of portraiture: its "honorific" function. The unsteady combination of the "repressive" and the "honorific" contributed to the development of photographic arrest records in law enforcement. John Tagg has argued that such a history of photography's use, rather than any of its intrinsic properties, is what has made photography "realistic." Thus from police records, the photograph matured in institutions concerned with the establishment of truthful identities: security clearances, medical records, state permits, and the like, often in the service of institutional power.[10]

In this same composite mode, photography froze images of "primitive" people whom the universalizing and homogenizing tides of modernity were otherwise washing away. David Livingstone's instructions to his brother, a photographer, transpose William Holman Hunt's ideas into the incipient scientific language of the next era: he asked Charles Livingstone to "secure characteristic specimens of the various tribes," using a camera, "for the purposes of ethnology."[11] In 1888, the invention of the half-tone grid system allowed such photos to be reproduced by mechanical means in newspapers and books. The "10¢ magazine revolution" then began to let great numbers of urbanites see pictures of "the tribes of men" living far away from them, from Africa to the Orient. Until then, citizens curious for visuals had had to rely on mobile collections of artifacts or displays of exotic people. Like such traveling displays, photography transferred "the location of analysis" from distant places to the comfort of the middle-class West. Unlike "exhibitions" and museums, however, photographs were individually possessed.[12] Postcards, magazines, tobacco cards, white hunter's books, and illustrated travel stories all yielded their messages in the safety of urban living rooms and studies. The transition from painting to mechanical reproduction, whatever else it accomplished, clearly engineered a shift from public display to private viewing.[13]

Photography also emerged as a "scientific" mode of representing human types. As racial ideologues accommodated Charles Darwin's theory of evolution to their ways of thinking, the concerns of physical anthropology were joined to the power of photography in order visually to "type" indigenes in Australia, Africa, and Asia. The style of the police "mug shot" was adapted to anthropological photography and slowly replaced *cartes-des-visites* style poses. Photography was also used to measure people's bodies. John Lamprey adopted the measuring grid of eighteenth-century anthropometry as a background to full-body images. Carl and Frederick Damann's portfolios of 1873–76, released in an edited English-language version as *Ethnological Photographic Gallery of the Various Races of Man*, began with romantic portrait genres of individuals and segued into stark profiles for its typed "lower" races.[14] Further examples can be seen in Gustav Fritsch's *Drei Jahre in Süd-Afrika* (1868), in coffee-table books such as *Africa Illustrated: Scenes from the Dark Continent* (1895), and in serious studies such as the philologists W. H. Bleek and Lucy Lloyd's *Specimens of Bushmen Folklore* (1911). Some of the same photographs even appear in Isaac Schapera's *The Khoisan Peoples of Southern Africa*, published in 1930.[15]

Photographic anthropometry had only limited success in typing "races." Technical difficulties inhered in the practice, and no clear pictorial commonalities emerged in the categorization of "human types." Despite Francis Galton's singular attempts to overlay photographs in his 1883 study *Inquiries into Human Faculty and Its Development*, the specificity of photography undercut generalizations based on social affinities. More important, the boundaries around aggregations of measurable traits (long labias, short arms, skin color) did not accord with the imperatives of colonial governance.[16] The problems of administration were more clearly in mind during the compilation of the massive colonial study *The People of India* (1868–75). The eight-volume work replaced the Company School's paintings of Indian "types" with over 400 photographs and descriptions of every Indian group and caste. For Africa, Sir Harry Johnston's *British Central Africa* (1897) used photographs to demonstrate Africans' "racial" differences; in contrast, Dudley Kidd's *The Essential Kafir* (1904) presented Africans in South Africa as a variegated but single "race," depicted in his own somewhat random photos. In the text in these treatments, racial and ethnic hallmarks were expressed as departures from a familiar Western norm—from the white, male, and middle-class self—and as reflections of colonial interests, registering the difficulty or usefulness of a population. All such observations were figured as insights into the immutable "natures" of different natives, which photographers sought to make visible at a glance.[17]

Mobile photographers tried to illuminate what had previously gone unseen by the growing middle class not only in Africa but in American and European working-class city slums. In 1890, Jacob Riis published his famous exposé of the conditions of the poor in New York. Some of his pictures derived from near-military attacks, with Riis and the police charging in, Riis firing his gun-shaped flash, the cops discharging their revolvers into the night air.[18] The violence that literally lay behind his depictions of the underclass in the West overlapped with the violence in modes of representing Africans. Elsewhere, from Walker Evans to August Sander, photographers preserved images of populations that were subject to policing, clearance, or economic hardship, and could be approached en masse. Appalachian farmers, German peddlers, lower-class Cockneys, befeathered "American Indians," and Kalahari Bushmen were all "dying out." And when evangelists traveled to working-class European neighborhoods to give salutary magic lantern lectures about Christianity or temperance, they would sometimes project pictures of Africans or Polynesians on the screen.[19] Exotic peoples might be preserved in visual records, but modernity, whether driven by reform or not, raged against them. In the words of the Austrian ethnologist Rudolf Pöch in 1910, the Kalahari's primitives had "stopped on a lower step of cultural evolution," a description that middle-class reformers also applied to tavern-going Europeans, to America's poor, and to women.[20]

Since such categories of humanity shaded into one another or even overlapped, it is remarkable that the classificatory criteria of botany or zoology were thought to provide the controlling paradigm. In fact, as James Ryan argues, in many nineteenth-century studies, "the terms of racial classification" were confused, even in the context of the state of ethnographic knowledge at the time. The major work titled *The Peoples of India*, for instance, mixed "tribe, race and caste" indiscriminately.[21] Vastly disparate human capacities, qualities, and ascriptions were juxtaposed as equivalent within the same pictorial frames, in the same type of nomenclatures. In natural history museums, there were, and in some there still are, dioramas in which both non-white human and animal "families" are displayed virtually side by side, the one in sculpture, the other in stuffed skin. The form of plates of reproductions of Africans, Asians, and Indians verge toward the trophy wall in a hunter's study.

Other writers have deplored the juxtaposition of animal and human images. Here, I would like to suggest that both sorts of collections might usefully be approached through the history of their assembly. As we shall see, the use of modern firearms in big game hunting established the technology, and the practices, that accommodated the production of photographs of Africans and other colonized people. Photography became a tool of empire by following the gun into Africa.

SHOOTING TYPES AND TROPHIES

"In an interview today, Mr. Harvey recounted how he and his colleagues followed [Princess] Diana relentlessly for years, taking pictures of her at the gym, on the street, on vacations, with boyfriends," according to a 1997 *New York Times* article. "With words that evoke the brutal language of sexual assault, they use 'doing Di' to mean 'taking pictures of Diana;' 'to bang,' 'to blitz,' 'to hose,' 'to rip,' 'to smudge,' or 'to whack' are all ways of saying 'to take pictures rapidly.' "[22]

Susan Sontag has pointed out that the vocabularies of photography and hunting overlap. Loading, stalking, aiming, cocking, and clicking are all appropriate examples of their shared linguistic and conceptual terrain. Even "snap shot" designated a military technique before it meant an off-hand photo. Sontag traces this correspondence between "shooting" and shooting to the great appetite of photography for capturing the world. There are however also more specific connections between violence, guns, and camera work in the period of the new imperialism, which allow us to extend Sontag's observations further.[23]

The photography of Africa shared some of the same personnel, techniques, and even technology with hunting. By hunting African big game, men of leisure asserted their domination of nature and by extension, the manly, European domination of Africa.[24] Toward the end of the nineteenth century, their hunting retreated from its openly commercial purposes and began to assume the essential features of visual collection. By the 1920s, a "simple hunting trip" might somehow turn into "a scientific enterprise of a certain magnitude," replete with photographers, for which extra funding could be secured.[25] Full-body and mounted animal trophies were crafted by skinners and taxidermists to hide their own restorative labor. They fashioned them to look untouched. The photography of animals achieved a similar feat: the labor of porters, guides, and gun-bearers almost always fell outside the frame of vision of the white traveler and his photographs and so was excluded from notice.

Styling themselves as conservationists, big game hunters forged new ties to the expanding middle class through museums and cinema. Their efforts to represent the vanishing herds of wildlife in Africa to paying Western audiences were widely understood as unimpeachable. It scarcely mattered whether the job was done with skins or with photographs and film. Like the photographs of "tribal types" that David Livingstone asked his brother to make, their trophies became "specimens," and indeed categories of animals and people were often depicted in the same books and films.[26] Western conservationists freely decried Africans' supposedly wanton destruction of game, but beyond that, they had little reason to interrogate the political and economic structures responsible for changing the environment; after all, their hunting was a part of the problem. The simple mimesis of animals did not invite introspection. Colonial regimes founded protected parks when wild beasts became dependent on the "stewardship of men" and lost their apparent nastiness.[27] Pictures and trophies were selective in what they revealed and obscured about the forms of agency underwriting colonial rule.

The technologies of the gun and the camera themselves evolved in lockstep. The 1860s saw the perfection of the breech-loading rifle and shotgun, using chemicals enclosed in a casing with an interior striking pin, which prevented the emission of gasses into the face and hands of the user. The 1860s also saw the development of dry-plate photography. Previously, most photographers had had to hand-coat their plates with collodion, a volatile compound first made in Germany by combining ether with guncotton (cellulose trinitrate), which was itself the inflammable result of dissolving cotton wool in nitric acid. Such chemicals were unpleasant, and when pre-prepped gelatin dry-plates became available in 1871, they found an immediate market, for much the same reason rifle cartridges had. Within a few years, cameras like the Scovill, the Blair, the Anschutz, and the Eclipse could take faster shots.[28] In gunnery, the British Martini-Henry rifle, derived from the American Peabody, set a new breech-loading standard and became the favorite of white hunters in Africa from the 1890s on, and the Remington and Soper were close competitors. Repeating rifles held multiple ammunition readied for even faster firing, the best makes being the Spencer, Colt, Kropatschek, and Winchester.[29]

In all these guns, ready-made cartridges, produced by factories, left the shooter free to spend time stalking and setting up his shot. Some of the most innovative dry-plate cameras were based explicitly on the mechanism of the Colt revolver, and cinema cameras would later draw elements of their design from the machine gun.[30] The founder of Eastman Kodak, George Eastman, was familiar with guns, and he had a regular shooting box near Norfolk, Virginia. But in contrast to the ease with which the sporting traveler prepared a shot, photographing was still a cumbersome process in 1870. Eastman himself, for instance, cancelled a visit to Santo Domingo because of the "bulk of the paraphernalia" required to take a picture. "It seemed that one ought to be able to carry less than a pack horse-load," he later wrote.[31] The casual traveler could bring along field glasses and a gun without much difficulty, but a tripod and heavy boxes of coated glass plates were a different matter.

In 1881, Eastman formed a partnership with William Walker, the first camera maker to adopt the manufacturing methods pioneered by gun makers in the United States, which permitted the use of interchangeable parts. As Roland Barthes suggests in describing photography's "revelatory" function, however, its chemistry was of greatest importance.[32] In 1885, Eastman and Walker developed a flexible photographic medium, a paper negative substrate coated in guncotton, which permitted twenty-four serial exposures. In a parallel development in 1886, a French inventor rolled pure gelatinized guncotton into sheets, cut it into narrow strips, and made the first modern smokeless gunpowder. In 1888, Eastman released the Kodak Camera, which took 100 exposures on a medium of paper-backed sheets of dry, etherized guncotton.[33] In March 1889, Eastman's chief chemist Henry Reichenbach added amyl acetate (a mild solvent, $C_7H_{14}O_2$) to guncotton, and created "celluloid," a tenuously stable and transparent medium that could be poured out into separable sheets and cut into strips. That same year, two Englishmen added nitroglycerine and acetone (C_3H_6O) to guncotton, and made the explosive, cordite.[34] Thus breech-loading guns and the Kodak Camera not only drew on the same language; they both sealed the same sort of chemicals in their cartridges.

The camera owner sent the whole Kodak Camera to the Eastman Company, which developed the pictures and mailed everything back. The watchwords of Kodak advertisements from 1888 onward were "caught" and "instantaneous."[35] The subject was to be "caught on the fly," snagged like a fish or trapped like an animal. For taking pictures of people without asking, as one would if one wished to shoot another person with a gun, one used "detective" cameras, and the early ads for the "pocket Kodak" presented it in the visual vocabulary of the pocket revolver. It yielded twelve shots, two barrelsful. The event of the snapshot and the resulting picture were both credited to the shooter, who "captured" the defining moments of significant experiences or occasions. A single instant of travel could then become the visual metonym of the entire holiday. Eastman's first effort to write a slogan for the Kodak roll-film camera was "You pull the trigger, we'll do the rest."[36]

No longer a "pack horse-load," Kodaks—and subsequently Leicas and Minoltas and so on—fit easily into travelers' bags. Even more important, photography had been redesigned, Eastman's copy told customers, so that the "mechanical work can be entirely separated from the chemical work."[37] Breech-loading guns and the Kodak camera kept the hands of the shooter clean. In 1888, Eastman told Walker, perhaps a bit optimistically, that he would rather keep the patent to roll film than own the patent to the telephone. In England, the most industrialized nation in the world, one out of four families bought a camera by 1900.[38] The whole range of services once offered by the studio—the backdrop cloth, the Sunday suit, the furniture, the braces for support, the box of plates, the professional operator—was eventually done away with, just as the telephone demoted the courier, the clerk, and the typist. Even more, since the amateur's brief click of the shutter was all that counted in "taking" a picture—much as the click of the trigger was "enough" to produce a hunting trophy—the Kodak revolution caused the apparent erasure of Kodak's own factory workers. Skilled and semi-skilled chemists, contractors, packagers, and service people were no longer encountered by the customer, and so, effectively disappeared. Eastman refigured the consumer as a producer. The photograph was attributed to the shooter, just as paid safaris gave the trophy to the rifleman with the first clean shot.

The development of modern photography in Africa thus followed several paradigms central to hunting. In both endeavors, consumers stalked and stopped elements of the world, and a wonderfully wide capacity to signify was granted to their pictures and trophies. Nevertheless, the skilled aid behind the scenes and the political and economic context for both projects were obscured in both media. While lived experience in Africa embarrassed such pretenses, as the immense local infrastructures for every colonial activity could hardly be ignored, images and ideologies served to shore them up. The constancy of such repair work was indispensable to modern colonial rule.

THE IMAGE AND COLONIAL UNDERSTANDING

Photography affected the practices and institutions that composed empires because of its imagery. Yet historians have hardly begun to consider the practical involvement of visual images in the structures of power that composed imperialism. How should they do so? It might be best to begin by examining the circulation of images in itself, as opposed to their placement in judicial or administrative forums. Cinema and still photography carried messages to and from Africa and the West, and their images were repeated and reproduced in ever new and distant contexts. For instance, Carl Akeley's and Kermit Roosevelt's images of the Nandi (Kalenjin-speakers in western Kenya) directly influenced Edgar Rice Burroughs's *Tarzan* stories, and later also informed Osa and Martin Johnson's many films.[39] At least two of those films, the Johnsons' *Congorilla* (1927) and *Simba* (1928), which included further Akeley footage, in turn influenced Irving Thalberg's *Tarzan the Ape Man* (1932) and Merian Cooper's *King Kong* (1933)—not to mention the Pygmy-modeled Ewoks of George Lucas's *Return of the Jedi* (1983) and the jungle chieftains of his *Phantom Menace* (1999).[40] The depictions of good and bad African kings in the Korda brothers' *Sanders of the River* (1935) can be found again in *King Solomon's Mines* (1937) and *Zulu* (1963). Stately, cattle-keeping Africans appeared in Underwood and Underwood's stereoscope cards in 1909, and the same figures still tracked for *Mutual of Omaha's Wild Kingdom* in the 1960s, which was hosted by Marlin Perkins—a close friend of Osa Johnson's.[41] Minstrelsy begat the loose-limbed cartoon "native" in *Tintin*, *Betty Boop*, and *Bugs Bunny*, who then became the witch doctor in Disney's hugely successful *The Lion King* (1996), this time in the guise of a baboon.

The connections between such lines of popular representation, and the history of actual colonialism, are rather more difficult to outline. Ethnography, the administration of "tribes" under colonial rule, and photography and cinema, all impinged on one another's domains.[42] My general sense of the current literature is that there is little consensus beyond the idea that they were gendered, racist, contemporary, and thus in some way mutually constituted phenomena. Some scholars, striving to go further than this, have granted immense power to the Western "gaze," and approach the position that seeing itself is tantamount to state control. The idea derives from a strange misreading of Michel Foucault.[43] It is clear enough that action and the essence of picturing are different things when we consider representations of underdogs outwitting the powerful. Tintin flummoxes hostile Congolese in the frame of a comic strip; an African figure defeats a white man in a game of chess in a sculpture fronting a Ghanaian women's cult; a "white colonial" masquerader is a figure of fun in a Gure dance performance in Harare. The same kind of distinction must also be drawn when white people photographed and catalogued Africans in books and reports: such acts of control were located in the domain of signs.[44]

Yet the "virtual" and "actual" of colonial engagements did affect one another. After all, one can learn about history from photographs, as several recent treatments have demonstrated, which would hardly be possible otherwise.[45] But the overlap was also instrumental. This was so first in the intuitive sense that the manipulation of people in the mechanics of colonial administration supplied the grounds for representing ethnic groups on paper. Indeed, the very notion of tribe derived from the process by which individuals in indigenous hierarchies, some of which were quite complex, were grouped into types subsequently seen as recognizable. In the basement of the University of the Witwatersrand's medical school, one can still find a library of Bushmen's skulls, Professor Raymond Dart's "Gallery

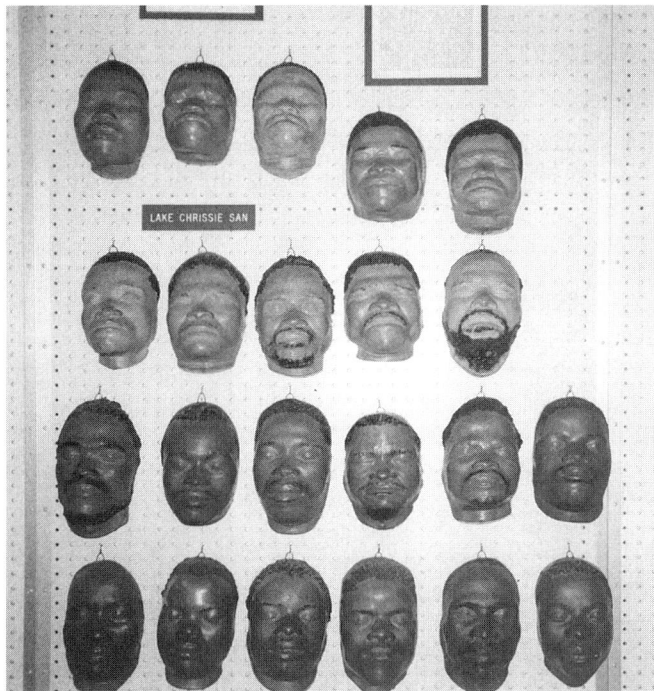

Figure 5.2. "Lake Chrissie San." Part of Professor Raymond Dart's "Gallery of African Faces," University of Witwatersrand Medical School. Photograph by Paul Landau.

of African Faces" (a trophy wall of plaster-cast life masks collected in the 1920s), and other photographic examples of the dynamic. Ethnic distinctions in medicalized tableaux are presented as if they were analogous to the divisions among biological species; but in fact, skulls, facial masks, and plates of photographed "types" are grouped together in this bizarre museum according to the logic of conquest and administration.[46] The same arrogance defined the aggregated nature of even the individual pictured subject. In most colonial-era photographs that achieved circulation, Africans were organized into administrative categories, either ethnic or otherwise: dock worker, weaver, krio; Wolofs, marimba players, youths. One need not push the point too far, since photographers were diverse in their aims and their affiliations: there were important differences among missionaries' didactic photographs, fashion and commercial images, cinematic propaganda, and major motion pictures.[47] Yet much of the time, with good photographers and with hacks, Africans in pictures were and are deindividualized and nameless.[48] In Allan Sekula's terms, they were framed within the "honorific" paradigm of portraiture, but they were homogenized according to photography's "repressive" function, that of possession or control.

This reduction of differences to the level of variations in genera was not simply a taxonomic expedient. It was a function of distance. For while "scientific" typological studies were of limited use to colonialism, the remote command structure of metropolitan overrule made the idea of an authentic and timeless Africa extremely appealing. It crystallized after the era of first-person accounts of exploration. This imaginary place not only helped compensate for the ugliness of genuine colonial encounters, but suggested that Africans who appeared carnal and impure and devious had been corrupted by colonialism. What is authentic always lies at a safe remove from the experience of the observer; Africans that exist in the pristine mode for Europeans are by definition still unfamiliar, still far away. It might seem as if distant people are again, by definition, people who are not yet understood very well: this would be a commonsense view. In fact, however, Europeans have often purported to know authentic Africans quite well, and to do so even from their mere pictures.

Because images of deindividuated people were and nearly always are images of the disempowered, the pinnacle of authenticity in colonial representations of Africans would be a "revealing" portrait of a distanced and generalized figure. Again, this is a contradiction, but it nevertheless perfectly describes a great deal of colonial photography and most portraiture. The impacted idea was so compelling to Margery Perham, the biographer of Frederick Lugard, that she used a photograph of a nameless elderly African man as a frontispiece to her book *Ten Africans*, a work which aimed at revealing the individuality of the persons she described. The photograph's caption is "The Authentic Sculpture."[49] Only if an individual's personal identity is denied can he or she be such a sculpture: an image to be experienced as potent, authentic, knowable, and reproducible.

Massed and distant types such as Pernham's "authentic sculpture" can mean many things. They have an aura of authenticity about them. In a much-cited essay, "The Work of Art in the Age of Mechanical Reproduction," Walter Benjamin elaborated this concept of "aura." He discussed aura as the quality of art's handwrought originality, as an effect similar to what Marx saw as the initial impulse toward commodity fetishism. In Benjamin's terms, the aura of an original work of art was the meaning created in situ by the tradition of the apprehension of that art: it was its "historical testimony," which was read back into the artwork as an intrinsic quality of it.[50] Perhaps because authenticity is always in retreat, Benjamin describes aura almost entirely in the past tense. It is something that recedes from view: we may encounter it, but we cannot quantify or contain it. It is "a unique phenomenon of distance."[51]

In much the same way, the "authentic" African is also unpossessable, wordless, and distant, and so always subject to contamination. By the turn of the century, the colonial traveler had to make an effort to get behind the scenes, off the tourists' path; yet once he reached the hoped-for setting, his own intercourse began at once to transform it and dispel its aura. The establishment of genuine intimacy erased all authenticity, and the search for authentic primitives can and could never be fulfilled. It seems to me that photography in Africa has often been a technique for

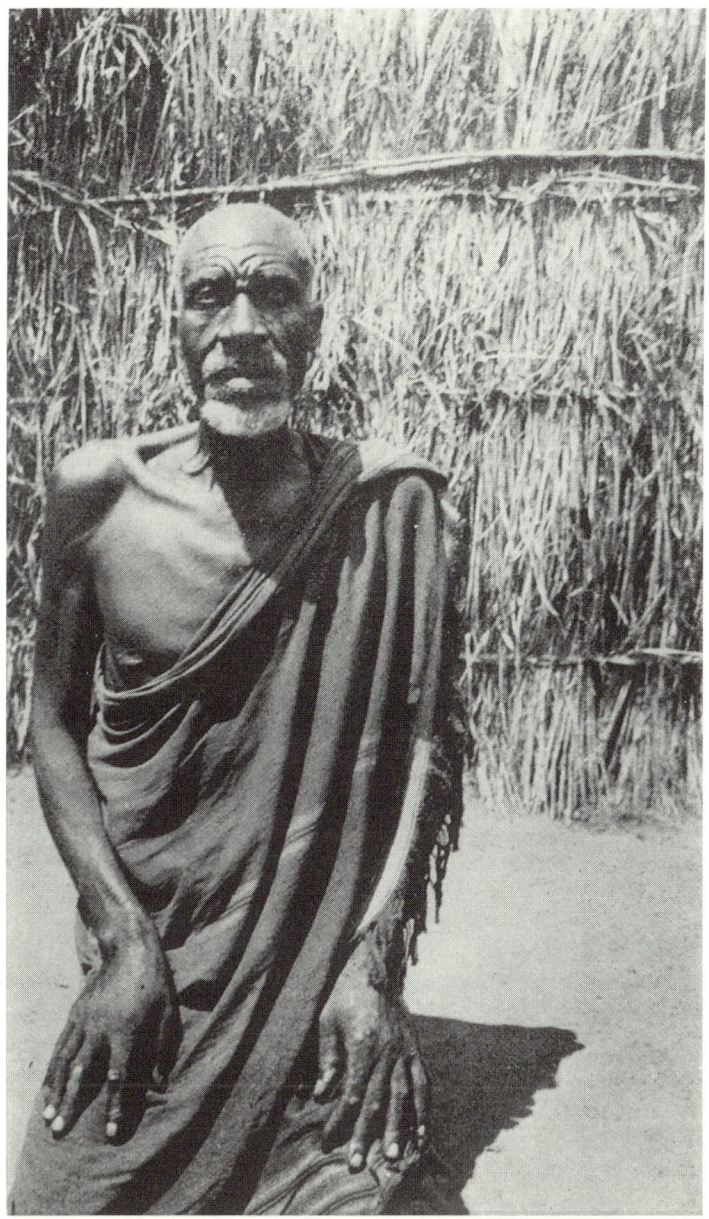

Figure 5.3. "The Authentic Sculpture." Frontispiece in Margery Perham, *Ten Africans* (London: Faber and Faber, 1936). Reproduced by permission.

derailing just this effect. In other words, the photography of the authentic was an assertion of a permanent aura, a permanent "intrinsic distance." The more "remote" from Western experience a photographed person appeared to be, the "truer," because more "authentic," he was, regardless of the circumstances of the taking of the picture. When images of the "Pygmy" and "Bushman" became icons in books, slides, magazines, and postcards, they perpetuated aura in direct proportion to its erasure in the lives of people called Pygmies and Bushmen.

In this sense, photography was much better than direct observation. Martin Johnson and Carl Akeley proved the point in their arrangement and filming of a "Lumbwa lion hunt" in Tanzania in 1925. They paid for young Kipsigis men—close relations of the Nandi—to walk all the way down into the Serengeti from Narok, Kenya, and then, with motor cars, they helped drive the quarry into the Kipsigis men's spears. The footage appeared in the Johnsons' successful 1928 movie *Simba*, as well as in Johnson's book *Safari*, backed up by a phony story explaining the background to the "traditional" hunt, which just "happened" to be captured on film. Pictures from the same series subsequently appeared in other books with yet other inventive captions, some flatly contradicting Johnson's.[52] Such photographs could maintain their authenticity against all odds. Photography also exceeded observation in the ubiquitous "expeditions" that worked their way through the Kalahari Desert distributing tobacco to everyone they met. Writing in 1925, Ernest Cadle commented on the anachronistic purity of the Bushman, writing: "I think the most fundamental thing in bushman life is that he is pristine . . . he is always giving expression to the elements that were first, when consciousness dawned upon man as a sentient being."[53]

The photography of Bushmen in coffee-table books could show this authenticity better than life ever would. The author Laurens van der Post became widely known for his elaboration of the nature of Bushmen's authenticity. Bushmen were, like other primitives, "everywhere undergoing revolutions" (as William Holman Hunt had put it). Their purity would be ruined or they would "vanish" altogether, ringing their images with aura. We now know that not even the most authentic bushmen were untouched. The nineteenth-century figure of the South African "Bushman" only came into being after the dispossession and murder of diverse Khoe- and San-speaking peoples in the first place. The Bushmen whom the 1925 "Denver African Expedition" of Ernest Cadle encountered were old pros in their dealings with whites. By 1950, even the most "remote" of them begged cigarettes from Western travelers.

After Elizabeth Marshall Thomas's *The Harmless People* was published in 1958, camera-toting travelers continued to erase authenticity everywhere outside the photographic frame. It was but a short step to ask Bushmen to perform their photographed "type" for the pleasure of tourists. This is indeed the daily routine at Kagga Kamma Park in South Africa, where Bushmen exhibit the skin-clad image of their own authentic lost selves.[54] They can then reappear in tourists' photo albums of exotic holidays, which further frame the experience of faraway, indigent peoples by cropping from memory the deadweight of travel and the discomfort of extraneous visuals such as brandy bottles and Coke cans. In the end, the image of "the Bushman" attained its mature form by completely erasing the historical circumstances of its own production.

The extreme examples cited above involving the Kipsigis and people called "Bushman" point to the general function of photography as a tool of empire.

PHOTOGRAPHY AND COLONIAL ADMINISTRATION

The most recent treatment of photography in southern Africa underscores the complexity of the relationships between picturing and colonialism, the difficulty in pinning them down. It focuses on the "haphazard" photographic traces left in Namibia by a defeated colonial power, Germany, and by a regional subcolonial power, South Africa. In the end, it shows that "the processes of producing [visual] knowledge were very strained and ambivalent and did not necessarily feed into the colony itself."[55] While the volume goes on to some excellent analyses, it is also worth suggesting that the very inattentiveness to African particularity that characterizes the pictorial archive in Namibia was a condition of the making of the visual sign of the tribe, which was so useful to colonial rule.

In magazines and books from the turn of the century onward, the emblem of the African tribe was an adult man in authentic and customary regalia. His image offered white colonial culture some grounds for cooperation with the gerontocratic patriarchy—leadership of senior men—of many African societies.[56] From the 1890s through the 1930s, the stereoscopic "Zulu warrior," the equestrian Fulani, the hunter "San" in Duggan-Cronin's beautiful photographs, all accompanied by explanatory captions, metonymically identified their "tribes."[57] The visual infatuation with pastoralists was manifested most of all by the popularity of East–Central African Maasai, mainly *murran* (male youths) draped in skins and leaning on long spears. At the same time that they were recollected in pictures and memoirs, Maasai *murran* lost their hunting grounds to whites and assisted colonial officials in "maintaining order" among the Luo and Kalenjin peoples. Maasai iconography had no place at all within it for the Maasai "loose women" who were supposedly corrupting Nairobi by the 1890s, just as the picture of the warlike Zulu did not reflect second- or third-generation Christians like George Champion or Albert Luthuli.[58]

Pictures of "traditional" Africans moreover supported the view that the "tribal economy" operated independently of the "colonial economy." It followed that mobile, male tribesmen might form a bridge between the two, taking up wage labor and returning home to "develop" their tribes. From the colonial standpoint, the 1935 film *Sanders of the River* represented the ideal alliance between paunchy white men and noble-formed black men. Paul Robeson is an African chief who, unlike his howling neighbors, is interested in "progress" and therefore cooperates with Sanders, the unassuming, steady district officer.[59] In actuality, colonial economies had always relied on African labor. They secured it largely through state legislation and subsequent interventions of chiefs, merchants, and district officers in the labor market. Mining, plantations, and cash-cropping used corvée (forced) labor from their beginnings.[60] The ideology of "the tribe" worked to mask such dependence. It ensured, for instance, that there was "no formal means of acknowledging that the entity called 'customary law' had been altered"—while colonial industries relied on "customary" African authorities to deliver workers to them and to govern over increasingly impoverished rural domains. The performed or photographed "tribesman" was the visual manifestation of the phony stasis of custom, neatly concealing the dependence of whites on the coerced or semi-coerced labor of Africans.

The "tribesman" also cloaked the increased burdens in farming and child-care that fell on African women. Behind the ethnic face, chiefs fought to formalize their control over their statutory minors. Often enough, therefore, the "unprogressive nature" of "tribes" was represented by images of women. In *National Geographic Magazine* for instance, social life, labor, beauty, and domestic space were often represented as female and perennial domains. Because African women occupied the "traditional economy" from which men could supposedly come and go with ease, they were doubly alienated from colonial policy makers, as Africans and as women.[61] Catherine Lutz and Jane Collins have subjected *National Geographic* to a close reading, for instance, and suggest that the magazine showed women of color in a similar manner to postcards of North African "harems" at the turn of the century, with much display of brown-skinned female breasts. In both media, the camera is aimed from a public, employing, pedagogical, male point of view, and African women are simultaneously sexualized and made to stand for cultural difference. If pictures of "tribesmen" concealed the economies of African men, those of "tribeswomen" obliterated those of women.[62]

Even beyond these senses, the pictured African "type" had a politically repressive function. Christraud Geary tells us that even before 1914, the German Reichskoliatamt demanded first rights to any photograph snapped by government personnel. Soon enough each colonial power had its own photographic service, not to mention the de facto ability to censor undesirable news pictures.[63] Most profoundly authentic Africana obfuscated local politics for metropolitan publics and policy makers. By infiltrating the circuits of money and power in the colonial era, images of deindividuated Africans became part of what James Scott has called the "public transcript" of domination, the acceptable presentation of the colonized. It was a transcript that imperialism relied on even more than Africans.[64] As the Western image of Africa matured in the 1920s and 1930s, the only mode of African national discourse that many colonial authorities tolerated was that reflected in the typological photograph: "traditionalism." Thus in Swaziland, the British and South African governments foreclosed on the progressive strategies of King Sobhuza, leaving him with no choice but to model his authority on a frozen picture of the world of his parents.[65] Because tradition meant homogenization, such strategies could cut both ways, and "public transcripts" were indeed used by subject peoples to dissimulate and to conceal. Thus when the Bechuanaland Protectorate tried to insinuate "offices" of administration into chiefdoms, some rulers in Botswana insisted, in response, that they only had undifferentiated "tribal councillors."[66] More often, however, images of authentic African culture militated against political activity and so favored the state. They were most often taken in rural areas, and so they obscured urban spaces; they were anachronistic, and so they disabled Africans from speaking from within their own time. In Zaire, Sese Seko Mobuto's "authenticity" policy asserted the primacy of a living past, disguising the origins of the Zairean state and marginalizing debates about contemporary life.[67] Malawi's Dr. Banda and Kwazulu's Chief Buthelezi similarly experimented with ways of replacing political debate with monolithic recreated traditions. Images played a role in all these substitutions.

The origins of such efforts lay in imperial rule. Metropolitan European control over Africa required that the "traditional" domain of governance be relied upon, and at a distance. This necessity was developed into the theory of "indirect rule" by the first governor of northern Nigeria, Frederick Lugard.[68] Officials resident in Africa took their most general orders from distant officials, in the Foreign Office in London and the Colonial Ministry in Paris. After the turn of the century, when the telegraph had reduced intervals of communication from several weeks to a matter of minutes, metropolitan authorities involved themselves more in their African possessions, but the chief aim was to limit expenditures. European offices used maps, reports, and ledgers to organize their policies, which were only imperfectly implemented by local officials.[69] Closer to the ambit of ordinary Africans, bureaucrats in colonial capitals such as Lagos or Mafeking mediated between utterly dissimilar constituencies, and often saw no profit in questioning the supposed homogeneity of tribal law, custom, and personality. The regular predictability of distant types was a useful fiction.

Most European administrators and (quite obviously) Africans knew better. Actual engagements between Europeans and Africans were full of contingency, and colonial personnel prided themselves on their "insider" knowledge. To adopt (and adapt) James Scott's terminology once again, from the point of view of the metropole, there were multiple "hidden transcripts" in Africa. Some lay side by side, others one behind the next like the layers of an onion. The integration of district officers and resident magistrates into *African* politics, for example, played according to transcripts hidden beneath that half of Lugard's "dual mandate" that specified the improvement of African jurisprudence by example and by appeal. A Fulani emir's traffic in slaves or a clerk's reliance on "dashes" were best painted out of public discourse and hidden from metropolitan observers.[70] The bodily intimacy between whites and African servants created further representational problems. The "boy" who removed the mistress's night soil had to be trusted in quite another way than as a "tribesman." Clerks, cooks, medical aides, valets, and wet nurses were indispensable, and also found their way into images; businesses and missions both advertised with icons of *évolués*, some of which Africans transformed into liberatory ideals.[71] Yet they were unsettling figures, leaning to dandyism, mired in opaque tradition, tragic figures, unable to fit in. Africans concealed "transcripts" from Europeans on many levels, but Europeans also averted their eyes.[72]

My point is that *in the colonial metropole,* the uncomfortable knowledge of African realities, and the intimate reliance on real Africans, were, as much as possible, subordinated to depictions of qualities projected onto African types. The "public transcript" of the tribesman was a solution to the problem of underfunded imperial rule over diverse and numerous peoples. Not only did it provide an interface, however imperfect a one, for Africans to make themselves visible; it also, paradoxically, helped assuage the subterranean fears of whites.

> The pagans now sprang from hiding in all directions and, with blood-curdling yells, leapt in pursuit.... From my position beside Roddie, I could not repress a shudder at the bloodthirsty and menacing aspect of this dark and savage people. How very easily they could demolish the lot of us, I thought. And yet, such is the power of the white man, when Barkie raised his megaphone and shouted "Cut!" they immediately relaxed and peacefully awaited further instructions.[73]

The more Africans might be imagined to be locked into predictable habit, the better it was for everybody. The reduction of people to types even mandated the insistence, on occasion, that celluloid or paper was more real than people. How else can we understand the difficulty involved, for instance, in getting Africans to perform as "Africans"? In their guide to colonial and evangelistic filmmaking in Africa, L. A. Notcutt and G. C. Latham tell us that "Bantu women" were too self-conscious to act out their own "type," but Zanzibari Africans did better. "Our experience of native actors was that at least one in five can give quite a creditable performance of any action which is customary in his life.... One native actress [from Zanzibar] acted well the part of a woman of her own type."[74]

The degree to which an African could act like her type, as defined by others, could itself become a distinguishing feature of the type (or image) she portrayed. The absurdity of the above example should not obscure how common a process this was: as with Dart's "Bushman Faces," the colonial power in Africa elicited features from groups created by the compromises of its rule, and then countenanced those observations as the supposedly antecedent, organizing principles of its rule. As a result colonial and metropolitan officials sometimes ruled less over populations than over images, like the Queen of Hearts in *Alice in Wonderland.*

When the public transcripts of authenticity intersected with Africans' genuine politics, the results could be disastrous. The Kenyan government's draconian response to the Mau Mau uprisings was conditioned by the idea that "the Kikuyu" were exhibiting a kind of pathology resulting from their collective, tribal nature, in its encounter with modernity.[75] In Burundi and especially in Rwanda, complex forms of patronage were reduced to two massed identities, "Tuutsi" and

"Hutu," essentialized with sets of physical traits—and represented in photographs by Jacques Maquet and others. The utility of this "public transcript" contributed a necessary precondition for the genocidal conflicts in those countries, in some of which Hutu extremists claimed "authenticity" solely for themselves.[76] The nadir of the confluence between fixed images and malleable, discriminatory policies was perhaps reached in "separate development" in South Africa. Only "the tribe as a whole" might progress, so that in the official mind, articulate individuals—such as the Zulu chief Albert Luthuli—had no standing as Africans. "Progress" and "tribe" amounted to antithetical notions. Today, the South African Tourist Board continues to offer pictures of its ethnic plurality, replacing apartheid's language of control with happy talk of rainbows and identity.

THE BUFFERING EFFECT OF THE SPECTACLE

The idea that Western photographs objectified colonized peoples in Africa is correct, if also banal. Photographs, like perspectival paintings before them, can just as easily be said to have objectified observers.[77] The immobile perspective of the photograph cements the *viewer* in a single position: it holds the eye "static, unblinking, and fixated."[78] More important, when Africans were represented in a staged tableau, they had usually decided to participate in it, just as an African actress in a film profited from her collaboration in making her "public transcript." Christraud Geary has shown that the king of Bamun in Cameroon quickly learned what the camera was for, and mastered it for his own ends, displaying himself in staged poses and carefully selected clothing.[79] Male youths in Kenya, Botswana, or Zimbabwe were glad to sit together in solidarity for a portrait, and if paid a wage, were often willing to perform a caricature of their identities. None of these people had evident cause to worry about the effects of their depiction.[80]

The negotiations between Africans and Europeans in the creation of images also blurs the question of what constitutes a Western- versus an African-produced picture. Christraud Geary and Virginia-Lee Webb make an important point in this regard in their discussion of colonial-era postcards. Whether an image was made by a Senegalese Creole photographer such as Alphonso Lisk-Carew or a prominent Western photographer such as Volkmar Wentsel, "sponsors shipped scenes of the colonies to large cities and the centers of empire, where they were turned into postcards by specialized firms in Europe or by big companies in the United States.... [and] shipped back to the distant sponsors in foreign territories, [where] Westerners bought them."[81]

The forces that marshaled and distributed images were the same ones that propagated the dominant interpretations of what the images were taken to mean. In the end, the ethnic status or even the class affiliation of a given photographer was not that important. The dominance of an interpretation corresponded with power more generally. Lutz and Collins, in their already mentioned analysis of images of women's bodies in *National Geographic*, stress the importance of the particular choices

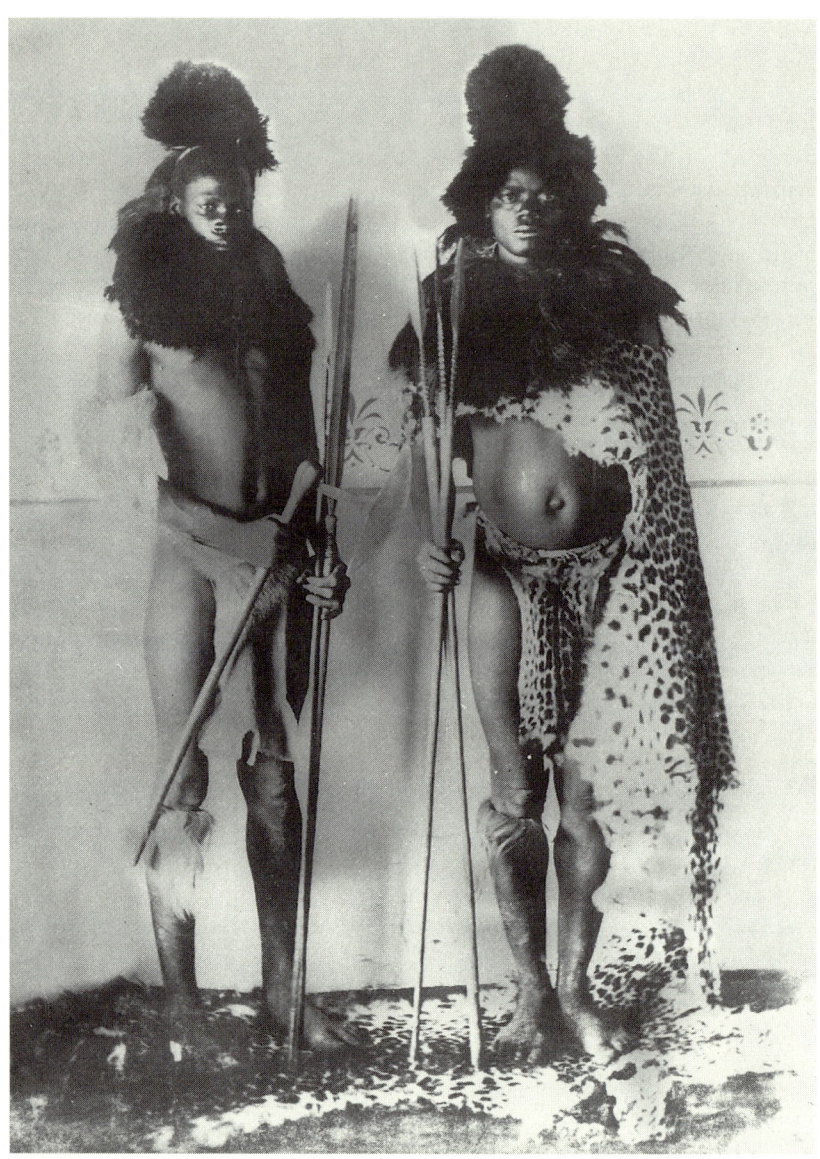

Figure 5.4. "Ndebele Warriors." Two young men in batttle dress, ca. 1890. Courtesy Zimbabwe National Archives. Photographer unknown.

made by magazine editors. Surely, however, the larger context for the circulation of the magazine did more to determine where the camera looked. Dark-skinned colonized people, who did not sexualize the seeing of breasts, were photographed; their images were brought home to midwestern American families in which glimpsing breasts was highly charged with sex; American money then encouraged the further photography of naked brown-skinned women in future *National Geographics*, and indeed in cinema and postcards, too.[82] Ultimately, the role of photography in the colonial project emerges not from who made images, nor even (and this is really the central point) from the graphic content of the images themselves. Rather, it lay in the appropriation of tribal images into structures of distribution and interpretation.[83] And it is precisely the constant possibility of appropriation that characterized mechanically reproduced images of Africans.

In this essay I have tried to suggest *how* visual iconography, and especially photography, was involved with colonialism in Africa. The mechanics and marketing of guns and cameras concentrated agency in a common way: they "shot" and "took" emblems of the wider world; they made claims to own the world by virtue of shooting and taking it; they reduced it to archetypes; and they subordinated and concealed the infrastructure necessary to the process. The seemingly objective visual presence of Africans, and the plangent specificity and realness of photographs, stabilized "authenticity" and obscured a world of politics and labor that people in Europe did not wish to see. Africans' modes of identity were complex, stacked and overlapping. Western colonial photography, suitably captioned and contextualized, flattened them into comparable "tribes." It reflected the ideology that modern economies were naturally divorced from tribes and created a buffering illusion of control, facilitating the "administration" of those tribes. A very political history has arrayed images of Africa in a widening gyre around Western urbanites, until politics and class have all but disappeared from view.

Finally, the traffic in images under colonial rule served the colonial project in Africa, alongside not only guns and steamships, but radio, newsreels, presses, and carbon paper. Images offered "the sympathetic magic of manipulating personhood through visual replicas."[84] Like other symbolic interfaces, visual images gave rise to the *appearance* of immediacy, while safely blocking the metropole from those elements of colonial life over which it had little control anyway. Walter Benjamin once predicted that moving pictures would allow common people to "calmly and adventurously go traveling" anywhere they liked.[85] A pioneering developer of the Internet predicts more to come: "Imagine some kind of a chair that's connected to this system that you sit in and fly around wherever you want to go."[86] In the same sense, the cumulative effect of pictures drawn from different parts of European empires was to give the Western eye a total mobility over the African landscape, to unmoor its locality in metropolitan bodies.

This was an illusion. Every beholder of prepared information is ensconced in a tendentious and finite "archive" of representations.[87] Both in Africa and in the West, the preferred visuals often obscured real politics, the struggles and compromises that operated according to undetected scripts. If we may think once more in terms of "tools of empire," we might say that images and actions impinged upon one another, and drove one another forward, but they never quite meshed. Modern imperialism in Africa inhabited their chronic misalignment.

NOTES

Thanks go to Patricia Hayes, Emily Epstein Landau, and Deborah Kaspin, for reading and commenting on parts of this essay; to Yale University, for financial support; to William Beinart, for helpful suggestions; and to Cathy Connor, the archivist at the George Eastman House in Rochester, New York. Epigraph: Margery Perham, *Ten Africans* (London: Faber & Faber, 1936), 73, quoting Ndansi Kumalo, who played the Ndebele king Lobengula in the film *Rhodes* (1936), recalling the 1896 uprising known as Chimurenga.

1. Daniel Headrick, *The Tools of Empire: Technology and European Imperialism in the Nineteenth Century* (New York: Oxford University Press, 1981).

2. See Peter Marzio, *The Democratic Art: Chromolithography, 1840–1900* (Boston: D. R. Godine, in association with the Amon Carter Museum of Western Art, Fort Worth, 1979); Jonathan Crary, *Techniques of the Observer: On Vision and Modernity in the Nineteenth Century* (Cambridge, Mass.: MIT Press, 1990), esp. 112, 149; A. D. Bensusan, *Silver Images: History of Photography in Africa* (Cape Town: Howard Timmins, 1966); *To Catch a Sunbeam: Victorian Reality Through a Magic Lantern*, ed. G. A. Household (London: Michael Joseph, 1979); Elizabeth Shepard, "Magic Lantern Slides in Entertainment and Education, 1860–1920," *History of Photography* 11, 2 (April–June 1987): 91–108; David Prochaska, "Fantasy of the Photothèque: French Postcard Views of Colonial Senegal," *African Arts* 24, 4 (1991): 40–47, 98; *Delivering Views: Distant Cultures in Early Postcards*, ed. Christraud M. Geary and Virginia-Lee Webb (Washington, D.C.: Smithsonian Institution Press, 1998); and recent special issues of *Cahiers d'Études africaines, African Arts,* and *African Research and Documentation.*

3. Leopold Senghor, "Preliminary Poem," *Prose and Poetry* (Oxford: Oxford University Press, 1965), 121. On Banania and its context, see Jan Nederven-Pieterse, *White on Black: Images of Africa and Blacks in Western Popular Culture* (New Haven, Conn.: Yale University Press, 1992), and Catherine Hodeir's chapter in this book.

4. Edward Said, *Orientalism* (New York: Vintage Books, 1978), 123 ff.

5. See Robert J. C. Young, *Colonial Desire: Hybridity in Theory, Culture and Race* (London: Routledge, 1995); Stephen Jay Gould, *The Mismeasure of Man* (New York: Norton, 1981); Joseph-Arthur, comte de Gobineau, *Essai sur l'inégalité des races humaines* (Paris: Firmin Didot, 1853–55); John Beddoe, *The Races of Britain: A Contribution to the Anthropology of Western Europe* (Bristol, U.K.: Arrowsmith, 1885); John Knox, *The Races of Men: A Philosophical Inquiry into the Influence of Race over the Destinies of Nations* (London: Renshaw, 1862). For the current state of scholarly knowledge on the relationship between biological differences and human societies, see Luigi L. Cavalli-Sforza, *Genes, Peoples, and Languages* (New York: North Point Press, 2000).

6. Martin Jay, "Scopic Regimes of Modernity," in *Vision and Visuality*, ed. Hal Foster (Seattle: Bay Press, 1988).

7. Bernard S. Cohn, *Colonialism and Its Forms of Knowledge: The British in India* (Princeton, N.J.: Princeton University Press, 1994), esp. 99–100; and Stuart Cary Welch, *Room for Wonder: Indian Painting during the British Period, 1760–1880* (New York: American Federation of Arts,

1978). Thanks to Jock McLane. See also the exhibition catalogue *The Raj: India and the British, 1600–1947,* ed. Christopher Bayly (London: National Portrait Gallery, 1991).

8. George P. Landow, "William Holman Hunt's 'Oriental Mania' and His Uffizi *Self-Portrait*," *Art Bulletin* 64, 4 (1982): 653 for both quotations. As the great critic John Ruskin wrote, "Preraphaelitism has but one principle, that of absolute, uncompromising truth in all that it does, obtained by working everything, down to the most minute detail, from nature, and from nature only"(quoted in Aaron Scharf, *Art and Photography* [1968; New York: Penguin Books, 1986], 70–71, and see also 74). See also Van Deren Coke, *The Painter and the Photograph* (Albuquerque: University of New Mexico Press, 1964). On Holman Hunt, see also Linda Nochlin, "The Imaginary Orient," *Art in America,* May, 1993, 127, cited by James Ryan, *Picturing Empire: Photography and the Visualization of the British Empire* (Chicago: University of Chicago Press, 1997), 120; and Mary E. Coleridge, *Holman Hunt* (London: T. C. & E. C. Jack; New York: F. A. Stokes, 1908).

9. Millais incorporated the use of daguerreotypes into his work, and Delacroix and Degas used photos in theirs.

10. Allan Sekula, "The Body and the Archive," in *The Contest of Meaning: Critical Histories of Photography,* ed. Richard Bolton (Cambridge, Mass.: MIT Press, 1989), 343–89; John Tagg, *The Burden of Representation: Essays on Photographies and Histories* (1988; Minneapolis: University of Minnesota Press, 1993).

11. David Phillips, "Art for Industry's Sake: Halftone Technology, Mass Photography and the Social Transformation of American Print Culture, 1880–1920" (Ph.D. diss, Yale University, 1996); and Ryan, *Picturing Empire,* 146, citing David Livingstone to Charles Livingstone, May 10, 1858, in *The Zambezi Expedition of David Livingstone, 1858–1863,* ed. J. P. R. Wallis (London: Chatto & Windus, 1956), 432.

12. Terence Wright, "Photography: Theories of Realism and Convention," in *Anthropology and Photograph, 1860–1930,* ed. Elizabeth Edwards (New Haven, Conn.: Yale, 1992), 21.

13. Reading similarly slowly shifted from a social activity, done out loud, to a private, internal act, Roger Chartier argues in "Texts, Printing, Readings," in *The New Cultural History,* ed. Lynn Hunt (Berkeley and Los Angeles: University of California Press, 1989), 154–75.

14. Melissa Banta and Curtis Hinsley, *From Site to Sight: Anthropology, Photography and the Power of Imagery* (Cambridge, Mass.: Peabody Museum of Archaeology and Ethnology, 1986); Ryan, *Picturing Empire,* 149, and Frank Spencer, "Some Notes on the Attempt to Apply Photography to Anthropometry during the Second Half of the Nineteenth Century," in *Anthropology and Photography, 1860–1920,* ed. Elizabeth Edwards (New Haven, Conn.: Yale University Press, 1992), 100; Ray McKenzie, " 'The Laboratory of Mankind': John McCosh and the Beginnings of Photography in British India," *History of Photography* 11, 2 (1987): 109–18; Elizabeth Edwards, "Representation and Reality: Science and the Visual Image," in *Australia in Oxford,* ed. Howard Murphy and Elizabeth Edwards (Oxford: Pitt Rivers Museum, 1988). See also Saul Dubow, *Scientific Racism in Modern South Africa* (Cambridge: Cambridge University Press, 1995); A. M. Duggan-Cronin, *The Bantu Tribes of South Africa: Reproductions of Photographic Studies* (Cambridge: Cambridge University Press, 1928–41), and id., *The Bushman Tribes of Southern Africa* (Kimberley: Alexander McGregor Museum, 1942) for further examples. John Lamprey published *Method of Measuring the Human Form* in 1869, and Carl Damann published *Anthropologisch-Ethnologisches Album in Photographien . . . Herausgegeben mit Unterstützung aus dem Sammelungen der Berliner Gesellschaft für Anthropologies, Ethnologies und Ungeschichte* in 1873–76.

15. Gustav Fritsch, *Drei Jahre in Süd-Afrika: Reiseskizzen nach Notizen des Tagebuchs zusammengestellt. Mit zahlreichen Illustrationen nach Photographien und Originalzeichnungen des Verfassers, nebst*

einer Übersichtskarte der ausgeführten Routen (Breslau: F. Hirt, 1868); W. H. I. and Lucy Lloyd Bleek, *Specimens of Bushman Folklore* [Spine: *Bushman Folklore*] (London: George Allen, 1911); Isaac Schapera, *The Khoisan Peoples of Southern Africa* (London: Routledge, 1930); Spencer, "Some Notes on the Attempt to Apply Photography to Anthropometry"; and in general, Banta and Hinsley, *From Site to Sight*.

16. South African apartheid stands as a major exception to this statement (see Saul Dubow, *Scientific Racism in Modern South Africa*), but even here, Deborah Posel's recent research (so far unpublished) suggests that the bizarre minutiae of color charts did not have much to do with the cataloguing of statuses under South Africa's 1950 Population Registration Act.

17. *Africa Illustrated: Scenes from the Dark Continent. From Photographs Secured in Africa by Bishop William Taylor, Dr. Emil Holub, and the Missionary Superintendents* (New York: Ross Taylor, 1895); and see also Duggan-Cronin, *Bantu Tribes of South Africa;* H. A. Bryden, *Gun and Camera in Southern Africa* (London: Edward Stanford, 1893); Sir Harry H. Johnston, *British Central Africa* (London: Methuen, 1897); and Dudley Kidd, *The Essential Kafir,* with sixty-three full-page illustrations from photographs by the author (1904; 2d ed., London: A. & C. Black, 1925). For difference as a matter of utility, see Nicolas Thomas, *Colonialism's Culture: Anthropology, Travel, and Government* (Princeton, N.J.: Princeton University Press, 1994). See also Sander Gilman, *Difference and Pathology: Stereotypes of Sexuality, Race, and Madness* (London: Routledge, 1985), and *Health and Illness: Images of Difference* (London: Routledge, 1995).

18. This does not do justice to the muckraker's particular goals. See Jacob A. Riis, *How the Other Half Lives: Studies among the Tenements of New York* (1890; New York: Penguin Books, 1997).

19. See James Agee and Walker Evans, *Let Us Now Praise Famous Men* (1939, 1941; Boston: Houghton Mifflin, 1988); and August Sander, *"In der Photographie gibt es keine ungeklärten Schatten!"* ed. Gerd Sander (Bonn: Kunstmuseum Bonn, 1995); Sander represented not only dying provincial and "farmer types" but also industrialists and scholars as types. Paul Augustus Martin's photos are discussed in Roy Flukinger, *The Formative Decades: Photography in Great Britain, 1839–1920* (Austin: University of Texas Press, 1985), 130. See also Christopher Lyman, *The Vanishing Race and Other Illusions: Photographs of Indians by Edward S. Curtis* (New York: Pantheon Books, 1982), and Daile Kaplan, "Enlightened Women in Darkened Lands: A Lantern Slide Lecture," *Studies in the Anthropology of Visual Communication* 10, 1 (1984): 61–77.

20. Paul Landau, "The Illumination of Christ in the Kalahari Desert," *Representations* 45 (Winter 1994): 25–39; Christopher Pinney, "Colonial Anthropology in the 'Laboratory of Mankind,'" in *The Raj*, ed. Bayly. Rudolf Pöch quoted in Christraud M. Geary, *Images of Bamun: German Colonial Photography at the Court of King Njoya, Cameroun, West Africa, 1902–1915* (Washington, D.C.: Smithsonian Institution Press, 1988), 31.

21. Ryan, *Picturing Empire*, 156.

22. Sarah Lyall, "Diana's Hunters: How Quarry Was Stalked," *New York Times*, September 10, 1997, 1.

23. See Susan Sontag, *On Photography* (New York: Dell, 1973), esp. 7. Snapping a shot meant the same thing as "to snipe," to shoot at a moving target: see the *Oxford English Dictionary* (1933), s.v. "snap-shot."

24. John M. MacKenzie, *The Empire of Nature: Hunting, Conservation and British Imperialism* (Manchester: Manchester University Press, 1988); and William Beinart, "Review Article: Empire, Hunting and Ecological Change in Southern and Central Africa," *Past & Present* 128 (August 1990): 162–86.

25. Dr. H. Lang to resident commissioner, Pretoria, February 14, 1930, Vernay Kalahari Expedition, 1930, DCF 1/25, Botswana National Archives (BNA). The expedition col-

lected "specimens" for the American Museum of Natural History (New York), the Field Museum (Chicago), the British Museum, and the Transvaal Museum.

26. I explore this logic more fully in "With Camera and Gun in Southern Africa," in *Miscast*, ed. Skotnes. The actual hunting of Bushmen, and occasionally the marketing of their skins as trophies, is also taken up in other essays in that book. Mimesis is in a sense the "skin" of the thing represented, Michael Taussig argues in another context in *Mimesis and Alterity* (New York: Routledge, 1993), ch. 4, and 102; and see Ryan, *Picturing Empire*, 112 ff.

27. Harriet Ritvo, *The Animal Estate: The English and Other Creatures in the Victorian Age* (Cambridge, Mass.: Harvard University Press, 1987).

28. Reese V. Jenkins, *Images and Enterprise: Technology and the American Photographic Industry, 1839 to 1925* (Baltimore: Johns Hopkins University Press, 1975); Brian Coe, *The Birth of Photography* (New York: Praeger, 1976).

29. See Paul Landau, "Hunting with Gun and Camera," in *The Colonising Camera: Photographs in the Making of Namibian History*, ed. Wolfram Hartmann et al. (Cape Town: University of Cape Town Press; Athens: Ohio University Press, 1999).

30. For instance, the naturalist Carl Akeley's famous "Akeley Camera" was modeled on a turret-mounted machine gun and was immortalized by the photographer Paul Strand in 1923. For Strand's photograph, see Sarah Greenough, *Paul Strand: An American Vision* (Washington, D.C.: National Gallery of Art, 1990), 57.

31. Eastman wrote this in 1877. See James Ackerman, *George Eastman* (Boston: Houghton Mifflin, 1930), 78 and passim; and Elizabeth Brayer, *George Eastman* (Baltimore: Johns Hopkins University Press, 1997). Eastman had a shooting box in the 1890s.

32. Roland Barthes, *Camera Lucida* (London: Jonathan Cape, 1982), 31. This must be understood in terms of Barthes's understanding of the photograph as a peculiarly "uncoded message," an unmediated imprint of part of the world.

33. P. Z. Adelstein, "From Metal to Polyester: A History of Picture-Taking Supports," in *Pioneers of Photography: Their Achievements in Science and Technology*, ed. International Museum of Photography (Springfield, Va.: Society for Imaging Science and Technology, 1987); and *Encyclopedia of Firearms*, ed. Harold L. Peterson (New York: Dutton, 1964), 304.

34. Coe, *The Birth of Photography*, 71, 88; Peterson, *Encyclopedia of Firearms*, 304; and George Eastman to W. H. Walker, March 3, 1889, Eastman House archives, Rochester, N.Y.

35. James E. Paster, "Advertising Immortality by Kodak," *History of Photography* 16, 2 (1992): 135–39.

36. Helmut and Alison Gernsheim, *The History of Photography from the Camera Obscura to the Beginning of the Modern Era* (1955; Oxford: Oxford University Press, 1969), 425. The Kodak "ought to be in every Christian home," Eastman wrote to his partner Henry Strong (April 11, 1895). The Kodak slogan "You pull the trigger, we'll do the rest" was cited by Elizabeth Brayer (pers. comm., 1994); it was eventually changed to "You push the button, we'll do the rest."

37. Ackerman, *George Eastman*, 26.

38. Patents would actually be more accurate than patent, since Eastman patented every step of the production process. Eastman to W. H. Walker, Rochester, March 22, 1889, Papers of George Eastman, Eastman House, Rochester, NY.

39. Burroughs first wrote his initial book *Tarzan of the Apes* (1912; New York: Ballantine Books, 1983) in serial form in 1911, a year after Teddy Roosevelt published *African Game Trails* (New York: Dutton, 1910), a partly photographic account of Roosevelt's famous hunting safari. Gail Bederman, "*Tarzan* and After," Cameron, *Africa on Film*, and also James Patterson, "Africa on Film," *African Research and Documentation* 68 (1995): 75–79.

40. Osa and Martin Johnson's films can be rented directly from the Osa and Martin Johnson Safari Museum, in Chanute, Kansas.

41. Prochaska, "Fantasy"; Neal Sobania, "But Where Are the Cattle? Popular Images of Maasai and Zulu across the Twentieth Century" (forthcoming in *Visual Anthropology*).

42. See the University of Manchester's excellent Studies in the History of Imperialism series. For relevant points on the professionalization of anthropology, see Henrika Kuklick, "Tribal Exemplars: Images of Political Authority in British Anthropology, 1885–1945," in *Functionalism Historicized: Essays on British Social Anthropology*, ed. George W. Stocking, 59–82 (Madison: University of Wisconsin Press, 1984); Edwards, *Anthropology and Photography*, "Introduction," 6 ff., and for missionary photos, see Rory McLachlan Bester, "Insecure Shadows: CPSA Mission Photographs from Southern Africa c. 1895–1945" (M.A. thesis, University of the Witwatersrand, 1997).

43. It is true that seeing may be an aspect or stage of control, as it was intended to be in Jeremy Bentham's proposed prison, the "Panopticon," as well as in Bentham's attempts to recognize the realities of human behavior and create a code of law in accordance with them. Knowing that one is being seen may also feel invasive and discomfiting. Unless some action on the body of the seen is implicated, however, seeing is a rather passive activity. Michel Foucault, *Discipline and Punish: The Birth of the Prison* (New York: Vintage Books, 1979). The problem is also approached by Chris Jenks, *Visual Culture* (New York: Routledge, 1995), "Introduction," 15–16.

44. Nancy Hunt, this volume; Kramer, *The Red Fez: Art and Spirit Possession in Africa* (New York: Verso, 1993), 210–11; and Eric Worby, personal communication. The same case has been made for oral performance by Leroy Vail and Landeg White, *Power and the Praise Poem: Southern African Voices in History* (Charlottesville: University Press of Virginia, 1991); a large literature on carnival, commencing with Emmanuel Le Roy Ladurie, is also relevant here.

45. See, e.g., Gwyn Prins, "The Battle for Control of the Camera in Late Nineteenth-Century Western Zambia," *African Affairs* 89 (January 1990): 97–106; *Fotografia e storia dell'Africa: Atti del Convegno internazionale, Napoli–Roma, 9–11 settembre 1992*, ed. Alessandro Triulzi (Naples: Instituto universitario orientale, 1995) (thanks to Moore Crossey); *Colonising Camera*, ed. Hartmann et al.; and Geary, *Images from Bamun*.

46. For more on the relationship between photography, "anthropometry," and colonial anthropology, see Christopher Wright, "Visible Bodies: Anthropology and Photography, 1850–1900" (M.A. thesis, School of Oriental and African Studies, University of London, 1987); and the essays by Pinney, Poignant, and others in *Anthropology and Photography, 1860–1920*, ed. Elizabeth Edwards (New Haven, Conn.: Yale University Press, 1992). *The Peoples of India* was compiled by John Forbes Watson and John William Kaye; see Roy Flukinger, *The Formative Decades: Photography in Great Britain, 1839–1920* (Austin: University of Texas Press, 1985), 53. Grace Sieberling and Carolyn Bloore, *Amateurs, Photography and the Mid-Victorian Imagination* (Chicago: University of Chicago Press, 1986), 47, describe the effect of such pictures as similar to an antiquarian's portfolio. For the milieu of Dart's and others' Bushmen collections, see the forthcoming work of Ciraj Rassool and Patricia Hayes, esp. "Gendered Science, Gendered Spectacle: /Khanako's South Africa, 1936–37," delivered at the Gender and Colonialism conference at the University of the Western Cape, January 1997.

47. See my introduction to this book, "An Amazing Distance: People and Pictures in Africa."

48. For instance, see Eliot Elisofon's work in *Life* magazine and Duggin-Cronin's lovely plates, cited above; but also the work of Senegalese photographers such as A. Lisk-Carew, discussed by Chris Geary in *Delivering Views* and in her paper, "Betwixt and Between: Postcard Representations by Western and African Photographers," delivered at the Images and Empires conference.

49. Photograph by Margery Perham from her book *Ten Africans* (London: Faber & Faber, 1936).

50. Walter Benjamin, "The Work of Art in the Age of Mechanical Reproduction," in *Illuminations: Essays and Reflections*, ed. Hannah Arendt (1968; New York: Schocken Books, 1969), 223. In Benjamin's argument, the attribution of aura to photographs and cinema is counted as a mystification and even as fascistic. I suggest something similar below.

51. Ibid., 222. Hannah Arendt comments: "unapproachability is indeed a major quality of the cult image" (ibid., 243 n. 5).

52. George Eastman, *Chronicle of an African Trip* (Rochester: private printing, 1927), 54; Mary L. Jobe Akeley, *Carl Akeley's Africa* (New York, Dodd, Mead, 1929), 130. See also Martin Johnson, *Safari: A Saga of the African Blue* (New York: Putnam, 1928).

53. Robert Gordon, *Picturing Bushmen: The Denver Africa Expedition of 1925* (Athens: Ohio University Press, 1997), 74, citing E. Cadle to L. Fourie, November 16, 1925, Fourie's Collection, Museum Afrika, Johannesburg. In addition, see Gordon's essay in this volume.

54. Gordon, *Picturing Bushmen*, passim. The preceding points about authenticity owe much to Gordon. On Bushmen, see further Edwin Wilmsen, *Land Filled with Flies: A Political Economy of the Kalahari* (Chicago: University of Chicago Press, 1989), and Robert J. Gordon, *The Bushman Myth: The Making of a Namibian Underclass* (Boulder, Colo.: Westview Press, 1992). For Kagga Kamma, I am drawing on Hylton White, "The Homecoming of the Kagga Kamma Bushmen," *Cultural Survival Quarterly* (Summer 1993), and Barbara Buntman, "Bushman Images in South African Tourist Advertising: The Case of Kagga Kamma," in *Miscast*, ed. Skotnes, 271–80.

55. Patricia Hayes, Jeremy Sylvester, and Wolfram Hartmann, "Introduction," 7 and passim, in *Colonizing Camera*, ed. Hartmann et al.

56. The point is a general one. "Gerontocratic" and "senior" are not really equivalent terms, since seniority was more often a matter of statutory kinship or wealth, rather than age.

57. See Duggan-Cronin, *Bushman Tribes of Southern Africa*.

58. A. E. Afigbo, "The Establishment of Colonial Rule, 1900–1918," in *History of West Africa*, ed. J. F. A. Ajayi and Michael Crowder (New York: Columbia University Press, 1974), 2: 424–83; G. W. B. Huntingford, *Nandi Work and Culture* (London: HMSO for the Colonial Office, 1950), para. 29; Sobania, "But Where Are the Cattle?" For examples of Maasai photographs in memoirs, see, e.g., Frederick Courteney Selous, *Travel and Adventure in South-East Africa* (London: Rowland Ward & Co., 1893); Sir Harry Johnston, *The Uganda Protectorate* (London: Hutchinson, 1902); and A. Blayney Percival, *A Game Ranger's Note Book* (London: Windham, 1924); and see *Being Maasai*, ed. Thomas Spear and Richard Waller (Athens: Ohio University Press, 1993). "Loose women": Luise White, "Domestic Labor in a Colonial City: Prostitution in Nairobi, 1900–1952," in *Patriarchy and Class in Africa*, ed. Sharon Stichter and Jane Parpart (Boulder, Colo.: Westview Press, 1988), 142; Champion and Luthuli: Shula Marks, *The Ambiguities of Dependence in South Africa: Class, Nationalism, and the State in Twentieth-Century Natal* (Baltimore: Johns Hopkins University Press, 1986).

59. Zoltan and Alexander Korda, *Sanders of the River* (1935). There are some anomalies in this example. For instance, the chief's wife favors a modern education for her son.

60. Giovanni Arrighi, "Labor Supplies in Historical Perspective: A Study of the Proletarianization of the African Peasantry in Rhodesia," in *Essays on the Political Economy of Africa*, ed. id. and John Saul (New York: Monthly Review Press, 1973), 80–236. (Since Arrighi's important essay there have been many more nuanced appraisals, and the consensus is that African laborers did exercise choice, albeit under extra-market constraints.) For "custom," see Terence Ranger, "The Invention of Tradition Revisited," in *Legitimacy and the State in Twentieth-Century Africa: Essays in Honour of A. H. M. Kirk-Greene*, ed. id. and Olufemi Vaughan (Basingstoke, U.K.: Macmillan, in association with St. Antony's College, Oxford, 1993), 101–2; Sally Falk Moore, *Social Facts and Fabrications: Customary Law on Kilimanjaro, 1880–1980* (Cambridge: Cambridge University Press, 1986), 317–18; Martin Chanock, *Law, Custom and the Social Order: The Colonial Experience in Malawi and Zambia* (Cambridge: Cambridge University Press, 1985); and Mahmood Mamdani, *Citizen and Subject: Contemporary Africa and the Legacy of Late Colonialism* (Princeton, N.J.: Princeton University Press, 1996), ch. 4.

61. Limiting ourselves to Bushmen in the matter of gender, see Edwin Wilmsen, "The Real Bushman is the Male One: Labour and Power in the Creation of Basarwa Ethnicity," *Botswana Notes & Records* 22 (1989): 21–35, and Donna Harraway, "Remodelling the Human Way of Life: Sherwood Washburn and the New Physical Anthropology, 1950–1980," in *Bodies, Bones and Behavior: Essays on Biological Anthropology*, ed. George Stocking (Madison: University of Wisconsin Press, 1988). The best discussion of the hidden gender of the "citizen" in the modern state is Carol Pateman, *The Disorder of Women: Democracy, Feminism, and Political Theory* (Cambridge: Polity Press, 1989).

62. Catherine Lutz and Jane Collins, *Reading National Geographic* (Chicago: University of Chicago Press, 1993), 115; Malek Alloula, *The Colonial Harem* (Minneapolis: University of Minnesota Press, 1986). Appearing too late for my full consideration is Laura Wexler's long-awaited book on photography and gender in America, *Tender Violence: Domestic Visions in an Age of U.S. Imperialism* (Chapel Hill: University of North Carolina Press, 2000).

63. Christraud Geary, "Photography: Development," in *Encyclopedia of Africa South of the Sahara*, ed. John Middleton (New York: Scribner, 1997), 404–9.

64. James Scott, *Domination and the Arts of Resistance: Hidden Transcripts* (New Haven, Conn.: Yale University Press, 1990). I am altering Scott's meaning somewhat. He writes about "public transcripts" to indicate performances that "create the appearance of consent among subordinates" (55; see also 70).

65. Christopher Lowe, "Swaziland's Colonial Politics: The Decline of Progressive South African Nationalism and the Emergence of Swazi Political Traditionalism, 1910–1939" (Ph.D. diss., Yale University, 1998), 36.

66. Michael Crowder, "Tshekedi Khama and Opposition to the British Administration of the Bechuanaland Protectorate, 1926–1936," *Journal of African History* 26 (1985): 193–214.

67. Bogumil Jewsiewicki, "Painting in Zaire: From the Invention of the West to the Representation of the Social Self," in *Africa Explores: Twentieth-Century African Art*, ed. Susan Vogel (New York: Center for African Art; Munich: Prestel, 1991), 138–39; K. A. Busia, *The Challenge of Africa* (New York: Praeger, 1962), cited in Victor C. Uchendu, "The Passing of Tribal Man: A West African Experience," *Journal of Asian and African Studies* 5 (1970): 51–65.

68. Lugard was high commissioner of the Protectorate of Northern Nigeria from 1900 to 1906, and the governor of Nigeria—which then included the south as well—from 1912 to 1919.

69. Andrew Roberts, "The Imperial Mind," in *The Colonial Moment in Africa: Essays on the Movement of Minds and Materials, 1900–1940,* ed. Andrew Roberts (Cambridge: Cambridge University Press, 1990), 26 ff. Robert Thornton, "Narrative Ethnography in Africa, 1850–1920: The Capture of an Appropriate Domain for Anthropology," *Man,* n.s., 8, 3 (September 1983): 502–19, usefully discusses the "discovery on paper" of Africans by Westerners. My discussion here is influenced not only by Scott's *Hidden Transcripts,* but by James Scott, *Seeing Like a State: How Certain Schemes to Improve the Human Condition Have Failed* (New Haven, Conn.: Yale University Press, 1998), especially Scott's discussion (chs. 1 and 2) of the state's imperative to see and organize space in a "synoptic" and "replicable" manner (81), and indeed by many conversations with Scott himself.

70. Sean Stilwell, "'Amana' and 'Asiri': Royal Slave Culture and the Colonial Regime in Kano, 1903–1926," in *Slavery and Colonial Rule in Africa,* ed. Suzanne Miers and Martin A. Klein (London: Frank Cass, 1999), 167–88; Frank Salamone, "Colonialism and the Emergence of Fulani Identity," *Journal of Asian and African Studies* 20 (1985): 193–202.

71. Bogumil Jewsiewicki, "Zaïrian Popular Painting as Commodity and as Communication," in *African Material Culture,* ed. May Jo Arnoldi, Christraud Geary, and Kris L. Hardin (Bloomington: Indiana University Press, 1996), 349; and see Hudita Mustafa, this volume. The artistic work of Santu Mofokeng in Johannesburg also makes this point; but one might also reference the sexy fashion photography in *Drum* magazine, Mike Nicol, *A Good-Looking Corpse* (London: Secker & Warburg, 1991); and see Timothy Burke, *Lifebuoy Men, Lux Women: Commodification, Consumption and Cleanliness in Modern Zimbabwe* (Durham, N.C.: Duke University Press, 1996).

72. See Nancy Hunt, *A Colonial Lexicon: Of Birth Ritual, Medicalization, and Mobility in the Congo* (Durham, N.C.: Duke University Press, 2000), esp. ch. 3; and Jock McCulloch, *Colonial Psychiatry and the "African Mind"* (Cambridge: Cambridge University Press, 1995), ch. 5.

73. Natalie Barkas, *Behind the Camera* (London: Geoffrey Bles, 1934), 183. The description refers to a Nigerian set piece in an unnamed film.

74. L. A. Notcutt and G. C. Latham, *The African and the Cinema: An Account of the Work of the Bantu Educational Cinema Experiment during the Period March 1935 to May 1937* (London: Edinburgh House Press for the International Missionary Council, 1937), 144.

75. John Lonsdale, "Mau Maus of the Mind: Making Mau Mau and Remaking Kenya," *Journal of African History* 31 (1990): 393–421.

76. Jacques J. Maquet, *Le système des relations sociales dans le Rwanda ancien* (Tervuren, Belgium: Musée royale du Congo belge, 1954); A. Barns, *The Wonderland of the Eastern Congo* (New York: Putnam, 1922); and see also the photographs in Jean Rumiya, *Le Rwanda sous le régime du mandat Belge, 1916–31* (Paris: L'Harmattan, 1992), and the discussion by Liisa Malkki in *Purity and Exile: Violence, Memory, and National Cosmology among Hutu Refugees in Tanzania* (Chicago: University of Chicago Press, 1995), esp. ch. 2; and finally, David Newbury, "Understanding Genocide," *African Studies Review* 41, 1 (1998): 73–97.

77. Images in the modern world no longer signify outside their disassociated chains of resonance and are lost to the real, Guy Debord argues in *The Society of the Spectacle* (1967; trans., 1970; New York: Zone Books, 1994). This section and the subhead draw from his work.

78. Jay, "Scopic Regimes of Modernity," 7. The growth of snapshot photography might then be said to have recapitulated the tradition of seventeenth-century Dutch painting, with its "unframed" images and lack of a "clearly situated viewer." See Norman Bryson, *Vision and Painting: The Logic of the Gaze* (New Haven, Conn.: Yale University Press, 1983), 94; Svetlana Alpers, *The Art of Describing: Dutch Art in the Seventeenth Century* (Chicago: University of

Chicago Press, 1983), 138, cited by Jay; and Suren Lalvani, *Photography, Vision, and the Production of Modern Bodies* (Albany: State University of New York Press, 1996), 22.

79. See Nicolas Thomas's discussion of photos of Andaman Islanders in *Colonialism's Culture*, ch. 1; and my discussion of the photographs of Osa Johnson in Paul Landau, "With Gun and Camera in South Africa"; and Christraud Geary, *Images from Bamun*. Two of my Nigerian students pointed out King Njoya's evocation of Hausa-ness in several full-dress photos, which Geary does not remark. Njoya apparently understood the camera's eye in a complex way, sometimes as public and formal, and other times as private and candid. See also Jan Vansina, "Photographs of the Sankuru and Kasai River Basin Expedition Undertaken by Emil Torday (1876–1931) and M. W. Hilton Simpson (1881–1936)," in *Anthropology and Photography, 1860–1920*, ed. Elizabeth Edwards (New Haven, Conn.: Yale University Press, 1992).

80. Kenya youths: see, for example, Martin Johnson and A. Blaney Percival, *Kenya Colony: Camera Studies no. 1* (Nairobi: Government Service, 1936). Other examples from Botswana and other countries may be found in picture books in every major European and American bookstore. South Africa: Ciraj Rassool and Leslie Witz, "South Africa: A World in One Country: Moments in International Tourist Encounters with Wildlife, the Primitive and the Modern," *Cahiers d'Études africaines* 143 (1996): 24–58.

81. *Delivering Views*, ed. Geary and Webb, "Introduction," 2; see also Philippe David, ed., *Inventaire général des cartes postales Fortier* (Saint-Julien-du-Sault: Fostier, 1986–87), and Raymond Corbey, *Wildheid en beschaving: De Europese verbeelding van Afrika* (Baarn, Netherlands: Ambo, 1989), cited by Geary and Webb (not seen by me). This is not to disparage efforts exemplified in the recent conference in St. Louis, Senegal (January 25–27, 1999), "The Preservation and Promotion of the Photographic Heritage of West Africa."

82. Sometimes Lutz's and Collins's analysis verges on self-parody: "the centrality of the race-gender code to decisions about whose breasts to depict cannot be denied," they write, even though it would have been absurd for *National Geographic*'s photographers to have asked Polynesian and Maasai women to cover themselves. See also Eric Savarese, "La femme noire en image," in *L'autre et nous: Scènes et types*, ed. Pascal Blanchard et al. (Paris: Association Connaissance de l'histoire de l'Afrique contemporaine and Syros, 1995), 78–84. I would in fact argue that the nonsexual attitude of photographed peoples exerted a real influence on photographers.

83. As a mode of record-keeping, photographs were important to the expansion of the United States in the American West, Alan Trachtenberg argues in *The Incorporation of America* (New York: Hill & Wang, 1982), 20, cited by Rosalind Krauss in her essay, "Photography's Discursive Spaces," in id., *The Originality of the Avant Garde and Other Modernist Myths* (Cambridge, Mass.: MIT Press, 1985), 133. I have omitted the photographing (and imagining, and painting) of landscapes from this discussion, but one should consult Ryan, *Picturing Empire*, chs. 1 and 2, and the forthcoming work of Hermann Wittenberg.

84. Allen Feldman, "Violence and Vision: The Prosthetics and Aesthetics of Terror," *Public Culture* 10, 1 (Fall 1997), 29, citing Michael Taussig, "Maleficium: State Fetishism," in *Fetishism as Cultural Discourse*, ed. Emily Apter and William Pietz (Ithaca, N.Y.: Cornell University Press, 1993).

85. Benjamin, "Work of Art in the Age of Mechanical Reproduction," 236. "[T]he high point in the diffusion of panoramas coincides with the introduction of [Paris shopping] ar-

cades," Walter Benjamin observes in "Exposé of 1935," in *The Arcades Project*, ed. Rolf Tiedemann (Cambridge, Mass.: Harvard University Press, Belknap Press, 1999), 5.

86. John Markoff, "An Internet Pioneer Ponders the Next Revolution: Talking the Future with: Robert W. Taylor," *New York Times*, December 20, 1999, C38.

87. On "archive," see Michel Foucault, *The Archaeology of Knowledge* (New York: Pantheon Books, 1972), and Sekula, "Body and the Archive." Whereas Edward Said implies in *Orientalism* that an actual Orient stood in opposition to the distortions of Orientalism, Timothy Mitchell argues in "The World as Exhibition," *Comparative Studies in Society and History* 31 (1989): 225, that colonial expositions created "an effect *called* the real world," rejecting the distinction between "a real of representations and the external reality which such representations promise." See Thomas, *Colonialism's Culture*, 21–27.

Chapter 6

Portraits of Modernity: Fashioning Selves in Dakarois Popular Photography

Hudita Nura Mustafa

PICTURING ETHNOGRAPHIC ENCOUNTERS

On my trips over the past several years between Senegal and the United States, my bags have been filled with photos on my way to Dakar and with rolls of exposed film on my way back to the United States. These photos are research documents and tools, as well as souvenirs for my friends and myself. They are seemingly innocent ways to navigate the social terrain of ethnographic research.[1] And yet, like other visual practices, photography is neither purely scientific nor politically innocent. As Jonathan Crary writes, "problems of vision . . . [are] fundamentally questions about the body and the operation of social power."[2] Postcolonial practices around visuality provide glimpses of reclamations of subjugated bodies and selves. Furthermore, according to Abigail Solomon-Godeau, "photography brought into being new configurations and articulations of the body, and new images of masculinity and (especially) femininity which intersect with older modes of representation to produce their own potent and transfiguring admixtures of modernity."[3] A modernist technique of archiving the body, photography is rife with contradictory potentials, as it reveals and conceals, fixes and transforms, subjugates and liberates.[4]

This essay examines the creation and distribution of popular photographic portraiture in Dakar. Defying easy classification, Dakarois portrait photographs are masks and gifts, archive and fetish, conformity and recuperation. Women collect and display photographs of themselves dressed as elegantly as possible, a practice called *sañse*. The wedding album is at the center of the practices that surround portraiture in Dakar, and fashion and comportment are at its center. Indeed, I came to this topic in the course of my fieldwork on the expansion of garment production and fashion in Dakar. As I cultivated friendships and developed a network, I studied the arts of self-presentation, while my interlocutors attempted to (re)form *me* through dress, bodily carriage, work habits, and social obligations. I began to take photographs at important social events to record the occasions for myself and my friends, and as my collection of photographs grew, my photo album became my introduction as a researcher. Eventually I realized the importance of photography in the lives I was studying.[5]

A defining moment in this regard came in 1993, when I attended a family gathering in a poor suburb of Dakar. I was introduced to the father of the house, an elderly man who, only a few months after a major stroke, was nonetheless dressed up in a sky blue boubou for the occasion. Family from around the country had gathered, as they did every three months, dressed in fine clothes and anticipating a lavish midday feast. At first I asked others to take pictures of myself and my friends as mementos. I then approached the younger women for permission to photograph their sañse.[6] They agreed and adopted formal poses for me, as they would for any photographer. As I had the only camera and plenty of film, soon I was asked to take pictures of everyone, individually and in groups. Still mentally alert, the father spotted me and struggled to raise himself up to join in the picture taking. His daughter called me in to his room as she tried to help him, but to no avail, and since there was not enough light by his bedside, we abandoned the effort. The image of the elderly man battling his crippled body to join the photo taking remained with me, a haunting illustration of the importance of pictures to this Senegalese family.

Today photographic collections are commonplace in Senegalese households, and an important form of cultural capital in the several spheres of local life that involve display and exchange. It is crucially linked to the practice of sañse, whereby Senegalese, especially women, craft their social personae. This essay examines such portraiture to show how bodies and selves, once subjugated within a colonial imaginary, have been reclaimed and reformed through postcolonial strategies of self-invention. I begin by sketching the historical trajectory of photography in Senegal, from the colonial era, when Europeans used the camera to catalog ethnic types, up to the postcolonial present, when Africans use the same technology to depict their own culture of distinction. Next I discuss the transformations of Dakar, from cosmopolitan showpiece to site of socioeconomic collapse, as the context of the indigenization and transformation of photographic imaging and its meanings. Against this background, I show how African photography broke with the history of colonial representations by imaging "ordinary" Africans as effective subjects who have mastered the conventions of being *civilisé*. Through these novel images, Africans incorporate photographs into their own commercial, ceremonial, and self-making practices, linking global and local circulations of goods and images. In this context, the photographic collection, in the form of the album, becomes an African woman's prize property and familial archive, continually reinvigorating sartorial display and distinctions. Finally, I argue that the subject's practices of portraiture subverts the colonial male gaze with its own techniques and reframes the feminine body.

Ultimately, I wish to argue that the photographs of well-dressed persons, rather than simply instancing "colonial domination" or the "postcolonial crisis," represent

Figure 6.1. Amateur portrait of a well-dressed person, illustrating *sañse*, Dakar. Photographer unknown, February 1997.

agents who deliberately engage with practices of wealth, transnationalism, and charisma.[7] Here I follow recent cultural critics who reject questions about authenticity and instead consider power and the institutional dynamics of image production, whether by Europeans or Africans.[8] I also concur with Stuart Hall, who reminds us to "think of how these cultures have used the body—as if it was, and it often was, the only cultural capital that we had. We have worked on ourselves as the canvases of representation."[9]

Sañse is a vigorous instance of such practice, the creation of an elegant and refined presentation of self. Portrait photography extended its reach into multiple modes and contexts. Today's photographic images are indeed complicit with local ideologies of wealth and status, colonial ideologies of civilization, and patriarchal ideologies of the feminine as the site and sight of family honor. In the context of socioeconomic crisis, women's strategies rely on complicities with hegemonic constructs of femininity and elegance and with local indices of distinction. It is through such complicities that I read the weave of power and ask, "Whose apparatus? Whose fantasies?"[10]

A BRIEF HISTORY OF PHOTOGRAPHY IN SENEGAL

The practice of photographic recordkeeping in French West Africa began with colonialism, when French settlers, officials, and ethnographers used photographs as documents and memorabilia for circulation in the colonies and in Europe. Photography shaped narratives of progress and brought the dark continent to light for purposes of order and terror, efficiency and pleasure. Photos documented "progress" and "savagery" by showing African land mastered by railroads and scarified African bodies still in need of taming. Photos became postcards, personal memorabilia, and ethnographic documents, tying home and colony together for the European officials and the middle classes to which they presented Africa. Colonial-era postcards, missionary photos, and ethnographic photos provide a wealth of images of persons, buildings, and landscapes.[11] Postcard images mostly document French installation in the four French West African communes (administrative sectors) of Gorée, Saint-Louis, Rufisque, and Dakar and expansion into rural peanut cultivation. Of the total estimated postcard production during the colonial period—8,740 for West Africa—7,210 were made between 1901 and 1918. During this period, postcards were produced by French photographers based mostly in the first and second colonial capitals, Saint-Louis and Dakar.[12] That such images are so plentiful and date from the early colonial period suggests an affinity between the purposes of photography and colonial installation under the rubric of *la mission civilatrice*.

The few archival photographs of Africans or their activities are of the *scène et type* genre of women in supposedly traditional dress.[13] These include 310 "studies" of women and young girls, many semi-nude and embellished with both romantic or racist commentary. One card of an African woman sitting on the ground next to a basket of local plants has the French caption "I remember the sweet smell of their hair." Another shows three young Serer women, uncharacteristically dressed only in loincloths, with the printed caption "West Africa-Senegal-Serer-Nones," while the written message reads, on front, "Samples of beauty," and on the back, "We can say without exaggeration that these are crocodile mouths."[14] Malek Alloula writes of the relationship between postcards of staged, semi-nude Arab women and the colonial gaze in Algeria that "though it be an atomized rerun of this (colonial) discourse, it is, in each instance, its total and accomplished expression, its ever renewed reiteration." The apparent triviality of the postcard, as a mere picture or a simple note, belies its force to circulate images and meanings between colonizer and his constituency at home.[15]

Photography entered African circuits of circulation and display through African-owned, urban studios. In Senegal, studios and presumably the display of portraits on walls, date from the 1920s, but most images that remain in studios' collections date from the 1950s. Exquisite studio portraits from the 1950s reveal objects, poses, and images that linger in today's portraiture. In these early images, European objects such as pens, phones, or flowers designate high status in the way that current images display exotic Swiss cloth, Paloma Picasso sunglasses, or Saudi gold.[16] By the 1950s, a practice called *xoymet* in Wolof had made portraits part of bridal transfers in Saint-Louis.[17] On her wedding night, a bride was carried to her husband's home. His room would be temporarily decorated with ornaments and portraits borrowed from her neighbors and relatives. This must have provided a kind of introduction of her social network to the new family. Portraiture accentuated local preoccupations with self-presentation and provided new forms of interior decoration as urban society developed and stratified.

The internationally acclaimed portrait photographer Seydou Keita of Bamako, Mali, has dedicated fifty years to this form. His work is very similar to that of early Senegalese studio photographers. "Women came in their fancy dress," he said. "So, I positioned them and then spread out the dress. Above all, the attire had to come out in the photo. Hands, long slender fingers, jewels . . . were very important. It was a sign of wealth, elegance, and beauty."[18] He kept European suits, pens, radios, plastic flowers, telephones, and chairs as props for his clients.[19] Clients chose from a variety of poses displayed in photos in the studio. These included standing poses with one hand on a chair, poses with hand held to chin as if musing, chin leaning on folded arms, head tilted to one side, speaking on a phone. Others recline in imitation of the leisurely women of Saint-Louis. Some shots are taken on a diagonal. Those who could, adorned their hair and bodies with gold jewelry, their own or borrowed.[20] Women's images did not rely on European props as much as those of men. The focus on the head, with elaborate African hairstyles and gold decorations, and the hand, with locally hewn gold rings and bracelets suggests that even though French cloth was often bought and sewn into large frocks, French aesthetics were never hegemonic in women's style. Keita claims that he spent time posing clients and guiding them away from bad choices of props and poses, suggesting that the studio portrait was a lengthy, negotiated affair. The works of Mama Casset, the first Senegalese studio photographer, use the same poses. Recent critics suggest that such positioning and shorter focal length in early African portraiture demonstrate a mutuality between sitter and photographer that is absent from colonial photos.[21]

In the 1980s, photography came out of the studio and arrived at everyone's door. The introduction of color laboratories in downtown commercial avenues made it widely accessible, even though few people own their own cameras. Only very affluent families engage professional photographers or studios. Improvising with borrowed 35-mm cameras, itinerant amateurs now dominate the market. Most images are standard facial portraits, and print quality has declined. Studios are usually empty, and their owners are obliged to hit the road in search of business. Everyday life and candid shots are of no interest as photographs. Usually, household interiors provide the settings for the multiple poses that the woman of honor requires. Behind very ordinary doors, vastly different agendas from those of colonial postcards bring photography into women's bedroom cupboards and social spheres. Africans have used a modern technology for their own purposes, defying the logic of colonial indexing in favor of their own version of cultural sophistication.

COSMOPOLITAN DAKAR: A SNAPSHOT

The history of photography in Senegal reflects and shapes larger processes of colonization, decolonization, and modernization. These processes, and their imprint upon photographic practice, are revealed in the development of Dakar as a cultural project. Dakar emerged through colonial investment as the capital of French West Africa. The trading enclaves of Gorée, Saint-Louis, Rufisque, and Dakar were for centuries part of coastal Eurafrican societies of Portuguese, French, Wolof, and Arab influence. They became French communes at the end of the nineteenth century, soon after French West Africa was declared a colonial holding. African residents in the communes became French citizens, while rural Africans were considered subjects. Dakar became a focal point of modernization with a solid infrastructure of schools, clinics, commerce, and military bases. This was to advance what was called in the early colonial period (until the 1920s) the "assimilation" of Africans to superior ways of life. A lively intellectual life, an elegant downtown, and a seaside location give Dakar the name, "the Paris of Africa." It is a regional and, indeed, African center of statecraft, trade, and cultural production. As such, Dakar is a gateway for colonial and transnational connections and projects. It is both a center of French modernization and civilization in Africa and a part of centuries-long trans-Saharan, Eurafrican, and regional exchanges.

But, as is often true of major metropoles, Dakar is also a center of crisis. Notwithstanding its cosmopolitan atmosphere, it exhibits deepening poverty, disintegrating buildings and infrastructure, and, according to residents, degraded social relations. The expanding metropolitan region is now home to a quarter of

Senegal's population. Since the 1970s, regional droughts have turned the city into a magnet for rural and regional migrants. Since the 1980s, the World Bank's structural adjustment programs have led to the dismantling of the educational and employment bases of the urban middle class. In middle-class urban communities, there is a crisis of class identity and patriarchy. Social relations, work, and morality, especially of women, are subjects of rapid change and of debate. Social networks have both proliferated and become more brittle, incapable of meeting deepening needs. As middle-class women became entrepreneurs, especially in garment production, they became pillars of familial survival and targets of moral critique. Their work in public spaces, their patterns of consumption, and their dress and ceremonies are seen as dangerous signs of autonomy and even narcissism.[22]

At the same time, new kinds of cultural capital have become important markers of class. As education becomes a less certain path to advancement, commerce and small business have become the new ground of the middle class. New commercial elites with rural Mouride origins are emerging as economic and cultural leaders,[23] their consumption habits and world travels setting the pace for the urban middle class.[24] Matters of distinction—cultural capital, cosmopolitan flair, specialized knowledge, hierarchies of objects and taste, prestige display, bodily excellence—are increasingly important. Within the domain of cultural capital, surface matters.

In the terrain of distinction, the body is a key site for developing various ideologies of propriety, civility, and elegance. Grounded in a regional as well as local Dakarois history of beauty, prevalent conventions of the elegant person include the distinct restraint and bodily adornment valued by Wolof society, norms of modesty said to be Islamic, and French standards of fashionability. It is no surprise that *civilisé*, French for "civilized," has entered the lexicon of urban Wolof to mean cleanliness, sophistication, and orderliness. The epitome of civilisé is the elegant, fashionable woman with her carefully tended and adorned body. Photographic portraits of these bodies have graced Africans' walls and picture albums since the 1920s. No longer solely a program of reform of Africans, civilization in the form of modern techniques like photographic imaging is now enmeshed in African communities and practices.

I situate photography in the long history of colonial civilizing projects and the recent emergence of what I call the "sartorial ecumene." By this I mean linkages between local and transnational circulations of images, objects, events, and discourses of dress and adornment. Women's circulation practices are critical to these linkages. Like fashion, photography has been amenable to women's strategies of self-representation, diversification of wealth forms, and status advancement. Rather than assimilating Africans to Europe, photography reinvigorated long-standing local contests for prestige and respectability. To be worthwhile, the dress and conduct of the civilisé must be recognized in collective efforts such as social events, visual records, and gossip. Furthermore, the popular practice of the civilisé is independent of education, language, and other signs of francophilic civilization, which barely reach ordinary women. Their images speak not to French interlocutors, but to local rivals, albeit with a lexicon partially wrought through the colonial experience.

WEDDINGS, TAILORS, AND TELEVISION

As Africans have taken photography into their spheres of circulation, photography has both restructured and been restructured by their practices. The culture of display involves the interweaving of images, commodities, bodies, stories, and performances in practices around photographs. In the sartorial ecumene, the photograph is both an image of a performance and an object with its own trajectory. Photographs are bought, collected, displayed, and exchanged like other prize commodities such as cloth.[25] As mementos of cloth and events, they fuel nostalgia, desire, rivalry, and commodification. This is most evident in ceremonial events, personal collections, and fashion circuits. As a new valued commodity and a mechanism of commodification, photography heightens the pace and allure of fashion and ceremonies throughout social networks. Men are peripheral to women's circuits of collection, gift-giving, and socializing, which now incorporate photos. In this way, photography invigorates African traditional practice, while inserting African communities into global trends such as fashion, and providing another element in women's spheres of exchange and representation. For the middle classes, this domain is critical for consolidating networks, claiming and distributing wealth, competing for status among peers, and contesting elite distinction. Women both control commodities and commodify themselves. Photographs extend the circulations of the sartorial ecumene to larger networks and over time.

Despite the crisis in marriage and patriarchy, marriage remains a formative institution in gender and familial relations and is relevant to issues of display and appearance in three ways. First, fashion, as competition among women, is seen as a direct result of a crisis of marriage. For young people, marriage is now only a distant possibility, because new households have increasingly become financially unfeasible. For young women this means competition for eligible bachelors, or at least for their resources in courtship. Prostitution in various forms is also prevalent. Second, a married woman's physical appearance is seen as a direct reflection of her husband's well-being and his esteem for her. Family reputation and access to credit and networks is linked to women's appearance and conduct. Three, and crucially, women's influence upon male authority is seen to occur privately and in part through the power of beauty and charm. This is encapsulated in the saying that men are the head of the household and women are head of the bedroom. This complex relationship between social reproduction, authority, influence, and appearance is widely recognized. Yet the rise of fashion is widely seen as part of a culture of narcissism and moral decay.

Photographic techniques have migrated through many contexts and purposes in Senegal. In order to answer the questions, "Whose apparatus? Whose fantasy?"

we must look at the specific practices for which photography is used. The staging, circulation, and interpretation of socialities and selves in Dakarois women's photography relates to what Rosalind Krauss calls the "discursive space of photography."[26] In the sartorial ecumene, a woman is allowed a day of unchallenged elegance and fame at her wedding or her first child's naming ceremony. In portraits, the social space that grounds beauty institutionally is represented not by its inclusion in the image (i.e., money changing hands, gifts of cloth being given) but through the extraordinary beauty of an individual. Such beauty is known to be possible only through either collective effort or, in the case of new businesswomen, commercial success.

Photography has restructured the funding and timing of social events to highlight individual displays of sartorial excellence. Today, the parade of entrances are also photo shoots with congregations of amateurs awaiting guest arrivals. For most guests, it is a time to appear, pay one's respects, and nothing else. In fact, the music is so loud and the crowds so great that intimate socializing is difficult. The woman of honor, in each of her two to four outfits, makes the rounds of her guests for photo shots. Young men circulate, offering to take portraits of guests seated. Then they rush off to one-hour labs and return to sell the photos, or, if they cannot make it back in time, deliver them to their customers the next day. In 1992–94, photos sold for CFA 500 each but could be bargained down to CFA 350 (U.S.$1.50). Before going to such ceremonies, women try to siphon coins off a male suitor, a friend, or the household budget to buy a photo. I have never been to a wedding or baptism without photographic recording.

I discovered that photos are a form of women's property in my interviews about wedding expenses and negotiations. Although the cost of visual recording is covered by the groom, the videos and photos are kept by the bride, to be brought out from locked cupboards and other hiding places on social occasions. Visual recording is expensive. One videotape taken over a day or evening, cost CFA 12,000 for the man and equipment and CFA 2,500 for the blank tape. This is a hefty price gauged against a small businessperson's income of CFA 40,000 per month or even a bureaucrat's salary of CFA 80,000. For amateurs, this can provide a family income. One man told me that he had long been unemployed and now supported his family with weekend photography, earning a modest but respectable CFA 30,000 a month. For consumers, the need for photos, like the need for feminine adornment, justifies claims made on another's income, not only for private enjoyment, but also for redistribution as gifts. Several of the photos in my own album were given to me as gifts. This pattern of claims and redistribution is often deemed wasteful, but, as with clothing demands, it gives those without income access to resources. For income-earning women, expenses related to display secure their reputation and are part of their own self-aggrandizement. Women traders display large portraits of themselves at home and in their shops, impressing guests and customers with their elegance.

While the most important use of photographs is the sartorial display of ceremonial life, other moments are sometimes documented. One unique image I was shown documents the process of gift exchange. This was an image of a young friend, sixteen years of age, whose fashion desires were subsidized by her wealthy sister and her mother. She proudly showed me her wardrobe of clothing and a photo album that was already full. Among the pictures was one of her on the family couch, draped only in a long, green cloth, with one bare shoulder, normally an improper demeanor. She explained to me that her sister had given her the cloth for a religious holiday and she loved it so much that she wanted a picture of it before it was cut. The cloth was subsequently embroidered as a ceremonial garment at an elite shop at her sister's expense. I took a photograph of her in the finished boubou and gave her a copy for her album. Her first album and emerging collection of garments marked her initiation into the fashion system with familial support. This was a rare case in which the sequence of exchanges leading to sartorial display was explicit rather than implicit.

Garment producers' albums present garments at another point in their circulation. In the domain of production in the market and atelier, garments are presented as a portfolio of styles for potential consumption, objects outside of a context of use. Clients choose styles from tailors' albums for copying or modification. Such images often show just the necklines with embroidery or garnishes. Garment producers are ambivalent about photography because itinerant photographers own the negatives, putting what we might call intellectual property at stake. Once the images are taken, they can be reproduced and sold for CFA 250. Even portraits taken at events are sold for the sake of the embroidery design, without the knowledge of the subject. Because this practice places original designs in public circulation, some tailors do not allow photographs of their work. Photography extends the circuit and pace of fashion but deprives artisans of control over their original products.

Visual culture pervades urban popular culture and contributes to the definitive role of sartorial practice. Like photography, television fuels local exchange and channels global images into local fashion. As I learned the lexicon of urban material culture, I began to see double in the saris and straight hair lifted from Indian films, and the slit skirts called "Alexis" after the character from the American soap opera *Dynasty*. Television disseminates the products of elite Dakar designers. They dress the nightly news broadcasters as well as political and religious elites for official functions.[27] Indeed, the televised fashion contests hosted by the national textile firm SOTIBA are credited with having intensified fashion in the 1980s. Old Paris fashion journals as well as those from Abidjan and Dakar also serve to internationalize local fashion. Other effects are not simply dissemination but the continual presence of images, which serve as models upon which their copies, actually realized styles, are judged. For instance, as I photographed a neighbor at a wedding, I realized that he was standing under a portrait of the family marabout, his own flowing white embroidered robe duplicating the picture. On another occasion, while observing the work process in a hair salon, I looked beyond to the wall calendar, which depicted the same hairstyle that the stylist was shaping in front of

Figure 6.2. Sotiba fashion show. Photo by Hudita Mustafa, 1992.

me. Such unplanned doublings demonstrate the pervasiveness of fashion as a cultural practice.

COLONIAL ARCHIVES, FAMILIAL ARCHIVES, FIELD NOTES

Crucial to the power of the image as object is the capacity for "both stimulating and channeling remembrance."[28] How, for whom, and with what consequences does this channeling occur? If African women have been subjugated through colonial regimes of visuality, they now actively position themselves through photography. In the practices around such image-objects, women turn an assigned responsibility, to appear, into a space from which to make intense demands on familial resources and to assert their own excellence and prestige. Their practice asserts a local vision of modernity that places its subjects thickly amid current events, global flows, and personal trajectories. Displacing the indexical body of ethnic types, they play with the body surface to weave truth and masking as self-mastery. Portraits position ordinary women as *civilité* enacted through the body. The colonial archive, always distant from African spheres of circulation, remains so even as its technologies have been mobilized for multiple local projects of making selves, hierarchies of distinction, and familial archives.

The collecting of photographs by women—under mattresses, in wallets, in albums—reinvigorates the power of beauty to celebrate individuals and communities as well as enforce hierarchies of distinction. Practices around photographs such as posing, borrowing money, dressing, collecting photos in albums, exchanging them as gifts, and scrutinizing them suggest that the power of the photographic script extends, in dispersed ways, to daily life. Although men maintain small collections of photographs, women collect, archive, and continually refer to photos in albums. The album as an archive extends the power of the portrait through time and extended networks. Albums, kept in cupboards, under beds, or under tables, are brought out for visitors as part of recounting recent events or even as a welcoming gesture to a less familiar guest. Older urban families hold old studio photographs from the 1950s and 1960s, which they keep and prize for their elegance and grandeur. "In Dar-Refayil's narrative memory, time is punctuated by the quotidian use of domestic objects and relationships," Joëlle Bahloul writes of family reunions in Algeria. "It is a slow time, interrupted only by imprecise dates.... The narration of family reunions is a verbal family reunion: time in domestic memory is woven into the structure of genealogical history." As performed memory, these reunions cover the system of objects, including wall photographs.[29] Old studio portraits often decorate walls in Dakar. In many homes, deceased male bureaucrats from the 1960s and 1970s have left impoverished widows and unemployed children. In these dark living rooms, which now double as sleeping quarters, portraits framed with peeling paint are reminders of the proper middle class status that should have been.

In everyday use, albums remind one both of days of splendor and times of sorrow. Not only clothing but personal fates are scrutinized and compared. During an interview of a friend about her wedding, she soon pulled out her ceremonial boubous, already relegated to everyday wear. Then she pulled out her album from the same locked cupboard. She described with pride the cloth, money, and gold that had been exchanged. As we went through the album, image after image of splendor and artifice, she remembered the fortunes of some of her guests. In examining photos and remembering persons, many lives are rehearsed, from divorce to death to rich suitors. Albums are also part of the circulation of gifts and of nostalgia. Photos are pulled spontaneously from albums and given away. Many album photos are given as mementos or paid for by friends or suitors. Several friends

Figure 6.3. Wall in the atelier of an old tailor, Dakar. Photo by Hudita Mustafa, 1993.

identified important relationships as we went through albums. Leafing through an album locates a viewer within the owners' personal history of courtship, ceremony, and sartorial practice.

Today's proliferation of portraits of African women relishes specificity and presence in contrast to the typologizing of the colonial archive. The form of images may be standardized, but their purpose is to memorialize specific moments in individual life histories. The portraits that fill albums and adorn walls today show women dressed in their finest ceremonial wear: embroidered boubous, gold jewelry, elaborate coiffures, and headscarves (see figure 6.1). As archives, photographs renew the beauty and charisma of the person portrayed and document the solidarity of communities that produce events and persons. They extend the magicality of dress and events through time, place, and networks. Souvenirs, writes Susan Stewart, are metonyms of the original object or event, and require supplemental narration.[30] Photographs operate in this manner to refer to an event and enable its continual retelling and dispersal. Sometimes, the fragility of lived experience is in poignant contrast to the commemorative capacity of photographs.

I had acquaintances who separated after a few months due to financial hardship. Yet the video of their week-long, Toucouleur wedding circulated and was replayed among relatives long after their marriage had deteriorated. In this case, visual images not only created memory, but were the last traces of a fleeting effort to found a household amid socioeconomic collapse.

The wedding album is the pillar of the system of objects that surrounds portraiture. In my view, it has its precedent in the *xoymet* (Wolof) practice in bridal transfer of the 1940s, 1950s, and 1960s. A friend, Deinaba, showed me a wedding album filled with her portraits. She wore three outfits with different hairstyles in the morning, afternoon, and night. For each outfit in a sequence, she was photographed in different poses and perspectives—head shots, torso, full length—and she also had group photos with guests. This portfolio with some 200 photos cost about CFA 40,000, again, a month's wage for a low-level bureaucrat or trader, two weeks' wages for the middle-class bureaucrats who indulge in them. This family lived in a village outside Dakar. The patriarch was a technical manager and first-generation urbanized. The wedding was acclaimed as one of the most lavish in recent times. She spoke to me not just of the effect, but of the labor and pain that it had required. When another friend showed me her wedding album, she detailed to me the cost of the cloth and the cost and time required for the hairstyle: "This was the evening dress, it cost CFA 6,500 a meter. Mati Gueye [an elite designer] made it.... I had to go to the salon three times to try it. The hair took two hours in the morning and it cost 15,000. I went to the salon in the morning and evening.... I was so, so tired, I was crying just before this photo." The photograph was still very poised, and it was impossible to tell the distress that she was experiencing.

The narratives structured through albums highlight personal mastery of the signs of beauty, fashion, and composure. In a wedding or baptism album, multiple poses of the woman honored occupy at least the first half of the album, while group shots might be placed in the second half.[31] Household spaces appear in images to display expensive bedroom suites, bridewealth, or the living room furniture of wealthier homes. Another popular pose is seated on a bed or stool facing a mirror or looking off into the distance away from the camera. Poses are copied throughout the range of educational and income ranks. Facial expressions were grave and yet indirect. Young women are most likely to smile or look straight at the camera. Head and shoulder shots, usually at a slight angle to the face, were common. The most common pose is of the subject seated in a chair at ceremonies. Reclining poses on beds or sofas recur in the 1950s images and even now as imitations of the *saint-louisienne* woman of leisure. Most group shots are of brides or new mothers with a group of guests. Shots of sisters, close friends, or, less frequently, co-wives are not uncommon. An album might contain one picture of a woman together with her husband or new baby. Mixed-gender images, candid shots, or scenes of everyday life are very rare.

Visual documents have powerful inculcative effects. They make community life—the dress, music, social events—accessible to children before they can understand

Figure 6.4. Wedding photo of a bride with guests in a living room. Photo by Hudita Mustafa, 1993.

language or attend such events. For instance, I had a neighbor who often played the video of her two-year-old's baptism. The child could not fully understand language, but she could already identify the video as her own baptism and recognize herself wrapped up in the ceremonial cloth. As children imitate their mother's hair care rituals in their own gestures, they also learn to pose correctly from seeing photos. In my own experience of picture taking, even young girls of ten who had not been to many ceremonies had already developed a sense of conduct and of posing for photographs. For a picture that I took, a young friend of mine adopted a grave face and carefully held her shoulders at an angle to the camera. Through visual mementos, children are inducted into fashion and ceremonial life as witnesses before they can participate. As girls are initiated into the fashion system, they start going to tailors, attending ceremonies and dances, and collecting photos. One young man said that he had noticed his teenage sisters starting albums, and dressing in fancy clothes and gold, and he realized that his mother's resources were now focused on their social advancement. Facing a collapsed university system and hoping to attend a school overseas, he looked upon his mother's investment of CFA 50,000 in fashion with sour disapproval.

PORTRAITS OF MODERNITY   187

Figure 6.5. Seated guests at a naming ceremony. Photo by Hudita Mustafa, 1993.

Again, my own inculcation into local life both came from and resulted in the formation of my own album. I began to take pictures, receive them as gifts, and buy them from itinerants. Without any strategizing on my part, this quickly became a very effective introduction and research tool, and I often carried it with me to interviews. After my first year, I bought the usual cheap, Taiwanese album in the market, its plastic cover showing a little blonde girl, playing grown-up in a big hat and pearls. (Other covers depicted what I thought would be controversial images such as couples walking on the beach, playing tennis, or kissing in a park.) My album began with pictures of myself, family, and friends, including informal and candid shots. I included landscapes of places that I frequented and scenes from my student life. I then started to collect photos of friends and events that I attended in Dakar. During my interviews I would often ask about a woman's wardrobe, to get a sense of what she owned, how she acquired it, what styles or colors she preferred. Women often showed me their clothing, and albums always accompanied any discussion of ceremonies or clothing. In short, photography, without my realizing, came to pervade my life as well.

REFRAMING THE BODY

Like masks, portraits are strategic presentations of partial truths:[32] women work on themselves as canvases of representation, navigating the relative risks of display and concealment to forge their social selves.[33] The loan asked for discreetly, the boubou balanced delicately on the shoulder, these are acts of mastery and dignity. Posing, whether in the mirror, during a ceremony, or for a portrait involves a positioning, both material and representational. "I lend myself to the social game, I pose, I know I am posing, I want you to know that I am posing," Roland Barthes writes. But where Barthes fears the alteration of his individuality, I see such moments of (self-)objectification neither as loss nor as figments of generic ideals or cloaks of true selves, but as self-transformations.[34] Dakarois women claim their proper place in the hierarchy of elegance with portraits.

In the postcolonial context, posing, as a deliberate performance of the self, points to what Okwui Enwezor calls a "negotiated space" between colonial and postcolonial identities. On the one hand, popular photography is complicit with colonial indexing insofar as it uses colonial techniques and lexicons for African purposes of self-definition and self-assertion. On the other hand, African and European photographic projects reveal different political intentions and ambitions, reflected in the focus on subjects who are naked or clothed, savage or sophisticated, anonymous or named. The image and its politics are consequential.[35]

Photos and fashion are bridges for the emergence of other selves. Photos enable women to inhabit themselves as elegant, dignified beings, outside of the grueling routine of housework, social relations, and financial hardship. Their portraits preserve the extraordinary. Again quoting Enwezor, "portrait photography is the record of the model's self-inquiry . . . [portraits are] archetypes, models for the way their sitters wanted to appear . . . the portrait is therefore the outcome of an elaborate constitutive process."[36] Photographer, sitter, and viewer not only bring preconceived ideas of the elegant to bear upon the image but produce such ideas through the image. Portraits reconstitute the body of labor, reproduction, and patriarchy into that of beauty, elegance, and wealth. In so doing, they both reveal and conceal the essential self.

The viewing of portraits is, therefore, as important as their creation. It involves what Allan Sekula calls the private sentimental moment of individuation and celebration of the individual, as well as a "look up" and a "look down" across social scales.[37] This is evident in the kinds of judgments that portraits elicit. While, typically, in the United States, one comments upon the likeness of the photo to the person, or on the beauty of eyes or hair, in Senegal the issue is the execution of the techniques of sañse. Assessments of the finesse of eye makeup are common, as are comments on the styling of satin bridal ensembles. With portraits, women thus situate themselves and one another in hierarchies of taste, placing themselves under public scrutiny in order to make and remake their public personae.

If extraordinary public selves are created through sañse, portraits locate these selves and their prototypes in multiple archives, from private wedding albums to local newspapers to international television shows. Photography has thus assisted the "sartorial ecumene" that links local and transnational circuits of exchange and has reinvigorated the social practices through which Senegalese women—and men—shape their lives. It has also assisted the redefinition of civilisé away from the mastery of neocolonial institutions, which are falling apart, to the mastery of public reputations, which can always be reclaimed and reformed. With dress and photos, Dakarois women construct selves that are as fashionable as European "others" and as sophisticated as the ensconced African elite, exemplars of distinction, composure, and creativity amid the social and economic dangers that surround them.

NOTES

1. This essay draws on fieldwork conducted in Dakar between 1991 and 1994 with primarily Wolof, Muslim, middle-class garment-producers and -consumers. Dissertation research was funded by the Wenner-Gren Foundation for Anthropological Research, and the Social Science Research Council Africa Program. I consider my transactions in the fieldwork context treacherous because they involve multiple agendas on both my part and my interlocutors' part. I offered my small gifts both in friendship and as compensation for assistance. The issue of compensation, as with any kind of monetary or gift exchange in that society, was complicated. While many persons were supportive of me and my work, it was also understood and brought up that my work was of no use to them.

2. This is the central argument of Jonathan Crary, *Techniques of the Observer: On Vision and Modernity in the Nineteenth Century* (Cambridge: Cambridge University Press, 1992). In a Foucauldian analysis, he argues that modern European practices of vision emerged as part of new disciplinary forms of power that reshaped the relationship between the subject's body and society.

3. Abigail Solomon-Godeau, "The Legs of the Countess," in *Fetishism as Cultural Discourse,* ed. William Pietz and Emily Apter (Ithaca, N.Y.: Cornell University Press, 1993), 270.

4. In a provocative formulation, Allan Sekula challenges liberal histories of the democratization of photography. He suggests that in the nineteenth century, it introduced the panoptic principle into everyday life. Allan Sekula, "The Body and the Archive," in *The Contest of Meaning: Critical Histories of Photography,* ed. Richard Bolton (Cambridge, Mass.: MIT Press, 1989), 376. I also recall here Stuart Hall, "What Is This 'Black' in Black Popular Culture?" in *Representing Blackness: Issues in Film and Video,* ed. Valerie Smith (New Brunswick, N.J.: Rutgers University Press, 1997), who characterizes diasporic black popular culture as internally contradictory because of its use of dominant forms to express resistance or self-definitions.

5. In another case, however, I faced vehement accusations that "You're going to take that back to Paris" by a woman trader as I tried to photograph the sheep trade during the 1993 Id-ul-Hajj season.

6. *Sañse*, which is actually Wolof-French Creole, refers to a total outfit of dress, hair, and jewelry.

7. I have argued elsewhere that the rise of fashion and ceremonial exchange indicates both the mediation of socioeconomic crisis by women and the use by women of a designated responsibility to secure resources and status for themselves. The navigation of economic hardship in a dignified manner is enabled through practices and principles that manage social relations and their own selves. Many people told me that appearances are deceiving in Senegal, and I found this to be the case. Elegance in appearance is not necessarily a sign of education, worldliness, or wealth.

8. See *Anthropology and Photography*, ed. Elizabeth Edwards (New Haven, Conn.: Yale University Press, 1992), on the intertwined histories of these two fields. See Malek Alloula, *The Colonial Harem* (Minneapolis: University of Minnesota Press, 1986), on French colonial postcards in Algeria.

9. Hall, "What Is This 'Black' in Black Popular Culture?"

10. "Who owns the image?" Okwui Enwezor asks in *In/Sight: African Photographers from 1940 to the Present* (New York: Guggenheim Museum, 1996), a catalogue of works by and discussions of modern African art photographers.

11. Each genre had its own circuits of producers, consumers, and exhibitions. See Chris Geary, "Missionary Photographs: Private and Public Readings," *African Arts* 24, 4 (1991): 48–59.

12. See David Prochaska, "Fantasia of the Photothèque: French Views of Colonial Senegal" in *African Arts*, 24, 4 (1991): 40–47. Prochaska tells us that there was a steady drop in such images in the early and mid twentieth century. He suggests that one or two photographers were working in Thiès, Rufisque, Ziguinchor, and Kayes, all regional centers or towns associated with the peanut trade. When World War II began, besides a couple of studios in Saint-Louis, all photo producers were to be found in Dakar.

13. There are no photos of urban elites, traditional elites, or mixed-race persons reported in the research from the Dakar archives so far. Geary's work on missionary and colonial photos does show many of royalty. I found several also of tailors, and of school children in classrooms.

14. Prochaska, "Fantasia of the Photothèque."

15. Alloula, *Colonial Harem*, 103. Even today there is a separate sphere of photography that is unavailable—or of no interest—to Africans. Tourist postcards and expensive coffee-table books are sold in the elite Plateau district. The pornographic imagination continues today in these books and cards with studio shots of bare-breasted African women, usually staged.

16. See Jean M. Borgatti and Richard Brilliant, *Likeness and Beyond: Portraits from Africa and the World* (New York: Center for African Art, 1990), for a review of portraiture across cultures, which place several African art forms in this genre.

17. Niang Fatou Niang Siga, *Reflets de modes et traditions saint-louisiennes* (Dakar: Éditions Khoudia, 1990). Such hybrid practices abound in Africa for ceremonial use, for instance in effigies or shrines.

18. André Magnin, "Seydou Keita," *African Arts* 28, 3 (1995): 90–95. An offshoot of this genre of portraits are the glass paintings Senegalese artists began doing in the 1950s, which duplicate studio photographs or other images. These are popular among the local elite, expatriates, and tourists.

19. One of my early snapshots of friends shows the grandmother of the house holding the phone receiver to her ear as if conversing. She did this as I was about to take the picture as a pose. Phones are still signs of wealth and modern lifestyles.

20. The editors were unable to secure permission to reprint an image that exemplifies this trend.

21. See Enwezor in *In/Sight*.

22. I have elsewhere argued that such practices can be better seen as stemming from deliberate strategies for increasing incomes; see n. 24.

23. The Mouride, an Islamic brotherhood, is a powerful social organization in Senegal. From a base in rural peanut cultivation during the colonial period, it has grown into a partner of the state. In response to ecological crisis in the region, it has expanded into urban and, since the 1980s, transnational bases in the informal sector and trade. Mourides now form a powerful and wealthy trade diaspora with enormous political clout in Senegal.

24. Hudita Mustafa, "Practicing Beauty: Crisis, Value and the Challenge of Self-Mastery in Dakar, 1970–1994" (Ph.D. diss., Harvard University, 1998), uses the case of garment production and fashion to examine these shifts.

25. Photographic amulets of religious leaders display yet another logic of charisma as the crystallization of dynastic power. The maraboutic leaders in Senegal all have their pictures made and sold in the form of photographs, posters, and amulets. There is a vigorous economy involving tithing, prayers, and amulets of various kinds, from washed Koranic fragments to photos. These circuits commodify the sacred and also extend maraboutic presence.

26. Rosalind Krauss, "The Discursive Space of Photography," in *The Contest of Meaning: Critical Histories of Photography*, ed. Richard Bolton (Cambridge, Mass.: MIT Press, 1989).

27. The most eminent woman designer in the city dresses the television newscasters. They are usually in embroidered robes, called *boubous* locally, which have spread her fame much further than the small circle of Senegalese and African elites that she regularly serves.

28. Joëlle Bahloul, *The Architecture of Memory: A Jewish-Muslim Household in Colonial Algeria, 1937–1962* (New York: Cambridge University Press, 1996), 135.

29. Ibid.

30. Susan Stewart, *On Longing: Narratives of the Miniature, the Gigantic, the Souvenir, the Collection* (Durham, N.C.: Duke University Press, 1993), 170.

31. Jean François Werner, "Produire les images en Afrique: L'example des photographies de studio," *Cahiers d'Études africaines* 36, 1 (1996): 81–112, discusses studios in Bouake, Ivory Coast. Werner sees portraits, outside of the ritual of studio staging, as signs of growing individualism. In this case, I see them as a sign of tension between a culture of narcissism and the collective effort that the event represents.

32. In Borgatti and Brilliant, *Likeness and Beyond*, Jean Borgatti identifies three overlapping genres of African portraiture. First, anthropomorphic portraits assemble objects, such as a deceased's possessions, to portray not the human figure but its accomplishments and social position. Second, representational forms present a physical likeness to the person such as life-size effigies. Third, emblematic portraiture uses objects or portions of a figure, such as tusks carved with symbols of a character trait. Photographs have been incorporated into these African forms of portraiture. Borgatti presents examples of their use instead of effigies, as replacements for twin statues, and in composite shrines that combine photos and local artistic products. In general, Borgatti claims that African portraits emphasize community ideals of beauty and conduct, whereas, while photographic portraits in the modern West also rely on conventions, they do so in celebration of the autonomous bourgeois individual.

33. I paraphrase here from Hall, "What Is This 'Black' in Black Popular Culture?" who writes of the excellence in diasporic black popular culture of using the body in cultural production.

34. Ritual masking stops with the Diola in the Casamance. There is no Wolof or Toucoleur practice of masking, where art instead relies on either performance or adornment such as jewelry, weaving, hair braiding, and cloth dying.

35. Roland Barthes, *Camera Lucida: Reflections on Photography* (New York: Hill & Wang, 1983), 11, 34.

36. *In/Sight*, 33.

37. Sekula, "Body and the Archive," 376. Every "look at the frozen gaze of the loved one" is shadowed by a "look up" and a "look down," evoking both ambition and fear.

Chapter 7

Mami Wata and Santa Marta: Imag(in)ing Selves and Others in Africa and the Americas

Henry John Drewal

Sometime soon after their first fifteenth-century encounters with European visitors from across the seas, people in Africa added to their ancient pantheons of water deities a spirit that has come to be know as Mami Wata, pidgin English for "Mother of Water." Since then they have been developing a complex and elaborate iconography, taking exotic (and indigenous) images and objects, interpreting them, investing them with new meanings, and then re-presenting them in inventive ways to serve their aesthetic, devotional, and social needs. Among those images were nineteenth-century European images of a snake charmer. More recently in the Americas, Voudoun devotees in Haiti and Santeria followers in the United States have taken that same image in order to define and represent an African Santa Marta / Saint Martha. This essay explores this circumatlantic visual history, tracing its evolution, contexts, and significances in shaping personal and community identities. Combining the object-orientation of art history, the contextual-orientation of anthropology, and the individual case study perspective of psychology, I consider three episodes in the visual history of Mami Wata: (1) a European representation of an exotic "other" that became implicated in Mami Wata's art history in Africa; (2) case histories of the assemblages of this European image and other alien objects on Mami Wata shrines in Africa; and (3) the re-presentation and transformation of Mami Wata into an African Catholic saint in the Americas.[1] Finally, I consider my own practices of analysis and interpretation of others' visual culture as homologous with those of Mami Wata followers and suggest what implications this may have for transcultural studies in general. In all these stories, I argue that images are expressions of agency and self-actualization.

By "agency," I mean the instrumentality of creating one's reality—the process of turning aspirations into practices and products. Such agency never occurs in a vacuum or by accident. Rather, it emerges out of what already exists. It is a response to events and situations, some that open up possibilities, others that close them off. Thus people shape culture and history, just as culture and history shape them in complex ways. In defining others, people simultaneously define themselves.

A people's visual culture consists of all images and objects used by them, whether locally produced or imported. Those from elsewhere—creations of other systems of thought and action that have been recontextualized—reveal as much about the users as objects produced by them. Moreover, people intentionally or unintentionally use the objects of others to define themselves. Museums, defined as institutions intended for the storage, analysis, and display of the objects of others, are good examples. As George Stocking explains, we as alien observers collect the objects of "others—of human beings whose similarity or difference is experienced... as in some profound way problematic."[2]

As we begin to reflect on our own uses of the objects of others in defining ourselves, we may explore how others engage in similar practices. For example, in Togo, the Ewe and Mina peoples have a number of societies (*tigari, goro, kunde*) for the detection and control of antisocial persons. When spirits come during possession trances, the Ewe or Mina devotees speak, dress, eat, dance, and sing as "foreigners," that is, as Hausa or Mossi. Thus Ewe and Mina mediums become outsiders in order to deal with antisocial insiders.

THE SNAKE CHARMER IMAGE IN EUROPE

The West has had a long and enduring fascination with exotic societies, which serves to satisfy its own internal needs. The romantic movement of nineteenth-century Europe was a form of escapism, a reaction against the harsh realities and social upheavals associated with the early Industrial Revolution. Material about the exotic appeared in many travelers' accounts, some of which, as Philip Curtin remarks, contain "an interest blending genuine intellectual curiosity with a libidinous fascination for descriptions of other people who break with impunity the taboos of one's own society."[3]

By the second half of the nineteenth century, the European interest in the exotic had spread beyond the upper and middle classes to a much wider audience. In the Victorian era of rigid social norms, strict moralistic tenets, and repressed desires, people turned to the exotic to provide a "temporary *frisson*, a circumscribed experience of the bizarre."[4] Institutions such as botanical and zoological gardens, ethnographic museums, and especially circuses provided the means of such an escape. One of the most important centers for these developments was the northern German port and trading center of Hamburg. Hamburg, in many ways, was Europe's gateway to the exotic. It was an important member and leader of the Hanseatic League, a group of wealthy independent city-states on the North Sea that developed powerful export/import companies, whose vessels plied the world's oceans. Hamburg's contacts with distant lands fed the popular European appetite for things exotic. For one, illustrated accounts of adventures abroad proliferated in books, magazines, and newspapers. For another, the exotic became literally tangible as a growing number of African, Asian, and Indian sailors appeared in the port of Hamburg and other maritime centers in Europe.[5] As the fascination with the exotic grew, so did the need to clarify it.

A man named Carl G. C. Hagenbeck realized the business potential of the situation. Hagenbeck was a fish merchant in the port area of Hamburg (St. Pauli) that was also noted as an "entertainment" center for sailors and others. In 1848, a fisherman who worked the Arctic waters brought some sea lions to Hagenbeck, who exhibited them as a zoological attraction. The immediate success of the venture led to a rapidly enlarged menagerie of exotic animals from Greenland, Africa, and Asia.[6]

Sensing the public's enormous appetite for things bizarre, Hagenbeck decided to expand his imports to include exotic people. The first, in 1875, were a family of Laplanders, who accompanied a shipment of reindeer. This was the modest beginning of a new concept in popular entertainment—the *Völkerschauen*, or "people shows."[7] In order to advertise these attractions, Hagenbeck turned to Adolf Friedlander, a leading printer, who quickly adapted the multicolored lithography techniques pioneered in Germany in the 1860s to cheaply reproduce posters advertising Hagenbeck's circuses and "people shows."[8]

Hagenbeck was soon producing a series of ambitious shows, involving a "Nubia Caravan" from the Gordon-Pascha expedition to the White Nile in 1876, Eskimos in 1878, and people from the Sudan, India, and Ceylon in 1880, and from Somalia in 1885. In 1886, Hagenbeck produced a minispectacle, trumpeted as his "International Circus and Ceylonese Caravan," which included seventy artists or craftspersons, jugglers and magicians, musicians, and many wild animals, and was seen by over a million people within a six-week period.[9]

In about 1880, Hagenbeck hired a famous hunter named Breitwiser to travel to Southeast Asia and the Pacific to collect rare snakes, insects, and butterflies. In addition to fauna, Breitwiser brought back a wife, who soon began to perform as a snake charmer in Hagenbeck's show under the stage name of "Maladamajaute." A photograph of her, taken about 1887 in a Hamburg studio, shows her attired for her performance.[10] In it, various accoutrements of dress and ornamentation duplicate the features of a well-known snake charmer chromolithograph, the original of which almost certainly came from the Freidlander lithography company. These include the style and cut of Maladamajaute's bodice, the stripes made of buttons, the coins about her waist, the armlets, the position of the snake around her neck and a second one nearby, the nonfunctional bifurcated flute held in her hand, and her facial features and coiffure.[11]

There can be little doubt that Maladamajaute was the model for the chromolithograph. Her light brown skin placed her beyond Europe, while the boldness of her gaze and the strangeness of her occupation epitomized the *otherness*, the mystery and wonder of the "Orient," a name cognate with the word "orientation" and deriving from the West's construction of "the East."[12] As Maladamajaute's

Figure 7.1. Snake charmer chromolithograph. Original is nineteenth-century. Probably Freidlander Lithography Company, Germany.

fame as a snake charmer spread, her image began to appear in circus flyers and on billboards in France. Soon afterward, and probably unknown to Maladamajaute, her image spread to Africa, but for other reasons, and with a new identity.

THE SNAKE CHARMER BECOMES MAMI WATA IN AFRICA

Mami Wata devotees in Africa are particularly concerned with alien things, because their water spirit is most often perceived to be "foreign." Their shrine rooms are filled with exotica from overseas intimately associated with Mami Wata. These intriguing or "problematic" objects provoke reflection and action. Densely packed and fastidiously arranged, the shrines are spiritual magnets to attract and please Mami Wata so that her presence and support are assured. While Mami Wata followers possess a certain awareness of foreign ways, they do not use alien objects primarily to analyze or understand the ideas or values of the "other," but rather to examine and define themselves and their own society. As persons who are often troubled by questions of self-identity, Mami Wata devotees evaluate and transform external forces to shape their own interior lives and the lives of those around them.

Not unlike anthropologists (or Africanist art historians), Mami Wata devotees "study" others—overseas visitors—and formulate generalizations about them from impressions, experiences, and other evidence as if they were produced by some external "thing." This invention is an objectification or reification of that "thing."[13] Their study of others' "ways," including lore, writings, possessions, or patterns of worship, is actually a resymbolization of them, transforming others' symbols into their own.[14] This essay is my own objectification of the process by which people, European audiences of snake charmers, devotees of Mami Wata in Africa, and followers of Santa Marta Africana in the Americas, shape their understandings of an exotic "other" for different reasons. That process is, at the same time, one of self-definition.

In Africa, Mami Wata generally represents a "free," unencumbered spirit of nature detached from any social bonds. She is broadly identified with Europeans rather than with any African ethnic group or ancestors. Although her name "Mami" is usually translated as "Mother," she has no children, nor family of any kind, and it may be this aspect of her that attracts those concerned with sexual matter: impotence, barrenness, and homo- or bisexuality. She is entirely outside any social system. Her appellation of "Mother" connotes her sexual identity, her domination over the realm of water, and those who come under her sway. Her relationship with her devotees is more as a lover than as a parent.[15] In Ghana, she is notorious for her jealousy. She is said either to drive a man's wives out of the house or to kill them. In the Congo, she demands total sexual abstinence in return for riches—profit in exchange for progeny.[16] Likewise, the benefit she brings, monetary wealth, is acquired rather than inherited and is, therefore, outside the kinship system. As a foreigner, she provides alternatives to established cultural avenues. Her otherness and her independence together legitimize novel modes of action.

She personifies unattainable, exquisite beauty, vanity, jealousy, sexuality, romantic not maternal love, limitless good fortune; not health, long life, or progeny, but material and monetary riches. She is thus very much part of the international trading system between Europe and Africa (and other regions of the world as well) that began in the late fifteenth century.

Substantial evidence suggests that the *concept* of Mami Wata has its origins in the very first encounters of Africans and Europeans in the fifteenth century. Her first representations were probably derived from European images of mermaids and marine sculptures. As an Afro-Portuguese ivory shows, an African sculptor (probably Sapi, on the coast of Sierra Leone) was commissioned to create a mermaid image for his European patrons as early as 1490–1530.[17] And an eighteenth- or nineteenth-century ship's figurehead now in Ijebu-Ode, Nigeria, is called Mami Wata by its owners.

By the second half of the nineteenth century, the establishment of colonial empires and the rapid expansion of trade linking Africa with both Europe and the East provided the setting for the rapid spread of the images and ideas about Mami Wata. Not long after its publication in Europe, the chromolith reached West Africa, where the snake charmer's skin color and long, straight black hair identified her for African viewers as someone from beyond Africa. In Africa, the print became the primary icon for Mami Wata, the pidgin English name for an African water spirit believed to come from "overseas," that is, Europe. A 1901 photo of a water spirit headdress taken in the Niger River Delta town of Bonny shows clear evidence of the print's inspiration. Note especially the long, black hair parted in the middle; the garment's neckline; the earrings; the position of the figure's arms and the snakes; and the low-relief rendering of the inset with a kneeling flute player surrounded by snakes.

The confluence of multiple factors helps to explain the print's rapid acceptance and dispersal in Africa. One is the correspondence between indigenous African images and ideas about water spirits and those of European explorers and traders who arrived along African shores in the fifteenth century aboard ships that were floating art galleries depicting reptilian creatures, fish-legged figures, and mermaids. These icons corresponded closely with those that many African peoples associated with water divinities—reptiles and amphibians such as turtles, frogs, crocodiles, and especially serpents, as well as half-human, half-aquatic creatures such as mermen and mermaids.

The mermaid seems to have been the primary icon for Mami Wata until the arrival of the Snake Charmer print, which quickly superseded the mermaid as Mami Wata's primary image in many parts of Africa. Both the style and iconography of

Figure 7.2. Water spirit headdress, Bonny, Nigeria, 1901. Photographer unknown.

the print help to explain its rapid, widespread acceptance. Its naturalism contributed to its interpretation as a "photography" of a foreign spirit by Africans. "Someone must have gone under the water to snap it," one priest told me. Being a product of Western technology, this "photography" was thus a medium that reinforced the message.

The snake is an important and widespread African symbol of water and rainbow deities.[18] The serpent linked Mami Wata with the rainbow deity complex among the Mina, Ewe, Aja, Fon, Yoruba, and Igbo in West Africa. The rainbow is regarded as a celestial serpent or, more specifically, the Royal Python. As a spirit, the rainbow controls the waters of the sky and unites them with the waters on earth, while Mami Wata dominates the seas and other bodies of water. Mami Wata followers therefore consider them an inseparable pair. The iconography of the European print perfectly reflected indigenous beliefs about rainbows, water snakes, and water spirits in this area. In the print, a multicolored python arches like the rainbow over the head of the snake charmer. Thus imported talcum powder containers with rainbow motifs are favorite decorations for Mami Wata shrines, uniting a sweet-smelling foreign product and an indigenous symbol of the Royal

Python. The print thus contributed to reshaping the rainbow complex and extending it to include a foreign spirit.

In addition, the thick black hair may have evoked associations with certain sacred children in the region of the Niger River Delta said to be "children of the sea" and identified by their abundant locks, which are likened to seashells.[19]

Other elements in the print linked it with myths and images of mermaids. The snake charmer shared the complexion, facial features, long, flowing hair, and breath-taking beauty of mermaids. Icons of wealth also contributed. Golden armlets, earrings, neckline, pendant, and waist ornaments combined to evoke the riches that Mami Wata promises to those who honor her. The theme of wealth that underlies much of Mami Wata worship is sometimes exaggerated in her sculpted images, specifically in Igbo masking headdresses from Onitsha and in some Ibibio sculptures.

Since Africans usually depict complete figures in their visual arts, the half-figure rendering of Mami Wata was taken to be significant by African viewers. Devotees in discussing this aspect of the print pointed out that Mami Wata in her mermaid manifestation was half woman, half fish. What was not shown became important. The unseen lower portion of the snake charmer conveyed to devotees that Mami Wata was "hiding her secret," the fishtail. The ambiguous rendering of the cloth below the waist, reminiscent of fish scales, probably reinforced this idea.

The use of an overall blue-green background and the absence of any contextual features, like landscapes or buildings, contributed to the impression of an underwater scene. In one Igbo shrine, the worshipper recreated Mami Wata's world by filling the aquamarine-colored space with mirrors, canoe paddles, fish nets, and low relief snakes floating across the walls. Near the center of the raised platform is a coiled-up stuffed cloth snake. In procession, the priestess wraps it around her torso, drapes it over her shoulders, and holds it aloft in her right hand, just as the snake charmer does in the print. Also imaging the print, the priestess wears a long black wig parted in the center, a profusion of golden bangles around her neck, and a European-style formal gown trimmed in gold.

The shrines of Mami Wata devotees express their unique and very personal relationship with the spirit and the history of this involvement. Frequently, this involves dreams and visions of journeys to Mami Wata's fabulous underwater realm. These excursions are evoked in shrines that recreate aquatic settings. The blue-green background and the absence of any contextual features in the snake charmer print contributed to the imagining of such underwater scenes. In one Igbo shrine, the priestess, Mrs. Margaret Ekwebelam, sits holding a fan with an image of Mami Wata based on the snake charmer chromolith. Behind her the space is transformed into Mami Wata's world by the blue-green color of the walls, so similar to the background of the print. In the back corner is a stack of basins, whose color blends with that of the wall and floor. In the center of this aquamarine environment, there is a blue model of a European steamer raised on two columns to give the impression

Figure 7.3. Contemporary Igbo shrine to Mami Wata. Photo by Henry Drewal.

Figure 7.4. Mrs. Margaret Ekwebelam and her Mami Wata shrine. Photo by Henry Drewal. With permission of Mrs. Ekwebelam.

of floating. The priestess's personal experiences with Mami Wata require its presence.

In the priestess's dreams Mami Wata came in human form, either flying or swimming through the water. Sometimes, she came in her canoe and took the woman on long voyages. Bothered by these frequent visitations, the latter consulted a diviner, who instructed her to get a European steamer to put in her house. The steamer dissuaded Mami Wata from insisting that the woman travel with her by canoe, a less prestigious vessel. As one Igbo man explained, "she has it in order to avoid riding in those spiritual canoes." She thus uses her steamer to control the spirit.

At Lomé, Togo, an Ewe priestess, Mamisi Walas, described her first encounter with Mami Wata as a vision of a seascape. She went on to explain how, instead of going to school as a child, she would go to the beach and remain there for hours, gazing into the water. When her father learned of her "unnatural" behavior, he punished her. Soon afterward, she became seriously ill. The following day, she went down to the sea again and this time went in, because she felt compelled to cover herself in water. Some fishermen had to rescue her. After this incident, her father took her to a priest, who divined her identity as a chosen one of Mami Wata. She was later initiated into the Mami Wata priesthood.

In Mamisi Walas's dreams, Mami Wata would tell her to collect clay, first from one river, then from another, and also from a third. Then Mami Wata instructed her to go to the sea. When she reached shore, the waters parted, making a road, and she went inside. She came to a door, opened it, and saw Mami Wata, who gestured to her with a sweeping arc over her head. Mami Wata told her to make a clay stool and then a figure of a girl. She made both, but when she saw someone coming to look at what she had made, she tried to chase her away. Then she woke up.

Since that dream, Mamisi Walas has had many others in which Mami Wata told her to make clay sculptures of what she sees. In one dream, she was told to gather leaves associated with the deity Dan—the celestial water serpent or rainbow—for they were powerful. The very next day, she began to gather them and put them in the statues. During her dreams, she saw water, Mami Wata with a snake, and leaves on the surface of the water. These leaves she represented on the shoulders or in the hands of some of her figures, and in this way depicted Mami Wata as she was coming out of the water. She also puts other plants in pots to decorate the space. The wavy lines in the clay-covered floor of her shrine evoke a beach, rivulets of water, and snakes—all central themes in her visions. Some of these dream visions represent Mami Wata as in the chromolithograph wearing costume jewelry. Others are beautiful women in brightly colored bikinis or seated men with snakes in their hands or wrapped around their necks.[20] Gin, Schnapps, and soft drink bottles line the walls, each filled with liquids to be used in ceremonies. The space is pristine—freshly swept and meticulously arranged. Bamboo painted white and

Figure 7.5. Contemporary Mami Wata clay sculptures by Mrs. Mamisi Walas. Photo by Henry Drewal. With permission of Mamisi Walas.

spotless white cloth constitute the walls of the shrine room, creating a space that is distinctly otherworldly.

In the century since the print's arrival in Africa, it has been reprinted in large numbers in India and, more recently, England, and it continues to be distributed widely in sub-Saharan Africa, where its influence can be discerned in at least fifty ethnically different areas in twenty countries.

Figure 7.6. Clay Mami Wata wearing costume jewelry. Sculpture by Mrs. Mamisi Walas. Photo by Henry Drewal. With permission of Mamisi Walas.

THE "SAINTIFICATION" OF MAMI WATA IN THE AMERICAS

As the worship of Mami Wata continues to change on the African continent, flourishing in some places and declining in others, her nineteenth-century "snake charmer" image—with new meanings—has reached and begun to influence viewers/believers in the Americas.

Sometime in the 1960s or early 1970s, the manufacturers of popular plaster statues of saints for sale in Latino religious goods stores, known as *botanicas*, added another to their inventory—Santa Marta, or Saint Martha. In contemporary popular

Catholic iconography, Santa Marta is identified with the medieval saint of Tarascon in Provence, France, who was canonized for having subdued a dragon that threatened her community. In one of her popular chromoliths, she is shown standing unafraid before a dragon.

At the same time, this European Saint Martha has an African double known under several appellations: Santa Marta la Dominadora ("Saint Martha the Dominator"), Santa Marta Africana ("the African Saint Martha"), and Santa Marta la Negra ("Black Saint Martha"). As numerous people explained to me, "There are two Saint Marthas, one white, and one black." The juxtaposition of African and Catholic sacred entities and icons has a long history in the Americas.[21] The African Saint Martha's image is based upon the Hamburg Snake Charmer *cum* African Mami Wata one in the form of a painted plaster statue.

The story of this figure's arrival in the United States associates it with a Havana, Cuba–New York City drug-running operation. It is said that it was first used to transport contraband and money and only later became a popular religious icon of an exotic saint.

The black or African Saint Martha is known as "La Dominadora"—"The Dominator"—because of her attributes and particular powers. She is called upon when one needs spiritual assistance in establishing, maintaining, or breaking relationships concerning one's "significant other." She is very much linked with matters of the heart. As the owner of a famous botanica in Miami told me recently, when you work with "*la dominadora,* you are working with fire . . . she can do bad as well as good. That's why offerings and prayers are at midnight, since she can go either way." A new addition to her paraphernalia is a brass medallion that has recently appeared for sale in botanicas. Around the perimeter is inscribed "Santa Marta la Dominadora." Its use was not explained to me.

In Haiti, Pierrot Barra, a Voodoo artist/priest and president of a Bizango secret society, created a work in her honor.[22] "Santa Marta is a spirit that comes from Santo Domingo," he says. "She works with the snake, who is not Danbala, but is very *hot* and cannot be stopped by secret societies." In Barra's picture, Santa Marta and the snake are shown on their sacred "mountain." There is a small figure on her right, perhaps a reference to the flute-player of the chromolith, who becomes a small child in some plaster statues in North America.

It appears that the iconography of the statue and other Santa Marta images, together with aspects of Islamic and Judeo-Christian ideologies, have combined to shape these ideas and attitudes. There is an unmistakably sensual and erotic treatment of Santa Marta Africana that is quite different from the image of the "white" Saint Martha, or any other female Catholic saint for that matter. Note especially her tight bodice, plunging neckline, and splayed legs (fig. 7.7). The snake—symbol of carnal knowledge, "original sin," as well as the phallus—has enormous evocative power, as it did for repressed Victorian viewers in the 1886 Hamburg image of the sensuous snake charmer.

Figure 7.7. Contemporary "Saint Martha." Manufactured object. Photo by Henry Drewal.

ENVOI—REFLECTIONS

What implications might the Mami Wata phenomenon hold for studies of visual culture in Africa or elsewhere? As stated at the outset, this essay is my own reification of some of the ways in which people—whether Europeans, Mami Wata and Santa Marta believers, or myself—objectify "others" in constructing themselves. The process is fundamentally the same, even though our motivations and goals may be very different. We are all engaged in creative constructions: I have selected fragments from my discussions with Mami Wata followers, my participation in their ritual performances, and my observations and interpretations of their shrines; they with their fragmented, personal encounters with foreigners from overseas and/or their visual culture. In other words, we all—as individuals, communities, groups, nations, or multinationals—are continually involved in the definition, the reification of others. In the process, we "resymbolize" aspects of the "other," translating and transforming them into our own symbols on our own terms. Defining others is thus inextricably implicated in self-definition. As Mikhail Bakhtin wrote, we "constantly and intensely... oversee and apprehend the reflections of our life in the plane of consciousness of [the] other."[23]

One of the revealing things about this history is that the "West" has no monopoly on the definition of selves in terms of others.[24] Mami Wata followers have been defining themselves in terms of overseas strangers all along, and I, being one, became part of that process. One particular conversation illustrates the point. In the winter of 1975, a Mami Wata priest was remarking how during certain seasons, large numbers of water spirits seem to gather at the Hotel Tropicana near Lomé, an expensive beachside resort hotel favored by European and American tourists. When I asked how he knew they were for Mami Wata, he seemed surprised at my naïveté and replied, "Go there and see for yourself!" It was then that I realized he was referring to people sitting or lying on the beach for hours facing the seas—just as in the life histories of many Mami Wata devotees, like Mamisi Walas of Lomé. My many questions about Mami Wata beliefs and practices were probably often interpreted as an expression of devotional involvement. And this research into the history and impact of Mami Wata and her spirit sisters in the Americas has, in fact, shaped my practices and beliefs in various ways—like this presentation, my own altar in her honor, and my performance of her at the 1996 Greenwich Village Halloween Parade in Manhattan. One might say I *am* truly devoted to her.

Mami Wata devotees are consciously and passionately engaged in self-definition. They are not denying their Ewe-ness or Igbo-ness, or trying to become European in their use of foreign objects, any more than Picasso tried to become African in adopting an African visual vocabulary in his own work—even though he did create "fetishes" that were venerated in the art world![25] Rather, Picasso (for various motives) used African images to define himself as an enfant terrible—a radical iconoclast whose actions fit his cultural model of an avant-garde artist. Mami Wata and Santa Marta believers are similarly creatively assessing and defining their position

Figure 7.8. Henry Drewal's personal altar to Mami Wata. Photo by Henry Drewal.

in the global colonial, neocolonial, postcolonial, and capitalist systems that are the outgrowth of long, complicated histories of African and Latin American interactions with "others" from across the seas, whether Europeans for Africans, or Europeans and Africans for Latinas and Latinos.

Yet a history of asymmetrical political, technological, and economic relations, compounded and magnified by deep-seated racist ideologies, has fostered authoritarian and authoritative accounts of other cultures, presenting them as static, passive, and powerless anachronisms in a worldview epitomized by such phrases of denigration or negation as, "the West and the rest" or "the non-Western world." Moving from such a mind-set to one of global interdependencies in constant flux, scholars are searching for ways to transcend culturally created prisms (some might say prisons) in a field of multiple perspectives.

Collaborative research of a new order may be required, intercultural as well as interdisciplinary, not simply the double regard of insiders working with outsiders on particular topics, but equivalences in dynamics. Another strategy might be to reevaluate the relationship between participation and observation in our research methods. Experiential knowledge may be crucial, especially in the understanding of expressive, that is, sensorial, culture—the products of processes that often must be experienced to be understood more fully. Yet observation (and theorizing and interpretation) have often been privileged at the expense of bodily experience.[26] Redressing this imbalance may have important implications for studies of visual culture. In these and other ways, ethnographies in general and studies of expressive culture in particular may shed light on the countless devices people design in order to define, assert, and empower themselves.

In closing, there would seem to be few popular images in the history of art that have had an impact comparable to the one we have considered here. Within a hundred years, a German poster for Europeans of an exotic "Oriental" snake charmer became both the principal icon for Africans of an exotic—that is, European—water spirit named Mami Wata *and* an exotic African-Catholic saint called Santa Marta la Dominadora in the American. The image has "charmed" many, allowing minds and imaginations to construct the reality of an "other" as an integral part of the process of self-definition and empowerment in three very different cultural worlds.

NOTES

I wish to acknowledge the following institutions and persons for their help in shaping this essay: the National Endowment for the Humanities (for grants F77-42 and RO-20072-81-2184); Cleveland State University; the Nigerian Museum; Obafemi Awolowo University; the University of Ibadan; the Metropolitan Museum of Art; the University of Wisconsin–Madison; the Martens family in Lomé, Togo, in 1975; Wilhelm Zimmermann, Margaret Thompson Drewal, and especially, the priestesses and priests of Mami Wata who shared their views and lives with me during the course of fieldwork. Some parts of this essay were previously published in *African Material Culture*, ed. Mary Jo Arnoldi et al. (Bloomington: Indiana University Press, 1996). The Wilhelm Zimmerman material is housed at the Circus Archive, Ellerbek, Germany.

1. For more on case studies of psychology, see Henry Drewal, "Art, History, and the Individual: A New Perspective for the Study of African Visual Traditions," in *Iowa Studies in African Art*, ed. C. Roy (Iowa City: School of Art and Art History, University of Iowa, 1984), 1: 87–114.

2. *Objects and Others: Essays on Museums and Material Culture*, ed. George W. Stocking Jr. (Madison: University of Wisconsin Press, 1985), "Introduction," 4; and see also *Anthropology and the Colonial Encounter*, ed. Talal Asad (New York: Humanities Press, 1973).

3. Philip Curtin, *The Image of Africa* (Madison: University of Wisconsin Press, 1975), 24. See, e.g., the Rev. John Adams's traveler's account in his *Curious Thoughts on the History of Man* (1789; reprint. Bristol, U.K.: Thoemmes Press, 1995).

4. James Clifford, "On Ethnographic Surrealism," *Comparative Studies in Society and History* 23 (1981): 542.

5. Urs Bitterli, *Die "Wilden" und die "Zivilisierten": Grundzüge e. Geistes- u. Kulturgeschichte d. europ.-überseeischen Begegnung* (Munich: C. H. Beck, 1976), and H. C. Debrunner, *Presence and Prestige: Africans in Europe: A History of Africans in Europe before 1918* (Basel: Basler Afrika Bibliographien, 1979).

6. G. Niemeyer, *Hagenbeck* (Hamburg: H. Christians Press, 1972), 247.

7. S. Benninghoff-Luhl, "Die Ausstellung der Klonisierten: Völkerschauen von 1874–1932," in *Andenken an den Kolonialismus: Eine Ausstellung des Völkerkundlichen Instituts der Universität Tübingen*, ed. Volker Harms et al. (Tübingen: ATTEMPTO, 1984).

8. Cf. R. Malhotra, *Manege Frei: Artisten- und Circusplakate von Adolf Friedlander* (Dortmund: Harenberg Kommunikation, 1979).

9. Niemeyer, *Hagenbeck*, 251.

10. Henry Drewal, "Performing the Other: Mami Wata Worship in West Africa," *Drama Review*, T118 (1988): 169, pl. 8.

11. The whereabouts of the original edition of this image are still unknown. 1,200 copies of the version illustrated here were printed in 1955 in Bombay, India, by the Shree Ram Calendar Company, "without changing a line even from the original" (manager of the Shree Ram Calendar Co., Bombay, India, pers. corresp., June 17, 1977).

12. James Clifford, *The Predicament of Culture* (Cambridge, Mass.: Harvard University Press, 1988), 13.

13. Roy Wagner, *The Invention of Culture* (1975; rev. ed., Chicago: University of Chicago Press, 1981), 26.

14. Ibid., 30.

15. See C. Gerrits, "Conceptions and Explanations of sii-Epilepsy—A Medical-Anthropological Study among the Bassa and Kpelle in Liberia," *Curare* 6 (1983): 36; R. M. Wintrob, "Mammy Water: Folk Beliefs and Psychotic Elaborations in Liberia," *Canadian Psychiatric Association Journal* 15 (1970): 150.

16. Johannes Fabian, "Popular Culture in Africa: Findings and Conjectures," *Africa* 48, 4 (1978): 319.

17. D. Fraser, "The Fish-Legged Figure in Benin and Yoruba Art," in *African Art and Leadership*, ed. id. and H. Cole (Madison: University of Wisconsin Press, 1972), fig. 14.10.

18. Cf. Wilfrid D Hambly, *Serpent Worship in Africa* (Chicago: Field Museum of Natural History, 1931; reprint. New York: Kraus, 1968).

19. Henry Drewal, "Flaming Crowns, Cooling Waters: Masquerades of the Ijebu-Yoruba," *African Arts* 20, 1 (1986): 32–41, 99–100.

20. Some Mami Wata pantheons of water spirits contain a Papi Wata as well, a complex subject for another study.

21. Roger Bastide, *The African Religions of Brazil* (Baltimore: Johns Hopkins University Press, 1978).

22. *Sacred Arts of Haitian Voudou*, ed. Donald Cosentino (Los Angeles: UCLA Fowler Museum of Cultural History, 1995), 381, pl. Q-6.

23. Mikhail Bakhtin, as quoted in Tsvetan Todorov, *Mikhail Bakhtin, The Dialogic Principle* (Minneapolis: University of Minnesota Press, 1984), 94.

24. Cf. *Occidentalism: Images of the West*, ed. James G. Carrier (New York: Oxford University Press, 1995).

25. Paul Landau, conversation, April 22, 1997.

26. Cf. James Clifford, *Predicament of Culture*, 31; and Mark Johnson, *The Body in the Mind: The Bodily Basis of Meaning, Imagination, and Reason* (Chicago: University of Chicago Press, 1987, 1990).

Chapter 8

"Captured on Film": Bushmen and the Claptrap of Performative Primitives

Robert J. Gordon

"Don't look now, death is dancing me ragged" is the haunting refrain in John Marshall's classic film *N!ai, the Story of a !Kung Woman*. If there is a single feature of indigenous life that has been the subject of the cinematographer—commercial, professional, academic, or tourist—it has been dancing. As far back as 1906, the Austrian ethnologist Rudolf Pöch, reflecting on his New Guinea experiences before making the first Bushman movies in the Kalahari, suggested that dances "are the simplest and most effective subjects for cinematography and the best means of practicing the medium since they enable one to record what is most visual and effective when reproduced."[1]

Fatimah Rony suggests that such a fascination with dance as spectacle arose out of the industrial world's interest in the bodies of indigenes, bodies that were to be watched at a distance. The "native" was identified with the body, and the "native's" dance was imagined as "frenzied movements by people lacking rationality," giving rise to an image that became common in commercial films.[2] It is perhaps not incidental that the one scene in *N!ai* that includes tourists has them photographing a trance dance; or, that the most recent Bushman documentary dealing with the relations between people and carnivores is titled *Dancing with the Future*. Faced with the problem of promoting tourism, the Northern Cape Tourist Association hired an American to develop a "Bushman tourist show" with the ex-military Bushmen of Smitsdrift.[3] Not unreasonably, he focused on healers and their associated trance dancing.[4] If there is one thing tourists expect when visiting Bushmanland, it is to see Bushmen dance. A dance, many tourists believe, allows Bushmen to shed their Western accoutrements and sham behavior and reveal an "authentic primeval Africa." Authentic Bushmen, these tourists believe, are those who dance exactly as they do in the countless (real and pseudo-) documentary films made about them. This essay is about these "performative primitives,"[5] about how they

Figure 8.1. N!ai. From *N!ai, The Story of a Kung Woman* (dir. John Marshall, 1980). Courtesy John Marshall and Documentary Educational Resources, Watertown, Mass.

have become caught up in a dance that contains steps of their own devising but is at the same time staged by colonialism.

"Death is dancing me ragged" also references dance as a form of language, of ritual communication, in which both Bushmen and Europeans participate.[6] A dance is preeminently a social gathering in which a series of "rhythmic and patterned bodily movements" are performed.[7] The performances we see in films in fact involve choreography and a complex grammar; yet they can also develop into what Edward Hall calls "entrainment," the process whereby two or more people become engaged in each other's rhythms until they synchronize. Like epic balladeers, those labeled Bushmen do not memorize all their steps, but rather combine stock phrases, formulas, and etiquettes in patterns improvised according to the responses of one another and their audience.[8] Each performative encounter creates a new route through old themes. And by using dance as a site for focused interaction with Europeans, indigenes are able to divert attention away from areas and concerns on which they would prefer the Europeans not to intrude.

In a larger sense, Bushmen are part of a "dance" that they only control partially. At the same time, the Western spectator/participant is, like Bushman dancers, placed under restrictions and forced to act the role expected of the tourist. Greg Dening points out that the roots of the distinction between observer and observed lie in the emergence of the theater during the Enlightenment, in which burlesques, pantomimes, and satires taught people to "perspectivize," to "see" the strange. Dening further adopts the term "claptrap" to signify the moment when a performer is "trapped in a clap when he or she evoked applause in the middle of a dramatic scene."

> By a gesture, a pose, a look, a pause, an actor drew the attention of the audience away from the part being acted to the acting of the part. Mimesis—the representation of reality—was broken or changed. [Claptrap] is the moment of theatricality in any representation . . . in which the audience . . . participates in the creative process of representing.[9]

Theatricality still runs deep in every cultural encounter between indigenes and Western strangers. In the "claptrap" of the representations of those labeled Bushmen, it influenced and redirected the nature of the relationship with the wider world.

One of the most important backdrops to the performance of Bushman dance is that created by the (cine-)camera, with its tendency to "frame" performances. The movie camera is a critical part of the legacy of the "Graphic Revolution," in Daniel Boorstin's phrase; it helped render the spectacle available for mass consumption.[10] In the late nineteenth century, "ethnographic exhibitions" were a popular form of "educational" entertainment, but the cinema proved to be a more cost-effective way of circulating "primitive bodies" in industrial society. The camera has provided a meeting place for science and fantasy, if only because the Western empirical tradition assumes that visualizing a society is "synonymous for understanding it."[11] Photography records experience very differently than language; a photograph cannot be "out of context," because photographs and other visual images create their own contexts. Visual images thus have the power to dismember reality and juxtapose events and things that have no historical or logical connection. They create pseudocontexts and give fragmented and irrelevant information an automatic utility.[12]

MOVIES AT HOME AND ABROAD

Visual images have different meanings for and impacts on different audiences. The cinema's central characteristic entails movement and changing images. The cinema takes us away from the where we are to the scene of the action; yet in a sense, it is too close to the real for us to inhabit it like a story. Cinema pulls us into the visible present, while still photographs are about the past. Movies hide their exploitative natures with a "self-told" quality.[13] One can gaze upon and contemplate a still photograph, whereas movies encourage not gazing but glancing: shallow, accumulative looks. As Walter Benjamin puts it, before a frame of a movie, no sooner has one's "eye grasped a scene than it is already changed."[14] It is glancing, not gazing, that has encouraged and shaped the way tourists now look at those they label Bushmen. The lack of depth, the inability to gaze, is what makes movies fundamentally different from both still photographs and texts.

Still photography has a longer history in the Kalahari than movies, and in the case of the Bushmen, it goes back to the 1860s, when James Chapman pioneered the use of stereoscopic pictures. Soon afterward came Gustav Fritsch, who in 1872 published his paradigmatic *Die Eingeborenen Süd-Afrika's* (Natives of South Africa), based on three years of travel in 1863–66. Fritsch acknowledged his disappointment at how indigenes reacted to his efforts at photographing them. In the first pages of his book, he remarks that Bushmen did not like removing their clothing for the camera: "[I]t was the feeling of shame that one had to struggle against. However, many natives, especially the chiefs and the students of the mission schools, showed themselves to be extraordinarily proud of the not-at-all-becoming rags that civilization draped upon them."[15]

As regards cinema, the pioneer was Rudolf Pöch, an Austrian ethnologist, who not only made the first movie about Bushmen (1909) but also amassed the world's largest Bushman skull collection.[16] After traveling from Swakopmund through Windhoek and the Kalahari to the Victoria Falls, Pöch returned to South Africa and then made a rapid foray up to the southern Kalahari. At the conclusion of his eighteen-month expedition, he gave a triumphal interview to the *Cape Times Weekly* of November 3, 1909. Entitled "The Bushman Tribes," the interview portrayed the anthropologist—long before Bronislaw Malinowsi—as a heroic figure. (Pöch advised that "the earnest student should learn the language of the people forming the subject of his inquiries, and do everything possible to obtain their confidence. Investigations of this description necessarily entail considerable time and no little amount of labour.") Pöch found that "the physical structure of the Bushmen was absolutely different from that of all the other low races he had previously seen." His researches into "the physical appearance of the Bushmen and their habits and customs" was facilitated by photography:

Not only were the camera and cinematograph requisitioned for this purpose, but the phonograph was utilized in order to aid the study of the Bushmen's language. The Bushmen did not object to being photographed, nor was any difficulty experienced in getting them to speak into the phonograph. By aid of the cinematograph pictures were taken showing the natives dancing.[17]

There are two grainy halftone photographs included with the article. One is of a Bushman speaking into a phonograph by Pöch's tent. On the far left is the cinematograph, and on the right, an assistant measures a young lady. The second picture is entitled "Colonial Bushman and Hottentot Location, Prieska." Far from portraying pristine primitives, the photograph shows Bushmen in rags. Yet in Pöch's film footage, all the Bushmen are decked out in loincloths, with no vestiges of "Western contamination" at all.

Even though his work was largely neglected by anglophone academics, Pöch set the parameters for film documentaries on Bushmen. His film work and his large collection of skulls was much discussed in the League of Nations's creation of the mandated territory of South West Africa after World War I. More significantly, Pöch epitomized what was to become an increasingly popular genre of juvenile literature and film, namely, the adventures of the "photographer explorer." Burton Holmes, the inventor of the travelogue, later made over $5 million in the 1930s from his eight thousand or so illustrated lectures. The same genre accommodated the likes of Robert E. Ripley ("Believe It or Not") and Lowell Thomas, the latter reputed to have had more friends among the powerful than anyone else in the world. A significant part of the audiences of these men were youths, for whom they became inspirational models. It is no surprise that one of the most popular interwar movies, *King Kong* (dir. Merian Cooper, 1933), begins with a scientific cinematographic expedition, which ends up capturing the giant ape.

By 1927, Kodak cine-cameras and "do-it-yourselfers" were all the rage. The interwar years were characterized by aggressive marketing by companies like Eastman Kodak and Bell & Howell of new camera technologies, and they used the forum of *National Geographic* to deliver advice on how to deal with camera-shy natives. This was the milieu of the trendsetting Denver African Expedition, which arrived in southern Africa in 1925 to discover and film what was termed the "missing link." The expedition made a film called *The Bushman* and took some five hundred still photographs. Through the successful commercial marketing of both movie and stills, the expedition had a major impact on creating and sustaining the "pristine" iconography of Bushmen that persists today. After the Denver African Expedition, practically every American, British, Italian, or French "expedition" to Namibia and the Kalahari included a cinematographer or at least a still photographer.[18]

Local settlers and officials were not always overawed by the credentials or aims of these expeditions. Dr. Louis Fourie, the South West African territorial

Figure 8.2. "Dr. Cadle and two average size Kalahari Bushmen." Also titled "Cadle and Kung Bushmen." Photo by C. L. H. Hahn. No. A 111. This image appeared in several publications in 1927, including *Municipal Facts, The Literary Digest,* and *Asia.*

medical officer, and the foremost authority on Bushmen of the time, was instrumental in guiding the Denver Expedition *away* from those he considered the "purest" Bushmen. In a letter to the South African guide to the expedition, Donald Bain, Fourie lamented that cinema's attempt to please its audiences would bring ridicule.

[The] only way to get good Bushman records is *not* to attempt to stage-manage them. [Native Commissioner of Ovamboland C. L. H. "Cocky"] Hahn has told me of the scene he witnessed. Where on earth have you ever heard of six Bushmen stalking the same animal in Indian file etc. etc. The whole affair is ridiculous. The boy ["August"] *I* gave you as guide knows... what stuff you require and drop the film.[19]

The micropolitics of filming needs to be placed in the settler context. How did settlers and officials see movies? How did the state frame perceptions and shape what was filmed and shown? In the colonies, and certainly in the mandated territory of South West Africa, there was much trepidation about what the cinema could do.[20]

WHITE MAN'S MAGIC

The battle of the bioscope in Namibia was long and tortured. In 1919, two colonial NCOs applied for a license to build a "native cinema" in the Windhoek location. "It is recognized by us that the native in this country is inferior in intelligence and by installing an entertainment such as herein suggested it would in our opinion have a tendency to raise them to a higher standard educationally" they wrote, and offered to show only pictures of "high educational value which had been previously scrutinized." The bioscope, they argued, would reduce native crime. Despite endorsements from officials, the administrator turned down their application because he felt that "the time was not yet ripe for such an experiment."[21]

The campaign was protracted, and a second issue that had to be resolved was who should control the cinema. "The personality of the person authorized to run the Bioscope is a very important one," one magistrate wrote. "The natives have impressionable minds and are in many respects like big uneducated children." Bioscopes, he felt, were best run by local authorities, who would be able to exercise better control; thus, too, "natives can be prevented from spending more than a reasonable portion of their earnings on this form of amusement." All this despite already existing censorship controls. It was only in 1939, after much legal wrangling, that a "Coloured" was granted a bioscope license to show films in Luderitz.[22]

It was not only apprehension about the bioscope's impact on indigenes that gave rise to official moral concern. Its alleged influences on whites were also contested. From about 1910, movies had been a regular staple in the larger towns of German South West Africa, and they continued to be even during World War I. After South African troops occupied South West Africa, the South African police in 1918 investigated complaints about the local movie fare:

> There can be no doubt that the usual kind of Bioscope display has a very undesirable, and in many cases highly detrimental effect on the minds and morals of children and of youths and girls.... human nature being what it is, it may readily be surmised that, following immediately upon a [Bioscope] display, nerve exciting at

the best, and often directly playing upon sexual instincts, these journeys home through dark streets and quiet lanes are not as free from danger as one would desire.[23]

Ten years later the principal of the Keetmanshoop Secondary School protested the screening of *Don Juan*, despite not having seen the film. As a matter of principle he did not frequent the cinema:

> I should have thought that any man or woman of only moderate education would have realised the unwisdom, nay more, the moral danger, of permitting boys and girls to witness a performance with this title, portraying as all must know it does, only the career and acts of a libertine.... the picture was not only suggestive but openly displayed immorality.... I do not deny that the cinematograph may frequently be of educational value ... [but] it is well known that the main purpose of most moving pictures is financial gain, and as long as human nature remains what it is, both those who make and those who show films will provide many that are sensational or suggestive.[24]

In 1928, the German consul evidently requested that one film, Charlie Chaplin's *Shoulder Arms*, be banned as it would "irreparably damage race relations" in the territory. A month later, citing expert opinion produced by the League of Nations on the social impact of the cinema, the administration moved to create a board of censors.[25] This board had to vet films directly imported to the territory, but most films had already been approved by the South African Board of Censors. The South African Entertainment (Censorship) Act of 1931 listed the following features that, if depicted in an offensive manner, might lead to a film being banned: (a) impersonation of the king; (b) scenes holding up to ridicule or contempt any members of the king's military or naval forces; (c) treatment of death; (d) nude human figures; (e) passionate love scenes; (f) scenes purporting to illustrate "night life"; (g) scenes containing reference to controversial or international politics; (h) scenes representing antagonistic relations between capital and labor; (i) scenes tending to disparage public figures; (j) scenes tending to create public alarm; (k) the drug habit, "white slave" (prostitution) traffic, vice, or loose morals; (l) scenes calculated to affect the religious conviction or feelings of any section of the public; (m) scenes calculated to bring in any section of the public into ridicule or contempt; (n) juvenile crime and, in the case of older persons, scenes of the technique of crime and criminality; (o) brutal fighting; (p) drunkenness and brawling; (q) pugilistic encounters between Europeans and non-Europeans; (r) intermingling between Europeans and non-Europeans; and (s) rough handling or ill-treatment of women and children.[26]

So all-encompassing were the South African censor's powers that the U.S. Department of Commerce complained that "exhibitors hesitate to offer films for review that may be rejected" by them. Films that were banned included *Viva Villa* ("too much brutality") and *Tarzan and His Mate* ("offensive to decency").[27] Clearly, the state was in awe of the magical power of film, or at least of its supposed effect on children and Africans.

The important question, as Michael Taussig points out in his discussion of the impact of the gramophone, is not so much the "native's" vulnerability to cinema and recorded sound as "the white man's fascination with their fascination with these mimetically capacious machines."[28] This is most clearly illustrated by "Bain's Bushmen," an "exhibit" of Bushmen put together by Donald Bain and brought to the 1936 Empire Exhibition in Johannesburg. Their "meeting with the wonders of the white man's civilization for the first time of their lives" provided much copy for the local press. "White Man's Magic Alarms Bushmen" a typical headline asserted:

> In the past few weeks the old patriarch Abraham has been through a life time of novel experiences, and his natural dignity and philosophy have enabled him to treat even such momentous occasions as his first flight in an aeroplane as if they were everyday occurrences in the Kalahari Desert.... His poise almost deserted him [when an] elevator proved altogether to much for his understanding... and he shrank back in terror from an apartment window and... he was bewildered at the mysteries of the bathroom having a hot and a cold water tap.[29]

Their alleged first view of movies led to another Cape Town headline: "Bushmen Rush Screen to See Where Talkie Comes From. They Like Mickey Mouse but Dancing Zulus Scared Them. Abraham Sees Himself in Kalahari Film."

> Abraham, the centenarian Bushman chief, will never be surprised again. Where the white man is, anything is possible, he now believes. He has seen and heard the greatest wonder of all—Mickey Mouse....
>
> Dancing in any form appeals to the Bushmen and it is impossible for them to keep their feet still in the presence of music [in this case, Zulu dancing]. Aniko, Abraham's fifty-year-old daughter leads the dancing.
>
> [When the Kalahari camp scenes were shown] they made a concerted rush forward. They looked under and behind the screen in an effort to find just where it all came from, but to no avail.

Indeed, as Taussig suggests, European settlers appear to have been more obsessed by the white man's magic than the Bushmen were. Whites were taken with the magic of mechanical reproduction itself, which restores "the mimetic faculty as mystery in the art of mechanical reproduction, reinvigorating the primitivism implicit in technology's wildest dreams, therewith creating a surfeit of mimetic power."[30] Technological gadgets promoted the illusion that colonizers had the means of controlling the colonized.

THE SAVAGE HITS BACK

Stories of Bushmen rushing movie screens should be read as morality plays that served the settlers' needs. From the fragmentary evidence, it is clear that Bushmen were not overawed by cinematography. On the contrary, they rapidly accepted movie makers and tried to exploit them in their turn, using strategies ranging from noncollaboration to mimicry.[31]

The Denver Expedition of 1925, after filming in Etosha, traveled through Ovamboland, where they met an old German transport-rider named Hartmann; when one of the territory's little magazines started up a few years later, Hartmann, who had a literary bent, wrote about their encounter. His essay, "Of Wild and Tame Bushmen," recalled how he welcomed the expedition as one of three in Ondangua in 1925. The Münchausenesque bragging of the "Yankees" was so bad it could have come from a Karl May Western: they claimed to have discovered an unknown tribe of Bushmen who had never seen a European; to have narrowly escaped from a Bushman attack when their car was mistaken for a wild animal; and to have been given a never-before-seen Bushman religious relic. They were extremely proud of their footage of wild war dances and secret religious rituals. Hartmann, for his part, with the attitude of an experienced "colonial hand," viewed such claims as naïve. The sacred Bushman religious relic turned out to be a common Ovambo doll.

On one of his trips through the Etosha Game Park, Hartmann hooked up with the Denver Expedition's interpreter, the "Bastard Jeremias" (Bastard, and Baster, in the parlance of the southern African frontier, meaning "of mixed descent"). When Hartmann asked Jeremias to show him the "wild Bushmen" encountered by the expedition, Jeremias gathered some Bushmen and staged a mock attack. After begging cigarettes from Hartmann, the Bushmen performed their war dance. Suddenly, Hartmann realized that he knew its melody: it was "Matiche," a Mexican song that had been popular with German troops during the Herero war of 1904–7. Hartmann also recognized one of the dancers. On insisting on seeing their living quarters, Hartmann was first taken to a "primitive encampment," clearly for tourist consumption, and only then to their real abode, which consisted of tin shacks (pondoks) and an old German military bed. Best of all, they owned an old phonograph, on which they played their only record—"Matiche"!

The Denver African Expedition was followed a year later by that of an Austrian anthropologist named Viktor Lebzelter. He too visited the Etosha Pan in search of Bushmen, but he was rather dismissive of what he found there. The Bushmen usually wore European rags and had European names. As if referring directly to the Denver Expedition, Lebzelter continued, "They are always prepared to put on old [traditional] clothes and to dance for distinguished guests and allow themselves to be photographed. They are in the best sense *Salon Bushmen* who are dependent upon foreign traffic."[32]

Other amateur ethnographers also filmed the Etosha Bushmen. Jan Gaerdes, for example, shot some eight hundred meters of film in 1927 en route to the Kunene River. Oliver Crosby, a "gentleman explorer" who frequented the adventurers' clubs of the East Coast of the United States, also made some films of Bushmen in Etosha and used them on the Washington, D.C., lecture circuit.[33] The De Schauensee

Expedition under the guidance of Donald Bain filmed the Etosha Hei//omn in 1930. Tourists to the Etosha Game Park in the interwar years were frequently surprised by "wild" Bushmen who would then gratefully accept cigarettes and thus reveal their "tameness." A visitor to Etosha in 1935 wrote how "one of those creatures of the wild,"

> complete with bow and arrow and pot belly, was well worth a photograph. The interpreter was requested to pass on our wishes to Mr Bushman, and, after a lot of tongue-clicking and unnecessary talking, the answer came, decisive and uncompromising: "I want a shilling first." So much of the backward Bushman; as this touch of sordid materialism of our civilisation had crept into the picture, we decided that he was not worth a photograph at all.

Later, "this man, complete with zebra-skin cap, sat on the mudguard" and served as their guide.

> [W]hen we had at last reached the semblance of a track, I drove over a piece of pointed bone, which immediately went right through the outer casing of a tyre.... It seemed that Mr 1/- Bushman had decided to get his own back on us for refusing to take his photograph, and crossing his palm with silver. The bone was definitely hand-carved.[34]

The practice of filming "wild Bushmen" hunting in the Etosha Pan Game Park continued even after World War II. Bushmen residing in the Game Park were expected by the park warden to cultivate and maintain a "wild" image for the benefit of tourists. For many Bushmen, engaging in such behavior was a successful foraging strategy.

A similar trajectory is to be found at the other major site where "wild Bushmen" were successfully imaged, the southern Kalahari. Some of the people measured and photographed by Pöch were later shown to the anthropologist Dorothea Bleek and, most important, were eventually taken by Donald Bain to the 1936 Empire Exhibition in Johannesburg. They became one of the exhibit's most successful attractions.[35] In part, this was because of Bain's campaign to save "the last Bushmen" by obtaining a reserve for them. In the face of official claims to their inauthenticity, Bain not only had their "racial purity" attested to by scientists such as Raymond Dart; but he also searched as far afield as Lake Ngami to find authentic artifacts and items of clothing for them. The use of Afrikaans, the creole lingua franca of South West Africa as of most of South Africa, was prohibited, and the Bushmen were made to speak Nama or /auni in public.[36] The Union Research Board paid A. M. Duggan-Cronin, a well-known photographer of Africans, to come and photograph them.[37] Although Bain's efforts to secure a reserve for "the last South African Bushmen" failed, these Khomani and /auni Bushmen were allowed to live in the newly proclaimed Kalahari Gemsbok Park as long as they did so "traditionally." That meant dressing up in skins and posing for tourists' cameras. The *Rand Daily Mail* reported that Bain's camp attracted "numerous coloured people, who try to pass themselves off as Bushmen," and local farmers complained that they were deprived of "farm hands."[38] The same complaint was to be heard at the Etosha Game Park right through the 1950s.

Not only had some of these same people been photographed by Pöch, but it is also possible that some of them might have had showbusiness experience going back to 1884, when "The Great Farini," a self-proclaimed showman, displayed a troupe of six "Earthmen" (Bushmen) brought over from the southern Kalahari. The Earthmen's "keeper," a Baster named Gert Louw, told Farini stories. He, Farini, and Farini's photographer son "Lulu" had searched for Kalahari diamonds. Despite an initial fear of Lulu's camera, the Bushmen of the southern Kalahari adapted to being photographed.[39] In 1913, Fred Cornell, a prominent prospector, also took a movie camera to this area and made a film of Bushmen that supposedly included remarkable footage of dancing; the film was regrettably spoiled by the "intense heat." Cornell's guide was apparently also none other than Gert Louw.[40]

By the 1930s, it is very likely that farm laborers like Bain's "last Bushmen" were well aware of what cinema was all about, since itinerant European hawkers with movie vans were a feature of rural South Africa in the interwar years. Saturday night at the bioscope was a major feature of the social scene on the Platteland. Farmers would think nothing of traveling fifty miles to the venue (perhaps a dining hall or country hotel), often bringing their black farmworkers along with them, who would watch through the windows from the outside. *Tarzan* and other "African" films were popular fare at these showings, which some local audiences at least delighted in dissecting for improbabilities and anachronisms.[41]

Thus the acculturation to the notion of performance was two-sided. Both Bushmen and whites participated in Dening's "claptrap," the shifting of mimesis from the habits being represented to the habit of representation. Tourists came and tourists filmed, and not only South Africans, but international figures such as Jens Bjerre and Marlin Perkins. The same has been true in Botswana. The refinements of performance continue to the present, with the Australian TV traveloguer Abby Mangels "doing the Bushmen" with himself dressed in a loincloth.[42]

GATE- AND GOATKEEPERS

Bushmen's "dances" or performances were mediated by experienced gatekeepers or cultural entrepreneurs. Pöch did not stagger blindly into the desert; he was guided there, probably by Gert Louw. For the Denver Expedition, we have Fourie swearing by the reliability of his "boy" August. In the case of Donald Bain, it is clear that the major facilitator was /khanako ("Aniko" above), or as she was referred to in the Afrikaans press, "Ou Fytjie" (Old Fig). Strong and independent-minded, /khanako assisted Bain in congregating what later became known as "Bain's Bushmen," and as a daughter of "Old Abraham" (!gurice), the putative patriarch of the collected Bushmen, she played a leading role in their governance.

This becomes clear in the way in which especially the Afrikaans press was enraptured by her. For example, after watching the annual intervarsity rugby match between Stellenbosch and Cape Town University, /khanako claimed to want to import rugby into the Kalahari. Obviously, she knew the way to a warm-blooded Afrikaner's heart![43]

After Bain went bankrupt while on tour with the Bushmen, they were repatriated back to the Gordonia district and /khanako emerged as their spokesperson. Reporting on their resettlement, the Upington magistrate noted: "Most of them confidently expect Mr Bain to visit them again and hope to be allowed to camp in the Game Reserve. The daughter of the old 'Chief' asked me to make representation to the Minister of Native Affairs so that some of the money which she says Mr Bain collected during their tour and which she alleges he collected for them, may be obtained from him and handed over to them."[44]

After the failure of Bain's controversial efforts, another person, Coenraad Frederik Macdonald, also took some southern Kalahari Bushmen on tour in 1939. Macdonald was charged under the censorship laws for illegally exhibiting Bushmen. His court case achieved a certain prominence, and from the record, it appears that his defense was that "Fytjie" (/khanako) had approached him, as a well-known person in the Gordonia district, to take the Bushmen on tour; she had helped collect the troupe, and he hoped to buy a farm for them to settle on with the profits. As he spoke, "Fytjie" was waiting outside the court to be called to give evidence.[45]

Two indigenes achieved a certain prominence as gatekeepers and interpreters in South West Africa. First, there was "Native Sergeant Saul" who was stationed in Gobabis and was touted as the expert on the eastern Bushmen. Not only did he facilitate Dr. Fourie's, and Bleek and Drury's, research in Sandfontein, but he had also apparently known Pöch. As a police tracker, he was closely involved in operations following the murder of the Gobabis magistrate van Ryneveld in 1922. The second was Ngani, a Hei/-om. Ngani's story is almost mosaic. Found under a bush, where his mother had abandoned him, he grew up in the household of the secretary for South West Africa, came to speak nine different languages, and was known to mix a good martini. Practically every travelogue on Namibia from the 1930s to the 1950s has a vignette or two about Ngani's mimicry, his linguistic capabilities, and his ability to anticipate one's wishes before one even became aware of them.[46] He also served as interpreter on a number of important anthropological expeditions, including P.J. Schoeman's, discussed below, and those of the Marshall family in 1952–53, 1957–58, and 1961.

Some whites choreographed their own interactions with Bushmen, as we have seen. Donald Bain was crucial, and he was followed by P.J. Schoeman, the warden of Etosha Game Reserve and chair of the "Bushman Preservation Commission." Schoeman successfully brought a troupe of !Kung to the van Riebeeck Festival commemorating three hundred years of white settlement in South Africa. White South West Africans also had an impact on this dance. Francois Stroh grew up on a farm with Bushmen and claimed to speak six Bushman "dialects." Working as an agent for one of the political groupings in South West Africa, Stroh took Bushmen on carefully staged trips to events like the Germiston Centenary Festival in South Africa and served as a self-appointed spokesperson for their interests.[47]

Undoubtedly the most important choreographer and gatekeeper was the South African government, supported by the press and its expanding middle-class readership. In the wake of Donald Bain's 1936 efforts to save the "Last South African Bushmen," the *Rand Daily Mail* editorialized: "[T]he plea.... should certainly be responded to, not alone in the interests of science but also because the picturesque, the unusual and the historic are national assets and matters for nation-wide concern. Every effort should be made to prevent this remarkable little people from disappearing."[48] There were also more pragmatic considerations. Already in 1952, when four parties applied for permits to study Bushmen in the Kavango River region, officials complained, "It would seem that the Bushmen are starting to resent the interference of so many Europeans."[49] Some of the expeditions were thought to be glorified hunting trips. The South African government, in defense of its policy of apartheid and its illegal occupation of the territory, was sensitive to any negative publicity that might be generated. Research visas thus became a major way of controlling the image of Bushmen, and until recently, only researchers with impeccable conservative credentials, or who were focusing on limited questions that would not embarrass the administration, were allowed to visit Bushmen. South Africa might then proclaim its support for "science." Better to do research on Bushmen as "pristine people" than to investigate the wider context in which they were located.

Officials at the lower level also helped to choreograph Bushmen's interactions. Writing about the Etosha Game Reserve in a pamphlet produced for the 1935 Wembley Exhibition, the game warden claimed: "In the precinct of these places a study can also be made of the wild Bushmen resident there. They form part and parcel of this sanctuary and afford an interesting study for those anxious to acquaint themselves with their life and pursuits."[50] But as Bushmen in both the Etosha Game Reserve and the Kalahari Gemsbok Park discovered to their dismay, refusing to behave in the manner that officials thought proper for "traditional Bushmen" led to their eviction from these ancestral places.

Today, government policy continues to shape the dance. The World Wide Fund, Ford Foundation, and USAID have, moreover, been promoting "natural resource management" in the name of "sustainable development." Bushmanland has been identified as a place eminently suitable for ecotourism, and they have tried, with some anthropological tinkering, to foist Western-style conservation concepts on the locals. Bushmen's behavior toward tourists is still molded by their version of "claptrap," their perceptions of government policies. In Namibia, a local ecotourist company has a contract for Nyae Nyae in the former Bushmanland. Tourists, carrying cameras, are escorted by locals on "traditional" hunting and foraging expeditions. One of their spokespeople-guides, Benjamin Xishe, justifies these performances in these terms: "We need the young people to see that our way of life is not always the one that loses.... If foreigners come here and pay to see our way of life, maybe the young people will keep learning the skills. Maybe the government will help us keep the Herero out."[51] The camera provides a site for contemporary indigenous political engagement, but the dance continues to mean different things to different people.

THE CAMERA AND THE AUTHENTIC

So far I have discussed the collaborative nature of the "dance" or performance of Bushmanness itself. Yet the overall strategy of the dance was not of Bushmen's devising, and the effects of its staging could not be determined by them. An important mechanism in removing this control has been the camera's reinforcement of "authenticity." Government policy insisted that while "Native Life" was an important tourist commodity, one could look, but not mix, with indigenes. Many anthropologists who were supposed to do fieldwork ran afoul of the regime allegedly for too much mingling. Indeed, "participant-observation," if it ever were a realistic research method, was discouraged in Afrikaans-language *volkekunde* (ethnology) departments.

This situation reinforced the virtues of photography, and especially movies. The camera, as Ed Bruner puts it, is the mask the tourist wears: it allows the tourist to be a voyeur without commitment, while the indigenes work as poseurs.[52] It is a prophylactic, preventing the indigene from returning the "gaze." The use of film and the video camera distinguishes the tourist from the ethnographer; tourism is preeminently concerned with "surrender" in the sense that one is "on vacation" and thus "gives oneself up to the power of another," the tour guide. Ethnography concerns writing and verbal interaction. Certainly, in Nyae Nyae, ecotourists are so busy snapping pictures or videoing that they have no time to get involved in the local life of the community.[53]

The use of photography in ethnography has been widely discussed and debated. While Americans have been much taken with the camera as a research tool, Europeans, and especially Germans, have been more skeptical. In his thorough overview of research methods, Hugo Bernatzik for example, emphasizes the importance of photography as documentary proof, but he is scathing about the use of cinematic film, since it is nearly impossible to shoot unposed sequences.[54] Undoubtedly, the film that has done most to promote the imagery of "pristine Bushmen" has been Jamie Uys's box-office hit *The Gods Must Be Crazy* (1980) which was not only the largest grossing foreign film in the United States but broke records in a number of European countries and Japan and spawned not only a sequel but a minor industry of similar films. Part of the success of *The Gods Must be Crazy* can be attributed to its successful blending of comedy with a pseudo-documentary narrative style. More than any other single factor, the film is widely held to have encouraged tourists to visit Bushmanland, where they hope to encounter "authentic" Bushmen as represented by Uys.

Philosophically, the ideology of "authenticity" is inimical to the age of modernity; yet a preoccupation with the increasing rarity of "true," "original," and "authentic" objects and experiences is one of modernity's key characteristics. In the case of Bushmen, it is anthropologists, documentarians, and, rather perversely, South African Parks Board scientists, who are the authoritative figures in deciding on the "authenticity" of their Bushman wards. To present this "reality" credibly, a number of strategies are employed. Authenticity, as Dean MacCannell points out, is not given, but is negotiable.[55] It varies from audience to audience. What whites in Grootfontein, Namibia, regard as corrupted or trivial in Bushman dance is accepted as authentic in Cape Town.

One device for establishing authenticity and credibility was obtained by looking off the "beaten track" and "beneath the surface." Authenticity or its lack is revealed by going off-stage or behind the scenes and being "in with the natives," or at least with white officials on extended patrols. This is part of the power of John Marshall's filmic corpus, in which the viewer feels constantly "back stage." But frequently this "insider," back-stage sensibility was achieved not after long and close relationships but through a "staging" of a back region. Donald Bain was accused of such staging by the National Parks Board, and he (along with a number of other scientists) argued that the practice was acceptable so long as "technical" problems required it. "Staged authenticity," where both audience and stagers realize that the performance is a performance, is also a common feature of the present age of postmodernity. Yet documentary films still support solid claims to the authentic. Worse, often the footage to be seen is valorized by the claim that the subjects are on the point of extinction, an assertion dating back to at least the middle of the nineteenth century.

The very frameworks by which documentary films establish their authenticity transform Bushman culture into a "tourist culture" that is progressively harder to live out in practice. Film, especially when shown on television, reaches a far wider audience than either photographs or written presentations. Documentaries, typically accepted as educational, are usually done with some authoritative narrator presenting opinion as fact.[56] Perhaps the most important element of ascribing authenticity to "dances," to performed representations, is the ubiquitous fairy tale that outside the "contaminating presence" of the West, there exist ecologically noble folk who live in complete harmony with nature. In many films, making "unspoiled" scenes meant removing all vestiges of Western clothing and other signs of "civilization." Thus, while Bushmen's "dancing" may be quite purposeful, and while it may engage a multitude of meanings, its repeated, command performance must ultimately be considered onerous. Fairy tales have happy endings, but not when Westerners impose them on people and demand they conform to them simply to survive.

CONCLUSION

Performance is very much part of the ideological genealogy of the people of Kagga Kamma, who have a achieved a certain touristic renown as South Africa's "Last Bushmen." Those so labeled are not only "prisoners of their reputation" but, in the view of some, are their own pragmatic agents of self-presentation. Hylton White, in his sensitive study of the Kagga Kamma Bushmen, quotes their leader Dawid Kruiper as saying, "I am an animal of nature. I want the tourists to see me and to know who I am. The only way our tradition and way of life can survive is to live in the memory of the people who see us."[57] The quotation is rapidly becoming canonic, and indeed it is common to find assertions of Bushmen's autonomy. For example, the recently released Namibian documentary *Dancing with the Future* focuses on natural resource–management in the erstwhile Bushmanland. One of the Bushmen interviewed says, quite matter-of-factly, that if the tourists want them dressed in loincloths, then so be it. Yet from the film, it is also clear that they dress in skins not out of a perceived unity with nature but in the hope that their evident poverty will persuade rich Westerners to help them. In a situation that Bushmen perceive as dire poverty, collaboration in maintaining the fairy tale is the easier option.[58]

To be sure, those labeled Bushmen have actively and successfully exploited the ambiguities of their imposed identities. But one must nonetheless be concerned about the voyeuristic quality of knowledge about them. The national identities of Bushmen have been reduced and simplified into a handy bit of shorthand, a salable image. Whatever their initial state, Bushmen are today "inevitably demeaned by tourism into the psychological and political inferiors of the tourists who view them."[59] Their maneuvers, survival gambits, and exercises of autonomy exploit a space of conceptual ambiguity within an overall discourse that is imposed from without. Bushmen play on the moral ambiguities inherent in the position of dominant outsiders, even while those outsiders can, and do, call the tunes. In the dance of the "pristine primitive," Bushmen are still being dispossessed of their complex identities today, just as they have long been of their land. Perhaps this is the ultimate meaning of N!ai's "Don't look at me now, death is dancing me ragged."

NOTES

1. Rudolf Pöch quoted in Fatimah Tobing Rony, *The Third Eye: Race, Cinema, and Ethnographic Spectacle* (Durham, N.C.: Duke University Press, 1996), 65.

2. Ibid., 65.

3. Smitsdrift is a settlement in the Cape for Bushmen who worked for the South African military in Namibia and Angola.

4. Thomas Riccio, " N!ngongiao: People Come Out of Here," *TheatreForum* 10, 1 (1997): 45–59.

5. Dean MacCannell, *Empty Meeting Grounds: The Tourist Papers* (New York: Routledge, 1992).
6. One perhaps thinks here of Erving Goffman's discussion of interaction ritual in *Relations in Public: Microstudies of the Public Order* (New York: Basic Books, 1971); see esp. "Preface."
7. *Webster's Ninth New Collegiate Dictionary* (1984), s.v. "dance."
8. Edward T. Hall, *Dance of Life: The Other Dimension of Time* (Garden City, N.Y.: Anchor Press / Doubleday, 1983).
9. Greg Dening, "The Theatricality of Observing and Being Observed: Eighteenth-Century Europe 'Discovers' the ? Century 'Pacific,' " in *Implicit Understandings: Observing, Reporting, and Reflecting on the Encounters between Europeans and Other Peoples in the Early Modern Era*, ed. Stuart B. Schwartz (New York: Cambridge University Press, 1994), 458.
10. Daniel Boorstin, *The Image: A Guide to Pseudo-Events in America* (New York: Macmillan, 1961).
11. Johannes Fabian, *Time and the Other: How Anthropology Makes Its Object* (New York: Columbia University Press, 1983), 106.
12. Neil Postman, *Amusing Ourselves to Death: Public Discourse in the Age of Show Business* (New York: Viking, 1985), 76. "[W]e have produced in this century a human mutation, a species that substitutes vicarious experience for the real thing," Nadine Gordimer writes of television in "Our Century," *Transition* 71 (1997): 21.
13. John Berger, *Keeping a Rendezvous* (New York: Pantheon Books, 1991); and see Alison Griffiths, "Knowledge and Visuality in Turn of the Century Anthropology," *Visual Anthropology Review* 12, 2 (1996–97).
14. Walter Benjamin, "The Work of Art in the Age of Mechanical Reproduction," in *Illuminations: Essays and Reflections,* ed. Hannah Arendt (1968; New York: Schocken Books, 1969), 238.
15. Gustav Fritsch, *Die Eingeborenen Süd-Afrika's* (Breslau: F. Hirt, 1872), 4.
16. Helga-Marie Pacher, *Anthropologische Untersuchungen an den Skeletten der Rudolf Pöch'schen Buschmannsammlung* (Graz: H. Böhlaus, 1961). These included sixty-six complete skeletons and over a hundred skulls.
17. See Walter Hirschberg, *Völkerkundliche Ergebnisse der südafrikanischen Reisen Rudolf Pöch's in den Jahren 1907 bis 1909* (Vienna: Anthropologischen Gesellschaft in Wien, 1936). It is quite probable that Bushmen were rounded up for Pöch by Cape authorities who had been instructed to render all possible assistance to his research.
18. The lineage is long and distinguished, and moves from Denver to De Schauensee, Vernay Lang, Ciprioti, Loeb, Morden, Panhard, Bjerre, and, most important, the Marshall and van der Post multiple expeditions, followed by Marlin Perkins with his made-for-TV quest.
19. Dr. Louis Fourie to Donald Bain, Tsumeb, December 10, 1925, Fourie Collection, MuseumAfrika, Johannesburg.
20. "The social impact of films upon newly literate Africans is likely to be more pronounced than upon Europeans, and it should be noticed that in all countries anxiety is expressed regarding the tendency of many films to glorify violent crime and erotic passion." Lord Hailey, *An African Survey: A Study of Problems Arising in Africa South of the Sahara* (London: Oxford University Press, 1938; rev. ed. 1957, 1968), 125.
21. Letter from Quarter-Master Watson & Sgt. Major Castle, October 27, 1919, SWAA A50/57 Films, National Archives of Namibia.
22. Magistrate, Swakopmund, March 29, 1934, SWAA A50/57 Films, National Archives of Namibia. The content of the film was not an issue as the South African Board of Censors had already developed a classification of films with the following viewing categories: (a) European, (b) Natives, (c) Children, (d) Females, (e) Males. National Archives of Namibia.

23. SWAA A50/57 Films, National Archives of Namibia.

24. File A183/9 Film Censorship: Cinematographic Film Ordinance, National Archives of Namibia. For contemporary debates on the impact of movies in the United States, see Herbert Blumer and Philip M. Hauser, *Movies, Delinquency, and Crime* (New York: Macmillan, 1933); Herbert Blumer, *Movies and Conduct* (New York: Macmillan, 1933).

25. By virtue of the 1928 ordinance, inspectors could reject films for any of the following reasons: (a) endangering the safety of the state; (b) contrary to good policy; (c) may cause a disturbance of public order; (d) calculated to offend the religious convictions or feelings of the public; (e) calculated to bring any section of the public into ridicule or contempt; (f) offends against ordinary decency; and (g) contrary to good morals. As "keepers of morals," women were appointed to this board in equal numbers to men. File A183/9 Film Censorship: Cinematographic Film Ordinance, National Archives of Namibia. See also William Marston Seabury, *Motion Picture Problems: The Cinema and the League of Nations* (New York: Avondale Press, 1929). Seabury was the former general counsel to the Motion Picture Board of Trade.

26. Thelma Gutsche, *The History and Social Significance of Motion Pictures in South Africa, 1895–1940* (Cape Town: Howard Timmins, 1972), 299–300.

27. Ibid., 302.

28. Michael Taussig, *Mimesis and Alterity: A Particular History of the Senses* (New York: Routledge, 1993), 198.

29. This and the next clipping are from the private ephemera collection of John Bain, Hawaii, and lack precise identifications and dates.

30. Taussig, *Mimesis and Alterity*, 208.

31. Taken from Julius Lips's classic work *The Savage Hits Back* (1937; New Hyde Park, N.Y.: University Books, 1966), which first examined how colonized peoples used art as a means of resistance. The following four paragraphs are derived from Robert J. Gordon, *Picturing Bushmen* (Athens: Ohio University Press, 1997).

32. Viktor Lebzelter, *Eingeborenenkulturen in Südwest- und Südafrika wissenschaftliche Ergebnisse einer Forschungsreise nach Süd- und Südwestafrika in den Jahren 1926–1928* (Leipzig: Karl W. Hiersemann, 1934), 82; my emphasis. As if to drive home the point, he continued: "These Bushmen are really protection officials who watch over the game, but they are also volunteer police who catch all Ovambo who try to avoid the Pass controls at Namutoni. Generally, they are still the most well-armed Bushmen" (my translation).

33. O. Crosby to L. Fourie, Fourie Collection, MuseumAfrika, Johannesburg.

34. F. W. Ahrens, *From Bench to Bench: Reflections, Reminiscences and Records* (Pietermaritzburg: Shuter & Shooter, 1948), 151–52.

35. Dorothea Bleek, for example, wrote to Maingard, "Dr Ballantine showed some photographs taken at Bain's camp. My sister and I both recognized the old 'voorman' as one of the men I had photographed when with Miss Wilman and Scotty Smith in 1911. He was then at Lentlands Pan further south than Witdraai.... I wonder whether... some [of them] are /auni from further north," Bleek to Maingard, July 23, 1936, Maingard Collection, UNISA, Pretoria. It is also likely that they were also measured and photographed by Pöch. For more on Bleek, see Skotnes, this volume.

36. Bain's "collection camp" some 215 miles north of Upington near the hamlet of Kyky attracted many journalists. The correspondent for *Die Burger* reported that "racially pure" Bushmen were scarce but that the Coloured in the area spoke an old style Dutch. Yet many of the "Bushmen" girls, unbeknown to many of the scientists, were singing songs in an Afrikaans dialect from a previous era. So much for authenticity. Nevertheless, "It is worth

the trouble to see a lot of Bushmen dance" (*Die Burger,* July 31, 1936, "Hoe Kalahari Boesmans Vriende Maak").

37. To quote Duggan-Cronin from the *Diamond Fields Advertiser* (undated, on file in the Maingard Collection, UNISA, Pretoria): "My great difficulty was the changing of photographic plates. This I had to do in a mud hut while two boys held blankets over me. Underneath the blankets I had a red lamp. The heat was terrible also and there was little shade.... These Bushmen are the easiest people in the world to work with. They have not yet learned to be mercenary."

38. *Rand Daily Mail,* July 2, 1936.

39. Shane Peacock, *The Great Farini: The High-Wire Life of William Hunt* (Toronto: Viking, 1995).

40. Fred C. Cornell, *The Glamour of Prospecting: Wanderings of a South African Prospector in Search of Copper, Gold, Emeralds, and Diamonds* (London: T. F. Unwin, 1920; reprint, Cape Town, 1989).

41. Gutsche, *History and Social Significance,* 176.

42. On Botswana, see, e.g., Nicholas Luard, *The Last Wilderness: A Journey across the Great Kalahari Desert* (New York: Simon & Schuster, 1981), who recalls finding Bushmen who were tending Tswana farmer's fields. "They'd encountered Europeans before, and they knew what they were expected to do: plait rope from fibrous leaves, carve beads from ostrich eggshells, make fire from sticks.... It was simply a ritual obligation on both sides—the San to demonstrate their skills, I the foreigner, to observe, which was what they'd learned foreigners wished to do" (203–4).

43. *Die Burger,* May 11 and 12, 1937.

44. Magistrate, Upington, to Sec. NAD, August 19, 1937, NTS 9587 382/400, Bushman Reserve, vol. 2, National Archives of South Africa, Pretoria.

45. NTS 9587 382/400, Bushman Reserve, vol. 2., National Archives of South Africa, Pretoria. After World War II, /khanako and her friends moved to the Botswana side of the Nossob River: Sec 108 S. 108/2/2, Botswana National Archives, Gaborone. Ciraj Rassool and Patricia Hayes are currently working on a biography of /khanako.

46. See, e.g., Margarethe von Eckenbrecher, *Was Afrika mir Gab und Nahm: Erlebnisse einer deutschen Frau in Südwestafrika* (Berlin: E. S. Mittler & Sohn, 1909; new ed., 1937, 1940); Negley Farson, *Behind God's Back* (New York: : Harcourt, Brace, 1941); Sidney Legendre, *Okavango, The Desert River* (New York: J. Messner, 1939); and Margareta Oldevig, *The Sunny Land* (Cape Town: Howard Timmins, 1944).

47. *Die Beeld,* May 4, 1986.

48. *Rand Daily Mail,* July 22, 1936.

49. South West Africa Administration (SWAA) A198/52–56, Nat. Arch. of Namibia, contains many examples of this.

50. File Native Administration Ovamboland NAO 33/1, October 15, 1935, Nat. Arch. of Namibia.

51. Rupert Isaacson, "Call of the Wild," *Daily Telegraph,* November 2, 1996.

52. Edward M. Bruner, "The Ethnographer/Tourist in Indonesia," in *International Tourism: Identity and Change,* ed. Marie-Françoise Lanfant et al. (Thousand Oaks, Calif.: Sage Publications, 1995). The relationship between tourist and anthropologist is complex, because, as Bruner points out: "Colonialism, ethnography, and tourism occur at different historical periods, but arise from the same social formation, and are variant forms of expansionism occupying the space opened up by the extensions of power" (E. M. Bruner, "Of Cannibals, Tourists and Ethnographers," *Cultural Anthropology* 4 [1989]: 439).

53. Isaacson, "Call of the Wild." In order to stop their obsessive photo snapping, local people sometimes make tourists carry firewood!

54. Hugo Adolf Bernatzik, *Afrika: Handbuch der angewandten Völkerkunde* (Innsbruck: Schlüsselverlag, 1947).

55. Dean MacCannell, *The Tourist: A New Theory of the Leisure Class* (New York: Schocken Books, 1976).

56. Janet Dixon Keller, "Schemes for Schemata," in *New Directions in Psychological Anthropology*, ed. Theodore Schwartz et al. (New York: Cambridge University Press,1992).

57. Hylton White, *In the Tradition of Our Forefathers: Bushman Traditionality at Kagga Kamma: The Politics and History of a Performative Identity* (Rondebosch, South Africa: University of Cape Town Press in association with the Centre for African Studies, 1995), 1, 17.

58. Keyan Tomaselli, pers. comm. (from an undated draft of a paper, 1997).

59. Stuart Hall, "What Is This 'Black' in Black Popular Culture?" in Michele Wallace, *Black Popular Culture: A Project*, ed. Gina Dent (Seattle: Bay Press, 1992; reprinted in *Representing Blackness: Issues in Film and Video*, ed. Valerie Smith [New Brunswick, N.J.: Rutgers University Press, 1997]), 24.

Chapter 9

Decentering the Gaze at French Colonial Exhibitions

Catherine Hodeir

"Curiosité, c'est ignorance," the organizers of the ethnographic exhibit on the French colonies proclaimed at the opening in May 1931 of the Exposition coloniale internationale in Paris, one of the most significant exhibitions of its kind. It was indeed an apt expression for the representation of Africa and Africans that European national and "universal" exhibitions promulgated in the late nineteenth century. The African mise-en-scène displayed in them entailed a complex interaction and distancing between the object and its presentation. Africa was the aphrodisiac of the unknown: it appealed greatly to the European urban public, but it was only a fragmentary and partially revealed object of study. What were the stakes of knowledge about Africa in the 1930s? And why were interactions between "dark" Africa and the Enlightenment gaze of the West framed by notions of authenticity and identity?

THE *FÊTE COLONIALE* AND THE STILL IMAGE

Four distinct roles were ascribed to Africans on display at the 1889 Paris Universal Exhibition. On the Champ-de-Mars, at the foot of the Eiffel Tower, the so-called "natives" appeared as entertainers (singers, dancers, musicians); as waiters in restaurants and bars; as shopkeepers and craftsmen; and finally, as "themselves," in which role they referenced a lost pastoral existence. In the aftermath of World War I, a new position emerged in the colonial spectacle, that of the *tirailleur sénégalais*. Known by his highly recognizable uniform, the French African colonial soldier, or *tirailleur,* was integrated with other colonial native roles to form a complete metropolitan spectacle. The result appeared in numerous European exhibitions (see the list on page 248).

The presentation of an "innocent" native African village can be tied to the exhibition of a "Senegalese Village" at the Champ-de-Mars in 1889. It was immediately a very popular attraction. Four years after the Conference of Berlin in 1885, the "great steeplechase" for the African continent had already begun.[1] France was already in a dominant position in Senegal and Gabon. The presentation of the "new primitives," fenced inside an imagined village and wearing leopard-skin loincloths, stimulated public curiosity and excitement.[2] Seeing them in their "natural habitat," the photographer, the portraitist, the journalist, and the simple tourist experienced the "innocent native" as a representative of a former stage of human development.

The Senegalese "natives" were to present themselves in this light before thousands of daily visitors. An easy task? Perhaps not as easy as it seems. The first rule of their performance was to repeat recognizable gestures continuously, gestures that were at once specific, unambivalent, and yet continually evolving. In the 1931 exhibition, "fisherman" and "oarsman" presented a show of "native techniques" every hour on the Seine and subsequently on Lake Daumesnil.[3] Women pounded millet with mortar and pestle and cooked a meal on an open fire three or four times a day. One of the most widely awaited spectacles was the Muslim prayer, which transpired in a situation of complete promiscuity among "infidel" visitors. A form of impromptu pastoralism was evoked by adults' interactions with African children. The children cast a watchful eye over imagined fields from a watchtower at the 1889 exhibition, but also jumped into a pond to retrieve coins thrown by amused visitors. The spectacle of the newborn, in some cases born during the exhibition itself, as in Rouen in 1896, was an inscription of a distinctly different cultural becoming. The infant wrapped behind the mother's back in a colorful piece of cloth was a constant source of fascination for passing spectators: it was never too early to take up the career of "native" performer at colonial exhibitions.[4]

Yet another fixture at the colonial exhibitions was the "native" artisan-shopkeeper. The African artisan was known for four distinct crafts: weaving, leather work, blacksmithing, and goldsmithing. At the 1889 exhibition, blacksmiths forged all kinds of African and Western objects: gun barrels, knives and daggers, swords and spurs, watch chains and key rings, tear-drop earrings, and scissors. A wooden fence at the 1900 exhibition shielded Senegalese artisan-shopkeepers from intrusive crowds (the scene evoking a zoo); looking over it, visitors saw another archetype, the Senegalese weaver with his assistant, probably his son. At an adjacent stand, a crowd gathered around a goldsmith, entranced by his dancing mallet fashioning the precious metal.[5]

The presence of native craftsmen in the context of displays of new instantaneous communication technologies reinforced the role of the universal exhibitions themselves as harbingers of modernity. Nineteenth-century exhibitions in Paris regularly featured a Galerie des machines, where French workers demonstrated their recently mechanized trades before the public. African artisans were also part of the overall spectacle. At the 1937 Universal Exhibition, the "native" craftsman stood alongside his metropolitan brethren, integrated into the broader realm of French craftsmanship, in an exhibit called "Arts et techniques de la vie moderne." African craftsman were intended to reflect the economic policy that French governments

Figure 9.1. Senegalese weaver and apprentice, Universal Exhibition, Paris, 1900. Collection iconographique Maciet, Bibliothèque des Arts décoratifs, Paris. Reproduced by permission.

of the 1930s wished to institute. This policy consisted in developing handicrafts, and not industries, in their colonies. French factories would be "protected" from African competition and would keep their privileged markets; and consequently, no dangerous "native" working classes would arise in the French empire. By political design, African crafts were represented as purely traditional. Thus a young girl from Ségou, Mali (formerly French Sudan), wove traditional motifs in the 1931 exhibition. Fifty years later, however, she revealed that visitors had asked her to copy motifs for them and that she had added them into her repertoire and brought them back to Africa.[6]

Musicians, singers, and dancers were the featured attractions at the exhibitions. In the 1931 exhibition, every Sunday night, from May to November, a procession appeared along the Grande Avenue des Colonies. The weekly parade presented a sample of the exhibits in the Colonial Exhibition, which, in turn, represented the larger tapestry of the French empire. The parade also publicized the theatrical presentations in the exhibition, such as "An African Fairy Tale," "Dancing and Singing

Figure 9.2. Senegalese jeweler's workshop, Universal Exhibition, Paris, 1900. Collection iconographique Maciet, Bibliothèque des Arts décoratifs, Paris. Reproduced by permission.

from the Colonial World," "Colonial Nights," and "Farewell to the Colonies." The numerous shows drew larger audiences than the regular Paris theater at the time. Although the "natives" who performed on stage had to be very professional, the shows they acted in were considered to be the quintessence of "primitivism." André Maurois, a member of the Académie française, whose popular book on the 1931 Colonial Exhibition was widely distributed at the time, wrote: "For the primitive, dance is the highest form of escapism. Like a member of a symphonic orchestra, a poet reciting an ode... the African subject, in flight from hostile surroundings, looks for solace in rhythmic movement.... Ahhhhh! How the monotony of the tom-toms calms the restless spirit."[7]

The revered tom-tom at the exhibition was a reversal of existing colonial rules in French West Africa, which often forbade it. "Administrators have forbidden celebrations along with tom-tom drums on the grounds that they find them bothersome."[8] On the other hand, what kind of music was really played? The label on the "Bambaras' Band" record from the 1931 exhibition lists the musical piece, "Coup de Chaleur," and under it, "Fox trot." It is true that a certain black African elite was already listening and dancing to Western music played on gramophones imported to Africa. The so-called "African primitive" shows of the Colonial Exhibition may well have been a *métissage*.

African dancers also participated in staging the evening fairy tales on the fairgrounds of the exhibition, while the Théâtre d'eau, held on the Daumesnil Lake, used elaborate modern technology. "At the beginning of each show, the atmosphere of magic was summoned by a demonstration on water in which a circle of canoes were disguised as floating huts.... Then on-stage, Africans carrying torches would move the flame to the rhythmic syncopation of the music."[9] If by 1900 the intimacy of the *kora*-playing griot had been established as a proper form of entertainment for metropolitan audiences, the water and light show combined "native" subjects with technological mastery in a "mass spectacle." It rehearsed the terms of an emergent political ideology, the dominance of European technology in evolutionary and productive terms.

The unknown identity and intrametropolitan interactions of the numerous African waiters and waitresses at the exhibitions are passed over in silence in the official literature. Guide books and book illustrations only punctuated this silence with servant-master dichotomies. The appearance of the tirailleur sénégalais, on the other hand, tended toward overexposure in its constant repetition. The popularity of what was known as *la force noire* dates to the trench warfare of the Great War and to stories of the steadfastness of the African tirailleur.[10] Since the tirailleur Bakary Diallo had appeared on the packaging of the French breakfast cocoa Banania, visitors to the exhibition could already identify the costume and were at ease with the military bearing of the Senegalese riflemen.[11] The tirailleurs were the official escort of government officials from the opening to the closing ceremonies of the 1931 exhibition, and as sentries guarding the French West African Pavilion, they would lower the flag from the "Bronze Tower," which represented the French Overseas Military Forces, in the official phrasing, "uniting the peoples of Empire under one flag to the trumpet's call."[12]

Images of the exhibition were multiplied thousands of times through the media of the day. French newspapers of all political persuasions maintained full daily coverage of the Colonial Exhibition through 1931. Conservatives and radical socialists alike could get their daily dose from *Le Figaro* or *L'Echo de Paris* as well as *L'Oeuvre* or *Le Populaire*. *Le Temps* and *L'Illustration* followed the exhibition most closely for their elite group of subscribers, but the more popular daily *Paris Soir*, with an average daily distribution of 130,000, also published daily photos and cover stories on the events at the exhibition.[13] A representative photo in *Paris Soir* depicts the African "native" alongside zebras and monkeys from the Vincennes zoo.[14] This association between African "natives" and African animals related not only to their mode of display, but to the evolutionary narrative of the civilizing process.

The encounter with the "authentic" African "savage" was a favorite subject in newspapers and guidebooks. Eugène Monod, in an illustrated volume, remarked on the ethos of maternal charity that Parisian women quickly established with Africans on display at the 1889 exhibition. "They would often bring sweets or candies, which were most appreciated by the African subjects. This form of nurturing underscored a belief among Parisians that these curious people were simply overgrown children. An accurate appraisal."[15] From time to time, there were accounts of reporters escorting Africans around Paris. These encounters would bring to light the usual stereotypes, which opposed the perceptions of the "primitive" African to the "civilized" complexity of the City of Light and Enlightenment. On other occasions, an imagined cannibalism resurfaced from a concealed savagery, as during the visit of some Gabonese Pahoins in 1889.[16]

There was a veritable mania for Africa in 1931. Songs, games, and advertisements were everywhere. The "Official March of the Colonial Exhibition" was composed, recorded and sold at the exhibition; it was entitled "Nenufar," or "water lily" (*nénuphar*), and represented the exoticized colonial male subject. Part of the song, in translation, went as follows: "Nenufar's conception of elegant dress was to put gloves on his feet; he was barely clothed and his hair gleamed like rough steel wool." Nenufar exemplified the masculine as fetish, which seduced Parisian women spectators.[17] A more degrading stereotype was the "Displayed African Woman," known as the "Négresse à Plateau." And among the toys inspired by the Colonial Exhibition was a basketball hoop for children featured in the 1931 window display at the Galeries Lafayette department store. Its hoop was the orifice created by the distended lower lip of an African woman. A political cartoon in a fashion magazine positions this same ubiquitous black female figure on her knees with an ashtray protruding from her lower lip in the middle of a Parisian salon, where fancy, chattering white women delicately ash their cigarettes.[18]

The advertisements for the exhibition were somewhat less spectacular, and many were anchored in the reality of African workers serving white settlers. Muscular black men were shown helping a recent French settler unload a truck of Englebert tires or carrying boxes of Vilmorin seed under the eye of a colonial foreman. Other advertisements featured the "resourceful African" who benefited from modern French technology such as the gas stove, which replaced open fires, or Lustucru pasta (to be prepared on such a stove), which provided food for a large family.

The stereotype of the African subject was a significant mode of address at the exhibition; its presentation implied an emplotment of humanity across a spectrum of increasing levels of civilization. In the dichotomy between nature and culture, the "white" European was culture personified, the "yellow" Asian in an upper middle range between nature and culture, the "Arab from North Africa" in a lower middle range, and the "black" African was closest to nature.

BEHIND THE SCENES

In spite of major shifts in the depictions of Africa in French anthropology, popular representations of African subjects displayed significant continuities in the fifty years from the 1880s to the 1930s. Modern anthropology was present at Paris exhibitions in 1931 and in 1937, albeit for a restricted audience in scientific conferences. At the

Figure 9.3. "Le gaz aux colonies." Advertisement, 1931. *L'Illustration* (Paris), May 23, 1931. Reproduced by permission.

time, anthropology was reconsidering its way of looking at "primitive" civilizations, while public perceptions were still being shaped by the presentation of racial and cultural stereotypes as scientific truths. We are thus led to further probe the intentions of the organizers at the exhibitions.

In 1889, the man behind the display of the Senegalese Village was Commandant Noirot, a colonial administrator and ethnographer who had spent an extended period of his life in Senegal. By bringing representatives of several African ethnic groups to Paris, Noirot attempted to provide a setting in which the public at large and anthropologists in particular could observe and study actual Gabonese and Senegalese subjects. "From head to foot, each 'specimen' is catalogued," wrote Eugène Monod. "The head is round, brahycephalic, dolichocephalic...." Such measurements "lead us to conclude that the Wolof ethnic group is intelligent.... Let us educate them, develop their natural propensities, and we shall make them into first-class auxiliaries of the colonial enterprise."[19]

The racial hierarchy established at the end of the nineteenth century was implemented by Louis Marin in the Ethnographic Section of the 1931 Colonial Exhibition. "The Negroid races of Africa and the Pacific Islands may be educated to a certain extent, but cannot be assimilated." A series of dioramas at the Musée des Colonies demonstrated the point. The first window represented a barely clothed

African student before the African teacher; the second display featured the same student, this time wearing a *pagne* (loincloth) at a French primary school; the third depicted the student wearing a *boubou* at a technical training school; and in the fourth and final display, the African pupil was transformed, dressed in pants and shirt, at a college-level technical school.[20]

Just a stone's throw away from the Musée des Colonies, Marshal Louis Lyautey, the commissioner of the 1931 Colonial Exhibition, opened the Congrès international et intercolonial de la Société indigène. In his opening address, which was aimed at influencing French public opinion, he proclaimed: "We must begin to understand that we are dealing with races that are not inferior, but different, left back by a civilizational deficit." Earlier that year, still in the conference hall at the Cité des informations,[21] the organizers of the first international conference on colonial history had written a preamble to their sessions: "[W]e can no longer uphold the distinction between superior and inferior races." Finally, at the exhibition in 1937, Paul Rivet, the founder of the rebuilt Musée de l'Homme, affirmed that "those peoples who have been labeled 'savage' and more recently called 'primitive' could be advanced" and might soon "have a history." "Do these peoples hailing from preindustrial societies retain a sense of authenticity? Are they less deprived than we have previously thought, less easily understood than imagined, and less receptive to outside intervention?"[22] By making this proclamation, Rivet distanced himself from "classical" racial typology. One of the pioneers of an emergent French Anthropology, Rivet in 1937 convoked a Congrès international de l'évolution culturelle des peuples coloniaux (International Conference on Colonial Peoples' Cultural Evolution). The name of this conference in 1937 can be compared with the title of a similar event six years earlier, the Congrès international et intercololonial de la société indigène, mentioned above. The titles of the two conferences emphasize the debate about the status of the "native" (*indigène*) developed over the course of the 1930s and revealed at the exhibitions. At the Congrès de la société indigène, in 1931, Louis Massignon was already drawing attention to the fact that *indigène* could be interpreted as pejorative. The day following his statement, the Paris newspapers published a proclamation to French troops in Tunisia ordering officers to refrain from using the term *indigène* and to say "Tunisian" instead.[23] Nonetheless, *indigène* continued to be used south of the Sahara until well after World War II.

Behind the scenes, the representation of the "native" was at once a complex performance and an ideologically loaded rendering. More and diverse kinds of roles were in the works. The reception of "native peoples on display" was perceived through their contextualization in a performative setting and an evolutionary narrative. From the beginning, organizers were caught in multiple contradictions: authenticity and glamour, attraction and comfort, pedagogy and limited space.

In 1889, the organizers of the first *village nègre* (the nickname of the Senegalese village) sought to inventory the various housing structures from different regions of Senegal, all assembled as part of a single, model African village. This condensation of Senegalese structures consisted of a "Coampan" habitation from

Saint-Louis, a "Toucouleur" cabin, a "Wolof" hut, a cabin from Fouta Djalon, a "Bambara" house, and so on. Such an architectural amalgam could never and would never exist, except in an exhibition. Nonetheless, the Paris public had the impression of being privy to an authentic African experience. The visitor's attention to the African architecture on display was focused on its stylistic vagaries and novelty, its exotic otherness.

An even more elaborate exhibition was assembled in Lyon in 1894. Two African villages were joined by a wooden bridge. The official catalogue of the Lyon exhibition, the *Livre d'or*, noted this scenic addition after describing the materials used to construct the two villages. The first village consisted of clay and mud, and the second village of lighter huts was built of branches and leaves. The significance of the construction materials corresponded to the natural resources of French West Africa, especially of the coast and in the French Sudan.

Representations of colonial urban spaces complemented the rural "authentic" African settings. At the 1894 Exposition universelle de Lyon, an "African street corner" harkened back to the rue du Caire at the 1889 Universal Exhibition, which also prefigured the rue de Djenné of the 1931 Colonial Exhibition. In the rue de Bakel at the Lyon exhibition, "one would enter a narrow winding street and be led toward small fenced enclosures made of rush plants, which formed small courtyards. Here and there, scattered aloe plants had taken root in the wall, yucca plants sprouted out of a chink in a house and the tendrils of watermelon plants would cling to the surface of a rough-textured wall."[24] The presence of what might be perceived as "African" plants—although all them could also be found on other continents, and were able to survive a season in Paris—offset the abundant European vegetation around Lake Daumesnil, authenticating the setting. Authenticity was not verisimilitude, however, and no mud, trash, dirt, dangerous animals, or poisonous insects were allowed. The model of a sanitized African village actualized ideas in colonial hygiene and offered an imagined African landscape for European visitors who might be discomfited by a real trip to Africa.

At an exhibition setting as large as the 1931 Colonial Exhibition, the pavilion was the preferred architectural choice. Sub-Saharan Africa was no exception. The French possessions were fragmented into several pavilions according to the colonial partition of the African territories: French West Africa (AOF), French Equatorial Africa (AEF), the Somali Coast and Madagascar, and Cameroon and Togo. The Belgian Congo pavilion represented various foreign colonial metropoles. The United Kingdom declined Lyautey's invitation to showcase British colonial possessions, but Portugal did not, using a fifteenth-century fortress to exhibit Portuguese activities in Mozambique and Angola.[25]

The organizers of the 1931 Colonial Exhibition as well as the architects of the pavilions kept four rules in mind: visibility, pedagogy, entertainment, and security. Adhering to these rules was challenging, and they were often upheld at the cost of "authenticity." Most of the African pavilions were in one distinct regional architectural style, but a hybrid approach was adopted in the joint Cameroonian-Togolese pavilion, in an interesting pedagogical-architectural synthesis. The pavilion itself was a rectangular-shaped building inspired by the clay huts, typical of the southern forest region, while the cone-shaped roof, made of straw, evoked the roundness of northern structures built on the savannah. Another device typically deployed to project an imaginary vision of sub-Saharan Africa was to enlarge various civilizational artifacts. For example, the pathway leading to the Belgian pavilion was lined with oversized shields and spears, evoking a larger-than-life heroic mythology. Welcoming the visitor at the entrance to the Malagasy pavilion, a gigantic tower was crowned with a series of four stylized Zebu cattle heads, vaguely resembling an American Indian totem pole. The tower was supposed to be an example of Malagasy funerary monuments, which, in Madagascar, are constructed on a human rather than a monumental scale; an actual Zebu skull is placed atop a pile of stones and branches.

Oversizing was also the technique used to display one of the best-known African architectural forms: the red, bricklike *tata*. The tata is a fortified palace from the Niger valley and in fact does exist on a monumental scale, and for this reason was used as the archetypal West African built form for colonial exhibitions in Marseille (1922), Wembley (1924), and Paris (1931). Tatas found in the Niger were never more than 20 meters high, but the West African pavilion at the 1922 Marseille exhibition was a towering 57 meters (nearly 180 feet). At the 1931 Colonial Exhibition, the tata was 45 meters (almost 150 feet) high and was designed with an elevator that carried visitors to the top in order to admire the panorama of the reconstructed colonial city—all while still on the outskirts of Paris.

This view contributed to the cinematographic effect built into the design of the exhibition itself. Upon arriving on the main thoroughfare of the exhibition, known as the Avenue des Colonies, visitors enacted a dolly shot, traveling from the modest Somali pavilion to the huge gray mass of the centerpiece of the exhibition, Angkor Wat. A little further along, built on the same scale, was the red brick tata of French West Africa, the final monument before the shot ended at the Bronze Tower. The ephemeral architecture of the exhibition was analogous to a film set, requiring limited construction time and even less time to dismantle. For the sake of durability, steel, wood, and ceramic lattice-work were used for construction. A rough mortar of cement and lime was used to reproduce an adobe-style texture, and the red brick color of the karite butter exterior was imitated with spray paint.[26]

The final effect was nonetheless striking. The West African Pavilion, designed by the architects Olivier and Lambert, was much talked about at the 1931 Colonial Exhibition, although it was judged second-best in comparison with Angkor Wat by the media. In press reports, the two were used as metonymic devices demonstrating the respective degree of civilization of the "Indochinese" and African peoples. Angkor Wat was described by one journalist as *the* peerless Khmer monument, "cut like a jewel, [and] covered with magnificent chiseled designs." The attendant press corps rated it as far more sophisticated than the simple red tata, which was

Figure 9.4. French Western African Pavilion, seen from the upper terrace of restaurant, International Colonial Exposition, Paris, 1931. Bibliothèque des Arts décoratifs, Paris. Reproduced by permission.

described as "roughly made and topped with enormous mud *chignons* bristling with stakes."[27]

Curiously enough, most journalists and guidebooks mistakenly described the West African pavilion as the mosque of Djenné, although every bar of the ornate grillwork doors was a fetish, which would be entirely unacceptable in a Muslim house of God. The 1931 Colonial Exhibition was the end of an era of architectural referencing that had begun with the Paris Universal Exhibition of 1900, which featured reconstructed mosques from Djenné and Timbuktu. By the 1931 exhibition, the ghost of the Djenné mosque as it appears in the press and the details of the tata evoked a collective memory of past exhibitions. The French West African Pavilion was certainly not the Djenné mosque, but rather an elaborate combination of Sudanese and neo-Sudanese architecture. Moreover, the original mosque at Djenné did not exist anymore, having been restored by French architects at the beginning of the century in a way not appreciated by the inhabitants of the region. So, was the pavilion a copy of a copy? Do we have a few remaining details from a reworked copy, transferred onto the tata at the 1931 Colonial Exhibition? Or do we simply have a neo-Sudanese piece of architecture created by the architects Olivier and Lambert?[28]

The African settings at the exhibitions were based on an architectural *ré-écriture* that responded to the exigencies of a metropolitan public spectacle and its site-specific logistics. The constructions were designed to be taller than the treetops for panoramic visibility. Next, the security and free circulation of thousands of visitors had to be ensured. Above all, however, the exhibitions' organizers sought to create symbols of an imagined Africa and to facilitate a popular colonial consciousness. French public opinion was not yet convinced of the need for a colonial empire before World War II, and it was precisely the function of the exhibitions to instill a popular will into and sense of collective responsibility for the colonial enterprise.[29]

Behind the scenes of the exhibition, another vision emerges. In the evening, the African performers left their "native villages" and went to their dormitories (if unmarried) or rooms (if they were couples), which were equipped with modern conveniences. After taking a shower, they put on European clothing provided by the organizers. (Even in front of the public, in 1900 Parisian African "natives" had to wear grey flannel when the temperature suddenly dropped.) A soup kitchen prepared the performers' preferred cuisine. They were either paid a salary or they received a percentage on the souvenirs and handicrafts they made and sold at the exhibition. For the most part, the African participants were hired on a contract of limited duration that stipulated a six-day work week. One of them acted as their spokesman in mediating the inevitable disputes with the exhibition's organizers over its six-month duration. In short, they were wage laborers.[30]

Many of the Senegalese who appeared as part of the Village nègre in 1889 were rehired for subsequent exhibitions in Europe. They thus became specialized performers. Their children and grandchildren were initiated into their theatrical tradition and appeared as part of reconstructed "native villages" in the 1920s and 1930s. Even though they belonged to different ethnic groups, African village performers developed into "family" businesses with contacts and trade secrets, like circus families. At the 1931 exhibition, the African performers were French-educated. A group of young Malagasy performers requested official authorization to continue their education in France, after having passed the *baccalauréat* school-leaving examination in Paris. The exhibitions' organizers also scheduled leisure activities for the African actors: trips to the Eiffel Tower and to Versailles were interspersed with shopping trips to French textile mills.[31] The already-mentioned weaver woman from Ségou, as a young girl at the 1931 exhibition, had been delighted by a boat ride on the Seine in a *bateau-mouche*.[32]

A small number of works of fiction refer to the African workers in the exhibitions. In Ousmane Socé's 1937 novel *Mirages de Paris* the main character is a man named Fara.[33] Shortly after he arrives in Paris from French West Africa in 1931, Fara takes the metro to visit the Colonial Exhibition, where he happens to meet a good friend. "Ambrousse was selling Moroccan rugs that were made, for commercial reasons, in the country of the *négresses à plateau*. He asked Fara to return the next day to work with him. He would take him on as an associate and share the profits."[34] This arrangement between Fara and Ambrousse is plausible enough. Whether or not the A.-O. F. (Afrique-Occidentale française) commissioner gave his authorization, who would pay attention to one more African rug seller?

Figure 9.5. "Coco Banania et les poissons-volants," 1931. *Coeurs Vaillants* (Paris), May 31, 1931. Reproduced with the kind permission of the Bibliothèque de Documentation internationale contemporaine (BDIC), Nanterre, France; and the Association pour la Connaissance de l'Histoire de l'Afrique contemporaine (ACHAC), Paris, France.

In May 1931, a popular children's magazine, *Coeurs Vaillants*, offered a short comic strip to its young readers: "Coco, Banania, and the Flying Fishes."[35] Two little African children, both named for chocolate consumer products, long for their parents, who have gone off to work as "natives" at the Paris Colonial Exhibition. The little girl weeps so much that her tears soon make an ocean ("J'ai fait pousser la mer," she says). All of a sudden, two flying fishes come out of the water and offer to take Coco and Banania on their backs and fly to the Eiffel Tower. In the happy ending of this "Colonial Exhibition tale," the children join their bewildered parents at Vincennes.

DECENTERING THE GAZE: OTHERNESS, SELF-REFLECTION, AND THE EUROPEAN SUBJECT

A less perceptible gaze can finally be addressed, if not fully elucidated: that of African participants in French colonial exhibitions. Their perspectives on the European visitors and administrators as well as on the status of their own presence in the exhibitions can only be partially recovered through absences in the historical documentation. As figures outside of the official discourse, their participation as imperial subjects represented a structured silence. They either belonged to the very small African elite that was considered to be assimilated (and who played the

French game very well) or they were people who hesitated to use the written word to protest against colonial domination. Only in 1937 did Paul Rivet invite the young Léopold Sédar Senghor—who would later become president of Senegal—to speak on the "Senegalese bourgeoisie and the French Colonial school system" at the Congrès des peuples coloniaux (and Senghor had not yet fully developed his theory of *négritude*). For the most part, therefore, we are forced to reinterpret the significance and orientation of the official commentary on the African participants from the margins.

In a commentary on the 1900 exhibition, one journalist noted that "representatives of the Wolof ethnic group are the most civilized of the Senegalese. They exhibit such pride in being considered French that they attempt to assume this identity as often as possible."[36] As curator of the colonial section at the 1900 Universal Exhibition, Jules Charles-Roux wrote, "these blacks quite understand our civilization and voluntarily seek a form of assimilation."[37] In the *Livre d'or* of the Lyon 1894 exhibition, it was claimed that the Senegalese inhabitants of the two reconstructed African villages "retained a profound respect and admiration for the French[,] which might further French influence in West Africa." These comments may point to a form of ideological masking, or a hegemonic consciousness in which domination works by tacit consent, but they might also be read as wishful thinking on the part of the Lyon exhibition commentators; or even, perhaps, as veiled expressions of contempt for the efforts of "natives" to become "French."

At all of these exhibitions, the organizers consciously sought to project a humanist vision of the French colonial enterprise and to convey a sense of trust and respect toward the Africans within it—albeit only on its own terms. And so it is not surprising that African people were among the visitors to the exhibition. Among the African delegations, forty village headmen from French Equatorial Africa were invited to the 1931 Colonial Exhibition. After spending a day at the exhibition, they were taken on a tour of the French countryside and instructed on agricultural methods suitable for Africa. A delegation from Madagascar, composed of a medical doctor, an archivist, and a midwife from the Red Cross, was greeted with elaborate ceremony. Some of these Africans were decorated with the Legion of Honor. What role did they play, other than as ambassadors of France to Africa? How did they contribute to a theatrics of a colonial enterprise that can neither be dismissed as inconsequential nor condemned as simply a form of imperial servitude?[38]

Perhaps we might render a partial vision of European visitors to the exhibitions by analyzing African sculptural forms. In 1889, a "Loango sculptor [from Gabon] carved ivory statues of the round- or top-hatted Europeans, dressed in jackets and long frock coats, walking with perfunctory canes." This caricature of the bourgeois European male subjects was of course complemented by a vision of their wives, "wearing flattened or turned up hats, which were either too big or too small for their heads." The Gabonese artist did not "forget the incredible protrusion, [the bustle, that] European women, enslaved by fashion, so proudly sported."[39] A statuette of a *colon* (colonist) shown in the Catholic Mission pavilion at the 1931 exhibition was probably as misread then as it would be today: it appears to be a naïve representation of a European missionary. This genre of sculpture, in the terms of *l'art nègre*, tends to highlight powerful symbols such as the cross, the pith helmet, and the clergyman's cassock. In fact, the statuette is a votive object, invested with power: it is a hybridizing appropriation of the missionary worker and, by extension, of Catholicism.[40]

What did the African artisan think of the rules imposed on him by the exhibition organizers, rules that forbade him to leave the fairgrounds without special permission during the day and never at night? Was he so well informed that he would take these paternalistic restrictions as a way of protecting him, the "naïve" African subject, from communism? Would he notice that they isolated him from the surrealist agitators who distributed tracts criticizing the legacy of colonial exploitation at the entrance of the 1931 exhibition? In one broadside, the surrealists called the exhibition "a carnival of skeletons," referring to the slaughter of African troops on the front lines in the Great War. The communist daily *L'Humanité* was unlikely to be read by African participants in the exhibition, but they would have discovered a series of stories on scandalous labor practice in the daily column *Derrière le décor*. Behind the scenes, the story of forced labor evoked the phrase coined by Albert Londres, "one Negro per crosspiece," which referred to the construction of the Congo Océan railroad line, in which so many African workers lost their lives. This served as a central theme in André Gide's *Voyage au Congo* and *Retour du Tchad*.[41]

In fact, the various dissonant voices at the 1931 Colonial Exhibition drowned out the voices of African protests to colonization. Who took notice of the French Sudanese militant Tiemoko Garan Kouyaté, the leader of the Ligue de Défense de la Race nègre, when he called on his African brethren to boycott the 1931 exhibition? Blaise Diagne, the assimilated Senegalese undersecretary of state for the colonies, was one of the organizers of the 1931 exhibition; Diagne supported certain forced labor provisions at the International Work Bureau (under the auspices of the League of Nations). Kouyaté called Diagne "the African Judas" and condemned the exhibition as a whole as a "commercial and epicurean zoo of caged African lackeys."[42]

That sentiment did not receive widespread acclaim during the course of the 1931 exhibition. The "International League against Imperialism and Colonial Oppression," based in Berlin, encouraged the French Communist party to organize a counterexhibition, which came to be known as the "Truth about the Colonies." This effort was only reluctantly realized and received little popular support. While 33,000,000 tickets were sold to the Colonial Exhibition, only 4,426 visitors saw the counterexhibition, which was held at the Soviet Pavilion of the old 1925 Art Deco Exhibition. Few Parisians in 1931 were seduced by an anticolonialism that celebrated the Soviet Union and an art nègre that recapitulated the flattest ethnological categories. Recalling the event several years later, the organizer of the art nègre exhibit, the poet Louis Aragon, insisted that his network of collectors had lent some unique works. The rough description made of the exhibition by the communist organizers gives a different impression: African objects were displayed with those from Oceania and the Americas, presenting an ethnographic rather than an artistic vision. For an added touch of panache, a number of ugly kitschy Virgin Mary statuettes were shown alongside the other artwork in order to demonstrate how French missionaries were leading the African artistic spirit astray.

"Il pleut, il pleut à verse sur l'Exposition coloniale" ("It's raining, it's pouring on the Colonial Exhibition"), Aragon wrote.[43] On November 15, the 1931 Colonial Exhibition closed its gates, and the era of the colonial exhibitions was over. Today, when you walk through the Bois de Vincennes looking for the Paris Buddhist Temple, you will in fact come upon the ruins of an imagined Africa of 1931, since the Temple is none other than the made-over former Cameroon-Togo pavilion. Rather than simply reading this transformation as the repackaging of an exotic trope, we might look upon it as a mythical journey. A productive form of spirituality and soul-searching still haunts the former fairground, in spite of its overdetermined historical conditions.

CHRONOLOGICAL LIST OF COLONIAL EXHIBITIONS (NOT EXHAUSTIVE)

1883	International Colonial Exhibition	Amsterdam
1885	Universal Exhibition	Antwerp
1886	Colonial Exhibition	London
1889	Universal Exhibition	Paris
1894	Colonial Exhibition	Lyon
1896	National Exhibition	Rouen
1900	Universal Exhibition	Paris
1906	Colonial Exhibition	Marseille
1922	Colonial Exhibition	Marseille
1924	Colonial Exhibition	Strasbourg
1924–25	International Colonial Exhibition	Wembley
1930	International Colonial Exhibition	Antwerp
1931	International Colonial Exhibition	Paris
1935	Universal Exhibition	Brussels
1936	Empire Exhibition	Johannesburg
1937	Universal Exhibition	Paris
1938	Colonial Exhibition	Glasgow
1958	Universal Exhibition	Brussels

Figure 9.6. Buddhist Temple of Paris, formerly the Cameroon-Togo pavilion at the International Colonial Exposition, Paris, 1931.

NOTES

I would like to express my gratitude to Peter Bloom and Hariett Rochefort, who translated this paper, and to Paul Landau, who edited it.

1. The phrase "great steeplechase" (*course au clocher*) was used by the nineteenth-century French prime minister Jules Ferry, a premier imperialist, to signify European nations' competition over African territory.

2. Whereas Native Americans were introduced into elite circles in Europe in the sixteenth through the eighteenth centuries, this "discovery" of African indigenes occurred as part of a mass media event.

3. The universal exhibitions took place along the Seine, in the wealthy western part of Paris. The 1931 Paris Colonial Exhibition took place in the Bois de Vincennes, on the eastern outskirts of Paris, a lower-income district. The colonial fairgrounds were around Lake Daumesnil.

4. Sylviane Leprun, *Le théâtre des colonies* (Paris: L'Harmattan, 1986), 184; Casimir Bathia, "L'Afrique noire à Rouen : L'Exposition nationale et coloniale de 1896," in *Pleins Sud* (Paris: Association Connaissance de l'histoire de l'Afrique contemporaine, 1993). Leprun points out that the same attraction was at the Lyon exhibition in 1894.

5. Sylviane Leprun, *Théâtre des colonies*, 184. Photographs taken at the Paris exhibition, 1900, collection of the Musée des Arts Décoratifs, Paris.

6. Interview of Thérèse Traoré, from Ségou, by Sylviane Leprun, in 1983, while conducting research in Mali for the Laboratoire d'Architecture et d'Anthropologie, Paris.

7. André Maurois, *Sur le vif: L'Exposition coloniale* (Paris: E. Dentu, 1931).

8. Commissariat général de l'Exposition coloniale de Paris, *Congrès international et intercolonial de la société indigène,* vol. 1 (Paris: L'Exposition coloniale, 1931), 170: Remarks by Mr. Hazoume, schoolteacher.

9. Catherine Hodeir and Michel Pierre, *L'Exposition coloniale, Paris 1931: La mémoire du siècle* (Brussels: Éditions Complexe, 1991), 79–80.

10. Lieutenant-Colonel Charles Mangin—later a noted army commander during World War I, in which "native" troops suffered massive casualties—introduced the term as the title of his book *La force noire* (Paris: Hachette, 1910), which sought to convince French opinion, and the French government, of the usefulness of trained colonial soldiers.

11. In 1912, at Courbevoie, a suburb of Paris, a pharmacist created Banania, an instant chocolate-drink breakfast. A few years later, while watching one of his employees who had served in the war as a tirailleur sénégalais, he had the idea manifested in the ubiquitous image and the slogan, "Y'a bon, Banania." This ad went on until the early 1970s. Banania still exists, although the African tirailleur icon has disappeared. (See fig. 5.1.)

12. Hodeir and Pierre, *L'Exposition coloniale,* 34. For more about the tirailleur sénégalais, see Myron Echenberg, *Colonial Conscripts: The Tirailleur Sénégalais in French West Africa* (Portsmouth, N.H.: Heinemann, 1991).

13. *Le Temps* was the predecessor of *Le Monde*; its sensibility was clearly conservative.

14. The Vincennes zoo was opened in 1931 to complete the Colonial Exhibition, the intention being to present animals in their "natural" environment, just as the "natives" were displayed at the exhibition. When the exhibition closed, the zoo was moved to another part of the Bois de Vincennes, where it is still welcoming visitors. Part of it, including "the monkeys' rock," has recently been restored as a piece of national patrimony.

15. Eugène Monod, *L'Exposition universelle de 1889: Grand ouvrage illustré historique, encyclopédique, descriptif* (Paris: E. Dentu, 1890), 2: 139.

16. Africans were "in competition" as supposed cannibals with the indigenes of New Caledonia, for in 1931 "cannibal" Kanaks were shown for profit in a cage at the Jardin d'Acclimatation in the Bois de Boulogne on the western outskirts of Paris. The so-called African "cannibals" all belonged to the petite bourgeoisie and the exhibit was strongly condemned by the organizers of the colonial exhibition.

17. "Nenufar," by M. Roger, R. Feéval, and J. Monteux (Pathé Frères, February 13, 1931).

18. Catherine Hodeir, Sylviane Leprun, and Michel Pierre, "Les Expositions coloniales: Discours et images," in *Images et colonies: Iconographie et propagande coloniale sur l'Afrique française de 1880 à 1962,* ed. Nicolas Bancel et al. (Nanterre: Bibliothèque de documentation internationale contemporaine; Paris: Association Connaissance de l'histoire de l'Afrique contemporaine, 1993), 138–39. In "The Politics of Bushman Representations," this volume, Pippa Skotnes documents a congruent case of parts of bodies literally being made into receptacles.

19. Sylviane Leprun, "Paysages de la France extérieure: La mise en scène des colonies à l'Exposition du centenaire," in *Mise en scène et vulgarisation: L'Exposition universelle de 1889,* special issue of *Le Mouvement Social,* ed. Madeleine Rébérioux, October–December 1989, 149; and Monod, *L'Exposition universelle,* 2: 217. "Craniometry was the leading numerical science of biological determinism during the nineteenth century," Stephen Jay Gould observes in *The Mismeasure of Man* (New York: Norton, 1981), 25.

20. Catherine Hodeir, "Une journée à l'Exposition coloniale," In *Le temps des colonies,* special issue of *L'Histoire,* 69 (July 1984).

21. The Cité des Informations was a pavilion inside the Colonial Exhibition fairgrounds, centered on communication facilities.

22. Paul Rivet, *Congrès international de l'évolution des peuples coloniaux* (Paris: Protat frères, 1937), 13

23. Commissariat général de l'Exposition coloniale de Paris, *Congrès international et intercolonial de la société indigène* (Paris: L'Exposition coloniale, 1931), 2: 59.

24. Ulysse Pila, *À l'Exposition universelle de Lyon: Livre d'or* (Lyon: A. H. Storck, 1894). The rue du Caire, rue de Djenné, and rue de Bakel are discussed by Leprun et al. in *Théâtre des colonies* and "Expositions coloniales."

25. Great Britain eventually had a simple stand at the Cité des informations. [On Portuguese exhibitions at the same exhibition, see Eric Allina, " 'Fallacious Mirrors': Colonial Anxiety and Images of African Labor in Mozambique, ca. 1929," *History in Africa* 24 (1997): 9–52.—Eds.]

26. The Indochina pavilion was a faithful reproduction of the central body of the Khmer temple Angkor Wat, in the original dimensions. See *Rapport général de l'Exposition coloniale et internationale de Paris 1931* (Paris: Imprimerie nationale, 1933–34), 5: 670.

27. Hodeir and Pierre, *Exposition coloniale*, 44.

28. Work remains to be done comparing the Olivier and Lambert's project to the original Djenné mosque, and to its restoration according to subsequent neo-Sudanese architectural rules later on.

29. Raoul Girardet argues persuasively in *L'Idée coloniale en France, 1871–1962* (Paris: La Table Ronde, 1972) that colonial exhibitions failed to anchor an imperial consciousness in French public opinion. It was left for World War II to raise imperial consciousness among the French, where the French colonial lobby and government had failed in the 1930s. After the shock of defeat in 1940, both the Vichy regime and de Gaulle's France Libre saw the empire as all that was left of France's grandeur. Imperial sentiment reached its apogee after the Liberation in 1944–45.

30. *Rapport général*, vol. 5, *Les sections françaises*.

31. Ibid.

32. Thérèse Traoré, from Ségou, interviewed by Sylviane Leprun in 1983.

33. Christopher Miller, in "Hallucinations of France and Africa," a chapter in a forthcoming book, offers an informed study of Ousmane Socé's *Mirages de Paris* (Paris: Nouvelles éditions latines, 1937).

34. Socé, *Mirages de Paris*, 36. Selling items from one part of the French Empire as "authentic objects" from another region was common practice at the exhibition.

35. "Coco, Banania et les poissons volants: Conte de l'exposition coloniale," *Coeurs Vaillants* (Paris), May 31, 1931.

36. Louis Rousselet, *L'Exposition universelle, 1900* (Paris: Hachette, 1901). Note that saying that an African ethnicity was "French" had no legal standing in the French Republic.

37. Jules Charles-Roux, who came from a very powerful Marseillaise bourgeois family, became general commissioner of the Marseille Colonial Exhibition in 1906 and lobbied for the Marseille Colonial Exhibition in 1922. No systematic research has been done to interview former "native" performers and visitors to the colonial exhibitions.

38. Catherine Hodeir, "Le non dit à l'Exposition coloniale" (Mémoire de maîtrise, Paris I, Sorbonne, 1977), a systematic study of French newspapers in 1931, showed that no Africans were interviewed by the mainstream press.

39. Monod, *Exposition universelle*, 2: 40.

40. See Eliane Girard and Brigitte Kernel, "La statuette colon," in *Images et colonies*, ed. Nicolas Bancel et al., 286–91, and Eliane Girard, Brigitte Kernel, and Eric Mégret, *Colons: Statuettes habillées d'Afrique de l'Ouest* (Paris: Syros alternatives, 1993).

41. Albert Londres in *Le Petit Parisien*, June 7, 1928. André Gide, *Voyage au Congo* (Paris: Gallimard, 1927), and *Retour du Tchad* (Paris: Gallimard, 1928).

42. Kouyaté was the most important francophone African militant in the 1930s. He had a close but conflictual relationship with the French Communist party. See Jean-Pierre Biondi, *Les Anticolonialistes (1881–1962)* (Paris: Robert Lafont, 1992).

43. Louis Aragon, "Persécuté, persécuteur" (1931), in *L'oeuvre poétique*, vol. 5: *1930–33* (Paris: Livre Club Diderot, 1975).

Chapter 10

The Politics of Bushman Representations

Pippa Skotnes

This essay examines three episodes in the history of the visual representation of South African "Bushmen." The first is the creation of an archive of /Xam traditions in the 1870s and 1880s; the second is the making of a diorama at the South African Museum in Cape Town, using casts made in the 1910s; and the third is my own installation of an art exhibit at the South African National Gallery in 1996, devoted to the subject of Bushman representations in South Africa. The archive was a collaborative project, in which the /Xam were offered a means to express themselves; the diorama was a European construction of the primitive hunter-gatherer; my exhibition at the National Gallery was a response to both the archive and the diorama, and an interpretation of the varied processes that created them.

THE DIORAMA

In the late 1980s, I spent some weeks studying fragments of Bushman rock paintings that had been cut out of their original settings in the mountains of the Eastern Cape and put on exhibit in the South African Museum in Cape Town. I was interested in trying to understand the iconography and the formal arrangement of these paintings, but I was also curious to know how they had ended up in a museum largely given over to the display of wild animals. The fragments are still part of the museum's archaeological exhibit, contained in a smallish room that displays objects and miniature dioramas representing the Early, Middle, and Later Stone Age, and a collection of rock art, which includes the well-known Linton painting.[1] Adjacent to this room is the ethnographic hall, comprising a series of discrete dioramas, each concerned with an "ethnic group." By far the most popular of these is the one set in the Karoo, depicting a Bushman camp at the turn of the nineteenth century.

Figure 10.1. Part of diorama depicting hunter-gatherer camp, ca. 1800, in the South African Museum, Cape Town. Courtesy South African Museum. Reproduced by permission.

This diorama consists of thirteen male and female figures cast from life in plaster and painted in realistic detail. Each figure is engaged in some kind of domestic activity: one gazing out at the landscape, bow and arrow in hand; one crouching, bowstring drawn, ready to shoot at some invisible animal; a couple of figures are returning to camp, digging sticks in hand; yet another is squatting, preparing plant food; while another lies in the shade of a lean-to. Each figure is dressed in "traditional" skins, which cover the genital areas, and some have karosses slung over their shoulders. The scene is framed by a beautifully painted stretch of the Nieuweveld mountains and lit with a "clear, neutral light, typical of the Karoo on a winter's day."[2]

During the weeks I spent in the museum, many thousands of visitors passed through these rooms: schoolchildren and teachers, tourists and guides, families from Cape Town, university students. The paintings I was studying attracted some attention, as did the archaeological displays, but nothing compared with the interest and fascination that the Bushman diorama generated. It was a site where teachers and tour guides stopped to lecture to their audiences, enthusiastically recreating the life and manners of "the Bushmen." Almost every talk began with a description of the Bushman body. The speaker would dwell on skin colour (yellow), height (four feet), hair (frequently described as wool), body shape (large buttocks, explained by one guide as a "storage place for fat and water in hard times"), and, presented as the most significant feature of Bushman anatomy, the genitals. "The male penis," bellowed one German guide speaking in English to his tourist group, "is peculiar in that it stands erect at all times when at rest. The women's labia can hang to the knees."

Hunting was also treated at length. Guides characterized Bushmen in the same way as one might predators such as lions or leopards, or omnivores such as baboons. Many suggested that the life of the Bushman was nothing more than an endless pursuit of food and water. One teacher told her pupils that "the Bushmen can run for three days nonstop in pursuit of game," and another guide suggested that "the Bushmen were nocturnal, and slept in hollows in the ground during the day, coming out at night to hunt." There were shades of the best-selling author Laurens van der Post in their descriptions of "the little people" whom even man-eating lions disdained, who "hardly ever walked but . . . travelled at an easy trot."

As I listened to these comments, I became increasingly interested in what it was about the diorama and the images it presented that so fired the imaginations of the viewers who spoke about it. Many of the ideas expressed by the guides and teachers were decades-old, colonial stereotypes from the nineteenth century, available only in texts long out of print. When Bushmen communities had first been observed by Europeans, they were described as "Earth People" and "African Pygmies" who resembled "monkeys," "cruelly deficient of all the attributes which belong to human beauty," "clucking," "dwarfishly savage," with minds stuck in "torpid darkness."[3] They were the pygmies in Homer who waged war on the Cranes. In short, they were the strangest people on earth.[4]

The concern of the tour guides with Bushman genitals also derived from earlier European obsessions. When the Bushman woman Saartjie Baartman was exhibited in Europe from 1810 to 1815, it was not only the "prodigious size of her buttocks" (in the words of Auguste de Saint-Hilaire of the Natural History Museum in Paris)[5] that fascinated, but the imagined shape of her genitals. In the eighteenth century, François Le Vaillant and other travelers depicted women flashing long pendulous labia. Captain Cook wrote that "Hottentot" women had labia that "resembled the teats of a cow,"[6] and other reports claimed that they hung to the knees like an apron.

By the end of the nineteenth century, Bushman bodies had been the subject of dozens of photographic "essays," most of them scientific projects examining racial difference. Many of these photographs survive in museum collections and archives. Typically, they depict men and women, standing naked against a measuring stick, in front and side views. Men's genitals were set in profile, while women were persuaded to grasp their labia. James Drury, the man who made the life casts for the South African Museum's diorama, spent much time in search of information about Bushman genitals, and in 1924 published an article with his colleague Matthew Drennan in which he described some of his successes: "On asking a woman of these tribes to remove her loin cloth or apron, one could not at first detect any difference between her and an ordinary woman. . . . On separating the lips of the vulva it was easy to grasp the labia minora with a pair of forceps and pull them out for examination. This increased exposure gave rise to a distinct accession of shyness."[7] The diorama was built to preserve for posterity what was believed to be a discrete, disappearing racial type.[8] In 1905, A. C. Haddon issued a renewed call for an investigation of Bushmen and Khoikhoi ("Hottentots"), who were "very primitive varieties of mankind" and were "rapidly diminishing."[9] The British and South African Associations for the Advancement of Science agreed that making life casts of these "disappearing" races should be a priority.

In 1910, Drury and others traveled to Bushmanland in search of specimens of "undiluted blood"[10] suitable for casting. The director of the museum was particularly clear that the "specimens" should include the features that were understood at the time to be most characteristic of Bushmen, the male's semi-erect penis and the woman's elongated genitals.[11] Their cultural practices or social conditions were unimportant. Their physical copies would then be understood as images of hunter-gatherers connected to Europeans' own distant past, displaced from current culture and politics.

This was ironic, for at the time the Bushmen selected to be cast were survivors of one of the bloodiest wars in South African history. They were living in poverty, on land that had been stripped of its natural bounty, dispossessed of their independence, many no longer speaking their original language, most having lost all memory of the oral traditions of their parents. One of the people accompanying Drury was the anthropologist Dorothea Bleek. She lamented that while "fifty years ago every adult Bushman knew all his people's lore," at least in the northern parts of the Cape Colony, by 1910 "not one of them knew a single story... the folklore was dead."[12] Yet her interest too was also in these people as "specimens," and with some difficulty she managed to photograph some of her subjects naked, their tattered clothes lying in piles beside them.

The museum itself has acknowledged the deceit and the stereotypes that the Bushman diorama perpetuates. In the late 1980s, responding to a "flawed anthropological notion of racial typology," two smaller displays were mounted alongside the diorama.[13] One visually explained the technical methods used to make the life casts, the other provided a historical context for the casting project and offered photographic evidence of the actual circumstances of the individuals who were selected to portray the timeless Bushman, circumstances that had been deliberately excluded from the original project.

Nevertheless, despite these new exhibits, far older ideas still thrive today. These ideas are to be found neither in books nor in documentaries, nor in information presented by the museum itself, but rather, in the "folklore" supported by the diorama and passed down by tour guides and indoctrinated visitors to friends and children. Much of the power of this oral tradition resides in the compelling visual drama of the diorama itself, encouraging a voyeurism that borders on the erotic. Sidney Kasfir, in her review of my own exhibition, for instance, allowed that the diorama is "utterly ahistorical and fictionalized" but also wrote that it is "the kind of image everyone (including their present-day descendants, the museum-going public, the government, and this author) frankly loves."[14]

Figure 10.2. /Xam from the Prieska district, 1910, used as models for the casting project at the South African Museum. They comprise, from the rear, "the [four] sons of old Klaas, the bare headed man at the back. Having been brought up on farms, the lads are much taller than their parents. Their mother is seated front centre, half in front of Guiman, who sits with Rachel and two grandchildren. Janiki, the other old woman, is to the right front, some younger women and children make up the group." Dorothea Bleek, "Notes on the Bushman Photographs," *Bantu Studies* 10 (1936): 200. Courtesy South African Museum.

THE BLEEK/LLOYD ARCHIVE

In 1911, at the very time Drury's team was selecting individuals to cast for the diorama, a book by two remarkable scholars, Lucy Lloyd and Wilhelm Bleek (Dorothea's father), was published. Behind *Specimens of Bushman Folklore* lay a project that had begun in the middle of the nineteenth century and had produced, in addition to numerous drawings and objects, a written archive of some 13,000 pages, recording the oral traditions and folklore of Cape Bushmen. Like the diorama, the archive was an objectification of a people, but the archive was in part created by the people themselves (as in the image shown in fig. 10.3), and focused on their intellectual and cultural legacy, rather than on their supposedly aberrant bodies.

The project began in the late 1860s, when Bleek and Lloyd, both linguists, began to interview /Xam prisoners who had been jailed in the Breakwater Convict Station in Cape Town. The /Xam occupied much of the area that became the Cape Colony, living in distinct communities and speaking different dialects. When

Figure 10.3. A page of paintings of animals and plants, from a notebook made by a Bushman informant for Lucy Lloyd. Courtesy South African Museum.

Bleek and Lloyd began their work, Europeans knew little about Khoisan languages and peoples and virtually nothing about the /Xam. And, not long after their project ended, the language and cultural practices of the /Xam did in fact disappear forever.

Wilhelm Bleek was born into a family of scholars in 1827 in Germany. He earned his doctorate in linguistics at the University of Bonn, and after a visit to East Africa, he came to South Africa to work on a Zulu grammar. In 1861, he met Jemima Lloyd in Cape Town, whom he later married. The following year, Bleek took a post at the Sir George Grey Collection at the South African Library. For some time he had been fascinated with the possibility of studying Bushman languages, and in his words, "in 1870, the presence of twenty-eight Bushmen at the Breakwater afforded an unprecedentedly rare opportunity of obtaining good instructors."[15] Two of the prisoners, /A!kunta and //Kabbo, were placed in his custody.

Jemima's sister, Lucy, joined Bleek in his studies from their inception and worked with Bleek until his death in 1875.[16] Lucy Lloyd was born in 1834 in England. The daughter of a prominent Anglican clergyman, she was educated privately, first in England and later in South Africa, where she worked as a schoolteacher. After Bleek's marriage to Jemima, Bleek invited Lucy to live with them in Mowbray, a suburb of Cape Town. Neither Bleek nor Lloyd had been trained as an ethnographer or anthropologist.

The larger context in which Bleek and Lloyd did their work was dire for the Cape Bushmen. Drought had always been a possibility in the dry Karoo, but in the time before the coming of the Dutch-speaking farmers, natural resources were diverse. The oral literature of the /Xam describes a landscape rich in tortoises, rabbits, ostriches, birds, wild cats, hyena, lion, springbok, and other big antelope. Springbok in particular are at the center of many tales and descriptions of hunting lore, and until the late 1870s there were large herds of them. Then the Boers shot them out, "The springbok resemble the water of the sea. . . . [they] come in numbers to the place which is here, the springbok cover the whole place. Therefore the Boers' gunpowder becomes exhausted, that and the balls."[17] Boers not only destroyed the /Xam's game, but hunted down people as well. The Kenhardt and Prieska districts, from which most of Bleek and Lloyd's informants came, was effectively a war zone even before the 1870s. Thousands of Bushmen died at the hands of Boer commandos. Families of /Xam were hunted down and killed, or captured and distributed among the farmers of the district as laborers or servants. Tobacco pouches were made from women's breasts; children were dragged from their mothers arms, their heads smashed on stones; in one recorded case, a shepherd was tied to a wagon-wheel and beaten to death.[18] Not only Boers, but other African peoples such as Xhosa, Korana, and Bastaards hunted down the /Xam, whom missionaries often ignored as living beyond salvation. In 1863, the sympathetic magistrate of Namaqualand, Louis Anthing, reported to the Cape Parliament that there were few Bushmen left around the Orange River, and that those who had escaped the Boers were starving to death. The government did nothing.[19]

The /Xam bitterly resisted this invasion of their land and the slaughter of their people. As Nigel Penn has shown, they learned about their enemy and exploited Boers' weaknesses as best they could.[20] One of the /Xam who worked with Lloyd, Dia!kwain, had been convicted on a charge of killing a farmer who had threatened to murder his family. Others belonged to gangs that attacked farmers' property. Some of them told stories of how they used shamanism to transform men into lions and kill farmers' stock. Still, the /Xam communities disappeared. As their resistance failed, they abandoned everything that made them uniquely who they were. This, Anthony Traill argues, is the only way to explain the rapid and complete demise of the /Xam language by 1910.[21]

And this is, in part, what makes the Bleek and Lloyd archive so extraordinary. In the bloody history of interactions between Europeans and Bushmen, it stands alone as a product of cooperation, allowing the recording of what made /Xam people uniquely /Xam: their intellectual world and their traditions. The archive thus engages with a debate argued by Bleek and Lloyd themselves, one that is still very much alive today: whether the category "Bushman" is largely an artifact of colonial processes, or whether it signifies a prior, meaningful ethnic category. Reading the archive itself, it seems inescapable that at least the /Xam of the 1870s saw themselves as ideologically and historically separate from their neighbors. Not only did they draw powerful distinctions between themselves and stockkeepers—"the bloody-handed," the "ticks on the backs of sheep"— but between themselves and other groups living further north along the Orange River.[22] "[S]ome [of us] dress in cheetah and leopard skins, and differ from those who live in the mountains who wear catskins, and near the river who wear dassie [rock-rabbit] and jackal skins. Still others, wear red and white skins and resemble the beads which they wove," /Han≠kass'o told Lucy Lloyd.[23]

In the /Xam system of representation, shamanism was understood to be their most effective weapon of resistance. Their understanding of the world, Penn suggests, may well have inhibited a more useful understanding of the consequences of colonial invasion.[24] Their narratives combine events from an early mythical period, from personal narratives, and from trance visions and emanations, in a seamless time frame. They seem to have had a multilinear relationship to the past and the present. And at a time when their communities were most violently besieged, they chose to devote what were for many of them their final years to recording their narratives and oral traditions.[25] When the record of /Xam testimonies are set beside the South African Museum diorama's static representation of Bushmen, the Bleek and Lloyd archive can be read as the /Xam's most successful act of defiance. Bleek saw the project as one of retrieving and preserving not merely a few "sticks and stones, skulls and bone" as relics of the aboriginal races of this country, but also something of that which is most characteristic of their humanity, and therefore most valuable—their mind, their thoughts and ideas.[26] While Bleek's peer scientists assembled Bushmen's skulls and bones for the animal collections of museums, the /Xam who worked with Bleek and Lloyd were aware of the significance of their participation. Often full of nostalgia for their ancestral homes and anxious to return to their families, each stayed on beyond the end of his jail sentence, some returning at great cost to continue the work.[27] Lloyd recorded that //Kabbo, the oldest of the narrators, particularly valued the idea that his stories would become known by means of books, and Lloyd's efforts to see this achieved were made in the face of financial hardship.[28]

The Bleek/Lloyd archive can thus be seen as a collaborative document through which the /Xam were able to represent themselves. In it they acknowledged the forces that were destroying their communities, while foregrounding their rich oral traditions. In the Bleek/Lloyd archive, the physical shape of the /Xam was irrelevant. As Stephen Watson has commented in the introduction to his collection of poetic interpretations of /Xam oral literature, "In a world in which nature was hardly benign, human nature never simply given, death an ever-present shadow, there is little doubt that the /Xam's various myths gave them some universal, living cosmological order, that the structures of psyche and cosmos were bound tight in a web in which nothing was meaningless, no death final."[29]

The invisibility of the archive is in a sense proportional to the visually realized presence of the diorama. The Bleek and Lloyd records received no attention by anyone outside of the Bleek family for almost 100 years. In the 1970s, they became the subject of a thesis by Roger Hewitt, and they were also used by David Lewis-Williams for his groundbreaking thesis on rock art in the 1980s. Others, including myself, gained access to them, and in 1991, they were the subject of an international conference in Cape Town, resulting in the publication *Voices from the Past*.[30] The voluminous records themselves, however, are largely unpublished and are still relatively unknown.

MISCAST: THE POLITICS OF AN ART EXHIBIT

Miscast opened at the South African National Gallery in April 1996.[31] The perceptual contrast, not to say abyss, between the dioramas at the South African Museum, which objectified Bushman people, and the archive, in which some Bushmen expressed themselves, became one of the motivating factors in my curating the installation and editing its accompanying volume. But there were other factors at work, too. At the time, exhibitions of Bushman artifacts and lifeways were all remarkably deficient.[32] I had discovered that the storerooms of museums around the country, their libraries and archives, as well as state and university archives, were crammed full of objects, historical and visual material, which somehow had never become part of permanent displays. Nowhere in any of the exhibits I saw was there any evidence of the history and lore, the photographs, documents, narratives, and drawings that were richly present in the museum storerooms; nor was there any acknowledgment of the horrors of the encounter between settlers and Bushmen. Objects were never presented for their creative worth, nor were insights offered into the fragments of rock paintings that had been hacked out of shelters or the engraved stones that had been collected from the landscape. Not a trace was to be found of the oral literature recorded by Bleek and Lloyd. On the contrary, each exhibit focused on the physical characteristics of the "Bushmen" as a distinct racial type that, at least within the borders of South Africa, had become "extinct." The irony is that the biological material of Bushmen survives today in South Africa's diverse peoples, but it is /Xam culture that has disappeared.

By the time I came to planning my exhibit, I intended to do two things: to confront the dioramas visually and to put both "the archive" and "the storeroom" on display. I chose the South African National Gallery for the venue. Traditionally a bastion of white "high" art, the gallery had recently begun to show more African material. I wanted to get as far away as possible from an ethnographic or natural history context. I also realized that I had an enormous amount of information that was not in itself particularly visually exciting. I needed as much freedom as possible to design a contextual space for not only objects and photographs but historical documents, reports, and court records.

In some early meetings with interested parties, it became clear that certain material associated with Bushman history would be contentious. Although no scholar or museum professional could argue unequivocally why some things should be displayed and not others, most of them felt strongly about the issue. Some people found the possibility of displaying the nudity of the early casts to be problematic or even offensive, even if shown in an art gallery. Those who had casts or photographs of genitals wanted to keep them in their collections and prevent anyone but scholars and scientists from having access to them. I did not hear any convincing arguments as to why this should be. Doubtless, part of the reluctance to allow the material to be exhibited was the fear that it would be inadequately contextualized: the dignity of the individual photograph or cast would be insulted, the original humiliation repeated. Part lay in the fear of public censure: museum professionals were quite aware that some aboriginal people in America and Australia had been demanding that similar artifacts be returned to them or destroyed.

The display of human remains was a highly contentious issue. The British Museum (the Natural History section) allowed me to examine a collection of "trophy heads," heads of Bushmen that had been collected in the nineteenth century and stuffed by a taxidermist, but refused to let me to draw or photograph them. The museum's position was that the heads might "cause offense."[33] Before it would even consider giving me photographs of them for display, I would have to obtain the permission of "the Khoisan" of South Africa. At the same time, the curators saw no difficulty in permitting the heads to be used for scientific experiments, for example for DNA samples. The condition they imposed on me was extremely difficult to comply with. There are no known descendants of the individuals whose heads now lie in cardboard boxes in the Natural History Museum in London. We do not know which Khoisan group they came from, which language they spoke, or even exactly where they might have lived. Until recently, few people in South Africa claimed Khoisan ancestry.

Nevertheless, I wrote to the legal representative of the few ≠Khomani-speakers in the northern Cape; to the newly established Khoisan Representative Council (KRP), and the Griqua National Conference, both in the Cape; to the Kuru Development Trust in Botswana, and to the Working Group of Indigenous Minorities in Southern Africa (WIMSA), and I canvassed their opinion on the exhibition of human remains. The people I consulted in Botswana did not wish to see the heads themselves but believed they should be shown so that the world would know what happened. Similarly, the ≠Khomani and the Khoisan Representative Council wanted the heads, or photographs of them, exhibited. In an interview with the London *Observer*, Martin Engelbrecht of the KRP said, "I see no reason why the British are preventing us from exposing what happened to our people. We want to know how these remains came to be in the museum."[34]

The board of the South African National Gallery decided they could not exhibit human remains. This was a strange ruling given recent art exhibits by Alvim of Angola, Orlan, and a number of South African artists who have all used human material. Marilyn Martin, the director of the museum, did however make a formal request to the British Museum for photographs of the heads. The British Museum never responded.

Finally, the National Gallery rejected my own title for the exhibit, which was *Miscast: Negotiating the Presence of the Bushmen*. The gallery refused to allow the word "Bushmen" to be used. *Boesman*, the Afrikaans equivalent of "Bushman," has always been a pejorative term, in keeping with Afrikaner attitudes toward the people to whom it referred. In the Western Cape, most people classified as "Coloured" under apartheid, many of whom are of Khoisan extraction, are native Afrikaans speakers and understand *Boesman* as an insulting label. Because my purposes in the exhibit concerned the colonial apprehension of different groups of people, I wanted to keep the English version of the term and use "Bushmen," but the gallery refused.[35]

I began to anticipate that the installation would become a tool in the politics of identity in the Western Cape. I had wanted to confront the stereotype "Bushman," but now the installation would have to engage the loose, politically volatile term "Khoisan." Interestingly, I received an anonymous telephone call after *Miscast* opened. The caller, speaking in English and Afrikaans, said, "It is bad that you have put the Khoi and the San together. We Coloureds in the Western Cape are descended from the Hottentots [Khoi], not from the Bushman [San] . . . my people were never cattle thieves."

REPRESENTATIONAL DECISIONS AND THE ARTICULATION OF GALLERY SPACE

The space in *Miscast* was divided into discrete areas, each of which characterized an important function of the museum: to create displays, to curate collections (and store parts of them), and to educate. On the other hand, the spatial arrangement of the objects and cases was intended to suggest "science" and "church," powerful symbols and modes in European thought. This was in line with the contention of the exhibit that, aside from the Bleek/Lloyd archive, the history of the "Khoisan" as we know it from museum collections and historical records, and even from rock art, is the history of contact with Europeans, seen from the perspective of Europeans. In a review of the exhibit, Tony Morphet wrote: "The sad truth which sits in the shadows of the main exhibition is that there is no independent Bushman archive—and there is no access to an untouched historical current of brown or black experience . . . no privileged inheritance through blood or culture. . . . The Bushman archive was the land itself—fragments of it still exist in the rock art—but as a coherent source of record it is no more."[36]

In a second principle of spatial organization, the main room was divided into two sections. In the "front" section, designating the display area, two sets of thirteen opposing items faced one another. On the wall hung thirteen cases, each containing objects of Khoisan manufacture. The twelve smaller ones were dedicated to various known individuals, many of them contributors to or characters in the Bleek and Lloyd archive, and the larger central case (also distinguished by its brilliant red colour) was dedicated to Lucy Lloyd. The collection of cases symbolized a Last Supper in which individuals are sacrificed in the interests of the pervasive display of a collective racial type. Framing this part of the exhibit on the wall above, was a quotation from Greg Dening, describing the encounter between what he terms "the native" and "the stranger": "No one can hope to be mediator ... nor can anyone speak just for the one, just for the other. There is no escape from the politics of our knowledge, but that politics is not in the past, that politics is in the present."[37]

Facing this wall was a semi-circle of thirteen body casts. Each was a resin cast of a body section (legs, torsos, etc.). Each was headless. They had been produced in the 1980s from Drury's original field molds, which had not been previously cast. These represented the countless, nameless individuals reduced to racial types—a symbolic last supper in which the "Bushman" body was the sacrifice. Continuing the theme, there was, at the center of the room, a gray brick structure, based on the ground plan of a centrally planned church of the Renaissance (the beginning of the period of the "voyages of discovery"), but that, iconically, referred also to a fort, a jail, and a tomb. Twelve rifles, with a taller metal flag in their midst, again thirteen objects, were in a central circle, a visual suggestion of the Eucharist. Five books, spelling TRUTH, lay on one side of the structure, referring to the truth claims of both the church and science. Also half buried in a gray gravelly soil on other sides were gardens of cacti and a box containing a collection of (cast) human remains. The box of human remains referred both to issues of reburial and Catholic practices of enshrining and trading relics. The cacti referred to a crown of thorns and to the subject of aboriginality; cactus is popularly thought to be indigenous to South Africa, but is exogenous. All these objects were chosen for the range of associations they might provoke. While some people criticized the installation in the visitors' book for not revealing my own agency clearly enough, in fact the Catholic icons and structures in the exhibit drew strongly on my own background and convent schooling. They carry great power for me as symbols of sacrifice, betrayal, and transubstantiation.

In the back section of the main room were two piles of casts, six metal shelves with cardboard boxes, and two cabinets of objects and scientific instruments associated with nineteenth- and early-twentieth-century physical anthropology. The cardboard boxes were designed to resemble those found in many museums for the storage of human remains, and some of the labels drew attention to the problem of displaying "sensitive" material. Each one was dated for a particular event, so that together they represented multiple voices extracted from academic histories,

Figure 10.4. Pippa Skotnes's *Miscast* installation, main room. Photo by Pippa Skotnes.

Figure 10.5. Another view of the *Miscast* installation, main room. Photo by Pippa Skotnes.

Figure 10.6. Section of the semi-circle of resin casts, *Miscast* installation. Behind them: the shelves of cardboard boxes and the "time-line," the ladders intended to aid visitors in reading the higher labels. Photo by Pippa Skotnes.

from archives, and from comments and stories by //Kabbo, Diä!kwain, and others involved in the Bleek/Lloyd project. On each one there was also the date of the publication of the fragment of text, locating the writers as characters in their own narratives. Together, they made a nonlinear "time line," suggesting the contingency of the ordering of information into narratives and the fragmentary, mutable nature of the result. Their lack of chronology was also intended to evoke the sense of time present in /Xam testimonies in the Bleek/Lloyd archive.

A second room leading off the main room was hung with a series of photographs by Paul Weinberg, taken between 1984 and 1995 with the cooperation of Bushmen subjects in Botswana, Namibia, and Smitsdrift. The floor in this room was covered with vinyl tiles printed with documents and with photographs, mainly of Bushmen. The intention, as with other parts of the exhibit, was to make the experience of viewing active, rather than passive. The third room of the installation was set up as a library, reflecting the educational function of museums. A selection of the hundreds of documents and newspaper articles that were part of the research for this exhibition were laid out on a table for scrutiny. On the walls were mainly copies of rock paintings done variously over the years by Walter Battiss, George Stow, J. M. Orpen, Patricia Vinnecombe, and the Spatial Archaeology Research Unit at the University of Cape Town.

Figure 10.7. Part of the *Miscast* installation. The vinyl flooring of this room reproduced newspaper articles, archival photos, and reports of "commando" raids, and other official documents. Three cameras are in cases on the floor. Photo by Pippa Skotnes.

OVERALL PUBLIC REACTION

The *Miscast* exhibition stimulated a great deal of commentary, much of it very positive. Many people in the visitor's book, for instance, commented on the power of the visual to communicate differently than text and said they had known nothing of the history of Bushmen in South Africa. A resident diplomat from the Netherlands Embassy, for example, remarked that few of his countrymen knew anything about early Dutch "encounters with the Khoi and San people. They—we—should." Another visitor thanked me for offering "the opportunity to confront our images/conceptions of a people who rarely have a chance to represent themselves to a Western view. It challenges our knowledge—and the way that knowledge has been acquired about African peoples." And referring to the Truth and Reconciliation Commission in South Africa, which began its work in the first part of 1996, another person wrote, "This exhibit should be permanent—it is important that all South Africans see the genocide that was perpetuated. No truth and reconciliation commission is possible for the 'Bushmen.'" Overall, I believe, the *Miscast* installation succeeded in its aim of challenging the ahistoricity of the diorama and putting the archive on display. The majority of viewers and commentators, including those identifying themselves as Khoisan, left with a sense that they had confronted an untold or suppressed history. In her review, Carmel Schrire wrote that *Miscast* offered "a series of images that catapult right into the darkest heart of the anthropological venture, to conflate science and sorrow, archives and agony."[38]

It is also true that the exhibit opened a host of new dilemmas and problems, and that some reactions were hostile. Very few people understood the exhibit as installation art. My intentional references in the spatial arrangement and color relationships to installation artists such as Greenaway, Kosuth, and Haake, were entirely sidelined, and hardly anyone invoked any art-historical precedents in analyzing the exhibit. Many people did not understand the nonlinear presentation of historical information on the cardboard boxes and some were irritated by what they saw as an attempt to confuse. In one review, the writers ignored much of the material in the exhibits to better make a tendentious argument.[39] Some reviewers, having read some pre-opening publicity, were determined not to be disappointed in their expectation of finding stuffed heads and bottled genitals and claimed to have actually seen some of them in the cabinets.[40]

The installation became a rallying point and a focus of both Khoisan unity and disunity. At the opening, a group of ≠Khomani came in traditional dress. They attracted a great deal of attention in the press and were berated by the !Hurikamma Cultural Group, who said they were "sick and tired of naked brown people being exposed to the curious glances of rich whites in search of dinner-table conversation."[41] A Griqua group expressed the concern that there were "too many Bushmen." One of the Bushman representatives suggested that Afrikaans speakers could not claim to be Khoisan at all, and a number of white Afrikaners claimed that they were of Khoisan descent—angering some other Afrikaans speakers, who had been damagingly classified as "Coloured" under apartheid. Some groups, such as the Kleurling Weerstandsbeweging (the Coloured Resistance Movement, or KWB), were angered that a white person, and worse, a white academic, had "represented" them. At the forum held after the opening, one KWB member called out, "Give us the money so that we can make our own exhibit in our own way."[42] In contrast, the Khoisan Representative Council valued the installation as a "wake-up call" for Khoisan communities. Some individuals simply expressed dismay at the developing equation of "Coloured" with "Khoisan," a "tribal" category they had been at pains to escape. I had wanted to implicate viewers in a "politics of knowledge" (to this end I had installed mirrors, laid images, and mounted cameras on the floor). That understanding of politics was, to some extent, hijacked by the politics of the renewed South African search for racial "authenticity."

The use of the resin casts in the *Miscast* exhibit accounted for a great deal of the controversy about the installation. Inevitably, some people were offended by the nudity. Some Nharo asserted that there should have been separate viewings for men and women, since men and woman should not see nudity together. Others were critical of the opportunity for voyeurism that they felt the casts provoked. One reviewer raised issues of who is entitled to represent whom, claiming the exhibit showed "white" disrespect for "brown" people.[43] One visitor from Smitsdrift expressed shock and horror at the forum after the opening,[44] saying, "I do not believe that these things are true. All this plastic, they could have made it just to shock us. Showing these naked bodies is a very, very bad thing . . . to show these things here is just as bad as the people who did those things long ago. It is continuing the bad thing." The speaker however finished in a somewhat different vein. "We are not angry with the people who are showing us these things," he said, "but with the people who have done it to us." Sixpense Hunter, a viewer from Kuru in Botswana, said: "We are shocked . . . these things are true. . . . Although we are shocked and it is painful, we think it is good that people should see it. It strengthens our young people to stand up . . . the whole world should get a message from this exhibition. This should not happen to people ever again."[45]

Many people found the casts both beautiful and tragic. Tony Morphet characterized this view: "[N]one of the moulds is a whole person; the truncations, which were a necessary technical part of their making, represent symbolically an awful mutilation. Yet staged as they are, glowing from within on the underlit boxes, they stand as well for the inextinguishable beauty of the naked body in its parts, and its wholeness."[46]

The floor of the second room was another area of concern for visitors. While many found it engaging, some were offended at having to walk over photographs of Bushmen, of being drawn into the process of trampling history underfoot. One archaeologist wrote that this floor was "the most disturbing" part of the installation, as he was forced to reconsider his own practice: "Just as the texts and images on the floor represent the debris of a particular history, so too do the artefacts strewn across the surface of a site. Yet archaeologists, in trying to define sites and their history, feel they can tread on the debris of their own or others' ancestors with equanimity, colonizing the space for themselves."[47]

Another person writing in the visitors' book saw it differently: "Interesting to 'walk' on a museum exhibit—we came in to see a baby crawling on the tiles—

trying to grasp the pictures—somehow that shows clearly the continuity of life.... We cannot escape our past—but maybe we can have the freedom to come to terms with it."

One anthropologist also evoked children, but in defense of the diorama:

> When they were small my children delighted in these casts and saw real magic in them. When walking in the bush later they remembered these people whose casts made [them] visually real for them, and thus participated in something of the positive, seriously experienced heritage of the Bushmen.... I enjoyed seeing so much space [in the exhibit] devoted to the Bushmen [but I regret] that the issues of violence and loss are so much in the foreground.[48]

The body casts in the *Miscast* installation were, however, intended to argue that the very image of a beautiful people advanced by the diorama, and repeated throughout popular culture, has helped the suffering of Bushmen populations go largely unnoticed and unpoliticized. It is true that the *Miscast* installation did have one important feature in common with the diorama. Both take "real evidence," the body casts, and (in the case of *Miscast*) documents and photographs, and place them in invented contexts. The relationship between the genuine and the imaginary creates a powerful space where meaning and significance can be created by the viewer. The difference, however, is that the installation was designed expressly to deflect the kinds of easy projections that the diorama allows. Some evaluations of *Miscast* appear to regret this complication.[49]

CONCLUSION

The display of Bushman rock art in the third room of the installation was the most difficult part of the exhibit for me to resolve. Bushman rock art is the only "voice" of Khoisan people that in a sense reaches us in unmediated form, straight from the distant past. However, no unbroken painting tradition has survived, and no interviews with painters of Bushman rock art were recorded. All interpretations of rock art are the impressions of others. At best, the images can be read in conjunction with the Bleek/Lloyd archive and later ethnographies, but more often, as displayed in many museums, they stand perfectly silent, bearing witness only to the act of tearing them out of the landscape.

Even if it were possible to recover the "original" meaning of rock paintings, however, we would still have to admit that they were created in a landscape that shaped the lives of countless generations of people and painted in caves that saw hundreds, sometimes thousands of years of occupation by different communities. The "voice" of rock paintings therefore belongs to the landscape where the paintings were made. Paintings were renewed, repainted, added to. They were surely capable of sustaining a range of meanings that were constructed at different times and by different communities. The search for "original" meaning after all only makes sense if the intention of the artist is privileged over all others.

A comparison to my own installation here seems possible. How can a visual display be offered as a process, rather than an already established body of the known? *Miscast* created, by South African standards, a prodigious and unanticipated range of discussion and debate. Thousands of people supplied their own interpretations of *Miscast*'s material, and attendance at the National Gallery rose to an unprecedented level. Numerous articles and critical papers were written on the exhibit's content and reception, and I was subjected to an exhausting, five-month-long barrage of telephone calls, requests for interviews, praise, and criticism. My intentions were accepted by some but rejected by others, and my authorship as artist and curator determined only one part of what the exhibit came to mean.

NOTES

My research has been funded by the Research Committee of the University of Cape Town, the Centre for Science Development, the Anglo American Chairman's Fund, the Royal Netherlands Embassy and the Consulate of the Federal Republic of Germany, as well as a number of South African corporations. To all of them I am extremely grateful. Many friends and colleagues have shared with me their understanding of the Miscast installation, shedding light on the many ways in which it has been received. In particular, I must thank Stephen Watson, whose own poetic interpretations of /Xam literature have retrieved this tradition from literary obscurity, for his insights and comments; my fellow artists David Brown, Terry Kurgan, and Malcolm Payne; and Jos Thorne, my assistant curator, David Chidester, Martin Hall, Paul Landau, Tony Morphet, Sandra Prosalendis, and Carmel Schrire. Paul Landau and Deborah Kaspin made many useful comments on this essay. Archives consulted were the Lucy Lloyd MSS BC151 and Wilhelm Bleek and Lucy Lloyd MSS in the Jagger Library, University of Cape Town.

1. The Linton painting, extracted from a rock shelter in the Maclear district of the Eastern Cape, is a particularly fine example of what has been understood to be shamanistic art. It was recently exhibited as part of the "Africa: Art of a Continent" exhibition, which toured in Europe and the United States in 1995.

2. A. Schweizer and C. Thorn, "Bushman Diorama," *South African Museum Association Bulletin* 7, 10 (1961): 234.

3. See, e.g., *History of the Bosjesmans, or Bush People; The Aborigines of Southern Africa* (London: Chapman Elcoate, 1847).

4. See, e.g., "Opinions of the London Press," in *History of the Bosjesmans*.

5. P. R. Kirby, "The Hottentot Venus," *Afrikaner Notes and News*, 6, 3 (1949): 55–62. [See also Saul Dubow, *Scientific Racism in Modern South Africa* (Cambridge: Cambridge University Press, 1995), and Sander Gilman, "Black Bodies, White Bodies: Toward an Iconography of Female Sexuality in Late Nineteenth-Century Art, Medicine, and Literature," in *Race, Writing, and Difference*, ed. Henry Louis Gates (Chicago: University of Chicago Press, 1985).—Eds.]

6. See, e.g., Robert Gordon, "The Venal Hottentot Venus and the Great Chain of Being," *African Studies* 51, 2 (1992): 187.

7. J. Drury and Matthew R. Drennan, "The Pudendal Parts of the South African Bush Race," *Medical Journal of South Africa* 22 (1926): 113.

8. Patricia Davison, "Human Subjects as Museum Objects: A Project to Make Life-Casts of 'Bushmen' and 'Hottentots', 1907–1924," *Annals of the South African Museum* 102, 5 (1993): 165–83.

9. Ibid., 168.

10. Walter Rose, *Bushman, Whale and Dinosaur: James Drury's Forty Years at the South African Museum* (Cape Town: Howard Timmins, 1961), 46.

11. Davison, "Human Subjects as Museum Objects," 169.

12. Dorothea Bleek, "Bushman Folklore," *Africa* 2 (1929): 311–12.

13. Davison, "Human Subjects as Museum Objects," 171, 173–74.

14. Sydney Kasfir, "Cast, Miscast: The Curator's Dilemma," *African Arts*, Winter 1997, 8.

15. W. H. I. Bleek, *A Brief Account of Bushman Folklore and Other Texts: Second Report Concerning Bushman Researches, Presented to Both Houses of the Parliament of the Cape of Good Hope, by Command of His Excellency the Governor* (Cape Town: Juta, 1873), 2.

16. Ibid., 2.

17. /Han≠kass'o, Informant VIII in the unpublished manuscripts of Lucy Lloyd, book 14, 1878, 7226r. Jagger Library, University of Cape Town.

18. Diä!kwain, a /Xam man, tells the story of Ruyter, who had been "brought up by white men [and who had] died while he was with white men." He died at the hand of his employer, a farmer who had accused him of not herding sheep well and beat him while tied to a wagon wheel. Diä!kwain, in the unpublished manuscripts of Lucy Lloyd, book 23 (University of Cape Town, 1876), 5872–80.

19. For breathtaking accounts of the Northern Frontier and the destruction of Khoisan groups, see Nigel Penn, "The Northern Cape Frontier Zone, 1700–c.1815" (Ph.D. diss., University of Cape Town, 1994). Facsimiles of two of Louis Anthing's letters are reproduced in the parallel text in *Miscast: Negotiating the Presence of the Bushmen*, ed. Pippa Skotnes (Cape Town: University of Cape Town Press, 1996), 162–78.

20. Nigel Penn, "Fated to Perish: The Destruction of the Cape San," in *Miscast*, ed. Skotnes.

21. Anthony Traill, "!Khwa-Ka Hhouiten Hhouiten, 'The Rush of the Storm': The Linguistic Death of /Xam," in *Miscast*, ed. Skotnes, 183.

22. //Kabbo, Informant II, in the unpublished manuscripts of Wilhelm Bleek and Lucy Lloyd, book 32, 1873, 2926: "The Mantis takes away the sheep's ticks." Jagger Library, University of Cape Town, 1873.

23. /Han≠kass'o, Informant VIII, in the unpublished manuscripts of Lucy Lloyd, book 22 (1878), 7970–74. Jagger Library, University of Cape Town.

24. Penn, "Fated to Perish."

25. Diä!kwain was murdered by farmers on his return home, and //Kabbo died shortly after he had joined his wife in Bushmanland.

26. Bleek, *Brief Account of Bushman Folklore*, 2.

27. "Still studying with might and main ... in fear of losing our Bushmen ... they are very homesick," Bleek wrote to Sir George Grey in November 1872. /Han≠kass'o, for example, lost his small child, who died in Beaufort West, as well as his wife who was assaulted by a policeman en route to Cape Town. He worked with Lloyd for nearly two years, despite his anxiety to return to his remaining son, who had been left with friends. See Bleek and Bleek, "Notes on the Bushmen," in *Bushman Paintings*, ed. M. H. Tongue (Oxford: Clarendon Press, 1909), 36–44.

28. After Bleek's death, Lucy Lloyd was offered his post at the South African Library at half his salary, but she was fired five years later when the library appointed Theophilus Hahn to her position. She appealed to the trustees, who supported her on the basis of her excellent work, and took the case to the Supreme Court, where the matter was not decided. Hahn resigned in 1883, and his post was left vacant. Lloyd had eventually to abandon her work and return to Europe. After struggling for years to find a publisher, she finally managed to publish *Specimens of Bushman Folklore* in 1911. Two years later, she became the first woman to be awarded an honorary doctorate in South Africa. She died in 1914 in Cape Town. See W. D. Maxwell-Mahon, "Lucy Catherine Lloyd," *Dictionary of South African Biography*, vol. 4 (Pretoria: Nationale Boekhandel, 1981), 315–16, and South African Library, manuscript collection MSB 223 3 (102).

29. Stephen F. T. Watson, *Song of the Broken String: After the /Xam Bushmen: Poems from a Lost Oral Tradition* (Riverdale-on-Hudson, N.Y.: Sheep Meadow Press, [1991], 1996), 19.

30. Roger Hewitt, *Structure, Meaning and Ritual in the Narratives of the Southern San*, Quellen zur Khoisan-Forschung, 2 (Hamburg: H. Buske, 1986); J. David Lewis-Williams, *Believing and Seeing: Symbolic Meanings in Southern San Rock Paintings* (New York: Academic Press, 1981); *Voices from the Past: /Xam Bushmen and the Bleek and Lloyd Collection*, ed. Janette Deacon and Thomas Dowson (Johannesburg: University of Witswatersrand Press, 1996).

31. The Miscast installation was designed and curated by myself, assisted by Jos Thorne, an architect. It was officially opened by /'Angn!Ao/'Un from the Farmers Cooperative in Nyae Nyae, Namibia, and ran for five months.

32. Most other southern African museums have repeated the display format of that of the South African Museum. Bushmen displays are unvaryingly focused on food gathering and hunting, and the majority employ the use of body casts or models. Some displays link the casts with rock painting activities, but the more powerful association is always with the natural environment, and the nakedness of the casts focuses attention on the body.

33. Robin Cox, personal communication, November 2, 1995.

34. Philip van Niekerk, "Skeletons in White Man's Cupboard," *Observer* [London], February 18, 1996.

35. Some Namibian "Bushmen" were currently rehabilitating the term "Bushmen" in any case. See *Miscast*, ed. Skotnes, 338.

36. Anthony Morphet, "Miscast," *Pretexts: Studies in Writing and Culture* 6, 1 (1997): 99.

37. Greg Dening, *Mr Bligh's Bad Language: Passion, Power and Theatre on the Bounty* (New York: Cambridge University Press, 1992).

38. Carmel Schrire, "Miscast," *South African Review of Books* 44 (1996): 13–15.

39. In their reading of the cardboard boxes, Douglas and Law ignored the many labels that emanated from a Khoisan perspective. They also argued that the apartheid era did not feature in the installation by ignoring the vast amount of information on the boxes, the floor, and in the "library" section that came from that period. Stuart Douglas and Jennifer Law, "Beating Around the Bush(man!): Reflections on 'Miscast: Negotiating Khoisan History and Material Culture,'" *Visual Anthropology* 10 (1997): 85–108.

40. I corrected a number of these misapprehensions in drafts of articles that were sent to me to comment on.

41. R. Roussouw, "Setting History Straight—or Another Chance to Gape," *Mail and Guardian*, April 19, 1996. The same group expressed distaste for a white woman handling "naked" casts.

42. The forum was planned for the day after the opening of the exhibition (April 14, 1996) to hear and discuss concerns common to many Khoisan groups. It was attended by over seven hundred people. Delegates from the Working Group of Indigenous Minorities in Southern Africa (WIMSA) included people from the Kuru Development Trust in Ghanzi, and from Nyae Nyae, Bagani, and the Aminuis Corridor 17 in Namibia; the South African San Institute (SASI), the Griqua National Conference and South African Griqua Research and Development (SAGRAD), the Khoisan Representative Council, which has Khwe, !Xu, and Griqua representatives; the Khomeni of the southern Kalahari; people from the Richtersveld; the !Hurikamma Cultural Movement, and the rightist Kleurling Weerstandsbewegung (KWB), the Coloured Resistance Movement of the Western Cape.

43. See Yvette Abrahams, "Miscast," *South African Review of Books* 44 (1996): 15–16, Rustum Kozain, "Miscast," ibid., 14–15, and miscellaneous letters in vol. 45 of the same, including my responses.

44. Smitsdrift is a camp of !Xu and Khwe communities in the Cape created for ex-mercenaries who worked for the South African army in Namibia and Angola. The representative for the Smitsdrift community at the forum was a Dutch Reformed minister, Mario Mahongo. His (and others') objections to nude casts were grounded in contemporary Christian objections to exposing the naked body.

45. Sixpense Hunter at the forum held after the opening of the *Miscast* exhibit.

46. Morphet, "Miscast," 96.

47. Paul Lane, "Breaking the Mould? Exhibiting Khoisan in Southern African Museums," *Anthropology Today* 12, 5 (1996): 7.

48. The writer continues: "It is very difficult to retain the memory of the beauty of a skin bag or the sublimity of face, in the context of the medical instrument on display and the detailed instructions for cutting off and preserving a Bushmen's penis or ear for posting to the 'scientist.'"

49. See, e.g., Steven Robins in the *Sunday Independent*, May 26, 1996, 23.

Chapter 11

Omada Art at the Crossroads of Colonialisms

Paula Ben-Amos Girshick

This essay focuses on the court art of the Edo Kingdom of Benin in present-day Nigeria during the last half of the nineteenth century, a period of historical transition when that kingdom, an imperial power in its own right, fell to British colonial domination. It addresses the questions: what are the artistic implications of such a transition from colonizer to colonized? And, how—and in what artistic contexts—are issues of colonial power and identity explored?

The answers to these questions will emerge from the analysis of the social position and artistic production of one group of palace artists, the Omada, an organization of young men who were personal and domestic servants of the king. Their official duty was to carry the state sword, or *ada*, when accompanying the king in his public appearances. In this position, as the late Ovia Idah explained, "The Omada were to the Oba [king] like the angels to Jesus."[1] It was forbidden for them to leave the palace grounds without the Oba. When not escorting the king, they performed general maintenance jobs, such as sweeping the place, and in their spare time, they played at wrestling or learned how to carve. The Omada rather than the better-known guild carvers (Igbesanmwan) or casters (Igun Eronmwon) are the focus of my analysis because they occupied a unique interstitial position within palace art production and this marginality provided them—and no other Benin court artists—with the space to explore the issues of power, domination, and identity that are central to the colonial experience, whether of the colonizers or the colonized. As Homi Bhabha has argued, it is those "'in-between' spaces that provide the terrain for elaborating strategies of self-hood—singular or communal—that initiate new signs of identity, and innovative sites of collaboration, and contestation, in the act of defining the idea of society itself."[2]

Although Homi Bhabha's intent is to investigate the interstices *between* cultures (and subcultures), it is equally valuable, I would argue, to examine *internal* differences, that is, to look within one culture at the in-between spaces where identities, interests, and values are negotiated and strategies of representation are formulated.

The last half of the nineteenth century, a period that encompassed the reigns of Obas Adolo (ca. 1850) and Ovorranmwen (ca. 1889), was a time of crisis for the Benin kingdom. The net of control it had cast over its tributaries began to unravel. At the same time, the British imperial presence was threatening the long-standing trade patterns and, indeed, the very sovereignty, of Benin and its neighbors. In this time of transition, as we shall see, it was the Omada artists—and not those in the guilds—who expressed the complexities and ambiguities of Benin's precarious position.

FROM COLONIZER TO COLONIZED: BENIN IN THE LAST HALF OF THE NINETEENTH CENTURY

Any discussion of colonialism in relation to Benin cannot be limited to the moment of British conquest—February 18, 1897—and its immediate aftermath. Instead, it must take into account that imperial domination was not a new experience for Benin or its neighbors in that region of the Guinea Coast. And it must recognize that the British capture of Benin was the outcome of a colonizing process that actually had its beginnings forty years earlier.

From at least the fifteenth century on, the Benin state was organized around warfare and tribute extraction based on its superior military organization, political power, and economic wealth. The exact nature and extent of Benin's rule varied over time and through space.[3] In early nineteenth-century Lagos, for example, Benin suzerainty involved the collection of annual tribute and control over the investiture of rulers and chiefs but little interference beyond that.[4] Conquest was an accepted, ongoing aspect of the political system. According to the local Benin historian Jacob Egharevba, it was the custom for kings to declare war in the third year after their succession to the throne.[5] Ruling princes of the empire who refused to pledge their allegiance at that time were considered rebels, and war was declared against them and their towns. In Benin oral traditions, the commencement of their empire-building was associated with the fourteenth- or fifteenth-century Oba Ewuare, who was credited with establishing the political structure of the kingdom and giving it its basic nature and divine underpinning. Thus, warfare and conquest were built into the state structure and were a key element of the kingdom's self-definition.[6]

By the nineteenth century, however, the political focus of the empire had shifted to maintenance and consolidation rather than conquest.[7] The kings who ruled then—Oba Osemwede (ca. 1816–51), Oba Adolo (ca. 1850–88), and Oba Ovorranmwen (ca. 1889–97)—were faced with a serious erosion of their political power by other local polities as well as by the British. At the beginning of the century, Benin trade with the interior was disrupted by civil wars in the Yoruba kingdoms to the west and north and by Itsekeri assumption of control over the river approaches to Benin territory to the south and east. In the second half of the nineteenth century, the Muslim emirate of Bida raided the northern territories of Benin for slaves and forced them to stop paying tribute to Benin. By the 1880s, Benin armies were preoccupied with villages on the northwestern and southeastern borders of the kingdom that were in a state of rebellion. On all sides, then, the political and economic control of the Oba was increasingly weakened.

The greatest threat to Benin was the British, whose ever-escalating encroachment from the 1840s on menaced the livelihood and well-being of the kingdom. Initially, British interest in the area centered on the slave trade and, after its abolition, on palm oil. As the trade expanded during the 1840s, the Benin River became an important center and traders living on the coast lobbied the British government to establish a permanent representative, resulting in the appointment of a consular official in 1849. Two years later, the British established a protectorate in Lagos and thus ended Benin's authority over that polity. As an outcome of the Berlin conference of 1885, the British were granted a "sphere of influence" that covered the coast between Cameroon and Lagos Colony as well as the middle and lower Niger (under charter to the Royal Niger Company), effectively surrounding the southwestern and southeastern flanks of the kingdom. The establishment of the Oil Rivers Protectorate in 1891, followed by its ominous renaming as the Niger Coast Protectorate in 1895, brought more administrators and a sizable constabulary.

The drive was clearly on to control more territory inland. A station was set up at Sapele, right on Benin's doorstep, and its resident officer went to Benin City in 1892 and successfully negotiated a treaty placing the Oba under the protection of the British Government. As Alan F. C. Ryder points out, the treaty clearly established "a new acquisitive interest in Benin by the Protectorate."[8] At the same time that they were placing themselves under British protection, the Oba and chiefs could observe the British taking forceful action against independent polities in the area, from their subjugation of the independent Yoruba state of Ijebu-Ode to the overthrow of powerful local leaders such as Chief Jaja of Opobo and Chief Nana of Brohimi. In the 1890s, the British Foreign Office was clearly stating its interest in annexing Benin.[9] All this finally culminated in February 1897, when a British expeditionary force captured the capital and sent Oba Ovorranmwen into exile.[10]

The processes that led to Benin's colonization were thus set in motion at least forty years before the actual imposition of British rule. The issues that colonialism raises were consequently also present before 1897: questions of domination and subordination, power and powerlessness, culture and control. Even though these issues had been part of Benin's version of colonial domination, they took on a new light as Benin faced its own probable conquest. The handwriting was on the wall, but who was going to see it? The answer to this question lies in Homi Bhabha's suggestion, put forward at the beginning of this essay, that in moments of historical transformation, one should look to the margins.[11] In the main part of this essay, I explore the centers and margins of nineteenth-century Benin court art in order to demonstrate that it was at the margins of royal artistic production that the handwriting was read and inscribed, that questions of cultural difference were raised, and that established boundaries were challenged and realigned.

CENTERS AND MARGINS IN NINETEENTH-CENTURY BENIN COURT ART

At the center of nineteenth-century artistic production were the hereditary craft guilds: the wood and ivory carvers, Igbesanwman, the brass casters, Igun Eronmwon, the iron smiths, Igun Ematon, the weavers, Owina n'Ido, the carpenters, Owina, and the leather workers, Isekpokin.[12] These guilds traced their origins back in dynastic time, some to the fifteenth- and sixteenth-century warrior kings, others to those who laid the foundations of the kingdom itself. In the case of the carvers' guild, some traditions ascribe its founding to Ogiso Ere, the second ruler in a previous dynasty. Members of the craft guilds lived in wards adjacent to one another not far from the palace. They shared a common artisan status in Benin society, higher than that of farmers because of their special skills and knowledge, their service to the Oba (and his economic support of them), and their urban residence. However, the prestige of artisans was never equal to that of chiefs, priests, or war leaders, because they had to work with their hands.

Guild members saw themselves as devoted servants of the monarch, rooted in the life of the court. Their monopoly of artistic production for the king, and through him the aristocracy of chiefs and priests, was maintained in principle by the threat of death. In reality, this threat was rarely carried out; instead, the monopoly was maintained by the practice of adopting into the guild anyone found in violation.

Internally, guilds were divided into age grades. In the carvers' guild—the focus of this discussion—there were three grades: the youngest, the Iroghae, consisting of young men just learning their craft, who performed menial tasks but were not allowed to go with their elders to the palace to perform ritual duties for the king; the middle grade, Urhonigbe, consisting of the young men who did the actual carving and as a result of entering this grade were introduced to *itaemwin*, secret palace activities; and, lastly, the senior grade, Ekhaemwe-Oba, consisting of the title holders, the senior men who held one of the three titles possessed by the guild. These titles were based on appointment by the Oba. The individual who possessed the highest ranking of these was the leader of the guild and his home was the religious center for the members. The shrine located in his home was devoted to the patron deity, Ugbe n'Owewe, the ancestral protector of the guild. The grades of Igbesanmwan were not age grades in the strictest sense but were a religious-political hierarchy through which individuals advanced in relation to their ritual preparedness and the willingness of the Oba to promote them.

Although they owned and managed farms in the villages around Benin City, the members of Igbesanmwan viewed carving as their full-time occupation. Carving was considered to be "in the blood" of all males born into the guild and every young man was expected to carve. A newly born male child was taken before the group ancestral shrine by his parents, who prayed to the patron deity, "Whatever act of carving is taught in Igbesanmwan, this child must know it." For the members of the guild, carving was a ritual activity inspired by their patron deity, Ugbe n'Owewe, who came to them in dreams and taught them designs. Each act of carving was a sacred act for which the individual had to be prepared through ritual cleansing.

The members of Igbesanmwan saw themselves as possessing a set of patterns that had been handed down from generation to generation by Ugbe n'Owewe. These patterns were what set them apart from other craft groups in society, particularly the Omada, and they were dependent on their protective spirit to provide and maintain their inspiration. They were similarly dependent on the Oba and felt that they existed solely to serve him. They relied on him not only for economic recompense for their carving but for their social standing, since any respect that they had within the social system came from their being servants of the king.

The carvings, castings, and other art forms created by the guild were used variously to establish communication with the spirit world, commemorate important personages and events, and decorate shrines, houses, and ceremonial attire. Their use was strictly regulated by sumptuary laws, which provided the support for a complex hierarchical aristocratic system. As I have explained elsewhere:

> Looked at synchronically, possession of art forms by an individual was a visual objectification of his position in the ranking system. Looked at diachronically, over the life time of this same individual, such possession was an expression of his progress towards self-completion. [Grant] McCracken has suggested (1988: 88) that we look at consumption as a "cultural project", the purpose of which is to complete the self—or, to put it in terms more congenial to Edo culture, to fulfill one's social destiny. It was through the possession and display of art objects that individuals attained the goals of social achievement they had set for themselves.[13]

Thus, the objects created by the guild artists were central to the social system and to the individual's sense of where he was in that system.

At the margins were the Omada, a term that is usually translated as "pages." These were young men who served as personal and domestic servants of the king. In contrast to the case of the guilds, oral historical information about the Omada is hard to come by in Benin. During my research in 1966, I was unable to find traditions about when the Omada organization was created and, especially, when its members began to carve. Informants claim only that the Omada started carving "a very long time ago."[14] However, it was possible to utilize the family traditions of ex-Omada and chiefs to establish that Omada carving existed during the period that is the focus of this essay—the reigns of Oba Adolo (ca. 1850) and Ovorranwmen (ca. 1889–97). This lack of any traditions of origin is significant. In Benin society, nearly every important organization, and every culturally meaningful object has its own story of origin, including—in fact, especially—guild art forms.[15] The absence of Omada history is a clear indication of their marginal artistic position.

This marginality or interstitial position can be seen in reference to three central components of the palace art system: the Oba, the chiefs, and the carvers' guild.

The Omada and the Oba

Recruitment to the Omada in the nineteenth century was open to all Edo youth. Boys were usually entered by their parents between the ages of six and ten, when they would otherwise have been trained by their fathers to farm or follow a craft. Boys were sent for a variety of reasons: to foster good relationships with the king, to promote advancement for a child from a disadvantaged family, or to provide a solution to family conflicts such as custody disputes or cases of child neglect. Boys whose behavior was deviant and uncontrollable were given to the Omada for disciplinary action, much as such boys in American society may be sent to military academies. There is some evidence as well, however, that rulers of subject states sent their sons to be "finished" at the Benin court.[16] In short, the composition of the Omada at any given time might be heterogeneous in terms of its members' socioeconomic backgrounds, urban or rural origins, and possibly even ethnic ancestry.

Being inducted into a period of servitude placed Omada in a marginal position, not as absolute slaves, but as persons no longer rooted in their own kin and neighborhood. Their social definition at that point totally depended upon the king. Their marginality was further emphasized by the fact that they were expected to go about naked during their time in the palace. Upon entrance to the Omada, youths pledged a sacred oath of loyalty to the king, swearing on the altars of Ogun, the god of iron and the enforcer of strict oaths, and on that of the Oba's ancestors, never to harm anyone in the palace and to keep all that they learned a secret on threat of death. Once this oath was taken, Omada were expected to be totally loyal to the king; in fact, during their stay in the palace, they were expected not to "serve any juju" (in other words, venerate any deity), as this would interfere with their total commitment. Some Omada, however, secretly made sacrifices to Ogun whenever they carved, in order to keep their tools "cool."

When youths had time off from their royal duties, they were expected to keep busy and some were instructed in carving by more senior members. The learning situation was similar to the modern classroom. There were no ritual preparations or prayers before commencing carving, nor did they work in isolation, like the guild. In fact, sons of chiefs who had accompanied their fathers to the palace sometimes joined in the training sessions. After a group of novices had been in the palace for a few years, the king could request that the senior members give them a carving proficiency test. Those who showed sufficient skill were freed from further learning and became established experts, which meant they were qualified to teach others and could also accept commissions from the Oba and chiefs. The economic benefits that accrued to these carvers in the form of payment by the king and chiefs in goods, cowries, and food was seen as an important way to accumulate capital for later use in purchasing a title or otherwise advancing one's status. Thus, as the late Oba Akenzua II explained, "Things were sold out by the Omada long before the arrival of the Europeans."[17]

The competition implicit in the system of examination was an important mechanism for maintaining the quality of carvings. In the guild, members felt responsible for upholding the good name of their organization, and the quality of their work was controlled by the assignment of the objects to experts and by the criticism of the elders. The Omada had no need to keep up a reputation as good carvers; their concern was to be good servants of the king. The motivation for acquiring proficiency in carving, then, was the hope of monetary reward and the chance to attract the attention of the king, and these could only be achieved through success in competition. In contrast, Igbesanmwan was a family organization whose relationships were based on kinship. For them, service to the Oba was a ritual duty, not a means to advancement. The belief that all could carve by divine inspiration militated against the development of a competitive spirit, as did the religious nature of the carving activity itself.

In their capacity as palace servants, the Omada were well situated to improve their status. Occasionally, a superior carver would come under the personal auspices of the Oba and would receive particularly valuable assignments, and upon leaving the Omada would receive a minor title, Oba's craftsman (*owin'oba*). But whether or not they received this special attention, all Omada benefited from the king's obligation to set them up well upon their release from service. Graduation from the Omada, a ceremony called "clothing the Omada," also initiated them into the Ibierugha, the initial grade within the Iweguae palace association, which was the preliminary step for moving up in the palace hierarchy. Once out of the Omada, men rarely carved again. Instrumentality was at the heart of Omada art production and thus ensured its marginality. With the explicit requirement that Omada "not serve any juju," their creations were removed from the sphere of creativity that derived from and served supernatural powers. From the standpoint of the Oba and palace, carving was a way to keep idle hands busy and at the same time acquire attractive decorative objects; from that of the Omada, carving was a means to the end of social advancement.

The Omada and the Chiefs

The Omada were able to take advantage of their position to maneuver in the tangle of political alliances and enmities, both among chiefs and between chiefs and the king. As pages, they functioned as "gatekeepers," controlling access to the king. Moreover, the Omada were allowed to move around throughout the entire palace, whereas chiefs were restricted to the quarters belonging to their particular palace association. They therefore had access to a wide range of people and activities, and gained possession of valuable knowledge. By offering gifts of their carvings and their services, they were able to develop relationships that would aid them after they left the palace.

Thus, politically astute carvers could use both their art and their access to negotiate themselves into positions that the status hierarchy did not normally allow.

Omada and Igbesanmwan

It is generally believed by members of both the Omada and Igbesanmwan that the Omada initially learned carving from guild artists. Because of their freedom of movement, they were able to observe the guild members carving in their special workroom in the palace. Although observation is an acceptable mode of learning in Benin, it is not always favored by those being watched, and as a consequence the relationship between pages and guild members was fraught with tension. Guild members complained to me in conversation that the Omada had stolen their designs, while ex-Omada argued that by virtue of their royal service, they were entitled to utilize whatever they had learned in the palace.

COURT ART AND ICONOGRAPHY, CA. 1850–1897

Guild Carving. In the mid nineteenth century, guild carvers created decorated royal altar tusks, ivory horns, gongs, figurines, bracelets, and other ornaments and wooden commemorative heads, altars of the hand, boxes, rattle staffs, commemorative heads, and other shrine objects. On decorated objects, the majority of figures are usually in frontal, static poses in a symmetrical, often hieratic composition. The central figure is the king or a particularly high-ranking chief, queen mother, or priest, flanked by lesser chiefs and retainers and surrounded by symbols of power (ceremonial swords, leopards, crocodiles, etc.). The monarch is always represented in full coral bead regalia. When Europeans appear, often in profile, they are depicted in sixteenth-century Portuguese attire and shown in positions of support for the monarchy, recalling the time when Benin so benefited from the trade and military assistance of the Portuguese.

Royal altar tusks—the epitome of nineteenth-century guild art—abound with images of power. Some refer to the occult powers and divine ancestry of kings, especially Obas Ozolua and Esigie, the great warriors of the fifteenth and sixteenth centuries; to palace ritual specialists like Osa and Osuan, who controlled devastating supernatural forces to harm enemies of the state; and powerful symbolic animals such as the leopard and the elephant.[18] Guild art was aimed at the promulgation and reinforcement of royal hegemonic ideology. Benin kings used these art forms to shape history, that is, to ensure that significant events in their own reigns and those of their ancestors would be remembered as they wished. Since Igbesanmwan carvings were created directly in response to royal commissions, and could be rejected by the king if he were not satisfied, they quite naturally reflected the concerns and political agendas of royalty, as the detail of the carving below shows. Guild art did not therefore lend itself very well to confronting the changing fortunes of the king, or the weakness of kings vis-à-vis their chiefly rivals or foreign threats.

Figure 11.1. Carved royal altar tusk, late nineteenth century. 44 inches. Courtesy the Metropolitan Museum of Art. Gift of Mr. and Mrs. Klaus Perls, 1991 (1991.17.104).

Figure 11.2. Detail of carved royal altar tusk shown in figure 11.1, showing Ozolua the Conqueror. Drawn by Joanne Wood. Courtesy the Metropolitan Museum of Art.

Omada carving. During this same period, Omada carvers were making prestige objects, which included rectangular wood kola nut boxes, stools and chairs, beams, doors, panels, and incised coconuts and coral beads, all decorated with bas-relief designs.[19] As I have pointed out elsewhere, "the relative positioning of the figures with the total carvings tends to be informal and unordered, without the strict emphasis on symmetry, balance and hieratic composition so characteristics of objects made by Igbesanmwan. Moreover, the figures themselves are frequently portrayed in profile and can be seen in poses of movement or even relaxation, while those represented on [guild-produced objects] are mainly in frontal and static positions."[20]

Most important, the distinctive social proportion of king to attendants is often violated, with the Oba appearing below and sometimes smaller in size than the chiefs and attendants around him; for example, on the top of a stool now in the Metropolitan Museum of Art a supporting chief looms over the Oba.[21] While these violations of stylistic canons might derive in part from the type of training and variable skill of the Omada carvers, they also reflect a more distant and perhaps even ironic view of royal power.

To a large extent, the Omada employed the same artistic vocabulary as Igbesanmwan: Obas in full coral regalia, sometimes with mudfish legs, supportive palace chiefs and a variety of attendants, including Omada themselves, symbolic animals and reptiles, and power objects. Yet their interstitial position—their marginal status, heterogeneous origins, and instrumental attitude toward art production—opened up a space for the Omada to create very different types of imagery from that of the guild. Kate Ezra discusses the "strange hybrids of form and imagery" in Omada carving:

> The palace pages create[d] ancient, ritually sanctioned types of objects, such as the *agba* [ceremonial stool], as well as newly introduced foreign ones, such as the chair. In decorating them they [drew] on the time-honored motifs devised long ago by Igbesanmwan to express deep, philosophical concepts, but they also depict[ed] people and things that had only recently appeared in Benin, and had no spiritual connection to the concept of kingship. They often juxtapose[d] those images in odd but amusing ways, crowding them in off-beat, asymmetrical compositions. Omada works are a witty and lighthearted contrast to the solemn, tradition-bound nature of much of Benin art.[22]

Indeed, their art is striking in its violation of the norms of guild art, whether casting or carving. On the Omada-made stools, boxes, and coconuts are a range of images that never appear in guild art, either because they are totally secular or because they are tabooed. Thus we find scenes from daily life: a European shopkeeper seated on a chair before a table propped up on a casket, with rows of bottles and wine glasses laid out in front of him and bolts of fabric hung above, an iron worker at a forge, a palm wine tapper, a young girl carrying a tray with food on her head.[23] This latter image is particularly interesting because on her left is a kind of metacommentary—a representation of carved rattle staffs and a commemorative head on an ancestral altar (perhaps a playful reference to the handiwork of their rivals, the Igbesanmwan guild). Even more unusual are the depictions of naked couples, in one case in the act of sexual embrace, a subject matter that never appeared in guild art.[24] With such images, Omada art pushed at the boundaries of the artistically permissible and thinkable.

At the same time, Omada work began to deal with the changing fortunes of the kingdom. The iconography of Omada carving, far more than that of the guild, expresses the unraveling of Benin hegemony, its political instability, and its vulnerability to British expansion. This is most evident in the depiction of Europeans, whose threatening presence loomed on the Benin horizon.[25] Omada art communicates a deep ambivalence toward Europeans, a mixture of enchantment with their material culture combined with distaste and even ridicule.

The Edo have a long history of contact with Europeans and their material culture; indeed, many terms for material culture in the Edo language are Portuguese loan words.[26] Five centuries of trade with the Portuguese was followed by trade with the Dutch, French, and English, a commerce that involved headgear, horsetails, shirts and cloaks, coral and glass beads, luxury fabrics, and brass pans and bowls. Hats and other items of regalia were incorporated into Benin guild art and were

Figure 11.3. Omada wood carving of a European shopkeeper, part of a box, 28 inches long. Courtesy the Brooklyn Museum of Art. Gift of Arturo and Paul Peralta-Ramos (56.6.63 A+B).

Figure 11.4. Omada carving of young girl with tray, drawn by Debra Wilkerson.

"Edoized," as several scholars have demonstrated by tracing of European prototypes for Benin regalia.[27] Sixteenth-century Portuguese costumes and weapons are the primary unmediated representations of European material culture in guild art.[28] What is unique about nineteenth-century Omada iconography is that, for the first time, the predominant material signs of prosperity and power are imported objects: boats, barrels, parasols, bottles, jugs, coffers, tables, cannons, guns and other weapons, and other everyday European objects.[29] For example, Felix von Luschan illustrates a wooden box belonging to a Frau Erdmann (quite probably the wife of the German merchant whose pre-1897 photographs of the palace Benin appear in von Luschan's book) on which are depicted two Europeans stretched out in lounge chairs, while another kneels in front of a long row of casks and boxes. Representations of writing also appear on the boxes.[30] The fact that these material objects now so clearly announce their origins suggests an awareness of—and even an abdication to—more powerful forces understood to come from outside the kingdom.

In Omada art, Europeans are conventionally depicted as single male figures, although in a few cases, a European stands in the hieratic pose reserved for Obas and high-ranking chiefs, between two smaller European supporters holding parasols.[31] White men are typically depicted holding an umbrella with a crooked handle in the left hand and a curved sword in the right. Their faces, frequently bearded, often have puffy cheeks and upward slanting eyes. They are always dressed in what looks like striped pajamas, with a gun or other weapon at the waist. The only bit of variation in their costume is in their brimmed hats, which have either a rounded or a flat crown. When not lounging or sitting, they stand, perhaps atop a horse or on a crescent-shaped boat.

Figure 11.5. Omada wood carving of a European in a boat, 15-1/2 inches. Courtesy the Metropolitan Museum of Art. Gift of Mr. and Mrs. Klaus Perls, 1991 (1991.17.63ab).

Figure 11.6. Omada wood carving criticizing European manners. Courtesy the Field Museum, Chicago, Illinois (neg. no. A99516).

These depictions of Europeans are rife with humor and sometimes even ridicule. While parasols, swords, boats, and horses are all status objects, there is often a clear element of mockery involved. For instance, the European is shown forced to hold his own parasol, which implies a loss of status; or he is placed in a peculiar position, for instance, standing on, rather than riding, his horse. On a carved stool in the Field Museum, what may at first glance appear to be a straightforward depiction of the custom of pipe smoking is in fact a criticism of European manners. The Edo consider it highly improper to appear in public with something in one's mouth. The same sort of ridicule is even more explicit in a carved chair in the Metropolitan Museum of Art. It shows a representation of a European lying sprawled on the ground, a nearby wine goblet suggesting that he is drunk.

The frequent representation of Europeans in profile is yet another example of mockery. The frontal pose is the most exemplary in Benin art; the king *never* appears in profile. Those shown that way are lacking in social graces or aesthetic appeal. In fact, profile highlights the very features of Europeans that Edo consider the most unattractive: their pointy noses, thin lips, and flat behinds.

When Edo and Europeans figures are depicted in the same space, the depth of the ambivalence in the treatment of Europeans and European material culture is best revealed. On a stool top in Hamburg, a king stands on a coffer.[32] To his immediate left and right are neither Omada, nor chiefs, but rather two profiled Europeans, who are casually seated and facing him. One has his knees crossed, which is an improper

Figure 11.7. Omada carved chair depicting a drunk European. Courtesy the Metropolitan Museum of Art. Gift of Mr. and Mrs. Klaus Perls, 1991 (1991.17.62).

public position, and his chin rests nonchalantly on his hand. The other holds a pistol pointed jauntily upward. Compared with the rigid formality of Edo royal accompaniment (see fig. 11.1), this depiction crosses boundaries to the point of disrespect.

Yet in other depictions of Europeans together with the king, the foreigners are sometimes of equal height with the monarch, a striking violation of Edo status perspective. Even more, in figure 11.6, the stool in the Field Museum, the European figure is in the central hieratic position. He is flanked by Edo kings, who are possibly two versions of Oba Ozolua.[33] Is this striking and ambiguous image to be read as Europeans being contained by the ancestral power of warrior kings, or are the Edo themselves being overpowered?

So it was at Benin's own fin de siècle that Omada art opened up the possibilities of imagining the kingdom in new and highly disturbing ways. In both its style and its imagery, Omada art speaks of disorientation, of a world flooded with powerful foreign objects, a world in which the central focus—the divine king—can be overshadowed and displaced. In 1891, a Yoruba trader, significantly named Thompson Oyibodudu, which means, literally, "black white-man," was captured violating Benin trade restrictions. Oyibodudu was then brought to Benin to be sacrificed. As the executioners went to cut off his head, Oyibodudu reportedly called out: "The white men that are greater than you or I are coming to fight and conquer you." Six years later a British military expedition captured Benin City and sent the king, Oba Ovorranmwen, into exile.[34]

NOTES

The research on which this essay is based was supported by a grant from the Foreign Area Fellowship Program, for which I am very grateful. I thank the late Oba Akenzua II, the late Ovia Idah, and the numerous other carvers, from Igbesanwman and the Omada, who generously shared their knowledge. Lastly, my thanks go to my daughter, Ilana Gershon, whose comments helped in the formulation of this essay.

1. Ovia Idah, personal communication, 1966.
2. Homi K. Bhabha, *The Location of Culture* (New York: Routledge, 1994), 1–2.
3. Very little attention has been paid to Benin's relations with its colonized neighbors. See Biodun Adediran, "Pleasant Imperialism: Conjectures on Benin Hegemony in Eastern Yorubaland," *African Notes* 15, 1–2 (1991): 83–95, for a discussion of Benin imperialism in the eastern Yoruba corridor, and Isidore Okpewho, *Once upon a Kingdom: Myth, Hegemony, and Identity* (Bloomington: Indiana University Press, 1998), on images of Benin's colonial power among its former tributaries.
4. Alan F. C. Ryder, *Benin and the Europeans, 1485–1897* (London: Longmans, 1969), 241.
5. Jacob Egharevba, *Benin Law and Custom* (Lagos: C.M.S. Niger Press, 1949), 35.
6. Sandra Barnes and Paula Ben-Amos, "Ogun, the Empire Builder," in *Ogun, Old World and New*, ed. Sandra T. Barnes (Bloomington: Indiana University Press 1989), 44.
7. The following historical discussion is drawn mainly from R. E. Bradbury, *Benin Studies*, ed. Peter Morton-Williams (New York: Oxford University Press for the International African Institute, 1973), and Ryder, *Benin and the Europeans*.
8. Ryder, *Benin and the Europeans*, 21.
9. Ibid., 266.
10. Ibid., 22–23.
11. Bhabha, *Location of Culture*, 2.
12. The following discussion of Igbesanmwan and Omada is drawn from my work in the early 1970s, esp. Paula Ben-Amos, "Social Change in the Organization of Woodcarving

in Benin City, Nigeria" (Ph.D. diss., Indiana University, 1971), and "Professionals and Amateurs in Benin Court Carving," in *African Images: Essays in African Iconology*, ed. Daniel McCall and Edna Bay (New York: Africana Pub. Co., for the African Studies Center, Boston University, 1975), 170–89.

13. Paula Ben-Amos Girshick, *Art, Innovation, and Politics in Eighteenth-Century Benin* (Bloomington: Indiana University Press, 2000).

14. Henry Ling Roth, *Great Benin: Its Customs, Art and Horrors* (1903; London: Routledge & Kegan Paul, 1968), 196, citing the British trader Cyril Punch, who visited Benin in the late 1880s and 1890s and reported seeing a "court official" carving an ivory tusk, who may have been an Omada. Brass plaques from the sixteenth century depict naked young men standing alongside kings and holding swords. Whether these are the forerunners of today's Omada is impossible to determine.

15. For stories of the origin of Igbesanmwan-created objects, see Ben-Amos, "Professionals and Amateurs in Benin Court Carving," 176.

16. Rowland Abiodun cites the Owo tradition that the sixteenth Olowo, Osogboye, was "sent to Benin as a crown prince by his father to learn the court arts and customs and bring them back to Owo." Abiodun, "The Kingdom of Owo," in *Yoruba: Nine Hundred Years of Art and Thought*, ed. Henry Drewal and John Pemberton (New York: Center for African Art, 1989), 96.

17. Oba Akenzua II, personal communication, 1966.

18. For the dating of tusks and the analysis of their iconography, see Barbara Blackmun, "From Trader to Priest in Two Hundred Years: The Transformation of a Foreign Figure on Benin Ivories," *Art Journal* 47, 2 (1988): 128–38, and "Oba's Portraits in Benin," *African Arts* 23, 3 (1990): 61–69, 102–4.

19. Scholars have not yet established a chronology for Benin objects made of wood, as they have for the brasses and ivories, and therefore the dating of Omada carving is uncertain. Philip J. C. Dark, *The Art of Benin: A Catalogue of an Exhibition of the A. W. F. Puller and Chicago Natural History Museum* (Chicago: Field Museum of Natural History, 1962); William B. Fagg, *Nigerian Images* (London: Percy Lund, Humphries & Co., 1960). Stylistic and iconographic correspondences with nineteenth-century guild ivory carvings suggest that a mid nineteenth-century date for many of the Omada works considered here is plausible. For the purposes of this essay—but with the clear understanding that future research may prove me wrong—I consider Omada carvings that are found in European collections formed from objects removed in 1897 to date from the nineteenth century. See C. H. Read and O. M. Dalton, *Antiquities of the City of Benin and from Other Parts of West Africa in the British Museum* (London: William Clowes & Sons, 1899); and Felix von Luschan, *Die Altertümer von Benin* (Berlin: Vereinigung wissenschaftlicher Verleger, 1919; reprint, New York: Hacker Art Books, 1968). For further discussions of Omada art, see Ben-Amos, "Professionals and Amateurs in Benin Court Carving"; id., *Art, Innovation, and Politics;* Justine M. Cordwell, "Some Aesthetic Aspects of Yoruba and Benin Cultures" (Ph.D. diss., Northwestern University, 1952); Kate Ezra, *Royal Art of Benin: The Perls Collection in the Metropolitan Museum of Art* (New York: Metropolitan Museum of Art, 1992); and Catherine Hess, "Unconventional Carving: Stools and Coconut Shells," in *The Art of Power / The Power of Art: Studies in Benin Iconography*, ed. Paula Ben-Amos and Arnold Rubin (Los Angeles: Museum of Cultural History, 1983), 41–49.

20. Girshick, "Professionals and Amateurs in Benin Court Carving," 171.

21. Ezra, *Royal Art of Benin*, 263, pl. 128. For other examples, see Luschan *Altertümer*, figs. 846, 849.

22. Ezra, *Royal Art of Benin*, 266–67.

23. Luschan, *Altertümer*, fig. 842, p. 489. The palm wine tapper: Ezra, *Royal Art of Benin*, fig. 127.

24. Luschan, *Altertümer*, pl. 124, lower left. Nude images and representations of sexual relations do appear in Yoruba wood carving from this period (Roy Sieber, personal communication, 1997), and the Omada inclusion of similar motifs may reflect Yoruba influence.

25. For a discussion of European portrayals in guild art, see Kathy Curnow, "Alien or Accepted: African Perspectives on the Western 'Other' in Fifteenth and Sixteenth Century Art," *Studies in Visual Anthropology* 13, 1 (1990): 38–75.

26. See Hans Melzian, *A Concise Dictionary of the Bini Language of Southern Nigeria* (London: Kegan Paul, Trench, Trubner & Co., 1937).

27. Ryder, *Benin and the Europeans* .

28. Luschan, *Altertümer*, and Donna Kathleen Abbass, "European Hats Appearing in Benin Art" (M.A. thesis, Southern Illinois University, 1972).

29. See Maria Helena Mendes-Pinto, Introduction, *Os descobrimentos portugueses e a Europa do Renascimento* (Catalogue of the XVII Exposição Europeia de Arte, Ciencia e Cultura in Lisbon. Lisbon: Conselho de Ministros, 1983).

30. Luschan, *Altertümer*, figs. 842, 846, 858–59, pl. 124.

31. For instance, *ART/artifact*, ed. Susan Vogel (New York: Center for African Art, 1988), 54, and Museum für Völkerkunde Dresden, *Benin: Europäerdarstellungen der Hofkunst eines afrikanischen Reiches, aus dem Staatlichen Museum für Völkerkunde Dresden*, ed. Siegfried Wolf (Leipzig: Prisma-Verlag, 1972), pl. 32.

32. Luschan, *Altertümer*, pl. Y.

33. Barbara Blackmun has pointed out the distinguishing characteristics of Oba Ozolua in Benin art. For another example of the same pose, see Luschan, *Altertümer*, pl. 124.

34. Thompson Oyibodudu quoted in Robert Home, *City of Blood Revisited: A New Look at the Benin Expedition of 1897* (London: R. Collings, 1982), 17.

Chapter 12

Bad Copies: The Colonial Aesthetic and the Manjaco-Portuguese Encounter

Eric Gable

In this essay, I look at the ways in which Africans and Portuguese in late colonial-era Guinea-Bissau copied each others' bodies to visualize themselves. I focus on two sets of images produced at roughly the same time by people on opposed sides of the colonial encounter. One consists of carved wooden figures that look like caricatures of Portuguese colonial officers, but that chiefs and rulers in the Manjaco ethnic group used to commemorate their ancestors. The other is an obsessively thorough series of photographs of Manjaco women's scarified torsos that one such colonial officer, Artur Martins de Meireles, collected in order to illustrate an anthropological monograph on Manjaco customs of "bodily mutilation" he published in 1960.

In the mid twentieth century, the Manjaco "figurative innovation" became the fashion of choice among members of an emerging Manjaco aristocracy—the families of rulers and chiefs who held traditional positions of authority while acting as intermediaries between the Manjaco and the colonial administration. Manjaco chiefs installed these seemingly parodic figures in household ancestor shrines—shrines that up to this point had been populated by wholly abstract carved shapes. At the same time that Manjaco elites were copying images of Salazarist administrators for an indigenous ancestor cult, colonial officers were compelled to replicate the scholarly study of (what Portuguese characterized as) a fast-disappearing traditional culture, and anthropological study became one element in an administrator's official training. Meireles, who had served as an administrator in the Manjaco region for fifteen years, used the authority of his office to undertake a study in which he and his assistants recorded the presence or absence of scarification patterns on the torsos of over 20,000 Manjaco women—the vast majority of the post-pubescent female population—and to photograph ("dorsal and ventral") hundreds of them to illustrate his thesis that Manjaco traditional culture, as epitomized by scarification, was in decline.

What are we to make of Manjaco copies of Portuguese faces as commemorative "portraits" of ancestral Manjaco? What are we to make of Meireles's contemporaneous meticulous documentation of Manjaco "mutilation"? A convenient way to explore such questions is to begin with the historical context from which these images emerged. Both sets of images are clearly products of a particular colonial encounter. Contextualized in that encounter, they also illustrate a more pervasive colonial aesthetic.

The particular historical moment might be called the climax of colonialism in Guinea-Bissau, then known as Portuguese Guinea. The Salazarist regime, also called the New State government (1926–59), with its peculiar combination of nostalgic paternalism and futuristic modernism, finally began to make good on its claim to be "civilizing" its poor little patch of West Africa. In other words, at least the possibility opened for schools, hospitals, roads, bridges, and wells to proliferate as they had in neighboring French colonies. Because the New State was inaugurated just as much of the world was plunged into the Depression, at first Portugal had left its colonial governments to fend for themselves. What is more, Guinea, in contrast to Mozambique and Angola, had only a miniscule expatriate European population, which was almost exclusively employed in government. But with the end of World War II, an increased prosperity came even to such impoverished colonies.

The 1940s were also the first decade that the Salazarist administrators could credibly claim that their "oldest" African colony had been fully secured. Since the sixteenth century, Portuguese "government" had maintained a presence in *praças*, or coastal entrepôts, and therefore had long interacted with the Manjaco and other coastal peoples. Nonetheless, even regions just beyond the praças' walls succumbed to Portuguese military control only in the twentieth century. While Manjaco and most other ethnic groups were conquered by force of arms between 1913 and 1915, sporadic resistance persisted in some regions into the 1930s. Portuguese political security would moreover be very short-lived. In July 1959, around the time Meireles's monograph was going to press, African dockworkers in Bissau went on strike, in violation of New State laws. In the ensuing repression, fifty African workers were killed, including many Manjaco. Within three years, the Guinean nationalist party (known by its acronym as the PAIGC), under the leadership of Amilcar Cabral, began an armed struggle for independence. In 1974 , the PAIGC decisively defeated Portuguese troops. This, along with the wars in Angola and Mozambique, catalyzed the overthrow of the dictatorship in Portugal and the end of Portuguese colonialism abroad.[1]

During the brief climax of Portuguese colonialism in Africa, the New State made anthropology a central component of colonialism administrative training. A discipline that had never had a place in the Portuguese academy became, arguably, more important to New State colonial officials than to their counterparts in the French and English colonial systems they often tried to emulate.[2] During this brief era of New State economic prosperity and relative political stability, the Manjaco were perhaps both the most studied and the least subordinated of Guinea's subjects.[3] They were considered to be the most politically stratified and centralized of coastal wet-rice farming "animists" (as opposed to the Muslim Fula and Mandinga in the interior). While the Portuguese made mutually productive military alliances with interior peoples, they found that the peoples of the coast—the Balanta, Papel, Bramé, and Manjaco, for instance—were much less tractable.[4] The Portuguese, especially in the New State era, blamed this on the essential egalitarianism of the "animists," who were generally seen as acephalous. Because the Manjaco had an elaborate federation of rulerships or "lands," however, they appeared to be an exception to the rule, or at least to the ethnographic rules that Portuguese in the colonial era were given to writing.[5]

To the Portuguese, the typical Manjaco was "a worker who had escaped, for the most part, the atavistic indolence inherent in the great mass of the negro population."[6] The Manjaco region was rich in resources to be exploited for the benefit of the colony and its civilizing mission. Its forests were virtual oil-palm plantations. Its cultivated upland fields already produced more of the colony's leading export crop—peanuts—than any other region. But Manjaco had the disturbing propensity to vote with their feet against local chiefs and the colony and for greater freedom and better economic prospects in French Senegal or British Gambia. By the mid 1940s, when Meireles became a colonial officer in the region, roughly a fifth of them in any given year were hard at work in neighboring Senegal, their labor adding nicely to the French balance sheet. The more cosmopolitan Manjaco became, Portuguese New State administrators constantly repeated, the less likely they were to remain colonial subjects. Meanwhile, Manjaco rulers tended to be a disruptive rather than a constructive influence—becoming tyrants and getting deposed with alarming regularity. By Meireles's time, as many as a third of Manjaco chiefships were either vacant or the current officeholders were embroiled in litigation. Because political "perturbations" caused "great unrest," Manjaco had "little attachment for their land."[7] Manjaco were a particular embarrassment in a colony that—because it had been so hard to rule, so hard to "fix" as specifically Portuguese—was routinely characterized by New State authorities as an insult to Portuguese identity.[8]

The difficulties Manjaco posed exacerbated a certain ambivalence among New State administrators. At times they evinced a nostalgia for dream natives governed by tradition, and at times they wanted modern Manjaco unfettered by custom; all the while, they were becoming more entangled as gatekeepers in local politics. As a result, for Manjaco, the ability to manipulate the forms and technologies of bureaucracy became more and more a necessity of political life, a manifestation and instantiation of power. A carved "portrait" of a Manjaco chief in the guise of a colonial officer makes perfect sense in such a context. So, too, does a photograph of a naked Manjaco girl, whose scarified skin is a sign of an essential and exciting difference, the disappearance of which was paradoxically at once a goal of Salazarist colonialism and a threat to its reason for being. The mutilated girl is both a beauty and a savage.

Figure 12.1. Photograph of a scarified Manjaco woman by Artur Martins de Meireles, from his *Mutilações étnicas dos Manjacos*, Publicações do Centro de Estudos da Guiné Portuguesa: Memórias, 22 (Bissau, 1960), p. 241.

The two sets of images, carved and photographed, complement each other in what amounts to a generic colonial aesthetic. On the one hand, the carved figure and the modern Manjaco who commissioned such figures represent the "bad copy" that V. Y. Mudimbe notes is the objectification of colonialist disgust. On the other hand, the scarified torsos of Manjaco women, understood as prurient images, are a typical objectification of colonialist desire. In the generic colonialist aesthetic, the good native is invariably a woman, and the bad copy is inevitably a man. She is

Figure 12.2. Two Manjaco ancestor posts, one of them by Jon Biku Pinambe. Photo by Eric Gable.

the woman fettered by tradition, needing to be released or protected from its savagery and yet promising that she will not be, and that she will instead invite you into it. He is the visible product of your civilizing mission. He is the native who wears your suits, but the style is a little too flamboyant, and you laugh at his imperfect attempts at imitation. Yet you are often anxious because you are never quite sure whether he mimics you to make fun of you.[9]

It has long been argued that nothing bothered the settler more than such bad copies, "savvy boys," "trousered Africans," because they upset the implicit paternalism of the colonial enterprise.[10] But the bad copy has also upset the enemies of colonialism, for the "black man who wants to be white" is proof positive of colonialism's pathological effect.[11] For both camps, the bad copy is often an aesthetic abomination—an embodiment of a troubling inauthenticity.

The bad copy is a problem in the colonial aesthetic. It continues to echo in the way *colon* art (most often statuettes of European colonials) is assimilated into a Western aesthetic premised on a misplaced authenticity—and, by extension, in how Westerners come to imagine people like Manjaco in the Western cultural universe. I shall return to the problem of the bad copy at the end of this essay in order to suggest how the particulars of the Manjaco version of mimicry might allow us to break this particularly encumbering frame. Along the way I also use the images that the Portuguese generated to supply a particular context for my appraisal of a generic colonialist aesthetic.

THE COLONIALIST'S DRESS CODE

In the archive in Bissau are a couple thousand ethnographic photographs taken from the mid 1940s to 1974.[12] Hundreds of them appeared in the *Boletim Cultural da Guiné Portuguesa*, a journal launched on what the New State claimed was the 500th anniversary of colonization. The *Boletim* published on a wide variety of subjects, including history and even imaginative fiction. Its main purpose, however, was to display the supposed Salazarist commitment to modernizing science, and it featured numerous ethnographic reports and speculative essays written by officials like Meireles.[13] The collection of ethnographic photographs supplied their illustrations.

What struck me immediately in looking through this accidental ensemble of pictures was the sheer number of images of bare-breasted nubile girls. It was as if I had found the Portuguese version of what Malek Alloula calls "the colonial harem." Although this harem had been gathered for scientific reasons, and the photos had all been taken as an ethnographic record of a colony's people, they were clearly a skewed record, "fixed" by a particular frame, an all-too-familiar, even predictable gaze.[14] In addition to the photographs that appear in Meireles's studies, there were dozens of others that remained unpublished. The camera angle in these shots is level with the women's navels and tilts upward toward their exposed breasts. Some of the more alluring images of nubile torsos later appeared as an oddly out-of-place feature of the generally scholarly *Boletim* called "Scenes and Types of Guinea." It juxtaposed photographs of roads and bridges with picturesque images of the "natives," mostly girls, and was at once an advertisement for the colony's modernity and for its bucolic charms. Thus some of Meireles's photographs ended up shorn of their scientific pretenses and used merely as illustrations of the colonial idyll.

The Portuguese were notorious among colonizers for copulating and cohabitating with their subjects. The British travel writer Archibald Lyall, who visited Guinea "between the wars," repeats what amounts to the common wisdom about the Portuguese and "colonialist desire": "I met dozens of Portuguese officials all through Guiné and better hosts one could not wish to find. They are gay and friendly and hospitable. They are very good judges of whiskey and they make no pretense of indifference to the luscious and well-displayed charms of their younger female subjects."[15]

Portuguese themselves often reveled in this reputation, for it proved that they did not discriminate, that they were not racist.[16] This image of the Portuguese—this way of "fixing" them as distinct from their colonizing peers—is also a kind of stereotype. But it illuminates, as it were, the peculiar focus of the ethnographic ensemble. It "explains," perhaps, why so many images of nubile girls ended up in "Scenes of Guinea" as advertisements for the colony.

Something else struck me about the accidental gallery of images in Bissau. It bore very little resemblance to what was contained in the bulk of the documents that made up the archive. These documents were the stuff of "administrative anthropology," the effluvia of a colonial bureaucracy. When ethnography appeared at all, it was pragmatic and allusive. The gap between such words and the stock of pictures distributed among them raises a crucial issue for any study of empire. Words and pictures work in different ways. Pictures, while nominally "fixed" in their specificity, can also migrate in order to dovetail or contradict what words say. Thus while the images of exposed torsos Meireles used for his monograph are not necessarily erotic, they arguably become erotic as they are appropriated in different contexts.

This is perhaps most obvious if one compares Meireles's images to images of similarly scarified "Manjaco maidens" taken by the Austrian Hugo Bernatzik.[17] Bernatzik's "maidens" are at once more erotic and more appealing, and in giving them a romantic aura, he also humanized them. On the other hand, Meireles's photographs are less brutal than a set of images his administrative superior, António Carreira, took to illustrate his own brief ethnographic essay on Manjaco scarification. Carreira's images are clinically cropped at the neck and pudenda, preserving the anonymity of his subjects but turning them into scientific specimens. Carreira was Guinea's most prolific and scrupulous scholar, and as much of a modernizer as the Portuguese colonial service produced. According to the stories Manjaco tell today, Carreira had the eccentric reputation for touring the district capital market and ordering bare-breasted women to cover themselves with a blouse or brassiere. Yet almost all Carreira's ethnographic works are illustrated at the front and back of each chapter with art deco lithographs of "village scenes": thatch-roofed huts and palm trees; a stylized silhouette of a near-naked maiden pounding millet; a young woman bare to the waist, bending over a fishing net.

Figure 12.3. Art deco lithograph of "village scenes" from António Carreira's ethnographies in *Boletim Cultural da Guiné Portuguesa*.

The images that filled the margins of so many of the texts produced under New State auspices had a life of their own. To tie the meaning they convey to the authorial intent of the officials who used them is to bypass a perhaps crucial question about what they reveal, and about whom. Are we to "read" such images—that is, supply them with discursive meaning? (And isn't this what we invariably do?) Or are we to interpret them as a kind of "exposure" of what cannot quite be put into words—what goes without saying?

A "NUCLEUS APART"

The anthropology in the administrative documents served tangible ends in the paternalistic culture of New State, Salazarist policy. Colonial officers needed to make Manjaco political practice make sense and to institute some version of indirect rule. Officially, at least, New State administrators were uncomfortable with indirect rule: it was a stopgap measure, a temporary pause in the long march toward managed modernity. But in Portuguese Guinea, they quickly recognized, and thenceforth defended on pragmatic grounds, the need for some form of "native" rule. They were forever alluding to Manjaco "habits and customs"—rarely given in any detail—in order to make pronouncements about why this or that chief was or was not a "duly constituted authority," why one pretender to office had to be reinstated, another deposed. In discovering stable "duly constituted authority," they were, they constantly complained, monumentally unsuccessful.

The upshot was that administrators such as Meireles, in collusion with Manjaco chiefs and their families—particularly those who had some education, who had connections in the colonial bureaucracy, who had emigrated to urban areas, or who had (in the then-current Manjaco idiom) "seen France"—invented a Manjaco tradition that might be termed "the pecuniary polity." The Portuguese envisaged the dozens of Manjaco lands as a single congeries of "rulerships," each ruler receiving his title from the "ruler of rulers" in Bassarel, and each ruler, in turn, having the right to install in office sometimes dozens of chiefs in any given "land." In this invented tradition, rulers could install anyone they chose to, and indeed the Portuguese emphasized that Manjaco competed for political titles by bribing the rulers, for with each particular office went the lifetime usufruct rights to valuable wet-rice fields and palm groves.

In enshrining the pecuniary polity as a Manjaco "tradition" the colonial officials legitimized corruption as normal political practice. But they were also not above breaking the rules of the system they arguably played a large part in inventing. A particular nuisance for them were the "tangled roots of superstition" that surrounded the selection of the paramount ruler in Bassarel. As a result, the "ruler of rulers" was not really an effective leader from the Portuguese perspective, and various colonial officers often found themselves supporting chiefly candidates who were not the Bassarel king's choice. Conversely, Portuguese officials seemingly accepted as temporary officeholders men they themselves called "usurpers," but then wrote endless memoranda to their superiors about their attempts to replace them with legitimate candidates. In effect, they normalized a quiet subversion of the rules, of saying one thing in documents intended for superiors and doing something else "on the ground," all in pursuit of their primary goal: to get Manjaco to stay put and farm in "Guiné" for the profit of the colony.

In the words of their documents, Portuguese administrators come across as diligent and disinterested managers of traditional authority, perplexed and enervated by conniving natives. The colonial officer is always on the side of "duly constituted authority" and against "usurpation," even when so-called "usurpers" remained in office for years. Manjaco whom I interviewed in the 1980s were certain that the Portuguese sided with the usurpers, who had bought them off. Indeed, the Portuguese admitted the existence of corruption. Meireles, summing up the mess in one of the rulerships, noted that the usurper in question would not have been so persistent had he not been encouraged by someone "of influence" who was on the take: "I am certain that it would not be far from the truth to say that with the promise of the transfer of the administrator and allusions to personal influence, the petitioner must have sucked from [the usurper] at least a dozen thousands of escudos. [A]nd this is what would be easy to verify."[18] The "petitioner" here is a Manjaco, albeit a government official. In the documents, it is always a native who suffers the accusation and a Portuguese official who makes the effort to distance himself from corruption's polluting taint.

If we can conclude anything, it is that these natives are the ones whose voices were clearly heard in the villages, for it was they who relayed and read the "letters" that contained the administration's proclamations. Yet it is these voices—and their power to influence, cajole, even, perhaps control—that is totally erased in the managed accounts of the documents. These people became the Portuguese sorcerers' apprentices, sometimes doing their superiors' bidding, sometimes making a messy situation worse. In most official memoranda, they appear euphemistically, if at all, but occasionally one gets a glimpse of what was probably the common view. For example, in

1936, António de Carvalho Viegas, the Portuguese governor of the colony, warned future colonial officers about the Manjaco. They were a particular nuisance because they constantly crossed the border into Senegal and as a result were no longer pure:

> In general, the colonizer judges the Manjaco from individuals of the race who live together with the white. Nothing is more misleading. The smart Manjaco—putting on the air of civilization that is belied by his ridiculous taste in fashion—constantly questioning, shrewd in small matters, is only the Manjaco who has lived in the urban centers.... The other, the one that represents the majority, the one of economic value, the one that works and gathers the palm nut is as savage [as any primitive].[19]

Viegas wanted to dismiss cosmopolitan Manjaco as anomalous, and he did so in two typical, yet discursively opposed ways. On the one hand, those Manjaco who might appear civilized were not so, as evident from "their ridiculous taste in fashion." They were bad copies. On the other hand, "those who had been to Dakar or Bissau"—those who had learned to read and write and "petition"—were not "the majority." To Viegas such "constantly questioning, shrewd" Manjaco were a dangerous aberration, a kind of cancer in the body politic. They were "like a nucleus apart, which does not represent, in the sector of native politics and economics, a valuable element."[20]

MANJACO MUTILATIONS

As Meireles tried to resolve the vexing problems of the "usurpations" in the Manjaco territory, he was constantly finding himself entangled with members of this "nucleus apart." Viegas's wish to deny cosmopolitan Manjaco an explicit place in contemporary village life also characterizes Meireles's monograph. Meireles wrote his monograph and took the photos that illustrate it at the end of a long, frustrating association with the Manjaco. Like so many colonial-era ethnographies written by New State administrators, it has a beside-the-point quality to it.[21] Not only was its research conducted just before the revolution was about to begin, but it scans as inadvertent parody—as a kind of bad copy. A pretension to science overwhelms the subject: the science is big, its product small.

To conduct his inquiry of mutilations as completely and comprehensively as possible, Meireles used the opportunity another study provided. He had been ordered to "concentrate" the local population so that a medical team could assess the extent of sleeping sickness among the Manjaco. Once the doctor, sitting at one table, was through examining each patient, each subject moved to another table, where Meireles's assistant asked each Manjaco to face him and then turn around so that the assistant could record on a "sheet" whether scarification was present or absent and where on the torso the scarification occurred. In a short time, Meireles was able to collect data on 42,224 Manjaco, 18,452 of which were males and 23,772 females, or roughly 56 percent of the total population. The tables he compiled were a map, as it were, covering the territory they codified.

 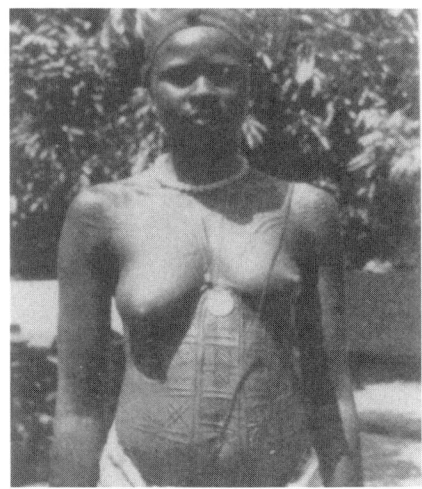

Figure 12.4. Two photographs from Artur Martins de Meireles, *Mutilações étnicas dos Manjacos,* Publicações do Centro de Estudos da Guiné Portuguesa: Memórias, 22 (Bissau, 1960), figs. 6 and 7, p. 26, both captioned "Rapariga de Pecixe tatuada."

Meireles felt compelled to argue that such an exhaustively illustrated sample was as complete as practically possible. The tone he takes is one of defensive apology, as if he were anticipating an audience that might doubt his science. In defending his sample he emphasized:

> It could possibly be objected that the numbers presented do not possess the value [of completeness] attributed to [them], by virtue of the fact that there are, outside of the borders of the Province, some two dozen thousand Manjaco. It must be said that . . . those who remain definitely residing abroad, whose number must run around 12,000, have begun to detribalize and lose, therefore, interest for an ethnographic study.[22]

The "modern" Manjaco thus remained for Meireles in 1960, as for Viegas in 1936, a "nucleus apart"—people who were recognized but only in order to be explained away.

Meireles's thesis about tattooing or scarification was simple. As with many other "unevolved peoples," Manjaco had a kind of skin that was perfect for tattooing. Tattooing was an adolescent preoccupation based on "coquetry and fashion." The lines and marks had no "ideographical" significance; they were merely decorative, "a kind of geometry."[23] Yet scarification was also the quintessential sign of their primitive cultural identity. As Manjaco modernized, as they came into "contact with evolved populations," then "this primitive fashion" went out of style. By tabulating the incidence of tattooing among women by age, Meireles was able to prove beyond a shadow of a doubt that this fashion was indeed in steep decline.[24] Meireles concludes his observations with a clichéd profundity aimed at those who might find such "savageries" unusual or odd:

> [I]n the supercivilized cities of Europe and America, there are numerous beauty salons, that, to remove the hairs off the legs of women use a sticky paste.... Now the pain provoked by such a depilatory must be a close cousin to the pain produced by the incisions of tattooing.... What can we conclude? That whatever the latitude, women subject themselves to suffering in order to embellish their bodies.[25]

As Homi Bhabha remarks, following Edward Said, fixing the colonial subject is a twofold process.[26] Thus Meireles fixes tattooing. There must be a certain freezing in time—the creation of timelessness. Here all female bodies are alike; they are the universal degree zero. Female bodies are always torturing themselves, turning authentic charms into unnatural attractions.[27] Then, there must be an allowance for a lapse of time, usually involving a loss. Here a fashion recedes into the past at the moment Manjaco become more evolved and modern, and turn into bad copies.

THE MANJACO DRESS CODE

From the perspective of local Manjaco political practice, in order for individuals to claim that they were a "duly constituted authority" in the competitive scramble for local political titles, they had to point to an ancestor who had held the office before them. Contrary to the Portuguese view, political titles were not open to the highest bidder, but were restricted to a circle of families who shared the title in a roughly equitable, albeit constantly contested, succession. Every Manjaco "court," like every Manjaco "house" *(kato)*—the indigenous landholding group—had a cluster of ancestor "posts" *(pitchap)*, enshrining previous caretaker-shareholders in the estate.[28] These posts were the material manifestations of the history of the competitive circulation of titles among a restricted group of households. Most such posts are, as the name literally implies, merely a wooden stake stuck in the ground. They are planted so as to be publicly visible—at the entrance to a compound courtyard or under the veranda of the compound's most permanent and prominent building. Most such stakes are carved (often perfunctorily) in aesthetically pleasing abstract shapes. A cluster of such forms—a stack of inverted cones, a vertical yet slightly curved form culminating in two outstretched armlike projections—look like a collection of sculpture by Brancusi.

Within local genres, which were characterized by abstraction, the figurative images used by many Manjaco as posts were a double innovation. Not only were they representational in form, but the status of their producers in relation to their consumers was also different. Most commemorative carvings were and are made by a kinsman of the ancestor to be enshrined—specifically someone who counts as a sister's son. The person is selected by divination and that person can in turn ask a

Figure 12.5. Cluster of Manjaco ancestor posts, showing abstract and figurative forms. Photo by Eric Gable.

more dexterous family member to do the actual work, but the point is that the object produced itself is of less significance than the web of sociality its production entails. The carver is "paid" for his work, but again the payment is a part of an explicit ritualization of kinship, for he returns part of the payment later to complete a cycle of reciprocity. By contrast, the figurative commemorative carvings were clearly objects in a system of conspicuous consumption. Notably, cash and cattle figured in the transaction, and carvers developed reputations that were if not transethnic at least translocal.

Figurative carvings were specifically marketed to colonial-era chiefs and rulers and their families—the duly constituted authorities of colonial neo-tradition. Three carvers are today remembered as the innovators of three distinct, yet imitated, styles. I briefly met the most renowned of these carvers—Soga Mendes—and interviewed the family of the another—Jon Biku Pinambe—who died in 1984. Of the third innovator, Uut, I learned very little. He may have begun carving as early as the 1920s. His sculptures are birdlike figures that resemble the styles of the Nalu and Baga in southern Guinea-Bissau and Guinea.[29] He may have continued carving into the 1950s, and he is the only Manjaco artist to have one of his pieces on display at a European museum—a piece more than likely appropriated from an ancestor shrine by Portuguese troops during the revolution.

Soga Mendes initially imitated a figurative style from a neighboring ethnic group, the Bijagos, where he had spent years working on a large German oil-palm concession. Soga supplemented his income making kitschy images of Africans and parodies of Portuguese for sale to Europeans. Soga began to reach a wide audience when he was invited to produce and sell his work as part of the events commemorating the "500th Anniversary of the Discovery of Guinea," which was, again, a key element in the Salazarist administration's attempt to put Portugal's oldest enclave and most peripheral possession on the modern colonial map. The celebration involved the creation and display of traditional culture, and indigenous craftspeople were organized by the Catholic Church to make works to sell at kiosks in the recreated villages. It was there that Soga first sold his stereotyped tourist-art renderings of "A Manjaco Ruler and His Wife"—the king in toga and top hat, the queen carrying a gourd bowl on her head. Soon, however, such figures became popular among chiefs in the southern Manjaco "lands," where the top hat style was indeed an official "uniform" and where it continues as such on formal occasions to this day. Soga also began to get commissions for similar icons of tradition from rulers in lands where such a royal uniform had never been the fashion. At the 500th anniversary celebration, Soga also made carvings imitating the bronze busts of the Portuguese governors of the colony, both in uniform or in mufti, and he sculpted at least one bust of "Doutor Salazar."[30] Versions of these also found their way into Manjaco shrines.

Jon Biku Pinambe began his carving career making wooden shoes in the northern European "traditional" style for Africans who had never had the opportunity

Figure 12.6. Manjaco ancestor posts by Uut. Photo by Eric Gable.

of visiting these exotic locales. Later, following Soga's lead, he began working on European figures. He suffered from leprosy and had, according to family members, only stubs for fingers, making it impossible for him to clutch the fulcrum shovel and cultivate the wet-rice fields as most Manjaco men should. He had taken up carving while on an extended convalescence (possibly at a missionary hospital) in the southern town of Catio. There he "learned to carve" from the Nalu—an ethnic group whose carved work is, like that of the Bijagos, well represented in European collections. He is responsible for the carvings of the figures in military uniforms,

Figure 12.7. Manjaco ancestor posts by Soga Mendes. Photo by Eric Gable.

and those in suits and fedoras. Like Soga's, his style was widely, if more briefly, imitated.

The images these men made became the fashion of choice among the local aristocracy. Today, such figurative posts seem ironically incongruous: a plump colonial officer in a white tunic, his face and hands painted pink, the pockets of his tunic festooned with brightly colored medals; a dapper little white-faced man with long black sideburns and a Hitlerian moustache dressed in a black suit with a white

Figure 12.8. Cluster of Manjaco ancestor posts, including some by Jon Biku Pinambe. Photo by Eric Gable.

handkerchief and a row of pens peeking out of the pockets; a severe birdlike avatar decked out in a top hat, clutching a tax book under one arm and holding a fountain pen in the other hand.

They do not seem to belong in a peasant village. And indeed nowadays they are, like scarification, artifacts of past "traditions," for there are no longer any carvers making figurative images for money in Manjaco lands.[31] Most posts carved today are in the abstract style and by a kinsman in the appropriate relationship to the deceased. Occasionally, someone will fashion a figurative image—a head mounted on an unembellished trunk. More rarely, the family will bypass the kinsman to go "across the river" to neighboring Ziguinchor to buy airport art and then return to "plant" these generic images of "primitive" Africans or crude knockoffs of colon figures as posts in home villages. I once encountered a carving commissioned in Dakar; the carver had used a photograph of the deceased as a model. But this was the exception to the general postcolonial "reversion" to abstraction.

Manjaco posts, whether figurative or abstract, are obviously anthropomorphic, but they are not in a primary sense "portraits." In the abstract "post," what is being signaled is a moment in a life-cycle and a relationship. The shape the post takes and the manner in which it is planted signals the moment when a young man asserts his right to build a conjugal hut around the courtyard of the corporate house.[32] It marks the moment when a youth becomes a man with domestic responsibilities. The planting of such a post is normally done by sons to honor a father once these sons become elders and have mature and married, or about-to-be married, sons of their own. It heralds the elder's right to be a stakeholder in house corporate property—to distribute use rights to house rice fields, for example, to newly married sons. In a sense the post—and indeed the ancestor it ostensibly enshrines as a continuing presence in household affairs—is a kind of proxy, an effigy of the living elder who plants it.

This was even more directly the case where claims to the corporate properties of royal or chiefly "titles" were concerned. It was a common practice in the climax of colonialism for families to put forth candidates who were old enough ostensibly not to care whether they personally suffered supernatural reprisals for holding a title for which their qualifications were dubious. Such men, however, could act as fronts for family corporate interests—younger men who received from them various "titled fields" that were the titleholder's right to parcel out.

Thus it makes sense that figurative carvings did not so much resemble an individual as the congeries of "technologies" that the various subalterns functionaries needed to master in order to work behind the scenes to ensure that a family could claim and hold a political title. What seems to have occurred in many cases is that sons and grandsons—the stock boys, the clerks, the returned emigrants—commissioned images of ancestors that enshrined their powers and attributes in what Anthony Appiah labels a "neo-tradition." Discussing a Yoruba carving that curators called "Man on a Bicycle," Appiah argues that it was "produced by someone who does not care that the bicycle is the white man's invention: it is not there to be other to the Yoruba Self."[33] The Manjaco sculptures of ancestor figures reveal this same matter-of-fact and pragmatic appropriation, an old icon incorporated new, but also ephemeral, iconography.[34]

COPYING?

Thus far I have suggested that colonial-era political unrest—the scramble for chieftaincies that went on after the scramble for this part of Africa redefined the technologies of power and authority in Manjaco villages—was the historical framework for carvings of Manjaco ancestors in suits and photographs of scarified Manjaco maidens. Both the figurative carving and Meireles's photos of scarified torsos are visible refractions of the same, by and large invisible, subject. This subject remained invisible by a form of collusion between the colonizer and the colonized. This subject is the so-called "nucleus apart" who had the bureaucratic means to get their figurehead in office or someone else's figurehead out of office, so that family members could enjoy the usufruct rights to rice fields, and the access to village labor that possession of such titles entailed. These shadowy operators are the local versions of the universally derided "bad copy."

As such, these juxtaposed imagic genres reveal a widely remarked upon paradox inherent in colonialist practice and discourse.[35] Colonialists needed to modernize backward Africans in order to make the colonial enterprise a success. But to do away with their backwardness, get Africans to become *evolués*, to "assimilate," as the Portuguese put it, is to destroy the foundations of colonialism. The problem for the colonialist inevitably became: what to do with the *assimilado*? One widely invoked solution, and the Portuguese were hardly unique here, was to ignore their presence—they were inauthentic no matter how many of them there were or how long they had existed—and substitute images of a "timeless Africa."[36] This is the assertion of the "illuminations" bracketing the articles in *Boletim Cultural da Guiné Portugugesa* and the function of the "Types and Aspects of Guinea" photo gallery at the back of each issue, and just as Portugal was hurrying to institute modernizing schemes at the level of the village—wells, schools, clinics—in the so-called "Guiné Melhor" campaign. Such imagery became even more prevalent as Portugal was losing control of its oldest African colony. As the revolution reduced Portuguese "zones of control" to urban areas and a few patches of countryside, "Scenes of Guinea" hid their erasure behind the mask of a smiling maiden.

Portuguese administrators, official Salazarist "assimilation" policy aside, needed naked Manjaco to practice a self-validating paternalism. And it could be argued that, for Portuguese, this generic colonial need was exacerbated by a long history of insecurity about their own modernity as compared to other colonialist powers. This insecurity underwrote the unintentional parody of the scientific enterprise that Meireles undertook.

The way I have supplied a narrative frame for these images, not to mention the images themselves, is doubtless familiar. For at least the past fifteen years, scholars in art history, anthropology, and history have made creative use of the kinds of the colonial-era aesthetics that governed the production of art objects on both sides of the encounter to critically appraise that encounter.[37] Indeed, one result of scholarly interest has been that kitsch—the colon figure, postcolonial "genre" painting, tourist art—has increasingly become of interest to museums.[38] Just as actual colonial imagery is displayed in order to parody or criticize the ideas of their makers, when we look at colon figures such as the Manjaco ancestor carvings, we like to read into them parodies and caricatures of colonial administrators, and by extension, a colonial critique.[39] But such a reading is hard to sustain, and is inevitably destabilizing, precisely because of the ambiguities inherent in copying or mimicry.[40] Ultimately, we need to know how these figures were read by Manjaco and Portuguese at the time of the colonial encounter. We would hope that not only would Manjaco have recognized their figurative innovation as a form of "appropriation," in the sense that artists and critics today use the term, but that Portuguese recognized it in that way too and felt its sting.

It is unfortunately not possible to recover what Manjaco wished to communicate about their Portuguese colonial rulers when they planted these figures in local chiefly shrines. During the 1950s and 1960s, however, Manjaco invented praise names for their shadowy sepoys and clerks, names beaten out on funeral drums, which continue to be used today for their contemporary analogues. One such name was "White's Ears Are Whiter." It became a popular, in fact, generic praise name for any of the Manjaco of the time who worked in the colonial government. Praise names are aphorisms—they begin as frozen fragments of dialogue, often a recollection of an insult flung in one direction and reclaimed as a compliment. In this case, so I was told by the chief of the funeral drummers in the village where I did fieldwork in the late 1980s, "White's Ears Are Whiter" originated as mockery—one Manjaco accusing another, a low-level clerk, of having put on airs because he wore "a white's clothes" or could "write in the white's words." In Manjaco, "ears" can simply be a synecdoche for appearance, but "ears" is also a metaphor for intelligence. The clerk responded to the insult by claiming that "the white's ears may be whiter"—that is, that a white will always look more white than any Manjaco—but that he, in fact, was smarter, more educated, than his ostensible superiors. In short, "White's Ears Are Whiter" is at once a recognition of colonialism's inequities and an assertion that the condition is temporary. Copying is more than mimicry; it is doing the same thing, only better.[41]

If some Manjaco saw copying in that way, many Portuguese saw in the kinds of objects Manjaco copied evidence of an enduring inferiority. They used such objects to retrace the rhetoric of a timeless (and backward) Africa by employing aesthetic versions of the trope of the bad copy and the nucleus apart. Thus in an article called "Painting and Sculpture in Portuguese Guinea" that appeared in the *Boletim* in 1964, Fernando Rogado Quintino, using a work from Soga Mendes as an illustration, allowed that local carvers who "obey clearly Western conceptions betray dexterity in their preparations."[42] But Quintino emphasized that such copying of Western styles "inverts" a parallel borrowing by Western artists of African styles. "If the European artist modernizes his art in being inspired by the styles of African art . . . then the African artist, his way paved by the abandonment of his archaic notions, produces banal works in the European style."[43] When Europeans "copy" the cultural materials of colonial others they make originals. Their appropriation of the work of others is evidence of Europeans' intrinsic capacity to create. By contrast, Africans copy because they have abandoned or lost their cultural moorings (their "archaic notions") and the best they can produce as a result are "banal works."

For Quintino, this tendency to "copy" was prefigured in traditional culture itself. Artists, he wrote, "habituated to a blind subjection to patterns dictated by mystical belief, without the power to create, without the spirit of invention, search for subjects in Western art and produce the crudest imitations—without formal beauty, without expressiveness, without artistic value."[44]

Nowadays, Quintino's dichotomizing aesthetic might seem easy to disparage—a reflection of the safely distant mentality of Salazarist Portugal—our "bad copy," as it were. Yet when I show slides of Manjaco carvings to college students, most of them respond to them in ways that echo Quintino. Students find the colon African ancestor figures off-putting. What they see in the carved figures of white men in perfectly turned out suits and ties knotted just right, is yet more proof of Africa's current inauthenticity, of natives who have succumbed (out of weakness, out of slavish ignorance) to the charms of the West. I find it hard to change their minds even after I have detailed the long history of such appropriation by Manjaco, of its typicality: of appropriation as ethos.[45] Meanwhile, when I show them slides of the photographs of the naked African "maidens" the Portuguese took, these naked Africans are accepted as appropriately authentic. Students are often disturbed by the marks of scarification that etch these women's bodies. Someone will inevitably ask how a young woman could stand it—how could she let someone cut into her flesh like that? But they do not, as a rule, see the frame that makes the picture—the colonial power that forced these women to expose themselves to the lens, the colonial authority that imagined that such exposures were scientifically productive. In short, students often read the two genres in much the same way as colonialist would have. As with students, so with other audiences. There are authentic and inauthentic Africans, and Africans who seem to imitate "us" are diminished.

Thus it appears that the colonialist understanding of "the bad copy" persists as a vernacular aesthetics of authenticity, and that it underwrites a Western politics of identity today.[46] For my students, to copy is to condemn oneself to inferiority; to copy is to cheapen oneself, to turn oneself into a fake. In assuming this, many of my students are doubtless anxious that they themselves are unoriginal. But collectively they also exhibit a kind of confidence, or even pride, in the fact that they are inheritors of a civilization characterized by a long and varied genealogy of creativity.

To such a pedigree, it seems almost impossible to add the sort of creativity Manjaco evince when they copy, when they proudly let themselves be praised as "White's Ears Are Whiter," when they borrow busts of Portuguese governors in order to make commemorative carvings for their aristocrats. But such people are cosmopolitans. In a powerful critique of theories of "culture" in comparative studies of African and European philosophies, Paulin Hountondji argues that for Africans, the right to be unoriginal is an assertion of the right to be a fully enfranchised citizen of the world. Why, asks Hountondji, should Africans be denied the right to appropriate Western works and ideas, "while Westerners still have the right to extend their own curiosity to all continents and cultures without losing their identity?"[47] For Hountondji, certain ideas happen to be empowering or liberating, and to label them "Western" is a mistake; anyone can take them and use them. Good ideas do not belong exclusively to any one "culture," itself a spurious reification. "Cultural values are like venereal diseases: they flourish here and there, develop in one place rather than another according to whether the environment is more or less favorable; but this purely historical accident cannot justify any claim to ownership or, for that matter, immunity."[48]

I would suggest that Hountondji's eloquent argument would be congenial to the Manjaco I came to know in my brief sojourn in Guinea-Bissau. Such Manjaco are and have been for a very long time quick to take—from Portuguese, from Bijagos, from Nalu—whatever they find currently useful, not because they look up to others and look down on themselves, but because they know that the place that everyone inhabits may indeed only be a periphery. It is this kind of casual disregard for the proprieties of a misplaced authenticity that is the foundation for a true cosmopolitanism. To copy is to create.

NOTES

I received funding for research in Guinea-Bissau (from August 1986 through February 1988) and in Portuguese archives in Lisbon from the Wenner-Gren Foundation for Anthropological Research, the National Science Foundation, and the Carter G. Woodson Institute at the University of Virginia. I also received a grant from Mary Washington College to track down the photographic imagery on the Portuguese side of the colonial encounter. I thank the Urinque family for hosting me while I undertook research in the court-village of Catama. And I thank Jennifer Nourse, Peter Huber, Deborah Kaspin, and Paul Landau for helpful comments on versions of this essay.

1. For an excellent introduction to Guinea-Bissau in the revolution and after independence, see Joshua Forrest, *Guinea-Bissau: Power, Conflict, and Renewal in a West African Nation* (Boulder, Colo.: Westview Press, 1992).

2. Rui Pereira has begun the task of situating Portuguese ethnography in the context of New State politics. He argues that anthropology was taken far more seriously in the New State colonial administration than it ever was in similar regimes in Great Britain or France. See Pereira, "A antropologia aplicada na politica colonial portuguesa do Estado Novo," *Revista Internacional de Estudos Africanos* 4–5 (1986), 193–206; and id., "Colonialismo e antropologia: A especulação simbolica," ibid. 10–11 (1989): 269–81.

3. For an overview of colonial-era ethnographic efforts and their failure, see A. Teixeira da Mota, *Inquérito etnográfico, organizado pelo governo da colónia no ano de 1946* (Bissau, 1947). On several occasions between 1918 and 1946, the central government tried to organize the systematic collection of ethnographic data by devising questionnaires (based in part on consultation with museum-based anthropologists in Portugal) and ordering local administrators to compile reports based on them. The results were in general poor. Most administrators never bothered to submit reports. In 1918, only one response survived long enough to lodge itself in official archives. In 1927, six responses were collected; only two (one on the Manjaco) were published. In 1934, one response became available in printed form to officials in the colony. Moreover, the questionnaires themselves covered such a broad range of topics that the part dealing with local politics ended up as little more than footnotes in the few reports that were submitted. It is mainly due to the singular efforts of the prolific autodidact António Carreira (see bibliography) that Manjaco entered the colonial-era ethnographic record (see also the several entries for Artur Martins de Meireles).

4. See António Carreira, *Documentos para a história das ilhas de Cabo Verde e "Rios de Guiné": Séculos XVII e XVIII* (Lisbon: António Carreira, 1983).

5. A. Teixeira da Mota, *Guiné Portuguesa* (Lisbon: Agencia Geral do Ultramar, 1954), is the best typology of the colony's ethnic groups.

6. Luis António de Carvalho Viegas, *Guiné Portuguesa* (Lisbon: Imprensa Nacional, 1936–40), 135.

7. Ibid.

8. For more on Portuguese Guinea, see Luiz Nunes da Ponte, *A campanha da Guiné (1908): Breve narrativa* (Porto: Empreza Guedes, 1909); Carreira, *Documentos;* and Viegas, *Guiné Portuguesa*. R. S. Hammond, *Portugal in Africa, 1815–1910: A Study in Uneconomic Imperialism* (Stanford, Calif.: Stanford University Press, 1966), argues that the Portuguese were motivated to colonize Africa less by economic interest than by a sense of shame driven by inferiority—by nationalistic *vergonha*, explicit in Governor Honorio Barreto's (1847) exposé of colonial weakness and corruption. Barreto, "a negro with the soul of a white," became a revered ancestor in the Salazarist version of Portugal's civilizing mission in Africa, and his critique was republished in 1947 to censure the Portuguese for their lack of vigor in colonizing Guinea. Elsewhere, the *vergonha* theme was repeated by various governors, military officers, and visitors, bemoaning the tumble-down *praça* with its rusted cannon and drunken garrison; local chiefs visiting to collect tribute and wearing European clothes in improper ways, "savages" who claimed to be the "Portuguese senhores," or owners of the land, and so forth.

> Tall, strong... they live a lazy life of drunkenness and *souteneurs* [pimps]. They only fight. It is the women who work and sustain the men.... It is the women who come to the praça to sell water, fruit, eggs, milk.... The husband waits at the gates of Bissau.... After receiving the money, he goes to buy rum to get drunk, or buys gunpowder, which he uses to celebrate his dead or to fight us,

wrote Frederico Pinheiro Chagas, *Na Guiné (1907–1908)* (Lisbon: J. F. Pinheiro, 1910), xxx, in a typical refrain.

9. The idea of the "bad copy" comes from V. Y. Mudimbe, *The Surreptitious Speech: Présence africaine and the Politics of Otherness, 1947–1987* (Chicago: University of Chicago Press, 1992). Paul Landau sums up a parallel colonialist aesthetic for missionaries who "fostered 'educated' attitudes through their own teachings" yet "despised their students as inferior poseurs," who wanted natives to dress but were put off when they dressed up. Such people (the French called them *évolués*) were dangerously hybrid (see Homi K. Bhaba, "Of Mimicry and Man: The Ambivalence of Colonial Discourse," *October* 28 [1984]: 125–33) rather than comfortably other (see id., "The Other Question: The Stereotype and Colonial Discourse," *Screen* 24, 6 [1983]: 16–36). "[T]hey threatened a state of being that missionaries held as natural and undivided, but which, strangely, could never quite be put into words," Paul Landau observes in *The Realm of the Word: Language, Gender, and Christianity in a Southern African Kingdom* (Portsmouth, N.H.: Heinemann, 1995), 62. An aesthetic sensibility such as this is more completely revealed in images than it is glancingly perceived in textual asides. For characterizations of the colonialist aesthetic, see Dorothy Hammond and Alta Jablow, *The Myth of Africa* (New York: Library of Social Science, 1977); Abdul Jan Mohamed, *Manichean Aesthetics* (Boston: University of Massachusetts Press, 1983); and id., "The Economy of Manichean Allegory: The Function of Racial Difference in Colonialist Literature," *Critical Inquiry* 12 (1985): 59–87; Christopher Miller, *Blank Darkness* (Chicago: University of Chicago Press, 1985); and John Cullen Grueser, *White on Black: Contemporary Literature about Africa* (Urbana: University of Illinois Press, 1992).

10. In the now classic typology of British and French versions of indirect rule, Michael Crowder notes that while the British colonial officer usually "respected the [traditional] chief

as separate but equal . . . it was the educated African before whom he felt uneasy." He "openly expressed his contempt for the 'savvy boy' or the 'trousered African.' " Crowder argues that the British were more likely to have such an attitude than were the French—especially French colonial officers steeped in a republican and modernist ethos—but those with more direct experience under French rule would disagree. See Michael Crowder, "Indirect Rule—French and British Style," *Africa* 34, 3 (1964): 204; V. Y. Mudimbe, *The Invention of Africa: Gnosis, Philosophy, and the Order of Knowledge* (Bloomington: Indiana University Press, 1988); and Paulin J. Hountondji, *African Philosophy: Myth and Reality* (1983; 2d ed., Bloomington: Indiana University Press, 1996).

11. See Frantz Fanon, *Black Skin, White Masks* (New York: Grove Press, 1967), 11.

12. For a sense of the early chaotic years of the postconquest colony, see Lady Dorothy Mills, *The Golden Land: A Record of Travel in West Africa* (London: Duckworth, 1929); Archibald Lyall, *Black and White Make Brown: An Account of a Journey to Cape Verde and Portuguese Guinea* (London: Heinemann, 1938); Viegas, *Guiné Portuguesa*; and Mota, *Guiné Portuguesa.*

13. Henrique Pinto Rema, "O Centro de Estudos da Guiné Portuguesa lembra 25 anos de existencia," *Boletim Cultural da Guiné Portuguesa* 26, 101 (1971): 21–61, is an inventory of all the articles published in the journal in its first 25 years.

14. For good analyses of the imagery of the ethnographic gaze, see *Historical Photographs in Anthropological Inquiry*, ed. Joanna Cohen Sherer, special issue of *Visual Anthropology* 3, 3–4 (1990); and *Anthropology and Photography, 1860–1920*, ed. Elizabeth Edwards (New Haven, Conn.: Yale University Press, 1992).

15. Lyall, *Black and White Make Brown*, 213.

16. This was, for example, the argument Portugal's most influential anthropologist made: Antonio Jorge Dias, "Contribuição para o estudo da questão racial e da miscegenação," *Boletim da Sociedade de Geografia* 83 (1965): 63–72.

17. Hugo Adolf Bernatzik headed a research expedition to the colony and produced perhaps the most beautiful collections of photography in the service of ethnography ever published, in *Äthiopen des westens: Forschungsreisen in Portugiesisch-Guinea* (Vienna: L. W Seidel & Sohn, 1933).

18. Artur Martins de Meireles, *Mutilações étnicas dos Manjacos,* Publicações do Centro de Estudos da Guiné Portuguesa: Memórias, 22 (Bissau, 1960), 15.

19. Viegas, *Guiné Portuguesa*, 1: 131.

20. Ibid.

21. Despite the constant reiterations that administrators needed to assemble detailed ethnographies in order to run the colony better, the questions they asked slighted practical issues. Their flavor can be sampled from a few excerpts on "Family Life" from the 1946 inquiry in Mota's *Inquérito etnográfico,* 85–87: "Artificial deflowering before marriage. . . . The importance conceded to virginity. The social position of the wife: slave and beast of pleasure of the man, or free. . . . Indicate if there exists professional prostitution. . . . Degree in which marriage alienates the liberty of the woman . . . punishments, payments of indemnities. . . . Forms of marriage. . . . Individual marriage—polygamy and monogamy. Polygamy results from social progression and is linked to the implantation of the notion of individual property. The woman is the object of pleasure and of work, and therefore treated like any other property: the more women one has the richer one is."

22. Meireles, *Mutilações étnicas,* 15.

23. Ibid., 25.

24. Ibid., 34–35.

25. Ibid., 46.

26. Bhabha, "Of Mimicry and Man," 126.

27. In the New State imaginary, prostitutes removed leg and armpit hair.

28. See Eric Gable, "Women, Ancestors, and Alterity among the Manjaco of Guinea-Bissau," *Journal of Religion in Africa* 26, 2 (1996): 104–21. For the best descriptions and analyses of such corporate groups in neighboring wet-rice farming societies, see Olga F. Linares, *Power, Prayer and Production: The Jola of Casamance, Senegal* (Cambridge: Cambridge University Press, 1992), and Marc Schloss, *The Hatchet's Blood: Separation, Power, and Gender in Ehing Social Life* (Tucson: University of Arizona Press, 1978).

29. António Carreira, "Mutilações ethicas dos Manjacos," *Boletim Cultural da Guiné Portuguesa* 20 (1961): 151–54, offers this speculative sketch on Uut, as well as photographs of some of his work.

30. Ibid. Lampreia's inventory of objects collected in the ethnographic museum contains several such examples attributed to "Suga" (or Soga) Mendes. I have tracked down some of these works in storage at the national Ethnological Museum in Lisbon, but not, unfortunately, the very intriguing bust of Salazar. See Museu da Guiné Portuguesa, *Catálogo-inventário da Secção de Etnografia do Museu da Guiné Portuguesa*, por José D. Lampreia (Lisbon: Junta de Investigações do Ultramar, 1962).

31. It is tempting to link the decline in the figurative innovation to the end of colonialism. When Guinea-Bissau won its independence from Portugal in 1974, the government also abolished the "traditional" rulerships, treating them as exploitative relics of colonialism. Moreover, they abolished the Manjaco "title" system and privatized lands once controlled by the rulers and chiefs. Manjaco by and large accepted, even applauded, these mandates. See Eric Gable, "The Decolonization of Consciousness: Local Skeptics and the 'Will to be Modern' in a West African Village," *American Ethnologist* 22, 2 (1995): 242–57.

32. See António Carreira, "Simbolos, ritualistas, e ritualismos anima-fieticistas na Guiné Portuguesa," *Boletim Cultural da Guiné Portuguesa* 16, 63 (1961): 505–40, and Gable, "Women, Ancestors, and Alterity," for more thorough discussions of the iconography of Manjaco ancestor carvings.

33. Kwame Anthony Appiah, "Is the Post- in Post Modernism the Post- in Postcolonial?" *Critical Inquiry* 17 (1991): 357.

34. As I have argued in "The Decolonization of Consciousness," Manjaco are culturally polyglot and pragmatic, in a way "modern," and this is their "tradition." For another manifestation of Manjaco responses to modernity, see Eric Gable, "A Secret Shared: Fieldwork and the Sinister in a West African Village," *Cultural Anthropology* 12, 2 (1997): 213–33.

35. Hountondji, *African Philosophy*.

36. Christopher Miller, *Blank Darkness: Africanist Discourse in French* (Chicago: University of Chicago Press, 1985), 170.

37. See, e.g., Bennetta Jules-Rosette, *The Messages of Tourist Art: An African Semiotic System in Comparative Perspective* (New York: Plenum Press, 1984); Sally Price, *Primitive Art in Civilized Places* (Chicago: University of Chicago Press, 1989); Bogumil Jewsiewicki, "Painting in Zaire: From the Invention of the West to the Representation of the Social Self," in *Africa Explores: Twentieth-Century African Art*, ed. Susan Vogel (New York: Center for African Art; Munich: Prestel, 1991), 114–75; and Annie E. Coombes, *Reinventing Africa: Museums, Material Culture and Popular Imagination in Late Victorian and Edwardian England* (New Haven, Conn.: Yale University Press, 1994).

38. See, e.g., Herbert Cole, *Icons: Ideals and Power in the Art of Africa* (Washington, D.C.: Smithsonian Institution Press, 1989).

39. We tend to ventriloquize our own desire for subversion, as Graham Huggan argues in "Colonialism, Anthropology, Mimesis," *Cultural Critique* 38 (1998), his critique of Michael Taussig, *Mimesis and Alterity* (New York: Routledge, 1993). Fritz Kramer, *The Red Fez: Art and Spirit Possession in Africa* (New York: Verso, 1993) argues similarly against Julius Lips, *The Savage Hits Back* (1937; New Hyde Park, N.Y.: University Books, 1966), the originator of the theory that colon statues represent a critical satire. Kramer stresses that such African portraits of whites are not caricatures but efforts at mimetic mastery. Paul Stoller, *Embodying Colonial Memories: Spirit Possession, Power and the Hauka in West Africa* (New York: Routledge, 1995), 90, also criticizes Taussig for stressing mimesis as critique, arguing that colon images such as the Igbo *mbari* Taussig discusses were a mimetic attempt to "master whiteness... a way of tapping into circuits of colonial and postcolonial power." Yet Stoller ends up concluding that "embodied oppositions to whiteness in West Africa took on many forms: armed rebellions, individual defiance, remarkable ruses, mocking mascarades, and mimicking plastic arts" (ibid). In short "mastery" (one way of imagining copying) migrates into mimicry.

40. One of the destabilizing questions is audience reception. As Christopher Steiner argues in his wonderfully informative ethnography of contemporary "primitive" art production in the Ivory Coast, *African Art in Transit* (Cambridge: Cambridge University Press, 1994), 154, the colon figure is now an art object because "its very ownership signifies the reappropriation of Africa and is thus prized as an image which pays homage to the conquest of the continent." As such, it is "perhaps the ultimate postmodern creation." In Steiner's estimation, colon figures do not "achieve their value or authenticity by an emphatic denial of foreign contact" but instead are "interpreted by their buyers as a celebration of modern Western expansionism." See also Philip R. Ravenhill, "Baule Statuary Art: Meaning and Modernization," *Working Papers in the Traditional Arts,* 5 and 6 (Philadelphia: Institute for the Study of Human Issues, 1980).

41. Here I am following Huggan, "Colonialism, Anthropology, Mimesis."

42. Fernando Rogado Quintino, "A pintura e a escultura na Guiné Portuguesa," *Boletim Cultural da Guiné Portuguesa* 19, 75 (1964): 281.

43. Ibid., 283.

44. Ibid., 288.

45. For example, the Manjaco figurative innovation in carving is anticipated by a similar innovation in Manjaco textile design. Well before the beginning of the nineteenth century, Manjaco weavers created the "tradition" (see Appiah, "Is the Post- in Post Modernism the Post- in Postcolonial?") of incorporating abstract North African inspired motifs into elaborately woven textiles for a thriving local interethnic market. Since the early twentieth century, Manjaco weavers have increasingly incorporated figurative imagery—bottles, flags, ships—into these expensive prestige textiles. See António Carreira, *Panaria Cabo-Verdiano-Guinéense: Aspectos históricos e sócio-económicos* (Lisbon: Junto de Investigações do Ultramar, 1968).

46. See Price, *Primitive Art in Civilized Places.*

47. Hountondji, *African Philosophy,* xi.

48. Ibid., 177.

Conclusion

Signifying Power in Africa

Deborah D. Kaspin

The preceding chapters describe several roles played by visual images in the political landscapes of Africa. We have focused on images, not because they represent a uniquely efficacious medium of expression, but because they compress complex intentions in economical forms, and because, as Paul Landau notes in his introduction, they often move more easily than language across cultural boundaries. Thus visuals are not simply meaningful but diversely meaningful according to the variety of their social and historical contexts. By concentrating on images, then, we can concretely trace the movement of cultural artifacts across social circles and situations and assess the changes in meaning that accompany them. This means, too, that our project is not simply about visuality, but about cultural contact and political encompassment—peoples and power—engendered by European expansion in Africa.

I shall conclude this book, then, by reflecting on the cultural transformations our authors have described. This means shifting the discussion from images specifically to signifying practice more broadly, and from particular signs to the fabrics of meaning they presuppose. It also means giving special attention to those cultural media that normalize the polity in the public imagination. Thus the issue at hand is how the signs of imperialism are read and reformulated by its various subjects.

MYTH AND IMAGE

To echo issues raised in Landau's introduction, and to embrace the range of disciplinary backgrounds the preceding chapters represent, I find a theoretical point of departure in the culture critic Roland Barthes. Beginning in the 1950s, inspired by the American logician Charles Sanders Peirce, Barthes used semiotic theory to interrogate French popular culture and political consciousness.[1] He describes signs as vehicles of social values and judgments, conveying meanings that are public, irreducible, and morally freighted. They not only communicate (and conceal) information and intentions but distinguish virtue from sin, friend from foe, worth from worthlessness. Barthes goes on to demonstrate the ubiquity of signs in everyday life by exposing the ideological subtexts of commonplace things. He writes, for example, about the following image of empire:

> I am at the barber's, and a copy of *Paris-Match* is offered to me. On the cover, a young Negro in a French uniform is saluting, with his eyes uplifted, probably fixed on a fold of the tricolour. All this is the meaning of the picture. But, whether naively or not, I see very well what it signifies to me: that France is a great Empire, that all her sons, without any colour discrimination, faithfully serve under her flag, and that there is no better answer to the detractors of an alleged colonialism than the zeal shown by this Negro in serving his so-called oppressors.[2]

This portrait of the African as French patriot elicits nationalist sentiments by juxtaposing a few highly charged and contradictory images—the African soldier, the French flag, the military salute—and wrapping the African "other" in the moral fabric of the French nation-state. In so doing, the picture records, falsifies, and mystifies the French imperial landscape at one and the same time. While it accurately reflects the racial diversity of colonial France, it implies that national loyalties unify this diverse population, notwithstanding the rebellions of African colonies against French rule erupting at the same time. And it conceals its ideological inflections in the seeming objectivity of photography, appearing to the observer's eye as the benign depiction of a simple social fact.

Barthes refers to this type of sign as "myth," because it communicates a vision of the world and world order beyond the ostensibly neutral information it conveys. Similar myths, he argues, saturate popular culture in films, advertisements, entertainments, cuisine, and so forth, bringing national projects into the realm of mainstream consumption. By circulating widely and innocuously through public life, they naturalize imperial interests in the consciousness of the masses, eroding the diversity of identities and outlooks within a common "bourgeois mythology"— this even as the French empire disintegrates.[3]

Barthes's semiology provides a useful umbrella for this volume. Our authors share his interest in consumer goods as myths, in the commonplace as the political, and in the seemingly innocuous images that normalize imperial vistas in popular consciousness. At the same time, they complicate his concerns by addressing the frontiers of empire, as well as its center, and the arc of its history, as well as its end. Thus in effect they describe bourgeois mythology in the making, as colonialism creates new myth makers and brings new cultural repertoires into the polity. Indeed, they confront not a single bourgeois mythology, but, minimally, two— Africans' and Europeans'—and explore both the fragmentations and consolidations of public culture wrought by imperial expansion.

Arguably, then, our collective purpose is a kind of mytho-history, one that traces the collisions, collusions, and transformations of mythologies as imperial projects unfold over time. This means following two paths of analysis. First, our authors reveal the social interests and predicaments expressed in mythic form, and, in so doing, problematize Barthes's notion of a homogenizing bourgeois mythology. Accordingly, myths serve the interests of empire, publicly legitimating the official distributions of power and privilege by making them appear commonsensical (Burke, Landau, Gordon, Hodeir, Skotnes, Gable). Myths also provide the discursive media for challenging empires, using public fora and private spaces to scrutinize the instruments of authority and to expose hypocrisy in high places (Hunt, Olaniyan, Skotnes). More ambiguously and, perhaps most commonly, myths serve very personal interests, as ordinary citizens internalize and recast the signs of domination, and at the same time, resist and reform the circumstances of their disempowerment (Mustafa, Girshick, Gordon).

Second, our authors show how mythological systems fare as systems when political history radically alters the character of the material world. Sometimes mythologies accommodate new elements and environments, while retaining their interior logic as semiotic systems (Bunn, Landau, Drewal, Hodeir, Gable). Sometimes they give way in their entirety and are replaced by new mythologies along with new political economies (Gordon, Skotnes). And sometimes they undergo fundamental transformations, retaining aspects of their original character while revaluing their elements in new and surprising ways (Hunt, Olaniyan, Mustafa, Girshick). In other words, mythologies adjust to historical situations, and vice versa.

We are interested, then, in both the human predicaments that seek mythological expression, and the systemic transformations that take place in bodies of myth as political economies are transformed. These issues defy simplification and generalization, given the several cultural histories that colonialism brought together, and the ambiguous distributions of power that colonial and national states have wrought. Still, the many insights offered by the preceding chapters may be systematized by addressing the following problem: the fate of bourgeois mythologies as empires rise and fall.

MYTHOLOGICAL REPRODUCTIONS:
AFRICA OBSERVES EUROPE...

Although colonial and postcolonial studies today do not often examine the cultural elements of precolonial Africa that survived Western encroachment, the preceding chapters describe several African mythologies that have accommodated icons of and from foreigners without disrupting the myth systems qua systems. Henry Drewal's chapter on Mami Wata is a case in point. He begins with the snake charmer of European popular culture, a seductive woman of the Orient who can bewitch even the deadliest of creatures. When her lithographic image traveled to Africa, she inspired a new set of mythological elaborations based on local conceptions of femininity and power. Like her European counterpart, she is a mysterious "other," but as an African sign, she rises from the waters' depths to bring fertility and wealth to her devotees. An image of exotic femininity for both Europeans and Africans, she connotes eroticism to the first and abundance to the latter, indicative of the different fabrics of meaning into which she is woven.

Drewal's analysis of cultural diffusion reminds us that the impetus for cultural change does not arise from the flow of foreign goods and persons into new places. Rather mythologies can absorb new elements without fundamentally altering their internal logic, since the value of novelty lies in its familiarity as a mythic type: even the stranger is a familiar type found in well-traveled landscapes of "selves" and "others." Eric Gable makes a similar point in his study of colonial Guinea-Bissau. During Portuguese rule, Manjaco artisans began to produce statuary of white colonial officers to include among the ancestor figurines decorating important graves. Colonial whites (and Gable's own students) saw the new portraiture as evidence that Manjaco were seduced by Western culture and were rapidly losing their own. Gable, however, argues that the appropriation of outsiders is, among Manjaco, a long-standing cultural practice, whereby icons of foreigners are valued according to local matrices of meaning. Specifically, the mortuary figures represent powerful allies, who protect the lineage and ensure its durability across time and generation. Accordingly, it is the Manjaco who domesticated the European and not the other way around.

By illustrating the capacity of African mythologies to encompass novelty, Drewal and Gable demonstrate their intrinsic elasticity as meaning systems, whose logical integrity does not depend on their isolation and insulation. Evidently, social change, like cultural meaning, is in the eye (or myth) of the beholder. Paula Ben-Amos Girshick explores the flip side of this proposition, that mythologies generate their own transformations according to the social locations of their practitioners. Thus artisan guilds serving the Benin royal court relied on a conventional iconography of power (the front-facing pose, the towering figure, the animals symbolizing magical power, and so forth) to produce highly readable images of kingly charisma. Their work was very different from that of the Omada carvers, who also learned their craft in the king's court, but sought their clients among his subordinates and commoners. Using and abusing the iconography of guild art, Omada art sought to diminish the king, elevate his inferiors, and ridicule the Europeans who proclaimed themselves the new rulers of the realm. Two artistic traditions thus sprang from the same mythological repertoire and developed in tandem, one conservative, the other innovative, one the instrument of the state, the other of its competitors and critics.

By attesting to the vitality of African myth systems, these three chapters also afford us a glimpse of the mythological universe that Europeans entered and how they were perceived, at least in West Africa, early in the colonial era. Outsiders in all their guises—as men, mermaids, or wild beasts—were potential sources of power with positive and negative implications: they could bring fertility and strength, or sterility and death. The African might hope, therefore, not to vanquish the foreigner, but to secure his or her allegiance and to obtain this alien power as an aspect of one's own. Thus just as the Benin king claimed the leopard as his animal ally, a chief or merchant might claim a European in order to enhance his stature among his rivals—unless, as Omada artwork suggests, the European squandered his cultural capital by behaving boorishly. Outsiders acquired additional significance if they were associated with water, as illustrated by the crocodile familiars and mudfish legs attributed to Benin kings. Both Mami Wata and European colonial officers came from across or within the ocean, an "other" world whence life comes and whither it returns. The ocean was the semantic equivalent of the heavens, the grave, and the spirit world, all interchangeable as "other worlds" in the polarities of "self" and "other," substance and spirit, life and death. Life in this world could be enhanced only through one's connections to these other worlds, hence encounters with mysterious strangers were as necessary as they were risky.

...AND EUROPE OBSERVES AFRICA

Although many examples of mythological reproduction can be found in modern Africa, they are sometimes more evident when the topic is not African but European sensibilities. By this I mean the propensity of Europeans to represent Africa according to mythological schemas that predate European explorations there. For well over a millennium, the world in European imagination was divisible into realms of light and dark, Christendom and heathendom, civilization and wilderness. When Europe colonized Africa, the African became the newest figure in a familiar landscape, one in which a godlike, enlightened, masculine, and adult "self" is judged against a monstrous, backward, feminine, and childish "other."[4] The preceding chapters describe many reproductions of this old typology in European depictions of Africa and Africans (Landau, Burke, Mustafa, Skotnes, Hodeir, Gordon, and Gable).

Paul Landau's chapter on colonial-era photography, for instance, shows how a new technology of image making found its aesthetic parameters in this old mythology, notwithstanding its purported capacity to record "just the facts." Taking its semantic cues from big game hunting, the camera bore witness to European mastery of the African wilderness by "shooting" the exotic creatures who inhabited it. Naturalists exploited this new tool, since it facilitated their own efforts to devise and document taxonomies of the animal—including the human animal—kingdom for encyclopedias and museums. And colonial administrators followed on the heels of the naturalists, seeking typologies of the tribes they sought to rule, and turning to photography for the iconic images that could distinguish one tribe from another. For all these photography aficionados, the camera's value lay not only in its ease of operation but also in its apparent objectivity. And yet photographic images were as susceptible to mythological imaginings as painting or poetry. Thus the effort to record social types was forever compromised by the impulse to separate the civilized from the uncivilized, the enlightened from the naïve, the hygienic from the rude, in short, the fully human from the largely bestial. In European hands, the camera would relentlessly seek out those Africans who fit the primitive type, and whose physical features—like unusual genitalia or scarified bodies—evoked their affinity with the wilderness.

The durability of this mythology was due in part to the fact that its principal consumers were in Europe, where the ideal would never be judged against the actual. Here Africa entered European consciousness only by artifice, giving myth makers, from Henri Rousseau to Edgar Rice Burroughs, full rein to design Africa according to popular sensibilities. Often these mythic productions were driven directly by their marketability, as reflected in the ability of *King Kong* to pay for itself many times over. But sometimes they were contrived in order to enlist public interest in imperial projects. This was the case with the French colonial exhibitions described by Catherine Hodeir. These multimedia productions took up several city blocks, the sheer scale of the exhibition impressing the public with the breadth and grandeur of the empire it recreated. Within its confines, Africa and other exotic lands were portrayed according to the conventions of theater and the iconographies of primitivism with which French spectators were already familiar. Here sociological accuracy was sacrificed for mythological type by displaying only those cultural practices that suggested no European influences and evoked the simple, happy tribesman living close to nature. The exhibitions were thus able to assert Europeans' cultured superiority over the fascinating but childlike savage, while placing Africans within an evolutionary tableau vis-à-vis other exotic peoples. In so doing, they established the moral rectitude of colonialism by enlisting the spectators as subjects in its outward-looking paternalism.

European myths of Africa were easily fleshed out in Europe, where their elemental signs were already familiar and only their popular appeal was at stake. They were much harder to flesh out in Africa, not only—or even primarily—because the discrepancies between the mythical and the actual were too apparent, but because here the colonial enterprise itself was on the line. For the colonizers, bourgeois myths provided the models and shored up the resolve to create, not facsimiles of the wilderness in Europe, but a factual Europe in the wilderness. This meant bringing mythic models to life in ways that were simultaneously dramatic and mundane.

David Bunn described the urgency of this enterprise in evocative detail. South Africa's white settlers treated the frontier grave as the physical and moral boundary between the Christian community and the pagan wilderness. Death was an opportunity not only to commend the soul to Christ but to redraw the line between the saved and the savage. And while settlers used the churchyard to direct a moral lesson inward, soldiers used the unfenced frontier to direct a complementary lesson outward. To whit, the fallen soldier marked a step in an ongoing march to wrest the wilderness from savages and to bring it, but not them, into the embrace of Christendom.

So essential was this imagery to European domination that it was replicated in at least one national monument of white-ruled South Africa. This is the Voortrekker

Monument in Pretoria, which commemorates the victory of Afrikaners over Zulus at Blood River, an event read by Afrikaner nationalists as a sign that God intended whites to win the land from blacks. The monument is a large, block-shaped building reminiscent of a tomb or crypt, whose walls contain not the bodily remains but the sculpted images of heroic frontiersmen and -women. It is encircled by a low wall on which a bas-relief of ox wagons and pioneers forms the *laager* that protected white settlers from black warriors at Blood River. The monument thus depicts not only the battle but a circle of salvation around the Afrikaner nation, as the laager wall separates the souls of the heroic dead from the Kaffers ("Kaffirs," from Arabic, "infidel"), who are forever banished from the kingdom.[5]

As these monuments to European domination attest, the contrast between civilized selves and savage others is starkly drawn when the conquest of the wilderness is meant to be absolute, as it was in South Africa. Moreover, once the conquest is complete, it is possible to conscript Africans into the role of the savage, making the European mythology that much more convincing. This is the case with southern Africa's Bushman population, whose place in the colonial imagination is recounted by Robert Gordon and Pippa Skotnes. Perhaps the longest-suffering victims in African history, today's Bushmen have found their way into the global economy by playing the part of "pure primitives" for filmmakers, photographers, and even ethnographers according to a Western mythology of pristine Africa.

Gordon's chapter describes at length the role played by Western cinematographers in "capturing" Bushmen in an iconography of primitivism. Serving the interests of tourism and the South African state, the prototypical film Bushman replicates the cultural politics of Hodeir's colonial exhibitions, a prototype that is well known to (and cherished by) countless moviegoers from the hit film *The Gods Must Be Crazy*.[6] In an artful interweaving of comedy and sentimentality, the movie shows the "graceful little people of the Kalahari" living in paradisiacal isolation, far from the stresses of civilization. The artifice of the imagery is exposed, in turn, by the documentary film *N!ai, The Story of a !Kung Woman*.[7] Here we learn that the South African Defence Force restricted mobile Bushman groups to a fixed settlement, where they had insufficient resources to sustain a livelihood. These Bushmen were in desperate straits when the makers of *Gods* came to their community to fashion an image of Eden in the desert. Acting a part in a movie offered a path out of poverty, at least for a few, making *Gods* only one episode in a long history of conquest and conscription.

The brutality behind the making of *Gods* is part and parcel of the tragic point that Skotnes makes, that the myth of the living Bushman depended on the dismemberment of actual Bushmen. Thus, while Gordon describes the production and persuasiveness of celluloid images, Skotnes shifts our gaze to the body itself, whose parts and casts are preserved in the timeless venue of museum collections. In so doing, she also shows how Bushmen were differently imagined as colonial history unfolded. During periods of territorial expansion, whites saw Bushmen as savages who should be hunted down like vermin to clear the way for civilization. But once the territory was securely in their hands, and the Bushman population decimated, the innocent, but exotic primitive replaced the savage as the dominant sign in a mythology of benign governance.

MYTH-EDUCATING AFRICANS

It should come as no surprise that the most vivid portraits of savage Africa are produced where settlers most aggressively advance and maintain their territorial claims. But Europeans did not uniformly share this territorial ambition or the belief that Africans were irredeemably alien. For many, Africans were the newest members of their moral universe and were to be enlisted in its mythologies of power and order. Thus their mission was not to force Europe onto the wilderness but to draw Africa into civilization, a task that required African participation as political subjects and as Christians.

Colonial histories are replete with examples of the "myth-education" of Africans.[8] Christian missions, for instance, not only provided religious teachings but also ran primary schools, clinics, and model farms for the Africans they hoped to convert. As Jean and John Comaroff detail, Methodist missionaries not only offered religious instruction but demonstrated a range of cultural practices, from landscaping to literacy, to the Tswana among whom they lived and preached.[9] And as Nancy Hunt describes in this volume, Catholic missionaries used a variety of tools, including cartoons, to instruct Congolese in the proprieties not only of worship but of marital conduct and personal hygiene.

Similarly, many administrative policies imposed European cultural habits upon Africans in the belief that this would improve their quality of life. In Nyasaland, for instance, agricultural policy forced Africans to adopt a quintessentially British aesthetic of land use—single crops planted in straight, parallel lines—purportedly to improve crop production.[10] And in Zimbabwe, as Timothy Burke reports, public health officers and commercial advertisers used films and cartoons to teach a new body aesthetic in the name of health and hygiene. In similar fashion, Africans throughout the continent learned elements of European work culture, from clock watching to collar starching, as they fulfilled the monetary obligations imposed on them through taxation and land and labor policy.

Europeans throughout colonial Africa set out to civilize "the savage," and yet this effort was fraught with ambiguities. Only by preserving the mythological status quo could Europeans claim authority over Africa, for by civilizing Africans, they were grooming their own replacements as rulers: elevating the "other" necessarily meant diminishing the "self," like the king who rears his own usurper. Timothy Burke explores this dilemma in his discussion of white ambivalence about African education. On the one hand, colonial teachers and marketing agents used pictures to inculcate Western practices in Africans, on the assumption that Africans could and should be civilized. Yet these same whites suspected that Africans were unable to read the images correctly, given incapacities of perception rooted in their essential nature as primitives: the intellectual sophistication involved in symbolic thought was simply beyond their ken. White farmers, in contrast, feared that Africans were not only educable but too intoxicated with European achievements to remain content with their status as savages. Thus these whites believed that educators and advertisers were giving Africans the means and motives to rise above their station and overturn the status hierarchies on which the settlers depended.

As Eric Gable points out, this kind of ambivalence is the inevitable ideological by-product of colonialism. European empires needed the primitive as their essential justification and therefore saw what francophone colonizers called the *évolué* as both their best ambition and worst nightmare, for the westernized African meant that colonialism had succeeded and that European preeminence was over. To preserve the colonial endeavor, then, évolués would always be regarded as poor imitations ("bad copies") of whites and, therefore, the exceptions to alterity that proved the rule.[11] Only then could Europeans create oases of authentic civilization surrounded by what remained, at least by comparison, a savage land. Then, too, signs of savage Africa—decorative masks, animal skin hearthrugs, woven baskets, and so forth—could selectively enter European homes as evidence that the domestication of the wilderness was under way, but forever incomplete.[12]

AFRICAN APPROPRIATIONS AND TRANSFORMATIONS

While Europeans contemplated the risks and benefits of civilizing Africans, Africans contemplated the risks and benefits of associating with Europeans, given their own cultural predilection to seek out strangers and obtain the valuables they might offer. But if each was drawn to the other, it was neither for the same reasons nor with the same understandings. Africans evidently did not, for example, share the Europeans' desire to refashion the other, either in their own image or as their mythological opposite. Many, in fact, were more than willing to mimic these strangers, whether in admiration or revulsion, in celebration or satire. On the face of it, the African propensity to imitate complemented the European impulse to acculturate and may have persuaded some colonizers that their impact on Africans was considerable. But imitation, like missionization, is culturally motivated and cannot be taken at face value as evidence of conversion or assimilation. The more pertinent issue is how Africans put European cultural materials to their own uses.

Certainly, many political myth-signs in Africa—as elsewhere in the postcolonial Third World—were introduced during colonial rule and are reproduced today as the insignia of independent nations: the high-flying flag, the military salute, and the presidential motorcade are all elements of a national political culture that Europe brought to Africa along with the notion (and necessity) of the nation-state.[13] Notwithstanding their ideological convenience to the French public, African soldiers really did salute the French Tricolore, prefiguring their many successors and cultural cousins who salute the flags of independent Africa today.[14] More complexly, European and American missionaries introduced Christianities to Africa under the aegis of domesticating the savage and left behind a legacy of myth signs that connoted civility, modernity, and authority. According to Landau, for instance, nineteenth-century Ngwato royals saw Christ's kingdom and their own as isomorphic and therefore required their subjects to convert to Christianity or risk denunciation as enemies of the state.[15] Protestantism is similarly implicated in contemporary African class structures. In Malawian professional circles, I continually meet devout Presbyterians who attend church every Sunday, recite grace at every meal, and decry non-Christians as backward, immoral, and potentially dangerous. In the political arena and the private home, the city and the farm, African Christians identify faith with virtue and achievement, paganism with sin and incivility, and understand salvation—in this world or the next—to be the destiny of the observant.

Still, if Africans have mastered European codes of value, they have also reinvented them to reflect and amplify their own concerns and circumstances. Hudita Mustafa's chapter is a case in point. She begins by reviewing the conventions of portraiture that European photographers brought to Senegal, conventions that separated civility from savagery and rulers from ruled. She then recounts how, in Dakar (the "Paris of Africa"), these conventions came to connote sophistication and rudeness to urban Africans as they fashioned their social personae. A colonial representational style thus informed the portraiture of their urban Senegalese clientele by local photographers, with, however, a crucial revision: Africans rejected the beautiful savage and instead adopted the postures of haute culture. Ultimately, wedding albums became prized documents of Senegalese cosmopolitanism, depicting subjects who are clothed, rich, and sophisticated, rather than naked, poor, and simple.

The development of a local industry in portrait photography thus accompanied (and recorded) both the indigenization of a European mythology and a shift in its frame of reference. Civilization and savagery came to imply less the distance between Europeans and Africans than the differences between categories of Africans—between the urban and the rural, the affluent and the indigent, life's successes and its failures. The European virtually disappeared from the semantic set, whose contrasting images reflected class strata and social aspiration more often than race.

Nancy Hunt makes a similar point in her chapter on Congolese cartoons. She begins with the figurative styles of Hergé's *Tintin au Congo* and follows their development through several generations of Belgian and African cartoonists. Many of the stylistic conventions remained constant, such as the mischievous twins, the dandified évolué, even the thick-lipped blackface of minstrelsy. But as the artist's perspective changed, the sympathetic self was identified in new figures and opposed to a new array of others. In M'Pila's *Mbu and Mpia*, for instance, the heroes are two delinquent black boys, while their antagonist is the sometimes minstrelesque évolué. Europeans, on the other hand, are rarely depicted at all, reflecting their relative unimportance in the artist's imagination. For him, the significant selves and others are not opposite races, but opposite classes, ages, and ethnicities—neighbors in a world where white people rarely enter the field of vision.

African image makers became equally adept with the civilized sophisticate and the uncivilized primitive. This is perplexing, for while the emblems of civilization were abundant everywhere in colonial Africa, those of primitivism were not and had to be contrived by the photographers and filmmakers who posed African subjects for the postcards, picture books, and popular movies that circulated among Europeans. And yet, despite its artifice and its circumscribed spheres of consumption, the mythic primitive was taken up by African image makers, such as the entrepreneurs who set out to market icons of tribal culture to those who sought an encounter with the exotic. Like the actors Gordon describes, these businessmen and -women honed their skills as performers and artisans according to the mythology of authentic Africana that their (primarily white) customers expected to find.

I saw this enterprise close at hand when I worked as a lecturer for a tour group in Kenya and Tanzania. I was struck by the extent to which local culture was molded to fit the requirements of the tourist trade. Nothing entered the tourist market in original form; rather, cultural artifacts were revised, even wholly invented, to appeal to foreign buyers. Tribal dances were choreographed for the stage and performed at museums, cafes, and hotels where spectators could watch in comfortable anonymity. Bus tours were available to Maasai villages, where the family patriarch lectured on local culture, while his wives sold home crafts. And numerous colorful "tribesmen" appeared on the highways throughout the day, selling photo-ops to passing motorists. All of these images were replicated in the many postcards, books, and videos on sale in hotels and gift shops, forming a hermeneutic circle that embraced buyers and sellers, Europeans and Africans alike.[16]

The tourist industry is not, however, the best evidence that the prototypical primitive has been embraced within African social imaginations. For this we must look at cultural transactions among and between Africans to see if savages figure as pervasively and complexly as sophisticates in their own discourses of identity. Hunt suggests that they do, as illustrated by M'Pila's cartoon buffoon Monoko, who is both the pretentious évolué and the black-faced fool; and by Lukembo's schoolteacher, "an apelike savage" who speaks broken French to his more urbane pupils. In both cases, the savage within the "wannabe" is exposed by youngsters—rascals in one instance, sophisticates in another—who, because of their youth, must be true to themselves, and whose authenticity reflects badly on the artifice of adults.

But perhaps the more pointed re-creations of these contrasting images are described by Tejumola Olaniyan in his chapter on Akinola Lasekan. A Nigerian nationalist, Lasekan drew political cartoons to fuel public interest in the independence movement and developed a pictography of social types that pitted a "muscular" Nigerian nationalism against a "corpulent" British colonialism. These figures drew, in part, on the mythology of savagery and civilization, by juxtaposing a semi-nude African and an elaborately dressed European. At the same time, they inverted the political values encoded in that mythology, by portraying the African as robust, virile, adult and virtuous, and the European as flabby, weak, childish, and immorally dependent. Lasekan found an icon for Nigerian nationalism by giving the undercivilized African a positive inflection in pointed contrast to his acutely civilized oppressor.

By making use of a European bourgeois mythology, Africans realized the best ambition and greatest fear of these colonizers, surpassing them in their own game of cultural sophistication and moral authority. Indeed, while Africans drew on imperial mythologies to orient themselves as colonial subjects, they drew on these same myths to disrupt colonial authority and reorient the polity. Lasekan is a case in point, for he used the images and media that colonialism introduced—as a means of acculturation, no less—to incite public opinion against the colonial state. Of course, his success in mobilizing the Nigerian public may have owed less to the content of his cartoons than to the fact of them: like Benedict Anderson's print capitalism, he created in his readership an imagined community of Nigerians, in itself a sentiment incompatible with colonial rule.[17] Still, the instruments and images of imperial control provided the means of its undoing, precisely because the colonized became so adept at using them, and because they represented the most direct route from the margins to the centers of political power.[18]

THE MORE THINGS CHANGE

Images and empires have intersected in many ways in colonial and contemporary Africa. Empire building has coincided with the reproduction of essentially stable mythologies; the erosion and replacement of local mythologies by imperial mythologies; and the transformation of local and imperial mythologies as empires are built and rebuilt. This demonstrates the many dimensions of African modernities and serves as a caveat against oversimplification in larger debates about domination and resistance, globalization and localization, change and continuity. Still, some readers may object that I have listed here not three outcomes of imperialism but three aspects of one outcome, namely, transformation. Thus the mythologies that accommodate colonial incursions and retain their internal coherence can also engage their social environment in new ways. This is illustrated by the royal portraiture of Benin kings, whose form never changes, but whose significance to the community it inhabits can vary radically, depending on whether the king is successful in war or diminished by rivals. Similarly, the indigenization of European mythemes in Africa suggests that colonized Africans are reproducing the cultural universe of their colonizers. But it also reflects that Africans have the discursive means to engage and confront structures of power in ways that money- and powerbrokers cannot misconstrue. Some Africans, for example, are sufficiently practiced in Western body arts (fashion, tourism, sports, and so on) to make careers in the global media industry. Others successfully use the institutional centers and resources of elites, like churches and the civil service, to mobilize political pressure against those same elites.

It will, however, come as no surprise to other mytho-historians that reproduction and transformation occur simultaneously. As Marshall Sahlins observed almost two decades ago, these are two sides of the same coin, for signs are revalued through their usage, and reused for the communicative possibilities they permit.[19] Cultural continuity is not, therefore, a sterile concept but complexly entailed in cultural revision.

At the same time, this volume offers some surprising revelations about the limits and loci of transformation, as Europeans seem singularly unwilling or unable to revise their own mythologies. Although many colonial Africans became Christians, colonial Europeans did not similarly become Muslims or "animists." Although the linguistic horizons of Africans have expanded dramatically, those of Europeans have not, aside from the inclusion of a few new words into established European languages. And although contemporary Africans, like their colonial predecessors, combine indigenous and imported cultural practices, their European counterparts adhere, for the most part, to European models of dress, cuisine, architecture, and so forth. Inverting the dichotomy of "hot" and "cold" cultures proposed by Claude Lévi-Strauss, or of "peoples with and without history" as disparaged by Eric Wolf, Europeans relentlessly reproduce the same old mythology of cultural supremacy, even while Africans innovate.

This is not to say that transformations never take place on the upper side of colonial class strata. Skotnes, for example, used her position as a museum curator to expose and subvert the cultural politics of museum collections. Not only did she direct the public eye to the violence underlying South Africa's presumptive multiculturalism, but she also revealed that her own politics were not constrained by the history of the institution that employed her. Gable expressed similar, albeit more modest, ambitions in his efforts to educate new generations of students about the politics of representation. This sentiment is echoed throughout this volume, all of whose contributors mean to expose the underbelly of colonial encounters and the multiple responses among Africans.

Still, we must be circumspect about the cultural authority of scholars on issues of grave public importance. True, the *Miscast* exhibit provoked a vibrant public debate, but the exhibit and the surrounding discussion were symptomatic of a more profound radicalism originating outside the museum, as South African statesmen and stateswomen tore down the old order and replaced it with a racially inclusive democracy. The state that had required the pristine primitive in order to legitimate itself no longer existed, giving public institutions the latitude—indeed, the moral mandate—to expose the abuses of the deposed regime. This is cultural revision, to be sure, but it is permitted by the political revolution that preceded it.

Gable's classroom represents an alternative scenario. In the relative stability of American college life, his students are seldom persuaded that the "authentic primitive" is a Western invention or that nudity is not an indicator of African cultural integrity. Here, what is at stake is not a system of governance, but simply the right to believe in one's own apperceptions. Yet even (especially?) when the stakes are so low, the professor as myth-critic can be left whistling in the dark about the hidden politics of signifying practice. Evidently, the heirs of colonialism do not abandon their mythologies easily—or what is hegemony for?

Still, it is curious that Western hegemonic myths about primitive Africa are so intractable, given the fact that the empires those myths supported collapsed over thirty years ago. And yet, standardized images of Africa are still part of Western public culture, as a glance across the media reveals. The "United Colors of Benetton" advertising campaign, which purported to celebrate cultural diversity, sunk to familiar depths in the early 1990s with the photo of an anonymous (because headless) African man holding a human leg bone. With characteristic enthusiasm for exoticism, the popular television show *The X-Files* has also portrayed Africans as sorcerers and vampires, alongside its regular fare of (mostly white) space aliens, shape-shifters, and mutants. The 1993 movie *The Air Up There* recasts the missionary as a basketball coach, who goes to Kenya to find a natural athlete among its tribesmen and bring him into the light of civilization. Not coincidentally, the coach wins the affections of a missionary who shares his parental feelings for this raw but beautiful land.[20]

If images of primitive Africa endure long after colonialism in Africa ended, it is perhaps because the images are not fundamentally about Africa at all. They arise from a Western bourgeois mythology of any and all wildernesses, inhabited by creatures who are, alternatively, innocent and savage, naked and hairy, dark-skinned and ghostlike. The mythology is ubiquitous. The *Star Wars* series and a host of imitators recreate the imagery of unchartered lands as undiscovered solar systems, with subtexts about civilized selves, primitive others, and at least implicit ethnic stereotypes. Landau and I have both used these movies in the classroom to demonstrate modern myth making and recommend the exercise to other teachers. Or invite your students to watch the television show *Buffy the* [blond] *Vampire Slayer* (1992) as a group of white youth do battle with demons—played by black and white actors—in a curiously areligious version of Christian soldiers in the heart of darkness. These are variations of the same mythology of alterity that gave Africa a meaningful outline in the European imagination. The mythology persists, because it is fundamentally about the self—unknowable, unseeable, unshapeable, except in relation to an imaginary opposite to draw it—me—into focus.

In the meantime, the imperial signs and systems that colonialism introduced in Africa were already domesticated (that is, Africanized) when the postcolonial era began. Today's African mythologies are as varied as the social situations they inhabit, having acquired, during the several decades of independent rule, new textures and intentions in the hands of new creators and consumers. We are not, however, prepared to speak of African bourgeois mythologies with the same confidence that we speak of European ones. This may reflect that bourgeois mythologies, as Barthes conceived of them, are part of a specifically Western imperial history, or—and this, I think, is more likely—that the concentrations and distributions of power that sustain bourgeois myths are harder to pin down and systematize across Africa and its histories. In other words, one is hard-pressed to find a population that is dispersed across the continent, or a large stretch of it, and yet ideologically drawn into the imagined community of an elite. Still, this does not mean that such communities do not exist in Africa, bound, in part, by their own mythologies of self and other. It means only that the work is cut out for mytho-historians to seek the sites and signs of African social imaginaries, and to write them into historiography alongside the mythologies that underpinned Western imperial expansion. Africanists of several disciplines and nationalities are now undertaking this task, and we are pleased to contribute this volume to the effort.

NOTES

1. My principal source is Roland Barthes, *Mythologies* (New York: Noonday Press, 1992). See also Terence Hawkes' *Structuralism and Semiotics* (Berkeley and Los Angeles: University of California Press, 1977) for an account of Barthes's significance vis-à-vis Ferdinand de Saussure, Charles Sanders Peirce, Claude Lévi-Strauss, and the field of semiotics.

2. From "Myth Today," reprinted in Barthes, *Mythologies,* 116.

3. When Barthes wrote "Myth Today" in the late 1950s, French forces had been driven out of Indochina and were facing similar nationalist movements throughout Africa. For Barthes, French bourgeois mythology and the crisis in French colonialism were centrally implicated in each other, the one serving to conceal the other.

4. The deeper history and contemporary applications of this mythology are discussed in detail by Gustav Jahoda in *Images of the Savage: Ancient Roots of Modern Prejudice in Western Culture* (New York: Routledge, 1999).

5. In a longer version of his chapter, Bunn discusses the political use of mortuary monuments or ancestor shrines by black homeland rulers, who use a similar sign system as Afrikaners to legitimate their political authority. The monuments were as persuasive as the rulers were popular, hence both were dismantled when apartheid ended.

6. *The Gods Must Be Crazy,* directed by Jamie Uys (1980).

7. *N!ai, The Story of a !Kung Woman,* directed by John Marshall (1980).

8. The whole of European history contains episodes of cultural reeducation alongside imperial expansion. Rome built temples to Caesar throughout Europe, introducing not only an iconography of divine kings to German and Arab peoples but also the large-scale architectural interiors that came to signify the majesty of the ruling class. Later, the Catholic Church replaced pagan rites with Christian rites, which not only turned savages into Catholics but egg-laying rabbits and evergreen trees into Christian symbols. When European nations performed ceremonies of state to impress the majesty of European rule upon their colonial subjects, they were following a well-honed cultural tradition, with much the same effect: the empire fell, but its insignia remained.

9. John and Jean Comaroff, *Of Revelation and Revolution,* vols. 1 and 2 (Chicago: University of Chicago Press, 1991, 1998).

10. I discuss the aesthetics of agricultural practice in Nyasaland in "Kings into Commoners: The Reinvention of Chiefship in Central Malawi," a manuscript in preparation.

11. As Gable points out, this argument originates with African intellectuals, Paulin Hountondji in *African Philosophy: Myth and Reality* (1983; Bloomington: University of Indiana Press, 1996), and V. Y. Mudimbe in *The Invention of Africa: Gnosis, Philosophy and the Order of Knowledge* (Bloomington: University of Indiana Press, 1988) and *The Surreptitious Speech:* Présence africaine *and the Politics of Otherness, 1947–1987* (Chicago: University of Chicago Press, 1992).

12. I have spent many (very pleasant) hours in these "oases of civilization" created by British expatriates in Malawi. Their households and social networks are organized around routines of commensality, observing the same cycles of food and drink every day, and preparing standard ritual fare for holiday meals, such as turkeys for Christmas dinner, hot cross buns for Good Friday, and roasts on Easter Sunday. Their ambivalence toward Africans surfaces in domestic discourse about household staff. Typically, the cook/housekeeper is the celebrated *évolué*, whose crisp clothing, proficiency in English, and skills in the kitchen are heralded as a sign of a happy marriage between European employers and African employees. The reciprocal is the gardener, whose limited skills in English and ragged work clothes make him the butt of many jokes, usually about his stupidity when faced with European technical sophistication.

13. Benedict Anderson, *Imagined Communities: Reflections on the Origin and Spread of Nationalism* (New York: Verso, 1991). Eric Hobsbawm and Terence Ranger, *The Invention of Tradition* (Cambridge: Cambridge University Press, 1986).

14. Barthes, *Mythologies*.

15. Paul Landau, *The Realm of the Word: Language, Gender and Christianity in a Southern African Kingdom* (Portsmouth, N.H.: Heinemann, 1995).

16. Deborah Kaspin, "On Ethnographic Authority and the Tourist Trade: Anthropology in the House of Mirrors," *Anthropological Quarterly* 70, 2 (1997): 53–57.

17. Anderson, *Imagined Communities*.

18. Scholars have yet to examine the uses of primitivism in postcolonial identity politics, a curious oversight, given the intensity of interest in ethnicity as a political strategy. And yet, as Jomo Kenyatta's *Facing Mount Kenya* (New York: Vintage Books, 1965) attests, Africans have long undertaken projects of ethnographic self-discovery to assert their membership in moral communities that predate colonialism and have survived its demise. Sometimes these projects serve the interests of political opportunism, such as Gatsha Buthelezi's Inkatha Freedom Party, which raised the specter of tribal warfare in the 1990s in an attempt to scuttle South Africa's democratic transition. But more often, the formalization of ethnic categories is simply the needful reformulation of signs of identity that are at once African and modern. Although this volume cannot provide any answers, we can at least pose the question: do ethnic politics incorporate the mythologies of primitivism that colonialism brought to Africa?

19. Marshall Sahlins, *Historical Metaphors and Mythical Realities: Structure in the Early History of the Sandwich Islands Kingdom* (Ann Arbor: University of Michigan Press, 1981) and *Islands of History* (Chicago: University of Chicago Press, 1985).

20. *The Air Up There*, directed by Paul Glaser (1993).

BIBLIOGRAPHY

Abbass, Donna Kathleen. "European Hats Appearing in Benin Art." M.A. thesis, Southern Illinois University, 1972.
Abiodun, Rowland. "The Kingdom of Owo." In *Yoruba: Nine Hundred Years of Art and Thought*, ed. Henry John Drewal and John Pemberton III. New York: Center for African Art, 1989.
Abomo, Marie Rose Maurin. " 'Tintin au Congo,' ou la stratégie d'une demarche coloniale." In *Tintin, Hergé et la belgité*, ed. Anna Soncini Fratta. Bologna: Cooperativa libraria universitaria editrice Bologna, 1994.
Abrahams, Peter. *Tell Freedom: Memories of Africa*. New York: Knopf, 1954.
Abrahams, Yvette. "Miscast." Reviews. *South African Review of Books* 44 (1996): 15–16.
Ackerman, Carl W. *George Eastman*. Boston: Houghton Mifflin, 1930.
Adams, John, Rev. [1750?–1814]. *Curious Thoughts on the History of Man; Chiefly Abridged or Selected from the Celebrated Works of Lord Kaimes, Lord Monboddo, Dr. Dunbar, and the Immortal Montesquieu... Designed to Promote a Spirit of Enquiry in the British Youth of Both Sexes*. London: G. Kearsley, 1789. Reprint. Bristol, U.K.: Thoemmes Press, 1995.
Adediran, Biodun. "Pleasant Imperialism: Conjectures on Benin Hegemony in Eastern Yorubaland." *African Notes* 15, 1–2 (1991): 83–95.
Adelstein, P. Z. "From Metal to Polyester: A History of Picture-Taking Supports." In *Pioneers of Photography: Their Achievements in Science and Technology*, ed. International Museum of Photography. Springfield, Va.: Society for Imaging Science and Technology, 1987.
Adorno, Theodore. *Minima Moralia*. Translated by E. F. N. Jephcott. London: Verso, 1974.
Afigbo, A. E. "The Establishment of Colonial Rule, 1900–1918." In *History of West Africa*, ed J. F. A. Ajayi and Michael Crowder, 2: 424–83. 2 vols. New York: Columbia University Press, 1972–73.
Africa Illustrated: Scenes from the Dark Continent. From Photographs Secured in Africa by Bishop William Taylor, Dr. Emil Holub, and the Missionary Superintendents. New York: Ross Taylor, 1895.
Agee, James, and Walker Evans. *Let Us Now Praise Famous Men*. 1939, 1941. Boston: Houghton Mifflin, 1988.
Ahrens, F. W. *From Bench to Bench: Reflections, Reminiscences and Records*. Pietermaritzburg: Shuter & Shooter, 1948.

Akeley, Mary L. Jobe. *Carl Akeley's Africa: The Account of the Akeley-Eastman-Pomeroy African Hall Expedition of the American Museum of Natural History.* New York: Dodd, Mead, 1929.

Alberti, Ludwig. *Account of the Tribal Life and Customs of the Xhosa in 1807*, Translated by Dr. William Fehr from the Original Manuscript in German of The Kaffirs of the South Coast of Africa [Nähere und augsgebreitetere Nachrichten von denen einen Theil der Südlichen Küste von Afrika bewohnenden Kaffern]. Cape Town: Balkema, 1968.

Alexander, Jocelyn. "Dissident Perspectives on Zimbabwe's Post-Independence War." *Africa* 68, 2 (1998): 151–82.

Allina, Eric. " 'Fallacious Mirrors': Colonial Anxiety and Images of African Labor in Mozambique, ca. 1929." *History in Africa* 24 (1997): 9–52.

Alloula, Malek. *The Colonial Harem.* Translated by Myrna Godzich and Wlad Godzich. Minneapolis: University of Minnesota Press, 1986.

Alpers, Svetlana. *The Art of Describing: Dutch Art in the Seventeenth Century.* Chicago: University of Chicago Press, 1983.

Anderson, Benedict. *Imagined Communities: Reflections on the Origin and Spread of Nationalism.* London: Verso, 1983.

Apostolidès, Jean-Marie. *Les métamorphoses de Tintin.* Paris: Seghers, 1984.

Appadurai, Arjun. *Modernity at Large: Cultural Dimensions of Globalization.* (Minneapolis: University of Minnesota Press, 1996.

Appiah, Kwame Anthony. *In My Father's House: Africa in the Philosophy of Culture.* Oxford: Oxford University Press, 1992.

———. "Is the Post- in Post Modernism the Post- in Postcolonial?" *Critical Inquiry* 17 (1991): 336–57.

Apter, Emily, and William Pietz, eds. *Fetishism as Cultural Discourse.* Ithaca, N.Y.: Cornell University Press, 1993.

Aragon, Louis. "Persécuté, persécuteur." In *L'oeuvre poétique*, vol. 5, *1930–33*. Paris: Livre Club Diderot, 1975.

Ariès, Philippe. *The Hour of Our Death.* Translated by Helen Weaver. New York: Knopf, 1981.

Arnoldi, Mary Jo, Christraud Geary, and Kris L. Hardin, eds. *African Material Culture.* Bloomington: Indiana University Press, 1996.

Arrighi, Giovanni. "Labor Supplies in Historical Perspective: A Study of the Proletarianization of the African Peasantry in Rhodesia." In *Essays on the Political Economy of Africa*, ed. id. and John Saul, 80–236. New York: Monthly Review Press, 1973.

Asad, Talal. *Anthropology and the Colonial Encounter.* New York: Humanities Press, 1973.

Assouline, Pierre. *Hergé: Biographie.* Paris: Plon, 1996.

Aumont, Jacques. *The Image.* Translated by Claire Pajackowska. London: British Film Institute, 1997.

"Les aventures de Mbumbulu." *Nos Images* 1–7, no. 1–82 (July 15, 1948–1954).

"Les aventures de la famille Mbumbulu." *Nos Images* 7–8, nos. 83–126 (1954–December 20, 1954).

Ayliff, Rev. John. *Memorials of the British Settlers of South Africa.* Grahamstown: Godlonton, 1985.

Azikiwe, Nnamdi. *Renascent Africa.* London: Frank Cass, 1937.

Bahloul, Joëlle. *The Architecture of Memory: A Jewish-Muslim Household in Colonial Algeria, 1937–1962.* Translated by Catherine du Peloux Ménagé. New York: Cambridge University Press, 1996.

Bain, Donald. *The Kalahari Bushmen.* Johannesburg: Tillet & Sons, 1936.

Baldassari, Anne. *Picasso and Photography: The Dark Mirror.* Houston: Houston Museum of Fine Arts / Flammarion, 1997.

Bancel, Nicolas, Pascal Blanchard, and Laurent Gervereau, eds. *Images et colonies: Iconographie et propagande coloniale sur l'Afrique française de 1880 à 1962*. Nanterre: Bibliothèque de documentation internationale contemporaine; Paris: Association Connaissance de l'histoire de l'Afrique contemporaine, 1993.

Bande dessinée et Tiers monde. Special issue of *Vivant Univers*, no. 367, and *Coccinelle: La BD à bon dieu: Revue d'information et d'analyse sur la bande dessinée*, no. 11 (January–February 1987).

Banta, Melissa, and Curtis Hinsley. *From Site to Sight: Anthropology, Photography and the Power of Imagery*. Cambridge, Mass.: Peabody Museum of Archaeology and Ethnology, 1986.

Barber, Karin. "Popular Arts in Africa." *African Studies Review* 300 (1987): 1–78, 105–32.

———, ed. *Readings in African Popular Culture*. Bloomington: University of Indiana Press, 1997.

Barkas, Natalie. *Behind the Camera*. London: Geoffrey Bles, 1934.

Barnard, Alan. "Laurens van der Post and the Kalahari Debate." In *Miscast: Negotiating the Presence of Bushmen*, ed. Pippa Skotnes, 239–47. Cape Town: University of Cape Town Press, 1996.

Barnes, Sandra T. "The Many Faces of Ogun." In *Africa's Ogun, Old World and New*, ed. Sandra T. Barnes, 1–28. Bloomington: Indiana University Press 1989.

Barnes, Sandra T., and Ben-Amos, Paula. "Ogun, the Empire Builder." In *Africa's Ogun, Old World and New*, ed. Sandra T. Barnes, 36–64. Bloomington: Indiana University Press, 1989.

Barns, Thomas Alexander. *The Wonderland of the Eastern Congo: The Region of the Snow-Crowned Volcanoes, the Pygmies, the Giant Gorilla, and the Okapi*. New York: Putnam, 1922.

Baron-Carvais, Annie. *La bande dessinée*. Paris: Presses universitaires de France, 1985.

Barthes, Roland. *Camera Lucida: Reflections on Photography*. Translated by Richard Howard. New York: Hill & Wang, 1981.

———. *Mythologies*. Paris: Seuil, 1957. Translated by Annette Lavers. New York: Hill & Wang, 1972. Reprint, Noonday Press, 1992.

Baruti, Barly. "Souvenirs, avenirs . . ." In *Un diner à Kinshasa: Concours BD 96 Bruxelles-Kinshasa*, 12–13. Brussels: Édition Ti Suka asbl, 1996.

———. *La voiture! C'est l'aventure*. Brussels, 1985[?].

Bastide, Roger. *The African Religions of Brazil*. Baltimore: Johns Hopkins University Press, 1978.

Bathia, Casimir. "L'Afrique noire à Rouen: L'Exposition nationale et coloniale de 1896." In *Pleins Sud*. Paris: Association Connaissance de l'histoire de l'Afrique contemporaine, 1993.

Bayly, Christopher, ed. *The Raj: India and the British, 1600–1947*. Exhibition catalogue. London: National Portrait Gallery, 1991.

Bederman, Gail. *Manliness and Civilization: A Cultural History of Gender and Race in the United States, 1880–1917*. Chicago: University of Chicago Press, 1995.

Behrend, Heike, and Tobias Wendl. "Photography: Social and Cultural Aspects." In *Encyclopedia of Africa South of the Sahara*, ed. John Middleton, 3: 409–15. New York: Scribner, 1997.

Beinart, William. "Review Article: Empire, Hunting and Ecological Change in Southern and Central Africa." *Past & Present* 128 (August 1990): 162–86.

Ben-Amos, Paula [now Girshick]. "African Visual Arts from a Social Perspective." *African Studies Review* 32, 2 (September 1989): 1–53.

———. " 'À la recherche du temps perdu': On Being an Ebony Carver in Benin." In *Ethnic and Tourist Arts: Cultural Expressions from the Fourth World*, ed. Nelson H. H. Graburn. Berkeley and Los Angeles: University of California Press, 1976.

———. *The Art of Benin*. London: British Museum Press, 1995.

———. "The Powers of Kings: Symbolism of a Benin Ceremonial Stool." In *The Art of Power / The Power of Art: Studies in Benin Iconography*, ed. id. and Arnold Rubin. Los Angeles: Museum of Cultural History, 1983.

———. "Professionals and Amateurs in Benin Court Carving." In *African Images: Essays in African Iconology*, ed. Daniel F. McCall and Edna G. Bay, 170–89. New York: Africana Pub. Co. for the African Studies Center, Boston University, 1975.

———. "Social Change in the Organization of Woodcarving in Benin City, Nigeria." Ph.D. diss., Indiana University, 1971.

Ben-Amos, Paula, and Arnold Rubin, eds. *The Art of Power / The Power of Art: Studies in Benin Iconography*. Los Angeles: Museum of Cultural History, 1983.

Benjamin, Walter. "Exposé of 1935." In id., *The Arcades Project*, trans Howard Eiland and Kevin McLaughlin, ed. Rolf Tiedmann, 3–13. Cambridge, Mass.: Harvard University Press, Belknap Press, 1999.

———. *Illuminations: Essays and Reflections*. Translated by Harry Zohn. Edited by Hannah Arendt. 1968. New York: Schocken Books, 1969.

———. "The Task of the Translator." In id., *Illuminations: Essays and Reflections*, ed. Hannah Arendt. 1968. New York: Schocken Books, 1969.

———. "The Work of Art in the Age of Mechanical Reproduction." In id., *Illuminations: Essays and Reflections*, ed. Hannah Arendt, 217–52. 1968. New York: Schocken Books, 1969.

Benninghoff-Luhl, Sibylle. "Die Ausstellung der Kolonialisierten: Völkerschauen von 1874–1932." In *Andenken an den Kolonialismus: Eine Ausstellung des Völkerkundlichen Instituts der Universität Tübingen*, ed. Volker Harms, Klaus Barthel, et al. Tübingen: ATTEMPTO, 1984.

Bensusan, A. D. *Silver Images: History of Photography in Africa*. Cape Town: Howard Timmins, 1966.

Berger, John. *Keeping a Rendezvous*. New York: Pantheon Books, 1991.

Bergh, J. S., and J. C. Visagie. *The Eastern Cape Frontier Zone, 1660–1980: A Cartographic Guide for Historical Research*. Durban: Butterworths, 1985.

Berglund, Axel-Ivar. *Zulu Thought Patterns and Symbolism*. Uppsala: Swedish Mission Institute, 1976.

Berlage, Jean. *Répertoire de la presse du Congo belge (1884–1958) et du Ruanda-Urundi (1920–1958)*. Brussels: Commission belge de bibliographie, 1959.

Berman, Bruce. "Ethnicity, Patronage and the African State: The Politics of Uncivil Nationalism." *African Affairs* 97 (1998): 305–41.

Bernal, Martin. *Black Athena: The Afroasiatic Roots of Classical Civilization*. 2 vols. New Brunswick, N.J.: Rutgers University Press, 1987.

Bernatzik, Hugo Adolf. *Afrika: Handbuch der angewandten Völkerkunde*. 2 vols. Innsbruck: Schlüsselverlag, 1947.

———. *Äthiopen des westens: Forschungsreisen in Portugiesisch-Guinea*. 2 vols. Vienna: L. W. Seidel & Sohn, 1933.

Bester, Rory McLachlan. "Insecure Shadows: CPSA Mission Photographs from Southern Africa c. 1895–1945." M.A. thesis, University of the Witswatersrand, 1997.

Bhabha, Homi K. *The Location of Culture*. New York: Routledge, 1994.

———. "Of Mimicry and Man: The Ambivalence of Colonial Discourse." *October* 28 (1984): 125–33.

———. "The Other Question: The Stereotype and Colonial Discourse." *Screen* 24, 6 (1983): 16–36.

Bhabha, Homi K. "Signs Taken for Wonders: Questions of Ambivalence and Authority under a Tree outside Delhi, May 1817." *Critical Inquiry* 12, no. 1 (1985): 144–65.
Biondi, Jean-Pierre. *Les anticolonialistes (1881–1962)*. Paris: Robert Lafont, 1992.
Bitterli, Urs. *Die "Wilden" und die "Zivilisierten": Grundzüge e. Geistes- u. Kulturgeschichte d. europ.-überseeischen Begegnung*. Munich: C. H. Beck, 1976.
Blackmun, Barbara. "From Trader to Priest in Two Hundred Years: The Transformation of a Foreign Figure on Benin Ivories." *Art Journal* 47, 2 (1988): 128–38.
———. "Oba's Portraits in Benin." *African Arts* 23, 3 (1990): 61–69, 102–4.
Blanchard, Pascal, and Armelle Chatelier, eds. *Images et colonies: Nature, discours et influence de l'iconographie coloniale liée à la propagande coloniale et à la représentation des Africains et de l'Afrique en France, de 1920 aux indépendances: Actes du colloque organisé par l'ACHAC du 20 au 22 janvier 1993 à la Bibliothèque nationale*. Paris: Syros / Association Connaissance de l'histoire de l'Afrique contemporaine, 1993.
Blanchard, Pascal, Stéphane Blanchoin, Nicolas Bancel, et al., eds. *L'autre et nous: Scènes et types*. Paris: Syros / Association Connaissance de l'histoire de l'Afrique contemporaine, 1995.
Blaut, James. *The Colonizer's Model of the World: Geographical Diffusionism and Eurocentric History*. New York: Guilford Press, 1993.
Bleek, Dorothea. "Bushman Folklore." *Africa* 2 (1929): 302–13.
———. "Notes on the Bushman Photographs." *Bantu Studies* 10 (1936): 200–204.
Bleek, Edith, and Dorothea Bleek. "Notes on the Bushmen." In M. Helen Tongue, *Bushman Paintings*. Oxford: Clarendon Press, 1909.
Bleek, Wilhelm H. I. *A Brief Account of Bushman Folklore and Other Texts. Second Report Concerning Bushman Researches, Presented to Both Houses of the Parliament of the Cape of Good Hope, by Command of His Excellency the Governor*. Cape Town: Juta, 1875.
———. *Report of Dr. Bleek Concerning His Researches into the Bushman Language and Customs*. Cape Town, 1873.
Bleek, W. H. I., and Lucy Lloyd. *Specimens of Bushman Folklore* [Spine: *Bushman Folklore*]. London: George Allen, 1911.
Bloch, Maurice. "Death, Women and Power." In *Death and the Regeneration of Life*, ed. id. and Jonathan Parry, 211–30. Cambridge: Cambridge University Press, 1982.
Bloch, Maurice, and Jonathan Parry, eds. *Death and the Regeneration of Life*. Cambridge: Cambridge University Press, 1982.
Blumer, Herbert. *Movies and Conduct*. New York: Macmillan, 1933.
Blumer, Herbert, and Philip M. Hauser. *Movies, Delinquency, and Crime*. New York: Macmillan, 1933.
Boddy, Janice. *Wombs and Alien Spirits: Women, Men and the Zar Cult of Northern Sudan*. Madison: University of Wisconsin Press, 1989.
Boorstin, Daniel. *The Image: A Guide to Pseudo-Events in America*. New York: Macmillan, 1961.
Borgatti, Jean M., and Brilliant, Richard. *Likeness and Beyond: Portraits from Africa and the World*. New York: Center for African Art, 1990.
Boulard, Tristan. "Matamata et Pilipili." Brussels: Libération Films, 1996. 55 min.
Bourdieu, Pierre. *Distinctions: A Social Critique of the Judgement of Taste*. Translated by Richard Nice. London: Routledge, 1986.
———. *Outline of a Theory of Practice*. Cambridge: Cambridge University Press, 1977.
Bourdieu, Pierre, with Luc Boltanski et al. *Photography, a Middle-Brow Art*. 1965. Translated by Shaun Whiteside. Stanford, Calif.: Stanford University Press, 1990.

Bradbury, R. E. *Benin Studies*. Edited by Peter Morton-Williams. New York: Oxford University Press for the International African Institute, 1973.
Braeckman, Colette. "Barly Baruti: Dessiner envers et contre tous à Kinshasa." *Le Soir*, n.d. [1992?].
Brayer, Elizabeth. *George Eastman*. Baltimore: Johns Hopkins University Press, 1997.
Brett, Guy. *Through Our Own Eyes: Popular Art and Modern History*. London: GMP Publishers, 1986.
Brink, Yvonne. "Places of Discourse and Dialogue: A Study in the Material Culture of the Cape during the Rule of the Dutch East India Company, 1652–1795." Ph.D. diss., University of Cape Town, 1992.
Brontë, Emily. *Wuthering Heights*. 1847. New York: Oxford University Press, 1987.
Brownlee, W. T. *Reminiscences of a Transkeian*. Pietermaritzburg: Shuter & Shooter, n.d.
Bruner, Edward M. "The Ethnographer/Tourist in Indonesia." In *International Tourism: Identity and Change*, ed. Marie-Françoise Lanfant, John B. Allcock, and Edward M. Bruner. Thousand Oaks, Calif.: Sage Publications, 1995.
———. "Of Cannibals, Tourists and Ethnographers." *Cultural Anthropology* 4 (1989): 438–45.
Bryden, H. A. *Gun and Camera in Southern Africa*. London: Edward Stanford, 1893.
———. *Wild Life in South Africa*. London: Harrap, 1936.
Bryson, Norman. *Vision and Painting: The Logic of the Gaze*. New Haven, Conn.: Yale University Press, 1983.
Bunn, David. "'Our Wattled Cot': Mercantile and Domestic Space in Thomas Pringle's African Landscapes." In *Landscape and Power*, ed. W. J. T. Mitchell, 127–74. Chicago: University of Chicago Press, 1994.
Buntman, Barbara. "Bushman Images in South African Tourist Advertising: The Case of Kagga Kamma." In *Miscast: Negotiating the Presence of the Bushmen*, ed. Pippa Skotnes, 271–80. Cape Town: University of Cape Town Press, 1996.
Burke, Timothy. *Lifebuoy Men, Lux Women: Commodification, Consumption and Cleanliness in Modern Zimbabwe*. Durham, N.C.: Duke University Press, 1996.
Burroughs, Edgar Rice. *Tarzan of the Apes*. 1912. New York: Ballantine Books, 1983.
Cameron, Kenneth. *Africa on Film*. New York: Continuum Press, 1994.
Campagnoli, Ruggiero. "Présentation du quatrième numéro de *Beloeil*." In *Tintin, Hergé et la belgité*, ed. Anna Soncini Fratta. Bologna: Cooperativa libraria universitaria editrice Bologna, 1994.
Carreira, António. *Documentos para a história das ilhas de Cabo Verde e "Rios de Guiné": Séculos XVII e XVIII*. Lisbon: António Carreira, 1983.
———. "Mutilações ethicas dos Manjacos." *Boletim Cultural da Guiné Portuguesa* 16, 2 (1961): 151–54.
———. *Panaria Cabo-Verdiano-Guinéense: Aspectos históricos e sócio-económicos*. Lisbon: Junto de Investigações do Ultramar, 1968.
———. "Simbolos, ritualistas, e ritualismos anima-fieticistas na Guiné Portuguesa." *Boletim Cultural da Guiné Portuguesa* 16, 3 (1961): 505–40.
———. *Vida Social dos Manjacos: Publicação comemorativa do v centenário da descoberta da Guiné*. Publicações do Centro de Estudos da Guiné Portuguesa, Memórias, no. 1. Lisbon: Centro dos Estudos da Guiné Portuguesa, 1947.
Carretta, Vincent. "Olaudah Equiano or Gustavus Vassa? New Light on an Eighteenth-Century Question of Identity." *Slavery and Abolition* 20, 3 (1999): 96–105.
Carrier, J. G., ed. *Occidentalism: Images of the West*. New York: Oxford University Press, 1995.

Cavalli-Sforza, Luigi L. *Genes, Peoples, and Languages.* Translated by Mark Seielstad. New York: North Point Press, 2000.
Les cent aventures de la famille Mbumbulu. Leopoldville: Édition de la Revue *Nos Images,* 1956.
Certeau, Michel de. "Montaigne's 'Of Cannibals': The Savage 'I.' " In *Heterologies: Discourse on the Other,* trans. Brian Massumi, 67–79. Minneapolis: University of Minnesota Press, 1986.
Chagas, Frederico Pinheiro. *Na Guiné (1907–1908).* Lisbon: J. F. Pinheiro, 1910.
Chanock, Martin. *Law, Custom and the Social Order: The Colonial Experience in Malawi and Zambia.* New York: Cambridge University Press, 1985.
Chanson, Philippe. *Tintin au Congo, c'est quand même un peu* GROS! *Une relecture critique de l'imagerie nègre en perspective créole.* Cartigny, France: Tribune Libre, 1995.
Chartier, Roger. "Texts, Printing, Readings." In *The New Cultural History,* ed. Lynn Hunt, 154–75. Berkeley and Los Angeles: University of California Press, 1989.
Clifford, James. "On Ethnographic Surrealism." *Comparative Studies in Society and History* 23 (1981): 539–64.
———. *The Predicament of Culture.* Cambridge, Mass.: Harvard University Press, 1988.
Clifford, James, and George E. Marcus, eds. *Writing Culture: The Poetics and Politics of Ethnography.* Berkeley and Los Angeles: University of California Press, 1986.
"Coco Banania et les poissons volants: Conte de l'Exposition coloniale." *Coeurs vaillants* (Paris), May 31, 1931.
Coe, Brian. *The Birth of Photography.* New York: Praeger, 1976.
Coetzee, Colin. *Forts of the Eastern Frontier: Securing a Frontier, 1799–1878.* Alice, South Africa: University of Fort Hare, 1995.
Cohen, David William, and E. S. Atieno Odhiambo. *Burying SM: The Politics of Knowledge and the Sociology of Power in Africa.* Portsmouth, N.H.: Heinemann Educational Books, 1992.
Cohn, Bernard S. *Colonialism and Its Forms of Knowledge: The British in India.* Princeton, N.J.: Princeton University Press, 1994.
Coke, Van Deren. *The Painter and the Photograph.* Albuquerque: University of New Mexico Press, 1964.
Cole, Catherine. "Reading Blackface in West Africa: Wonders Taken for Signs." *Critical Inquiry* 23 (1996): 183–215.
Cole, Herbert. *Icons: Ideals and Power in the Art of Africa.* Washington, D.C.: Smithsonian Institution Press, 1989.
Coleman, James S. *Nigeria: Background to Nationalism.* 1958. Benin City: Broburg & Wistrom, 1986.
Coleridge, Mary E. *Holman Hunt.* London: T. C. & E. C. Jack; New York: F. A. Stokes, 1908.
Comaroff, Jean. *Body of Power, Spirit of Resistance.* Chicago: University of Chicago Press, 1985.
Comaroff, Jean, and John Comaroff. *Of Revelation and Revolution,* vol. 1: *Christianity, Colonialism and Consciousness in South Africa.* Chicago: University of Chicago Press, 1991.
———. *Of Revelation and Revolution,* vol. 2: *The Dialectics of Modernity on the South African Frontier.* Chicago: University of Chicago Press, 1998.
———, eds. *Modernity and Its Malcontents: Ritual and Power in Postcolonial Africa.* Chicago: University of Chicago Press, 1993.
Commissariat général de l'Exposition coloniale de Paris. *Congrès international et intercolonial de la société indigène.* 2 vols. Paris: L'Exposition coloniale, 1931.
Coombes, Annie E. *Reinventing Africa: Museums, Material Culture and Popular Imagination in Late Victorian and Edwardian England.* New Haven, Conn.: Yale University Press, 1994.

Corbey, Raymond. "Ethnographic Showcases, 1870–1930." In *The Decolonization of the Imagination: Culture, Knowledge and Power*, ed. Jan Nederveen Pieterse and Bhikhu Parekh, 57–80. Atlantic Highlands, N.J.: Zed Books, 1995.

———. *Wildheid en beschaving: De Europese verbeelding van Afrika*. Baarn, Netherlands: Ambo, 1989.

Cordwell, Justine M. "Some Aesthetic Aspects of Yoruba and Benin Cultures." Ph.D. diss., Northwestern University, 1952.

Cornell, Fred C. *The Glamour of Prospecting: Wanderings of a South African Prospector in Search of Copper, Gold, Emeralds, and Diamonds*. London: T. F. Unwin, 1920. Reprint, Cape Town, 1989.

Cornet, Joseph-Aurélien. "Histoire de la peinture zaïroise." In id., Remi De Cnodder, Ivan Dierickx, and Wim Toebosch, *Soixante ans de peinture au Zaïre*. Brussels: Les éditeurs d'art associés, 1989.

Cory, Sir George. *The Rise of South Africa*. London: Longman, Green & Co., 1926.

Cosentino, Donald, ed. *Sacred Arts of Haitian Vodou*. Los Angeles: UCLA Fowler Museum of Cultural History, 1995.

Crais, Clifton. *The Making of the Colonial Order*. Cambridge: Cambridge University Press, 1992.

Crary, Jonathan. *Techniques of the Observer: On Vision and Modernity in the Nineteenth Century*. Cambridge, Mass.: MIT Press, 1990.

Craven, Thomas. *Cartoon Cavalcade*. New York: Simon & Schuster, 1943.

Crone, G. R., trans. and ed. *The Voyages of Cadamosto and Other Documents on Western Africa in the Second Half of the Fifteenth Century*. Works issued by the Hakluyt Society, ser. 2, no. 80. London: Hakluyt Society, 1937; Nendeln, Liechtenstein: Kraus Reprint, 1967.

Crowder, Michael. "Indirect Rule—French and British Style." *Africa* 34, 3 (1964): 197–205.

Cullinan, Patrick. *Robert Jacob Gordon, 1743–1795: The Man and His Travels at the Cape*. Cape Town: Struik, 1992.

Curnow, Kathy. "Alien or Accepted: African Perspectives on the Western 'Other' in Fifteenth and Sixteenth Century Art." *Studies in Visual Communication* 13, 1 (1990): 38–75.

Curtin, Philip. *The Image of Africa*. Madison: University of Wisconsin Press, 1975.

Darian-Smith, Kate, Liz Gunner, and Sarah Nuttall, eds. *Text, Theory, Space: Land, Literature, and History in South Africa and Australia*. New York: Routledge, 1996.

Dark, Philip J. C. *The Art of Benin: A Catalogue of an Exhibition of the A. W. F. Puller and Chicago Natural History Museum*. Chicago: Field Museum of Natural History, 1962.

David, Philippe, ed. *Inventaire général des cartes postales Fortier*. 2 vols. Saint-Julien-du-Sault: Fostier, 1986–87. François Edmond Fortier (1862–1928) was a photographer and publisher of postcards at Dakar.

Davis, David Brion. "Constructing Race: A Reflection." *William and Mary Quarterly*, 3d. ser., 54, no. 1 (January 1997): 6–16.

Davison, Patricia. "Human Subjects as Museum Objects: A Project to Make Life-Casts of 'Bushmen' and 'Hottentots', 1907–1924." *Annals of the South African Museum* 102, 5 (1993): 165–83.

———. "Material Culture, Context and Meaning." Ph.D. diss., University of Cape Town, 1991.

Deacon, Janette. 1996. "A Tale of Two Families: Wilhelm Bleek, Lucy Lloyd and the /Xam San of the Northern Cape." In *Miscast: Negotiating the Presence of the Bushmen*, ed. Pippa Skotnes. Cape Town: University of Cape Town Press, 1996.

Deacon, Janette, and Thomas A. Dowson, eds. *Voices from the Past: /Xam Bushmen and the Bleek and Lloyd Collection*. Johannesburg: Witwatersrand University Press, 1996.

Debord, Guy. *The Society of the Spectacle.* Translated by Donald Nicholson-Smith. 1970. New York: Zone Books, 1994. Originally published as *La société du spectacle* (Paris: Buchet/Chastel, 1967).

Debrunner, H. C. *Presence and Prestige: Africans in Europe: A History of Africans in Europe before 1918.* Basel: Basler Afrika Bibliographien, 1979.

Delavignette, Robert. *Afrique équatoriale française.* Les Albums des Guides bleus, 29. Photographs by Michel Huet, Michel Mako, and Pierre Ichac. Notes by Jacques Vulaines. Paris: Hachette, 1957.

Dening, Greg. *Mr Bligh's Bad Language: Passion, Power, and Theatre on the Bounty.* New York: Cambridge University Press, 1992.

———. "The Theatricality of Observing and Being Observed: Eighteenth-Century Europe 'Discovers' the ? Century 'Pacific.'" In *Implicit Understandings: Observing, Reporting, and Reflecting on the Encounters between Europeans and Other Peoples in the Early Modern Era,* ed. Stuart B. Schwartz, 451–83. New York: Cambridge University Press, 1994.

Denis, Benoît. "L'Afrique à l'Amérique: L'odyssée mentale des héros chez Hergé et Céline." In *Tintin, Hergé et la belgité,* ed. Anna Soncini Fratta, 75–87. Bologna: Cooperativa libraria universitaria editrice Bologna, 1994.

Depelchin, H., and C. Croonenberghs. *Journey to Gubulawayo: Letters of Fr. J. Depelchin and C. Croonenberghs, J.J., 1879, 1880, 1881.* Translated by Maria Lloyd. Bulawayo, Zimbabwe: Historical Facsimiles, 1979.

Derrida, Jacques. "By Force of Mourning." Translated by Pascale-Anne Brault and Michael Naas. *Critical Inquiry* 22 (Winter 1996): 171–92.

———. *Spectres of Marx: The State of Debt, the Work of Mourning, and the New International.* Translated by Peggy Kamuf. New York: Routledge, 1994.

Detry, Robert. *Les mots français désignant les noirs du Congo belge (1920–1945).* Mémoire en philologie romaine, Université Catholique de Louvain, 1965.

Devisse, Jean, and Michel Mollat. *From the Early Christian Era to the "Age of Discovery."* Vol. 2 of *The Image of the Black in Western Art.* Translated by William Granger Ryan. New York: Morrow, 1979.

Dias, Antonio Jorge. *Boletim da Sociedade de Geografia* 83 (1965): 63–72.

Diawara, Mamadou. "Le cimitiere des autels, le temple des tresors: Reflexions sur les musées d'art Africains." In *Jahrbuch der Wissenschaftskolleg zu Berlin.* Berlin: Wissenschaftskolleg, 1997.

Diawara, Manthia. *African Cinema: Politics and Culture.* Bloomington: Indiana University Press, 1992.

Dineur, Fernard. *Tif et Tondu au Congo belge.* Brussels: Éditions Jonas, 1979.

Diouf, Mamadou. "Fresques murales et écriture de l'histoire: Le *Set/Setal* à Dakar." *Politiques Africaines,* June 1992, 41–54.

Doke, C. M., D. McK. Malcolm, and J. M. A. Sikakana. *English-Zulu Dictionary.* Johannesburg: University of Witswatersrand Press, 1958.

Douglas, Mary. *Purity and Danger: An Analysis of the Concepts of Pollution and Taboo.* 1966. Reprint. New York: Routledge, 1992.

Douglas, Roy. *The World War, 1939–1943: The Cartoonists' Vision.* London: Routledge, 1990.

Drechsler, Seymour. "The Ending of the Slave Trade and the Evolution of European Scientific Racism." In *The Atlantic Slave Trade: Effects on Economies, Societies, and Peoples in Africa, the Americas, and Europe,* ed. Joseph E. Inkori and Stanley Engerman, 361–96. Durham, N.C.: Duke University Press, 1992.

Drewal, Henry J. "Art, History, and the Individual: A New Perspective for the Study of African Visual Traditions." In *Iowa Studies in African Art*, ed. C. Roy, 1: 87–114. Iowa City: School of Art and Art History, University of Iowa, 1984.

———. "Flaming Crowns, Cooling Waters: Masquerades of the Ijebu-Yoruba." *African Arts* 20, 1 (1986): 32–41, 99–100.

———. "Mermaids, Mirrors, and Snake Charmers." *African Arts* 21, 2 (1988): 38–45, 96.

———. "Performing the Other: Mami Wata Worship in West Africa." *Drama Review* T118 (1988): 160–85.

Drewal, Henry, and Margaret Drewal. *Gelede: Art and Female Power among the Yoruba*. Bloomington: Indiana University Press, 1983.

Drury, James. and M. R. Drennan. "The Pudendal Parts of the South African Bush Race." *Medical Journal of South Africa* 22 (1926): 113–17.

Du Bois, W. E. B. "On Being Ashamed of Oneself (1933)." In *The Oxford W. E. B. Du Bois Reader*, ed. Eric J. Sundquist. New York: Oxford University Press, 1996.

Dubow, Saul. *Scientific Racism in Modern South Africa*. Cambridge: Cambridge University Press, 1995.

Duggan-Cronin, A. M. *The Bantu Tribes of South Africa: Reproductions of Photographic Studies*. 4 vols. Cambridge: Cambridge University Press, 1928–41.

———. *The Bushman Tribes of Southern Africa*. Kimberley: Alexander McGregor Museum, 1942.

Echenberg, Myron. *Colonial Conscripts: The Tirailleur Sénégalais in French West Africa*. Portsmouth, N.H.: Heinemann, 1991.

Eckenbrecher, Margarethe von. *Was Afrika mir Gab und Nahm: Erlebnisse einer deutschen Frau in Südwestafrika*. Berlin: E. S. Mittler & Sohn, 1909; new ed., 1937, 1940.

Eco, Umberto. *A Theory of Semiotics*. Bloomington: Indiana University Press, 1976.

Edwards, Bryan. *The History, Civil and Commercial, of the British Colonies in the West Indies*. 1793. 2d ed. 2 vols. London: John Stockdale, 1794.

Edwards, Elizabeth. "Representation and Reality: Science and the Visual Image." In *Australia in Oxford*, ed. Howard Murphy and Elizabeth Edwards. Oxford: Pitt Rivers Museum, 1988.

———. "Photography: A Reflexive Overview from Anthropology." *African Research and Documentation* 68 (1995): 18–35.

———, ed. *Anthropology and Photography, 1860–1920*. New Haven, Conn.: Yale University Press, 1992.

Egharevba, Jacob U. *Benin Law and Custom*. Lagos: C.M.S. Niger Press, 1949.

Elongo, Gabriel. "Correspondance de Stanleyville: Match Comte de Flandre—Duc de Brabant." *La Croix du Congo*, 3 September 1933, 4.

Equiano, Olaudah. "The Interesting Narrative of the Life of Olaudah Equiano, or Gustavus Vassa, The African. Written by Himself." In id., *The Interesting Narrative and Other Writings*, ed. Vincent Carretta. New York: Penguin Books, 1995.

Errington, Shelly. *The Death of Authentic: Primitive Art and Other Tales of Progress*. Berkeley and Los Angeles: University of California Press, 1998.

Ezra, Kate. *Royal Art of Benin: The Perls Collection in the Metropolitan Museum of Art*. New York: Metropolitan Museum of Art, 1992.

Fabian, Johannes. "Popular Culture in Africa: Findings and Conjectures," *Africa* 48, 4 (1978): 315–34.

———. *Remembering the Present: Painting and Popular History in Zaire*. Narrative and paintings by Tshibumba Kanda Matulu. Berkeley and Los Angeles: University of California Press, 1996.

———. *Time and the Other: How Anthropology Makes Its Object*. New York: Columbia University Press, 1983.
Fagg, William B. *Nigerian Images*. London: Percy Lund, Humphries & Co., 1960.
Fanon, Frantz. *Black Skin, White Masks*. Translated by Charles Lam Markmann. New York: Grove Press, 1967. Originally published as *Peau noire, masques blancs* (Paris: Seuil, 1952).
———. *The Wretched of the Earth*. Translated by Constance Farrington. New York: Grove Press, 1963. Originally published as *Les damnés de la terre* (Paris: François Maspero, 1961).
Farson, Negley. *Behind God's Back*. New York: Harcourt, Brace, 1941.
Fatou Niang Siga, Niang. *Reflets de modes et traditions saint-louisiennes*. Dakar: Éditions Khoudia, 1990.
Fettweis, Nadine. "Le phénomène Zamenga." In *Papier blanc, encre noire: Cent ans de culture francophone en Afrique centrale (Zaïre, Rwanda, et Burundi)*, vol. 2, ed. Marc Quaghebeur, E. van Balberghe, et al. Brussels: Éditions Labor, 1992.
Fieldhouse, D. K. *Merchant Capital and Economic Decolonization: The United Africa Company, 1929–1987*. Oxford: Oxford University Press, 1994.
Fish, Stanley. *Is There a Text in This Class? The Authority of Interpretive Communities*. Cambridge, Mass.: Harvard University Press, 1980.
Flukinger, Roy. *The Formative Decades: Photography in Great Britain, 1839–1920*. Austin: University of Texas Press, 1985.
Forrest, Joshua. *Guinea-Bissau: Power, Conflict, and Renewal in a West African Nation*. Boulder, Colo.: Westview Press, 1992.
Foucault, Michel. *The Archaeology of Knowledge*. Translated by A. M. Sheridan Smith. New York: Pantheon Books, 1972.
———. *Discipline and Punish: The Birth of the Prison*. Translated by Alan Sheridan. New York: Pantheon Books, 1977. Reprint. New York: Vintage Books, 1979, 1995.
Francart, Roland. *La BD chrétienne*. Paris: Éditions du Cerf, 1994.
François, Edouard. "Raoul et Gaston, le mythe africain," *Phénix: Revue internationale de la bande dessinée*, no. 13 (1970): 31–35.
Fraser, D. "The Fish-Legged Figure in Benin and Yoruba Art." In *African Art and Leadership*, ed. D. Fraser and H. Cole, 261–94. Madison: University of Wisconsin Press, 1972.
Frederickson, George M. *The Black Image in the White Mind: The Debate on Afro-American Character and Destiny, 1817–1914*. Hanover, N.H.: University Press of New England/Wesleyan University Press, 1971.
Freedberg, David. *The Power of Images: Studies in the History and Theory of Response*. Chicago: University of Chicago Press, 1989.
French, Jack H. "The Death and Burial of Sandile." *The Coelacanth* 18, 1 (April 1980): 30–43.
Freud, Sigmund. *On the History of Psycho-Analytic Movement, Papers on Metapsychology and Other Works*, vol. 14 of *The Standard Edition of the Complete Psychological Works of Sigmund Freud*, translated under the general editorship of James Strachey, in collaboration with Anna Freud. 24 vols. London: Hogarth Press and the Institute of Psycho-Analysis, 1953–74.
Fritsch, Gustav. *Drei Jahre in Süd-Afrika: Reiseskizzen nach Notizen des Tagebuchs zusammengestellt. Mit zahlreichen Illustrationen nach Photographien und Originalzeichnungen des Verfassers, nebst einer Übersichtskarte der ausgeführten Routen*. Breslau: F. Hirt, 1868.
———. *Die Eingeborenen Süd-Afrika's*. Breslau: F. Hirt, 1872.
Gable, Eric. "The Decolonization of Consciousness: Local Skeptics and the 'Will to be Modern' in a West African Village." *American Ethnologist* 22, 2 (1995): 242–57.

———. "A Secret Shared: Fieldwork and the Sinister in a West African Village." *Cultural Anthropology* 12, 2 (1997): 213–33.

———. "Women, Ancestors, and Alterity among the Manjaco of Guinea-Bissau." *Journal of Religion in Africa* 26, 2 (1996): 104–21.

Gainer, David. "Hollywood, African Consolidated Films, and 'Bioskoopbeskawing,' or Bioscope Culture: Aspects of American Culture in Cape Town, 1945–1960." M.A. thesis, University of Cape Town, 2000.

Gallagher, Catherine, and Thomas Laqueur, eds. *The Making of the Modern Body: Sexuality and Society in the Nineteenth Century*. Berkeley and Los Angeles: University of California Press, 1987.

Gates, Henry Louis, Jr., ed. *"Race," Writing, and Difference*. Chicago: University of Chicago Press, 1986.

Geary, Christraud. *Images from Bamun: German Colonial Photography at the Court of King Njoya, Cameroon, West Africa, 1902–1925*. Washington, D.C.: Smithsonian Institution Press, 1988.

———. "Photography: Development." In *Encyclopedia of Africa South of the Sahara*, ed. John Middleton, 404–9. New York: Scribner, 1997.

Geary, Christraud M., and Virginia-Lee Webb, eds. *Delivering Views: Distant Cultures in Early Postcards*. Washington, D.C.: Smithsonian Institution Press, 1998.

Gernsheim, Helmut, and Alison Gernsheim. *The History of Photography from the Camera Obscura to the Beginning of the Modern Era*. 1955. New York: McGraw-Hill, 1969.

Gerrits, C. "Conceptions and Explanations of sii-Epilepsy—A Medical-Anthropological Study among the Bassa and Kpelle in Liberia." *Curare* 6 (1983): 33–40.

Gibson, James J. *The Senses Considered as Perceptual Systems*. Boston: Houghton Mifflin, 1966.

Gide, André. *Retour du Tchad*. Paris: Gallimard, 1928.

———. *Voyage au Congo*. Paris: Gallimard, 1927.

Giedion, Siegfried. *Mechanization Takes Command: A Contribution to Anonymous History*. 1948. New York: Norton, 1969.

Gilman, Sander. *Difference and Pathology: Stereotypes of Sexuality, Race, and Madness*. London: Routledge, 1985.

———. *Health and Illness: Images of Difference*. London: Routledge, 1995.

Girard, Elaine, and Brigitte Kernel. "La statuette colon." In *Images et colonies: Nature, discours et influence de l'iconographie coloniale liée à la propagande coloniale et à la représentation des Africains et de l'Afrique en France, de 1920 aux indépendances: Actes du colloque organisé par l'ACHAC du 20 au 22 janvier 1993 à la Bibliothèque nationale*, ed. Pascal Blanchard and Armelle Chatelier, 286–91. Paris: Syros / Association Connaissance de l'histoire de l'Afrique contemporaine, 1993.

Girard, Eliane, Brigitte Kernel, and Eric Mégret. *Colons: Statuettes habillées d'Afrique de l'Ouest*. Paris: Syros alternatives, 1993.

Girardet, Raoul. *L'idée coloniale en France, 1871–1962*. Paris: La Table Ronde, 1972.

Giroud, Frank, and Barly Baruti. *Eva K.*, vol. 1: *Les hommes du train;* vol. 2: *Amina*. Toulon, France: Soleil/MC Productions, 1995–96.

Girshick, Paula [Paula Ben-Amos]. *Art, Innovation, and Politics in Eighteenth-Century Benin*. Bloomington: Indiana University Press, 1999.

Glassman, Jonathan. *Feasts and Riot: Revelry, Rebellion, and Popular Consciousness on the Swahili Coast, 1856–1888*. Portsmouth, N.H.: Heinemann, 1995.

Gobineau, Joseph-Arthur, comte de. *Essai sur l'inégalité des races humaines*. 4 vols. Paris: Firmin Didot, 1853–55.

Gombrich, Ernst. *Art and Illusion*. Princeton, N.J.: Princeton University Press, 1956.

———. "Image and Code: Scope and Limits of Conventionalism in Pictorial Representation." In *Image and Code,* ed. Wendy Steiner. Ann Arbor: University of Michigan, 1981.
———. *Relations in Public: Microstudies of the Public Order.* New York: Basic Books, 1971.
Goodman, Nelson. *Languages of Art: An Approach to a Theory of Symbols.* 1968. 2d ed. Indianapolis: Hackett, 1976.
Goody, Jack. *The Domestication of the Savage Mind.* Cambridge: Cambridge University Press, 1978.
Gordimer, Nadine. "Our Century." *Transition* 71 (1997).
Gordon, Robert J. *The Bushman Myth: The Making of a Namibian Underclass.* Boulder, Colo.: Westview Press, 1992.
———. *Picturing Bushmen: The Denver Africa Expedition of 1925.* Athens: Ohio University Press, 1997.
———. "The Venal Hottentot Venus and the Great Chain of Being." *African Studies* 51, 2 (1992): 185–201.
Gore, Charles, and Joseph Nevadomsky. "Practice and Agency in Mammy Wata Worship in Southern Nigeria." *African Arts* 30, 2 (Spring, 1997): 60–69, 95.
Gould, Stephen Jay. *The Mismeasure of Man.* New York: Norton, 1981.
Graburn, Nelson H. H., ed. *Ethnic and Tourist Art: Cultural Expressions from the Fourth World.* Berkeley and Los Angeles: University of California Press, 1976.
Greenough, Sarah. *Paul Strand: An American Vision.* Washington, D.C.: National Gallery of Art, 1990.
Griffiths, Alison. "Knowledge and Visuality in Turn of the Century Anthropology: The Early Ethnographic Cinema of Alfred Cort Haddon and Walter Baldwin Spencer." *Visual Anthropology Review* 12, 2 (1996–97): 18–43.
Grillenzoni, Rossella. "Bibliographie Hergé." In *Tintin, Hergé et la belgité,* ed. Anna Soncini Fratta. Bologna: Cooperativa libraria universitaria editrice Bologna, 1994.
Grueser, John Cullen. *White on Black: Contemporary Literature about Africa.* Urbana: University of Illinois Press, 1992.
Gutsche, Thelma. *The History and Social Significance of Motion Pictures in South Africa, 1895–1940.* Cape Town: Howard Timmins, 1972.
Hailey, William Malcolm [Lord Hailey]. *An African Survey: A Study of Problems Arising in Africa South of the Sahara.* Issued by the Committee of the African Research Survey under the auspices of the Royal Institute of International Affairs. London: Oxford University Press, 1938. Rev. ed. 1957, 1968.
Halen, Pierre. "Le Congo revisité: Une décennie de bandes dessinées 'belges' (1982–1992)." *Textyles,* no. 9 (1992): 291–306.
———. "Tintin, paradigme du héros colonial belge? (à propos de 'Tintin au Congo')." In *Tintin, Hergé et la belgité* ed. Anna Soncini Fratta. Bologna: Cooperativa libraria universitaria editrice Bologna, 1994.
Hall, Edward T. *Dance of Life: The Other Dimension of Time.* Garden City, N.Y.: Anchor Press / Doubleday, 1983.
Hall, Martin. "The Proximity of Dr Bleek's Bushman." In *Miscast: Negotiating the Presence of the Bushmen,* ed. Pippa Skotnes. Cape Town: University of Cape Town Press, 1996.
Hall, Stuart. "What Is This 'Black' in Black Popular Culture?" In *Representing Blackness: Issues in Film and Video,* ed. Valerie Smith. New Brunswick, N.J.: Rutgers University Press, 1997. Originally published in Michele Wallace, *Black Popular Culture: A Project,* ed. Gina Dent (Seattle: Bay Press, 1992).

Hambly, Wilfrid D. *Serpent Worship in Africa.* Field Museum of Natural History Publication 289, Anthropological Series 21, 1. Chicago: Field Museum of Natural History, 1931. Reprint. New York: Kraus, 1968.

Hamilton, Carolyn. "Ideology, Oral Traditions and the Struggle for Power in the Early Zulu Kingdom." M.A. thesis, University of the Witswatersrand, 1986.

———. *Terrific Majesty: The Powers of Shaka Zulu and the Limits of Historical Invention.* Cambridge, Mass.: Harvard University Press, 1998.

Hammond, Dorothy, and Alta Jablow. *The Myth of Africa.* New York: Library of Social Science, 1977.

Hammond, R. S. *Portugal in Africa, 1815–1910: A Study in Uneconomic Imperialism.* Stanford, Calif.: Stanford University Press, 1966.

Hammond-Tooke, W. D. *Bhaca Society.* Cape Town: Oxford University Press, 1962.

Hannerz, Ulf. *Transnational Connections: Culture, People, Places.* New York: Routledge, 1996.

Haraway, Donna. "Remodelling the Human Way of Life: Sherwood Washburn and the New Physical Anthropology, 1950–1980." In *Bones, Bodies, and Behavior: Essays on Biological Anthropology*, ed. George Stocking Jr. Madison: University of Wisconsin, 1988.

———. "Teddy Bear Patriarchy: Taxidermy in the Garden of Eden, New York City, 1908–36." In id., *Primate Visions: Gender, Race and Nature in the World of Modern Science.* New York: Routledge, 1989.

Harries, Patrick. "Exclusion, Classification and Internal Colonialism: The Emergence of Ethnicity Among the Tsonga-Speakers of South Africa." In *The Creation of Tribalism in Southern Africa*, ed. Leroy Vail, 82–117. London: James Curry; Berkeley and Los Angeles: University of California Press, 1989.

Hartman, Wolfram, Jeremy Sylvester, and Patricia Hayes, eds. *The Colonizing Camera: Photographs in the Making of Namibia History, 1915–1950s.* Cape Town: University of Cape Town Press; Athens: Ohio University Press, 1998.

Hawkes, Terence. *Structuralism and Semiotics.* Berkeley and Los Angeles: University of California Press, 1977.

[Hay, George]. "How We Buried Sandile." *Cape Mercury,* June 12, 1878.

Headrick, Daniel. *The Tools of Empire: Technology and European Imperialism in the Nineteenth Century.* New York: Oxford University Press, 1981.

Hecht, David, and A. Maliqalim Simone. *Invisible Governance: The Art of African Micropolitics.* New York: Autonomedia, 1994.

Hendrickson, Hildi, ed. *Clothing and Difference: Embodied Identities in Colonial and Post-Colonial Africa.* Durham, N.C.: Duke University Press, 1996.

Henningsen, Amelia de. *The Reminiscences of Amelia de Henningsen: Notre mère.* Edited by Margaret Young (Sister Anne Mary, M.S.A.). Cape Town: Maskew Miller Longman, 1989.

Hergé [Georges Rémi]. *Les aventures de Tintin: Reporter du Petit "Vingtième" au Congo.* Tournai, Belgium: Casterman, 1982. Facsimile of the original edition, Brussels: Editions du Petit "Vingtième," 1931.

———. *Les aventures des Tintin: Tintin au Congo.* 1946. Paris and Tournai, Belgium: Casterman, 1974.

Herman, Paul. "Bande dessinée et Congo: De la passion au flirt discret." In *Zaïre, 1885–1985: Cent ans de regards belges.* Brussels: Coopération par Education et la Culture, 1985.

Hertz, Robert. *Death and the Right Hand.* 1906. Translated by Rodney and Claudia Needham. Introduction by E. E. Evans-Pritchard. Aberdeen (?): Cohen & West, 1960.

Hess, Catherine. "Unconventional Carving: Stools and Coconut Shells." In *The Art of Power / The Power of Art: Studies in Benin Iconography*, ed. Paula Ben-Amos and Arnold Rubin, 41–49. Los Angeles: Museum of Cultural History, 1983.
Hewitt, Roger. *Structure, Meaning and Ritual in the Narratives of the Southern San*. Quellen zur Khoisan-Forschung, 2. Hamburg: H. Buske, 1986.
Hirschberg, Walter. *Völkerkundliche Ergebnisse der südafrikanischen Reisen Rudolf Pöch's in den Jahren 1907 bis 1909*. Vienna: Anthropologischen Gesellschaft in Wien, 1936.
History of the Bosjesmans, or Bush People; The Aborigines of Southern Africa. London: Chapman Elcoate, 1847.
Hobsbawm, Eric, and Terence Ranger, eds. *The Invention of Tradition*. Cambridge: Cambridge University Press, 1986.
Hochschild, Adam. *King Leopold's Ghost: A Story of Greed, Terror and Heroism in Colonial Africa*. Boston: Houghton Mifflin, 1998.
Hodeir, Catherine. "Une journée à l'Exposition coloniale." In *Le temps des colonies*, special issue of *L'Histoire*, 69 (July 1984).
———. "Le non dit à l'Exposition coloniale." Mémoire de maîtrise, Paris I, Sorbonne, 1977.
Hodeir, Catherine, and Michel Pierre. *L'Exposition coloniale, 1931: La mémoire du siècle*. Paris: Éditions Complexe, 1991.
Hodeir, Catherine, Sylviane Leprun, and Michel Pierre. "Les expositions coloniales: Discours et images." In *Images et colonies: Iconographie et propagande coloniale sur l'Afrique française de 1880 à 1962*, ed. Nicolas Bancel et al. Nanterre: Bibliothèque de documentation internationale contemporaine; Paris: Association Connaissance de l'histoire de l'Afrique contemporaine, 1993.
Home, Robert. *City of Blood Revisited: A New Look at the Benin Expedition of 1897*. London: R. Collings, 1982.
Hountondji, Paulin J. *African Philosophy: Myth and Reality*. Translated by Henri Evans. 1983. 2d ed. With an Introduction by Abiola Irele. Bloomington: Indiana University Press, 1996.
Household, G. A., ed. *To Catch a Sunbeam: Victorian Reality through a Magic Lantern*. From the collection of L. M. H. Smith. London: Michael Joseph, 1979.
Huggan, Graham. "Postcolonialism, Anthropology, and the Magic of Mimesis." *Cultural Critique* 38 (Winter 1997–98): 91–106.
Hunt, Nancy Rose. *A Colonial Lexicon: Of Birth Ritual, Medicalization, and Mobility in the Congo*. Durham, N.C.: Duke University Press, 1999.
Hunter, Monica. *Reaction to Conquest: Effects of Contact with Europeans on the Pondo of South Africa*. London: Oxford University Press, 1936.
In/sight: African Photographers, 1940 to the Present. Catalogue of an exhibition held May 24–September 29, 1996, at the Solomon R. Guggenheim Museum. New York: Guggenheim Museum, 1996.
International Museum of Photography. *Pioneers of Photography: Their Achievements in Science and Technology*, ed. Eugene Ostroff. Proceedings of the First International Congress, Pioneers of Photographic Science and Technology, held July 22–25, 1986, at the International Museum of Photography, George Eastman House, Rochester, N.Y. Springfield, Va.: Society for Imaging Science and Technology, 1987.
Isaacson, Rupert. "Call of the Wild." *Daily Telegraph*, November 2, 1996.
Ivy, Marilyn. *Discourses of the Vanishing: Modernity, Phantasm, Japan*. Chicago: University of Chicago Press, 1995.

Jacquemin, Jean-Pierre. "BD africaine: Masques, perruques." In *L'année de la bande dessinée 86–87*, ed. Stan Berts and Thierry Groenstein. Grenoble: Éditions Glénat, 1986.

———. "Jeunes pour jeunes et compagnie . . ." In *Un dîner à Kinshasa: Concours BD 96 Bruxelles-Kinshasa*, 20–21. Brussels: Édition Ti Suka asbl, 1996.

Jahoda, Gustav. *Images of the Savage: Ancient Roots of Modern Prejudice in Western Culture*. New York: Routledge, 1999.

JanMohamed, Abdul. "The Economy of Manichean Allegory: The Function of Racial Difference in Colonialist Literature." *Critical Inquiry* 12 (1985): 59–87.

———. *Manichean Aesthetics: The Politics of Literature in Colonial Africa*. Amherst: University of Massachusetts Press, 1983.

Jannone, Christian. "Les hommes-léopards et leurs dérivés dans la bande dessinée." In *L'autre et nous: Scènes et types*, ed. Pascal Blanchard et al., 197–200. Paris: Association Connaissance de l'histoire de l'Afrique contemporaine and Syros, 1995.

Jay, Martin. "Scopic Regimes of Modernity." In *Vision and Visuality*, ed. Hal Foster. Discussions in Contemporary Culture, no. 2. Seattle: Bay Press, 1988.

Jenkins, Reese. *Images and Enterprise: Technology and the American Photographic Industry, 1839 to 1925*. Baltimore: Johns Hopkins University Press, 1975.

Jenks, Chris, ed. *Visual Culture*. New York: Routledge, 1995.

Jewsiewicki, Bogumil. "Collective Memory and Its Images: Popular Urban Painting in Zaire: A Source of 'Present Past.'" *History and Anthropology* 2, 2 (1986): 389–96.

———. "Corps interdits: La représentation christique de Lumumba comme rédempteur du peuple zaïrois." *Cahiers d'Études africaines* 36 (1–2), 141–42 (1996): 113–42.

———. "The Formation of the Political Culture of Ethnicity in the Belgian Congo, 1920–1959." In *The Creation of Tribalism in Southern Africa*, ed. Leroy Vail, 324–49. Berkeley and Los Angeles: University of California Press, 1989.

———. "Painting in Zaire: From the Invention of the West to the Representation of Social Self." In *Africa Explores: Twentieth-Century African Art*, ed. Susan Vogel, 130–51. New York: Center for African Art; Munich: Prestel-Verlag, 1991.

———. *Chéri Samba: The Hybridity of Art / L'hybridité d'un art*. Westmount, Quebec: Galerie Amrad African Art Publications, 1995.

———. "Zaïrian Popular Painting as Commodity and as Communication." In *African Material Culture*, ed. Mary Jo Arnoldi et al., 334–56. Bloomington: Indiana University Press, 1996.

Johanssen, P. E. *Ruanda: Kleine Anfänge—Grosse Aufgaben*. Bielefeld: Bethel, 1915.

Johnson, Mark. *The Body in the Mind: The Bodily Basis of Meaning, Imagination, and Reason*. Chicago: University of Chicago Press, 1987, 1990.

Johnson, Martin, and A. Blaney Percival. *Kenya Colony: Camera Studies no. 1*. Nairobi: Government Service, 1936.

Johnson, Osa. *I Married Adventure*. New York: Lippincott, 1940.

Johnston, Harry H., Sir. *British Central Africa: An Attempt to Give Some Account of a Portion of the Territories under British Influence North of the Zambesi*. London: Methuen, 1897.

———. *The Uganda Protectorate: An Attempt to Give Some Description of the Physical Geography, Botany, Zoology, Anthropology, Languages and History of the Territories under British Protection in East Central Africa, between the Congo Free State and the Rift Valley and between the First Degree of South Latitude and the Fifth Degree of North Latitude*. London: Hutchinson, 1902.

Jones, Anna Laura. "Exploding Canons: The Anthropology of Museums." *Annual Review of Anthropology* 22 (1993): 201–20.

"Journal of an Officer Serving in Kaffirland from the Outbreak of the Present War." Part 3. *United Services Magazine*, 1851: 30–34.

Jules-Rosette, Bennetta. *The Messages of Tourist Art: An African Semiotic System in Comparative Perspective.* New York: Plenum Press, 1984.

Jullian, Philippe. *The Orientalists: European Painters of Eastern Scenes.* Translated by Helga Harrison and Dinah Harrison. Oxford: Phaidon, 1977.

Junod, Henri. *The Life of a South African Tribe.* 2 vols. 1912–13. 2d ed. New Hyde Park, N.Y.: University Books, 1962.

Kalibiona, Maurice. *Marie reine de la paix.* Louvain-la-Neuve, Belgium: Éditions du Moustier, 1989.

———. *Le triomphe du Coeur Immaculé de Marie.* Marquain, Belgium: Éditions Hovine, 1993.

Kaplan, Daile. "Enlightened Women in Darkened Lands: A Lantern Slide Lecture." *Studies in the Anthropology of Visual Communication* 10, 1 (1984): 61–77.

Kasfir, Sidney. "African Art and Authenticity: A Text with a Shadow." *African Arts* 25, 2 (1992): 41–53.

———. "Cast, Miscast, The Curators's Dilemma." *African Arts* 30, 1 (1997): 1–9.

Kaspin, Deborah D. "Chewa Visions and Revisions of Power: Transformations of the Nyau Dance in Central Malawi." In *Modernity and Its Malcontents: Ritual and Power in Postcolonial Africa*, ed. Jean Comaroff and John Comaroff, 34–57. Chicago: University of Chicago Press, 1993.

———. "On Ethnographic Authority and the Tourist Trade: Anthropology in the House of Mirrors." *Anthropological Quarterly* 70, 2 (1997): 53–57.

———. "Kings into Commoners: The Reinvention of Chiefship in Central Malawi." MS.

Keegan, Timothy. *Colonial South Africa and the Origins of the Racial Order.* Cape Town: David Philip, 1996.

Keller, Janet Dixon. "Schemes for Schemata." In *New Directions in Psychological Anthropology*, ed. Theodore Schwartz, Geoffrey M. White, and Catherine A. Lutz. New York: Cambridge University Press, 1992.

Kenyatta, Jomo. *Facing Mount Kenya: The Tribal Life of the Gikuyu.* New York: Vintage Books, 1965.

Key, Wilson Bryan. *The Clam-Plate Orgy, and Other Subliminal Techniques for Manipulating Your Behavior.* Englewood Cliffs, N.J.: Prentice-Hall, 1980.

Kidd, Dudley. *The Essential Kafir.* 1904. 2d ed., London: A. & C. Black, 1925.

King, Captain W. R. *Campaigning in Kaffirland.* London: Saunders & Otley, 1853.

Kirby, Percival R. "The Hottentot Venus." *Afrikaner Notes and News* 6, 3 (1949): 55–62.

Knight-Bruce, G. W. H. *Memories of Mashonaland.* London: Edward Arnold, 1895.

Knox, John. *The Races of Men: A Philosophical Inquiry into the Influence of Race over the Destinies of Nations.* London: Renshaw, 1862.

Kolb, Peter. *Description du Cap de Bonne-Esperance.* Amsterdam: Jean Catuffe, 1741.

Kozain, Rustum. "Miscast." *South African Review of Books* 44 (1996): 14–15.

Kramer, Fritz. *The Red Fez: Art and Spirit Possession in Africa.* Translated by Malcolm Green. New York: Verso, 1993.

Krauss, Rosalind E. "The Discursive Space of Photography." In *The Contest of Meaning: Critical Histories of Photography*, ed. Richard Bolton. Cambridge, Mass.: MIT Press, 1989.

———. *The Originality of the Avant Garde and Other Modernist Myths.* Cambridge, Mass.: MIT Press, 1985.

Krige, Eileen Jensen. *The Social System of the Zulus.* Pietermaritzburg: Shuter & Shooter, 1950.
Krige, Eileen Jensen, and Jacob D. Krige. *The Realm of a Rain Queen: A Study of the Pattern of Lovedu Society.* London: Oxford University Press, 1943.
Kukertz, Heinz. *Creating Order: The Image of the Homestead in Mpondo Social Life.* Johannesburg: Witwatersrand University Press, 1990.
Kuklick, Henrika. "Tribal Exemplars: Images of Political Authority in British Anthropology, 1885–1945." In *Functionalism Historicized: Essays on British Social Anthropology,* ed. George W. Stocking, 2: 59–82. Madison: University of Wisconsin Press, 1984.
Laband, John. *Rope of Sand: The Rise and Fall of the Zulu Kingdom in the Nineteenth Century.* Johannesburg: Jonathan Ball, 1995.
Lakeman, Sir Stephen. *What I Saw in Kaffirland.* Edinburgh: Blackwood & Sons, 1880.
Lalvani, Suren. *Photography, Vision, and the Production of Modern Bodies.* Albany: State University of New York Press, 1996.
Landau, Paul S. "George Eastman on Safari: The Camera and the Lumbwa Lion Hunter in Tanzania, July 1928." Forthcoming.
———. "Hunting with Gun and Camera." In *The Colonising Camera: Photographs in the Making of Namibian History,* ed. Wolfram Hartmann, Jeremy Sylvester, and Patricia Hayes, 151–55. Cape Town: University of Cape Town Press; Athens: Ohio University Press, 1999.
———. "The Illumination of Christ in the Kalahari Desert." *Representations* 45 (Winter 1994): 25–39.
———. *The Realm of the Word: Language, Gender, and Christianity in a Southern African Kingdom.* Portsmouth, N.H.: Heinemann, 1995.
———. "The Samuelites of Southern Africa: Colonialism and the Displacement of the Self." MS.
———. "With Camera and Gun in South Africa: Constructing the Image of Bushmen, ca. 1880–1940." In *Miscast: Negotiating the Presence of Bushmen,* ed. Pippa Skotnes, 129–41. Cape Town: University of Cape Town Press, 1996.
Landow, George P. "William Holman Hunt's 'Oriental Mania' and His Uffizi *Self-Portrait.*" *Art Bulletin* 64, 4 (1982): 647–55.
Landsberg, Steve. "The $10 Billion Man." *New York Times,* January 24, 1999, A21.
Lane, Paul. "Breaking the Mould? Exhibiting Khoisan in Southern African Museums." *Anthropology Today,* 12, 5 (1996): 3–10.
Larkin, Brian. "Indian Films and Nigerian Lovers: Media and the Creation of Parallel Modernities." *Africa* 67, 3 (1997): 406–40.
Lasekan, Akinola. "Problems of Contemporary African Artists." *Kurio Africana: Journal of Art Criticism* (Ile-Ife, Nigeria) 1, 1 (1989): 24–37.
Lawal, Kunle. "Britain and Nationalists' Conflicts in Nigeria in the Age of Transfer of Power: 1948 to 1960." African Studies Association conference paper, 1992.
Lebzelter, Viktor. *Eingeborenenkulturen in Südwest- und Südafrika wissenschaftliche Ergebnisse einer Forschungsreise nach Süd- und Südwestafrika in den Jahren 1926–1928.* Leipzig: Karl W. Hiersemann, 1934.
Legendre, Sidney. *Okavango, The Desert River.* New York: J. Messner, 1939.
Lembede, Anton Muziwakhe. *Freedom in Our Lifetime: The Collected Writings of Anton Muziwakhe Lembede.* Edited by Robert R. Edgar and Luyanda ka Msumza. Athens: Ohio University Press, 1996.

Leprun, Sylviane. "Paysages de la France extérieure: La mise en scène des colonies à l'Exposition du centenaire." In *Mise en scène et vulgarisation: L'Exposition universelle de 1889*, special issue of *Le Mouvement Social*, ed. Madeleine Rébérioux, October–December 1989.
———. *Le théâtre des colonies: Scénographie, acteurs et discours de l'imaginaire dans les expositions, 1855–1937*. Paris: L'Harmattan, 1986.
Lewis-Williams, J. David. *Believing and Seeing: Symbolic Meanings in Southern San Rock Paintings*. New York: Academic Press, 1981.
Leyder, Jean. *Le graphisme et l'expression graphique au Congo belge*. Brussels: Société royale belge de Géographie, 1950.
Linares, Olga F. *Power, Prayer and Production: The Jola of Casamance, Senegal*. Cambridge: Cambridge University Press, 1992.
Lindfors, Bernth, ed. *Africans on Stage: Studies in Ethnological Show Business*. Bloomington: Indiana University Press, 1999.
Lips, Julius E. *The Savage Hits Back*. Translated from the German by Vincent Benson. 1937; New Hyde Park, N.Y.: University Books, 1966.
Liu, Alan. *Wordsworth: The Sense of History*. Stanford, Calif.: Stanford University Press, 1989.
Livingstone, David. *The Zambezi Expedition of David Livingstone, 1858–1863*. London: Chatto & Windus, 1956.
Lothrup, Eaton S., Jr. *A Century of Cameras (From the Collection of the International Museum of Photography at George Eastman House)*. New York: Morgan & Morgan, 1982.
Lovejoy, Paul. *Transformations in Slavery: A History of Slavery in Africa*. Cambridge: Cambridge University Press, 1983.
Low, David. *A Cartoon History of Our Times*. New York: Simon & Schuster, 1939.
Lowe, Christopher. "Swaziland's Colonial Politics: The Decline of Progressive South African Nationalism and the Emergence of Swazi Political Traditionalism, 1910–1939." Ph.D. diss., Yale University, 1998.
Luard, Nicholas. *The Last Wilderness: A Journey across the Great Kalahari Desert*. New York: Simon & Schuster, 1981.
Luschan, Felix von. *Die Altertümer von Benin*. 3 vols. Berlin: Vereinigung wissenschaftlicher Verleger, 1919. Reprint. New York: Hacker Art Books, 1968.
Lüsebrink, Hans-Jürgen. " 'Le Congo belge s'ouvre à la littérature': Impact et contexte historique des concours littéraires de *La vox du Congolais* en 1940–1951." In *Littératures de Congo-Zaïre: Actes du colloque international de Bayreuth, 22–24 juillet 1993*, ed. Pierre Halen and Janos Riesz. *Matatu* 13–14. Amsterdam: Rodopi, 1995.
Lutz, Catherine, and Jane Collins. *Reading National Geographic*. Chicago: University of Chicago Press, 1993.
Lyall, Archibald. *Black and White Make Brown: An Account of a Journey to Cape Verde and Portuguese Guinea*. London: Heinemann, 1938.
Lyall, Sarah. "Diana's Hunters: How Quarry Was Stalked." *New York Times*, September 10, 1997, 1.
Lyman, Christopher. *The Vanishing Race and Other Illusions: Photographs of Indians by Edward S. Curtis*. New York: Pantheon Books, 1982.
MacCannell, Dean. *Empty Meeting Grounds: The Tourist Papers*. New York: Routledge, 1992.
———. *The Tourist: A New Theory of the Leisure Class*. New York: Schocken Books, 1976.
MacGaffey, Wyatt. "Dialogues of the Deaf: Europeans on the Atlantic Coast of Africa." In *Implicit Understandings: Observing, Reporting, and Reflecting on the Encounters Between Europeans*

and Other Peoples in the Early Modern Era, ed. Stuart Schwartz, 249–67. Cambridge: Cambridge University Press, 1994.

———. "Zamenga of Zaire: Novelist, Historian, Sociologist, Philosopher, and Moralist." *Research in African Literatures* 13 (1982): 208–15.

Mackay, James. *Reminiscences of the Last Kafir War.* Grahamstown: Richards, Glanvile & Co., 1871.

MacKenzie, John M. "Chivalry, Social Darwinism and Ritualized Killing: the Hunting Ethos in Central Africa up to 1914." In *Conservation in Africa: People, Policies and Practice,* ed. David Anderson and Richard Grove, 41–62. Cambridge: Cambridge University Press, 1987.

———. *The Empire of Nature: Hunting, Conservation and British Imperialism.* Manchester: Manchester University Press, 1988.

———, ed. *Imperialism and Popular Culture.* Manchester: Manchester University Press, 1986.

Magnin, André. "Seydou Keita." *African Arts* 28, 3 (1995): 90–95.

Malhotra, R. *Manege Frei: Artisten- und Circusplakate von Adolf Friedlander.* Dortmund: Harenberg Kommunikation, 1979.

Malkki, Liisa H. *Purity and Exile: Violence, Memory, and National Cosmology among Hutu Refugees in Tanzania.* Chicago: University of Chicago Press, 1995.

Malti-Douglas, Fedwa, and Allan Douglas. *L'idéologie par la bande: Héros politiques de France et d'Egypte au miroir de la BD.* Cairo: Centre d'études et de documentation économique, juridique et sociale, 1987.

Mamdani, Mahmood. *Citizen and Subject: Contemporary Africa and the Legacy of Late Colonialism.* Princeton, N.J.: Princeton University Press, 1996.

Mandel, Ernest. *Delightful Murder: A Social History of the Crime Story.* Minneapolis: University of Minnesota Press, 1984.

Manning, Patrick. *Slavery and African Life.* Cambridge: Cambridge University Press, 1990.

Maquet, Jacques J. *Le système des relations sociales dans le Rwanda ancien.* Tervuren, Belgium: Musée royale du Congo belge, 1954.

Mark, Peter. *Africans in European Eyes: The Portrayal of Black Africans in Fourteenth- and Fifteenth-Century Europe.* Foreign and Comparative Studies: Eastern Africa, 16. Syracuse, N.Y.: Maxwell School of Citizenship and Public Affairs, Syracuse University, 1974.

Markoff, John. "An Internet Pioneer Ponders the Next Revolution: Talking the Future with Robert W. Taylor." *New York Times,* December 20, 1999, C38.

Marks, Shula. *The Ambiguities of Dependence in South Africa: Class, Nationalism, and the State in Twentieth-Century Natal.* Baltimore: Johns Hopkins University Press, 1986.

———. "Rewriting South African History; or, The Hunt For Hintsa's Head." University of Natal History Seminar paper, April 1996.

Maroun, J. E. "Second Address, 'Bantu Market' Session." In *Third Advertising Convention in South Africa: The Challenge of a Decade.* Johannesburg: Statistic Holdings Ltd., 1960.

Martirossiantz, Anouche. "L'Afrique centrale vue par la bande dessinée: Notes de lecture." In *Papier blanc, encre noire: Cent ans de culture francophone en Afrique centrale (Zaïre, Rwanda, et Burundi),* vol. 2, ed. Marc Quaghebeur, E. van Balberghe, et al. Brussels: Éditions Labor, 1992.

Marzio, Peter. *The Democratic Art: Chromolithography, 1840–1900.* Boston: D. R. Godine, in association with the Amon Carter Museum of Western Art, Fort Worth, 1979.

Masagha [Masogha], Joseph. "South African Agent." *Negro World,* September 27, 1924.

Mata Masala, Catherine M. "Zamenga Batukezanga: Anatomie d'un succès populaire." In *Littératures de Congo-Zaïre: Actes du colloque international de Bayreuth, 22–24 juillet 1993,* ed. Pierre Halen and Janos Riesz. *Matatu* 13/14. Amsterdam: Rodopi, 1995.

Maurois, André. *Sur le vif: L'Exposition coloniale.* Paris: E. Dentu, 1931.

Maxwell-Mahon, W. D. "Lucy Catherine Lloyd." *Dictionary of South African Biography,* 4: 315–16. Pretoria: Nationale Boekhandel, 1981.

Mba, Nina E. "Olufunmilayo Ransome-Kuti." In *Nigerian Women in Historical Perspective,* ed. Bolanle Awe, 133–48. Lagos: Sankore Publishers; Ibadan: Bookcraft, 1992.

Mbembe, Achille. "The 'Thing' and Its Doubles in Cameroonian Cartoons." In *Readings in African Popular Culture,* ed. Karin Barber, 151–63. Bloomington: University of Indiana Press, 1997.

McCall, Daniel, and Edna Bay, eds. *African Images: Essays in African Iconology.* New York: Africana Pub. Co., for the African Studies Center, Boston University, 1975.

McClintock, Anne. *Imperial Leather: Race, Gender, and Sexuality in the Colonial Contest.* New York: Routledge, 1995.

McCloud, Scott. *Understanding Comics: The Invisible Art.* Northampton, Mass.: Kitchen Sink Press, 1993. New York: HarperPerennial, 1994.

McCracken, Grant. *Culture and Consumption: New Approaches to the Symbolic Character of Consumer Goods and Activities.* Bloomington: Indiana University Press, 1988.

McCulloch, Jock. *Colonial Psychiatry and the "African Mind."* Cambridge: Cambridge University Press, 1995.

McCully, Marilyn. "The Fallen Angel?" Review of *The Picasso Papers,* by Rosalind E. Krauss. *New York Review of Books,* April 8, 1999, 18–24.

McKenzie, Ray. " 'The Laboratory of Mankind': John McCosh and the Beginnings of Photography in British India." *History of Photography* 11, 2 (1987): 109–18.

McLuhan, Marshall. *The Gutenberg Galaxy: The Making of Typographic Man.* Toronto: University of Toronto Press, 1962.

Medhurst, Martin J., and Michael A. DeSousa. "Political Cartoons as Rhetorical Form: A Taxonomy of Graphic Discourse," *Communication Monographs* 48, 3 (September 1981): 197–236.

Meireles, Artur Martins de. "Baiu (Gentes de Kaiu) I—Generalidades." *Boletim Cultural da Guiné Portuguesa* 3, 11 (1948): 607–38.

———. "Baiu (Gentes de Kaiu) II—Kambaxe." *Boletim Cultural da Guiné Portuguesa* 4, 1 (1949): 7–27.

———. *Mutilações étnicas dos Manjacos.* Publicações do Centro de Estudos da Guiné Portuguesa: Memórias, 22. Bissau, 1960.

Melzian, Hans. *A Concise Dictionary of the Bini Language of Southern Nigeria.* London: Kegan Paul, Trench, Trubner & Co., 1937.

Mendes-Pinto, Maria Helena. Introduction and captions, *Os descobrimentos portugueses e a Europa do Renascimento.* Catalogue of the XVII Exposição Europeia de Arte, Ciencia e Cultura in Lisbon. Lisbon: Mosteiro Dos Jeronimos, 1983.

Merleau-Ponty, Maurice. *The Prose of the World.* Edited by Claude Lefort. Translated by John O'Neill. Evanston, Ill.: Northwestern University Press, 1973.

Messaris, Paul. *Visual Persuasion: The Role of Images in Advertising.* Thousand Oaks, Calif.: Sage Publications, 1997.

Mfumu'eto. "Nguma ameli Muasi na Kati ya Kinshasa." *Mensuel de Bandes dessinées* 1, no. 1 (April 1990). Kinshasa: Éditions Mpangala Original and Offest MGS.

———. "Nguma ameli Muasi na Kati ya Kinshasa." *Mensuel de Bandes dessinées et de détente* 1, Super Spécial Choc no. 2 ([May?] 1990). Kinshasa: Offest MGS and Union Chrétienne, Le journal des petits pour l'éducation et le savoir vivre.

Middleton, John. "Lugbara Death." In *Death and the Regeneration of Life*, ed. Maurice Bloch and Jonathan Parry, 134–54. Cambridge: Cambridge University Press, 1982.

Miller, Christopher. *Blank Darkness: Africanist Discourse in French*. Chicago: University of Chicago Press, 1985.

———. *Theories of Africans: Francophone Literature and Anthropology in Africa*. Chicago: University of Chicago Press, 1990.

Miller, Joseph C. "History and Africa / Africa and History." *American Historical Review* 104, 1 (1999): 1–32.

———. *Way of Death: Merchant Capitalism and the Angolan Slave Trade, 1730–1830*. Madison: University of Wisconsin, 1988.

Mills, Lady Dorothy. *The Golden Land: A Record of Travel in West Africa*. London: Duckworth, 1929.

Mitchell, Timothy. "The World as Exhibition." *Comparative Studies in Society and History* 31 (1989): 217–36.

Mitchell, W. J. T. *Iconology: Image, Text, Ideology*. Chicago: University of Chicago Press, 1986.

Mkele, Nimrod. *Advertising to the Bantu: Second Advertising Convention in South Africa*. Durban: Society of Advertisers, 1959.

Moliterni, Claude, Philippe Mellot, and Michel Denni. *Les aventures de la BD*. Paris: Découvertes Gallimard, 1996.

Monk, Ray. *Ludwig Wittgenstein: The Duty of Genius*. New York: Free Press, 1990.

Monod, Eugène. *L'Exposition universelle de 1889: Grand Ouvrage illustré historique, encyclopédique, descriptif*. 2 vols. Paris: E. Dentu, 1890.

Montaigne, Michel de. "Of Cannibals." Essay 31 in Montaigne, *Complete Essays*, trans. Donald M. Frame, 150–59. Stanford, Calif.: Stanford University Press, 1958.

Moorman, Marissa. "Film, Gender and the Nation in Postcolonial Angola: On the Possibilities of Cinema as an Historical Source." Forthcoming.

Morphet, Anthony. "Miscast." *Pretexts: Studies in Writing and Culture* 6, 1 (1997): 95–99.

Mostert, Noël. *Frontiers: The Epic of South Africa's Creation and the Tragedy of the Xhosa People*. New York: Knopf, 1992.

Mota, A. Teixeira da. *Guiné Portuguesa*. 2 vols. Lisbon: Agencia Geral do Ultramar, 1954.

———. *Inquérito etnográfico, organizado pelo governo da colónia no ano de 1946*. Bissau, 1947.

Mount, Marshall W. *African Art: The Years since 1920*. 1973. Bloomington: University of Indiana Press, 1989.

Mphahlele, Ezekiel. *Down Second Avenue*. New York: Anchor Books, 1971.

Mudimbe, V. Y. *The Idea of Africa*. Bloomington: Indiana University Press, 1994.

———. *The Invention of Africa: Gnosis, Philosophy, and the Order of Knowledge*. Bloomington: Indiana University Press, 1988.

———. *The Surreptitious Speech*: Présence africaine *and the Politics of Otherness, 1947–1987*. Chicago: University of Chicago Press, 1992.

Munn, Nancy D. "Excluded Spaces: The Figure in Australian Aboriginal Landscape." *Critical Inquiry* 22 (Spring 1996): 446–65.

Museu da Guiné Portuguesa. *Catálogo-inventário da Secção de Etnografia do Museu da Guiné Portuguesa*. Por José D. Lampreia. Lisbon: Junta de Investigações do Ultramar, 1962.

Museum für Völkerkunde Dresden. *Benin: Europäerdarstellungen der Hofkunst eines afrikanischen Reiches, aus dem Staatlichen Museum für Völkerkunde Dresden.* Die Schatzkammer, 28, Edited by Siegfried Wolf. Leipzig: Prisma-Verlag, 1972.

Mustafa, Hudita. "Practicing Beauty: Crisis, Value and the Challenge of Self-Mastery in Dakar, 1970–1994." Ph.D. diss., Harvard University, 1998.

Nasson, Bill. " 'She preferred living in a cave with Harry the snake-catcher': Toward an Oral History of Popular Leisure and Class Expression in District Six, Cape Town, c. 1920s–1950s." In *Holding Their Ground: Class, Locality and Culture in Nineteenth- and Twentieth-Century South Africa*, ed. Philip Bonner, 285–306. Johannesburg: Ravan Press, 1989.

Nederven-Pieterse, Jan. *White on Black: Images of Africa and Blacks in Western Popular Culture.* New Haven, Conn.: Yale University Press, 1992.

Newbury, David. "Understanding Genocide." *African Studies Review* 41, 1 (1998): 73–97.

Ngubane, Harriet. *Body and Mind in Zulu Medicine.* London: Academic Press, 1977.

Nicol, Mike. *A Good-Looking Corpse.* London: Secker & Warburg, 1991.

Niemeyer, G. *Hagenbeck.* Hamburg: H. Christians Press, 1972.

Nochlin, Linda. "The Imaginary Orient." *Art in America*, May 1993, 127–39.

Notcutt, L. A., and G. C. Latham. *The African and the Cinema: An Account of the Work of the Bantu Educational Cinema Experiment during the Period March 1935 to May 1937.* London: Edinburgh House Press for the International Missionary Council, 1937.

Ofoegbu, Ray. "Azikiwe's Intellectual Origins." In *Azikiwe and the African Revolution*, ed. Michael S. O. Olisa and Odinchezo M. Ikejiani-Clark, 53–71. Onitsha: African-Fep Publishers, 1989.

Okeke, Uche. "History of Modern Nigerian Art." *Nigeria Magazine* 128–129 (1979): 100–118.

Okpewho, Isidore. *Once upon a Kingdom: Myth, Hegemony, and Identity.* Bloomington: Indiana University Press, 1998.

Oldevig, Margareta. *The Sunny Land.* Cape Town: Howard Timmins, 1944.

Olisa, M. S. O. "Azikiwe's Political Ideas: The Dream of the African Revolution." In *Azikiwe and the African Revolution*, ed. id. and Odinchezo M. Ikejiani-Clark, 72–89. Onitsha: African-Fep Publishers, 1989.

Omu, Fred I. A. *Press and Politics in Nigeria, 1880–1937.* Atlantic Highlands, N.J.: Humanities Press, 1978.

Onishi, Norimitsu. "Tintin at 70: Colonialism's Comic-Book Puppet?" *New York Times*, Friday, January 8, 1999, A4.

Ouedraogo, Jean-Bernard. "La figuration photographique des identites sociales: Valeurs et apparences au Burkino Faso." *Cahiers d'Études africaines* 141–42 (1996): 25–50.

———. "Scénographie d'une conquête: Enquête sur la vision plastique d'un colonial." *Cahiers du LERSCO: Iconographie et Sociologie* (1991).

Pacher, Helga Maria. *Anthropologische Untersuchungen an den Skeletten der Rudolf Pöch'schen Buschmannsammlung.* Graz: H. Böhlaus, 1961.

Pagden, Anthony. *The Fall of Natural Man: The American Indian and the Origins of Comparative Ethnology.* New York: Cambridge University Press, 1982.

Palmié, Stephan. *Wizards and Scientists: Explorations in Afro-Cuban Modernity and Tradition.* Durham, N.C.: Duke University Press, 2002.

Panofsky, Erwin. "Die Perspektive als 'symbolischen Form.' " *Vorträge der Bibliothek Warburg* 4 (1924–25): 258–331.

Parker, Andrew, Mary Russo, Doris Sommer, and Patricia Yaeger, eds. *Nationalisms and Sexualities.* New York: Routledge, 1992.

Paster, James E. "Advertising Immortality by Kodak." *History of Photography* 16, 2 (1992): 135–39.
Pateman, Carol. *The Disorder of Women: Democracy, Feminism, and Political Theory.* Cambridge: Polity Press, 1989.
Patterson, James. "Africa on Film." *African Research and Documentation* 68 (1995): 75–79.
Peacock, Shane. *The Great Farini: The High-Wire Life of William Hunt.* Toronto: Viking, 1995.
Pedler, Frederick. *The Lion and the Unicorn in Africa: A History of the Origins of the United Africa Company, 1787–1931.* London: Heinemann, 1974.
Peeters, Benoît. *Tintin and the World of Hergé.* London: Metheun, 1989.
Peirce, Charles S. "The Icon, Index, and Symbol." In *Collected Papers of Charles Sanders Peirce,* ed. Charles Hartshorne and Paul Weiss, vol. 2. 8 vols. Cambridge, Mass.: Harvard University Press, 1931–58.

———. *The Philosophy of Peirce: Selected Writings.* Edited by Justus Buchler. New York: Harcourt, Brace, 1940.

Peires, J. B. *The Dead Will Arise: Nongqawuse and the Great Xhosa Cattle-Killing Movement of 1856–7.* Johannesburg: Ravan Press; Bloomington: Indiana University Press, 1989.
Pemberton, John. *On the Subject of "Java."* Ithaca, N.Y.: Cornell University Press, 1994.
Penn, Nigel G. "'Fated to Perish': The Destruction of the Cape San." In *Miscast: Negotiating the Presence of the Bushmen,* ed. Pippa Skotnes. Cape Town: University of Cape Town Press, 1996.

———. "The Northern Cape Frontier Zone, 1700–c. 1815." Ph.D. diss., University of Cape Town, 1995.

———. "The /Xam and the Colony, 1740–1870." In *Sounds from the Thinking Strings,* ed. Pippa Skotnes. Cape Town: Axeage, 1991.

Perchuk, Andrew, and Helaine Posner, eds. *The Masculine Masquerade: Masculinity and Representation.* Catalog of an exhibition at the MIT List Visual Arts Center, January 21–March 26, 1995. Cambridge, Mass.: MIT Press, 1995.
Percival, A. Blayney. *A Game Ranger's Note Book.* London: Windham, 1924.
Pereira, Rui. "A antropologia aplicada na politica colonial portuguesa do Estado Novo." *Revista Internacional de Estudos Africanos* 4–5 (1986): 193–206.

———. "Colonialismo e antropologia: A especulação simbolica." *Revista Internacional de Estudos Africanos,* 10–11 (1989), 269–81.

Perham, Margery. *Lugard,* vol 1: *The Years of Adventure, 1858–1898;* vol. 2: *The Years of Authority, 1898–1945.* 1956. Reprint. Hamden, Conn., Archon Books, 1968.

———. *Ten Africans.* London: Faber & Faber, 1936.

The Periplus Maris Erythraei: Text with Introduction, Translation, and Commentary. Translated and annotated by Lionel Casson. Princeton, N.J.: Princeton University Press, 1989.
Peterson, Harold L., ed. *Encyclopedia of Firearms.* New York: Dutton, 1964.
Phillips, David. "Art for Industry's Sake: Halftone Technology, Mass Photography and the Social Transformation of American Print Culture, 1880–1920." Ph.D. diss., Yale University, 1996.
Phillips, Ruth B., and Christopher B. Steiner, eds. *Unpacking Culture: Art and Commodity in the Colonial and Postcolonial Worlds.* Berkeley and Los Angeles: University of California Press, 1999.
Picart, Bernard. *Ceremonies et coutumes religieuses de peuples idolatres representées par des figures dessinées de la main de Bernard Picard.* Amsterdam: J. F. Bernard, 1729. Translated as *The Ceremonies and Religious Customs of the Various Nations of the Known World; Together with Historical Annotations, and Several Curious Discourses . . .* 7 vols. (London: Claude Du Bosc, 1733–39).

Pierre, Michel. "Un certain rêve africain." *Cahiers de la bande dessinée,* no. 56 (February–March 1984): 83–86.
Pietz, William. "The Problem of the Fetish, I." *Res* 9 (1985): 5–17.
———. "The Problem of the Fetish, II: The Origin of the Fetish." *Res* 13 (1987): 23–45.
———. "The Problem of the Fetish, IIIa: Bosman's Guinea and the Enlightenment Theory of Fetishism." *Res* 16 (1988): 105–23.
Pifer, Drury L. *Innocents in Africa: An American Family's Story.* New York: Harcourt Brace, 1994.
Pila, Ulysse. *À l'Exposition universelle de Lyon: Livre d'or.* Lyon: A. H. Storck, 1894.
Pinney, Christopher. "Colonial Anthropology in the 'Laboratory of Mankind.'" In *The Raj: India and the British, 1600–1947,* exhibition catalogue, ed. Christopher A. Bayly. London: National Portrait Gallery, 1991.
Pontalis, J. B. *Frontiers in Psycholanalysis: Between the Dream and Psychic Pain.* Translated by Catherine Cullen and Philip Cullen. New York: International Universities Press, 1981.
Ponte, Luiz Nunes da. *A campanha da Guiné (1908): Breve narrativa.* Porto: Empreza Guedes, 1909.
Post, Laurens van der. *The Lost World of the Kalahari.* Harmondsworth, U.K.: Penguin Books, 1958.
Postman, Neil. *Amusing Ourselves to Death: Public Discourse in the Age of Show Business.* New York: Viking, 1985.
Pratt, Mary Louise. "Fieldwork in Common Places." In *Writing Culture: The Poetics and Politics of Ethnography,* ed. James Clifford and George Marcus, 27–50. Berkeley and Los Angeles: University of California Press, 1986.
———. *Imperial Eyes: Travel Writing and Transculturation.* London: Routledge, 1992.
Price, Sally. *Primitive Art in Civilized Places.* Chicago: University of Chicago Press, 1989.
Pringle, Thomas. *Poems Illustrative of South Africa.* 1834. Edited by John Robert Wahl. Cape Town: C. Struik, 1970.
Prins, Gwyn. "The Battle for Control of the Camera in Late Nineteenth-Century Western Zambia." *African Affairs* 89 (January 1990): 97–106.
Prochaska, David. "Fantasy of the Photothèque: French Postcard Views of Colonial Senegal." *African Arts* 24, 4 (1991): 40–47, 98.
Quintino, Fernando Rogado. "A pintura e a escultura na Guiné Portuguesa." *Boletim Cultural da Guiné Portuguesa* 19, 75 (1964): 277–89.
———. *Prática e utensilagem agrícolas na Guiné.* Lisbon: Junta de Investigações do Ultramar, 1971.
Rabb, Theodore K., and Jonathan Brown. "Image and Text." *Journal of Interdisciplinary History* 17, 1 (Summer 1986): 1–6.
Radhakrishnan, R. "Nationalism, Gender, and the Narrative of Identity." In *Nationalisms and Sexualities,* ed. Andrew Parker et al., 77–95. New York: Routledge, 1992.
Ramirez, Francis, and Christian Rolot. *Histoire du cinema colonial au Zaïre, au Rwanda et au Burundi.* Tervuren, Belgium: Musée royale de l'Afrique centrale, 1985.
Ranger, Terence. "'Great Spaces Washed with Sun': The Matopos and Uluru Compared." In *Text, Theory, Space: Land, Literature, and History in South Africa and Australia,* ed. Kate Darian-Smith et al., 157–71. New York: Routledge, 1996.
———. "Taking Hold of the Land: Holy Places and Pilgrimages in Twentieth-Century Zimbabwe." Paper presented at conference on "Culture and Consciousness in Southern Africa," September 1986.

Ranger, Terence, and Olufemi Vaughan, eds. *Legitimacy and the State in Twentieth-Century Africa: Essays in Honour of A. H. M. Kirk-Greene.* Basingstoke, U.K.: Macmillan, in association with St. Antony's College, Oxford, 1993.

Rankin, A. M., and P. J. Philip. "An Epidemic of Laughing in the Bukoba District of Tanganyika." *Central African Journal of Medicine* 9, 5 (May 1963): 167–70.

Rapport général de l'Exposition coloniale et internationale de Paris, 1931. Presented by Governor-General Olivier. 7 tomes, 9 vols. Paris: Imprimerie nationale, 1933–34.

Rassool, Ciraj, and Leslie Witz. "South Africa: A World in One Country: Moments in International Tourist Encounters with Wildlife, the Primitive and the Modern." *Cahiers d'Études Africaines* 143 (1996): 24–58.

Rassool, Ciraj, and Patricia Hayes. "Gendered Science, Gendered Spectacle: /Khanako's South Africa, 1936–37." MS, 1997.

Ravenhill, Philip R. "Baulé Statuary Art: Meaning and Modernization." *Working Papers in the Traditional Arts*, 5 and 6. Philadelphia: Institute for the Study of Human Issues, 1980.

Read, C. H., and O. M. Dalton. *Antiquities of the City of Benin and from Other Parts of West Africa in the British Museum.* London: William Clowes & Sons, 1899.

Reis, A. P. van der. *The Response of Urban Blacks to Colours.* Pretoria: Bureau of Market Research, 1980.

Rema, Henrique Pinto. "O Centro de Estudos da Guiné Portuguesa lembra 25 anos de existencia." *Boletim Cultural da Guiné Portuguesa* 26, 101 (1971): 21–61.

Riccio, Thomas. "N!ngongiao: People Come Out of Here." *TheatreForum* 10, 1 (1997): 45–59.

Richards, Paul. *Fighting for the Rain Forest: War, Youth and Resources in Sierra Leone.* Portsmouth, N.H.: Heinemann, 1996.

Richards, Thomas. *The Commodity Culture of Victorian England.* Stanford, Calif.: Stanford University Press, 1990.

Ricoeur, Paul. *Oneself as Another.* Translated by Kathleen Blamey. Chicago: University of Chicago Press, 1992.

Riis, Jacob A. *How the Other Half Lives: Studies among the Tenements of New York.* 1890. New York: Penguin Books, 1997.

Ritvo, Harriet. *The Animal Estate: The English and Other Creatures in the Victorian Age.* Cambridge, Mass.: Harvard University Press, 1987.

Rivet, Paul. *Congrès international de l'évolution culturelle des peuples coloniaux.* Paris: Protat frères, 1938.

Roberts, Andrew. "The Imperial Mind." In *The Colonial Moment in Africa: Essays on the Movement of Minds and Materials, 1900–1940*, ed. id., 24–76. Cambridge: Cambridge University Press, 1990.

———. "Review Article: Photographs and African History." *Journal of African History* 29, 2 (1988): 301–11.

———, ed. *Photographs as Sources for African History: Papers Presented at a Workshop Held at the School of Oriental and African Studies, London, May 12–13, 1988.* London: SOAS, 1988.

Rodney, Walter. *How Europe Underdeveloped Africa.* Washington, D.C.: Howard University Press, 1972.

Rony, Fatimah Tobing. *The Third Eye: Race, Cinema, and Ethnographic Spectacle.* Durham, N.C.: Duke University Press, 1996.

Rose, Walter. *Bushman, Whale and Dinosaur: James Drury's Forty Years at the South African Museum.* Cape Town: Howard Timmins, 1961.

Roth, Henry Ling. *Great Benin: Its Customs, Art and Horrors.* 1903. London: Routledge & Kegan Paul, 1968.
Rousselet, Louis. *L'Exposition universelle, 1900.* Paris: Hachette, 1901.
Rumiya, Jean. *Le Rwanda sous le régime du mandat belge, 1916–31.* Paris: L'Harmattan, 1992.
Ryan, James R. *Picturing Empire: Photography and the Visualization of the British Empire.* Chicago: University of Chicago Press, 1997.
Rydell, Robert. *All the World's a Fair: Visions of Empire at America's International Expositions, 1876–1916.* Chicago: University of Chicago Press, 1984.
Ryder, A. F. C. *Benin and the Europeans, 1485–1897.* London: Longmans, 1969.
Sadowsky, Jonathan. "Imperial Bedlam: Institutions of Madness and Colonialism in Southwest Nigeria." Ph.D. diss., Johns Hopkins University, 1996. Revised and published as *Imperial Bedlam: Institutions of Madness in Colonial Southwest Nigeria.* Berkeley and Los Angeles: University of California Press, 1999.
Sahlins, Marshall. *Historical Metaphors and Mythical Realities: Structure in the Early History of the Sandwich Islands Kingdom.* Ann Arbor: University of Michigan Press, 1981.
———. *Islands of History.* Chicago: University of Chicago Press, 1985.
Said, Edward. *Orientalism.* New York: Vintage Books, 1978.
Saint-Martin, Fernande. *Semiotics of Visual Language.* Bloomington: Indiana University Press, 1990.
Salamone, Frank. "Colonialism and the Emergence of Fulani Identity." *Journal of Asian and African Studies* 20 (1985): 193–202.
Sander, August. *August Sander: "In der Photographie gibt es keine ungeklärten Schatten!"* Edited by Gerd Sander. Bonn: Kunstmuseum Bonn, 1995.
Santner, Eric. *Stranded Objects: Mourning, Memory, and Film in Postwar Germany.* Ithaca, N.Y.: Cornell University Press, 1990.
Santos Rufino, José dos. *Albuns fotográficos e descritivos da colónia de Moçambique. Photographic and descriptive albums of Portuguese East Africa. Albums photographiques et descriptifs de la colonie portugaise de Mozambique.* 10 vols. Hamburg: Broschek & Co., 1929.
Saussure, Ferdinand de. *Course in General Linguistics.* 1959. Translated by Wade Baskin. Edited by Albert Sechehage. New York: McGraw-Hill, 1966.
Savarese, Eric. "La femme noire en image." In *L'autre et nous: Scènes et types,* ed. Pascal Blanchard et al., 78–84. Paris: Association Connaissance de l'histoire de l'Afrique contemporaine and Syros, 1995.
Schapera, Isaac. *The Khoisan Peoples of South Africa.* London: Routledge, 1930.
Scharf, Aaron. *Art and Photography.* 1968. New York: Penguin Books, 1986.
Schildkrout, Enid, Jill Hellman, and Curtis Keim. "Mangbetu Pottery: Tradition and Innovation in Northeast Zaire." *African Arts* 22, 2 (February 1989): 38–47, 101.
Schloss, Marc. *The Hatchet's Blood: Separation, Power, and Gender in Ehing Social Life.* Tucson: University of Arizona Press, 1978.
Schrire, Carmel. "Miscast: Reviews." *South African Review of Books* 44 (July–August 1996): 13–15.
Schultze, Leonard. *Aus Namaland und Kalahari.* Jena: Gustav Fischer, 1907.
Schweizer, A., and C. Thorn. "Bushman Diorama." *South African Museum Association Bulletin* 7, 10 (1961): 230–36.
Scott, James. *Domination and the Arts of Resistance: Hidden Transcripts.* New Haven, Conn.: Yale University Press, 1990.

———. *Seeing Like a State: How Certain Schemes to Improve the Human Condition Have Failed.* New Haven, Conn.: Yale University Press, 1998.

Seabury, William Marston. *Motion Picture Problems: The Cinema and the League of Nations.* New York: Avondale Press, 1929.

Segall, M. H., D. T. Campbell, and M. J. Herskovits. *The Influence of Culture on Visual Perception.* New York: Bobbs-Merrill, 1966.

Sekula, Allan. "The Body and the Archive." In *The Contest of Meaning: Critical Histories of Photography,* ed. Richard Bolton, 343–89. Cambridge, Mass.: MIT Press, 1989.

———. "On the Invention of Photographic Meaning." In *Thinking Photography,* ed. Victor Burgin, 84–109. London: Macmillan, 1982.

Sekyi-Otu, Ato. *Fanon's Dialectic of Experience.* Cambridge, Mass.: Harvard University Press, 1996.

Selous, Frederick Courteney. *Travel and Adventure in South-East Africa; Being the Narrative of the Last Eleven Years Spent by the Author on the Zambesi and Its Tributaries; with an Account of the Colonisation of Mashunaland and the Progress of the Gold Industry in That Country.* London: Rowland Ward & Co., 1893.

Senghor, Léopold Sédar. "Preliminary Poem." In *Prose and Poetry.* Oxford: Oxford University Press, 1965.

Seremetakis, C. Nadia. *The Last Word: Women, Death and Divination in Inner Mani.* Chicago: University of Chicago Press, 1991.

Shaw, Margaret, and N. J. van Warmelo. "The Material Culture of the Cape Nguni (Part 4)." *Annals of the South African Museum* 58 (March 1988): 447–499.

Shepard, Elizabeth. "Magic Lantern Slides in Entertainment and Education, 1860–1920." *History of Photography* 11, 2 (April–June, 1987): 91–108.

Sherer, Joanna Cohen, ed. *Historical Photographs in Anthropological Inquiry.* Special issue of *Visual Anthropology* 3, 3–4 (1990).

Shone, Thomas. *The Albany Journals of Thomas Shone.* Edited by Penelope Silva. Cape Town: Maskew Miller Longman for Rhodes University, Grahamstown, 1992.

Sieberling, Grace, and Carolyn Bloore. *Amateurs, Photography and the Mid-Victorian Imagination.* Chicago: University of Chicago Press, 1986.

Silverman, Kaja. *The Subject of Semiotics.* New York: Oxford University Press, 1983.

———. *The Threshold of the World.* New York: Routledge, 1996.

Sima Lukombo [*dessinateur*], and Inampunde [*scénariste*]. "Apolosa Moniteur." *La revue des jeunes,* no. 25 (n.d.), 21–27.

Sisé, Mongo Awai. *Les aventures de Mata Mata et Pili Pili: Le portefeuille.* Kinshasa: Mongoproduction and Éditions Mama-leki, 1978.

——— [*dessinateur*]. *Bingo en ville: Les aventures d'un enfant africain.* Brussels: AGCD, 1981.

——— [*dessinateur*]. *Bingo à Yama-Kara: Les aventures d'un enfant africain.* Brussels: AGCD, 1982.

———. *Le Boy: Les aventures de Mata Mata et Pili Pili.* Ecaussines, Belgium: Euraf Éditions, 1982.

Skotnes, Pippa, ed. *Miscast: Negotiating the Presence of Bushmen.* Cape Town: University of Cape Town Press, 1996.

———. "Running Before That Wind: A Parallel Text." In *Miscast,* ed. id.

Sloane, David Charles. *The Last Great Necessity: Cemeteries in American History.* Baltimore: Johns Hopkins University Press, 1991.

Snowden, Frank, Sr. *Blacks in Antiquity.* Cambridge, Mass.: Harvard University Press, 1970.

Sobania, Neal. "But Where Are the Cattle? Popular Images of Maasai and Zulu across the Twentieth Century." *Visual Anthropology.* Forthcoming.
Socé, Ousmane. *Mirages de Paris.* Paris: Nouvelles éditions latines, 1937.
Soga, Tiyo. *The Journal and Selected Writings of the Reverend Tiyo Soga.* Cape Town: A. A. Balkema, 1983.
Solomon-Godeau, Abigail. "The Legs of the Countess." In *Fetishism as Cultural Discourse,* ed. William Pietz and Emily Apter. Ithaca, N.Y.: Cornell University Press, 1993.
Sontag, Susan. *On Photography.* New York: Dell, 1973.
Soumois, Frédéric. *Dossier Tintin: Sources, versions, thèmes, structures.* Brussels: Jacques Antoine, 1987.
Spear, Thomas, and Richard Waller, eds. *Being Maasai.* Athens: Ohio University Press, 1993.
Spencer, Frank. "Some Notes on the Attempt to Apply Photography to Anthropometry during the Second Half of the Nineteenth Century." In *Anthropology and Photography, 1860–1920,* ed. Elizabeth Edwards, 99–107. New Haven, Conn.: Yale University Press, 1992.
Spicer, M. W. "The War of Ngcayecibi (1877–1878)." M.A. thesis, Rhodes University, Grahamstown, 1978.
Sprague, Steven. "Yoruba Photography: How the Yoruba See Themselves." *African Arts* 12, 1 (1978): 52–59, 107.
Stapleton, T. J. *Maqoma: Xhosa Resistance to Colonial Advance, 1798–1873.* Johannesburg: Jonathan Ball, 1994.
Steedman, Andrew. *Wanderings and Adventures in the Interior of Southern Africa.* Vol. 1. London: Longman & Co., 1835. Reprint, 1966.
Steiner, Christopher. *African Art in Transit.* Cambridge: Cambridge University Press, 1994.
———. "The Trend in West African Art." *African Arts* 34, 1 (January 1991): 38–43, 100.
Stewart, Susan. *On Longing: Narratives of the Miniature, the Gigantic, the Souvenir, the Collection.* Baltimore: Johns Hopkins University Press, 1984. Paperback reprint, Durham, N.C.: Duke University Press, 1993.
Stilwell, Sean. " 'Amana' and 'Asiri': Royal Slave Culture and the Colonial Regime in Kano, 1903–1926." In *Slavery and Colonial Rule in Africa,* ed. Suzanne Miers and Martin A. Klein, 167–88. London: Frank Cass, 1999.
Stocking, George W., Jr., ed. *Objects and Others: Essays on Museums and Material Culture.* Madison: University of Wisconsin Press, 1985.
Stoler, Laura Ann. *Race and the Education of Desire: Foucault's History of Sexuality and the Colonial Order of Things.* Durham, N.C.: Duke University Press, 1995.
Stoller, Paul. *Embodying Colonial Memories: Spirit Possession, Power and the Hauka in West Africa.* New York: Routledge, 1995.
———. "Regarding Rouch: The Recasting of West African Colonial Culture." In *Cinema, Colonialism, Postcolonialism: Perspectives from the French and Francophone World,* ed. Dina Sherzer, 65–79. Austin: University of Texas Press, 1996.
Strother, Z. S. *Inventing Masks: Agency and History in the Art of the Central Pende.* Chicago: University of Chicago Press, 1998.
Stubbs, Thomas. *The Reminiscences of Thomas Stubbs, Including Men I Have Known.* Edited by W. A. Maxwell and R. T. McGeogh. Cape Town: A. A. Balkema for Rhodes University, Grahamstown, 1978.
Sundkler, Bengt. *Bantu Prophets in South Africa.* 1948. London: Oxford University Press, 1961.

Sundquist, Eric J., ed. *The Oxford W. E. B. Du Bois Reader.* New York: Oxford University Press, 1996.
Szombati-Fabian, Ilona, and Johannes Fabian. "Art, History, and Society: Popular Painting in Shaba, Zaire." *Studies in the Anthropology of Visual Communication* 3, 1 (1976): 1–21.
———. "Folk Art from an Anthropological Perspective." In *Perspectives in American Folk Art,* ed. Ian M. G. Quimby and Scott T. Swank, 167–88. New York: Norton, 1980.
Tagg, John. *The Burden of Representation: Essays on Photographies and Histories.* 1988. Minneapolis: University of Minnesota Press, 1993.
Tantala, Renée. "Verbal and Visual Imagery in Western Uganda: Interpreting the 'Story of Isimbwa and Nyimawiru.'" In *Paths Toward the African Past: African Historical Essays in Honor of Jan Vansina,* ed. Robert W. Harms, Joseph C. Miller, David S. Newbury, and Michele D. Wagner, 223–43. Atlanta: African Studies Association, 1994.
Taussig, Michael. *Mimesis and Alterity: A Particular History of the Senses.* New York: Routledge, 1993.
Thomas, Elizabeth Marshall. *The Harmless People.* New York: Knopf, 1958.
Thomas, Nicolas. *Colonialism's Culture: Anthropology, Travel, and Government.* Princeton, N.J.: Princeton University Press, 1994.
Thompson, Harry. *Tintin: Hergé and his Creation.* London: Hodder & Stoughton, 1991.
Thompson, Robert Farris. *African Art In Motion: Icon and Act in the Collection of Katherine Coryton White.* Catalog of an exhibition, National Gallery of Art, Washington, D.C.; Frederick S. Wight Art Gallery, University of California, Los Angeles. Los Angeles: University of California Press, 1974.
———. *Flash of the Spirit: African and Afro-American Art and Philosophy.* New York: Random House, 1983; Vintage Books, 1984.
Thornton, Robert. "Narrative Ethnography in Africa, 1850–1920: The Capture of an Appropriate Domain for Anthropology." *Man,* n.s., 8, 3 (September 1983): 502–19.
"Tintin revient au Congo." Editorial. *Zaïre,* December 29, 1969, 3.
Todorov, Tzvetan. *The Conquest of America: The Question of the Other.* 1984. Norman: University of Oklahoma Press, 1999.
———. *Mikhail Bakhtin: The Dialogic Principle.* Minneapolis: University of Minnesota Press, 1984.
Traill, Anthony T. "!Khwa-Ka Hhouiten Hhouiten, 'The Rush of the Storm': The Linguistic Death of /Xam." In *Miscast: Negotiating the Presence of Bushmen,* ed. Pippa Skotnes, 161–84. Cape Town: University of Cape Town Press, 1996.
Triulzi, Alessandro, ed. *Fotografia e storia dell'Africa: Atti del Convegno internazionale, Napoli–Roma, 9–11 settembre 1992.* Naples: Instituto universitario orientale, 1995.
Tshibanda Wamuela Bujitu, and Nsenga Kibwanga. *Alerte à Kamongo ou un accident dans la mine.* Lubumbashi: Éditions Lanterne and Imprimerie Saint Paul, 1989.
———. *Les refoulés du Katanga.* Zaire [Brussels?]: Impala, n.d. [1995?].
Turner, Victor. *The Forest of Symbols: Aspects of Ndembu Ritual.* Ithaca, N.Y.: Cornell University Press, 1967.
Ukadike, Nwachukwu Frank. *Black African Cinema.* Berkeley and Los Angeles: University of California Press, 1994.
United Kingdom. War Office. *Musketry Instructions, Martini-Henry Rifle and Carbine.* London: British War Office, 1892.
An Universal History, from the Earliest Account of Time. Articles by George Sale, George Psalmanazar, Archibald Bower, George Shelvocke, John Campbell, John Swinton, and others. 21 vols. London: T. Osborne, 1747–68.

Vaes, Benedicte, and Ignace M'Boma. "Rendez-vous chez Tintin." *Zaïre*, January 11, 1971, 26–39.
Vail, Leroy, ed. *The Creation of Tribalism in Southern Africa*. London: James Curry; Berkeley and Los Angeles: University of California Press, 1989.
Vail, Leroy, and Landeg White. *Power and the Praise Poem: Southern African Voices in History*. Charlottesville: University Press of Virginia, 1991.
Van de Kerchove, Marcel. "Tintin en voyage: Une vision 'belge' des mondes exotiques?" In *Tintin, Hergé et la belgité*, ed. Anna Soncini Fratta. Bologna: Cooperativa libraria universitaria editrice Bologna, 1994.
Van Opstal, H. *Tracé RG: Le phénomène Hergé*. Brussels: Lefrancq, 1998.
Van Wyke Smith, M. "'The Most Wretched of the Human Race': The Iconography of the Khoikhoin (Hottentots), 1500–1800." *History and Anthropology* 5, 3–4 (1992): 285–330.
Vandromme, Pol. *Le monde de Tintin*. Paris: La Table Ronde, 1994.
Vansina, Jan. *Art and History in Africa*. Madison: University of Wisconsin Press, 1984.
———. "Photographs of the Sankuru and Kasai River Basin Expedition Undertaken by Emil Torday (1876–1931) and M. W. Hilton Simpson (1881–1936)." In *Anthropology and Photography, 1860–1920*, ed. Elizabeth Edwards. New Haven, Conn.: Yale University Press, 1992.
———. "Venture into Tio Country: Congo, 1963–1964." In *In Pursuit of History: Fieldwork in Africa*, ed. Caroline Keyes Adenaike and Jan Vansina, 113–126. Madison: University of Wisconsin Press, 1996.
Vaughan, Megan. *Curing Their Ills: Colonial Power and African Illness*. Stanford, Calif.: Stanford University Press, 1991.
Vellut, Jean-Luc. "La peinture du Congo-Zaïre et la recherche de l'Afrique innocente." *Bulletin des Séances de l'ARSOM* 36, 4 (1990): 633–59.
Vidal, Gore. "Twain on the Grand Tour." *New York Review of Books,* May 23, 1996, 24–30.
Viditz-Ward, Vera. "Photography in Sierra Leone, 1850–1918." *Africa* 57, 4 (1987): 510–17.
Viegas, Luis António de Carvalho. *Guiné Portuguesa*. 3 vols. Lisbon: Imprensa Nacional, 1936–40.
Virilio, Paul. *The Aesthetics of Disappearance*. Translated by Philip Beitchman. New York: Semiotext(e), 1991.
———. *Speed and Politics: An Essay on Dromology.* Translated by Mark Polizzotti. Foreign Agents Series. New York: Semiotext(e), 1986.
Vogel, Susan, ed. *Africa Explores: Twentieth-Century African Art.* New York: Center for African Art; Munich: Prestel-Verlag, 1991.
———. "Always True to the Object, in Our Fashion." In *Exhibiting Cultures: The Poetics and Politics of Museum Display*, ed. Ivan Karp and Steven D. Lavine. Washington, D.C.: Smithsonian Institution Press, 1991.
———. *Baulé: African Art, Western Eyes*. New Haven, Conn.: Yale University Press, 1997.
———, ed. *ART/artifact*. New York: Center for African Art, 1988.
Wagner, Roy. *The Invention of Culture*. 1975. Rev. ed. Chicago: University of Chicago Press, 1981.
Wallis, J. P. R., ed. *The Zambezi Expedition of David Livingstone*. London: Harmondsworth, 1856.
Ward, Harriet. *Five Years in Kaffirland*. 2 vols. London: Henry Colburn, 1848.
Washbrook, David. "Ethnicity and Racism in Colonial Indian Society." In *Racism and Colonialism: Essays on Ideology and Social Structure*, ed. Robert Ross. The Hague: M. Nijhoff for Leiden University Press, 1982.

Watson, Stephen. *Song of the Broken String: After the /Xam Bushmen: Poems from a Lost Oral Tradition*. Riverdale-on-Hudson, N.Y.: Sheep Meadow Press, [1991], 1996.
Webb, Colin de B., and John Wright, eds. *The James Stuart Archive of Recorded Oral Evidence Relating to the History of the Zulu and Neighboring Peoples*. Killie Campbell Africana Library, vols. 1–3. Pietermaritzburg: University of Natal Press, 1976–82.
Webster, Alan C. "Land Expropriation and Labour Extraction under Cape Colonial Rule: The War of 1835 and the 'Emancipation' of the Fingo." M.A. thesis, Rhodes University, Grahamstown, 1991.
Webster's Ninth New Collegiate Dictionary, ed. Frederick C. Mish. Springfield, Mass.: Merriam Webster, 1984.
Weinberg, Paul. *In Search of the San*. Johannesburg: Porcupine Press, 1997.
Weiss, Brad. " 'Buying Her Grave': Money and AIDS in Northwest Tanzania." Seminar paper, Department of Anthropology, University of Chicago.
Welch, Stuart Cary. *Room for Wonder: Indian Painting during the British Period, 1760–1880*. New York: American Federation of Arts, 1978.
Welsh, David. *The Roots of Segregation: Native Policy in Colonial Natal, 1845–1910*. Cape Town: Oxford University Press, 1971.
Wendl, Tobias. *Mami Wata: Oder ein Kult zwischen den Kulturen*. Kulturanthropologische Studien. Munster: Lit, n.d. [1991?].
Wendl, Tobias, and Heike Behrend, eds. *Snap Me One! Studiofotografen in Afrika*. Munich: Prestel, n.d. [1998?].
Wendl, Tobias, and Nancy Du Plessis. *Future Remembrance: Photography and Image Arts in Ghana*. Berlin: Institut für den Wissenschaftlichen Film, 1997.
Werner, Jean François. "Produire les images en Afrique: L'example des photographies de studio." *Cahiers d'Études africaines* 36, 1 (1996): 81–112.
Wexler, Laura. *Tender Violence: Domestic Visions in an Age of U.S. Imperialism*. Chapel Hill: University of North Carolina Press, 2000.
White, Hylton. "The Homecoming of the Kagga Kamma Bushmen." *Cultural Survival Quarterly*, Summer 1993.
———. *In the Tradition of the Forefathers: Bushman Traditionality at Kagga Kamma: The Politics and History of a Performative Identity*. Rondebosch, South Africa: University of Cape Town Press in association with the Centre for African Studies, 1995.
White, Landeg. *Magomero: Portrait of an African Village*. Cambridge: Cambridge University Press, 1987.
White, Luise. "Domestic Labor in a Colonial City: Prostitution in Nairobi, 1900–1952." In *Patriarchy and Class in Africa*, ed. Sharon Stichter and Jane Parpart, 139–60. Boulder, Colo.: Westview Press, 1988.
Williams, Eric. *Capitalism and Slavery*. Chapel Hill, N.C.: University of North Carolina Press, 1944.
Wilmot, R. A. *A Cape Traveller's Diary*. 1856. Friends of the University of the Witwatersrand Library, no. 2. Johannesburg: Ad. Donker, 1984.
Wilmsen, Edwin. *Land Filled with Flies: A Political Economy of the Kalahari*. Chicago: University of Chicago Press, 1989.
———. "The Real Bushman Is the Male One: Labour and Power in the Creation of Basarwa Ethnicity." *Botswana Notes & Records* 22 (1989): 21–35.
Wintrob, R. M. "Mammy Water: Folk Beliefs and Psychotic Elaborations in Liberia," *Canadian Psychiatric Association Journal* 15 (1970): 143–57.

Wittgenstein, Ludwig. *On Certainty*. Translated by G. E. M. Anscombe. New York: Blackwell, 1969.
———. *Philosophical Investigations*. Translated by G. E. M. Anscombe. New York: Blackwell, 1958.
———. *Philosophical Occasions, 1912–1951*. Edited by James Klagge and Alfred Nordman. Indianapolis: Hackett, 1993.
Woodburn, James. "Social Dimensions of Death in Four African Hunting and Gathering Societies." In *Death and the Regeneration of Life*, ed. Maurice Bloch and Jonathan Parry, 187–210. Cambridge: Cambridge University Press, 1982.
Wren, Percival Christopher. *Foreign Legion Omnibus: Beau Geste, Beau Sabreur, Beau Ideal*. New York: Grosset & Dunlap, 1925.
Wright, Christopher. "Visible Bodies: Anthropology and Photography, 1850–1900." M.A. thesis, School of Oriental and African Studies, University of London, 1987.
Yekela, Drusilla. "The Sandile Dynasty." South African Museums Association Annual Conference (Eastern Cape Branch) paper, October 1985.
Yoka, Lye. *Lettres d'un Kinois à l'oncle du village*. In *Cahiers Africains* 15. Brussels: Institut Africain; Paris: L'Harmattan, 1996.
Young, Robert J. C. *Colonial Desire: Hybridity in Theory, Culture and Race*. London: Routledge, 1995.
Zamenga, B. [*scènariste*]; and Alain-Mata and A. Mushabah 'Mass [*dessinateurs*]. *Pourquoi tout pourrit chez nous?* Luozi, Zaire: Éditions Zola-Nsi, 1990.
Zamenga, B. [*scènariste*], and Masioni [*dessinateur*]. *Belle est aussi ma peau noire*. Luozi, Zaire: Éditions Zola-Nsi, n.d. [1995?].
Žižek, Slavoj. *Tarrying With the Negative: Kant, Hegel, and the Critique of Ideology*. Durham, N.C.: Duke University Press, 1993.
Zwide, Gordon Ndodomzi. "Burial and Funeral Practices in the Ciskei: An Enquiry into Present-Day Practices and Associated Ideas." M.A. thesis, University of Fort Hare, 1984.

CONTRIBUTORS

David Bunn is chair of history of art and head of the new Wits School of Arts at the University of the Witwatersrand in Johannesburg and academic director of the University of Chicago anthropology study abroad program in South Africa. He has written widely on visual theory and history, landscape, memory, and trauma, and contemporary South African culture.

Timothy Burke is associate professor of history at Swarthmore College. He received his Ph.D. in history from Johns Hopkins University. He is interested in commodification, domesticity, colonialism, popular culture, and cyberculture. His books include *Lifebuoy Men, Lux Women: Commodification, Consumption, and Cleanliness in Modern Zimbabwe* and *Saturday Morning Fever: Growing Up with Cartoon Culture* (with Kevin Burke).

Henry John Drewal is professor of art history and Afro-American studies at the University of Wisconsin at Madison. He has investigated and written about the arts of Africa and the African diasporas, and especially about Yoruba traditions in Africa, Brazil, and Cuba. His books include *Gelede: Art and Female Power among the Yoruba* and *Beads, Body, and Soul: Art and Light in the Yoruba Universe*. He is working on an exhibition and book about Mami Wata.

Eric Gable is associate professor of anthropology at Mary Washington College. He has studied the intersection of religion and politics in Sulawesi, Indonesia, and Guinea-Bissau and examined the production of public history in the United States. He is the author of *The New History in an Old Museum: Creating the Past at Colonial Williamsburg* (with Richard Handler).

Paula Ben-Amos Girshick is professor of anthropology at Indiana University at Bloomington. She has written *The Art of Benin* and *Art, Innovation, and Politics in*

Eighteenth-Century Benin. She is the coeditor (with Arnold Rubin) of *The Art of Power/The Power of Art: Studies in Benin Iconography.*

Robert J. Gordon is professor of anthropology at the University of Vermont. He has spent time researching and teaching in Papua New Guinea, Namibia, Lesotho, and South Africa. His books include *Law and Order in the New Guinea Highlands: Encounters with Enga* (with Mervyn J. Meggitt), *The Bushman Myth: The Making of a Namibian Underclass* (with Stuart Sholto-Douglas), and *Picturing Bushmen: The Denver African Expedition of 1925.* He is currently working on a film about non-Nazi Germans in Namibia.

Catherine Hodeir holds a Ph.D. in history from Paris I Sorbonne. Her book on the history of colonial big business and the movement toward independence in the French colonies will be published in 2002. She is currently coordinating an international conference on the economic evolution of France from 1973 to the present and directing a project to write the history of Sodexho, the world leader in catering. She is the coauthor of *L'exposition coloniale, 1931: La mémoire du siècle* (with Michel Pierre).

Nancy Rose Hunt is associate professor of history and obstetrics/gynecology at the University of Michigan. In 2000 she received the Herskovits Prize for her first book, *A Colonial Lexicon: Of Birth Ritual, Medicalization, and Mobility in the Congo.* She has written historical essays about medical equipment, colonial domesticity, bicycles, meaning, and power in colonial central Africa and is currently working on a book about manhood and infertility scares.

Deborah D. Kaspin is currently working on *Culture by Contrast,* a book about theories of culture and contemporary public policy debates in the United States. She holds a Ph.D. in anthropology from the University of Chicago. She was a lecturer in African and Afro-American Studies at the University of Virginia and an assistant professor of anthropology at Yale University. She has written about tourism in Africa and religion, ritual, and ethnicity in Malawi and drafted a book, provisionally entitled *Kings into Commoners: The Reinvention of Chiefship in Central Malawi,* about the transformations of Chewa chiefship in colonial and contemporary Malawi.

Paul S. Landau is associate professor of history at the University of Maryland at College Park. He has written essays about Botswana, slide shows, and Bushmen, as well as screen fiction and a book called *The Realm of the Word: Language, Gender, and Christianity in a Southern African Kingdom.* He is working on a book about landless peasants, mistranslations, and displaced identities under colonial rule, called *The Samuelites of South Africa.*

Hudita Nura Mustafa is assistant professor of anthropology at Emory University. She received her Ph.D. from Harvard University in 1998. She is interested in globalization and urban life, the informal sector, fashion, and gender in West Africa.

Her forthcoming book is called *Practicing Beauty: Crisis, Value, and the Challenge of Self-mastery in Contemporary Dakar.*

Tejumola Olaniyan is professor of English and African languages and literature at the University of Wisconsin at Madison. He is completing a book about political cartooning in Africa. His scholarship and teaching concern African and diasporic culture, literature, and popular culture and the theory, history, and sociology of drama.

Pippa Skotnes is an artist and the director of the Michaelis School of Fine Art and professor of fine art at the University of Cape Town. She has created works in the genres of book art, printmaking, and photography and contributed scholarship on the people called Bushmen. She edited *Miscast: Negotiating the Presence of the Bushmen* and wrote *Sound from the Thinking Strings, Heaven's Things: A Story of the /Xam,* and */Kaggen's Grief* (forthcoming).

INDEX

Action Group, 133–34
Administration générale de la coopération au développement, 109
Adorno, Theodore, 24
Advertising, 41–55
Africa: European image of, 2–6; artists in, 110–12, 171
African art, 6–9; sculpture of Europeans in, 246–47. *See also* comics; Mami Wata; Manjaco; Omada
Africans: appropriations and transformations of, 328–31; "authentic," 152–54, 158–59; color perception and, 52; in movies, 150; types/categories, 142–46, 150–52, 154, 156, 158
Air Up There, The, 333
Akeley, Carl, 150
Alloula, Malek, 176
alterity, 1
ancestors, 23
Anthing, Louis, 259
anthropology: at colonial exhibitions, 238–40; Portuguese colonialism and, 295, 300, 315n3
anthropometry, 145
"Apolosa moniteur," 114, 115
Appiah, Anthony, 311
Aragon, Louis, 248
"art," 7, 8; resemblance and signification in, 10–11. *See also* African art
aura, 23, 152
authenticity, 152–54; African politics and, 158–59; of Bushmen, 154–55, 212; photography and, 152–55; staging, 227

Ayliff, John, 58
Azikiwe, Nnamdi, 124–25, 133, 138

Baartman, Saartjie, 255
Bahloul, Joëlle, 183
Bain, Donald, 222–24, 227
Baines, Thomas, 76
Bamba, Amadou, 9, 26
Banania, 142, 143, 237, 250n11
bandes dessinées (BDs). *See* comics
Bantu Educational Cinema Experiment, 43
Barkas, Natalie, 158
Barra, Pierrot, 206
Barreto, Honario, 316n8
Barthes, Roland, 188, 320–22
Baruti, Barly, 90–91, 109, 116, 123n87
Baulé, 8, 22, 23, 26
Beau Geste, 5
Behrend, Heike, 23
Belgian Congo. *See* comics; *Tintin au Congo*
Belgium, *Tintin au Congo* in, 90–93
Benin state. *See* Edo Kingdom
Benjamin, Walter, 6, 23, 152
Bernatzik, Hugo, 226, 300
Bhabha, Homi, 275
blackface, 24–25; characters in comics, 97, 98, 103, 114
Blanchard, Pascal, 5
Bleek, Dorothea, 230n35, 256, 257
Bleek, Wilhelm, 257–61
Bloch, Maurice, 65, 75, 84n3
Body art, 253–74, 294–319

375

Boletim Cultural da Guiné Portuguesa, 299–300, 301, 312
Bond, James, 26–27
Borgatti, Jean, 191n32
Botswana, 25
Bourdieu, Pierre, 12
Bowler, Thomas, 77
boys' adventure stories, 4
British Museum (Natural History), 262, 263
Brontë, Emily, 86n22
Brownlee, Frank, 67
Bruner, Edward M., 231n52
Burroughs, Edgar Rice, 4
Bushmen: Abraham, 220; acceptance of movie makers by, 220–23; authenticity and, 154–55, 212; dance of, 212–14, 227; diorama at South Africa Museum of, 253–56; genitals of, 254–55; Jeremais, 221; /khanako, 223–24; ≠Khomani, 262; movies of, 215, 218, 221–22, 223, 326; as pejorative term, 263; phonograph and, 216; photographs of, 215–16, 217, 222; tourism and, 154–55, 223, 225–26, 228; white man's magic and, 220; /Xam, 257–61. See also *Miscast; names of specific individuals*
Butler, Henry, 73, 74

Cadle, Ernest, 154, 217
cannibal humor, 98, 113–14
"cannibals," 1, 3
captions, 15
caricature, 124–40, 275–93
Carreira, António, 300, 301
cartoons: African, 329, 330–31; dandy figures in, 100; realism in, 139n4. See also comics
Casset, Mama, 177
categories, human, 142; photography and, 144–46
censorship, of films: in Namibia, 219, 230n25; in Southern Rhodesia, 47
Cetshwayo, King, 66–67, 69
Chagas, Frederico Pinheiro, 316n8
Charles-Roux, Jules, 246
Christianity, 328–29, 330–31. See also missionaries, Catholic
Churchill, Winston, 129, 130
cinema: contrasted with still photography, 215; introduction into Africa of, 43, 45–48; misunderstandings of, 45–47; in Namibia, 218
"claptrap," 214, 223, 225
Coca-Cola, 18
Coeurs Vaillants, 245
Coleman, James, 135, 138n2

Colonial Exhibition 1931, 233; advertisements for, 238, 239; African visitors to, 246; architecture at, 241–43; dioramas at, 239–40; dissonant voices at, 247; entertainment at, 235–37; fiction about, 244–45
colonial exhibitions: African settings at, 240–44; craftsmen at, 234–35, 236; entertainers at, 235–37; list of, 248; Senegal at, 233–34, 240–41, 244. See also Colonial Exhibition 1931; Universal Exhibition 1889; Universal Exhibition 1894; Universal Exhibition 1900; Universal Exhibition 1937
colonialism: images and, 142, 149–55; photography and, 155–58, 161; unnaturalness of, 127–29; writing and, 141–42
colonialist aesthetic, "bad copy" in, 297, 299, 314
comics, 14–15; in Belgian Congo, fifties, 105–8; in Belgian Congo, since independence, 108–16; in Belgian Congo, interwar, 98–102; in Belgian Congo, postwar, 103–5; blackface characters in, 97, 98, 103, 114; Catholic influence on, 110–11; central aspects to, 97; Congolese drawn, 98, 99, 106–10, 114–16; dandy figures in, 100, 113–14; street, in Kinshasa, 112. See also *Tintin au Congo*
Congrès international et intercolonial de la société indigène, 240
Cook, James, 255
Coombes, Annie, 5
Coq Chante, Le, 100, 101
Cornell, Fred, 223
Cosmo-Kin, 100, 101, 102
Crary, Jonathan, 172
Croix du Congo, La, 100, 102, 111
Crosby, Oliver, 221
Crowder, Michael, 316–17n10
Curtin, Philip, 2, 194

Dakar, 172–73, 177–78; fashion shows in, 181, 182; photography of social events in, 180–81, 185–87
dance, 8, 212–14; of Bushmen, 227
Dart, Raymond, 150–51
Degrelle, Léon, 118n14
Dening, Greg, 214, 264
Denver African Expedition, 216, 221, 223
De Schauensee Expedition, 221–22
Diagne, Blaise, 247
Diawara, Mamadou, 7–8
Dillon, Roger, 41
Drawing, 90–123, 124–40

Dress, 178–80, 189
Drewal, Margaret, 8
Drury, James, 255–56
Du Bois, W. E. B., 29n14
Duchamps, Marcel, 9
Duggan-Cronin, A. M., 222, 231n37

Eastern Cape, South Africa: conflict in, 61–62; European and military graves in, 58, 60–61, 73, 75–78; map of, 59; settlement of, 57–58. *See also* Nguni, mortuary practices of; Sandile; Xhosa, Ngqika
Eastman, George, 148
Edo Kingdom (Benin, Nigeria), 20–21, 276, 285; British conquest of, 277; craft guilds of, 278–79. *See also* Igbesanmwan; Omada
Egharevba, Jacob, 276
Ekwebelam, Margaret, 200, 202
Elliott, William, 60
Elongo, Gabriel, 98
Engelbrecht, Martin, 263
Enwezor, Okwui, 188
Equiano, Olaudah, 2–3, 28–29n9
Etosha Game Park/Reserve, 222, 223, 225
Europeans: depicted in African sculpture, 246–47; depicted in Benin art, 285, 286, 287, 288, 289–91; image of Africa of, 2–6; intractibility of, 332–33; mythological representation of Africa by, 324–27
Ewe, 203, 204, 205
exhibitions, 233–52, 253–74
Ezra, Kate, 285

Fabian, Johannes, 8, 90, 96
Fanon, Frantz, 111–12
Farini, The Great, 223
Films, 41–55, 141–70, 212–32
Fordyce, Colonel, 75, 76–77, 78
Fortier, Edmond, 12
Fourie, Louis, 216–18, 223
France. *See* Colonial Exhibition 1931; colonial exhibitions; Universal Exhibition 1889; Universal Exhibition 1894; Universal Exhibition 1900; Universal Exhibition 1937
Fritsch, Gustav, 215

Gable, Eric, 21, 323, 328, 332
Gaerdes, Jan, 221
Geary, Christraud, 5, 159
Girshick, Paula Ben-Amos, 20–21, 323
Godlonton, Robert, 79, 81

Gods Must Be Crazy, The, 226–27, 326
Gombrich, Ernst, 10–11
Goodman, Nelson, 11
Gordimer, Nadine, 229n12
Gordon, Robert Jacob, 62, 63
Graburn, Nelson, 8
graves/graveyards, 56–57; Durkheimian theory and, 84n3; Hertzian theory and, 84n3; indexical nature of, 57, 60; as landscape signifiers, 56–57, 71–73; Manjaco, 296–98; modernity and, 87n35; Nguni, 64, 66; as signs, 57; unquiet, 64–65; Xhosa vs. European, 64–65; Zulu, 64, 65, 66–67
Gray, Thomas, 57
Guinea-Bissau. *See* Manjaco

Haddon, A. C., 256
Hagenbeck, Carl G. C., 18, 195
Haggard, Rider, 4
Hahn, C. L. H., 217, 218
Hailey, Lord, 229n20
Hall, Edward T., 214
Hall, Stuart, 175
Hamburg, Germany, 194–95
Han≠kass'o, 260
Hannerz, Ulf, 5
Hauka, 24
Hay, George, 78, 82, 83
Headrick, Daniel, 142
Hecht, David, 8, 23
Hergé. *See* Rémi, Georges
Herskovits, M. J., 11
Hertz, Robert, 66, 84n3
Holmes, Burton, 216
"Hottentots," 62, 63. *See also* Khoisan
Hountondji, Paulin, 314–15
Huggins, Godfrey, 48
Hunt, Nancy, 329, 330
Hunt, William Holman, 144
Hunter, Monica, 66

iconic signification, 11
icons, 10, 18; decontextualized, 26–27; Tintin as, 94
Ife, 10
Igbesanmwan, 278–79, 281; iconography of carvings of, 282, 283, 284
Igbos, 3, 200, 201
image-Africa, 2–6
indexical signification, 10, 57
indigène, 240

Jacquemin, Jean-Pierre, 114
Jeunes pour Jeunes, 114
Jews, 3
Jewsiewicki, Bogumil, 96–97
Johnson, Martin, 150, 154
Johnson, Osa, 150
Joseph's Holiday Adventure, 135–37, 138
Jules-Rosette, Benetta, 8
Junod, Henri, 23

Kalibiona, Maurice, 110
Kasfir, Sidney, 256
Kasongo, Baudouin-Freddy, 94
Keita, Seydou, 176
/khanako (Old Fig), 223–24
Khoisan, 262, 263. See also Bushmen; *Miscast*
≠Khomani, 262
King Kong, 216, 325
Kinshasa, 9, 90–116
kitsch, 312
Kleurling Weerstandsbeweging (Coloured Resistance Movement), 268
Kodak Camera, 148–49
Kouakou, Koffi, 9
Kouyaté, Tiemoko Garan, 247
Kramer, Fritz, 24
Krauss, Rosalind, 16
Krige, Eileen, 67
Kruiper, Dawid, 228
Kukertz, Heinz, 66
Kumalo, Ndansi, 141

Lane, Paul, 169
Lasekan, Akinola: early cartoons of, 126, 127; European models of, 125, 130–31; nationalism and, 124, 130–31; party politics and, 132–34; realism of, 15, unnaturalness of colonialism and, 127–29
Last Supper, The, 18
Latham, G. C., 158
Lebzelter, Viktor, 221, 230n32
Le Fleur, A. A. S., 25
Lembede, Anton, 11–12
Leonardo da Vinci, 18
Lips, Julius, 20
Livingstone, David, 144
Lloyd, Lucy, 257–61, 264, 273n28
Lomami Tchibamba, Paul, 98, 99, 120n45
Londres, Albert, 247
Lotcutt, L. A., 158
Louchet, 98, 99

Louw, Gert, 223
Luard, Nicholas, 231n42
Lugard, Frederick, 157
Lukombo, Sima, 114, 115
Lumumba, Patrice, 106
Lyall, Archibald, 300
Lyautey, Marshal Louis, 240
Lye, Yoka, 96, 116

Macdonald, Coenraad Frederik, 224
Magic, 21–23
"Maladamajaute," 195, 197
Mali, 7, 8
Mami Wata, 18, 193, 322–23; dreams/visions of, 200, 203; origin of, 197–98; rainbow deity complex and, 199–200; self-definition of followers of, 208, 210; shrines, 200, 201, 202, 203–4, 205, 209; uses of, 197–98. See also Santa Marta/Saint Martha
Mangels, Abby, 223
Manjaco, 296; ancestor posts of, 298, 305–11; appropriation of outsiders by, 323; bodily scarification by, 294, 297, 299–300, 303–5; copying by, 312–15; figurative innovation of, 294, 319n45; "pecuniary polity" of, 301–2
Maqoma, 71
Marc, Frère ("Masta"), 103, 104, 121n56
Marin, Louis, 239
Maroun, J. E., 52
Marshall, John, 212, 213
Matamata and Pilipili, 105
Maurois, André, 236
M'Bila, P., 106, 107, 108
Mbu and Mpia, 106–8, 112, 114
Mbumbulu, 103–5, 112, 113
McCloud, Scott, 97
Meireles, Artur Martins de, 302; study of scarification by, 21, 294, 297, 299–300, 303–5
memorials, 56–89, 294–319
Mendes, Soga, 307, 309, 313
Merle, Paul, 106
Merleau-Ponty, Maurice, 7
Mfumu'eto, 114
Mickey Mouse, 26
Miller, Joseph, 2
mimesis, 24, 319n39
mimetic images, 14, 27
Miscast (exhibition on Bushmen), 261–63, 332; organization of 263–67; public reaction to, 267–70; rock art in, 270

missionaries, Catholic: comics and, 110–11; films produced by, 105; representation of, 247
Mitchell, W. J. T., 11
Moffat, John and Mary, 14
Monod, Eugène, 237–38
Montaigne, Michel de, 1, 2, 3, 18, 26
Morphet, Tony, 263, 269
Mota, A. Teixeira da, 317n21
Mount, Marshall W., 9
movie camera, 214
Mpondo, 66
Mudimbe, V. Y., 9
museums. *See* exhibitions; *Miscast*
myths: Barthes on, 321; bourgeois, 333; educating Africans in, 327–28; representation of Africans by Europeans in, 324–27

N!ai, The Story of a !Kung Woman, 212, 213, 326
Namba, 70–71
National Council of Nigeria and the Cameroons, 124, 125, 130, 132–34
National Geographic Magazine, 156, 159, 161
Nederveen-Pieterse, Jan, 5
Ngani, 224
Ngonga, 100, 102
Ngubane, Harriet, 64, 69
Nguni, mortuary practices of, 62, 64, 65, 66
Nigeria, political cartoons of, 124–38. *See also* Edo Kingdom
Noirot, Commandant, 239
Nos Images, 103, 105
Novels, 4
Nqeno, Chief, 72

Omada, 279, 323; depiction of Europeans by, 285, 286, 287, 288, 289–91; Igbesanmwan and, 282; the kings and, 275, 280–82
Oyibodudu, Thompson, 291

paintings, 193–211
Panofsky, Erwin, 10, 14
Parry, Jonathan, 65, 84n3
Peirce, C. S., 10, 57
Peires, Jeff, 64
Pende, 8
Penn, Nigel, 259, 260
performance, 172–92, 212–32, 233–52
Perham, Margery, 152, 153
photographs: commemorative capacity of, 183–85; as indexical signs, 16; magical quality of, 22–24; manipulation of, 17; "realism" of, 11, 16–17, 144–45; studio portraiture, 176–77; universal power of, 51; viewing of portraits, 188–89
photography: the body and, 172; ethnography and, 226, 231n52; guns and, 146–49; "honorific" and "repressive" function of, 144; hunting vocabulary of, 146, 149; influence on movies of, 150; mythological imaginings of, 324–25; representation of human types by, 144–46; technology of, 148. *See also under* Dakar
Picart, Bernard, 62, 63
Picasso, Pablo, 12, 208
Pinambe, Jon Biku, 298, 307–8
Pöch, Rudolf, 212, 215–16, 222, 223
portraiture, 141–71, 172–92
Portugal: anthropology and colonialism of, 295, 300, 315n3; Benin state and, 285, 287; in Guinea-Bissau, 295, 312
postcards, 175, 176
primitivism, 7; magical powers of, 22; in postcolonial politics, 335n18
Pringle, Thomas, 58

Quintino, Fernando Rogado, 313–14

Rambo, 27
realism, 24; of Akinola Lasekan, 15; in cartoons, 139n4; of photographs, 11, 16–17, 144–45
religion, 56–89, 193–211
Rémi, Georges (Hergé), 91–92, 93–94, 109, 118n14. See also *Tintin au Congo*
Reni, Guido, 14, 17
Renton, Henry, 72–73
Ricoeur, Paul, 6, 27
Riis, Jacob, 145–46
Rivet, Paul, 240, 246
Roberts, Andrew, 5
Rockefeller family, 16
Rony, Fatimah, 212
Ruskin, John, 163n8
Ryan, James, 5
Ryder, Alan F. C., 277

Sahlins, Marshall, 331–32
Said, Edward, 2
Saint Paul Afrique, 109, 111
Samba, Chéri, 112, 113
Sandile, 72, 78–83
sañse, 172–75, 188
Santa Marta/Saint Martha, 205–7

Sao, 106
Saussure, Ferdinand de, 26
"savages," 328–32
Schoeman, P. J., 224
Schrire, Carmel, 268
sculpture, 193–211, 275–93
Sekula, Allan, 11, 144, 188
Senegal: at colonial exhibitions, 233–34, 240–41, 244, 246; history of photography in, 175–77; importance of pictures in, 173, 179; marriage in, 179. *See also* Dakar
Senghor, Léopold Sédar, 142, 246
Seremetakis, Nadia, 65
Shone family, 60–61
signs, 320–21
Simone, A. Maliqualim, 8, 23
Sisé, Mongo Awai, 109
slave trade, 2–4
snake charmer image, 195–98, 206
Socé, Ousmane, 244
Soga, Tiyo, 70, 71
Solomon-Godeau, Abigail, 172
Sontag, Susan, 147
South Africa. *See* Bushmen; Eastern Cape; *Miscast*
South African Entertainment (Censorship) Act of 1931, 219
South African Museum, 253–56
Stanley, Henry Morton, 4
Stocking, George, 194
Stoller, Paul, 319n39
Stroh, Francois, 224–25
Strother, Zoe, 8
Swahili, 4
"symbol," 10
Szombati-Fabian, Ilona, 8

Taussig, Michael, 220, 319n39
Thompson, Harry, 93
Thompson, Robert Farris, 8
Thonga, 23–24
Tintin au Congo, 15, 90; in Belgium, 90–93; as icon, 94; reception in Belgian Congo of, 93–97, 110, 111–12
tirailleur sénégalais, 142, 233, 237
tourism: Bushmen and, 154–55, 223, 225–26, 227–28; local culture molded to fit, 330; photography and, 226
Traill, Anthony, 259
"Truth about the Colonies" exhibition, 247–48
Truth and Reconciliation Commission, 268

Tshibanda Wamuela Bujitu, 123n92
Tshibumba Kanda Matula, 90, 96
Tswana, 14, 23, 25
Twain, Mark, 14, 15, 17

United Africa Company (UAC), 135–38
Universal Exhibition 1889, 233–34, 240–41
Universal Exhibition 1894, 241, 246
Universal Exhibition 1900, 235, 236
Universal Exhibition 1937, 234–35
Uut, 307, 308
Uys, Jamie, 226–27

van der Post, Laurens, 4
Van Haelst, Father, 121n57
Vaughan, Megan, 41
Viegas, António de Carvalho, 303
visual advertising: in Belgian Congo, 105; misinterpretations of, 13, 51–53; restrictions on, 49; subliminal images in, 53; in Zimbabwe, 44, 48–51, 52, 53
Vogel, Susan, 8
Voortrekker Monument, 325–26

Walas, Mamisi, 203, 204, 205
Walker, William, 148
Wallez, Abbé Norbert, 91–92
Ward, Harriet, 68
Watson, Stephan, 260–61
Webb, Virginia-Lee, 159
Weinberg, Paul, 266
Wendl, Tobias, 23
West African Pilot, 125, 126, 138n2
White, Hylton, 228
Wittgenstein, Ludwig, 26
Wolof, 178, 246

/Xam Bushmen, 257–61
Xhosa, Ngqika, 61–62; colonial rhetoric and graves of, 72; desecration of grave of, 73; European antipathy to burial practices of, 68–69; mortuary practices of, 13, 64, 65–73. *See also* Sandile
Xishe, Benjamin, 226
X rays, 12

Zaïre, 94
Zimbabwe (Southern Rhodesia): introduction of film in, 47; visual advertising in, 48–51, 52, 53
Zulu, 24, 27; mortuary practices of, 64, 65, 66–67

Compositor:	Impressions Book and Journal Services, Inc.
Text:	Monotype Baskerville
Display:	10/12 Baskerville
Printer and binder:	Edwards Brothers, Inc.